Pebble® Plus

Bugs, Bugs, Bugs!

Spiders

by Margaret Hall

Consulting Editor: Gail Saunders-Smith, PhD

Consultant: Gary A. Dunn, MS, Director of Education
Young Entomologists' Society Inc.
Lansing, Michigan

Capstone press®
Mankato, Minnesota

Pebble Plus is published by Capstone Press,
1710 Roe Crest Drive, North Mankato, Minnesota 56003.
www.capstonepub.com

Library of Congress Cataloging-in-Publication Data
Hall, Margaret, 1947–
    Spiders/by Margaret Hall.
    p. cm.—(Pebble plus: Bugs, bugs, bugs!)
    Includes bibliographical references and index.
    ISBN-13: 978-0-7368-2591-7 (hardcover)   ISBN-10: 0-7368-2591-6 (hardcover)
    ISBN-13: 978-0-7368-5099-5 (softcover pbk.)   ISBN-10: 0-7368-5099-6 (softcover pbk.)
    1. Spiders—Juvenile literature. [1. Spiders.] I. Title. II. Series.
QL458.4.H34 2005
595.4′4—dc22   2003024967

Summary: Simple text and photographs describe the physical characteristics and habits of spiders.

Editorial Credits
Sarah L. Schuette, editor; Linda Clavel, series designer; Kelly Garvin, photo researcher; Karen Hieb,
      product planning editor

Photo Credits
Ann & Rob Simpson, 7
Bill Johnson, 4–5
Bruce Coleman Inc./David Lushewitz, 16–17; Gary Meszaros, 10–11; Michael Fogen, 15
David Liebman, 20–21
DigitalVision/Gerry Ellis & Michael Durham, 1
Pete Carmichael, cover, 8–9, 12–13, 19

Note to Parents and Teachers

The Bugs, Bugs, Bugs! series supports national science standards related to the diversity
of life and heredity. This book describes and illustrates spiders. The images support
early readers in understanding the text. The repetition of words and phrases helps early
readers learn new words. This book also introduces early readers to subject-specific
vocabulary words, which are defined in the Glossary section. Early readers may need
assistance to read some words and to use the Table of Contents, Glossary, Read More,
Internet Sites, and Index/Word List sections of the book.

Word Count: 99
Early-Intervention Level: 11

Printed in the United States of America in North Mankato, Minnesota.
012013
007134R

Table of Contents

Spiders 4
How Spiders Look 6
What Spiders Do. 16

Glossary 22
Read More 23
Internet Sites. 23
Index/Word List 24

Spiders

What are spiders?

Spiders are arachnids.

5

How Spiders Look

Many spiders are black, brown, or gray. Some spiders have furry bodies.

Some spiders are about
the size of a fist. Other
spiders are about the size
of a dime.

9

Spiders have eight legs.
They feel sounds with
their legs. Spiders do not
have ears.

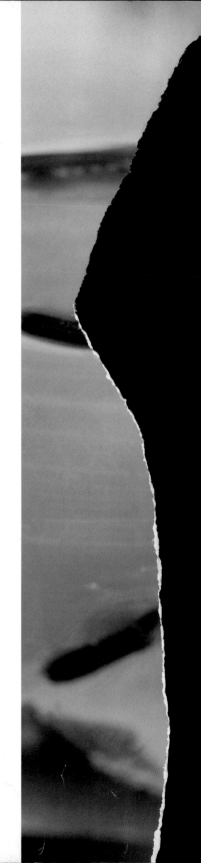

Spiders have many eyes.

Most spiders have

eight eyes.

13

Spiders have two fangs.

The fangs are hollow.

What Spiders Do

Some spiders spin webs.

They eat food that gets

stuck in the webs.

Some spiders jump on their food. They eat insects.

Some spiders go fishing.

They catch and eat fish.

Glossary

arachnid—a small animal with eight legs, two body sections, and no wings or antennas; spiders, scorpions, mites, and ticks are arachnids.

fang—a long, hollow tooth; a poison called venom flows through fangs.

insect—a small animal with a hard outer shell, six legs, three body sections, and two antennas; most insects have wings.

web—a fine net of silky threads

Read More

Houghton, Gillian. *Spiders, Inside and Out.* Getting Into Nature. New York: Rosen, 2004.

Hughes, Monica. *Spiders.* Creepy Creatures. Chicago: Raintree, 2004.

Tagliaferro, Linda. *Spiders and Their Webs.* Animal Homes. Mankato, Minn.: Capstone Press, Pebble Plus, 2004.

Internet Sites

FactHound offers a safe, fun way to find Internet sites related to this book. All of the sites on FactHound have been researched by our staff.

Here's how:

1. Visit *www.facthound.com*

2. Type in this special code **0736825916** for age-appropriate sites. Or enter a search word related to this book for a more general search.

3. Click on the **Fetch It** button.

FactHound will fetch the best sites for you!

Index/Word List

arachnids, 4

bodies, 6

catch, 20

dime, 8

ears, 10

eat, 16, 18, 20

eight, 10, 12

eyes, 12

fangs, 14

feel, 10

fist, 8

food, 16, 18

furry, 6

hollow, 14

insects, 18

jump, 18

legs, 10

size, 8

sounds, 10

spin, 16

stuck, 16

webs, 16

important contextual issues related to secondary education, and it develops their abilities to think analytically about their chosen profession. We hope the book will give future teachers a sense of personal and professional confidence as they take up their new responsibilities.

Acknowledgments

We would like to recognize those who provided valuable assistance to us during the development of the third edition of *Secondary Education: An Introduction*. Many people reviewed early drafts of many of the chapters. In particular, we would like to thank Harold W. Arnett, Missouri Western State College; Jean Dennee, Eastern Illinois University; James Dick, University of Nebraska at Omaha; Lydia Carol Gabbard, Eastern Kentucky University; Michael Lindsay, University of Wisconsin–Eau Claire; Kim Metcalf, Indiana University; and Gayle A. Wilkinson, University of Missouri–St. Louis. Leanne South and Jill Webb devoted many hours to the preparation of the instructor's manual that accompanies the text, and we thank them for their persistence and dedication. Finally, our wives merit special thanks for the tolerance and help they extended to us while we worked on this revision.

DGA
TVS

REFERENCE

One Student at a Time. Report of the State Board of Education Task Force on High School Education. Austin, TX: Texas Education Agency, October 1992.

Contents

Part **I**

Orientation to Secondary Education 1

1 Secondary Schools and Students 5

Introduction 6
The Senior High School 6
The Junior High School 8
The Middle School 9
Influences on Enrollment Patterns 11
Enrollments of Minority-Group Students 12
Patterns of Physical Development 14
Patterns of Intellectual Development 17
    Sensorimotor Stage: Ages Birth to 2 17
    Preoperational Thought Stage: Ages 2 to 7 17
    Concrete Operations Stage: Ages 7 to 11 17
    Formal Operations Stage: Ages 11 to 16 18
    Implications of Piaget's Stages for Teachers 18
Review of Key Ideas 22
Follow-Up Questions and Activities 24
    Questions 24
    Activities 24
References 25

2 Secondary Teachers' Diverse Roles 29

Introduction 30
The Instructional Role 30
    Diagnosing Students 31
    Developing Objectives 32
    Choosing and Implementing Instructional Approaches 33
    Evaluating Students' Progress 35
The Counseling Role 35
The Management Role 37
The Curriculum-Development Role 38
The Public Relations Role 40
The Professional-Development Role 41

Non-School Roles   43
Review of Key Ideas   47
Follow-Up Questions and Activities   48
    Questions   48
    Activities   48
References   49

3   Teaching as Decision Making   51
Introduction   52
Factors Influencing Instructional Decisions   53
    Information About Self   53
    Information About Teaching and Learning   54
    Reflective Practice   57
Using Research-on-Teaching Findings   57
    Beliefs About Students   57
    Stimulating Student Interest   59
    Using Student Contributions   61
    Making Wise Use of Time   62
    Presenting Good Lessons   63
Review of Key Ideas   68
Follow-Up Questions and Activities   69
    Questions   69
    Activities   70
References   71

Part II
Planning   73
4   Content Selection and Organization   77
Introduction   78
Some Influences on Content-Selection Decisions   80
Content-Breadth and Content-Depth Decisions   82
The Breakdown of Academic Content   84
    Facts   84
    Concepts   84
    Generalizations, Principles, and Laws   86
    The Role of the Structure of Knowledge in Content-Selection Decisions   87
Matching Students and the Instructional Program   88
Sequencing Content   89
    Part-to-Whole Sequencing   89
    Whole-to-Part Sequencing   90
    Chronological Sequencing   91
    Non-Sequential Topic Sequencing   91
    External Constraint Sequencing   91

Review of Key Ideas   94
Follow-Up Questions and Activities   96
    Questions   96
    Activities   96
References   97

5   Writing Objectives   99
Introduction   100
Relationship of Objectives to Goals and Aims   100
    Goals   101
    Aims   101
    Objectives   103
Objectives as Intended Learning Outcomes   105
    Identifying Observable Student Behaviors   106
    Defining Student Performance   106
    Other Components of Objectives   107
The ABCD Format for Preparing Instructional Objectives   107
    A or Audience   108
    B or Behavior   108
    C or Conditions   108
    D or Degree   109
    Putting the Elements Together: The Complete ABCD Format   110
Moving from Aims to Instructional Objectives   110
Instructional Objectives and Evaluation   111
Types of Instructional Objectives   111
    Objectives in the Cognitive Domain   112
    Objectives in the Affective Domain   114
    Objectives in the Psychomotor Domain   119
Review of Key Ideas   124
Follow-Up Questions and Activities   124
    Questions   124
    Activities   125
References   125

6   Preparing Units and Lessons   129
Introduction   130
Planning Stages   131
    Long-Term Planning   131
    Intermediate-Term Planning   131
    Short-Term Planning   132
Variables That Influence Planning   132
    Teacher Characteristics   132
    Student Characteristics   134
    The Learning Context   134
    Available Time   135

Learning Resources   135
Instructional Units   135
  Elements of an Instructional Unit   136
  The Unit Planning Process   142
  Formatting the Unit   143
Lesson Planning   150
  The Lesson Planning Process   152
  Historical Lesson Plan Models   153
  Modern-Day Lesson Plan Formats   154
  Formatting Lesson Plans   156
Review of Key Ideas   160
Follow-Up Questions and Activities   160
  Questions   160
  Activities   161
References   162

7   Preparing for the Multicultural Classroom   165
Introduction   166
School Learning of Minority Group Students   167
Why Have Minorities Often Done Less
Well in School Than White Students?   168
  Historic Views of Minorities   169
  Appreciating the Cultural Context Minorities Bring to School   170
School Programs That Make a Difference   172
  Comer-Model Schools   172
  Characteristics of High Schools Serving Hispanics Well   173
Helping Minority Students Succeed: Teachers and Teaching   174
  Assuming That All Students Can Learn   174
  Providing Good Teachers   175
  Teachers' Awareness of Their Own Perspectives   176
  Avoiding Favoritism in the Classroom   177
  Mixing Minority Group and Majority Group Students in Groups   178
  Responding to Varying Learning Styles   179
  Establishing Relationships with Students' Families   179
Multicultural Perspectives: Information Sources   180
Review of Key Ideas   183
Follow-Up Questions and Activities   184
  Questions   184
  Activities   185
References   186

8   Planning for Exceptional Students   189
Introduction   190
A Brief History of Programs for Exceptional Students   191
Slow Learners   192

Students with Disabilities   194
    Public Laws 94–142 and 101–476   195
    Kinds of Disabilities   196
Gifted and Talented Students   204
    Identifying Gifted and Talented Students   206
    How Gifted and Talented Students See Themselves   206
    Enrichment and Acceleration   207
    Working with Gifted and Talented Students   209
Review of Key Ideas   213
Follow-Up Questions and Activities   214
    Questions   214
    Activities   214
References   215

Part **III**
Organizing the Learning Environment   217

9   Management and Discipline   221
Introduction   222
Classroom Management   224
    Teacher Leadership and Authority   225
    Teacher Consistency   228
    Managing the Physical Environment   228
    Managing Time   230
Preventing Problems   233
    The Purpose Is Self-Control   233
    Respect the Student's Dignity   233
    Treat the Causes of the Misbehavior   234
Responding to Problems: Two Key Principles   235
    The Benefits of Private Correction   235
    Choosing Misbehavior Means Choosing the Consequences   236
Responding to Problems: A Range of Responses   237
    Responses Supporting Self-Control   237
    Providing Situational Assistance   239
    Implementing Severe Consequences   240
    Corporal Punishment   242
Review of Key Ideas   245
Follow-Up Questions and Activities   246
    Questions   246
    Activities   247
References   247

10   Individualizing for Learning   251
Introduction   252
Altering Variables to Accommodate Individual Differences   253

Altering the Rate of Learning   254
Altering the Content of Learning   256
Altering the Method of Learning   258
Altering the Goals of Learning   259
Learning Activity Packages   261
    Title   262
    Overview   262
    Rationale   262
    Objectives   262
    Pretest   263
    Instructional Program   263
    Posttest   263
Learning Centers   264
    General Guidelines for Using Learning Centers   264
    The Alternate-Materials Center   266
    The Enrichment Center   267
    The Reinforcement Center   267
Learning Stations   267
    General Guidelines for Using Learning Stations   268
Computers and New Technologies   269
Review of Key Ideas   272
Follow-Up Questions and Activities   273
    Questions   273
    Activities   274
References   274

11   Enhancing Learning Through Technology   277

Introduction   278
Rationales for Use of Up-to-Date Technologies in School Programming   278
The Nature of the New Technologies   280
Forces Opposing the Spread of New Technologies in the Schools   281
Examples of Technologies and Their Uses in Secondary Schools   285
    Personal Computers   285
    CD-ROM   288
    Interactive Videodisks   289
    Interactive Distance Learning   290
    Videocassettes   291
    Optical Disks   291
    Electronic Satellite Links   293
Review of Key Ideas   296
Follow-Up Questions and Activities   297
    Questions   297
    Activities   297
References   298

Part IV
Promoting Learning and Thinking   301

    12   The Elements of Effective Instruction   305

        Introduction   306

        Proactive Teaching   308

        Goal-Directed Teaching   308

        Taking Prior Knowledge into Account   309

        Using the Social and Cultural Dimensions of the Class   309

        Scaffolding   310

        Balancing Depth and Breadth   311

        Motivating   312

            Needs and Interests   313

            Perceived Effort Required for Success   316

            Probability of Success   316

            Causal Attributions   317

        Clear Communication   318

        Teacher Questioning   320

            Question Purpose   320

            Question Clarity   322

            Nature of Student Responses   324

            Wait Time   324

        Reinforcement and Praise   325

            Reinforcement   325

            Praise   325

        Practice   326

        Monitoring and Adjusting   327

        Lesson Conclusion   328

        Self-Evaluation   328

        Review of Key Ideas   331

        Follow-Up Questions and Activities   333

            Questions   333

            Activities   333

        References   334

    13   Direct Instruction   337

        Introduction   338

        What is Direct Instruction?   339

        Basic Characteristics: An Elaboration   340

            Academic Focus   341

            Formal Delivery to the Whole Class   341

            Constant Monitoring to Check for Understanding   342

            Controlled Classroom Practice   342

        Appropriateness of Direct Instruction   343

A Model for a Complete Direct Instruction Lesson   344
  Daily Review   345
  Presentation of New Material   345
  Guided Practice   348
  Provision of Feedback and Correctives   349
  Independent Practice   350
  Periodic Reviews   351
This Chapter as an Example of Direct Instruction   353
Review of Key Ideas   355
Follow-Up Questions and Activities   356
  Questions   356
  Activities   356
References   357

14   Indirect Instruction   359
Introduction   360
Metacognition   361
  Teacher Modeling   361
  Visualizing Thinking   362
Inquiry Teaching   365
  Basic Steps in Inquiry Teaching   366
  Comparing, Contrasting, and Generalizing   369
  Building a Basis for Sophisticated
  Thinking Through Delimiting and Focusing   371
Creative Thinking   373
Critical Thinking   375
Problem Solving   378
Decision Making   380
Review of Key Ideas   387
Follow-Up Questions and Activities   388
  Questions   388
  Activities   388
References   389

15   Small Groups and Cooperative Learning   391
Introduction   392
Preparing for Small-Group Learning   394
  Two by Twos   394
  Inside and Outside   395
Scheduling Small-Group Learning   397
Examples of Small-Group Learning Experiences   399
  The Investigative Role Group   399
  The Tutorial Group   402

The Team Learning Group   403
Cooperative Learning   405
    Student Teams-Achievement Divisions (STAD)   406
    Teams-Games-Tournaments   408
    Jigsaw   409
    Learning Together   412
Review of Key Ideas   417
Follow-Up Questions and Activities   418
    Questions   418
    Activities   419
References   419

16   Affective Learning   423
Introduction   424
    Attitudes Toward Subject and School   426
    Personal Values   426
    Morality   426
Developing Positive Attitudes Toward Subjects and the School   427
    Nondirective Teaching   427
    Classroom Meetings   429
Values and Value Analysis   433
    Issues, Values, and Consequences Analysis   434
    Values Clarification   436
Morality   438
    James Rest's Framework   438
    Moral Discourse   440
    Kohlberg's Moral Reasoning   441
    Moral Dilemma Discussion   443
Review of Key Ideas   447
Follow-Up Questions and Activities   448
    Questions   448
    Activities   448
References   449

Part V
Measuring and Evaluating   451
17   Measuring Student Progress   455
Introduction   456
Authentic Evaluation   458
Traditional Data-Gathering Techniques   460
    Informal Approaches   460
    Formal Approaches   464

Review of Key Ideas   480
Follow-Up Questions and Activities   481
Questions   481
Activities   482
References   482

18   **Evaluating Teachers' Performance   485**
Introduction   486
Purposes for Evaluating Classroom Performance   487
Categories of People Providing Evaluation Data   488
Self-Evaluation   489
Peer Evaluation   491
Supervisor Evaluation   494
Data Sources for Teacher Evaluation   496
Data About Student Learning   496
Data from Student Opinions   497
Data from Classroom Observations   498
Portfolios   503
Material Prepared by the Teacher   503
Material Gathered from Others   504
Examples of Student Work   504
Assessing Portfolios   504
Review of Key Ideas   507
Follow-Up Questions and Activities   508
Questions   508
Activities   509
References   509

Part **VI**
Professional Concerns   511
19   **Legal Issues Affecting Students and Teachers   515**
Introduction   516
Legal Issues Affecting Students   517
In Loco Parentis   517
Freedom of Speech and Expression   518
Students' Freedom of Conscience   520
Student Dress and Appearance   521
Due Process   521
Gender Issues   524
Search and Seizure   525
Family Rights and Privacy   527
Legal Issues Affecting Teachers   528
Conditions of Employment   528

Teachers' Contracts   530
Teacher Dismissal and Due Process   532
AIDS and Drug-Abuse Testing   533
Reporting Suspected Child Abuse   534
Legal Liability   534
Academic Freedom and Freedom of Expression   536
Copyright Law   538
Teachers' Private Lives   540
Review of Key Ideas   545
Follow-Up Questions and Activities   548
Questions   548
Activities   548
References   549

20   Professional Development   551
Introduction   552
Preparation for Entry into Teaching   552
The Pretraining Phase   553
The Preservice Phase   554
Growing as a Teacher   557
The Induction Year   558
General and Specialty Organizations   562
General Organizations   562
Specialty Organizations   563
Career Options   567
Merit Pay and Career Ladders   567
Department Chair   568
Curriculum Coordinator   569
School Administrator   569
School Counselor   570
State Education Agency Employee   570
Teacher Educator   571
Opportunities Outside Education   572
Final Comments   573
Review of Key Ideas   576
Follow-Up Questions and Activities   579
Questions   579
Activities   579
References   580

Name Index   581
Subject Index   585

Secondary Education
An Introduction

I

Orientation to Secondary Education

The nation's middle schools, junior high schools, and senior high schools enroll about half of the nation's total population of students. Until this century, relatively few students continued their studies in secondary schools after completing their elementary school years. Today, there is a general assumption that all young people will go on to secondary schools, and the overwhelming majority of those who do so stay until they finish high school.

Secondary schools come in all shapes and sizes. Some are dilapidated brick piles that evidence years of deferred maintenance. Others are sparkling modern plants that are magnificently kept and that include every conceivable amenity. The diversity of these school buildings make a mockery of attempts to generalize about "what secondary schools are like."

A lack of uniformity also increasingly characterizes the secondary school student body. Students from racial, ethnic, and language backgrounds represent a growing percentage of the total population of secondary students. The changing student population challenges secondary educators to develop programs and procedures that respond effectively to these students' needs.

Content in Part 1 provides answers to questions people often have about where secondary schools came from, what they have been expected to do, and how secondary teachers ought to approach their tasks. Among these questions are:

- What are the historical origins of secondary schools?
- Why did junior high schools develop later than senior high schools, and how do they differ from middle schools?
- What are some of secondary teachers' roles?
- How can research findings influence decision making as they seek to meet students' needs in the classroom?

Discussion related to these questions is introduced in the three chapters in this section:

Chapter 1: Secondary Schools and Students

Chapter 2: Secondary Teachers' Diverse Roles

Chapter 3: Teaching as Decision Making

1

Secondary Schools and Students

AIMS

This chapter provides information to help the reader to:

- Identify patterns in the development of the nation's high schools.
- Point out considerations that led to the establishment of junior high schools.
- Suggest some reasons that help explain the development of the middle school as an institution.
- Point out some enrollment trends in secondary education.
- Characterize the population of today's secondary schools in terms of the ethnicity of the students.

FOCUS QUESTIONS

1. Historically, was as much attention give to secondary education as to elementary education?

2. What was the importance of the *Kalamazoo* case of 1874 for the future growth of the nation's secondary schools?

3. Why do you suppose there were no junior high schools in the middle nineteenth century and earlier?

4. What are some reasons that middle schools have grown in popularity in recent years?

5. Is the enrollment in the nation's secondary schools likely to increase or decrease during the 1990s?

6. What are some ethnic characteristics of today's secondary schools?

7. What are some developmental characteristics of secondary students in different age groups?

Introduction

Diversity is an apt word to describe the population of the nation's secondary schools. Students in middle schools, junior high schools, and senior high schools represent a range of characteristics that reflect those present in our society as a whole. Students differ in their physical characteristics, aspirations, intellectual capacities, interests, and values.

Secondary students attend the nation's senior high schools, junior high schools, and middle schools. Though all three of these school types are familiar to us today, they are all relative newcomers to the American educational scene. Elementary schools have been around much longer than senior high schools, junior high schools, or middle schools. Of the three types of secondary schools, the senior high school is the oldest.

The Senior High School

The first public high school in the United States, established in 1821, was the Boston English Classical School. Its curriculum emphasized useful and practical subjects. Less attention was given to subjects having fewer clear connections with the demands of daily living.

Interest in the high school as an institution developed slowly. Even as late as 1860, there were only about 40 public high schools in the country (Barry, 1961). Lack of money was a barrier to the popularity of public high schools. The principle of public support for elementary schools had been established in early colonial times. However, for many years the legality of using tax money to support secondary schools was doubtful. A key decision that clarified this situation was handed down in the famous *Kalamazoo* case of 1874 [*Stuart v. School District No. 1 of the Village of Kalamazoo*, 30 Mich. 69 (1874)], which supported the right of state legislatures to pass laws permitting local communities to levy taxes to support secondary as well as elementary schools.

Box 1.1

The Sophomore Year in High School as Proposed by the 1893 Committee of Ten

In 1893, the Committee of Ten proposed that all high school sophomores should take these subjects (National Education Association, 1893, p. 4).

Latin

Greek

English Literature

German (continued from the freshman year)

Algebra (could be replaced by bookkeeping or commercial arithmetic)

Botany

English History to 1688

What Do You Think?

1. How would citizens today react if a local school board attempted to implement this program?

2. How would most students fare if this were the established program of study?

3. How would you have reacted if you had faced this program of study during your sophomore year of high school?

Once the legality of public financing of high schools was assured, the number of high schools in the country increased rapidly. By 1900, there were over 6,000 high schools serving over half a million students. Today, more than 11 million students attend the nation's high schools (Ogle and Alsalam, 1990; p. 58).

The latter years of the nineteenth century and the first decades of the twentieth were a time of great debate about the nature of the high school program. In its simplest terms, the argument concerned whether the high school's primary role should be to prepare students for the world of work or for the academic world of the university.

In the 1890s, the National Education Association's Committee of Ten issued a report suggesting that the high school should be almost exclusively devoted to preparing students for college-level work. The Committee recommended that all high school students take (1) Latin, (2) Greek, (3) English, (4) a modern foreign language, (5) mathematics, (6) sciences, including physics, astronomy, and chemistry, (7) natural history, (8) history, civil government, and political economy, and (9) geography (National Education Association, 1893; Tanner and Tanner, 1980).

This view quickly came under attack by those who had noted the tremendous enrollment growth of high schools. These critics suggested that high schools were taking in many students who would be entering the work force immediately following graduation. A purely academic program, they argued, would not adequately prepare students for the survival skills they would need in the world of work. Positions of these critics were reflected in the final report of the National Education Association's Committee of Nine issued in 1911. The Committee of Nine contended that high schools had a responsibility to produce "socially efficient" individuals, by which it meant persons who were committed to funda-mental American values and were capable of making real contributions to the technical and social development of the country (National Education Association, 1911).

In 1918, a grand compromise was struck that bridged the gap between those favor-ing a college-preparatory high school and those favoring a practical, world-of-work-ori-ented high school. The report of the National Education Association's Commission on the Reorganization of Secondary Education of 1918 is widely regarded as a seminal document in the development of the American high school. It promulgated the view that the public high school should be "comprehensive."

In its inspired use of the word *comprehensive*, the Commission suggested that the high school should serve multiple purposes. This broad view of the high school was expressed in the Commission's description of these "cardinal principles" of secondary education:

- Health
- Command of fundamental processes
- Worthy home membership
- Vocational preparation
- Citizenship
- Worthy use of leisure time
- Ethical character

The comprehensive high school and its associated cardinal principles have been guiding assumptions of high school education for more than 70 years. The promise to provide something for every kind of student usually has allowed school leaders to main-tain working majorities in support of this general approach.

At the same time, this arrangement has bred resentment on the part of some com-munity members. Certain critics have felt that the comprehensive high school has emphasized breadth of services provided at the expense of quality.

These criticisms have spawned several initiatives to improve high schools. The America 2000 proposals introduced in the early 1990s call on secondary schools to develop a more limited focus and to place greater emphasis on a smaller number of key content areas (*America 2000*, 1991). Theodore Sizer (1992) has argued for a high school program that introduces students to fewer subjects in more depth, focuses on helping them develop thinking skills, graduates individuals only after they demonstrated mas-tery of the academic program, personalizes instruction, and vests significant authority in the hands of principals and teachers in individual schools.

The Junior High School

Junior high schools did not appear until the early years of the twentieth century. The movement to establish them began late in the nineteenth century, when large numbers of public high schools were being built. Academic programs offered in the high schools generally were quite demanding compared to those in the elementary schools. Some people saw the junior high school as an institution that would help learners prepare for the academic rigors of high school.

Others were attracted to the idea that a special school could respond to the unique physical and emotional needs of preadolescents and early adolescents. The views of those who saw the junior high school primarily as a training ground for the intellectual challenges of high school and those who saw it as an institution to serve the developmental needs of learners often generated heated debates. These controversies have continued unabated since the first junior high school in the country was established in Berkeley, California, in 1909.

The school organizational pattern developed in Berkeley was copied by many school districts throughout the country. This 6-3-3 scheme featured a six-year elementary school, a three-year junior high school, and a three-year senior high school (Popper, 1967). Most often, the junior high school was designed to serve students in grades 7, 8, and 9. However, some junior high schools included other grade-level groupings.

By the end of World War I, the debate between those who saw the junior high school as an academic preparatory institution for the high school and those who saw it as a school to serve students' special developmental needs had largely been won by supporters of the academic preparation position. Although some lip service continued to be paid to serving special needs of preadolescents and adolescents, mastery of subject matter had become the order of the day.

Junior high schools drew teachers from college and university preparatory programs that were oriented toward the senior high schools. With few exceptions, junior high school teachers were expected to have secondary rather than elementary certificates. Large numbers of junior high school teachers saw teachers in high school as their professional role models. Many of them hoped to teach at the senior high school level. Ever sensitive to negative comments that might come their way from teachers in the senior high school, many junior high school teachers worked hard to demonstrate that there was nothing "academically soft" about junior high school programs.

One consequence of all this was to divert attention from personal needs of junior high school students. This situation had always prompted criticism from people concerned about growth and development issues. These critics became more numerous in the years following the end of World War II. Drawing on the work of developmental psychologists and physiologists as an intellectual rationale, critics of the junior high school in the early 1960s were proposing the establishment of a new kind of school to serve preadolescents and early adolescents. They proposed that the new school be called a *middle school*, a term borrowed from European education.

The Middle School

The middle school concept began to catch on during the 1960s. In general, middle schools spanned three to five grades, always including grades 6 and 7 (Lounsbury and Vars, 1978).

Box 1.2

How Should a School System Be Organized?

Throughout the twentieth century, there have been recurring debates about how grades K through 12 should be divided among different school types. These arguments continue even today.

What Do You Think?

1. Do you like the idea of having a system featuring either a junior high school or a middle school to serve students between their elementary and senior high school years? If so, what features of this scheme do you find attractive? If not, what alternative might you propose?

2. Some taxpayers believe it would be more economical if we adopted a system featur-

ing only two kinds of schools, a K-to-8 elementary school and a 9-to-12 high school. What strengths and weaknesses do you see in this proposal?

3. What kind of a school or schools did you attend between your elementary and senior high school years? What features of this school arrangement did you like and dislike?

4. What do you predict the dominant pattern of grade distributions in different school types such as elementary schools, middle schools, junior high schools, and senior high schools will be in the year 2000? Why do you think so?

Supporters of the middle school were concerned not so much with grade levels as with age levels of students—from about 11 to about 14 years (Egnatuck et al., 1975).

Many middle school educators were committed to the idea that high school preparation should not be the primary focus of the school program. They argued that certain psychological and physiological characteristics of students in the 11- to 14-year-old group require a special set of educational conditions.

Since they first began to appear in the 1960s, middle schools' popularity has continued to increase. Middle schools have displaced junior high schools to become the dominant intermediate school type.

The specific arrangement of schools between the elementary school and the senior high school varies considerably from place to place. Some communities have only middle schools. Others have only junior high schools. Still others have both middle schools and junior high schools. This inconsistent pattern sometimes becomes even more confusing when programs offered by these schools are considered.

As originally conceived, middle schools were supposed to be schools heavily oriented toward serving students' special developmental needs. Many institutions called middle schools do reflect this kind of concern. On the other hand, many other middle schools are organized very much along the lines of senior high schools. They reflect an orientation toward academic content that differs little from that of some of the junior high school programs that initially prompted the establishment of middle schools.

Similarly, some junior high schools continue to see their role to be primarily as academic preparation institutions for senior high schools. However, other junior high schools have student-oriented curricula that are every bit as responsive to learners' developmental needs as those in similarly oriented middle schools. It is simply not accurate today to suggest that "middle schools care about students," whereas "junior high schools care about subjects." There are too many place-to-place variations. Conclusions about schools must be based upon an examination of their individual programs, not on whether they are called middle schools or junior high schools.

Influences on Enrollment Patterns

Since becoming widely available, birth control technology has resulted in changes in the age makeup of our population. This technology came to be almost universally available in the United States by the middle to late 1950s. Its dissemination contributed to a dramatic decline in the birthrate. This decline stood in marked contrast to the period of very high birthrate during the 15 years following the end of World War II. One important consequence of a declining birthrate is that the American population, on average, is growing older.

Effects on school enrollments of the change in American birthrates present a complex pattern. In general, from the 1960s to about 1988, this change resulted in a reduction in the total number of students enrolled in schools. In the last two years of the 1980s and continuing on into the 1990s, this pattern seemed to reverse and enrollments began to climb (Ogle and Alsalam, 1990; p. 58). The rise in enrollments occurred because large numbers of people who were born after World War II had children of their own, who were beginning to enter school. Although fertility rates for this group has remained relatively low, the extremely large number of females of child-bearing age has resulted in a large total population of children. Stated in another way, the increase in the number of children results not because individual mothers are having many children but, rather, because there are so many mothers.

The increase in overall school enrollment that began in the late 1980s was first noticed in the elementary schools. This, in time, will lead to substantial growth in the total number of secondary school students. Much of this growth will not be felt until the middle 1990s. When it comes, increases in numbers of secondary students are likely to be substantial. For example, it is estimated that more than a million and a half more students will attend the nation's secondary schools by the year 2000 than attended in 1988. In terms of actual numbers, about 13.4 million secondary students are expected to be enrolled by the year 2000 (Ogle and Alsalam, 1990; p. 58).

Increases in numbers of secondary school students will translate into a demand for many more secondary school teachers during the decade of the 1990s. The demand for new secondary teachers was expected to grow from about 95,000 a year in 1991 to about 114,000 a year in 2000 (Ogle and Alsalam, 1990; p. 92). School districts may be hard pressed to find numbers of qualified teachers to fill all vacant positions.

Box 1.3

As America "Grays," How Will Attitudes Toward Young People Change?

On average, the American population is getting older. By the year 2000, it is estimated that 35.6 percent of the population will be 45 years old or older (Hoffman, 1988). This represents an increase over the 1990 figure of 31.3 percent. Some people speculate that this aging population may have varying views of young people. Here are two possibilities.

A

As more and more people get closer to retirement, they will increase their interest in and support for education. They will do so out of self-interest. Educated workers will be better paid. Their high salaries will generate sufficient tax revenues to fund programs that benefit senior citizens. Senior citizens, then, will tend to be more supportive of education as they come to see how it will benefit them personally.

B

The higher percentage of older people will use their new political muscle to direct tax dollars to programs that benefit them personally. This will result in a diversion of money away from education. Money will be spent, instead, on improved medical care for the aged, special parks and recreational facilities for older citizens, and constructing community centers for retired people. Educational facilities for the young will be a low priority.

What Do You Think?

1. What are your reactions to argument A?

2. What are your reactions to argument B?

3. What counterarguments might you make to each?

4. Can you think of an outcome different from both argument A and argument B that will result from the trend toward an aging American population?

Enrollments of Minority-Group Students

Population growth among minorities is much higher than population growth of the nation's white majority. It is estimated that minorities will account for 60 percent of the total population growth of the United States. This figure is particularly impressive considering that minorities constitute only about 20 percent of the total national population (Marshall, 1990; p. 15). This increase in the growth of minorities in the general population is changing the ethnic makeup of the school population. The two largest minority groups in schools are African Americans and Hispanics.

Birthrates among African Americans and Hispanics are somewhat higher than among whites (non-Hispanics). As a result, both groups are a growing percentage of the total school population. For example, in 1960, African Americans represented about 13.4 percent of the total school population (Stern and Chandler, 1988; p. 50). By the late 1980s, African Americans accounted for 16.1 percent of those enrolled (Ogle and

Alsalam, 1990; p. 62). In 1960, Hispanics accounted for 6.5 percent of students in school (Stern and Chandler, 1988; p. 50). By the late 1980s, Hispanics accounted for about 10 percent of the school population (Ogle and Alsalam, 1990; p. 62).

Both the African-American population and the Hispanic population are overwhelmingly urban. African Americans who live in rural areas tend to be concentrated in the states in the Southeast. Rural Hispanics tend to live relatively close to the Mexican border. Though many Hispanics have ancestral roots in Mexico, large numbers, too, have ancestors who came to this country from Cuba, Puerto Rico, and other areas in Central America, the Caribbean, and South America. Many Hispanics of Cuban descent live in Florida. Many with family ties to Puerto Rico live in New York City.

Both African-American and Hispanic students experience more academic difficulty in schools than do white (non-Hispanic) students (Marshall, 1990). Many explanations have been proposed. Certainly, the economic circumstances of African Americans and Hispanics and language problems seem to be among the contributing factors. Additionally, there may be unintended cultural biases in some tests used to measure school achievement. Reading scores reflect the general tendency of African-American and Hispanic learners to do less well than white (non-Hispanic) students.

Because proficiency in reading is so critical to school success in many other subjects, researchers have been working hard to develop better tests to assess students' abilities in this area. Tests developed by the National Assessment of Educational Progress focus not only on basic reading skills but also on students' abilities to derive sophisticated understandings from written material. Recent results have suggested that most older secondary students are able to derive surface-level understandings from their reading; however, fewer than one-half of them are able to analyze and explain more sophisticated information (Ogle and Alsalam, 1990; p. 9). African-American and Hispanic students have been found to fall well below the national averages in terms of their ability to summarize and explain relatively complicated information they have been asked to read (Stern and Chandler, 1988; p. 58).

A number of explanations have been suggested for the failure of African-American and Hispanic students to perform well on tests requiring them to demonstrate more sophisticated reading abilities. One factor appears to be the kind of community a student lives in. In general, students from disadvantaged communities have tended not to do as well on these tests as students living elsewhere. Since a higher percentage of African-American and Hispanic students than white (non-Hispanic) live in impoverished economic conditions, this environmental variable may contribute to their lower test scores.

It has also been noted that students who are enrolled in academic, college-bound curricula (which tend to require students to do a great deal of reading) score higher on tests of more sophisticated reading skills. Smaller percentages of African-American and Hispanic students than white (non-Hispanic) students are enrolled in these programs. This raises a troubling question about advisement practices. Do counselors, knowingly or unknowingly, recommend "general" or "vocational" courses more frequently to African-American and Hispanic students than to white (non-Hispanic) students?

Percentages of African-American and Hispanic students who drop out of school are higher than those for white (non-Hispanic) students (Marshall, 1990). Students who leave school early represent a sad waste of intellectual capital. Their vocational prospects are limited. The extremely high dropout rate among Hispanic students, about twice as high as that for white (non-Hispanic) students, is particularly trouble-some. Today, Hispanics are the nation's fastest growing minority. Unless something can be done to increase the school retention rate among Hispanic students, the nation faces a future where millions of its citizens will lack important economic survival skills.

Because of the growing importance of Hispanic and African-American students as a percentage of the total secondary school population, important efforts are underway to better serve these young people. One thrust of the drive to help more of these students do better in school focuses on language. In a few places, black English programs have been established. The idea is to establish initial communication with African-American young people using a form of English that they know and to use it as a bridge to stan-dard American English. These programs have spawned heated controversies both within and outside the nation's African-American community. Some argue that black English programs will be the salvation for many African-American students. Others contend that these programs delay these students' acquisition of patterns of standard English and, hence, act as a barrier to their rate of academic progress.

The issue of language is also important for the population of Hispanic students in the schools. The federal government has taken an interest in the problems of students who come to school speaking languages other than English. Federal law requires schools to provide initial school instruction to students in their home language. This instruction must continue until students' proficiency in English approximately equals their proficiency in their home language. Bilingual programs in the schools have been controversial. Some feel they accelerate the adjustment of non-native speakers of English to the school program. Others believe that they delay the rate at which these learners acquire English.

The language issue is not limited to concerns about school learning of African-American and Hispanic students. Today's schools enroll students from many other cultural and lan-guage backgrounds. In recent years, for example, hundreds of thousands of students of Asian heritage have entered the schools. From the late 1970s to the late 1980s, enrollments of Asian students in the schools increased by more than 116 percent (Ogle and Alsalam, 1990; p. 62). This increase has resulted from heavy immigration from Asia over the last two decades. Some children of Asian immigrants speak little or no English when they come to school for the first time. School districts have had problems finding certified teachers who also are fluent in an Asian language to work with this growing population of Asian-heritage learners. Given that large numbers of newcomers will continue to enter the United States from Asia, schools probably will continue to face this problem for some time.

Patterns of Physical Development

Physical differences among secondary students of the same age often surprise begin-ning teachers. Fifteen-year-old boys may vary by eight inches in height (sometimes even more). There may be weight differences in excess of 30 pounds. These differences result in tremendous variations in the coordination, physical strength, and general appearance of individual students.

To some extent, these differences are accompanied by differences in interests. A group of 14-year-olds in a ninth-grade class may have enthusiasms ranging from those

Some of these eighth-graders have already had their "growth spurt"; others have not.

of typical middle-grade elementary school students to interests more characteristic of adults.

Some differences in interests have clear connections to physical differences. Large, early-maturing boys who do well in sports are more likely to find athletics exciting than late-maturing students who are not successful athletic competitors. Early-maturing girls, who at age 13 or 14 may look much like 17-, 18-, or 19-year-olds, tend to be treated differently by adults than their later-maturing age-mates. Interests of early-maturing girls often closely parallel those of girls who are three or four years older.

Delayed physical maturation can affect students psychologically. For example, late-maturing boys may not be able to compete successfully when there is considerable social payoff for students who are larger, stronger, and more coordinated. Learners in school often identify their leaders during quite early school years. This frequently means that leaders are drawn from among early-maturing students.

CASE STUDY

Students' Treatment of Other Students

Rhonda Kim is in her first year of teaching U.S. history to eighth-graders at Martin Van Buren Junior High School. She is having some problems with her second period class. Two students, Eric Greenbaum and Leroy Birdsong, weigh only about 85 pounds each.

They have slight frames, are three to five inches shorter than other boys in the class, and have feet that have to stretch to hit the floor when they sit down. Both Eric and Leroy would blend in almost invisibly in a typical class of fourth- or fifth-graders.

Some of the larger boys in the class constantly make Eric and Leroy the target of their jokes. They threaten to put them in hall lockers and to toss them around "like footballs." Sometimes they tell Eric and Leroy that someone has made a terrible mistake and that the two of them should be shipped back to elementary school "where they belong."

As a result of all this, Eric and Leroy have become withdrawn and shy. They rarely volunteer in class. When the period is over, they try to slip out quickly and quietly to avoid attracting any unwelcome attention from others in the class. They are becoming increasingly alienated from their own age group, and this alienation is being sensed by some of the less-sensitive (and much larger) boys in the class who sense that they have these two "on the run."

Ms. Kim is very concerned about this situation. She knows that Eric and Leroy are bright young people. She understands, too, that in time they will get their growth spurt and not look much different from their age-mates. She is worried that present behavior of others in the class is undermining whatever self-confidence Eric and Leroy had at the beginning of the year, and she has noticed that recent work the two have done has not been up to earlier levels of performance.

■ ■ ■

What should Rhonda Kim do? Are there others she should consult before taking any definite action? Is there a particular sequence of responses she should follow? Is the situation she is facing similar to anything you have faced personally or any episode you might know about? How successful do you think Ms. Kim's responses to this situation might be in resolving the problem she faces? Why do you think so?

Rates of physiological development vary by sex. Girls, in general, mature physically at an earlier age than boys. On average, girls in the 11- to 14-year-old range tend to be taller than boys in this age group. Between the ages of about 9 or 10 through about 14 to 14½, the average girl tends to be heavier than the average boy. What people in casual conversation sometimes call the adolescent "growth spurt" typically begins for girls somewhere in the 9½ to 14½ age range. For boys, this occurs somewhat later, typically falling somewhere between 10½ and 16.

In individual classes, teachers often find physiological differences among learners to be greater than expected in students of a given age. For example, although the typical ninth-grader is about 14 years old, many ninth-grade classes include a much broader age range. There may be learners as young as 12 and a few learners as old as 16 or even 17. Elective courses in high schools are particularly likely to include an extremely wide range of ages among the students who are enrolled.

Patterns of Intellectual Development

Students' intellectual development does not follow a random pattern. The kinds of thinking in which individuals can engage seems to follow a predictable, age-related sequence. Learners of certain ages, in general, have thought processes that are clearly different from those of learners in other age groups. For the teacher, this implies that a given student's failure to learn may not necessarily result from his failure to "try." An intellectual task may demand thinking at a level that is too sophisticated given the individual's present level of intellectual development.

The late Swiss psychologist Jean Piaget has been widely recognized for his work in identifying levels of intellectual development. Piaget suggested that young people pass through a series of four stages as their intellectual capacities grow toward those of mature adults. Let's look at each of these stages.

Sensorimotor Stage: Birth to Age 2

Intellectual activity during this first intellectual stage involves almost exclusively phenomena that can be perceived directly through the senses. As the young child matures and begins acquiring language skills, there is some preliminary application of language labels to concrete objects. The child starts to understand the connection between the name of an object and the object that is referenced by the name.

Preoperational Thought Stage: Ages 2 to 7

Language development occurs at a rapid rate during this stage. Increasingly, the child uses verbal symbols to reference concrete objects. Decisions tend to be made on the basis of intuition, not rational analysis. Young people at this stage frequently amuse adults by examining unfamiliar situations and arriving at bizarre conclusions. In part, this results from their tendency to focus exclusively on only a selected part of a total situation and to generalize excessively from limited information. For example, a child in this age group may conclude that airplanes are small objects about 12 inches in length because that is how they appear as they fly across the sky at high elevations.

Concrete Operations Stage: Ages 7 to 11

Rational logic begins to appear during these years. Young people increasingly are able to use systematic reasoning to arrive at solutions to certain kinds of problems. The kinds of problems for which they develop this facility are called *concrete problems*. That is, they involve phenomena that can be perceived directly through the physical senses. These young people are much less adept at using logical reasoning to analyze abstract problems.

Learners at this stage have great difficulty in "going beyond the givens" to make sense of a school task that demands more than a simple explanation of immediately available evidence. For example, they frequently become frustrated when asked to search for "hidden meanings" in literary selections. They tend to be very literal-minded. In general, school instructional programs that demand much sensory contact with tangible objects are successful with learners at this stage. They like problems that have answers. They are not at all happy when confronted with ambiguity.

Formal Operations Stage: Ages 11 to 16

As they move into the formal operations stage, the stage characterizing adult thought, young people are able to apply rational logic to all categories of problems. They can deal with content that requires them to go beyond the givens. They tend to resist taking any less than a formal logical explanation as evidence that something is either true or false. Sometimes, particularly when young people have just entered this stage, they become so enamored of the power of logic that they become upset when they feel they have discovered contradictions between what logic suggests to them the world should be like and what they perceive it to be. Many young people are extremely idealistic at this time of life. The differences between their idealistic view of the characteristics of a "logical and perfect" world and what they observe going on around them sometimes makes these young people suspicious of the motives of adults, whom they see to be defending an unjust or unfair society on illogical grounds.

■ ■ ■

To recapitulate, Piaget's stages suggest that human beings' intellectual development follows a predictable sequence. Each ascending stage is in all cases preceded by the stages that come before. The order of stages a person goes through en route to the formal operations stage is constant from individual to individual. The age ranges given are general guidelines. Some people enter and exit stages at ages somewhat younger or somewhat older than the mentioned age points. Again, though the specific ages at which individuals enter and leave stages vary, the general pattern of ascending from sensorimotor stage through the formal operations is thought to be common to all.

Implications of Piaget's Stages for Teachers

Particularly during the early junior high school years (or middle school or late middle school years), many students will still be functioning at the concrete operations stage (remember, this stage runs roughly from about age 7 through age 11). These students still are highly dependent on concrete learning experiences. Their teachers often feel their ingenuity is taxed as they try to devise large numbers of hands-on learning experiences. Difficulties these teachers face are exacerbated because the same classroom may include other students who have passed into the early parts of the formal operations

"And just what could I do to *avoid* being featured prominently in your forthcoming book titled *The Tyranny of Homework*?"

stage. Many of these students are extremely idealistic and potentially suspicious of adults (including the teachers), whom they see as too often defending a real world that is not "logical."

It is important for secondary school teachers, particularly those who work with younger secondary students in middle schools and junior high schools, to be aware of needs and attitudes associated with learners' developmental levels. An appreciation of the nature of these developmental levels can be a great asset in planning learning experiences for students that are consistent with their individual developmental levels. Students will succeed when lessons are properly targeted toward their abilities and interests. Success breeds confidence, improves attitudes toward the school in general and the teacher in particular, and acts to reduce classroom control problems. Finally, beginning teachers need to understand that students *do* change over time. Experienced

Table 1.1 Summary Table

Topics	Key Points
Diversity	Learners in secondary schools exhibit a broad range of characteristics. They vary in physical size, aspirations, intellectual characteristics, and values.
Senior High Schools	
Origins	Senior high schools developed later than elementary schools. In part this was true because there was doubt as to the legality of using tax money to support them. This issue was resolved in the famous *Kalamazoo* case of 1874. The court held that governments could legally tax to support secondary as well as elementary schools. Growth in numbers of high schools accelerated dramatically after this precedent was established.
Purposes	Initially, many people felt high schools should basically prepare students for colleges and universities. Others argued that they should prepare people for the world of work. The famous cardinal principles, promulgated in 1918 by the National Education Association's Commission on the Reorganization of Secondary Education, laid the groundwork for the idea of the "comprehensive" high school. The comprehensive high school was to be an institution to serve multiple purposes. This view of the high school continues to dominate even today.
Junior High Schools	The first junior high school did not appear until 1909. Initially, this school developed because of the discrepancy between the learning students had when leaving elementary school and entry-level expectations of high schools. In time, some critics came to believe that junior high schools should focus heavily on developmental needs of students and not so heavily on academic preparation for high school. In time, many junior high schools tended to grow to be more like high schools than elementary schools. In part this trend prompted support for a new kind of school, the middle school.
Middle Schools	Middle schools began to grow in popularity in the 1960s. Today, there are more middle schools than junior high schools. Grade levels in middle schools vary, but most include grades 6 and 7. Supporters of middle school argue that needs of early and preadolescents who attend are very special and that school programs should respond to them. Often these people have contended that the traditional junior high school had become too focused on academics and too much like the senior high school.

Topics	Key Points
Population of the Schools	For a variety of reasons, secondary schools are anticipating growth in overall enrollment during the 1990s. This growth will prompt a strong demand for new secondary school teachers.
Minority Students	Minorities are increasing as a proportion of the total school population. This is true because minority group birthrates are higher than those of the majority white (non-Hispanic) population and because of migration. The fastest growing minority group consists of Hispanics. Many minority group learners have traditionally not performed as well in school as white (non-Hispanic) students. Educators are very interested in trying new approaches that will help these students do better in school.
Physical Development	Rates of physical development vary greatly from student to student. There may be significant differences in relative physical development in secondary classrooms where most of the students are about the same age. Differences in attitudes and interests of individual students often are associated with their rates of physical development. Teachers need to be aware of these differences as they plan learning activities for individuals in their classes.
Developmental Stages	Jean Piaget identified four developmental stages through which people pass en route to adulthood. These are (1) the sensorimotor stage, (2) the preoperational thought stage, (3) the concrete operations stage, and (4) the formal operations stage. There are limitations on intellectual functioning associated with the first three stages. This is important for secondary school teachers because many learners in middle schools and junior high schools are still operating at the concrete operations stage. This puts some limitations on kinds of assignments teachers make and kinds of expectations they should have about what these young people can do.

teachers are able to share dozens of stories about happy, well-adjusted adults who as seventh and eighth graders appeared to their teachers as stubborn, intractable, and totally convinced that "the world had been ruined" as a result of people's failure to take actions based on logic.

Review of Key Ideas

- The first public high school in the United States was the Boston English Classical School, established in 1821. Public high schools were relatively late arrivals on the American educational scene. In part, this was due to concerns about the legality of using public tax money to support them. The principle of taxing citizens to fund secondary schools was supported in a landmark decision of 1874 that is popularly known as the *Kalamazoo* case. This case prompted rapid growth of high schools. Today, more than 11 million students attend these institutions.

- Throughout much of the latter part of the nineteenth century and on into the first two decades of the twentieth, there was much debate about the "proper" function of high schools. Some people felt that high schools should serve exclusively as college-preparatory institutions. Others felt that they should provide programs to prepare graduates for vocations and the world of work. In 1918, the National Education Association's Commission on the Reorganization of Secondary Education laid out a position that came to be regarded as a grand compromise between partisans of contending positions. The Commission suggested that high schools should be regarded as comprehensive institutions responsible for fulfilling a number of important missions.

- The NEA's Commission on the Reorganization of Secondary Education in 1918 identified seven cardinal principles of secondary education. These were (1) health, (2) command of fundamental processes, (3) worthy home membership, (4) vocational preparation, (5) citizenship, (6) worthy use of leisure time, and (7) ethical character. These seven principles were seen as objectives of the secondary school curriculum. They have continued to be the guiding principles of most public high school education in the United states.

- Junior high schools began to appear only after the beginning of the twentieth century; the first one was opened in 1909. The junior high school was a response to a recognition that ever-increasing numbers of students were seeking to continue their education beyond the elementary school level. There was a concern that the ending point of instruction in many elementary schools did not match up well with entry-level expectations of many high schools. The junior high school was seen as a "bridge" institution that could prepare students for a successful transition from elementary school to senior high school.

- Throughout much of the history of junior high schools, educators and citizens interested in these schools have debated whether these institutions should be regarded (1) primarily as schools to prepare students for the academic rigors of high school, or (2) primarily as institutions designed to respond to the unique personal emotional and developmental needs of preadolescents and early adolescents. By the end of World War II, many people felt this argument had been won by those who saw junior high schools as primarily designed to prepare students for senior high school.

- Middle schools began to be popular during the 1960s. Much of the impetus for interest in these institutions came from people who felt junior high schools were failing to provide programs well suited to the special emotional and developmental needs of preadolescents and early adolescents. Middle schools were organized to include at least three but rarely more than five grades that nearly always included grades 6 and 7. Today, these popular institutions outnumber junior high schools.

- It is important to note that there are great differences among individual junior high schools and individual middle schools. Some junior high schools are organized so that developmental needs of learners are a higher priority than academic content. Similarly, some middle schools are organized to emphasize academic content and to respond relatively superficially to learners' developmental needs.

- For a variety of reasons, school enrollments began a general pattern of increase in the late 1980s. It is expected that this increase will be especially noticeable in the nation's secondary schools during the 1990s. This pattern probably will stimulate a strong demand for new secondary school teachers throughout the 1990s.

- Population growth among minorities is higher than for the population as a whole. Minority group students are making up an ever larger proportion of the total school population. Growth in numbers of Hispanic students has been particularly high in recent years. There is evidence that, in general, Hispanic students and African-American students do less well in school than white (non-Hispanic) students. This pattern is of great concern to today's educators.

- One thrust of the general effort to develop programs to assist students from ethnic and cultural minorities has focused on the issue of language. Black English programs have been instituted in some places to assist some African-American students. Federal legislation mandates bilingual education programs that provide initial school instruction to students in their home language until their proficiency in English is roughly equivalent to that of native speakers. These programs have attracted both derisive comments and applause. They continue to be controversial, and debates about their relative merits seem certain to continue.

- Dramatic physical differences can be found among secondary school students of the same chronological age. Teachers need to be alert to potential psychological problems among learners whose physical development lags behind that of their age-mates. Physical maturation occurs at different rates for boys and girls: Girls tend to reach physical maturity earlier than boys.

- Developmental psychologist Jean Piaget discovered that intellectual development progresses through a series of stages that are roughly tied to chronological age. The first of these stages, the sensorimotor stage, occurs between birth to age 2. It features intellectual activity that involves almost exclusively phenomena that can be perceived directly through the senses. Stage two, the preoperational thought stage, occurring between the ages of 2 and 7, represents a time of rapid language development. Decisions tend to be made more on intuition than on the basis of rational thought. The third stage, the concrete operations stage, occurring between ages 7 and 11, witnesses the appearance of systematic reasoning. Reasoning, however, tends to be restricted to situations that are not abstract, but that can be perceived directly through the senses. The fourth stage, the formal operations stage, occurring between ages 11 and 16, represents development toward mature, adult thinking. At this stage young people begin to apply rational logic to all situations, including relatively abstract problems requiring them to "go beyond the givens." Piaget's work suggests a need for teachers to consider learners' developmental stages when planning lessons and assigning intellectual tasks. There should be some congruence between what learners are asked to do and what their level of intellectual development permits them to do successfully.

Follow-Up Questions and Activities

Questions

1. Why did interest in the senior high school develop rather slowly in this country?

2. What was the *Kalamazoo* case?

3. What is meant by the term *comprehensive high school*?

4. What factors led to the establishment of the junior high school?

5. How do you explain the rapid growth of middle schools over the past 30 years?

6. Why are school enrollments climbing during the 1990s?

7. How have minority group students' performances in school compared with those of white (non-Hispanic) students, and what are some factors that seem to be associated with any differences?

8. In what ways do rates of physical development of individual students influence their interests and their attitudes about school?

9. What stages of physiological development were described by Jean Piaget?

10. Some people argue that teachers need to be familiar with learner characteristics associated with each of Piaget's developmental stages. Why might this information be useful to secondary school teachers?

Activities

1. Examine a program of study from a local high school. To what extent does the school program seem to respond to each of the famous cardinal principles? Which ones seem to be emphasized more than others? What might this tell you about local priorities? Present your findings in a short paper.

2. Organize a classroom debate on this topic: "Resolved that today's middle schools and junior high schools should place more emphasis on academics than on personal and social development of students." Present your debate in class, and ask your instructor to critique arguments made both by supporters and opponents of this proposition.

3. Invite a panel of middle school and junior high school teachers to your class. Have them talk about their roles. Ask them to comment on special rewards and frustrations of working with these younger secondary-level students.

4. Conduct some library research to gather information about levels of achievement in various subject areas by minority group students. Then, find several articles suggesting approaches educators are making to enhance performance levels of these students. Ask your instructor for suggestions regarding sources of information. Present findings to your class in an oral report.

5. Diversity within today's classrooms often comes as a surprise to beginning teachers. Invite to your class a teacher who teaches a high school course that draws a cross section of learners. (Classes that are required for high school graduation tend to do this.) Ask the teacher to describe the variety of interests, capabilities, and attitudes represented among members of one of his or her classes.

References

America 2000: An Education Strategy. Washington, DC: United States Department of Education, 1991.

BARRY, T. N. *Origin and Development of the American Public High School in the Nineteenth Century.* Unpublished doctoral dissertation. Stanford University, 1961.

EGNATUCK, T; GEORGIADY, N. P.; MUTH, C. R.; AND ROMANO, L. G. *The Middle School.* East Lansing, MI: Michigan Association of Middle School Educators, 1975.

HOFFMAN, M. S. (ED.). *The World Almanac and Book of Facts, 1988.* New York: World Almanac, 1988.

LOUNSBURY, J. H. AND VARS, G. E. *Curriculum for the Middle Years.* New York: Harper & Row, 1978.

MARSHALL, R. (CHAIR). *Education That Works: An Action Plan for the Education of Minorities.* Cambridge, MA: Quality Education for Minorities Project, The Massachusetts Institute of Technology, 1990.

NATIONAL EDUCATION ASSOCIATION. *Addresses and Proceedings.* Washington, DC: July 11, 1911.

NATIONAL EDUCATION ASSOCIATION. *Report of the Committee of Ten on Secondary School Studies.* Washington, DC: NEA, 1893.

NATIONAL EDUCATION ASSOCIATION COMMISSION ON REORGANIZATION OF SECONDARY EDUCATION. *Cardinal Principles of Secondary Education.* Washington, DC: United States Government Printing Office, 1918.

OGLE, L. T. (ED.) AND ALSALAM, N. (ASSOC. ED.). *The Condition of Education, 1990: Volume 1—Elementary and Secondary Education.* Washington, DC: National Center for Education Statistics, 1990.

POPPER, S. H. *The American Middle School: An Organizational Analysis*. Waltham, MA: Balaisdell Publishing Company, 1967.

SIZER, T. R. *Horace's School: Redesigning the American High School*. Boston: Houghton Mifflin, 1992.

STERN, J. D. (ED.) AND CHANDLER, M. O. (ASSOC. ED.). *The Condition of Education*. Washington, DC: U.S. Department of Education, Office of Educational Research and Improvement, Center for Education Statistics, 1988.

Stuart v. School District No. 1 of the Village of Kalamazoo, 30 Mich. 69 (1874).

TANNER, D. AND TANNER, L. N. *Curriculum Development: Theory Into Practice*. 2nd ed. New York: Macmillan Publishing Company, 1980.

Secondary Teachers' Diverse Roles

AIMS

This chapter provides information to help the reader to:

- Describe the diversity of roles played by secondary school teachers.
- Identify examples of duties associated with teachers' instructional role.
- Explain specific teacher responsibilities in areas not related to transmission of academic content.
- Point out problems teachers sometimes face because of the many roles they must play.
- Explain how out-of-school responsibilities can have both positive and negative influences on teachers' abilities to discharge their duties at school.

FOCUS QUESTIONS

1. What are some things teachers have to do when discharging their instructional responsibilities?
2. What purposes are served by several of the roles teachers must play?

3. What are some things teachers do when discharging their counseling and adminis-
    trative responsibilities?
4. What public relations tasks often are assumed by secondary teachers?
5. What sorts of things do teachers do when involved in curriculum-development
    work?
6. Why is continuing professional development important for secondary teachers?
7. Why do teachers' varied role responsibilities have the potential to produce stress?

Introduction

The diversity of the roles they are expected to play often comes as a surprise to beginning secondary teachers. University-level preparation of educators places a heavy
emphasis on development of prospective teachers' instructional skills. In the real world
of the school, though instructing learners is a central obligation of teachers, they also
must discharge many other responsibilities. A fairly comprehensive list of teachers'
roles would include the following duties:

- Instruction
- Counseling students
- Administration
- Curriculum development
- Public relations
- Professional development
- Non-school related obligations

Demands associated with each of these roles can be heavy. Teachers often find
themselves pressed for time as they struggle to strike a balance among competing
obligations. Though there will always be occasional "difficult" days, a broader understanding among newcomers to teaching about the many roles they will be expected to
play can greatly reduce general levels of anxiety and enhance their abilities to discharge multiple duties confidently.

The Instructional Role

Although schools assume other obligations as well, providing instruction more than
anything else defines their identity. Schools evolved to serve the instructional function.
Of all the roles teachers play, delivery of instruction is the most important.

Although all secondary teachers play an instructional role, how this role is discharged and the specific purposes it serves vary considerably. Some teachers and school programs emphasize transmission of academic content. Others place a high priority on preparing learners for the world of work. Others seek to develop students' pride in citizenship. Still others focus heavily on helping students to solve personal problems and to function more effectively in social settings of all kinds.

Instructional practices of most teachers represent a blending of several of these emphases. Though the "ends" of instruction may vary, there are certain commonalities in the instructional practices of large numbers of teachers. Among common planning tasks are those associated with:

- Diagnosing students
- Developing objectives
- Choosing and implementing instructional approaches
- Evaluating students' progress

Diagnosing Students

Secondary school students are becoming an increasingly varied group. This diversity reflects ethnic and cultural differences as well as differences in physical and mental capabilities and in attitudes. Diagnosis for instructional purposes involves teacher actions that seek information about individual students. The idea is for the teacher to gather information that will help design lessons to enhance students' prospects for success.

For example, a high school English teacher might have in mind a lesson that would require students to comment on writing style differences of James Fenimore Cooper and Ernest Hemingway. The success of such a lesson would depend on students already having some understanding of the writing style of each author. (If this were not the case, students would be unable to complete the lesson's central learning task.) Before beginning this lesson, the teacher might wish to gather diagnostic information regarding students' levels of understanding of the writing styles of the two authors. If large numbers of them were unable to describe these styles confidently, the new lesson would have to be approached with this situation in mind. In such a case, the teacher might begin the lesson by reviewing stylistic characteristics of each author. Students would need this information to succeed when doing the compare-and-contrast part of the lesson.

In addition to gathering information about academic content, teachers often engage in diagnostic activities designed to find out something about students' interests. It is much easier to motivate students if lessons are organized to take advantage of pre-existing student enthusiasms. Of course, not all topics can be introduced in ways that respond to burning interests of students, but quite often parts of lessons can be planned to take advantage of what students like. Skillful teachers use areas of initial student enthusiasm as entry points to instruction on new topics.

Diagnostic information also helps teachers to pinpoint learning problems of specific students. For example, this information may identify characteristics of individuals related to such issues as their general levels of understanding of previously introduced material, their reading or computational abilities, their preferred learning styles, and the nature of problems associated with such exceptionalities as visual, auditory, or physical impairment.

Teachers gather diagnostic information in many ways. Personal observation of individual students is an important information source. Teacher-student conferences, though time consuming, give teachers excellent insights into characteristics of individual class members. Examination of previous samples of student work also often yields important information. Teacher-made tests, attitude inventories, and other pencil-and-paper procedures sometimes also provide useful information.

In summary, teachers use whatever procedures are appropriate to gather diagnostic information that will allow them to prepare lessons to help students experience success. Success is important. Young people who do well in the classroom develop higher levels of interest in school. They become easier to motivate. They grow in self-confidence. They tend to profit more from the entire school experience (Good and Brophy, 1991).

Developing Objectives

Instructional objectives identify what students are expected to be able to do as a result of their exposure to what has been taught. Objectives guide teachers as they make decisions about which learning resources to use and which instructional techniques to implement.

Identification of objectives helps teachers develop a clear understanding of their expectations of students. When the teacher knows precisely what she wants students to learn, lessons tend to be developed with more clarity, and students are better able to understand what the teacher wishes them to do.

For example, before establishing a clear learning objective, a high school history teacher might have a rather vague notion that "the students should be able to discuss causes of World War I." Lessons planned with this general idea in mind may include relevant information, but there is little to cue the teacher to highlight specific details, nor is there anything to suggest to students what they might be expected to include in their "discussions."

If the teacher takes this general idea and refines it into a more precise learning objective, the teacher will have a clearer focus for planning, and students will be better able to understand the teacher's expectations. For example, this teacher could develop a learning objective that might look something like this: "Each student, in an essay, will compare and contrast views of (1) Great Britain and its allies and (2) Germany and its allies regarding causes for the outbreak of World War I. Specific reference will be made to views of both Great Britain and Germany respecting (a) political causes, (b) social causes, and (c) economic causes." Developing objectives of this kind add a valuable dimension of specificity to lesson planning. Teachers who use them develop instructional plans more confidently, and their students tend to do better on tests.

Box 2.1

What Kind of Diagnostic Information Is Needed?

Think about a specific lesson you would like to teach. Then, respond to these questions:

1. What related content do you assume students already know? Why do you believe they must know this content to understand what you propose to teach in your lesson?

2. Point out at least three things you could do to test the accuracy of your assumption.

3. Describe how you might modify your lesson depending on what you found out after using the diagnostic approaches you identified in your response to question 2.

Objectives also help teachers to assess the success of their instruction. In preparing a test over a series of lessons on a topic, the teacher develops questions that relate to individual objectives. When students do well on test items tied to a particular objective, the teacher will know that procedures used to teach related content were appropriately designed and implemented. On the other hand, when large numbers of class members do poorly on questions related to a particular objective, a review of instructional procedures may be in order. When this happens, the teacher knows that he needs to spend additional time with the class reviewing content related to this objective. It may also be desirable for the teacher to revise procedures used to introduce this material before it is taught again to another group of students during a subsequent semester or school year.

Choosing and Implementing Instructional Approaches

Deciding what to do in the classroom and implementing these plans are key ingredients in a successful instructional program. A number of planning frameworks, sometimes called instructional models, have been developed to highlight tasks teachers must plan and implement in delivering instruction.

A model that has been adopted by many school districts was initially developed by Madeline Hunter and Douglas Russell (1977). Their model calls for teachers to take actions associated with each of the following:

- Anticipatory set (teacher actions designed to focus students' attention on the instruction to follow)

- Objective and purpose (teacher actions to communicate the purpose of the lesson and to indicate to learners what they should be able to do as a result of this instruction)

- Instructional input (actions taken to convey relevant content to students)

- Guided practice (monitoring students' work as they engage in activities requiring them to apply what they have learned)
- Independent practice (requiring students to complete assignments requiring new knowledge under conditions where teacher help is not available) (Hunter and Russell, 1977; pp. 86–88)

Another sequencing framework was introduced in 1980 by Jon Denton, David Armstrong, and Tom Savage. Their model drew heavily on the work of learning and instructional design specialists Robert Gagné and Leslie Briggs (1974). According to the Denton, Armstrong, and Savage (1980) model, teachers need to take these actions to plan and implement instruction:

- Emphasize objectives (teacher efforts to let students know what they will be able to do as a consequence of instruction)
- Motivate learning (actions taken to interest students in lesson content)
- Recall previous learning (efforts by the teacher to help students see a connection between previously mastered content and new material)
- Present new information (actions taken by the teacher to introduce new content)
- Recognize key points (teacher efforts to help students focus on essential parts of newly introduced content)
- Apply new information (opportunities for students to use what they have learned)
- Assess new learning (actions taken to evaluate what students have learned and to provide them with comments designed to assure that they have properly mastered new content) (Denton et al., 1980; pp. 10–14)

These two frameworks are the results of centuries of efforts to describe what teachers should do to maximize learning of their students (Posner, 1987). Nearly all of them specify categories of tasks teachers ought to accomplish. None specifies exactly which techniques a teacher should use to teach specific content to specific learners.

Researchers who have been concerned about the issue of "effective teaching" (teaching that results in high rates of learning among students) have found that there are no specific instructional techniques that will be successful irrespective of the makeup of the student population, the content being taught, the general milieu of the particular school, and the background of the individual teacher (Good and Brophy, 1991). This is *not* to say that there are no general principles of effective teaching. Researchers have established, for example, that direct, highly teacher-centered instruction works well when basic skills are being taught to young learners (Good and Brophy, 1991). In general, though, "what works" depends on many situational variables. This is why, initially, newcomers to the profession often do not feel particularly good about their ability to plan and deliver effective lessons to students. It simply takes time to assess students' needs, construct materials, and implement procedures that are well fitted to a particular group.

Evaluating Students' Progress

Evaluation of students' work is one of teachers' most important responsibilities. One important purpose of evaluation is to determine whether students have mastered objectives associated with what has been taught.

Evaluation of individual students requires teachers to maintain good records. These provide the evidentiary basis for grades. In the event a student (or his parent or guardian) question a grade, it is critically important for the teacher to have documentation available to support the decision that was made. Courts and school authorities almost always uphold grading decisions of a teacher who can document student performance by reference to a written record.

Teachers frequently use examinations or tests of various kinds to assess students' learning. Formal examinations, however, are certainly not the only available options. Term papers, projects of various kinds, performance tasks (e.g., making a pot on a potter's wheel or making a certain percentage of baskets from a free-throw line), one-on-one conversations, and a wide variety of other alternatives can provide information useful in evaluating levels of understanding and competence. Specific evaluation procedures vary greatly depending on teachers' interests, the nature of subjects being taught, and the kinds of students in a particular class.

The Counseling Role

As members of one of the helping professions, teachers' work involves intense interactions with those they serve, the students. Effective teachers have good interpersonal relations skills. These are particularly important when they discharge responsibilities associated with the counseling role.

Though nearly all secondary schools have professional counselors on their staffs, their presence by no means diminishes the importance of the counseling that teachers do. In secondary schools, relatively few professional counselors must serve large numbers of students. This means that these counselors spend much of their time dealing with students having extremely serious personal, family, or academic problems. These well-trained and well-intentioned professionals simply are unable to spend time working with all students in the school.

Further, individual students tend to become quite well acquainted with their teachers. Many of them feel comfortable sharing a wide variety of personal concerns with them. Teachers often are approached by students who are looking for a sympathetic ear. Prospective secondary teachers need to be prepared for students who seek advice, and they need to understand their own limitations as counselors. It is particularly important for them to know when a student should be referred to the professional counseling staff for help. Most professional counselors will provide suggestions about this matter to new teachers.

Effective teacher counseling does not imply that the teacher should strive to become a close friend of each student who comes in to chat. A student asking for help

Box 2.2

A Teacher Should Not Have to Be a Counselor, Too

Malcolm Smith, who has taught chemistry at Augustus Ford Senior High School for many years, recently made these comments to one of his colleagues.

"I was hired to teach chemistry. My people have always done pretty well on standardized tests. Lots of them have gone on to college and done well, and a few of them have even majored in chemistry. The way I see it, my purpose here is to teach what I know and that's it.

"Sure, some of these young folks have problems. A few of them probably need some hand-holding and cozy talk. But I'm not the person to do that. Those counselors who sit around their office and never have to teach a class or correct a paper are paid to deal with personal problems of students.

They should do their job, and let me do mine. I just don't want to deal with personal problems. I'm a teacher, not a counselor."

What Do You Think?

1. Why do you think Mr. Smith has arrived at this position? Do you think his view has been shaped by the particular work environment in his school, by his own personality, or by still other factors?

2. Contrast strengths and weaknesses of Mr. Smith's argument as you see them.

3. How do you think others on the school staff would respond to what he says?

---

with a problem is looking for guidance, not for a new friend. The student seeks advice from the teacher out of a conviction that the teacher is a mature adult who may be able to help. If the teacher misinterprets a call for help as an invitation to personal friendship, the credibility of the teacher may be undermined.

Many things teachers do have some connection to the counseling function. The ways they talk to students, the respect they show them in conversation, and the kinds of nonverbal signals they display all send messages to the student. Collectively, they "tell" individual students what the teacher thinks about them as people. These teacher actions can build or destroy rapport with students. Students' views of how their teachers perceive them greatly influence their interest in school and their patterns of behavior in the classroom. When students think teachers view them positively, they tend to be more interested in what they are being taught and more responsive than when they think teachers view them negatively.

Teachers who are particularly good at counseling students have mastered the skill of attending. *Attending* means listening carefully to what another person is saying and attempting to see the world through that person's eyes. Teachers who are good attenders often are able to help students identify critical features of problems and to assist them in working out solutions.

To discharge the counseling function successfully, a teacher must be mature and personally secure. He or she must have a positive self-concept. The purpose of the teacher-counseling function is to help young people develop into confident, self-assured problem-solvers. To be credible in discharging this role, teachers themselves must model this kind of behavior.

The Management Role

For many teachers, the management role is one of their least favorite responsibilities. Complaints often focus on the time that is lost attending to paperwork that could be better spent preparing lessons and working with individual students.

From time to time, efforts are undertaken to reduce teachers' paperwork load. Even so, teachers everywhere find they must discharge many important administrative responsibilities. For example, they must keep records on individual students. They have to order materials. Requests for films, software, and other technological support equipment and related materials have to be filed. Special state and federal programs require them to complete certain forms. Papers related to referral to counselors and

"Listen carefully as I share with you some thrilling and inspirational information on our superintendent's favorite topic ... good paperwork management."

administrators need to be completed. Students must be provided with hall passes, library passes, and other kinds of authorizations. Grades and other information about student performance must be entered into grade books. These managerial chores, though not particularly exciting, collectively help the school program to run smoothly.

Another administrative responsibility that deserves special mention is teachers' need to keep accurate attendance records. In many parts of the country, school districts receive money from the state based in part on the number of students in attendance. Districts have a financial interest in assuring that numbers of students attending classes are well documented. Teachers are almost always responsible for providing this information. If there are serious errors in teachers' records, a district may suffer an enormous loss in state funding.

Taking attendance accurately and *quickly* is important. Beginning teachers who do not develop a good system for doing this waste valuable time. Researchers have found a clear relationship between the amount of time students spend on tasks related to instruction and levels of achievement (Good and Brophy, 1991). A few unnecessary minutes spent taking attendance each day can add up to a tremendous amount of time over a school semester or a year. The accompanying loss of instructional time can result in diminished learning.

In time, most secondary teachers develop managerial skills that allow them to accomplish tasks quickly and efficiently. Today, teachers can use computer programs to reduce the tedium of entering and averaging grades, keeping attendance records, and taking care of other managerial chores. These technological aids allow teachers to accomplish these tasks more quickly. It may be that as these technologies become more sophisticated and more widely available there will be an overall reduction in time teachers must spend on administrative tasks, particularly those involving routine record keeping. This may result in a general increase in time available for instruction.

The Curriculum-Development Role

Newcomers to education sometimes have difficulty making a clear distinction between the terms *curriculum* and *instruction*. *Curriculum* refers to a general plan or framework for selecting and organizing content. *Instruction* refers to procedures followed to transmit content that has been selected and organized. Teacher preparation programs tend to place more emphasis on instruction than on curriculum. This is true because beginning teachers often have more concerns about their abilities to teach lessons and manage classes, topics that are more instructional than curricular in their orientation. These concerns are important, but they by no means suggest that all teachers, including beginners, do not have important curriculum-related responsibilities as well.

Curriculum operates at many levels. Some school districts may have large centralized curriculum operations staffed with numerous specialists. These individuals may lead curriculum-development efforts (activities that nearly always include some classroom teachers) that result in the development of scope and sequence documents and other materials that describe general patterns of what is taught at each grade level and in each subject.

Curriculum activities also take place at the building level. Teams of individual teachers within secondary school departments often work together to design courses and select basic instructional materials. Finally, individual teachers engage in curriculum work in their own classrooms when they plan individual units of work and lessons. This kind of curriculum planning is important because it allows each teacher to plan learning experiences that are appropriate for the specific group of students being taught.

In their curriculum-development role, teachers often work on district-level curriculum revision projects (developing a new secondary mathematics or English program, for example) or on committees charged with determining the appropriateness of various student learning materials. Curriculum revision projects often allow members of the development team to try out new materials and approaches in their own classrooms. These experiences broaden the expertise of these teachers and give them more options as they plan lessons for their students.

Much curriculum development work occurs late in the day after students have been dismissed, on evenings, on weekends, or during the summer months. Many school districts pay teachers for the curriculum work they do when school is not in session. After-hours work during the school year may or may not be paid, depending on local school

These teachers are working on a curriculum-revision project.

district policy. Individuals who become particularly interested and proficient in curriculum work often take advanced courses in this area. Graduate-level curriculum courses are commonly featured in master's degree programs in education.

The Public Relations Role

Secondary school teachers' behaviors can greatly influence the level of community support for schools and school programs. It is particularly important for professional educators to maintain good working relationships with parents. As the members of the voting public who have the most direct contact with the schools, parents' views greatly influence others in the community. Consequently, school leaders often encourage secondary school teachers to establish and maintain positive relationships with parents. This is not easy.

By the time their children begin attending secondary schools, some parents have put in many years as faithful participants in elementary school support groups. School is no longer the novelty it was when their children were just beginning to go to school. Generally, secondary school teachers and administrators find it difficult to sustain the levels of parent involvement that are common in many elementary schools.

Today, many elementary schools continue to draw large numbers of pupils from areas located reasonably close to the school. Secondary schools draw from a much broader geographic area. This situation becomes even more pronounced in areas of the country where students are bussed from widely separated parts of the community to assure an appropriate racial and ethnic mix in the student body. In short, it simply is not convenient for many parents to visit secondary schools.

To compensate for these difficulties, some secondary school principals actively encourage their teachers to maintain frequent and written communication links with parents of students. They are particularly eager for teachers to reach parents when they have good news to report. Many parents rarely have heard from anyone at the school except when their child has misbehaved or has been having particularly severe academic difficulties. A call from a teacher about something positive a student has done generates good feelings toward the teacher and the school. Parents who receive this kind of a call or a brief letter with the same information often pass on this information to friends. Teachers who make an effort to contact parents to share the good news contribute greatly to the development of supportive community feelings toward the secondary schools.

Teachers also communicate with parents indirectly. At home, students often talk about what goes on at school. When parents hear about interesting things going on in the classroom and about teachers who seem to care about their children's progress, they develop positive attitudes toward the school.

Parents often see comments teachers write on student papers. Comments that are excessively negative or that feature numerous grammatical and spelling mistakes can undermine their confidence in the teacher (and the school). Secondary teachers need to understand that what they write on papers may be seen by others and that the nature of these comments can influence how the community at large views educators.

In summary, the public relations role teachers play centers on maintaining sincere, open, and personable relations with community members, particularly parents. Teachers' public relations role does not require the kind of slick packaging of messages that might impress a professional advertising executive. The teacher's responsibility is simply to act in ways that help community members to understand that educators are effectively meeting the intellectual and emotional needs of the school's clients, its students.

The Professional-Development Role

Professional development for teachers is a career-long obligation. Some states and school districts require teachers to take classes and participate in other professional growth opportunities to maintain their eligibility for continued employment. Even where these kinds of pressures are absent, teachers feel a need to augment what they already know about student development, instructional techniques, and subject-matter content.

Professional-development activities take many forms. Taking formal courses is an avenue many teachers choose. They enroll in these courses during summer terms as well as during the school year. During the school year, many colleges and universities offer classes for teachers in the evening. Many school districts offer special courses and programs of their own. Sometimes teachers and administrators from the sponsoring district who are especially familiar with topics that are treated serve as instructors. Because these learning experiences often are planned by individuals who know about the specific concerns of district teachers, content is often highly relevant to the needs of participants.

Participating in professional groups provides teachers with opportunities to extend their expertise. Local, regional, state, and national meetings of these organizations allow them to rub shoulders with others sharing similar interests and to attend sessions presented by leaders in the field. Meetings, too, often feature exhibits of outstanding new learning resources, including a range of materials from traditional texts to sophisticated electronic technologies, such as CD-ROM.

The following list includes names of some prominent professional organizations in education. You may wish to write to one or more of these groups regarding membership information, publications, annual meetings, and other services they provide. Many of these groups make reduced-rate memberships available to college and university students who are preparing to teach. Additional information about these groups, including mailing addresses, is provided in Chapter 20, "Professional Development."

- American Alliance for Health, Physical Education, Recreation, and Dance (AAHPERD)
- American Vocational Association (AVA)
- Association for Childhood Education International (ACEI)
- Council on Exceptional Children (CEC)

Box 2.3

Do All Teachers Need Additional Professional-Development Experiences?

Two teachers recently had this discussion:

TEACHER A
"I have been teaching 20 years. When I first started, I needed to take some more history courses to give me more background. Some of the inservice sessions on instructional techniques were helpful too. But now I don't really think I need more professional development. I can learn whatever I need from observing how students in my own classes react to my teaching and by making appropriate adjustments."

TEACHER B
"I think everybody needs professional development training, no matter how long they've been teaching. I've been teaching a long time

too, and I fear sometimes that I'm getting out of touch with new ideas. I know I can learn a lot from thinking about how my own students react to my instruction, but maybe there are some other things I should be learning about too."

What Do You Think?
1. How might the individual experiences of these two teachers have influenced their positions on this issue?

2. Compare and contrast strengths and weaknesses of the two teachers' arguments.

3. Suppose you were asked to make the strongest possible case in support of each position. Describe briefly what you would say.

- International Council for Computers in Education (ICCE)
- International Reading Association (IRA)
- Music Teachers National Association (MTNA)
- National Art Education Association (NAEA)
- National Association for Gifted Children (NAGC)
- National Council for the Social Studies (NCSS)
- National Council of Teachers of English (NCTE)
- National Council of Teachers of Mathematics (NCTM)
- National Science Teachers Association (NSTA)

Publications produced by these groups as well as many other publications of interest to teachers are referenced in the *Education Index*. This publication is found in many university, college, and public libraries. In addition to reading journal articles, many teachers read books on education-related topics. Scores of new ones appear each year.

There is a trend today for teachers to be assigned to somewhat different roles as they gain experience. For example, teachers who have been successful in the classroom, who work well with others, and who are believed to be up-to-date professionally may be selected to serve as department chairs. Responsibilities associated with this position involve coordinating teaching schedules, managing departmental budgets, handling purchase orders, distributing supplies, and facilitating cordial working relationships among faculty members in the department. To discharge these responsibilities, teachers must develop expertise that goes beyond what they had when they first entered the profession.

Other teachers are given special responsibilities for developing programs for student teachers and coordinating activities for them when they are in the schools. Still others are given important curriculum-development responsibilities. Because of the diverse array of potential assignments for teachers, a commitment to continuous personal professional development is implicit in a decision to become an educator.

Non-School Roles

Teachers have challenging and varied roles they must discharge as part of their responsibility as professional educators. They also have personal lives beyond the world of the school. Family obligations, political interests, social memberships, hobbies, and other activities compete for a share of teachers' out-of-school hours. Many of these activities require considerable time. Managing time to accommodate these out-of-school demands with obligations associated with their professional responsibilities as teachers is difficult. Many teachers experience stress, for example, when they have to make a choice between meeting the needs of family members and doing an adequate job of preparing for their classes (or working through a huge stack of student papers that need to be corrected and returned).

CASE STUDY

Now Everybody's Mad

Ruben Sanchez teaches four government classes and one U.S. history class at Walton Creek Senior High School. He has been teaching for four years. As an undergraduate, he developed a high interest in politics, and he was active in student government. This enthusiasm for public affairs has continued. He avidly follows local, state, and national political debates, and he stresses to his students the importance of getting involved.

Ruben's principal, Carmen Smith-Hill, strongly supports what Ruben is doing in the classroom. She applauds his commitment to develop graduates who will take their citizenship responsibilities seriously. During this past year, she has encouraged Ruben to volunteer his time to work on several local citizens' committees. She points out that this kind of work builds important public relations bridges to the community and, at the same time, gives him credibility in the classroom when he stresses the importance of involvement.

Early this fall, she asked Ruben to volunteer for a citizens commission looking into changes in local zoning ordinances. He agreed to do so, but now he is having some second thoughts about the wisdom of this decision. He recently shared these thoughts with one of his colleagues:

"These meetings are just killing me. I never realized zoning was such a hot potato. We have people wanting to get changes that will allow them to build gas stations in areas that are now restricted to residences. People living in those areas get up in meetings and scream at the gasoline people. They are even angrier at those of us on the Commission. They think we have 'sold out' to unnamed 'special interests' that are hellbent on destroying their neighborhoods. I feel that I'm alienating everybody. To make things worse, the group has started meeting twice a week, and some of the meetings go on to midnight. I'd like to get out of this mess, but I'm afraid I'll get on Ms. Smith-Hill's bad list if I do."

■ ■ ■

What should Ruben Sanchez do? Describe two or three alternative options. What are the likely results should he decide to follow each of your suggestions? Why is he so concerned about the reactions of the school principal? What might this suggest about relationships between teachers in this school? Are there some other people he might wish to consult before making a final decision? Has anyone you have known been caught in this kind of a situation? If so, how was it resolved? Specifically, what do you think you would do if you were faced with a similar dilemma?

Though time obligations associated with non-school activities can be heavy, there often are important benefits. For example, they afford opportunities for teachers to broaden the range of their acquaintances in the community. This gives them a better perspective on how non-educators see the world and makes them more sensitive to unique features of the local community. Additionally, teachers and school programs get more widely known and appreciated when teachers are seen actively participating in community affairs. This can generate positive attitudes toward the schools.

Teachers must strike a reasoned balance between responsibilities associated with the school and the responsibilities of out-of-school obligations. This balance point will vary depending on personal characteristics, family circumstances, interests, and other circumstances of the individual teacher. Most teachers work out ways of balancing their professional and personal obligations. This is not something that is overwhelmingly difficult to do, but newcomers need to be prepared to face the challenge of allocating their time in ways that are professionally responsible and personally satisfying.

Table 2.1   Summary Table

Main Points	Explanation
The Instructional Role	Delivery of instruction is teachers' most important responsibility. It involves a number of important planning tasks.
Diagnosing Students	This instructional planning task requires teachers to seek specific information about individual students. This information is used to plan learning activities well suited to individual student needs.
Developing Objectives	This instructional planning task seeks to specify in precise language what students should be able to demonstrate as a result of their exposure to instruction on a selected topic. The objectives provide a framework teachers use in selecting instructional techniques and in making assignments.
Choosing and Implementing Instructional Approaches	This phase of classroom instruction requires teachers to select specific instructional procedures from among available alternatives and to implement them in the classroom.
Evaluating Students' Progress	Evaluation tells teachers something about what each student has learned and about the general effectiveness of the instruction that has been provided.
The Counseling Role	Teachers often have intense interpersonal interactions with students. If an appropriate trust relationship has been established, students sometimes will seek advice from teachers about personal problems. In discharging the counseling function, teachers need to recognize the limits of their own expertise and know when to refer an individual student to a member of the school's professional counseling staff.
The Management Role	Teachers perform many managerial and administrative functions. They keep student records of all kinds, report attendance figures, file paperwork associated with requests for learning materials, supply information required by certain state and federal agencies, provide hall and library passes, and fill out forms referring individual students to counselors or administrators. Though many of these functions continue to be seen as tedious and time-consuming, technological aids such as personal computers are making some management tasks less burdensome.

Table 2.1   Summary Table *(continued)*

Main Points	Explanation
The Curriculum-Development Role	Teachers may be involved in curriculum-development activity at one or more levels. Some curriculum work goes on within the individual school. Other projects involve teachers from several schools and, sometimes, from the entire school district. Curriculum work tends to be done after school, on weekends, or during the summer months. Beginning teachers often do not have a great deal of academic preparation in curriculum development. Those who become interested in this area often take graduate-level courses in the subject.
The Public Relations Role	Teachers' actions can greatly influence attitudes of the general community toward its schools. It is particularly important that positive relationships be maintained with parents. Their comments tend to taken very seriously by others in the community. Teachers' communication with parents when their children have done good work can generate positive feelings toward teachers and the entire local educational program.
The Professional-Development Role	Professional development of teachers is a career-long enterprise. Teachers work to keep current and to expand their range of expertise by (1) taking formal college and university courses, (2) attending professional-development sessions sponsored by state education officials or local school districts, (3) participating in various professional groups, and (4) reading widely in the professional literature of education.
Non-School Roles	Teachers have important identities outside of their roles as professional educators. They have family responsibilities. They may have a variety of responsibilities due to their affiliations with religious, social, and fraternal organizations. They may have keen political interests. They may pursue certain hobbies and other avocational interests with great enthusiasm. Teachers must find ways to allocate their time in ways that a fair share is allocated to school-associated responsibilities and non-school obligations. There is no universal formula for doing this. Each teacher must work out an arrangement that satisfies both professional and personal needs.

Review of Key Ideas

- Teachers must play many roles as they discharge their responsibilities in the schools. Demands associated with each can be heavy. Competing demands require teachers to make decisions about how their professional and personal time should be spent.

- Teachers' most important responsibility in school centers around their instructional role. Some specific tasks associated with the instructional role include (1) diagnosing learners, (2) developing objectives, (3) choosing and implementing instructional approaches, and (4) evaluating students' progress.

- Teachers also play a counseling role. Students often seek their advice about personal as well as academic problems. Teachers who are particularly helpful in assisting students to work out solutions to their problems are good listeners who have an ability to see the world through the perspective of the student and to suggest workable alternatives to resolve difficulties. Most teachers lack the professional training to deal with particularly severe problems students may be experiencing. Most schools have professional counseling staffs who assist students with problems beyond the limits of teachers' expertise.

- Teachers also function as managers. They maintain student performance records of all kinds, including grades. They take care of attendance. They order and inventory supplies. They fill out special forms enabling students to be in the hallways while classes are in session, to go to the library, or to see a counselor or an administrator. They provide data to comply with important state and federal regulations. Today, computer programs can take the tedium out of some of these administrative tasks.

- Teachers also often do curriculum-development work. This may involve building-level projects or projects embracing teachers from several schools (or even the entire school district). Teachers who develop serious interests in curriculum making often take advanced course work in the subject. Graduate courses in curriculum development are a common feature of master's degree programs in education.

- Teachers play an important public relations role. Their actions can greatly affect how community members view the school and its programs. Positive relationships with parents are critical. Parents' reactions often greatly influence how others regard teachers and administrators. Some schools encourage teachers to write or telephone parents when their children have done something good. These kinds of contacts can generate much goodwill.

- Professional development is a career-long obligation of professional educators. It can take many forms. Teachers often take formal course work or attend workshops sponsored by local districts or state education agencies that are designed to increase their levels of expertise. Involvement in various professional organizations also provides opportunities for professional growth. Programs of professional reading are used by many teachers as a way of enriching their understanding of their chosen field.

- Out-of-school activities also demand attention from teachers. These are widely varied and include family obligations of all kinds, activities associated with religious groups, work with social and political organizations, and political activities of all kinds. These out-of-school activities are important. They can be powerful growth experiences, but, at the same time, they can be very time-consuming. Teachers must strike a reasoned balance between time allocated to school-related work and time allocated to important out-of-school obligations.

Follow-Up Questions and Activities

Questions

1. How important is the instructional role of teachers compared to other roles they play?

2. What are some examples of tasks teachers must accomplish as part of their instructional role?

3. What are some components of models or frameworks that have been developed that sequence instructional tasks?

4. Since many secondary schools have professional counselors on their staffs, why do teachers still have a counseling role of their own?

5. Why do large numbers of teachers dislike many of the managerial and administrative aspects of their jobs? Are there ways in which schools and school programs could be revised to reduce the amount of time teachers must spend on these tasks? What might stand in the way of any suggested changes you might like to make?

6. How is instruction differentiated from curriculum?

7. Presently, most teacher preparation programs place more emphasis on learning experiences related to instruction than to curriculum. Why is this so? Argue pluses and minuses of the tendency to emphasize instruction more than curriculum.

8. Public schools work hard to win the respect and support of the communities they serve. Why is this so important, and how can teachers become involved in the school's public relations activities?

9. Some people contend that a person who commits to a career in teaching at the same time commits to career-long professional development. Is this really true, or is this just a politically expedient statement designed to convince the public that teachers all work hard to keep up to date?

10. How can teachers' non-school roles interfere with their school-related obligations, and how can they resolve these potential conflicts? What kinds of time commitment should school districts reasonably demand of their teachers?

Activties

1. Observe a teacher in the classroom. Using either the Hunter-Russell model or the framework introduced by Denton, Armstrong, and Savage, take notes indicating specific kinds of instructional tasks the teacher accomplished. (Use labels included

in Hunter-Russell or in Denton, Armstrong, and Savage.) Approximately how much time was devoted to each task? Compare your findings with similar information gathered by others in your class. In general, do some of these instructional tasks appear to have consumed more time than others?

2. Invite several teachers to visit your class. Ask them to comment on the administrative or managerial tasks they must take care of as part of their job. How do they like the administrative or managerial part of teaching? Are there some tasks they simply wish they did not have to do? Do they use computers in any of their administrative or managerial work?

3. Interview a secondary school principal regarding his or her expectations of teachers in the area of public relations. Are there specific things teachers need to do? Are there particular public relations expectations of teachers who are new to the building? If so, what are they? Share your findings in an oral report to your class.

4. Interview several teachers about kinds of professional development opportunities that are open to them. Are some of these sponsored by the school district? Does the district require all teachers to attend periodic professional-development sessions? If so, what are the specific requirements? What college and university courses are offered for teachers during the evenings in the local area? Present your findings in a short paper.

5. Interview several secondary school teachers who are relatively new to the profession. Ask them about any problems they may have faced regarding balancing out-of-school obligations and their school-related responsibilities. How have they resolved these problems? Do these people have any advice to share with prospective teachers? Present your findings as part of your contribution to a general class discussion of the topic: "How teachers cope with important non-school obligations."

References

DENTON, J. J.; ARMSTRONG, D. G.; AND SAVAGE, T. V. "Matching Events of Instruction to Objectives." *Theory Into Practice* (Winter 1980), pp. 10–14.

GAGNÉ, R. M. AND BRIGGS, L. J. *Principles of Instructional Design.* New York: Holt, Rinehart & Winston, 1974.

GOOD, T. AND BROPHY, J. *Looking in Classrooms.* 5th ed. New York: Harper Collins, 1991.

HUNTER, M. AND RUSSELL, D. "How Can I Plan More Effective Lessons?" *Instructor* (September 1977), pp. 74–75, 88.

POSNER, G. "Pacing and Sequencing." In M. J. Dunkin (ed.). *The International Encyclopedia of Teaching and Teacher Education.* Oxford, England: Pergamon Press, 1987, pp. 266–272.

3

Teaching as Decision Making

AIMS

This chapter provides information to help the reader to:

- Explain the importance of decision making in teaching.
- Point out the importance for performance in the classroom of a teacher's pedagogical personality, pedagogical assumptions, and pedagogical repertoire.
- Describe strengths and weaknesses of various sources of information about effective teaching and learning.
- Point out characteristics of reflective practice.
- Explain some general approaches to stimulating students' interest in lessons and using students' contributions as lessons are taught.
- Distinguish between allocated time, engaged time, and academic learning time.
- Point out some way teachers can enhance the clarity of their presentations and establish an appropriate lesson pace.

FOCUS QUESTIONS

1. What is involved in becoming a successful teacher?
2. What is the role of practical experience in learning how to teach?
3. What place should theory and research play in teachers' decisions about instruction?
4. How do individuals' beliefs and biases influence their decisions?
5. In what ways do teachers' expectations of students influence the way they interact with students?
6. What might be done to increase the amount of academic learning time?
7. How should teachers react to students' contributions to lessons (answers to questions, comments on what has been said by the teacher, and so forth)?
8. How can lesson clarity be increased?
9. What can teachers do to model effective thinking processes?
10. Are test grades always a good form of feedback?

Introduction

"What do I need to know to be a successful teacher?" is a question prospective educators ask often. Even experts vary on the answers they give. For example, some argue that the most important ingredient of effective teaching is a solid grounding in academics. Others suggest that mastery of a wide variety of instructional approaches and effective classroom management skills are the twin keys to success. Still others point to the importance of a sensitive and caring teacher personality as the main ingredient for success in the classroom.

There are elements of truth in each response, but none adequately describes what teachers must do to achieve success. The "what" does not involve a simple prescribed set of "good" teacher behaviors. Characteristics of students, communities, schools, and even teachers themselves vary so widely that a common approach to the challenges of instruction has no chance of succeeding. The settings of practice and the personalities involved are simply too diverse. What *is* required of the effective teacher is a commitment to the view that difficult professional decisions have to be made in light of unique individual circumstances. Effective teaching above all requires good decision making abilities (Shavelson, 1973).

Decisions often must be made that respond to questions such as these:

- What should be taught?
- How should content be sequenced?

- How can content be tied to student interests and aptitudes?
- What instructional techniques will be most effective in a given situation?
- At what pace should instruction be delivered?
- What should be done if students don't understand?

Factors Influencing Instructional Decisions

Teachers' decisions are based on several categories of beliefs and understandings. Some of these are closely associated with their own convictions and personalities. Others relate to the store of information they have about teaching and learning. Still others stem from the degree of analysis or reflectivity they are willing to apply to their daily instruction.

Information About Self

What should teachers know about themselves? One authority who has investigated this question suggests these three categories (Millies, 1992):

- Pedagogical personality
- Pedagogical assumptions
- Pedagogical repertoire

The term *pedagogy* is a root word in each of these ideas. This is because the intent is to identify certain characteristics of an individual when he is engaged in the teacher's role. He may well display other behavior patterns outside of school when interacting with family members, friends, and others.

Pedagogical Personality
The *pedagogical personality* refers to a person's self-concept, confidence, and bias in terms of how these characteristics affect interactions with students. To gain an appreciation of one's own pedagogical personality, these questions might be asked: "What do I believe about myself and my abilities as a teacher?" "How well do I know my subject?" "How confident am I in my ability to control members of the class?" "What are my biases regarding what a teacher 'ought to be' like?"

Pedagogical Assumptions
The phrase *pedagogical assumptions* refers to the basic values and beliefs that guide an individual teacher's practices in the classroom. Questions that might be asked as part of a self-diagnostic exercise focused on this dimension might include: "What is the purpose of education?" "What do I believe about teaching?" "How do I feel about students

from different social, economic, and ethnic groups?" "What learning principles are most important and should guide my instruction?" Answers to these questions help shape how an individual teacher organizes for instruction and interacts with students.

Pedagogical Repertoire

The term *pedagogical repertoire* refers to an individual teacher's knowledge of and appreciation for alternative approaches to managing students and introducing content. Questions such as these provide insights to an individual teacher regarding the extent of her pedagogical repertoire: "What are the best approaches to managing students in the classroom?" "What alternatives are available to me to teach this content?" "In which instructional approaches do I have the most confidence?" "What are some of my ideas for motivating members of this class?" "With which instructional techniques am I not comfortable?" "Of the instructional approaches I know and value, which one (or ones) make the most sense given what I must do next?"

■ ■ ■

The act of answering questions associated with pedagogical personality, pedagogical assumptions, and pedagogical repertoire can help individual teachers think through alternative approaches to teaching specific content to specific students. Thinking about possible responses prompts teachers to challenge their assumptions and think carefully about choices when several options seem to have promise. The hope is that, over time, this process will broaden their willingness to try new things. Problems some teachers face result because the untested assumptions they hold prevent them from choosing potentially successful instructional and management approaches.

Information About Teaching and Learning

In addition to knowledge about themselves, teachers need to know about basic principles of teaching and learning. Teachers who consistently provide sound instruction do so because they make informed instructional decisions. There are several sources of information about this kind of professional knowledge; one source is past experiences of successful teachers.

These experiences sometimes can be learned through direct consultation with a successful teacher. Often this happens to beginners when they are paired with especially good teachers for student teaching. Another source of this kind of information is collections of case studies or self-reports of teachers. One particularly good title of this sort is *Teacher Lore: Learning From Our Own Experiences* (Schubert and Ayers, 1992).

There are problems with relying *only* on professional judgment as a source of professional knowledge about teaching. For example, some outstanding teachers have developed patterns gradually over the years that have become so embedded in their own personalities that they are unable to describe to others what they do. In response

Box 3.1

Identifying Effective Teachers

Recall some teachers you had in middle school, junior high school, or senior high school. What were some characteristics of the best ones you had? Think about this issue as you respond to these questions.

What Do You Think?

1. What are two or three things about these teachers that stand out?

2. How do you think these people would respond to this question: "What makes a teacher successful?"

3. What kind of relationships did these teachers have with students, and how did they establish these relationships?

4. What sorts of teaching approaches did these people use?

5. How did they handle management and discipline problems?

6. Was your interest in becoming a teacher influenced by any of these people? If so, how?

7. Would you like to follow the teaching patterns used by any of these people? If so, which ones, and why?

---

to a "why did you do that?" kind of question, they may just respond, "I can't really tell you; it just felt right."

Another obvious limitation on professional judgment as a source of information is that teachers have very different personalities and styles. Something that works splendidly for one person may be a disaster when someone else tries it.

Finally, professional judgment sometimes is just plain wrong. Behaviors that may seem right to a given individual and that may even have a lot of intuitive logic behind them may be undesirable. For example, common sense would seem to dictate that the more praise a teacher gives to a student, the better that student's academic performance might be. Researchers have found that this is not true. In fact, praise that is not tied clearly to a specific correct accomplishment with a given academic task may have little or no impact on students' learning (Good and Brophy, 1991; Levin and Long, 1981).

Learning theory is another source of information about teaching and learning. Individual learning theories explain relations among variables in the teaching-learning process. Thinking about the implications of a given learning theory for a particular instructional problem sometimes helps teachers develop a feel for what might work.

However, learning theory is not always as helpful as one might suppose. The theories themselves are grounded on a tremendous volume of research and analysis. They attempt to frame general principles that are consistent with this scholarly work. However, they make no guarantees that these general principles provide guidelines that will fit *every* instructional situation. Hence, it is quite possible that some instructional approaches that are completely compatible with a given learning theory will not produce expected results.

Individual research studies represent another source of information about teaching. There has been an enormous increase in research focuses on classroom instruction over the past two decades. Organizations such as the American Educational Research Association publish reviews of research in specific areas. One journal that sums up great quantities of research on topics of interest to teachers in each issue is the *Review of Educational Research*. It is available in most university libraries and many public libraries.

Regrettably, research rarely speaks with a unitary voice on a given issue. It is not uncommon for several studies of the same question to come up with quite different results. Beginning teachers need to beware of the phrase "Research says." Research rarely "says" just one thing. It is important to know how much research has been done and what the general trend of the findings is. (Generally, a trend is all that can be hoped for. All studies of a given question almost never yield common results.)

This teacher considers previous experience with a similar lesson as a new lesson plan is developed. This kind of reflection often results in instruction leading to improved student performance.

Reflective Practice

The actual act of teaching, itself, can be a powerful teacher. To be useful as a vehicle for promoting additional professional growth, teaching must be reflective. This means that the teacher must think about what he did with a view to analyzing what worked well and what did not. This kind of reflection can lead to improved instruction (Reynolds, 1992). Reflective teachers seek answers to questions such as: "What accounted for the interest students had in parts of this lesson?" "What could I do to interest them in areas that did not 'turn them on'?" "What made the overall lesson successful (or unsuccessful)?" "If I had an opportunity to teach this lesson again, what would I change?"

When reflecting on lessons, effective teachers focus on different things than ineffective teachers. They tend to concentrate on issues associated with student understanding; less competent teachers are apt to think back more on superficial events that occurred during the lesson (Reynolds, 1992).

Reflective teaching takes time. James Henderson (1992), a leading proponent of this approach, points out that good reflection takes the form of a spirited internal debate. It involves considering strengths and weaknesses of alternative instructional techniques. This kind of analysis is sometimes referred to as a constructivist approach to teaching. The central idea here is that the teacher creates, or constructs, her own approach to teaching by considering personal experience, alternative instructional approaches, the unique features of the individual classroom, formal learning theories, and various philosophies of education.

Using Research-on-Teaching Findings

Information in this section has been divided into these five categories:

- Beliefs about students
- Stimulating student interest
- Using student contributions
- Making wise use of time
- Presenting good lessons

Beliefs About Students

The most important variable teachers work with is student characteristics. It makes no sense to plan instruction without good information about the backgrounds, abilities, interests, and general behavior patterns of students. Decisions teachers make in response to their views of students and student abilities greatly influence the overall impact of their instruction.

Some researchers suggest that teachers' most important beliefs about students concern why students behave as they do. Teachers' expectations of individual students are strongly tied to their beliefs about what students can do (Good and Brophy, 1991). Students for whom teachers have high expectations tend to achieve more than students for whom expectations are lower.

Teachers have been found to form their expectations of students based on their analysis of several key variables. Among these are student appearance, intelligence and achievement test scores, student behavior, and, sometimes, even on how students' older brothers and sisters have done in school (Braun, 1987).

These perceptions often result in patterns of teacher behavior toward some students that do not facilitate the maximum personal development of some class members. Braun (1987) has described a cycle of behavior that teachers often develop as a result of their beliefs about what individual students can do.

1. The teacher establishes a level of expectations for a student based on what he believes to be true of this individual.

2. Student behaviors are interpreted in light of these expectations.

3. As a result of how the teacher reacts, the student begins to develop a self-concept that is consistent with the teacher's beliefs about her.

4. As a result, the student's performance begins to reflect the teacher's expectation. This means students for whom the teacher has higher expectations do well, and students for whom the teacher has lower expectations do poorly.

Abundant research evidence supports the idea that certain kinds of teacher beliefs about students result in specific patterns of teacher behavior. Researchers Jere Brophy and Thomas Good (1986) have gathered together many of these studies. Some of the following patterns are consistent with research results in this area (Brophy and Good, 1986):

- Teachers are less responsive to students for whom they hold low expectations. They smile less and have less eye contact with these students. They provide these students with fewer signals to tell them they are doing well.

- Teachers call on learners less when they hold low expectations for them.

- Teachers provide less corrective feedback to low-expectation students than to high-expectation students.

- Teachers wait a shorter period of time for students for whom they hold low expectations to respond to questions than for students for whom they hold high expectations.

- Teachers criticize students for whom they hold low expectations more than students for whom they hold high expectations.

- High-expectation students receive more teacher praise than low-expectation students.

Box 3.2

Have a Teacher's Expectations Ever Influenced You?

Teachers' expectations for students sometimes are more obvious to the students than to the teacher. Without realizing they are doing so, teachers sometimes communicate to some students that they have little confidence in their abilities. At the same time, teachers may communicate to others that they expect great academic work for them. Reflect on some of your own experiences as a secondary school student as you respond to these questions.

What Do You Think?

1. Can you recall times when a teacher's behavior prompted you to do more? To do less? What happened in each case?

2. Do you recall any students who could have done better work but were "turned off" by what they perceived to be a lack of teacher confidence in their abilities?

3. If you remember times when teachers seemed to have preconceived notions about what individuals could do, how do you think these teachers got these ideas?

- More drill and practice activities are provided to low-expectation than to high-expectation students. Lessons, generally, have more interesting features when the audience consists of high-expectation students.

- Teachers give the benefit of the doubt when there is some question about the accuracy of a student's answer when he is a high-expectation rather than a low-expectation student.

How should teachers deal with the possibility that their perceptions of individual students are affecting their patterns of teacher-learner interaction? There is no easy answer. It is human nature to make certain inferences about others. However, self-monitoring efforts can help teachers to check on the accuracy of these inferences and assure that they are not prompting irresponsible patterns of behavior. Periodic efforts to take stock of what is going on often are helpful. As part of their reflection about how they are interacting with students, many teachers think seriously about any biases they might have that are resulting in unproductive patterns of working with certain individuals.

Stimulating Student Interest

Disinterested students tend to misbehave and disrupt learning of others. The key to prompting student interest, according to theorist James Henderson (1992), is to plan learning experiences that connect students' past experiences and views regarding what is important to the school curriculum. This implies a need for teachers to know their students well. They also must know their subject matter well enough so they can adapt and explain it to students in an understandable way (Reynolds, 1992).

WHAT SCHOLARS SAY

How Important Is Subject-Matter Knowledge?

Researchers have confirmed that knowledge of the subjects they teach is an important characteristic of effective beginning teachers. Interestingly, what seems to make a difference is not a general knowledge of the subject, but the particular nature of the teacher's understanding of and orientation toward her specialty area.

Individuals who have a great store of factual information related to their subjects and who simply provide these details one after the other to students do not communicate effectively. More successful teachers seem to have a depth and clarity of understanding of their subjects that gives them insights into possible problems students might have in mastering content.

They are able to provide students with many examples, to use appropriate analogies, and to connect information to students' lives in ways that differ from less successful teachers. These teachers know the major themes and principles that tie together vast quantities of information in their subject areas, and they are able to plan lessons in light of these broad understandings. They tend to view the purpose of instruction as helping students to grasp the key generalizations or findings of their disciplines. This planning helps them convey to students a purpose for learning the content that goes beyond the need for them to master isolated fragments of information.

Source: A. Reynolds. "What is Competent Beginning Teaching?" *Review of Educational Research* (Spring, 1992). *62*, pp. 1–35.

In planning for motivation, it is important to remember that it does not only occur at a lesson's beginning. Effective teachers plan for motivation during three distinct phases of a lesson: (1) at the beginning, (2) as the new material is introduced, and (3) at the conclusion of the lesson.

Motivation often results when students' curiosity is aroused. Frequently this happens when they are introduced to something unique or novel (at least unique or novel to them). Sometimes students react positively to information regarding the personal importance of mastering content that is about to be introduced. Variety during the lesson also tends to prompt continued student interest. The same can be said for encouragement and praise from the teacher.

Many effective teachers are careful to take time at the end of a lesson to highlight what students have learned. This practice gives students more self-confidence as they realize they have encountered and understood substantial amounts of new material. Feelings of success and accomplishment tend to build students' levels of self-esteem. As a result, they become more highly motivated to study material introduced in subsequent lessons.

Additional information related to motivation is introduced in Chapter 13, "Direct Instruction."

"Like you, Mr. Burbank, I am convinced that humor can be a valuable motivational tool in teaching. However ..."

Using Student Contributions

How should the teacher use student contributions? No answer to this question fits every occasion. Much depends on the specifics of the situation. The key principle is that the reaction to the student's contribution should encourage continued student participation, provide appropriate feedback to the student, and, at the same time, assure that the central focus of the lesson is not lost (Emmer, Evertson, Sanford, Clements, and Worsham, 1989).

When should the teacher challenge students' ideas? In general, if a challenge to a student's idea will cause this person to do more thinking about the issue and develop more sophisticated reasoning skills, the challenge may make sense. However, if the student is likely to see the challenge as a "put down" by the teacher, little good will come of it, and another approach ought to be considered. If a challenge is deemed appropriate, it is important that it be delivered in a tone of language that implies, "I may disagree with what you have said, but I still think highly of you as a person."

Making Wise Use of Time

Time available for instruction is limited. As a result, there is a need to use it wisely. It is particularly important that sufficient time be allocated for students to work on academic tasks. Unless teachers plan carefully, administrative tasks such as roll taking, distributing and collecting materials, and making announcements can significantly reduce the time students spend learning. A reduction in learning time, not surprisingly, results in reduced levels of academic performance (Good and Brophy, 1991). Careful planning of administrative tasks that saves even a few minutes each day can provide a teacher with many additional hours of instructional time over an entire academic year.

Time decisions teachers make can be sorted into three distinct categories. They are:

- Allocated time
- Engaged time
- Academic learning time

Allocated Time

Allocated time refers to the amount of time the teacher sets aside for students to learn specific material. Researchers have found that different teachers allocate very different quantities of time for teaching the same content (Good and Brophy, 1991). Why is this so? In part, these differences result from class-to-class differences in students. Interestingly, another determinant seems to be the teacher's personal interest in and feelings of competence with the topic being taught. Teachers tend to allocate more instructional time to topics they like and about which they believe themselves to be particularly well informed.

It is possible that some students may be educationally disadvantaged by time allocation decisions based on teachers' personal preferences. Properly, allocation decisions also need to consider the relative importance of a given topic in the context of the major aims of the course. Time provided for each topic needs to be sufficiently long to allow students to learn the material, but not so long that they become bored and motivation becomes a problem.

Engaged Time

Just because a teacher allocates a given amount of time for students to work on an assigned task does not guarantee they will do so. The term *engaged time* refers to that proportion of allocated time when students are actually studying assigned material. There are great classroom-to-classroom differences in proportions of engaged time (Good and

Box 3.3

Was Your Development Hindered Because of Insufficient Opportunity to Learn?

Researchers have found that teachers tend to spend more time on parts of their subjects that are of particular interest to them. For example, teachers who are Civil War buffs may spend weeks on this topic, but perhaps only a few days on the Great Depression. An English teacher who enjoys Melville may devote much more class time to his works than to those of Hemingway, Cather, or Oates. As a result, in later years some students find they have only a minimal understanding of content about which they wish they knew more.

What Do You Think?

1. Were there times when your teachers spent too much time on topics that interested them at the expense of covering other material well? Has the lack of attention to some topics ever caused a problem for you?

2. How do you react to the view that it is better for teachers to spend time on topics they like because they are most likely to motivate student interest in these topics?

3. What ideas do you have regarding providing students with genuine opportunities to learn all critical components of subjects you will be teaching?

Brophy, 1991). In general, teachers seek to increase the total engaged time. More engaged time correlates with more student learning (Berliner, 1984). Engaged time can be increased when teachers are well organized and attend efficiently to tasks such as roll taking, clear explanations of assignments, and monitoring students as they work.

Academic Learning Time

Academic learning time is that portion of engaged time when students are not only working on the assigned task but are experiencing success. Research has found that academic achievement is associated with an increase in academic learning time (Berliner, 1984). Teachers who are interested in increasing academic learning time must know their students very well. Assignments must be provided that are well matched to students' prior levels of knowledge, aptitude, and (to the extent possible) interests. Careful monitoring of students to assist them with problems is also important (Reynolds, 1992). When problems are spotted, the teacher needs to reteach part of the lesson, modify it, or otherwise take action to assure that student learning gets back on track.

Presenting Good Lessons

Good planning is a hallmark of the effective secondary teachers. Well-planned lessons feature clarity, variety, good modeling of appropriate practice, feedback to students, and appropriate pacing.

Clarity

Clarity implies a clear and precise use of language and a presentation style that moves logically and smoothly from point to point. There are many threats to clarity. Among them are teacher use of vague and ambiguous terms.

Vague terms fall into a limited number of categories. These include: (1) approximations (*about, sort of, roughly*, and so forth), (2) probability statements (*frequently, generally, often*, and so forth), (3) possibility statements (*chances are, could be, maybe*, and so forth), and (4) bluffing (*everybody knows, it's a long story*, and so forth).

These phrases have become so much a part of our ordinary speech that they cannot be eliminated entirely. However, overuse of these statements can cause confusion. Students' understanding is enhanced by more specific terms and phrases. For example, the phrase "20 years ago" communicates much more effectively than "some time ago."

Clarity can also be undermined by teachers who use false starts and verbal mazes. False starts are lessons that a teacher starts, gets diverted, and then starts again. Teachers who do this too often find students fail to pay close attention when a lesson is first begun. They have learned that the teacher will be going over the same material a second time.

Verbal mazes are teacher explanations that fail to communicate information in a clear, concise manner. Sometimes information provided fails to tie meaningfully to other things the teacher has said (at least no tie is evident in the minds of students). Most secondary students find it very difficult to sort coherent meaning from a teacher presentation that follows an excessively meandering course. They do far better when information moves smoothly from point to point and when the teacher pauses periodically to highlight key ideas.

Digressions are another threat to clarity. Teachers sometimes have attempted to insert high-interest digressions into their lessons as a means of capturing student interest. Some research evidence suggests that this practice fails to have the intended effect and actually can reduce what students otherwise would learn (Hidi, 1990).

Clarity can be enhanced through the use of advance organizers. An advance organizer basically is a brief overview or organization of important content to be presented. It provides students with a map they can follow as a lesson progresses. In addition, it gives them a way to pinpoint key points and to relate them to previously learned information.

Internal summaries also enhance clarity of lesson presentation. These are nothing more than stopping points during a lesson where the teacher pauses to recapitulate what has already been covered. These summaries help students to focus on key points and to see interrelationships among important ideas.

Marker expressions draw students' attention to important ideas. These are verbal cues the teacher makes to help students appreciate the importance of what is to follow. These are some examples: "This is important." "Write this down." "I want you to remember this." "Listen carefully to this point."

Clarity is improved when teachers' lessons feature a well-organized conclusion. This kind of a conclusion summarizes what has been covered and draws particular attention to important ideas. Key content often is repeated briefly during this summary, and this repetition aids student learning.

Enhancing Student Achievement

Student achievement generally improves when teachers provide appropriate feedback. This kind of feedback communicates information about the appropriateness or correctness of their responses. Feedback information helps students avoid errors and focus on important dimensions of content.

Praise is often used as part of feedback. Researchers have found that effective praise is specific and genuine. Further, it must be used in moderation (Good and Brophy, 1991). The term *specificity*, as applied to appropriate use of praise, means that students should be told precisely what they did that was praiseworthy. Further, the praiseworthy behavior should relate to content to be learned. If the teacher gives general praise that has no clear connection to a desirable academics-related behavior, it tends to have little impact on student performance.

Criticism also has its place when teachers provide feedback to students. Proper criticism focuses on helping a student resolve an academic difficulty. It is designed not simply to indicate student errors, but rather to suggest appropriate ways of correcting mistakes. Good criticism never demeans students as people. It focuses on enhancing their self-esteem by helping them to master content.

Grades on student work are also a form of feedback. However, they often are not as effective as some other approaches. One reason for this is that grades tend to represent a summary judgment over a considerable quantity of student work. Hence, they do not provide very specific information to a student about exactly what he or she has done that was either "well done," "average," or "poorly done." Written teacher comments that accompany letter grades often provide much more useful feedback information for students. These comments help them understand why a grade was awarded and focus their attention on how well they have mastered certain elements of content.

Providing a model for learners during a lesson improves student performance. There are many kinds of models teachers can supply. For example, a teacher's personal enthusiasm for a topic often is "catching" and tends to enhance students' interest. Many effective teachers are also good at modeling thinking processes that are appropriate for a particular task. These teachers often solve a problem similar to ones the students will be asked to do by thinking out loud with members of the class. ("Now if I found myself faced with this situation, the first thing I would look at would be. . . . Next, I would compare _____ and _____. If they seemed consistent, I probably would decide to. . . .")

In addition to thinking through an approach to a problem with a class, effective teachers sometimes find it useful to develop an example of a product of learning similar to what is expected of students. For example, if a group of students is expected to write a short paper comparing and contrasting positions of two individuals, the teacher might prepare a sample of such a paper. When making the assignment to the students, this material could be shared, and attention of class members could be drawn to various features the teacher would like to see included in the papers to be produced by students. An example of this kind greatly reduces the possibility students will fail to understand what the teacher expects of them.

Table 3.1   Summary Table

Main Points	Explanation
Teaching as Decision Making	Teaching cannot be reduced to a series of prescriptions or sure-fire formulas. It requires teachers to monitor what they do, to think about unique features of their instructional circumstances, to analyze options, and to make carefully reasoned choices.
Factors Influencing Instructional Decisions	
Information About Self	Teachers' personal beliefs and biases influence how they interact with students. It is important for teachers to develop an awareness of their personal perspectives and an appreciation for how they influence instructional decisions.
Pedagogical Assumptions	Teachers' educational philosophies and views of the learning process influence their instructional decisions. The nature of this influence is best appreciated by teachers who take time to reflect on the nature of their pedagogical assumptions.
Pedagogical Repertoire	The total number of instructional approaches an individual teacher knows well enough to implement in the classroom constitutes his or her pedagogical repertoire. Knowing a variety of techniques can increase options available to teachers as they attempt to respond to students' needs.
Information About Teaching and Learning	One source is experience of other teachers. A problem with this source is that conditions vary from setting to setting, and there are also profound differences in personalities of individual teachers. Hence, experiences of one person may not provide useful information to a teacher working in another setting. Learning theory also provides some guidance. However, learning theory rarely provides highly specific sets of guidelines pertinent to a specific instructional setting. Findings from the research also provide potentially useful information. However, such findings often hint at what happens most of the time; they rarely claim a specific procedure will succeed with every teacher in every classroom environment.
Reflective Practice	Reflective practice refers to teaching that is guided by careful thought about strengths and weaknesses of previous lessons, about the purposes to be achieved in a new lesson, about available learning materials, and about students' existing levels of expertise and motivation. Highly effective reflective teachers think intensively about which aspects of their instruction most affected student learning. The intended outcome of this kind of reflection is a lesson that responds to students' needs, interests them, and conveys content that they master.

Main Points	Explanation
Beliefs About Students	Teachers' beliefs about students affect how they interact with individuals in their classes and how much individual students learn. Students whom teachers expect to learn more *do* learn more than students for whom teachers hold lower expectations.
Stimulating Student Interest	A key to prompting interest is tying new learning to students' past experiences. Motivational experiences ought to be planned and delivered (1) at the beginning of a lesson, (2) as the body of the lesson is being taught, and (3) at the conclusion of the lesson.
Using Student Contributions	The guideline in this area is that the teacher's reaction to a student contribution should (1) encourage the individual's continued participation, (2) provide appropriate feedback to the student about what she has said, and (3) maintain a focus on the central theme of the lesson.
Making Wise Use of Time	Time is a scarce commodity in the classroom. It is particularly important that administrative and management duties do not detract unnecessarily from the total time for instruction.
Allocated Time	Allocated time is the total time the teacher sets aside for students to learn specific material.
Engaged Time	Engaged time is the amount of allocated time when students are actually working on an assigned task.
Academic Learning Time	Academic learning time is the part of engaged time when students are both working on the assigned task and mastering the material they have been asked to learn.
Presenting Good Lessons	
Clarity	Clarity implies an instructional style featuring precise use of language and an organization that features smooth point-to-point transitions. It involves use of precise terminology ("12 years ago," *not* "some time ago"). Clarity is enhanced when teachers avoid false starts (beginning a lesson, getting diverted, then beginning again) and verbal mazes (rambling discourse that gives students little sense of direction). Advance organizers (statements that cue students to categories of information to be covered), internal summaries (pauses to recapitulate what has been covered and to highlight key points), and use of marker expressions (phrases that cue students to pay attention to special points) enhance the overall clarity of a presentation.

Table 3.1   Summary Table *(continued)*

Main Points	Explanation
Presenting Good Lessons, *cont'd.*	
Enhancing Student Achievement	Achievement tends to improve when teachers provide students with appropriate feedback. This kind of feedback speaks with great specificity about the adequacy of the students' performance. It does *not* consist of vague statements that fail to provide students either with a clear idea of what they have done well or failed to do well. Teacher modeling of expectations also helps students do better. Grades have only limited effects on achievement because they tend to summarize work over a broad area and often fail to cue students to specific things they might do to improve.
Lesson Pacing	Researchers have found that lessons should move at a fairly brisk pace. In general, they should move along as fast as possible, consistent with students' ability to learn. Pacing should vary depending on the nature of the content being covered, the adequacy of the materials available to support instruction, and the abilities of students in the class.

Lesson Pacing

Researchers have found that lessons should move at a brisk pace, but a pace that is accompanied by high levels of student understanding (Good and Brophy, 1991). This does not mean effective teachers race to cover the material. Rather, they move along as quickly as possible given the abilities of students to keep up and profit from the provided instruction.

Pacing decisions place heavy demands on teachers. They must be made at the same time a lesson is being taught. This requires teachers to monitor student understanding closely to assure that students are grasping the new material. Many teachers find it useful to pause frequently to ask questions. This allows them to make quick judgments about how well students are following the instruction.

Review of Key Ideas

- Decision making is an essential ingredient of teaching. Teaching is a complex act. It cannot be reduced to formulaic prescriptions that are passed on to newcomers to the profession with the assurance that "these things are guaranteed to work." Teachers must reflect on many variables to make sound instructional decisions that effectively promote student learning.

- Teachers' decisions are influenced strongly by their own personalities, biases, and general world views. It is important that teachers develop an awareness of their own personal perspectives. Such an awareness helps them to avoid making decisions that are too strongly tied to personal biases and that, in some cases, may not be best for students.

- Researchers have found an important connection between teachers' expectations of students and students' levels of performance. In general, students do better when teachers hold higher expectations for them.

- Teachers gather information for decision making from many sources. Personal experiences of other teachers may provide some useful information, but because of differences in individual teacher personalities, in students to be served, and in other variables, these experiences may not be useful to other teachers. Learning theory offers some guidance. However, principles derived from learning theory may not be applicable in every instructional situation. Individual research studies also provide some useful information. Again, studies may yield insights that are not universally applicable.

- Relating the school curriculum to students' needs and interests enhances students' levels of interest. Ideally, motivational activities should occur during three distinct phases of a given lesson: the beginning, as new information is presented, and at the end.

- Researchers have found that using student ideas during a lesson helps to maintain student interest and involvement. Ideally, the teacher should react to students in ways that (1) encourage their continued participation, (2) provide them with appropriate feedback, and (3) help them maintain a focus on the central content of the lesson.

- Effective teachers manage time wisely. It is particularly important to maximize the amount of classroom time actually devoted to instruction. Researchers who have looked at the issue of teachers' use of time have identified three important time concepts. Allocated time refers to time set aside for instruction. Engaged time refers to time when students are actually working on an assigned task. Academic learning time is time when students are both working on an assigned task and experiencing success. Increases in academic learning time tend to correlate with improved achievement levels.

- Good lessons do not happen by accident. They tend to feature recurring patterns of effective teacher behavior. These include teacher (1) efforts to assure clarity of communication, (2) attempts to enhance student achievement through provision of appropriate feedback and modeling, and (3) attention to establishing an appropriate lesson pace.

Follow-Up Questions and Activities

Questions

1. What general kinds of questions do teachers face as they seek to make responsible instructional decisions?

2. What is pedagogical personality, and how can it influence a teacher's behavior in the classroom?

3. What are strengths and weaknesses of various sources of information about effective instructional practices that are available to teachers?

4. How would you define reflective teaching, and why is it important?

5. In what ways do teachers' beliefs about students affect levels of student performance?

6. At what points during a lesson should the teacher take specific action to motivate students?

7. How would you distinguish among the terms *allocated time, engaged time*, and *academic learning time*, and what is the general importance of teachers' decisions regarding how time is used?

8. Why is clarity important as lessons are presented, and what can teachers do to enhance their clarity?

9. Some people argue that the more praise teachers give students, the better. Do you agree? Why or why not?

10. Why is lesson pacing important, and what can teachers do to establish an appropriate pace?

Activities

1. Several books have been compiled that relate teachers' classroom experiences. One good one is *Teacher Lore: Learning From Our Own Experiences* (Schubert and Ayers, 1992). Read several teachers' accounts from *Teacher Lore* or another source. Based on what you have read, what are some things you will want to consider as you go about the business of making decisions in your own classroom? Share your ideas with others as part of a general class discussion.

2. Prepare a personal inventory of your own assumptions about effective teaching approaches. Share your list with others. Ask for some reaction from your instructor regarding how your assumptions square with findings reported in the effective-teaching research literature.

3. Locate a research article in a professional journal that reports results of an investigation focusing on the relative effectiveness of a given instructional approach. Based on the results (and assuming other studies confirmed them), what kinds of things should teachers be doing in the classroom?

4. Teach and videotape a lesson you present to other students. Review the lesson privately. Identify aspects of your presentation that you think could have been done better. Prepare a written summary explaining precisely what you would do another time to improve your overall presentation.

5. During an observation in a secondary school classroom, keep track of the percentage of total class time that is devoted to instruction focusing on academic content. What is going on when actual instruction is not taking place? Of time devoted to

instruction, how much time would you judge is engaged time and how much is academic learning time? What might have been done to increase the amounts of both of these time categories? Prepare a short written report for your instructor.

References

BERLINER, D. C. "The Half-Full Glass: A Review of Research on Teaching." In P. L. Hosford (ed.). *Using What We Know About Teaching*. Alexandria, VA: Association for Supervision and Curriculum Development, 1984, pp. 51–77.

BRAUN, C. "Teachers' Expectations." In M. Dunkin (ed.). *The International Encyclopedia of Teaching and Teacher Education*. New York: Pergamon Press, 1987, pp. 598–605.

BROPHY, J. AND GOOD, T. "Teacher Behavior and Student Achievement." In M. C. Wittrock (ed.). *Handbook of Research on Teaching*. 3rd ed. New York: Macmillan Publishing Company, 1986, pp. 328–375.

EMMER, E.; EVERTSON, C.; SANFORD, J.; CLEMENTS, B.; AND WORSHAM, M. *Classroom Management for Secondary Teachers*. Englewood Cliffs, NJ: Prentice Hall, 1989.

GOOD, T. AND BROPHY, J. *Looking in Classrooms*. 5th ed. New York: HarperCollins, 1991.

HENDERSON, J. G. *Becoming an Inquiring Teacher: A Caring Approach to Problem Solving*. New York: Macmillan Publishing Company, 1992.

HIDI, S. "Interest and Its Contribution as a Mental Resource for Learning." *Review of Educational Research* (Winter 1990). *60*, pp. 549–571.

LEVIN, T. AND LONG, R. *Effective Instruction*. Alexandria, VA: Association for Supervision and Curriculum Development, 1981.

MILLIES, P. "The Relationship Between a Teacher's Life and Teaching." In W. Schubert and W. Ayers (eds.). *Teacher Lore: Learning from our Own Experience*. New York: Longman, 1992, pp. 25–42.

REYNOLDS, A. "What is Competent Teaching?" *Review of Educational Research* (Spring 1992), 62, pp. 1–35.

SCHUBERT, W. H. AND AYERS, W. C. (EDS.). *Teacher Lore: Learning From Our Own Experiences*. New York: Longman, 1992.

SHAVELSON, R. *The Basic Teaching Skill: Decision Making*. R & D Memorandum No. 104. Stanford, CA: Center for R&D in Teaching, School of Education, Stanford University, 1973.

II

Planning

Researchers have found that careful attention to instructional planning is particularly important for preservice and beginning teachers (Good and Brophy, 1991). Newcomers profit from planning that requires them to clearly delineate purposes of their instruction, identify techniques to be used in working with students, and lay out step-by-step development of lessons. The process of planning helps them develop a structure that they can use to deliver organized, purposeful instruction.

On the other hand, efforts to plan instruction should not be overdone. The intent is not to prepare a rigid script for the class that will result in mechanistic lessons that lack even a hint of spontaneity (Good and Brophy, 1991). The idea is for planners to arrive at a well-defined general view regarding how lessons will unfold and what kinds of interactions with students will be featured.

More experienced teachers do not find it necessary to do so much formal planning. Years of working with subject matter content and students have helped them internalize ways to deliver purposeful, organized, and responsive instruction. Many experienced teachers do automatically what beginning teachers must consciously think about as they prepare formal instructional plans.

Part 2 answers questions people often have about planning concerns that are relevant for beginning secondary school teachers. Among these questions are:

- How are content-selection decisions made?
- What are some guidelines for preparing objectives?
- How can lessons and units be formatted?
- How can the special needs of students from diverse ethnic and cultural backgrounds be met?
- What are some considerations in planning for students with different kinds of disabilities?

Discussion related to these questions is introduced in five chapters:

Chapter 4: Content Selection and Organization
Chapter 5: Writing Objectives

Chapter 6: Preparing Units and Lessons

Chapter 7: Preparing for the Multicultural Classroom

Chapter 8: Planning for Exceptional Students

Reference

GOOD, T. AND BROPHY, J. *Looking in Classrooms*. 5th ed. New York: HarperCollins, 1991.

4

Content Selection and Organization

AIMS

This chapter provides information to help the reader to:

- Describe teachers' content-selection role.
- Identify the influence of textbooks on teachers' content selection.
- Point out how state and district curriculum guides and policies influence teachers' content-selection decisions.
- Distinguish between content breadth and content depth.
- Differentiate among facts, concepts, and generalizations.
- Point out some things that teachers must consider when they attempt to match students and the curriculum.
- Identify several ways content can be sequenced.

FOCUS QUESTIONS

1. How involved are individual teachers in selecting the content they teach?

2. What influence on teachers' content-selection decisions should textbooks and curriculum guides have?

3. What is the structure of knowledge, and how does it affect instructional decisions?

4. What criteria should be used in deciding what facts should be taught?

5. How are concepts defined?

6. What is the importance of generalizations and principles in teachers' content-selection decisions?

7. How do standardized tests influence teachers' content-selection decisions?

8. What role does available instructional time play in decisions teachers must make regarding content breadth and content depth?

9. What are some alternative approaches to sequencing content?

10. Why do some kinds of content seem to lend themselves more naturally to some sequencing approaches than to others?

Introduction

Norman Daly, a new world history teacher at Carpenter High School, expressed these feelings at the end of his first few weeks of teaching:

> Three weeks of school behind me. A few battle scars to show for the effort, but nothing major. My enthusiasm remains high. I know I can control my classes. I am finding that I can now begin to think a little more about *what* I am teaching. It is nice to have moved beyond an elemental concern for physical survival.
>
> My classes and I are tromping our way through Ancient Greece. Six notebooks crammed with university lecture notes on the topic are on my desk at home. I have also gathered together some good reference books. The subject is just so deep.
>
> The text we're using is one of these "gems" that compacts 3,000 years of historical truths into 600 pages. It purports to do Ancient Greece in 10 pages. It seems so irresponsible. We flit by something and then dash madly on to something new. I just don't feel this quick "once-over-lightly" approach is producing much learning.
>
> To make matters worse, the text is too difficult for many students. Beyond problems with the book, many of them don't have much context for a lot of the material. I mean, some of them don't know where Greece is. One of them asked me the other day if Greece is in South America!
>
> I know I should be providing more, but I just don't know exactly what I should expect these students to be able to do. I'd like to be doing better by them, but I'm not sure where to begin.

The issues Norman raises are typical of those facing many new teachers. Questions such as these are common: "What should I be teaching my students?" "What do I do if the textbook coverage is inadequate?" "How can I transform my university notes into materials suitable for people in my classes?" "What should I do if my people can't read the textbook?" "How concerned should I be about what my students will be asked on standardized tests?"

These questions are difficult ones. Indeed, they vex even many experienced teachers. How to select important content that is well matched to students' capabilities is one of our profession's perennial challenges. This is true because what people are taught bears a clear relationship to what they learn.

In recent years, the influence of content selection on learning has been gaining in popularity as a research topic. International comparisons of student achievement have prompted much of this interest. Many international achievement comparisons have revealed that American students consistently score lower than students in other nations. One of these studies compared mathematics achievement of 11-year-olds in California, Australia, and England (Barr, 1987). The California students had the lowest scores.

What accounts for this? Part of the answer lies in an analysis of the content to which students were exposed in the three locations. It turns out that much of the achievement test focused on topics that were treated in English schools one or two years earlier than in American schools. Score variances, then, were probably better explained by content-selection differences rather than by "lower quality teaching" in California schools (as compared to those in England).

Researchers interested in content selection have focused some of their attention on a variable called *opportunity to learn*. They have found that student achievement tends to go up when (1) a given aspect of content is treated, and (2) sufficient time is allocated for students to master this aspect of content (Good and Brophy, 1991). Even when teachers have identified similar topics to cover in their courses, researchers have found tremendous teacher-to-teacher differences regarding how much class time is devoted to the topic (Good and Brophy, 1991). The amount of academic background a teacher has in a topic and his personal interest contribute to how much class time a teacher devotes to it.

Sometimes newcomers to the profession presume that content selection decisions have already been made by people writing textbooks and preparing curriculum guides. Not so. Characteristics of students in a given class and other variables associated with the individual teaching setting may well be different from the assumptions of the textbook and curriculum document writers. Further, any examination of a group of textbooks for a given secondary school course will reveal that textbook authors do not agree on how the content should be divided and sequenced. In addition, textbooks also tend to vary considerably in terms of the depth of treatment given to individual topics.

Notes from college courses also fall short as a totally dependable source of information regarding what elements of content should be taught. For one thing, the scope of many college and university courses is much narrower than the typical secondary school course. For example, only a small portion of the content presented in a university-level comparative anatomy course would be relevant for students in an introductory high school biology course. Further, the intended audience for university professors' lectures differs considerably from the students enrolled in typical secondary school classes.

In the end, the secondary school teacher is responsible for making many content decisions. Content selection by individual classroom teachers is the best guarantee that there will be an appropriate "fit" between what is taught and the needs of the students to be served.

Some Influences on Content-Selection Decisions

In making content-selection decisions, some teachers operate under important constraints. For example, in some states rigid regulations stipulate that certain kinds of content must be included in individual secondary school courses. Some local districts have similar requirements. Obviously, these legal guidelines place some limits on teachers' decision-making authority. However, even where guidelines are quite explicit, teachers still continue to have a great deal of autonomy in deciding the relative emphasis on mandated elements of content and in selecting content beyond the scope of what is required by state or local regulations.

Results of standardized tests are often reported in local news media. Schools and teachers whose students score poorly on these tests may come in for public criticism. As a result, the types of information assessed on standardized tests often influences teachers as they make decisions about which content to emphasize. Students' standardized test scores are likely to suffer if the provided instructional program fails to focus on tested information.

CASE STUDY

Teaching to the Test

On a Monday afternoon, Betty Lewis waited with her math colleagues in the faculty lounge for a mathematics department meeting with Ms. Walker, the high school principal. Ms. Walker called this special meeting on short notice, and there had been a good deal of talk all day about what it might be about.

When a grim-faced Ms. Walker entered the room, it became obvious that she was in no mood for pleasantries. She got right down to business:

> "We just received our standardized test scores from the state for the mathematics test our students took in the spring. Our school's average score is down six points from last year. To make it worse, average scores in the other high schools in the district went up. I've been called on the carpet by the superintendent. He was very blunt. He said the scores were an embarrassment to the district, and that members of the school board want to know what is wrong with our math department.
>
> "The superintendent let me know in no uncertain terms that he expects some immediate action to be taken. In response to his request, I am going to require that each of you teaching students who will be taking the test this year spend a minimum of 15 minutes in each class period drilling students on material likely to appear on the test. I have files of tests from previous years in my office. I want you to study them carefully and identify sample test items you can use to help your people practice for the test they will take in the spring. I will expect a weekly report from each teacher identifying precisely what has been done in every period to focus students' attention on content likely to be included on the standardized test."

Betty Lewis and the other teachers were stunned as they heard this announcement. One veteran teacher looked at Ms. Walker and commented, "Don't you think this policy is a somewhat drastic reaction to a one-year dip in our students' scores? Besides, if we do what you're asking, how will we cover the required course content?"

Another teacher said, "What about our academic freedom? As certified professionals, isn't it *our* responsibility to teach students what we consider to be important?"

Still another teacher protested, "I question the ethics of taking items from past tests and teaching the students to respond to them correctly. This is 'teaching to the test,' not teaching students how to understand the subject matter. It seems to me this is just plain wrong."

In response to these questions, Ms. Walker said:

> "I hear what each of you is saying. Let me make some particular comments about the issue of ethics. I would ask *you* whether it is ethical for our school to be evaluated on the basis of one standardized score. That is precisely what our community is doing to us. We depend on our community for support. We may not like the game that is being played, but that is the reality we are in. Basically, the curriculum is what the community demands. If this means that your academic freedom sometimes has to be compromised, that is just how it is. None of us is happy about all this. But I assure you, the superintendent and board of education members are extremely concerned about the decline in our scores. If our students don't do better next year, some even more drastic changes may have to be made."

■ ■ ■

How do you respond to the issue of teaching to the test to raise scores? What are pluses and minuses of this practice? What would you do if you were a member of this mathematics department? *Do* communities unfairly judge schools based on standardized test scores? If so, what might be done about this situation? What is the proper course of action when community desires and decisions teachers want to make as professionals conflict?

We by no means are suggesting that teachers should take a purely reactive stance when confronted with a situation where standardized test scores are considered to be very important. It may be that the tests being used are not doing an adequate job of sampling important kinds of content. As professional educators, teachers have an obligation to enlighten the general public about the limitations of standardized test scores. Teachers need to work for the adoption of student assessment programs that go beyond standardized testing and that embrace diverse measures of student learning.

Availability of instructional support materials often influences teachers' content decisions. If a teacher has to make a choice between two topics, one of which is supported by abundant learning resources other than the textbook and one of which is supported by few such materials, she often feels compelled to select the one supported by plenty of support resources. Since better funded districts tend to have more money to spend on instructional support materials, teachers in more affluent schools often feel fewer constraints when they engage in content-selection activities.

Actions of individual teachers may be influenced by decisions of district- and building-level curriculum committees. Decisions of committee members in some places may be binding on all teachers in a district or a school. In other places, these decisions are presented in the form of suggestions that individual teachers are invited to accept, modify, or reject. Sometimes these groups' decisions are reported in formal curriculum documents. These documents contain ideas for unit titles and instructional approaches that often influence teachers' individual content-selection decisions.

Content-Breadth and Content-Depth Decisions

When teachers make content-selection decisions, they face two distinct but related tasks. On the one hand, they must decide upon the *breadth* of content to be covered. This refers to the range of information to be introduced. (Are we interested in teaching students about political, social, and economic events from 1900 to World War II, *or* are we interested in teaching students the same information from 1607 to 1993?)

On the other hand, teachers make decisions related to content *depth*. Depth refers to the extent of coverage related to a single content element. A decision to treat a given topic in great depth implies a need to commit considerable class time to this effort.

"Fenway doesn't *select* content. He teaches it *all*."

Box 4.1

Identifying Content to Be Taught

Suppose you accepted a teaching position in a district that had no curriculum guides for your subject. Suppose, too, that a late-summer fire had destroyed all course textbooks and that no replacements would be available until the second semester. If the school principal asked you to design your own course, how would you respond to the following questions?

What Do You Think?

1. What major topics would you cover? How would you justify your selection?

2. In what sequence would you teach these topics? Why?

3. Suppose you had 18 instructional weeks to work with. How much time would you devote to each topic? Why?

4. What two or three major concepts would you expect students to learn associated with each topic? Are any of these more important than others? If so, which ones? Why?

There is an accompanying expectation that students will emerge from this experience with an ability to engage in quite sophisticated thinking about the topic.

In making content-selection decisions, teachers must strike a balance between breadth and depth. Since time is limited, a decision to provide too much breadth at the expense of depth can lead to very superficial treatment of many important topics. An error on the side of depth can produce students who are eminently well prepared in certain areas and woefully inadequate in others that received little or no emphasis. The basic idea is to achieve a compromise between breadth and depth of coverage that results in a program well suited to students' abilities.

It is clear that an appropriate relationship between breadth and depth can affect students' learning. Researchers in one study found that learners in some classes mastered as little as 57 percent of the introduced content, while learners in others mastered as much of 98 percent of the material (Barr, 1987). Content in classes where individuals mastered high percentages of what was introduced was well matched to the special characteristics of individuals in the class.

In another study, researchers found that a content-selection decision that reduced breadth of coverage to allow students to spend more time on a smaller number of topics helped below-average junior high school mathematics students to greatly improve their final test scores (Barr, 1987). This finding is consistent with a recommendation of teacher effectiveness researchers Thomas Good and Jere Brophy (1991) that sufficient time be allowed for slower students to complete their work. When the emphasis is on breadth and a hurried pace through the program, many of these students give up. This reinforces their feelings of inadequacy and, often, leads them to develop negative attitudes toward their teachers and the school.

Making good breadth and depth decisions is difficult. In every secondary school subject area, the volume of content that could be taught is enormous. Clearly priorities have to be established and choices made. How can this be done? One approach focuses on a breakdown of academic content into the basic structure of knowledge. Information about this general approach is introduced in the next section.

The Breakdown of Academic Content

Textbook writers, developers of curriculum guides, and others who attempt to organize content for instructional purposes seek to break down subject matter in a systematic way. One approach for doing this derives from the work of learning theorists Jerome Bruner (1960) and Hilda Taba (1962). This structure of knowledge scheme allows different content types to be scaled in terms of their relative importance. It is based on the assumption that a content type such as a generalization, which includes information applicable to diverse situations, is more important than a content type such as a fact, which includes information relative to a particular situation. The structure of knowledge features three basic content types. From narrowest (and least important) to broadest (and most important), these are (1) facts, (2) concepts, and (3) generalizations, principles, and laws.

Facts

Facts refer to a specific circumstance or situation. They have limited transfer or explanatory power. For example, that Mexico City has more people than New York City is a fact that has some significance. It might suggest a reason for pursuing an answer to a question such as "Why has Mexico City grown so large?" However, simply knowing this fact does not help a person understand general reasons cities grow or causes of economic, political, and social problems of cities.

The real value of facts in the curriculum lies in their ability to facilitate student understandings of concepts and generalizations. Appropriate selection of facts has long been an issue of concern to curriculum developers. One authority, John Jarolimek (1990), suggests these kinds of facts should be selected: (1) facts that are likely to remain important over a long period of time, (2) facts used frequently in everyday living, and (3) facts needed to develop or elaborate on important ideas and generalizations.

Concepts

Concepts are major ideas or categories that help us to organize information. Sometimes we simply refer to concepts as *terms*. The defining characteristics of a concept are called *attributes*. Less complex and simpler to learn concepts have relatively few

Box 4.2

The Structure of Knowledge

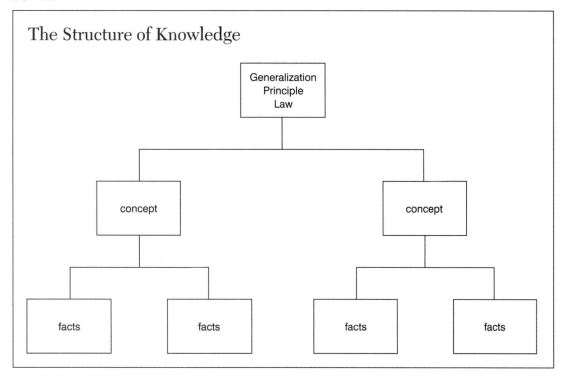

of these. On the other hand, an abstract concept such as "democracy" has a large number.

The fewer the attributes of a concept and the more concrete it is, the easier it is for students to learn. More complex concepts require more teaching time than less complex concepts. Often the extra teaching time can be justified because students need to master complex concepts as a prelude to learning the broad explanatory generalizations that will enable them to transfer learning to varied situations.

One way teachers help students learn a new concept is by presenting them with examples and non-examples of the concept. This helps students identify the concept's defining attributes. Obviously, for this kind of lesson to succeed the illustrations need to highlight the concept's key attributes, and the teacher must take action to assure that students pay attention to this information.

Concepts are organized in the mind into a hierarchy, or schema, that helps us to store and retrieve information. Some concepts, such as "reptile," are broad terms that help organize vast quantities of subordinate information. These broad concepts help organize more narrow, related concepts such as "snake," "turtle," and "lizard," which are much narrower in scope. Awareness of concept hierarchies and the connections between broad and related, narrower concepts helps teachers plan and sequence material for students.

Generalizations, Principles, and Laws

The third type of content goes by several names. Among those frequently used are *generalizations*, *principles*, and *laws*. Though they represent a common content type, there are some differences among generalizations, principles, and laws. In general, laws and principles are based on somewhat stronger evidence and are more universally applicable than generalizations. Some academic disciplines tend to use one of these terms more frequently than the others. For example, there are many "laws" in physics. Findings of social scientists often are reported as "generalizations." Specialists in art and music often cite "principles" of composition.

Generalizations, principles, and laws are statements that summarize what the best available evidence has revealed to be true or correct. They are expressed as statements of relationships among concepts. Here are some examples selected from different subject areas:

- Inherited characteristics of living organisms do not occur randomly; rather, they follow predictable patterns.
- Increased specialization in production has led to interdependence among individuals, communities, states, and nations.
- Survival in the earth's environment depends on the ability of people to interpret various phenomena that come to them through their senses.
- Descending temperatures result in contraction of objects; ascending temperatures result in expansion of objects.
- Areas and perimeter measurements of polygons do not occur in a random pattern; they can be determined by computations involving linear and angle measurements.
- Measures regarded as radical in one generation often are considered moderate in the next.
- Compositions of chemical compounds follow predictable patterns that can be discerned through the application of appropriate analytical procedures.
- A body immersed in a fluid is buoyed up by a force equal to the weight of the dispersed fluid.
- Since natural resources are limited and human wants are unlimited, every society has developed a method for allocating scarce resources.
- Different "moods" of paintings featuring common subjects and symbols result from differences in the sensory and compositional features of the individual work.

The "truth" of generalizations, principles, and laws is determined by reference to evidence. It is possible that some that are regarded as true today may be modified in the future when new evidence becomes available.

Existing generalizations, principles, and laws are constantly being challenged by experts doing pioneering work in their areas of specialization. Generalizations, therefore, should not be introduced to students as definitive answers. We want young people to understand that the search for new knowledge continues and that may of them can look forward to active participation in this exciting process.

Because generalizations, principles, and laws summarize the work of leading specialists and organize tremendous quantities of information, they function well as content organizers. These broad explanatory statements encourage students to place facts in their proper context and to grasp the importance of understanding relationships among concepts.

Because generalizations, principles, and laws describe relationships among concepts, students must grasp the concepts before generalizations, principles, and laws can be understood. Consider this social science generalization:

As a society becomes more educated and industrialized, its birthrate declines.

This generalization will make little sense to students who are unfamiliar with the concepts "society," "education," "industrialization," and "birthrate." Instruction focused on generalizations suggests to teachers key concepts that must be introduced to students.

Concepts often can be illuminated when students are introduced to specific facts. The need to explain the concepts, generalizations, principles, and laws associated with them provides a justification for selecting certain facts for emphasis in the instructional program.

All of this suggests a central role for generalizations, principles, and laws in the instructional planning process. Indeed, one of the teacher's first considerations in identifying content to be covered often is reflected in this question: "What generalizations, principles, or laws do I want my students to understand when this unit of study is completed?" Once these are identified, then the planning process moves on to identify key concepts and explanatory facts.

The Role of the Structure of Knowledge in Content-Selection Decisions

Focus generalizations, principles, and laws and related concepts are important for teachers to consider in making content-selection decisions. They provide an important organizational framework for instruction. In a sense, they serve as targets toward which teaching is directed.

Facts, too, play an important role. They serve as important building blocks that help students to grasp important concepts and the generalizations, principles, and laws to which they relate. The most important consideration in selecting facts is their relevance for helping students master concepts and focus generalizations, principles, and laws. When facts are selected with this purpose in mind, they help expand students' grasp of understandings that have broad transfer value. This approach to fact selection helps teachers prepare instructional programs that are internally consistent and that do not confront students with large quantities of fragmented and unrelated information.

For examples of the use of structure-of-knowledge components such as concepts and generalizations in formal instructional plans, see Chapter 6, "Preparing Units and Lessons."

Matching Students and the Instructional Program

In making content-selection decisions, the nature of students to be taught has an important influence on program planners. The idea that content should be selected so that it "fits" students is a statement of good intentions. Even within a single class, there are great differences among individual students' talents, interests, and motivations. Obviously, no content decision is going to result in a single program of study that is perfectly matched to each student. However, thought about general characteristics of the intended student audience can help teachers make content decisions that result in programs more suitable for students than those that might result without this consideration.

Even casual conversations provide teachers with important insights into students' interests and abilities. This information helps teachers select appropriate content and make assignments that are well suited to the needs of individual students.

A key point in considering student characteristics is that no single program, by itself, is ever perfectly matched to each student's needs. One of the teacher's most important responsibilities is to take the general content that has been selected and adapt it, as necessary, so that each student in the class has a reasonable chance to master it. This suggests that lessons often will introduce the same general content to different students in different ways.

A commitment to make the instructional program responsive to student characteristics requires teachers to know their students well. Gathering diagnostic information about members of a class is not a particularly difficult or time-consuming task. For example, careful attention to what individuals have done on previous assignments provides a great deal of information about what they can do and about where their interests lie. Individual teacher-student conferences have the potential to yield much information about problems individual students might be having and about their general levels of motivation.

Student characteristics are best identified by careful attention to students as individuals. It is not enough to become familiar with content to which students have been previously exposed. Introducing students to relevant prerequisite information by no means assures they have learned it. Given this reality, teachers must know their students well and develop a real understanding for what they have actually learned from previous instruction.

The intent of considering student differences is to make content decisions that will help students to master what is taught. Students who are successful develop better self-concepts and higher levels of self-confidence. These attitudes often translate into good motivation and high levels of achievement (Good and Brophy, 1991).

Sequencing Content

Decisions about what should be taught require more than simply selecting content. Once selected, elements of content also need to be sequenced. Content can be sequenced in different ways. The following are some examples (Armstrong, 1989; Posner, 1987):

- Part-to-whole sequencing
- Whole-to-part sequencing
- Chronological sequencing
- Non-sequential topic sequencing
- External constraint sequencing

Part-to-Whole Sequencing

In this approach, individual content parts are sequenced in such a way that simple parts are taught before more complex "wholes" that demand an understanding of the

Box 4.3

Fitting the Curriculum to the Students

It is important that the instructional program be fitted as closely to possible to the students for whom it is intended. Suppose you were hired to teach a class of tenth grade students in your subject area. Select a topic from your course, and think about how you might make this topic meaningful and interesting to your students.

What Do You Think?

1. What do you know about the general interests of tenth-grade students? How might this information help you interest them in your topic?

2. What prerequisite knowledge would they need to learn the new material?

3. How would you diagnose levels of prior knowledge about this topic in individual students?

4. What could you do before beginning instruction on the topic to find out personal interests of individual students, and how would you use this information to enhance their motivation to learn about the topic you propose to teach?

5. What will you do if some students have the needed background to begin study of the new topic and others do not?

individual parts. Some kinds of content lend themselves better to this kind of sequencing than others. Mathematics courses often are sequenced in this way. The internal logic of the discipline of mathematics strongly supports this sequencing scheme. It simply is not possible for students to grasp more complex parts of the subject without having first mastered less complex parts. The part-to-whole approach is also sometimes referred to as the simple-to-complex approach.

Whole-to-Part Sequencing

This approach is the direct opposite of part-to-whole sequencing. Here, students are first presented with "the big picture." Once this is done, they are introduced to the parts that, collectively, make up the whole. Some subject areas lend themselves more naturally to this arrangement than others. A subject that often is organized this way is geography. For example, world geography courses often begin with an overview of the entire globe. Frequently continents are introduced, as are global wind systems, weather systems, and ocean current systems. Following this overview, lessons often narrow their focus to deal in depth with large global regions. These, in turn, may be followed by lessons focusing on countries within regions and, perhaps, of regions within individual countries.

Chronological Sequencing

When this approach is taken, content elements are organized sequentially based on the variable of time. This scheme makes sense for some content areas, but not for others. History courses often are organized this way. When this is done, lessons focusing on earlier periods of time usually precede those focusing on later periods. (The chronological approach does not mandate an earliest-to-latest sequence, but it is more common than a chronological sequence running from latest to earliest.)

Subjects other than history sometimes also are organized chronologically. For example, some English courses arrange materials to be studied chronologically. A survey of American literature course may begin with a study of colonial era literature, proceed to a consideration of literature of the early republic, and use similar units of time to move students forward toward a concluding unit featuring present-day literature.

Non-Sequential Topic Sequencing

In some content areas, individual topics do not build on others in the course. For example, in a high school crafts course, basic information presented in a unit on tooling leather is not a prerequisite for units on making candles or using the potter's wheel. In courses of this kind, individual units logically can be sequenced in many different ways. Often teachers base sequencing decisions on their own interests and their feelings about what order of presentation might best serve student needs and interests.

External Constraint Sequencing

Sometimes sequencing decisions have little to do with a serious consideration of the substance of the content or of student needs. External constraints may require certain topics to be covered at certain times. For example, if a high school biology course regularly features a field ecology unit that is taught in an outdoor laboratory facility serving many schools, the date this facility will be available fixes the time in the instructional program when the unit will be taught.

Sometimes, availability of important support media also influences sequencing decisions. One of the authors once worked in a state with a small population that had only one centralized educational film library to serve every high school in the state. Teachers who wanted to use films had to schedule them months in advance, and often the dates of their availability exercised considerable influence over teachers' content-sequencing decisions.

External constraints often are frustrating for teachers. Fortunately, they usually affect a relatively small number of sequencing decisions that teachers must make. However, it is important that newcomers to the profession recognize that they may have to sequence some content in ways that, ideally, they would avoid.

Table 4.1   Summary Table

Main Points	Explanation
Content Selection Responsibilities	Though producers of textbooks and school curriculum guides have selected the content they contain, this selection may not be appropriate for students in a given class nor for the purposes an individual teacher hopes to achieve. Individual teachers must make many content selection decisions on their own.
Opportunity to Learn	This variable, much researched by scholars in recent years, refers to the issue of whether students have been exposed to particular information in their classes and, if they have, how much time has been devoted to its study. Not surprisingly, student achievement has been found to increase on standardized tests when content sampled includes that which students have had an opportunity to learn in their classes.
Influences on Teachers' Content-Selection Decisions	
State and Local Regulations	In some places, state and local regulations are quite explicit in their demands that certain information be treated as part of individual secondary school courses. These requirements place some limits on teachers' abilities to freely choose content. Typically, however, even where state and local guidelines are quite explicit, teachers retain considerable autonomy in terms of the relative emphasis they can give to required elements of content.
Standardized Tests	In some places, there is great interest in students' levels of performance on standardized tests. This public interest may pressure teachers to work with students to improve their scores. This may require teachers to select and emphasize content sampled by the standardized tests.
Availability of Instructional Support Materials	Once content-selection decisions have been made, teachers need instructional support materials to help them transmit information to their students. If teachers know that materials related to content area X are not available (or at least not available in sufficient quantity), they are unlikely to make a content decision that would require students to study area X. Availability of materials places some practical limits on the contents teachers select to treat in their courses.
Content-Breadth and Content-Depth Decisions	Breadth refers to the range of information to be introduced in a course. Depth refers to the intended sophistication of learning that is expected of students when they study a topic. Teachers must weigh breadth and depth decisions carefully. Because time is limited, priorities need to be established. This means that some high-priority topics will be studied in more depth (and more time will be devoted to them) than others. Not all topics can be studied in great depth. Such a decision would irresponsibly restrict the breadth of the course.

Main Points	Explanation
The Breakdown of Academic Content	The structure of knowledge framework represents one approach to breaking down knowledge. It stems from the work of Jerome Bruner and Hilda Taba. It provides a way for content types to be scaled in terms of their relative importance and explanatory power. From least encompassing and powerful to most encompassing and powerful, the three basic layers in the structure of knowledge are: (1) facts, (2) concepts, and (3) generalizations, principles, and laws.
Facts	Facts refer to a specific situation or circumstance and have limited explanatory power. Their most important function is to help students develop a better understanding of concepts and of generalizations, principles, and laws.
Concepts	Concepts are major ideas or categories that serve as organizers of vast quantities of information. Defining characteristics of concepts are called *attributes.* More concrete concepts with small numbers of attributes are easier for students to learn than more abstract concepts with large numbers of attributes.
Generalizations, Principles, and Laws	Generalizations, principles, and laws are statements of relationship among concepts. They summarize the best available evidence regarding what has been found to be "true" or "correct." These broad explanatory statements function well as major content organizers for program planners. They help teachers to identify key concepts that students must understand and to select facts to illuminate both the concepts and the generalizations, principles, and laws that have been selected as major program organizers.
Matching Students and the Instructional Program	There are tremendous differences among students from one school to another and from one class within a school to another. Further, even in the same class, individual students differ greatly from one another. This means that when they make content selection decisions, teachers need to think carefully about students who will be the consumers of instructional programs they design. Further, once basic content selection decisions have been made and the program is being delivered, some modifications in instruction are almost always necessary to meet special needs of certain students in the class. Students are simply too varied for one approach to fit all.
Sequencing Content	
Part-to-Whole Sequencing	This sequence introduces content from simplest to most complex. It sometimes is called simple-to-complex sequencing. It is most common in subject areas where students' subsequent progress requires them to master critical prerequisite information. Subject matter in mathematics classes often is sequenced this way.

Table 4.1   Summary Table *(continued)*

Main Points	Explanation
Sequencing Content, *cont'd.*	
Whole-to-Part Sequencing	In this approach, students are introduced to complex wholes before they study component parts more intensively. The idea is to present students with the "big picture" first. Sometimes world geography courses are sequenced this way. That is, they begin by considering global patterns before going on to study continents, regions, countries, and regions within countries.
Chronological Sequencing	Chronological sequencing is used when there is some logic in using time as an organizer. History courses frequently use this sequencing scheme. Chronological sequencing can go either from earliest to most recent or from most recent to earliest. The earliest to most recent pattern is by far the more common.
Non-Sequential Topic Sequencing	This sequencing pattern is used when individual topics in a course are relatively freestanding. This means that content in one topic is not essential for students to know before they can begin studying another one. When this is true, the adopted sequence is basically a matter of the teacher's personal preference.
External Constraint Sequencing	Sometimes sequencing of content is influenced by considerations that have little to do with specific demands of the content to be taught or with student needs. Necessary learning support resources may be available only at certain times. For example, it may be necessary to use a particular learning facility that is also in demand by other classes. The time when this facility is available will dictate when the unit requiring its use will be taught.

Review of Key Ideas

- Selecting content is one of teachers' most important responsibilities. Though some suggestions regarding what should be taught can be found in such diverse sources as school textbooks, state and local curriculum guides, and college and university course notes, the unique characteristics of individual classes and students require teachers themselves to play an active role in identifying what should be taught.

- Researchers have found that opportunity to learn is a variable that has much to do with student achievement. Unless content that is tested has been emphasized in class and students have had an opportunity to work with it, their test scores will not be high. Some differences in scores of American students and those in other countries may be attributable to differences in opportunity to learn the content referenced in the test.

- Teachers face some important constraints as they make content-selection decisions. In some places, state and local regulations require certain elements of content to be included in certain courses. The nature of content assessed on standardized tests also influences teachers' decisions. Test results, in many places, have assumed great political importance. Schools are under pressure to provide programs that give students the background needed to achieve high scores. Availability of instructional material also places some limits on the content-selection decisions teachers make.

- One aspect of teachers' content decisions focuses on breadth, or the range of information to be covered. Survey courses tend to have more breadth than courses that presume general knowledge and that are designed to develop more sophisticated information about certain topics within a broad content area.

- Another aspect of content decisions has to do with depth. Depth is the sophistication or extent of coverage of individual elements of content. When a decision is made to increase depth, the teacher is also making a decision to devote more time to a particular element of content. Such a decision also tends to be accompanied by an expectation that learners will develop more sophisticated levels of understanding than will be expected when they study other content elements in less depth. Good depth and breadth decisions require teachers to develop a clear view of their own instructional priorities.

- The structure of knowledge provides a content-breakdown framework that many teachers find useful. It includes three levels or layers of content. These content types include (1) facts, (2) concepts, and (3) generalizations, principles, and laws.

- Facts are content elements that refer to a specific circumstance or situation. They have limited transfer power. Facts should be selected in terms of their ability to help students grasp important concepts and focus generalizations, principles, or laws.

- Concepts are major ideas, terms, or categories that serve as major organizers for vast quantities of related information. For example the concept "automobile" is a descriptive term under which enormous quantities of related information can be subsumed. The defining characteristics of a concept are called its attributes. Less complex concepts have fewer attributes than more complex ones.

- Generalizations, principles, and laws are succinct distillations of the truths that have been found by professional scholars and researchers. They are expressed as statements of relationship among concepts. To understand generalizations, principles, and laws, students must understand the concepts embedded within them. The truth of a given generalization, principle, or law is based on the best available evidence. As new information becomes available, it may be necessary to modify the generalization, principle, or law.

- Student characteristics must be considered when content-selection decisions are made. It is never possible for a single content-selection decision to meet needs of every student in a classroom. Teachers always have to take the identified content and make some accommodations to meet special needs of individuals they teach. A key to fitting content to students is in-depth knowledge of the students who are to be taught. The more teachers know about their students, the better they are able to make content-selection decisions that will meet their students' needs.

- There are many approaches to sequencing content. Part-to-whole sequencing arranges content from simplest to most complex. Whole-to-part sequencing reverses this process and introduces complex wholes first; then, more intensive instruction is provided focusing on individual parts. Chronological sequencing uses calendar time as a sequencing mechanism. Usually, material is sequenced from oldest to newest. Non-sequential topic sequencing is used when individual topics are more or less free standing—that is, when topics do not build on one another in any systematic or predictable way. External constraint sequencing refers to situations that require teachers to teach specific elements of a course at a particular time because of some out-of-the-classroom situation that mandates a certain topic be covered at a specific time. For example, there may be only certain times of the year when certain resources needed to teach a topic are available.

Follow-Up Questions and Activities

Questions

1. Why are content decisions so important, and to what degree should teachers be involved in them?
2. What is the importance of opportunity to learn?
3. Why is it not a good idea for teachers to leave content selection to the experts who have written the course textbooks and prepared the adopted curriculum guides?
4. In what ways do standardized tests sometimes influence content-selection decisions?
5. What is meant by content breadth and content depth, and how do decisions related to breadth and depth influence the amount of time spent on a given topic in a course?
6. What is the structure of knowledge, and what does its use in content selection suggest about the proper role for facts?
7. What kinds of things contribute to the complexity of a given concept?
8. How is the truth of a generalization determined?
9. Why is important for teachers to consider student characteristics when they make content-selection decisions?
10. What are some alternative approaches to sequencing content?

Activities

1. Obtain a textbook in your subject area that is used in secondary schools. Analyze its content. Is the content consistent with what you think should be taught? Is material sequenced as you would sequence it? In general, how could the content selection and sequencing be improved? Present your reactions to your instructor in a short paper.

2. Ask your instructor for help in locating any guidelines or requirements for teaching your subject that may have been adopted either by your state or by a local school district. How constraining are these guidelines for the individual teacher? Do they pose any potential problems for you as you think about content decisions you might like to make? Share your reactions with others in a general class discussion.

3. Interview a secondary school teacher about how she selects specific content to be taught. Ask this teacher whether she places more emphasis on certain topics than others and, if so, why. Ask also where this person faces any troublesome rules, regulations, or guidelines that restrict the range of her content selection decisions. Share teacher reactions to your questions with others in your class in a brief oral report.

4. Several sequencing approaches are introduced in this chapter. Look through several secondary school textbooks. Are you able to identify the sequencing approaches used? Share your findings with others in your class as part of a discussion. (Hint: Some texts use a combination of the approaches introduced in the chapter.)

5. Select several topics you would teach in your own subject area. Sequence them in two different ways. Base your sequencing on one of the approaches introduced in the chapter. Share your plans with your course instructor. Be prepared to discuss the strengths and weaknesses of each approach.

References

ARMSTRONG, D. G. *Developing and Documenting the Curriculum*. Boston: Allyn & Bacon, 1989.

BARR, R. "Content Coverage." In M. Dunkin (ed.). *The International Encyclopedia of Teaching and Teacher Education*. New York: Pergamon Press, 1987, pp. 364–368.

BRUNER, J. *The Process of Education*. Cambridge, MA: Harvard University Press, 1960.

GOOD, T. AND BROPHY, J. *Looking in Classrooms*. 5th ed. New York: HarperCollins, 1991.

JAROLIMEK, J. *Social Studies in Elementary Education*. 8th ed. New York: Macmillan Publishing Company, 1990.

POSNER, G. "Pacing and Sequencing." In M. Dunkin (ed.). *The International Encyclopedia of Teaching and Teacher Education*. New York: Pergamon Press, 1987, pp. 266–272.

TABA, H. *Curriculum Development: Theory and Practice*. New York: Harcourt, Brace and World, 1962.

5

Writing Objectives

AIMS

This chapter provides information to help the reader to:

- Distinguish among goals, aims, and objectives.
- Describe general characteristics of instructional objectives.
- Point out each of the four elements included in a complete instructional objective.
- Write instructional objectives in the cognitive domain.
- Write instructional objectives in the affective domain.
- Write instructional objectives in the psychomotor domain.

FOCUS QUESTIONS

1. How much freedom do individual teachers have in selecting objectives?
2. How do the broad goals of education get translated into a form suitable for guiding classroom instruction?

3. How do teachers identify appropriate learning outcomes for their students?

4. How can instructional objectives be developed that encourage students to engage in higher-level thinking processes?

5. How can objectives be written that focus on students' attitudes?

Introduction

Teachers' instructional planning decisions do not end once content has been selected and sequenced. They must also consider what specific things they wish students to learn as a result of their exposure to instruction. Teachers' thinking about this issue results in the preparation of instructional objectives. These objectives specify in detailed terms what students are expected to do as a consequence of their exposure to given content in the classroom.

Teachers prepare instructional objectives in light of the kinds of content they wish students to learn, the level of sophistication they expect students to demonstrate at the end, and the abilities and interests of the students being taught. Instructional objectives function as guideposts for lesson planning and other kinds of instructional planning. (For specific information about unit and lesson planning, see Chapter 6, "Preparing Units and Lessons.") They establish a sense of direction for teachers. Instructional objectives are referenced by teachers as they select learning material to supplement what is provided in the course text, identify appropriate teaching strategies, and develop appropriate evaluation procedures.

Relationship of Objectives to Goals and Aims

Instructional objectives are the most specific of several categories of statements that give direction to instructional programs. Different authorities in education have devised various approaches for classifying these statements in terms of their specificity. One scheme includes these three basic categories.

* Goals
* Aims
* Objectives

Together, these categories function to identify large priorities of our society and to translate them into forms that provide direction for teachers planning programs for students in the schools.

Goals

Goals are broad statements of direction. They often are defined by national policy makers and important interest groups. For example, in the early 1990s concerns about the quality of the schools led the federal government to establish a set of goals in its America 2000 program. These three were among those included:

- By the year 2000, American students will leave grades 4, 8, and 12 having demonstrated competency in challenging subject matter, including English, mathematics, science, history and geography; and every school in America will ensure that all students learn to use their minds well, so that they may be prepared for responsible citizenship, further learning, and productive employment in our modern economy.
- By the year 2000, U.S. students will be first in the world in mathematics and science achievement.
- By the year 2000, every adult American will be literate and will possess the skills necessary to compete in a global economy and to exercise the rights and responsibilities of citizenship (*America 2000: An Education Strategy*, 1991; p. 3).

These goals describe a set of national priorities for school programs. They reflect important values and social concerns. Among these are the importance of preparing people who are literate in certain key subject areas (mathematics, science, English, history, and geography). The importance of preparing young people for citizenship is another value reflected in these goals. Still another value concern is implied by the importance attached to preparing individuals for productive employment.

Values implicit in educational policy statements such as *America 2000* suggest priorities for allocating resources in the school. However, these kinds of broad goal statements do not provide specific guidance for the classroom teacher. For example, a teacher working with the goals spelled out in the *America 2000* proposal would need answers to questions such as these before programs could be planned to implement these broad ideas in the classroom:

- What is meant by somebody being "literate" in mathematics, English, history, geography, and science?
- What do people need to know to be "vocationally competitive" on a global scale?
- What is required in preparing someone for "responsible citizenship"?

Aims

Aims are more specific and focused than goals. They provide a specific direction for a given subject. They represent an effort to take the intent of a general goal and refine its focus to relate specifically to expectations for students in a specific school course. One key question individuals ask themselves as they work to identify aims for secondary

Box 5.1

Applying Educational Goals to the Classroom

Translating broad social goals into ongoing school programs often leads to disputes. Look at some of the goals from the *America 2000* report that are referenced in this chapter.

What Do You Think?

1. Do you agree all of these should be high priority goals? If you disagree with the view that all should be seen as high priority goals, what is the basis for your disagreement?

2. What do each one of these goals imply about the kinds of things that might be taught in your subject area?

3. Do these goals imply anything about how teachers should teach and conduct their classrooms?

4. If you were to visit a high school, what would you look for as evidence the program there was consistent with these *America 2000* goals?

---

school subjects is: "What should students learn in these subjects that is related to major goals our society has established for the schools?"

For example, a goal calling for the schools to develop "responsible citizens" might result in the development of aims such as these for a high school government class.

- Students will understand how bills become laws.

- Students will know about power relationships as they are distributed among the executive, legislative, and judicial branches of government.

- Students will commit to the idea that citizens have an obligation to become informed on issues facing the nation and to express their preferences by voting.

- Students will understand how lobbying activities help bring perspectives of different groups to legislators' attention.

Aims for various subject areas often are adopted by groups of teachers, administrators, and community members. Sometimes these aims go through some kind of approval process and become the official aims of the school district. However they are developed and whatever their official standing, aims provide some important benefits to teachers. They help them to define the focus of their courses.

On the other hand, aims do *not* do some other things. For example, they do not include specific information about teaching strategies that might be employed, how students will be assessed, and specific elements of knowledge students will be expected to have as a result of their exposure to instruction. This kind of specificity is the province of the remaining category: objectives.

Box 5.2

From Goals to Aims

Developing school programs that are consistent with broad goals is difficult. The process requires content-related aims to be generated from the goals. The idea is to describe aims that flow logically from the goals. To illustrate what must be done, suppose the following broad goal had been adopted:

Each high school graduate will possess the knowledge and skill needed to exercise his or her rights and responsibilities as a citizen in a democratic society.

This broad goal must be translated into aims associated with the school's various curricular areas. This process might result in aims such as the following:

English:

- Students will identify bias in prose material.
- Students will be able to write and speak effectively.

Mathematics:

- Students will be able to recognize data distortions.
- Students will understand charts and graphs.

Business:

- Students will understand business ethics.
- Students will apply constitutional rights in the workplace.

Science:

- Students will understand ethical issues associated with applying science to social problems.
- Students will predict consequences of scientific actions.

Modern Languages:

- Students will be able to communicate effectively with people from diverse cultural groups.
- Students will recognize values of people from different cultures.

Objectives

Instructional objectives state in specific terms what students should be able to do as a result of their exposure to instruction. They are written in much more specific terms than aims statements. Additionally, they tend to be written by teachers of the students who are to be taught. Instructional objectives tie clearly to more general aims. Note this example:

Aim: Students will learn to use computer programs such as DAC Easy to Solve accounting problems.

Related Instructional Objective: Each student will input data on a spreadsheet, putting entries into the correct category with no more than two entry errors.

Note that the objective references much more specific behavior than the aim. Mastery of a behavior associated with a single instructional objective represents a stepping stone toward mastery of the much broader, much more general aim.

Instructional objectives are prepared by individuals with a good understanding of the abilities and needs of the students who will be the consumers of the instructional program that is designed to promote mastery of the objectives. The effort to modify objectives to achieve a "good fit" with students means that different teachers serving different students may develop quite different objectives related to the same general aim.

Instructional objectives help teachers in several ways. They provide guideposts for instructional planning. Once instructional objectives have been identified, teachers are able to tie selection of teaching techniques, learning materials, and evaluation procedures to the objectives.

Researchers have found that instructional planning that is guided by objectives results in better organized and purposeful instruction. Students whose instruction is guided by objectives have less confusion about what the teacher expects, and their levels of achievement tend to go up as compared to students taught by teachers who do not prepare objectives (Ferre, 1972; Morse and Tillman, 1973; Olsen, 1973). Benefits are especially likely to occur when the teacher shares instructional objectives with students and takes time to make certain they understand what they are supposed to be learning.

WHAT SCHOLARS SAY

How Effective Are Instructional Objectives?

Richard T. White and Richard P. Tisher (1986) reviewed large numbers of research studies that focused on the relationship between instructional objectives and students' achievement in science. In general, they found that students whose teachers used instructional objectives learned more than students of teachers who did not use them.

Their review also pointed out an interesting relationship between higher cognitive-level objectives and the kinds of information students had before instruction related to these objectives began. Students who had high levels of prior knowledge did much better when tested over content related to high cognitive-level objectives than did students who had low levels of prior knowledge.

This finding underscores the importance of teachers knowing entry-level abilities of students. Simply preparing high cognitive-level objectives and instructional activities to support them will not assure high levels of student achievement. Students must have the necessary background information to profit from the sophisticated instruction designed to support high cognitive-level objectives.

There also is some evidence that instructional objectives provide more learning benefits to some kinds of students than to others. Middle-ability students seem to benefit more from instructional programs guided by objectives than either low-ability or high-ability students.

Source: R. T. White and R. P. Tisher, "Research on Natural Sciences." In M. C. Wittrock (ed.), *Handbook of Research on Teaching* (3rd ed., pp. 874–905). New York: Macmillan Publishing Company, 1986.

"We will now consider pre-articulated, written, behavioral objective, clarified, instructional equipment selected, process orientation planned, teaching/learning strategy codifications. Or, as some people call them, lesson plan books."

Because objectives clearly state the kinds of behaviors students should be able to demonstrate at the conclusion of instruction, they help teachers develop appropriate evaluation tools. For example, if an objective clearly states that students should be able to "compare and contrast" something, the teacher is cued to avoid using an assessment tool, such as a matching test, that doesn't test students' abilities to engage in compare-and-contrast thinking. The behavior in the objective signals the teacher to consider an essay item or some other assessment vehicle that can measure this kind of thinking. (For more information about testing, see Chapter 17, "Measuring Student Progress.")

Objectives as Intended Learning Outcomes

There are two basic steps in preparing specific instructional objectives. First, the intended learning outcomes must be identified. Second, these must be described in terms of an observable student performance (Gronlund, 1991).

Identifying Observable Student Behaviors

In preparing objectives, it is important that the identified behavior reference what the *student* can do at the end of the instructional sequence, not what the *teacher* does as instruction is delivered. The following behaviors, which tell us what the teacher will be doing, are inappropriate instructional objectives:

- Demonstrate how to conduct an experiment.
- Lecture about causes of the break up of the former Soviet Union.
- Motivate students to read more short stories.
- Play music for the class to instill an appreciation for classical music.

Sometimes, writers of poor instructional objectives avoid referencing student behaviors, not by describing what teachers will be doing, but by describing what students will do to gain needed information. Examples of this kind of unacceptable instructional-objective behavior statement follow.

- The students will read the story.
- The students will discuss the causes.
- The students will view the film.
- The students will paint a scene.
- The students will listen to the music.

These statements tell us nothing about what the student has learned and what he should now be able to demonstrate as a result. Properly, behaviors in objectives reference student behaviors. Here are some examples:

- Describe steps followed in an experiment.
- Point out some events that led to the disintegration of the former Soviet Union.
- Interpret the meaning of a short story.
- Explain reasons for liking a particular piece of classical music.
- Interpret information on maps and globes.

Careful statements that reference expected student behaviors do not, by themselves, comprise a complete instructional objective. Something needs to be added that indicates the kind of evidence the teacher will take that students, indeed, are able to demonstrate these behaviors. This requires the writer of an instructional objective to make specific reference to the student performance that will be taken as evidence the behavior has been mastered.

Defining Student Performance

Teachers need evidence that will confirm students have mastered content referenced in instructional objectives. For this reason, objectives mention observable student behaviors that will be taken as evidence learning has occurred. The reference in objectives to observable behaviors is based on the principle that students should be able to act or perform differently as a result of instruction (Moore, 1992).

A wide variety of indicators are used in objectives as evidence of student learning. Here are some examples:

- Rewrites in his or her own words.
- Provides additional examples.
- Converts information to graphical form.
- Identifies implications.
- Predicts probable consequences.
- Lists possible inferences.

Note that these indicators use action verbs. Action verbs are verbs that refer to observable behavior. *List* is an action verb that can be observed directly; *appreciate* is not an action verb. This behavior cannot be observed directly; it must be inferred from other actions that can be observed.

Other Components of Objectives

In addition to information about expected student behaviors and what students must do to indicate they have mastered them, objectives often also include several other components. Frequently instructional objectives make clear reference to the specific students for whom the objectives are intended. Another common feature is information about how student proficiency will be assessed. Sometimes, too, instructional objectives provide information about how well students should do on assessments of proficiency for the teacher to conclude the objectives have been mastered.

A number of formats for preparing instructional objectives have been developed. One that includes information about students to be taught, expected behaviors, kinds of assessments to be done, and hoped-for levels of proficiency is introduced in the next section.

The ABCD Format for Preparing Instructional Objectives

The ABCD format for preparing instructional objectives is an easy one to use. The first four letters of the alphabet easily bring to mind its component parts. The A stands for *audience*—the specific students to be taught. B is for *behavior*—the observable student behavior that will be taken as evidence learning has occurred. The C stands for *conditions*. These specify the conditions of assessment or testing that will be used to measure students' abilities to perform the behavior described in the B component. The D refers to the *degree* of student proficiency the teacher expects to see as evidence that the objective has been mastered.

A or Audience

The A element of an instructional objective refers to the person or persons to whom instruction will be directed. This may be just one student, a small group of students, or an entire class of students. Because student needs differ, some objectives designed for certain class members may be different from those prepared for others.

The examples that follow typify the kinds of wording often found in the A or audience component of an instructional objective:

- Each student will . . .
- Louisa's group will . . .
- All students in all sections of Algebra I will . . .
- The fifth-period physics students will . . .
- Joanne, Inez, Maria, and LaShandra will . . .

B or Behavior

The B or behavior component of an instructional objective describes the observable behavior that students will be expected to be able to demonstrate as a result of their exposure to instruction. Action verbs are used to describe the required behavior. In planning this part of an objective, the teacher begins by asking, "What will I be able to see the student(s) do as a result of my instruction?"

The following fragments of instructional objectives illustrate kinds of wording often found in the behavior component.

- . . .list specific examples of . . .
- . . .describe characteristics of . . .
- . . .name . . .
- . . .apply the formula to a problem . . .
- . . .solve to find the unknown variable . . .
- . . .demonstrate the correct grip . . .
- . . .play the musical phrase . . .

C or Conditions

The conditions component describes the nature of assessment procedures to be used to determine whether the behavior has been mastered. This may include formal testing procedures requiring the use of essay items, multiple-choice items, true-false items, matching items, or completion items. There may be certain kinds of student "products" that may be reviewed. These might include such things as formal term papers, a bridge designed in a technology-education class, pots prepared using the coil method, or a set of mechanical drawings. Kinds of products referenced in the conditions component will vary depending on what is taught, teachers' preferences, and students' individual characteristics.

The following fragments of complete instructional objectives include wording often found in the conditions component:

- . . .on an essay examination . . .
- . . .on a 10-page term paper . . .
- . . .by preparing an original painting . . .
- . . .by constructing a model . . .
- . . .by throwing the discus . . .
- . . .during a formal recital . . .

D or Degree

The degree component makes explicit the minimum level of performance that will be taken as evidence of mastery. Setting an appropriate standard for student performance is not easy. For example, if a teacher decided that the conditions of assessment would consist of a 20-item multiple-choice test, it would be unlikely that the teacher would take only one correct answer as evidence the student knew the material. Many students would get one or more items right by guessing. On the other hand, insisting that all 20 items be answered correctly probably would set such a rigorous standard that few students would be credited with mastery of the material.

A good deal of teacher artistry is involved in deciding the degree of competency required for a given objective. The degree should take into account what is important for the future growth of the student as well as her past history and entry-level understanding. Students with a past history of failure may become discouraged if they believe the expected level of proficiency is beyond their capabilities.

For some kinds of items, for example those on true-false tests, degree is often indicated by specifying a minimum number or percentage of questions that must be answered correctly. This approach is not appropriate when some other kinds of assessment tools are used. For example, on an essay question, stating the degree in terms of percentage correct makes no sense; there is nothing to count. On essays, degree is often expressed in terms of specific categories of information that are to be included (e.g., "making specific references to (a) social conditions, (b) economic conditions, and (c) political conditions").

The following fragments of complete instructional objectives use language often found in the degree component:

- . . .respond correctly to at least 8 of 10 questions . . .
- . . .in an essay make specific references to at least three specific causes . . .
- . . .prepare a painting including six of the elements of composition presented in class . . .

Putting the Elements Together: The Complete ABCD Format

The instructional objectives provided here include each of the four basic components. Each component has been underlined and labeled:

       "A"   "B"   "D"
- Each student will solve correctly 8 of 10 mathematics problems

             "C"
presented on an exercise sheet.

         "A"   "B"   "C"
- Laura's cooperative learning group will compose a group essay that

                  "D"
includes at least three reasons why Swedish immigrants settled in

Minnesota.

        "C"   "A"
- On a multiple-choice test, the fifth period English class will

         "B"
identify correct examples of alliteration by responding correctly to

        "D"
at least 8 of 10 items.

Note that the audience, behavior, conditions, and degree components can appear in a variety of sequences. The order is not critical; the presence of each of the four components is.

Moving from Aims to Instructional Objectives

Once a general aim has been established, a first step toward developing an instructional objective involves identifying kinds of observable student behaviors that might suggest that students have acquired knowledge associated with the aim. Some teachers find that brainstorming to generate a list of possible behaviors is a good approach. To illustrate how this might work, consider this example:

Aim: Students will come to understand basic scientific terms.

List of Related Observable Behaviors:
- Writes definitions of terms.
- Matches term with appropriate definition.
- Supplies examples of terms.

- Draws a picture or diagram to illustrate the meaning of each term.
- Completes a crossword puzzle requiring recognition of meaning of terms.
- States relationships between meanings of pairs of terms.
- Distinguishes between proper and improper uses of terms.

A list of several observable behaviors provides the basis for decisions about the specific ones that will be included in the instructional objectives. In deciding which ones to include, the teacher will consider the time students have had to study the material and to take the test, the expected sophistication of thinking, and the general ability levels of students who will be taught.

Instructional Objectives and Evaluation

A common complaint among students is that teachers' tests often seem to bear little connection to what has been taught. Careful development and use of instructional objectives can resolve this problem. The objectives clearly identify what the teacher expects students to be able to do at the conclusion of an instructional sequence. They provide guidelines for the teacher to use in selecting material for students to study and instructional techniques to help them master the new content. They also reference the kind of testing that will be used at the conclusion of the instructional sequence. In short, instructional objectives provide teachers with a tool that allows them to develop a well-focused, internally consistent instructional program, in which evaluation has been designed in advance to assure its consistency with what has been taught. Use of instructional objectives helps teachers develop tests that students will see as relevant to the material they have studied (Popham, 1987).

Today, increasing attention is being given to the issue of authentic assessment. In short, this assessment is designed to evaluate students on their abilities to perform in ways consistent with what they have been taught. (See Chapter 17, "Measuring Student Progress," for a more detailed explanation.") Authentic assessment places heavy demands on students. Careful identification of intended evaluation procedures at the time objectives and the instructional programs that support them are planned helps students to perform better on assessment measures.

Types of Instructional Objectives

There are three basic types of objectives. Objectives in the cognitive domain focus on different kinds of intellectual behaviors, ranging from simple memory recall tasks to more sophisticated analysis and evaluation kinds of thinking. Affective domain objectives are used to plan instruction that is focused on attitudes and values. Objectives in the psychomotor domain describe skill behaviors requiring good control over the body's fine muscle system. There are several categories or levels of behavior within each of these domains. These levels tend to scale behaviors along a continuum from least complex to most complex.

Objectives in the Cognitive Domain

The cognitive domain is concerned with rational, systematic, or intellectual thinking. When we think about academic subject matter and what we expect students to learn, usually we have the cognitive domain in mind. Much of what we know about the cognitive domain stems from the work of Benjamin Bloom and others who set out during the 1950s to describe categories of cognitive domain thinking. Out of their deliberations came a seminal educational document, *Taxonomy of Educational Objectives: Handbook I: Cognitive Domain* (Bloom, 1956). Commonly referred to as Bloom's Taxonomy, this document introduced a six-level hierarchy of thinking, ranging from the most elementary to the most sophisticated thinking processes. Ordered from simplest to most complex, the elements of Bloom's Taxonomy are:

Knowledge

Comprehension

Application

Analysis

Synthesis

Evaluation

In preparing cognitive-level objectives, one consideration is the expected sophistication of students' thinking that will result from their exposure to instruction related to the objectives. To see how objectives can be designed to promote different levels of thinking, it is necessary to understand some basic characteristics of each of the levels in the cognitive domain.

Knowledge

Knowledge-level thinking involves the simple recall of previously learned information. The kind of behavior or performance mentioned in knowledge-level objectives call on students to reproduce or identify something to which they have been exposed. They are not asked to manipulate, analyze, think creatively about, or make sophisticated judgments concerning this material. The following are examples of knowledge-level instructional objectives:

- On a matching test, each student will identify capitals of selected countries of Europe by matching correctly at least 12 of the 15 capitals with the appropriate countries.
- Students will recognize titles of books written by Ernest Hemingway by responding correctly to 8 of 10 true-false items.

Comprehension

Comprehension-level thinking is somewhat more complex than knowledge-level think-ing. It requires a focus on more than a single piece of previously learned information. Understanding of important relationships and sequences may be required. It may also involve changing the form of previously mastered material or making simple interpre-tations. The following are examples of comprehension-level instructional objectives:

- Each student will develop literal translations from Russian to English for 10 sen-tences making no errors in at least 8 of the 10.
- Members of Laura's group will list the steps a bill must go through to become a law, including all steps and listing them in order, with no errors.

Application

Application-level thinking requires the use of previously learned material in an unfamiliar context. In the classroom, application requires students to "do something" with what they have learned. The following are examples of application-level instructional objectives:

- Each student in the geography class will compute correct air distances between 10 pairs of world cities using a tape measure and a 22-inch globe so that errors of no more than 50 miles short or long of the true distances are made on any more than two pairs of cities.
- Each biology student will correctly compute progeny ratios on at least 8 of 11 pro-vided problems.

Analysis

Analysis-level thinking requires the development of conclusions through study of the constituent parts of a phenomenon. In the classroom, analysis-level thinking helps stu-dents understand "wholes" by looking carefully at the parts that, collectively, make up the wholes. These are some examples of analysis-level instructional objectives:

- Each student will correctly identify the chemical composition of at least 15 of 18 provided unknown compounds.
- In an essay, each student will describe patterns of voting in the most recent presi-dential election on the part of voters of (a) very low income, (b) moderately low income, (c) average income, (d) moderately high income, and (e) very high income.

Synthesis

Synthesis-level thinking requires people to take several pieces of information and com-bine them to create something new (or at least "new" to the individual engaged in the thinking process). These are some examples of synthesis-level instructional objectives.

- On an essay, each student will describe at least six specific changes in the lives of residents of cities that would result from a law banning private automobiles from all streets lying within the city limits.

- Each student, in a three- to six-page paper, will describe at least three plausible differences in our lives today had settlement of the United States been from west to east by settlers coming predominantly from Japan and China.

Evaluation

Evaluation-level thinking requires people to make judgments in light of clearly identified criteria. It is essential that both the element of judgment and the element of clear criteria be present. Evaluation is *not* a simplistic sharing of unsupported personal opinion. The following are examples of evaluation-level instructional objectives:

- In a three- to six-page paper, each student will compare, contrast, and critique the plays of Racine and Corneille in terms of their adherence to the "rules" of classical drama.
- Each student will critique a selected painting by Gauguin and a selected painting by Van Gogh and determine which is the superior piece of work by completing an essay in which specific references are made to (a) the degree of coherence in each painting, (b) the degree to which each painting is "true" to the medium used, and (c) the degree of emotive pleasure or pain inspired by viewing each painting.

Cognitive Level and Teaching Time

There is a relationship between the cognitive level of an objective and the time required for students to develop the specified level of thinking. In general, as the cognitive level of an objective increases (e.g., goes from "knowledge" in the direction of "evaluation"), teaching time also increases. For example, it takes much more time to teach students to master content at the level of analysis than at the level of knowledge.

An important assumption of Bloom's Taxonomy is that every higher level of thinking presupposes an ability to function at every lower level. This means that a student cannot be expected to deal with analysis-level thinking about a topic until he has the background needed to handle knowledge-level, comprehension-level, and application-level thinking about the same issue. What all of this means is that there will not be time to teach students to function at high cognitive levels when dealing with *all* content in a given course.

Time considerations force teachers to establish priorities. Only important elements of content can be allocated the instructional time needed to enable students to develop extremely sophisticated levels of thinking. These high-priority topics require the teacher to sequence content carefully and to develop specific instructional plans that will help students to master all lower-level cognitive understandings related to topics selected for intensive study and targeted for student learning at the higher-cognitive levels. Some specific information regarding planning for sophisticated learning outcomes is introduced in Chapter 6, "Preparing Units and Lessons."

Objectives in the Affective Domain

The affective domain focuses on values, feelings, and attitudes. There is a relationship between affective and cognitive development of young people. Students who like and

Box 5.3

Sample Verbs for the Cognitive Domain

The following sample verbs are useful when writing objectives for each of the levels of the cognitive domain.

KNOWLEDGE
define, describe, list, name, label, recite, state, write, reproduce

COMPREHENSION
translate, transform, convert, illustrate, paraphrase, predict, rewrite, summarize, defend, explain, interpret, extrapolate

APPLICATION
solve, use, produce, compute, operate, prepare, perform, develop, transfer, demonstrate, assemble, find examples, predict, test

ANALYSIS
diagram, compare, subdivide, distinguish, differentiate, select, separate, relate, break down, infer, outline, illustrate, organize

SYNTHESIS
compose, create, devise, categorize, rearrange, build, revise, rewrite, generate, design, reconstruct, combine, compile

EVALUATION
judge, appraise, justify, criticize, discriminate, support, contrast, conclude

---

feel good about what they are doing in school tend to have better cognitive mastery of their courses than those who are unhappy in school. This makes a case for instructional planning that helps build students' sense of self-worth and positive attitudes toward the school program.

It is possible to develop programs that place heavy cognitive demands on students and, at the same time, help them develop feelings of self-worth. The hallmark of such programs is the assurance they provide to each student that they have a reasonable chance for success. So long as students feel they are succeeding, their attitudes toward school and their teachers will be positive.

In planning instructional objectives in the affective domain, certain cautions must be observed. For example, we must avoid establishing affective objectives that imply that certain attitudes, values, and feelings are "right," whereas others are "wrong." Although there may be a short list of attitudes, values, and feelings that everyone in our society endorses, most people in our democratic society have varied perspectives on important issues. A teacher who tends to prescribe particular values at the expense of others invites protests from students, parents, and others in the community.

In preparing affective objectives, we need to think carefully about an answer to this question: "In what area(s) do teachers have a legitimate 'need to know' about students' attitudes, values, and feelings?" An answer that has always made sense to us is that teachers more than anything else need to know how students are feeling about the instruction to which they are exposed in school. How do students like topics that have been selected? How do they react to this school subject as opposed to that one? Answers to questions such as these represent legitimate teacher concerns, and it is altogether appropriate for teachers to prepare affective objectives that will elicit information to provide answers.

In addition to attitudes, values, and feelings related to school subjects, another legitimate use of affective objectives relates to expanding students' commitment to fair play and other elements of democratic decision making. For example, our society generally expects schools to produce graduates who are willing to listen to diverse points of view and who are committed to the use of rational decision-making processes.

Information related to affective objectives should play no role in awarding grades to students. This information, properly, provides the teacher with evidence regarding how students are reacting to school in general and to some specific processes and content components characterizing their classes. Any attempt by the teacher to use such information for grading purposes undermines the reliability of the information obtained from students. Clever students will quickly begin to report attitudes (whether they truly hold them or not) that they believe the teacher wants to hear.

A widely used framework for thinking about objectives in the affective domain was developed by David Krathwohl and others in their *Taxonomy of Educational Objectives: Handbook II: Affective Domain* (1964). This work, often referred to as the Affective Taxonomy, scales attitudes, values, and feelings in terms of the degree to which they have been internalized. Ordered from least internalized to most internalized, the levels of the Affective Taxonomy are:

Receiving

Responding

Valuing

Organization

Characterization by a value or value complex

Teachers who wish to develop objectives in the affective domain can begin by reviewing characteristics of each level and by selecting the level of internalization most appropriate for their students. In general, it is more practical to focus on the lower levels of the Affective Taxonomy. Higher levels, for example, characterization by a value or value complex, reflect many years' growth and the influence of many factors. These are not levels teachers ordinarily expect to see in students as a result of their exposure to a single unit of study.

Receiving

Receiving refers to the willingness of a student to recognize that another point of view exists or to simply agree to look at something new. This means that he is willing to listen to information about, read about, or otherwise take in information about something new. At this level, there is no expectation that the student will give evidence of having accepted or "bought into" perspectives being promoted in the new information. Teachers are interested in the level of receiving because it implies students' willingness to at least allow themselves to be confronted with alternative points of view or perspectives. The following are examples of affective instructional objectives at the level of receiving:

- During the biology lesson, each student will listen attentively and ask at least one relevant question related to different views of the theory of evolution.
- When opportunities develop, each student will seek additional information on varying points of view concerning controversial political issues.

Responding

Responding requires the student not only to display a willingness to "take in" new information, but an additional willingness to react to it. The student reaction must be voluntary. It cannot in any way be coerced by the teacher or by pressure from other students. The following are examples of affective instructional objectives at the level of responding:

- When given an opportunity, at least once during the week each student will choose to participate in mathematics enrichment activities.
- When given free time during the physical education class, at least one-half of the class will choose to participate in a volleyball game.

Valuing

Valuing implies that the student has gone beyond responding and has freely chosen an attitude, value, or belief as his own. This internalization of attitudes, values, and beliefs is an important component of students' development. These internalized "guideposts" provide students with bases for making future decisions. The following are examples of affective instructional objectives at the level of valuing:

- The student demonstrates a concern for the environment by freely choosing to join an organization concerned with protecting the environment.
- Each student demonstrates a respect for the property of others by obtaining permission before using materials or other personal belongings of other students in the class.

Organization

Many decisions people make throughout their lives require them to resolve conflicts from two or more values or commitments they hold. The organization level of the affective domain is concerned with bringing together different values and organizing them into a value system or hierarchy. This system establishes priorities among values and serves as a valuable reference for people when they have to make choices among competing values. Lessons directed toward organization-level objectives seek to help stu-

Box 5.4

Sample Verbs in the Affective Domain

RECEIVING
listen, attend, notice, look, control, ask, follow, locate, reply

RESPONDING
read, answer, seek, help, practice, present, tell, perform, report, inform, discuss, assist, participate, comply, applaud, support, select

VALUING
share, initiate, act, join, invite, propose, participate freely, work, study, choose, volunteer

ORGANIZATION
arrange, prioritize, compare, contrast, generalize, integrate, synthesize, question

CHARACTERIZATION BY A VALUE OR VALUE COMPLEX
adhere to, influence, verify, defend, discriminate, serve, propose, practice, solve, display

---

dents to develop an awareness of the values they hold and the relative priorities they have assigned to each. The following are examples of affective instructional objectives at the level of organization:

- When confronted with a decision that calls upon them to choose among competing values, students will be able to make a choice and to identify the value priority that led them to make it.
- Each student will identify at least three value priorities that seem to have been given precedence over others by the signers of the Declaration of Independence.

Characterization by a Value or Value Complex

At the level of characterization by a value or value complex, individuals have so internalized a set of values or beliefs that their actions are consistent with them, even without their being consciously aware these actions are guided by a particular set of values and beliefs. Indeed, these individuals may not personally be able to name their priority values, but they will be recognized readily by others who infer them from observing what these people do. Lessons related to objectives at this level of the Affective Taxonomy often focus on helping students recognize that their actions reveal their values and on helping them narrow the gap between what they say they believe and how they act. The following are examples of affective instructional objectives at the level of characterization by a value or value complex:

- Students who choose to participate in a voluntary Saturday afternoon effort to help poor elderly residents do their shopping will identify three values that help to explain why they have decided to spend their Saturday in this way.

- Students will compare and contrast their responses on a requirement to list "five things I prefer to do on Sunday afternoons" with short written responses in a personally kept diary regarding what they actually did on four successive Sundays, and they will identify values implied by items on the original list and will comment on the consistency of their actual behaviors with behaviors that were listed.

Additional information regarding the affective domain and suggestions for instructional approaches that can be used to help students achieve objectives in this domain are included in Chapter 16, "Affective Learning."

Objectives in the Psychomotor Domain

The psychomotor domain includes behaviors that require coordinated use of the body's muscular system. Specific behaviors in this area cover a broad range, from activities such as running that require intensive use of large muscles to precision-drawing activities that require good control of the body's fine-muscle systems. The degree to which

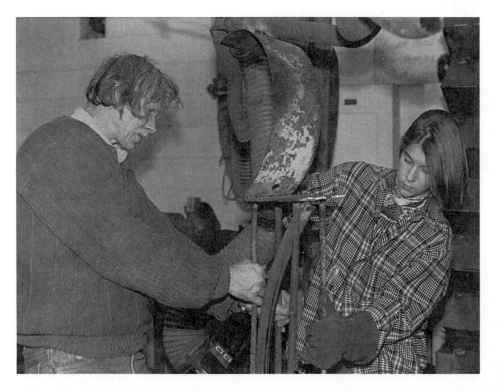

Many art projects require students to have excellent control of the body's muscular systems as well as keen cognitive insights.

teachers use psychomotor objectives depends on the extent to which the subjects they teach require students to demonstrate motor control (control of the body's muscular systems).

Instructional objectives in this domain can be organized under four basic levels of psychomotor activity. Listed from least sophisticated to most sophisticated, these are:

- Awareness
- Performance of individual components
- Integration
- Free practice

Awareness

The level of awareness is similar to the level of knowledge in the cognitive domain. At this level, all that is required is for the student to be able to identify movements required to properly perform an activity. For example, someone who is learning to play a stringed instrument needs to be aware of where strings are to be fingered for individual notes. A person learning a new dance must have a basic understanding of basic steps and the order in which they are to be accomplished. A person learning how to type must know where fingers should be placed on the keyboard. The following are examples of psychomotor instructional objectives at the level of awareness:

- Each student will orally describe to the teacher, with no errors, where fingers are to be placed on the violin to play a chord named by the teacher.
- Each student will describe the correct sequence of steps for preparing a clay pot using the coil method.

Performance of Individual Components

At the performance of individual components level, students can actually perform specific parts of a complex motor task. Teaching at this level requires breaking down a task into small steps and introducing the skill one step at a time. For example, someone who is learning dance first must learn correct body posture, then the correct sequence of steps, then the sequence when it is accompanied by music, and finally specialty turns and other embellishments. The following are examples of psychomotor instructional objectives at the level of performance of individual components:

- In front of the instructor, each student will demonstrate the proper body posture and the steps for a beginning-level dive with no errors.
- When given a practice model, each student in the biology class will make no mistakes in demonstrating the proper techniques for making an incision on a specimen.

Integration

At the level of integration, an individual is able to perform an entire sequence of motor behaviors associated with a given task, with some teacher guidance. The individual

Box 5.5

Sample Verbs in the Psychomotor Domain

AWARENESS
describe, detect, identify, isolate, select, relate, choose, recognize, diagnose

PERFORMANCE OF INDIVIDUAL COMPONENTS
demonstrate, imitate, follow, repeat, dissect, manipulate, fasten, sketch, model, mix, measure

INTEGRATION
operate, perform, act, construct, coordinate, rebuild, combine, assemble, play, react, arrange

FREE PRACTICE
adapt, alter, compose, originate, rearrange, revise, vary, create, design

---

steps have become so internalized that they are done almost automatically. The following are examples of psychomotor instructional objectives at the level of integration:

- When provided with an opportunity to use woodshop equipment and to choose appropriate wood, each student will construct an end table, under the supervision of the teacher, that has no more than two construction flaws.
- While supervised by the teacher, each student will use the potter's wheel to raise a clay pot at least eight inches high that has no cracks or other major flaws.

Free Practice

At the level of free practice, a person can perform a motor task frequently and in different settings with no guidance or prompting from the teacher. At this level, a person has become so proficient that she can modify the behavior so that it can be performed under a variety of circumstances. The following are examples of psychomotor instructional objectives at the level of free practice:

- Each student will properly dissect a frog on at least three separate occasions.
- In two or more recitals, each student will perform piano concertos with no more than two errors on each occasion.

■ ■ ■

It is important for teachers interested in planning psychomotor activities to know their students well. If students are asked to perform tasks at levels they have already mastered, they may become bored. If they are asked to do things far in excess of their ability levels, they may refuse to participate out of a belief that they have no chance to succeed. This can result in the development of very negative attitudes toward the teacher and toward school in general.

Table 5.1 Summary Table

Main Points	Explanation
Goals	These broad statements of direction describe, in very general ways, what policy-makers and important interest groups see as important outcomes of schooling. Goal statements reflect certain priorities that some groups have identified for emphasis in school programs.
Aims	Aims are more specific and focused than goals. They attempt to express the intent of goal statements in ways that more clearly delineate what is expected of students enrolled in specific school courses.
Objectives	These succinct statements describe what students should be able to do as a consequence of their exposure to instruction. They function as guideposts for instructional planning.
The ABCD Format for Preparing Instructional Objectives	This is a format for writing instructional objectives. The A refers to the audience component of the objective, the student or students for whom related instruction is designed. The B refers to behavior. This specifies in observable terms what the student will be able to do as a consequence of exposure to the related instruction. The C refers to the condition, the kinds of assessment procedures that will be used to ascertain whether the target behavior has been mastered. The D refers to the degree of proficiency that will be expected of students deemed to have mastered the objective.
Cognitive Domain	The cognitive domain is concerned with rational, systematic, or intellectual thinking.
The Cognitive Taxonomy	Developed by Benjamin Bloom and others, the cognitive taxonomy attempts to scale categories of cognitive thinking from least complex to most complex. Each higher level is thought to include every lower level.
Knowledge	This lowest level of the cognitive domain requires simple recall of previously learned information.
Comprehension	This level is one step higher than knowledge. It requires a focus on more than a single piece of previously mastered information, and it may require students to describe important relationships and/or to identify sequences of events.
Application	One step higher than the level of comprehension, application requires the use of previously learned material in a new or unfamiliar context.
Analysis	This level is one step higher than application. It involves thinking that requires consideration of the various parts of a whole as a means of determining the general character of the whole.
Synthesis	Synthesis level thinking, one step higher than analysis, involves the creation of new information by considering pieces of information that, in the experience of the person doing the thinking, have not previously been joined together. Creative thinking often involves synthesis.

Main Points	Explanation
The Cognitive Taxonomy, *cont'd.*	
Evaluation	Evaluation, the most sophisticated level of the cognitive taxonomy, requires making judgments in light of clearly identified criteria.
Cognitive Level and Teaching Time	In general, as the cognitive level of an instructional objective increases, the time required and content needed to help students master the objective also increases.
The Affective Domain	The affective domain focuses on values, feelings, and attitudes.
The Affective Taxonomy	The Affective Taxonomy, developed by David Krathwohl and others, features the levels of receiving, responding, valuing, organization, and characterization by a value or value complex.
Receiving	Receiving refers to a willingness to recognize that another point of view exists or to simply agree to look at something new.
Responding	Responding requires a willingness not just to take in new information, but also a willingness to react to it.
Valuing	Valuing implies a decision to freely choose a given attitude, value, or belief and claim it as one's own.
Organization	Organization refers to bringing together different values and organizing them into a value system or hierarchy that results in the establishment of priorities.
Characterization by a Value or Value Complex	At this stage, an individual has so internalized a set of values or beliefs that actions are consistent with them, even without the individual being aware they are guiding his actions.
The Psychomotor Domain	This domain includes behaviors that require coordinated use of the body's muscular system.
Levels of the Psychomotor Domain	Several schemes have been adopted to establish levels of behavior in the psychomotor domain. One of them includes the levels of awareness, performance of individual components, integration, and free practice.
Awareness	This level is somewhat similar to the cognitive level of knowledge. It requires an individual to identify movements necessary to properly perform an activity.
Performance of Individual Components	At this level, individuals can successfully perform specific parts of a complex motor task.
Integration	At this level, an individual can perform the entire sequence of motor behaviors associated with a given task, with some teacher guidance.
Free Practice	At this level, an individual can perform the task frequently and in different settings with no guidance or prompting from the teacher.

Review of Key Ideas

- Instructional objectives specify in quite detailed terms what students are expected to be able to do as a result of their exposure to instruction. Objectives help teachers to decide which aspects of content to emphasize, and they specify with considerable precision how students will be assessed and what levels of proficiency will be expected. They typically are prepared by teachers as part of their instructional planning.

- Instructional goals are broad policy statements developed by a governmental body or special interest groups that, in very general terms, describe hoped-for outcomes of school programs. Goals help establish general priorities for school programs.

- Instructional aims represent refinements of instructional goals. They express desired outcomes of individual courses as they relate to broader goals of schools and schooling.

- There are many formats for preparing instructional objectives. One that has been widely used is the ABCD format. The A or audience component refers to the student or students for whom the objective is intended. The B or behavior component describes, in observable terms, what the student or students should be able to do as a result of exposure to instruction. The C or conditions points out the nature of assessment or evaluation that will be used to determine whether new content has been learned. The D or degree describes the proficiency level that will be required for a judgment to be made that the material has been mastered.

- Instructional objectives in the cognitive domain focus on rational, systematic, and intellectual thinking. Bloom's Taxonomy scales levels of the cognitive taxonomy from simplest to most complex. Levels include knowledge, comprehension, application, analysis, synthesis, and evaluation.

- Instructional objectives in the affective domain focus on values, attitudes, and feelings. Levels of the Affective Taxonomy include receiving, responding, valuing, organization, and characterization by a value or value complex.

- Instructional objectives in the psychomotor domain focus on behaviors that require coordinated use of the body's muscular system. One scheme that establishes psychomotor levels from simplest to most complex includes the levels of awareness, performance of individual components, integration, and free practice.

Follow-Up Questions and Activities

Questions

1. What are the characteristics of goals, aims, and objectives?
2. Who decides what the goals of schools and schooling should be?
3. What are some kinds of information teachers need to have as they write instructional objectives for their students?

4. Why should teachers prepare instructional objectives?

5. Why are writers of instructional objectives encouraged to describe varieties of hoped-for student behaviors that can be directly observed?

6. What are the categories of the ABCD format for preparing instructional objectives?

7. What are some things teachers typically consider as they decide what levels of expected proficiency to include in the instructional objectives they are writing?

8. What is the concern of the cognitive domain, and what levels of cognitive knowledge are described in Bloom's Taxonomy?

9. What is the focus of the affective domain, and what levels of the affective domain were identified by David Krathwohl and others?

10. What is the focus of the psychomotor domain, and what levels have been identified to classify psychomotor behaviors in terms of their complexity and sophistication?

Activities

1. Review some articles, reports of speeches, editorials, or other sources in which concerns are raised about the quality of education in the United States. Identify what seem to be some implied goals for schools. Organize a panel to discuss the adequacy of these implied goals. As a concluding activity, try to identify four or five goals that a large majority of your class would agree to support.

2. Take one of the goals from a source such as the *America 2000* report and prepare three or four related aims for a school subject you would like to teach. Ask your course instructor to critique your list of aims.

3. Take one of the aims identified in the exercise described in item two. Get together with one or two other people who are interested in teaching the subject for which the aims were prepared. Prepare three to five instructional objectives related to the aim. Follow the ABCD format. Share your work with your instructor.

4. Working with some others who are interested in teaching your major subject, identify some appropriate affective-domain outcomes for a course you might teach. Prepare two affective-domain instructional objectives related to the outcomes you identify.

5. Organize a class debate on this topic: "Resolved that instruction based on pre-planned instructional objectives lacks spontaneity and results in low quality classroom instruction."

References

America 2000: An Education Strategy. Washington, DC: United States Department of Education, 1991.

BLOOM, B. (ED.). *Taxonomy of Educational Objectives: Handbook I: Cognitive Domain*. New York: David McKay, Inc., 1956.

FERRE, A. "Effects of Repeated Performance Objectives upon Student Achievement and Attitude." Doctor of Education dissertation. Las Cruces, NM: New Mexico State University, 1972.

GRONLUND, N. *How to Write and Use Instructional Objectives.* 4th ed. New York: Macmillan Publishing Company, 1991.

KRATHWOHL, D; BLOOM, B.; AND MASIA, B. *Taxonomy of Educational Objectives: Handbook II: Affective Domain.* New York: David McKay, 1964.

MOORE, K. *Classroom Teaching Skills.* 2nd ed. New York: McGraw-Hill, 1992.

MORSE, J. A. AND TILLMAN, M. H. "Achievement as Affected by Possession of Behavioral Objectives." *Engineering Education* (June 1973), pp. 124–126.

OLSEN, R. "A Comparative Study of the Effect of Behavioral Objectives on Class Performance and Retention in Physical Science." *Journal of Research in Science Teaching* (vol. 10, no. 3, 1973), pp. 271–277.

POPHAM, W. J. "Instructional Objectives Benefit Teaching and Testing." *Momentum* (May 1987), pp. 11–16.

WHITE, R. T. AND TISHER, R. P. "Research on Natural Sciences." In M. C. Wittrock (ed.). *Handbook of Research on Teaching.* 3rd ed. New York: Macmillan Publishing Company, 1986, pp. 874–905.

Student Characteristics

Students have vastly different interests, abilities, and academic backgrounds. Successful planning requires teachers to know their students well. Lessons that are based on unwarranted assumptions about students' mastery of prerequisite information (and about other critical student characteristics) will fail.

In thinking about the student-characteristics variable, it is useful to ask such questions as these:

- "What previous knowledge and background in this topic do these students have?"
- "What are these students interested in?"
- "Do some of these students have special needs? If so, how can they best be accommodated?"
- "Are there ways to take instructional advantage of some special characteristics of students in this class?"

The Learning Context

There are enormous differences among the nation's secondary schools. The character of individual schools is shaped by the general nature of the communities they serve, the characteristics of their students, the actions of school administrators, and state and local school policies. Taken together, these variables help give each school its own learning context.

Because of differences in the learning context, expectations of teachers sometimes vary considerably from school to school. For example, some administrators may be extremely sensitive to public reaction to students' standardized test scores and may pressure teachers to pay particular attention to content likely to be sampled on these tests. In other buildings, teachers may have to carefully document what they do, and administrators may require every teacher to submit detailed lesson plans for every class session that is taught.

The prevailing teacher evaluation system can also pressure teachers to behave in certain "preferred" ways. For example, if the scheme used in a school rewards teachers who have quiet classrooms, teachers are unlikely to opt for instructional techniques that involve spirited but noisy student interactions.

The learning context in an individual school almost always tends to be more supportive of some kinds of teacher behavior than others. For this reason, in deciding whether to accept a position that has been offered to them, teachers often ask themselves questions such as these:

- "What does the community expect of teachers and the schools?"
- "What will I need to do in this school to please administrators?"
- "How are teachers evaluated in this school?"
- "Is my teaching style compatible with what people expect here?"

Available Time

Time affects planning in several ways. The most important time consideration in planning for instruction is the amount of time actually available for instruction. A fixed number of instructional days and class periods is available. Difficult decisions have to be made regarding how this precious time should be allocated among the many topics that may merit attention.

The planning process, itself, takes time. Beginning teachers often feel stress as they work in the evening to plan new instructional experiences, correct student work, attend to committee obligations, and still maintain some semblance of a family and social life. For many of them, planning proficiency grows with experience, and they find they can complete unit planning and lesson planning obligations more efficiently.

Learning Resources

Kinds of resources available to support instruction place some limits on instructional planning. Teachers who are well trained in certain approaches and enthusiastic about using them cannot do so unless necessary support materials are available. Instructional plans need to be prepared in light of accurate information about the availability of needed learning resources.

Learning resource problems sometimes pose particular difficulties when state regulations or even local administrative policies change suddenly. For example, a guideline calling on all science teachers to spend at least 40 percent of their time in class doing laboratory work will produce nothing but frustration if appropriate laboratory facilities and other materials are not in place to support this kind of teaching.

Instructional Units

Organizing instruction into well-planned units has several advantages. When lessons are grouped together and systematically sequenced in an instructional unit, each lesson can build on content introduced previously. These interrelated lessons help develop an instructional scheme that promotes students' abilities to see relationships and to draw conclusions from analyses based on large quantities of information.

The process of unit planning also alerts the teacher to the need to gather certain kinds of learning resources. For example, as a teacher plans a unit, he may recognize a need for videotapes and maps. These materials may have to be ordered from a centralized media facility several weeks in advance. Since the unit ordinarily is planned some time before it is presented, typically there is time to obtain the learning materials needed to support instruction.

Unit planners need to be particularly sensitive to the intended audience. Information about students is used to identify an appropriate place for beginning instruction. Teachers often rely on their personal knowledge of students' past performance in mak-

This librarian/instructional media specialist is making a suggestion to a middle school teacher.

ing the where-to-begin decisions. Sometimes diagnostic tests are used to provide this information.

Unit plans tend to give teachers a sense of direction and security as they deliver instruction. They eliminate uncertainty about "what should be done tomorrow." They help establish a sense of order and routine that conveys to students that the teacher knows what she is doing and that tends to be associated with high levels of student achievement.

Elements of an Instructional Unit

Instructional units can be formatted in many ways. Many of them include these parts:

- Unit title
- Rationale and major goals

- Mandated content
- Major generalizations and concepts
- Instructional objectives and a tentative time line for teaching content related to each
- Instructional strategies for each objective
- Plans for the beginning and ending
- Evaluation procedures
- List of needed learning resources

The Unit Title

The unit title should communicate the essence of the content to be covered in the unit. Unit titles ordinarily are short. Sometimes even one word suffices. Examples of unit titles include: "The Halogens" (chemistry), "The Lake Poets" (English), "Factoring" (mathematics), and "The Progressives" (history).

Rationale and Goals

A unit rationale is a statement designed to establish the unit's importance. Writing the rationale helps the unit developer explain why the unit's content needs to be taught. The rationale helps convince others that the material to be covered is important.

Goals in unit plans are statements that describe general learning outcomes. Sometimes they describe relationships between unit content and the entire school subject of which they are a part. Goal statements provide other teachers, administrators, parents, students, and others with an appreciation of the basic purposes of instruction associated with the unit. Suppose a secondary school English teacher were preparing a unit titled "The Epic Hero Theme." This teacher might produce a goal statement something like this:

> This unit seeks to introduce students to the form, extent of use, and the purposes of "epic hero themes" as vehicles for communicating a culture's values.

Mandated Content

In some states, regulations specify the content that must be taught in individual courses. Some local school districts have similar rules. Where these mandates are in place, teachers often are required to provide evidence of where in their instructional programs required content is being covered. Some teachers find it convenient to develop a notation system to identify places in their instructional units where content required by state or local regulations is treated.

Major Generalizations and Concepts

Generalizations in instructional units summarize in a succinct way key ideas that students should master as a result of their exposure to unit content. (Chapter 4 provides more information about generalizations.) Concepts are terms. Generalizations take the form of a statement of relationship among concepts. Hence, to understand a generalization, students must also grasp the concepts that are associated with it. Consider this generalization from sociology:

Box 6.1

Selecting Unit Titles

It isn't easy to select good unit titles. Each unit represents a segment of a course. The unit should bring together content elements that share some common features. Often unit titles reflect a theme that functions as a useful organizer. If too much content is organized in one unit, students may be overwhelmed. On the other hand, if information is divided into too many units, content can become excessively fragmented. This, too, poses difficulties for students.

Suppose you were assigned to prepare units for one semester's work in a middle school, junior high school, or senior high school. (You choose the course.) There are about 16 instructional weeks in a semester. Identify titles of five or six units you would use, and indicate how much time you would devote to each.

1. How did you decide on unit titles?

2. What are other ways of dividing the semester's content into units?

3. How did you decide on time allocations? What are some alternative time arrangements?

UNIT TITLES   TIME ALLOCATION

_____   _____

_____   _____

_____   _____

_____   _____

_____   _____

_____   _____

When urbanization occurs rapidly in a country, differences in status among people in various social classes become more pronounced.

This generalization would be impossible for a student to comprehend who did not know the meaning of such concepts as "urbanization," "country," "status," and "social class." One of the teacher's tasks in planning units is to identify concepts associated with guiding generalizations that students are unlikely to know. Instructional experiences need to be included that will help them grasp meanings of these concepts.

Some concepts are more difficult for students to master than others. Characteristics that define a given concept are referred to as its *attributes*. Less-complex and simpler-to-learn concepts have relatively few of these. Consider the concept "triangle." Its attributes are (a) a two-dimensional closed plane figure that has (b) three sides and (c) three interior angles. Consider the small number of attributes associated with this concept as opposed the much larger number associated with more complex and difficult-to-learn concepts such as "democracy" or "socialization."

Instructional units containing large numbers of generalizations with complex concepts require more instructional time than those dealing with less-complex concepts. This reality requires unit developers to consider the sophistication of the content students are expected to learn as they make suggestions regarding how much time ought to be devoted to the unit (and even to individual parts of a each unit).

Instructional Objectives and Suggested Time Lines

Instructional objectives describe behaviors students are expected to demonstrate as a result of their exposure to instruction. The objectives tie closely to the generalizations and related concepts that the unit developer has selected to guide overall unit planning. Numbers of instructional objectives vary from unit to unit. Unit developers try to strike a balance between providing too many objectives (a situation which means each covers a very restricted range of content) and too few (a situation which may stretch an individual objective across an excessively large and complex body of information). In a unit designed to cover about three weeks, there might be between 6 and 10 instructional objectives.

Learning content associated with each objective varies depending upon the sophistication of the intended learning outcome. If the objective calls upon students to demonstrate only low-level knowledge and comprehension levels of thinking, little instructional time may be required. On the other hand, an objective requiring students to engage in sophisticated analyses of complex information may require the teacher to spend considerable instructional time preparing students to demonstrate their ability to engage in this kind of sophisticated thinking.

Time required to teach an individual unit also varies for reasons other than complexity of the intended learning outcome. The nature of students in a given class will influence a teacher's pacing decisions. In addition, there often are differences depending on the time of the school year when the unit is taught. Often units introduced early in a school year, when students are getting reacclimated to doing school work, take longer to teach than those introduced later in the year.

Instructional Strategies

An instructional strategy consists of systematically organized instructional techniques that are directed toward helping students master an objective. There needs to be an instructional strategy for each unit objective. Because some objectives are intended to develop more sophisticated student thinking than others, some instructional strategies are more complex than others. The "worth" of any instructional strategy is determined in terms of its ability to help students master the objective to which it relates.

Typically, instructional strategies are not described in great detail in instructional unit plans. A sentence or two describing the general instructional approach to be taken for each objective suffices. Instructional strategies are presented in much greater detail in lesson plans. The lesson plans provide the guidance for what teachers do in the classroom on a given day, and it is appropriate that detailed information about instructional strategies be provided in these important documents.

Box 6.2

The Beginning Steps in Planning a Unit

Identify a unit you might like to prepare in your subject area. Choose a unit title, write a rationale, identify one or more generalizations or principles that will serve as a focus, and write four or five instructional objectives. (Your instructor may have a preferred format for the objectives. Ask.)

Unit Title: _____

Rationale: _____

_____

_____

Generalizations: _____

_____

_____

_____

_____

_____

Instructional Objectives:

1. _____

_____

2. _____

_____

3. _____

_____

4. _____

_____

5. _____

_____

When referring to an objective focusing on student comprehension of the coefficient of expansion principle, a physics teacher might write the following information about an intended learning strategy in a unit plan outline:

> Conduct an inquiry lesson on the unequal rate of expansion in response to heat of different metals using the bi-metallic knife.

A related daily lesson would develop this strategy into a series of clearly defined steps.

Plans for the Beginning and Ending

Instructional unit plans often feature quite detailed descriptions of how the teacher intends to introduce the unit to students. The introduction is critically important to the success of the unit. If the initial activity captures students' interest, it will be easier for the teacher to sustain their enthusiasm as the body of the unit content is introduced.

Good unit introductions accomplish several purposes. They stimulate initial student interest and give students a general overview of unit content. They also provide them with a clear idea about what they will be expected to do.

Conclusions or suggested culminating activities often are also written into instructional unit plans. Their purpose is to help students to draw together the key ideas that have been introduced. Often these activities call on students to engage in application activities that require them to use some of the information they have learned. A good culminating activity can build students' confidence by providing them with opportunities to verify for themselves that they have mastered challenging new material.

Evaluation Procedures

Information about approaches to evaluating student progress on unit content is included in the instructional unit plan. Evaluation procedures often are provided not just for the culminating assessment at the conclusion but also for interim assessments that are made from time to time as the material is being taught.

It is important that selected evaluation procedures be consistent with the unit's objectives. For example, if an objective calls for students to engage in analysis-level thinking, the recommended evaluation procedure must have the capability of assessing this kind of thinking.

Many evaluation procedures are available to teachers. For more information about the general issue of assessment of students, refer to Chapter 17, "Measuring Student Progress."

List of Needed Learning Resources

Well-designed units are supported by a variety of learning resources. These resources need to be identified as units are planned. They may involve such items as supplemental readings, software, video and audiotapes, compact disks, maps, laboratory equipment, and resource people who may be invited to the class. Individual teachers often design their own learning materials to supplement the text and other basic instructional resources.

Today, budgets rather than materials' availability place more limits on the kinds of learning resources teachers can obtain. Catalogs containing an incredible variety of support materials regularly arrive at school district offices, at individual buildings, and in faculty mail boxes of classroom teachers. These catalogs taken together with district- and building-level library, media, and instructional resource centers help teachers develop a feel for the range of available materials. In well-funded school districts and schools, teachers may be allowed to purchase substantial quantities of instructional-support materials for units they develop. In others, budgetary limitations severely restrict teachers' ability to purchase these materials, and obviously their instructional options are more limited than those of teachers who work where more money is available.

The Unit Planning Process

Some educational methods textbooks and teacher education programs recommend a *linear* approach to instructional planning. Linear planning begins with (1) identifying the unit generalizations and objectives. It then moves on through the steps of (2) identifying appropriate content for achieving the objectives, (3) designing and sequencing learning activities related to the objectives, (4) identifying and gathering needed learning resources, and (5) identifying evaluation procedures.

Though this approach seems to make certain logical sense, researchers have found that few teachers follow this sequence. Secondary teachers more frequently begin the planning process with an identification of the content that needs to be taught. They tend to then move on to think about generalizations and objectives, activities, resources, and evaluation, but these elements are not considered one at a time. There is a moving back and forth among unit elements and a continuing process of readjustment until all pieces seem to fit together (Yinger, 1979). For example, in considering the issue of evaluation, if the teacher thinks about a possible essay examination that will require students to analyze an issue or a problem, the teacher may want to revisit plans for learning activities to be sure they will prepare students to do this.

WHAT SCHOLARS SAY

How Do Teachers Plan?

Researchers have found that many teachers develop executive planning routines (Clark and Peterson, 1986). These routines constitute a structure that helps them identify the specific management and instructional activities they will use during their lessons. Experienced teachers have been found to have better-developed ideas about productive planning routines than inexperienced teachers.

Well-conceived executive routines, when combined with a sound understanding of content to be taught, allow teachers to develop a clear view regarding how a lesson, ideally, should flow. This idealized image is modified as teachers consider such variables as (1) specific objectives to be mastered, (2) availability of instructional support materials, (3) time constraints, and (4) other contextual variables. Individual teachers vary the order in which these variables are considered.

The planning decisions of individual teachers have been found to exert a strong influence on such aspects of lessons as (1) content coverage, (2) grouping decisions, (3) the nature of opportunities provided for students to learn new material, and (4) allocation of time for specific classroom activities (Clark and Peterson, 1986). Planning, however, does not typically describe everything that will go on within a given lesson. Teachers use the planning process to establish a broad outline of what they intend to accomplish. Because there is some unpredictability once instruction begins, teachers tend to avoid excessive attention to detail in their plans, realizing that they need to retain their flexibility to respond to unanticipated situations as they occur in the classroom.

Source: C. Clark and P. Peterson, "Teachers' Thought Processes." In M. Wittrock (Ed.), *Handbook of Research on Teaching* (3rd ed., pp. 297–314). New York: Macmillan Publishing Company, 1986.

Formatting the Unit

There are many ways to format units. In some places, school districts have adopted a standard set of guidelines teachers are expected to follow in designing their instructional units. Administrators in some individual schools have developed formats that teachers in their buildings are supposed to use. In many other places (probably a majority of schools), teachers are allowed to make their own unit formatting decisions.

The sample unit introduced in this chapter features these eight headings:

- Unit title

- Rationale and goal statement

- Mandated content

- Focus generalization(s) and related concepts

- Instructional objectives and suggested time allocations

- Suggested teaching strategies

- Examples of evaluation procedures

- Suggested learning resources

A Sample Unit

Title

The American Revolution

Rationale and Unit Goal

The American Revolution was a key event in American history. An understanding of the Revolution helps explain the nature of Americans' basic beliefs and values. The goals of this unit are to help students grasp forces that led the American colonists to band together and to help students appreciate American values, beliefs, and institutions that, in large measure, are traceable to the American Revolution.

Mandated Content

State law requires that some attention be given during the unit to these content elements:

- Major events and forces leading to the Revolution
- Key military events and their consequences
- Important public personalities
- Lasting influences of the war

Focus Generalizations

Revolutions often occur when people believe that legitimate authority is insensitive to and unresponsive toward their needs.

Related Concepts
- Revolution
- Legitimate authority
- Wants and needs
- Responsive government

Revolutions challenge people to rethink their assumptions about the nature of the proper relationship between citizens and their government.

Related Concepts
- Role of citizenship
- Individual rights
- Role of government
- Governmental rights
- Loyalty
- Rebellion
- Independence

The values and beliefs of a given group of people have their roots in the pivotal events in the history of the people.

Related Concepts
- Values
- Beliefs
- Continuity and change over time
- Pivotal event
- Historical antecedents

Instructional Objectives and Suggested Time Allocation

- Each student will identify events leading to the American Revolution. *Suggested time allocation*: 1 day
- In an essay, each student will compare and contrast American and British advantages and disadvantages at the time of the outbreak of hostilities. At least two advantages and two disadvantages should be cited for each side. *Suggested time allocation*: 2 days
- Each student will identify American approaches to financing the war. *Suggested time allocation*: 1 day
- Each student will identify key military developments of the Revolutionary War and explain their importance. *Suggested time allocation*: 3 days
- Each student will analyze the results of the war with specific reference to its (a) political effects, (b) social effects, and (c) economic effects. *Suggested time allocation*: 4 days
- Students working in groups will identify values and beliefs that became important during the time of the American Revolution that are still highly valued and influential in the United States today. *Suggested time allocation*: 2 days
- Each student will profess an interest in learning more about the American Revolution. *Suggested time allocation*: No specific allocation. The instruction of the entire unit should be directed toward this objective.

Suggested Teaching Strategies

Beginning the Unit.   Bring in newspaper accounts of an ethnic or civil conflict occurring somewhere in the world. Ask students questions such as these:

- What do you think causes people to become so angry that they will fight and kill one another?
- What happens to a country when this kind of conflict occurs?
- Are there circumstances when it is right for people to rise up against the legal government?
- What about our own Revolutionary War? Did the colonists have legitimate reasons for rebelling against England, or were they just trying to serve their narrow, personal interests?
- In what ways do you think the Revolution might have changed ways people thought and acted?

Show parts of the filmstrip series, "The American Revolution: Two Views." Point out to students that questions noted above and those raised in the filmstrip will be investigated by the class over the next three weeks. Explain that the basic purpose will be to identify some reasons revolutions take place and to think about the nature of the proper relationship between a government and the citizens it serves. *Suggested time allocation*: 1 day

Recommended Teaching Approaches for Each Objective
OBJECTIVE 1:   Divide the class into several groups. Ask members of each group to conduct research and to report on how each of the following events contributed to the eventual outbreak of the Revolutionary War:

- Proclamation of 1763
- Sugar Act of 1764
- Stamp Act of 1765
- Declaratory Act of 1766
- Townshend Acts

Show the film, "Prelude to Revolution."

OBJECTIVE 2:   Divide the class into four groups.
   Assign each group to develop one of these lists:

- List of British advantages and disadvantages
- List of American advantages and disadvantages
- List of possible British arguments in support of and against going to war
- List of possible American arguments in support of and against going to war

Each group will share its list with the whole class. Allow students to work with the computer-based lesson titled, "Revolutionary War: Choosing Sides." Discuss.

OBJECTIVE 3:   Write the following information on the chalkboard: "It costs a great deal of money to conduct a war. How can this money be raised?"

Involve students in a brainstorming activity designed to provide answers to this question. Debrief. Go on to discuss ways money has been raised for recent conflicts (Desert Storm, Vietnam War, Korean War, and so forth). Assign students to read material explaining problems Americans faced in raising money to pay for the Revolutionary War and how money was actually obtained.

OBJECTIVE 4:   Lay out a time line for the years 1775 to 1781 in the front of the room. Assign groups of two or three students to conduct research on key events of the Revolutionary War. Ask them to place the event at its proper place on the time line and to write a description explaining what occurred and why the event was important. Ask students to view the videocassette titled, "The American Revolution." Discuss key events of the war.

OBJECTIVE 5:   Provide students with information about the Treaty of Paris of 1783. Divide class members into four teams. Ask each team to gather information about one of these questions:

- What were the issues of interest to France, and how did the treaty affect France?
- What were the issues of interest to Spain, and how did the treaty affect Spain?
- What were the issues of interest to Americans, and how did the treaty affect the former colonies?
- What were the issues of interest to the British, and how did the treaty affect Britain?

Conclude with a discussion of benefits and losses conferred by the treaty on the parties involved.

OBJECTIVE 6:   As a concluding activity, conduct a brainstorming activity in which students are challenged to identify basic values and beliefs held by the colonists during the Revolutionary War. Discuss the list generated by the class. Then, ask groups of students to take one of the identified values or beliefs and find examples of how it still influences the behaviors of present-day Americans.

OBJECTIVE 7:   Administer an interest survey on the last day the unit is taught to identify which aspects of the unit topic were most interesting to students. The survey should also elicit information about how students feel about learning more about the American Revolution.

Suggested Evaluation Procedures

Procedures for Individual Objectives
OBJECTIVE 1:   Use a matching test. Students will be required to match events leading up to the Revolution with a description of the event (knowledge- and comprehension-level evaluation).

Box 6.3

A Sample Evaluation Item for a Unit Objective

This item could be used with the sample unit. It is helpful to begin writing evaluation items as units are being developed. These can be placed in an "item bank" to be used when time comes for students to be assessed.

Instructional Objective 1: A Matching Item

Directions: The item on the left refers to an action taken by the British. On the right you will find a list of responses made by the American colonists. Match items by placing the letter of the action taken by the American colonists in the blank before the related action taken by the British.

British Action

_____ 1. Proclamation of 1763

_____ 2. Stamp Act, 1765

_____ 3. Townshend Acts, 1767

_____ 4. Tea Act gives East India Company a monopoly

_____ 5. "Intolerable Acts," 1774

_____ 6. Massachusetts declared to be in a state of rebellion, troops sent to Lexington and Concord, 1775

American Colonists' Action

a. Second Continental Congress convened, army established

b. First Continental Congress convened, Continental Association formed to boycott British goods

c. Parliament ignored, settlement of lands west of Appalachians continued

d. Cargo of tea destroyed by Boston Tea Party

e. Louis XVI invited to Boston for an emergency meeting

f. Boycott of British goods after violent protests by residents of Massachusetts

g. Boston Massacre results from clash between colonists and British troops

h. 12 of the 13 colonies refuse to import British goods

i. Colonists boycott British goods; colonists organize Sons of Liberty

(Key: 1 – c, 2 – i, 3 – f, 4 – d, 5 – b, 6 – a)

[Please note that more possible answers are provided than questions. This is a desirable design feature. If the number of possible answers in the right-hand column is exactly equal to the number of blanks in the left-hand column, a student who misses one item automatically also misses a second.]

OBJECTIVE 2:   Each student will be asked to prepare a written speech that might have been delivered by a colonist before the outbreak of the Revolutionary War. The speech may make a case either in support of or opposing going to war with the British. The written speech will be evaluated in terms of the quality of the arguments made, the correct identifications of potential advantages and disadvantages for each side, and its general persuasiveness (analysis- and synthesis-level evaluation).

OBJECTIVE 3:   Each student will respond correctly to 8 of 10 true-false items focusing on American attempts to finance the Revolutionary War (knowledge-level evaluation).

OBJECTIVE 4:   Each student will respond correctly to at least 80 percent of multiple choice items on a series of short examinations focusing on key events and other important developments associated with the Revolutionary War (knowledge- and comprehension-level evaluation).

OBJECTIVE 5:   Each student will prepare an essay focusing on social and economic consequences of the Revolutionary War. Each paper must include specific references to at least two social and two economic results of the War. Evaluation of the essay will take into account the quality of information cited and evidence that thinking goes beyond a recitation of material covered in class (analysis-level evaluation).

OBJECTIVE 6:   Each student will participate as a member of a team of four on a group activity that results in a "product" of some kind that illustrates and explains issues and values raised during the Revolutionary War that continue to be relevant for us today. These products or projects can take many forms. Art work, original plays, panel discussions, radio or television scripts, debates, and symposiums are among the possibilities.

OBJECTIVE 7:   Administer a simple attitude inventory on which students are asked to respond on a 1 to 3 scale (1 being highest or most positive and 3 being lowest or least positive) that asks them to record their interest in or feelings about various topics covered during the unit. Students need to be informed that their responses on the attitude inventory will have no bearing on their grades. Some teachers may prefer to give the same attitude inventory both at the beginning and the end of the unit. This will allow the teacher to look for shifts in interest in individual topics that may have resulted because of what students experienced as the unit was taught.

SUGGESTED LEARNING RESOURCES
General Reference Books
Bliss, George A. *The American Revolution: How Revolutionary Was It?* New York: Harper & Row, 1980.
Gephard, Ronald E. (ed.). *Revolutionary America*. Washington, DC: U.S. Government Printing Office, 1984.
Meltzer, Milton. *The American Revolutionaries: A History in Their Own Words*. New York: Harper & Row Junior Books, 1987.

Student Texts

Boorstin, Daniel J. and Kelley, Brooks M. *History of the United States*. Lexington, MA: Ginn & Company, 1986.

Patrick, John and Berkin, Carole. *History of the American Nation*. New York: Macmillan Publishing Company, 1987.

16MM Film

"Prelude to Revolution." 13-minute film available from Encyclopedia Britannica Educational Corporation, 425 N. Michigan Ave., Chicago, IL 60611.

Videocassette

"The American Revolution." Available from Guidance Associates, Communications Park Box 3000, Mt. Kisko, NY 10549.

Filmstrip

"The American Revolution: Two Views." 4 color film-strips and accompanying cassette tapes available from Social Studies School Service, P.O. Box 802, Culver City, CA 90232-0802.

Computer Software

"Revolutionary War: Choosing Sides." Computer-based role-playing exercise. One diskette available in either Apple or MS-DOS format from Social Studies School Service, P.O. Box 802, Culver City, CA 90232-0802.

Posters

"American Patriot Posters." A set of 10 color posters of Revolutionary-era patriots available from Social Studies School Service, P.O. Box 802, Culver City, CA 90232-0802.

Many unit-formatting options are available. The scheme introduced here is widely used. Another popular alternative features a layout that displays objectives, teaching approaches, and instructional materials in adjacent columns.

Lesson Planning

Instructional unit plans describe the general flow of instructional activity over a period of several weeks. Shorter-range instructional decisions are expressed in written form in teachers' lesson plans. A lesson plan might be looked at as the "script" the teacher follows in teaching students during a given period (or, in some cases, over one, two, or three successive periods: some individual lessons take more than one day to teach).

Typically, beginning teachers put more detail in their lesson plans than do more experienced teachers. Experienced teachers are able to keep many of the details in their heads, and they don't require as many written prompts as do newcomers to the profession who are still getting use to managing students and moving smoothly from one instructional point to another.

Box 6.4

An Alternate Scheme for Formatting an Instructional Unit

Unit Title:

Unit Rationale:

Generalization(s):

Objectives	Teaching Approaches	Materials

There are no precise rules governing how much detail a "good" lesson plan should contain. In general, there should be enough information to enable a substitute teacher to deliver the lesson without too much difficulty.

The Lesson Planning Process

As is true for unit planning, the process followed in developing lessons varies somewhat from individual to individual. Some begin by focusing on learning activities; others consider the objectives they are trying to achieve; others tend to start by thinking about the kinds of evaluation tools they will be using; still others begin at other points. Regardless of where the planning process begins, most teachers ultimately find themselves required to answer some key questions. Among them are the following:

- *What is the lesson objective?* The answer to this question is an important one. For one thing, it requires the teacher to weigh the importance of what he is contemplating and to determine that the purpose is a worthy one. Thinking about the objective sometimes also prompts ideas about possible teaching approaches.
- *What is a good entry point for instruction?* To answer this question, the teacher must have good information about the students to whom the lesson is to be taught. The entry point of any lesson should tie clearly to prior lessons and to what students already know.
- *How can I gain students' attention?* This question prompts the teacher to think about how students can be motivated at the beginning of a lesson. If an initial interest can be established, students are more likely to "stay with" the teacher for the duration of the lesson.
- *What is the best way to sequence lesson content and activities?* This is a difficult question because there is no answer that is "right" for all situations. In some cases, logic of the subject matter dictates the response. For example, in a mathematics lesson less complex content must precede more complex content. In other subjects, however, the sequencing decision is much more a matter of a teacher's personal professional judgment.
- *How can students become actively involved in the lesson, and what should they do to demonstrate they have learned?* Lessons requiring students to actively manipulate the new content tend to be more successful than those where they do little more than passively read or listen. Additionally, learning theorists tell us that new information is better remembered when people have had an opportunity to use it in some way. For this reason, it is important to include application activities in lesson plans, whenever possible.
- *How should students be grouped during the lesson?* Decisions need to be made regarding whether the students will be taught as members of one large group or as members of a number of small groups. If the decision is to have them divided into groups, specific thought must be directed toward how group members will be selected and how students will move smoothly (quickly and quietly) from the large group into the small groups. If it is important for groups to have leaders, decisions must be made about how they are to be selected and about how they will make their reports to the teacher. Plans also have to be prepared for distributing materials quickly and efficiently to all group members.

- *How can needs of students at different ability levels be met, and what should be done to monitor the progress of individual students?* Because all classes have individuals with vastly different levels of abilities and interest, plans must be made on the assumption that some students will need different learning materials than others and that some will finish more quickly than others. A system for keeping track of how individual students are doing also needs to be devised.

- *What kind of practice assignments need to be developed?* It is important to think carefully and to prepare in advance lesson assignments that call on students to apply what they have learned. Good assignments of this kind almost never can be created on the spur of the moment. They need to be carefully designed and prepared before lesson instruction begins.

- *How should the lesson be concluded?* It is as important to plan a sound lesson conclusion as a highly motivating lesson beginning. The conclusion should help students draw together major points that have been introduced. It is particularly important for the teacher to build in time for a lesson conclusion. The lesson should not "just stop." The ending needs to be a carefully planned and executed component that is treated as an essential feature of the lesson.

- *What materials are needed?* Some lessons fail because teachers have failed to think carefully about needed materials. Books, handouts, paper and pencils, and other needed items should be identified and gathered before the lesson begins. Some teachers find it useful to put together a "needed materials" checklist as part of their preparation. They check off individual items as they begin getting ready to teach the lesson and, in this way, assure themselves that any problems associated with the lesson will not be caused by materials-availability problems.

- *What rules and management guidelines should be adopted for this lesson?* Some lessons include activities that are designed to promote very active student involvement. To assure that students maintain a focus on the planned academic activity, the teacher needs to think through his or her expectations regarding what kinds of student behaviors are "appropriate" and to think about how these expectations will be communicated to students. Additional thought needs to be given to possible actions that will assure student compliance with these expectations.

- *How much time should be allocated to each part of the lesson?* Time is an extremely scarce commodity in the classroom. This resource needs to be expended wisely so as to assure the maximum possible learning benefit for students. Some parts of lessons clearly deserve more attention than others. Careful planners take time to make decisions about how much time they intend to devote to each part of a lesson.

Historical Lesson Plan Models

People have not always agreed on components needed in a lesson plan. Some lesson plans draw on long historical precedent: One was developed thousands of years ago by the ancient Spartans. In a model Spartan lesson, these four things were expected to happen (Posner, 1987):

- The teacher was expected to introduce the new material to the students.

- The students were asked to think about the material.
- The students were asked to repeat the new material aloud, and the teacher took time to work with students individually until each of them had memorized the material.
- The teacher then listened to each student recite the memorized material.

Many centuries later during the Middle Ages, the Jesuits developed another lesson plan model. It was designed for students attending cathedral schools. Several of its features would be endorsed by some educators today. It called on teachers to do the following (Posner, 1987):

- Present information slowly enough for students to take notes.
- Pause periodically to explain difficult parts of the new content.
- Relate the new content to other subjects.
- Ask students to memorize the new material.
- Assign monitors to work with individual students and to check on their recitations of memorized material.
- Conclude with a discussion and interpretation of the meaning of the new content.
- Reward the best performing students (for the purposes of giving all students incentives to learn).

In the nineteenth century, Johann Friedrich Herbart developed his *apperception* theory of learning (Meyer, 1975). According to this view, learning took place when ideas already in the mind were brought into contact with new information. If there was a logical relationship between what a person already knew and new information, the new information would be taken into the brain and would become part of the person's general store of knowledge. This theory placed a premium on the importance of diagnosing what learners already knew and establishing a connection between prior knowledge and new information.

A five-part lesson model was developed around the idea of apperception. According to this Herbartian lesson plan, each lesson should include these five key steps (Meyer, 1975):

- Preparation
- Presentation
- Association (tying new information to existing information)
- Generalization (stating broad applications of the new knowledge)
- Application

Elements of these lesson models from history are still found in many present-day lesson designs. In part this results because some of their features are consistent with modern theories of learning.

Modern-Day Lesson Plan Formats

Contemporary lesson plan formats vary. Virtually all of them call for a lesson title and a list of needed material. Other elements may differ from one scheme to another.

The Hunter and Russell Model

One set of guidelines for lesson planning that has been adopted by many schools was introduced by Madeline Hunter and Douglas Russell (1977). These elements are consistent with the Hunter and Russell model:

- *Lesson objective*:   This refers to the specific behavior the student should be able to perform at the conclusion of the lesson.
- *Behavioral standards*:   These include rules that need to be made clear before the lesson begins to prevent discipline problems.
- *Anticipatory set*:   This refers to the need to get students ready for a lesson. Anticipatory set includes such teacher actions as telling students about the purposes or objectives of the lesson, informing them in a general way about what they will learn, suggesting to them ways in which they will apply new information and how it may be used in other situations, and taking specific actions to enhance students' levels of motivation.
- *Instruction*:   The instruction component features actual introduction of new content to students. Important teaching processes during instruction include modeling for students what they are expected to do, checking periodically to assure students are understanding, and monitoring and adjusting the lesson pace to maximize learning.
- *Guided practice*:   This involves opportunities for students to apply new information under the watchful eye of the teacher. During this phase, the teacher has opportunities to correct any student misunderstandings and to provide supportive comments to students who do well. If, during the guided practice phase, large numbers of students make errors, the teacher can take time to reteach certain aspects of content that students have failed to understand.
- *Independent practice*:   During this phase of the lesson students are encouraged to apply what they have learned with a minimum of teacher guidance. In some instances, homework serves as independent practice. A lesson should not move on to the independent practice phase until students have demonstrated an ability to deal with the new content during guided practice.
- *Closure*:   During this lesson phase, the teacher summarizes what has been taught. Often students are actively involved in this process. For example, several of them may be called up to describe what has been learned or to demonstrate new knowledge in other ways.

The Hunter and Russell model has been adopted by many of the nation's school districts. It provides a useful format that prompts users to think seriously about several key components of their lessons.

The Gagné and Briggs Model

Another lesson-planning model derives from the work of Gagné and Briggs (1974). Some of its components are similar to several in the Hunter and Russell model. It includes the following elements:

- *Gaining attention*:   This opening part of a lesson requires the teacher to take action to prompt students' interest and to help them develop a "need to know" the new information.

- *Informing the learner of the objective*:   This step, closely paralleling step one in the Hunter and Russell approach, calls on the teacher to communicate to students clearly information about the lesson objective.

- *Stimulating recall of prerequisite information*:   This "instructional event" helps students see the link connecting information to be presented in the new lesson with what they have previously learned.

- *Presenting the stimulus material*:   This "event" is basically the same as the instruction category in the Hunter and Russell model. It features actions taken to transmit new material to students. Gagné and Briggs emphasize that presentation of new material should closely parallel the form in which students will encounter this information on application exercises, tests, or in other settings. The presentation should clearly highlight key points, and there ought to be variety in instructional methods used to introduce the material. It is particularly important for these methods to be closely matched to personal characteristics of individual students.

- *Eliciting the desired behavior*:   During this phase of the lesson, students are provided opportunities to demonstrate what they have learned.

- *Providing feedback*:   This element of the model calls on the teacher to provide feedback to students that helps them understand whether their responses to assigned tasks are correct. The idea is to shape students' behaviors in ways that will allow them to be successful when they are formally assessed on their mastery of lesson content.

- *Assessing the behavior*:   During this event, the teacher assesses what students have learned. Results of assessment help the teacher to evaluate both the quality of instruction (by ascertaining how well, on average, students have learned the material) and the relative levels of achievement of each student.

The Gagné and Briggs model can be used to plan lessons in many subject areas. One of its strong points is its inclusion of an assessment component. In our view, systematic planning of lesson assessment can yield extremely valuable information. We strongly recommend that such information be included in all lesson plans.

Formatting Lesson Plans

There are many acceptable ways to format a lesson plan. The sequence in which individual components are arranged often varies from teacher to teacher. What is important is for the lesson planner to give serious thought to the organizational scheme and to prepare the plan carefully once she has decided on an arrangement. The adopted scheme should allow the user to refer quickly to the completed plan to keep on track and to assure no planned parts of the lesson inadvertently have been omitted. Because of the need to use lesson plans while instruction is being delivered, it generally is not a good idea to make them too lengthy or to select a format that makes individual items difficult to find.

Box 6.5

An Example of a Lesson Plan Format

Unit Title: _____

Lesson Title: _____

    Lesson Plan Number: _____

Lesson Objective: _____

_____

Needed Prerequisites: _____

_____

_____

New Concepts: _____

_____

Behavioral Standards: _____

_____

Time	Lesson Sequence	Materials
	1. Gaining attention/inform students of objective	
	2. Presentation of new material	
	3. Checking understanding/ monitoring	
	4. Eliciting desired behavior/practice/feedback	
	5. Independent practice/application/ extension	
	6. Closure/evaluation of learning	

Teacher Evaluation of Lesson Effectiveness: _____

_____

_____

Table 6.1 Summary Table

Main Points	Explanation
Planning Stages	Long-term planning focuses on an entire school year or an entire school semester. Intermediate-term planning focuses on shorter periods of time, often two to six weeks. The most common document containing the results of intermediate term planning is the instructional unit. Short-term planning focuses on much shorter periods of time, often a single class period. The most common document used to record short-term planning decisions is the lesson plan.
Variables That Influence Planning	
Teacher Characteristics	Teachers' personal backgrounds, interests, and levels of knowledge influence decisions they make as they plan instructional units and lessons.
Student Characteristics	Students vary tremendously in terms of basic ability levels, interests, learning styles, and previous knowledge about topics to be taught. Instruction that is well fitted to individual students requires teachers to know characteristics of class members well.
The Learning Context	This refers to the general character or flavor of an individual school. The context is shaped by such things as the nature of the local community, the types of students who are served, the expectations of administrators, and the kinds of school policies adopted by local and state authorities. The learning context of an individual school tends to favor some kinds of teacher behaviors over others.
Available Time	Time available for both planning instructional experiences and teaching certain content affects teachers' decisions. Limited time requires teachers to establish priorities so this scarce resource is used wisely.
Learning Resources	Kinds of resources available to support instruction place some limits on instructional planning. Where certain types of resources are not available, teachers are disinclined to develop instructional plans that require these kinds of resources to be used.
Instructional Unit	An instructional unit is the written expression of intermediate-term planning decisions. An instructional unit provides a framework for systematically organizing a series of lessons around a common topic or theme.
Elements of an Instructional Unit	Instructional units can be formatted in many ways. Large numbers of unit formats include these elements: (1) a unit title, (2) a rationale and major goals, (3) mandated content, (4) major generalizations and related concepts, (5) instructional objectives and a tentative time line for teaching content related to each, (6) instructional strategies for each objective, (7) plans for beginning and ending the unit, (8) evaluation procedures, and, (9) a list of needed learning resources.

Main Points	**Explanation**
Instructional Unit, *cont'd.*	
Unit Planning Process	A typical linear approach to unit planning suggests that the planner follow these steps: (1) identify generalizations and objectives, (2) identify content needed to help students master objectives, (3) design and sequence learning activities related to objectives, (4) identify and gather learning resources, and (5) identify evaluation procedures. Experts who have studied what teachers actually do have found that different teachers start their planning at different places. They tend to shift back and forth among the five decision areas noted above until there is a good "fit" among all parts.
Unit Format	There are many ways to format units. In some places, local school districts provide a format for teachers to use. More commonly, teachers develop formats that fit their own needs. Whatever format is selected should provide for clarity of communication and should contain information seen as important by the unit developer.
Lesson Plans	Lesson plans are the written expression of teachers' short-term planning decisions. They might be regarded as a general outline or script that teachers follow in instructing students during a given period (or sometimes over one, two, or three successive periods).
The Lesson Planning Process	The process followed in planning a lesson varies from teacher to teacher. Some begin by focusing on learning activities. Others start with a consideration of objectives students are to master. Others begin by focusing on evaluation procedures they will be using. Still others begin their planning at other points.
Historical Lesson Plan Models	The idea that lessons should be planned systematically has been around for centuries. Among interesting historical models for planning lessons are those that were developed by (1) the ancient Spartans, (2) the Medieval Jesuits, and (3) Johann Herbart. Features of these lesson plan models from history are found in lesson plans developed today.
Modern-Day Lesson Plan Formats	Specific features of present-day lesson plan formats vary. Almost all of them call for a lesson title and for a list of needed materials. Two commonly used models are the one based on the work of Hunter and Russell and the one based on the work of Gagné and Briggs.

Review of Key Ideas

- Because of the unique characteristics of individual teaching settings, teachers must do much of their own instructional planning. Researchers have determined that effective teachers devote a great deal of time to planning.
- Teachers engage in long-term, intermediate-term, and short-term planning. Long-term planning embraces a time period of a semester or a full academic year. Intermediate-term planning focuses on time periods ranging from about two to six weeks in length. Instructional unit plans represent the written expression of intermediate planning. Short-term planning focuses on what goes on during one (and sometimes two or three) class periods. Short-term planning decisions are written in the form of lesson plans.
- Many variables affect specific decisions teachers make as they make instructional plans. Among variables that must be considered are (1) teacher characteristics, (2) student characteristics, (3) the general learning context, (4) available time, and (5) available resources to support learning.
- There are many ways to format instructional units. Many of them contain these key content categories: (1) unit title, (2) rationale and major goals, (3) mandated content, (4) major generalizations and concepts, (5) instructional objectives and an indication of time to be devoted to instruction related to each, (6) instructional strategies for each objective, (7) plans for beginning and ending the unit, (8) evaluation procedures, and (9) a list of needed learning resources.
- The idea that lessons should be planned in predictable ways is very old. Among interesting historical lesson-planning models are those developed by the ancient Spartans, the Medieval Jesuits, and the nineteenth century German, Johann Herbart. Herbart, in particular, developed a lesson plan format including some features that often are found in the lesson plans of many teachers today.
- Two contemporary frameworks for lesson plans are those developed by (1) Madeline Hunter and Douglas Russell and (2) Robert Gagné and Leslie Briggs. A lesson plan based on the Hunter and Russell model might include these components: (a) lesson objective, (b) behavioral standards, (c) anticipatory set, (d) instruction (guidelines related to introduction of new material), (e) guided practice, (f) independent practice, and (g) closure. A lesson plan based on the work of Gagné and Briggs might include these components: (a) gaining attention, (b) informing the learner of the objective, (c) stimulating recall of prerequisite information, (d) presenting the stimulus material, (e) eliciting the desired behavior, (f) providing feedback, and (g) assessing the behavior.

Follow-Up Questions and Activities

Questions

1. Why is it necessary for teachers to do instructional planning of their own when so much excellent information is available in curriculum guides, textbooks, and other learning materials?

2. What are some characteristics of long-term planning?

3. What are some similarities and differences between intermediate-term and short-term planning?

4. What is the importance of the learning context in instructional planning?

5. What are some typical components of instructional units?

6. Why is it important for teachers to have information about available learning resources when they plan instructional units?

7. Why is it often true that beginning teachers include more details in their lesson plans than do more experienced teachers?

8. What are some examples of historical lesson plan formats?

9. What are some components of a lesson plan that is consistent with the Hunter and Russell model?

10. What are some components of a lesson plan that is consistent with the Gagné-Briggs model?

Activities

1. Review some district or state-level curriculum guides. How many parts of the instructional unit format introduced in this chapter are included in the guides? What would need to be added to this material to make an instructional unit complete?

2. Interview a teacher about the process he follows in preparing an instructional unit. How does this person start this task? What goes into his decisions about sequencing content? Where is information about available materials found? What kind of format is used?

3. Visit two or more schools and compare how teachers in each approach a common subject. What differences are attributable to teacher variables and student variables? What differences seem to be caused by differences in the teaching context?

4. Get together with several others who are preparing to teach the same secondary school subject. Develop an instructional unit following the format introduced in this chapter. Share your unit with your instructor and request a critique. Be prepared to participate in a class discussion focusing on special difficulties you encountered and how you overcome them.

5. Write a lesson plan focusing on a topic you would like to teach. Use either the Hunter and Russell model or the Gagné-Briggs model to format your lesson. Be prepared to share answers to these questions with others in the class: How long did it take you to prepare the lesson? Do you think you would be able to accomplish this task more quickly were you to prepare another lesson? How comfortable would you feel in teaching this content?

References

CLARK, C. AND PETERSON, P. "Teachers' Thought Processes." In M. Wittrock (ed.). *Handbook of Research on Teaching*. 3rd ed. New York: Macmillan Publishing Company, 1986, pp. 297–314.

CLARK, C. AND YINGER, R. *Three Studies of Teacher Planning* (Research Series No. 55). East Lansing, MI: Michigan State University Institute for Research on Teaching, 1979.

GAGNÉ, R. AND BRIGGS, L. *Principles of Instructional Design*. New York: Holt, Rinehart & Winston, 1974.

HUNTER, M. AND RUSSELL, D. "How Can I Plan More Effective Lessons?" *Instructor* (September 1977), pp. 74–75; 88.

KAUCHAK, D. AND EGGEN, P. *Learning and Teaching: Research-Based Models*. Boston: Allyn & Bacon, 1989.

MEYER, A. E. *Grandmasters of Educational Thought*. New York: McGraw-Hill, 1975.

POSNER, G. "Pacing and Sequencing." In M. J. Dunkin (ed.). *The International Encyclopedia of Teaching and Teacher Education*. Oxford, England: Pergamon Press, 1987, pp. 266–272.

YINGER, R. A *Study of Teacher Planning: Description and Theory Development Using Ethnographic and Information Processing Methods*. Unpublished doctoral dissertation. East Lansing, MI: Michigan State University, 1979.

7

Preparing for the Multicultural Classroom

AIMS

This chapter provides information to help the reader to:

- Recognize the importance of responding to the special needs and perspectives of students from diverse cultural backgrounds.

- Point out the relationship between individuals' cultural backgrounds and the way they perceive reality, including schooling.

- Describe some rationales that have been used in the past to explain away the poor school performance of minority group students.

- Point out some demographic changes that underscore the importance of developing school programs that are responsive to minority students' needs.

- Identify some planning perspectives that can help white teachers develop instructional programs well suited to needs of African-American, Hispanic, Native American, Asian, and other minority group students.

- Name potential sources for information about perspectives of various minority groups.

1. What changes are occurring in the cultural and ethnic makeup of the schools?

2. How well have minority group students done in schools?

3. What trends are evident in high school graduation rates of students from different minority groups, and why is high school graduation considered so important?

4. How have some traditional views of minority group students stood in the way of serious efforts to educate these young people?

5. Why might parents of some minority group students be less supportive of schools and teachers than typical parents of non-Hispanic white students?

6. Why do educators consider students' cultural backgrounds to be important in planning instructional experiences to serve their needs?

7. What features of Comer-model schools explain their success in serving the needs of inner-city African-American high schools students?

8. What could high schools do to increase graduation rates of Hispanic students?

9. What can teachers do to better serve the needs of minority group students?

10. What are some sources of information that teachers might use in their efforts to become more knowledgeable about perspectives of students from different ethnic and racial groups?

Introduction

The entire American population is becoming more culturally diverse. Changes within the school population are occurring even more rapidly than changes within the population as a whole. By the year 2000, it is estimated that between 30 and 40 percent of learners in the schools will be nonwhite (Grant and Secada, 1989; p. 403). Further, "over the next decade in many schools the number of children speaking foreign languages and nonstandard dialects will become the majority, challenging the ability of schools to educate them" (Bowman, 1991; p. 17).

At the same time the student population of the schools is becoming more nonwhite, the nation's teachers, as a group, are becoming more white. More than 85 percent of all teachers are white (Grant and Secada, 1989). Despite efforts to encourage more minority students to pursue careers in teaching, fewer minorities are entering the profession today than in the past. These trends suggest that, in the years ahead, the large majority of white teachers will be instructing more and more students from ethnic and cultural backgrounds different from their own.

School Learning of Minority Group Students

Many minority students have not done well in school, as compared to the achievement of white students. However, there is some progress to report. For example, the percentage of African-American students completing high school has risen significantly since the middle 1970s. In addition, scores of African-American and Hispanic 17-year-olds on reading proficiency and writing proficiency tests have also improved (Ogle, Alsalam, and Rogers, 1991; pp. 28; 32–34).

Though achievement levels of African-American students continue to lag behind those of white students, the gap grows ever narrower. Regrettably, the same cannot be said for Hispanic students, whose achievement levels trail those of both white and African-American students by wide margins. Many Hispanic students do not finish high school. In a recent year, a national survey revealed that only 58.5 percent of 24- to 25-year-old Hispanics had completed high school. This figure compares with 90.3 percent for whites and 85.0 percent for African Americans (Ogle et al., 1991; p. 28).

Students' failure to complete high school greatly limits their future employability. One recent survey predicted a 35 percent increase between 1985 and 2000 in the number of jobs available for individuals with some college training, but only a 10 percent overall increase for high school graduates. Individuals lacking a high school diploma will find even smaller numbers of vacancies (Marshall, 1990).

Experts who have studied achievement of students in schools have identified a number of risk factors that characterize many individuals who do not do well. Among these risk factors are:

- Living with only one parent.
- Having parents who, themselves, lack a high school education.
- Limited proficiency in English.
- Coming from a household with an annual income below $15,000.
- Having a brother or sister who dropped out of school.
- Spending more than three hours a day home alone. (Ogle et al., 1991; p. 74)

Individuals having a single risk factor may not necessarily experience difficulty in school. Researchers, however, have determined that students having two or more risk factors are particularly likely to do poorly. Minority students are much more likely than white students to be in this situation. A recent survey of eight-graders revealed that 44 percent of African-American students, 39 percent of Hispanic Americans, and 36 percent of Native American students had two or more risk factors. These figures compare with a total of about 14 percent of white students (Ogle et al., 1991; p. 74).

With each passing year, nonwhite students make up a greater percentage of the total student population. The number of Hispanics in the schools—the group that has experienced especial difficulty in coping successfully with the school group—is increasing fastest of all. The changing makeup of the student population is forcing professional

Box 7.1

Percentage of Eighth-Graders with Selected Risk Factors by Race and Ethnicity

Race/Ethnicity	Living with One Parent	Limited English Proficiency	Income Below $15,000
White	17.7	6.2	14.1
African American	46.5	15.8	47.0
Hispanic	23.4	33.4	37.5
Asian/Pacific Islander	14.2	8.8	17.8
Native American	31.1	13.4	40.1
8th grade population as a whole	22.3	10.5	21.3

Source: Laurence T. Ogle, Nabeel Alsalam, and Gayle Thompson Rogers (Eds.), *The Condition of Education, 1991: Volume I—Elementary and Secondary Education* (p. 74). Washington, DC: U.S. Government Printing Office, 1991.

educators to reassess many school practices and to consider what can be done to improve achievement levels and graduation rates for minority students.

Why Have Minorities Often Done Less Well in School Than White Students?

That many minority students have failed to profit from school programs is not news. Why, then, have schools been slow to respond? Some traditional explanations have laid the blame on minorities themselves. Today, these "blame-the-victim" perspectives are widely discounted, but for many years, they allowed educators to escape professional responsibility for the poor performance of minority students. In more recent times, when there has been a more genuine commitment by school leaders to serve minority students better, a lack of understanding of special cultural perspectives of groups as diverse as African Americans, Hispanics, and Native Americans has undermined some good intentions. This blame-the-victim view, particularly when reinforced by discredited racist perspectives, has negative results not only for minority students but for whites as well.

Recently, B. D. Tatum observed that social practices based on racism have denied certain potentially valuable experiences to young people who are white. They have been denied opportunities to develop close personal relationships with African Americans who may have not been permitted to visit their homes. It has been observed that some young white adults "attribute the discomfort or fear they now experience in racially mixed settings to the cultural limitations of their youth" (Tatum, 1992; p. 4).

Historic Views of Minorities

An early explanation for minorities' failures to excel in school was the *genetic deficit* view (Savage and Armstrong, 1992). The premise of this position was that students from minority groups lacked the necessary intellectual equipment to do good work in school. This lack was ascribed to their status as sons and daughters of individuals who were not particularly bright. Hence, it was argued, an insufficient "capacity to learn" was passed on to their children. This mistaken belief provided a perfect rationale for schools to do little or nothing to improve instruction directed at minority students. Why, it was argued, should the schools commit scarce resources to programs designed to serve individuals who lacked the capacity to learn from them?

The genetic deficit view had been widely discounted by the middle of this century. In the 1960s, a new deficit view enjoyed some currency for a time. This was the *cultural deficit* position (Erickson, 1987). Individuals who were impressed by this idea felt that school problems of minority group students could be traced to their homes. It was alleged that their homes provided an intellectually sterile background that failed to give them attitudes and aptitudes needed for success in school. The cultural deficit argument allowed school leaders who were reluctant to commit serious resources to programs designed to help minority students to blame the home for failures of these young people to learn. Since many minority students came from impoverished home backgrounds, some argued that the hope that special programs for minority students might improve their performance in school was illogical.

Still another variant on the "blame-the-students, the-schools-can-do-nothing" theme was the *communication process* position. This view blamed poor minority student performance on language differences separating students and their teachers. It was alleged that these differences were so profound that minority students could not understand what was said in the classroom and what was expected of them at school. Their failure was attributed to this communication gap. Critics of this position pointed out that some minority students did extremely well in school despite economic and social backgrounds very similar to those of minority students who did poorly.

The genetic deficit, cultural deficit, and communication deficit views are now rejected by most educators. All three arguments are seen as weak attempts to excuse the school from being accountable for minority students' learning. Today, many people believe that minority students' failures in school have often resulted from the lack of a serious commitment on the part of educators to plan and deliver programs designed to help these young people learn. The rhetoric of concern has been there for many years, but a willingness to develop an intellectual and a financial commitment to help minority students in schools is relatively recent.

Appreciating the Cultural Context Minorities Bring to School

Success is a master motivator. When students experience it in school, their self-esteem soars. Their attitudes toward teachers and the whole school program becomes more positive. A key element, then, in any effort to improve the achievement of minority group students is the assurance of academic success. Planning such programs requires insight into the issue of important cultural differences and perspectives. It is important for teachers to understand these nuances as they plan programs that will result not only in superficial success but in a strong student commitment to the entire idea that schooling is important.

Individuals' attitudes toward school are shaped, in part, by the general attitudes they hold toward large social institutions. Many people believe our society in its present form is basically sound and that institutions designed to perpetuate the values that sustain it should be prized. These people see schools as worthy institutions that help to pass important information and values from generation to generation. Children of parents holding this view tend to be told that it is important to do well at school. High school graduation is likely to be held up as an worthy objective that is worth whatever effort is required to attain it.

On the other hand, some people do not see our society as basically just or fair. They may view the school as an agency dedicated to maintaining an unjust distribution of power and wealth. Education may be viewed as a plot to hold certain people down so others can rise. The school represents an agency dedicated to perpetuating inequities. People who subscribe to this view may be reluctant to hold high school graduation in particularly high esteem. Indeed, some particularly committed partisans of this position may see success in school as "selling out" to interests dedicated to perpetuating the more unjust aspects of our society.

People who view the school as basically a "good" institution and people who view the school as potentially "bad" are found among whites, African Americans, Native Americans, Hispanics, and other American ethnic groups. Each ethnic group includes individuals attracted to both views. However, because minority groups traditionally have not enjoyed the fruits of American society to the extent they have been enjoyed by whites, it is probable that more minority parents are suspicious of the motives of the school than white parents.

CASE STUDY

"Mr. Hobbs, Your History is Irrelevant"

Nolan Hobbs teaches United States history at Lee High School. He also occasionally is called on to teach economics classes and sociology classes. Recently, he shared these comments with Rafaela Sanchez, Lee High School's Vice Principal for Academic Programs.

"Things have gone just great this year. Well, that's generally the case, but there is a student in my fifth period class who has become a bit of a thorn in my side. I'm talking about Cassiella Birdsong. You'll remember she was in talking to you a few weeks ago about getting some bulletin board space in the hall for the Black Students Association.

"Well, anyway, Cassiella has convinced herself that I have absolutely nothing to teach her. She told me this morning that our history book was 'filled with a bunch of junk about dead white guys.' Even though I go out of my way to include information about contributions of African Americans, she still has it in her head that my whole course is dedicated to imposing a point of view she wants no part of.

"I know she's bright, and I am concerned that she's just not working up to her potential. I'm getting pretty frustrated with her telling me every day how 'irrelevant' everything in my course is. Her attitude is beginning to have a bad influence on some of the other students as well."

■ ■ ■ ■ ■

How do might you explain Cassiella's point of view? Is her reaction something Mr. Hobbs should be concerned about? If so, what should his next steps be? In addition to the Vice Principal, who else might he consult for advice? What would you do in this situation?

Some members of minority groups' negative attitudes toward school may trace to some disturbing evidence that minority students have often been treated less responsibly in schools than white students. For example, college preparatory classes in high schools enroll disproportionately high percentages of white students, whereas remedial courses enroll disproportionately high numbers of minority group students (Armstrong, Henson, and Savage, 1993). Minority group students have 1.6 times the likelihood of being assigned to special education classes than white students (Simon-McWilliams, 1989). Minority group students are much more likely to be assigned to school courses allowing little contact with the core academic program of high schools than are white students (Oakes, 1985). As noted previously, high school drop-out rates of minorities are higher for both African Americans and Hispanics than for whites. These data suggest that many minorities leave school ill equipped for jobs in a society that increasingly demands well-educated workers.

Given the failure of many school programs to serve minorities needs well, some minority students may reject academic achievement in school as a goal because the school has not acted as an institution truly dedicated to serving the interests of minorities (Ogbu, 1973). If the culture of these students reinforces the idea that the school has little to say to minorities, their attitudes will be affected. In this connection, Barbara Bowman (1991) has written:

> Culture includes the psychological process on which behavior rests, affecting how people perceive the world, how they understand the physical environment, events, and other people. Culture forms a prism through which members of a group see and create "shared meanings" for experience. (p. 18)

None of this is meant to suggest that all, or even a majority, of minority group students harbor negative attitudes toward the school. However, the data clearly support the idea that minority group learners have not always been well served by schools and that, consequently, among minorities who do not do well in school are those who question that school programs are really designed to help them.

Family attitudes toward the schools, historical experiences of minorities, and other influences help shape the reactions of individual minority students to the school program. Specific personal experiences in school also may affect how individual students respond to the program. For example, Hispanic students studying United States history who are exposed over and over again to the traditional presentation of the settlement of the United States as a European conquest that rolled relentlessly westward from its beginnings on the Atlantic seaboard may find little to connect to. Much Hispanic influence in this country has resulted from a south-to-north migration of Hispanics into the territory of the United States. The traditional course organization of United States history (east to west) makes little mention of Hispanic migrations or contributions.

Similarly, high school curricula that fail to mention contributions of African Americans, Native Americans, Asian Americans, and other minorities provide few human models with which younger members of these minority groups can identify. In short, schools that feature an old fashioned curriculum risk delivering academic knowledge that seems disconnected to the real lives of many minority students.

The obligation of educators who sincerely wish to serve *all* of the students (minorities included) is to develop programs that reflect a multicultural base. Such a broad base is needed if programs are to "connect" to the world views of students coming from the diverse ethnic and cultural groups that make up today's student population. The purpose is to get all young people to commit to the importance of the school program. This commitment, as we shall see, is heavily dependent on programming that builds the self-worth of all the students, not just students from the white majority.

School Programs That Make a Difference

Though it is generally accurate to say that many school programs have not served minority students well, certainly there are exceptions. Some efforts to improve school experiences of urban African-American students and to identify characteristics of secondary schools graduating high percentages of Hispanic students bear mention.

Comer-Model Schools

James Comer of the Yale Child Study Center and several of his associates commenced work over 20 years ago on a program to help African-American students in certain schools in New Haven, Connecticut. Enrollment in these schools was over 99 percent African American. Most students came from families with incomes below the national poverty level. When Comer's project began, students in these schools had the lowest scores and poorest attendance records of any schools in the city.

Comer and his associates developed an approach that features extensive shared decision making. This means that policies are made collectively and collaboratively by

Box 7.2

Shared Decision Making: How People Might React to This Change

Some approaches to educational reform, such as Comer-model schools, that seek (among other objectives) school programs that do a better job of meeting needs of minority students call for "shared decision making." This implies a pattern of decision making that is collaborative and that involves serious consideration of points of views of diverse constituencies, including parents and teachers as well as administrators.

What Do You Think?

1. Are teachers prepared to participate in making policy decisions related to the overall operation of schools and their programs? If not, how might they prepare themselves to take on this responsibility?

2. Is there a danger that parents will seek to divert school resources to the benefit of the racial or ethnic groups to which they and their children belong at the expense of others in the school? If "yes," what problems might ensue, and how might they be addressed?

3. What kinds of behavior changes do you think principals might have to make in schools that feature shared decision making? Do you think most principals will make these adjustments willingly?

---

principals, teachers, parents, and selected school support-staff people (particularly individuals concerned with students' mental health and personal development). These people function as a management team. They are trained to focus on developing solutions to problems students are having rather than on assigning blame.

A key premise from which management teams operate in Comer-model schools is that "all students can learn." This view, taken together with the highly participatory management scheme of Comer's approach, has had remarkable results. Fifteen years after the plan began, students in the Comer-model schools ranked close to the top of all schools in New Haven and were above national averages on standardized tests (Comer, 1988).

Characteristics of High Schools Serving Hispanics Well

More than 5 million students in our schools speak a language other than English as their first language (Borich, 1988). Most of these students are Hispanics, and many of them traditionally have not done well in high school. There has been a great deal of concern about the large numbers of Hispanic students who fail to complete 12 years of school. To provide information to school leaders wishing to better serve Hispanic students, Lucas, Henze, and Donato (1990) looked at a number of high schools with heavy enrollments of Hispanics that were graduating large numbers of these students and where the students were scoring well on standardized tests. They found these high schools had these characteristics (Lucas, Henze, and Donato, 1990; pp. 315–340):

- Value is placed on the home language and culture of the students.
- Teachers' expectations are high, and these expectations are communicated to students in concrete ways.
- School leaders have made the education of Hispanic students a priority.
- Staff-development activities are in place to help teachers and other staff people effectively serve Hispanic students.
- There are many different courses and programs of study available for students.
- A counseling program pays special attention to needs of Hispanic students.
- Parents are encouraged to become actively involved in the education of their sons and daughters.
- School staff members share a strong commitment to empowering Hispanic students through education.
- Efforts are made to develop students' levels of proficiency in *both* Spanish and English, something that is part of an overall effort to build pride in cultural heritage at the same time intellectual tools are honed that will allow for success beyond high school graduation.

Helping Minority Students Succeed: Teachers and Teaching

A number of guidelines have been suggested that have promise for promoting better learning and better attitudes toward school on the part of minority group learners. The following are some of the proposals that have been made:

- Assume all students can learn.
- Provide minority students with good teachers.
- Insist that teachers become aware of their own cultural perspectives.
- Encourage teachers to avoid favoritism in the classroom.
- Include students from varied ethnic and cultural backgrounds in each group when members of a class are divided into groups for instruction.
- Vary teaching methods to accommodate different learning styles.
- Develop close working relationships with students' families.

Assuming That All Students Can Learn

Minority group students (and, indeed, students in general), by the time they reach their secondary school years, are very sensitive to how they are seen by their teachers. If

Box 7.3

"All Students Can Learn?"

Recently, a citizen concerned about the academic program in a local high school made these comments.

"I see our political friends have been at it again. This week's slogan is 'all students can learn.' This alluring little phrase is being used to justify enormous expenditures for programs to serve students who have never done well in school.

"Let's be realistic. If these students have done poorly all through school, we're not going to 'save' them in high school. Some of them just *cannot* learn, no matter what we do. That is a cruel fact, but it's reality. We shouldn't be spending our scarce school dollars on these people. Too many good students deserve help, and we should spend money on programs to help them."

What Do You Think?

1. What are some strengths of this person's argument?

2. What are some weaknesses?

3. If you were to write a letter to a newspaper editor commenting on this position, what would you say?

they sense that those who teach them have little confidence in their abilities to learn, minority group students will be inclined to "live down" to the expectations of their teachers. Under the best of circumstances, the middle school, junior high school, and senior high school years are emotionally trying for many young people. The last thing they need is an adult teacher who reinforces students' suspicions of personal inadequacy. Students will not be motivated by a teacher who fails to convey to them a sincere belief in their ability to learn.

In addition to the negative psychological impact on students of teachers who convey to students an impression that they "cannot learn," such perceptions affect how these teachers interact with these students. In part, a teacher's commitment to prepare good lessons and deliver high-quality instruction ties to her belief that students can master the content. The personal conviction that instruction can "make a difference" with students is a strong motivator for the teacher. When this motivation is lacking, instructional quality diminishes, and so too do levels of student achievement.

Providing Good Teachers

Good teachers help students develop better attitudes toward school and learn more than do mediocre teachers. It is particularly critical that minority students be taught by individuals who are sensitive their special ethnic and cultural perspectives, respectful of them as individuals, and strongly committed to the view that they can and should learn. There is evidence that in some schools the better teachers have been assigned to teach classes enrolling relatively small numbers of minority students (Armstrong et al., 1993).

Often, teachers assigned to teach minority students are relatively new to the profession. Further, many of them are teaching subjects outside of their main areas of academic preparation. In this connection, a survey commissioned by the Quality Education for Minorities Project found that "teachers in predominantly minority schools were the least experienced, held the most emergency credentials, and were likely to be teaching outside of their fields" (Marshall, 1990; p. 43).

Teachers' Awareness of Their Own Perspectives

Members of the white majority, including teachers, live in a world where perspectives of their own group are so dominant that often they fail to recognize that they have a world view that may differ from that of members of other cultural and ethnic groups. In truth, all people are to a great extent conditioned to "make sense" of the world in ways consistent with the perspectives of the people with whom they interact. Teachers who have had few relationships with people from cultures other than the dominant white majority may

"Mirror, mirror on the wall, who is the most self-effacing, ethnically and culturally sensitive teacher of all?"

fail to recognize that in some instances minority group students come from groups whose ideas about "how the world is" and "how people should behave" vary from their own.

When people fail to recognize that there are multiple perspectives on these issues and erroneously assume that their own world view is the only one (or at least the only "correct" one), they may have difficulty communicating with people from other social and cultural orientations. This is particularly true for white teachers who find themselves teaching minority students. For example, in the dominant white culture when someone who is being addressed tries to avoid direct eye contact with the speaker, the speaker may conclude that the person is "shifty" or "guilty" or "ashamed" or "has something to hide." When a teacher gets this kind of reaction from a student, he may conclude that there is something wrong with the student. This conclusion makes sense, given the cultural orientation of the white majority.

However, not all cultures view eye contact in the same way. In some minority cultures, young people are taught that it is impolite to look adults in the eye. Hence, an attempt to look away from a teacher who is speaking may be intended as a polite gesture, as a recognition of the teacher's high status as an intelligent adult. A teacher who fails to recognize the cultural orientation of such a student and concludes the student has something to hide makes a mistake. Negative attitudes toward the student may develop. These may translate into lowered teacher respect for the student, lowered academic expectations for this individual, and unnecessarily strained interpersonal relations.

Avoiding Favoritism in the Classroom

By the time they arrive in secondary schools, minority group students are well aware that our society has different racial and ethnic groups. Some of them may have had experiences in school and elsewhere that have led them to conclude that sometimes members of minority groups are treated differently than members of the white, non-Hispanic majority. Additionally, nearly all middle school students are very concerned about the general issues of consistent and appropriate treatment. The credibility of the teacher is at risk when students suspect she "is not fair."

One way teachers demonstrate fairness is by avoiding favoritism in the classroom. It is particularly important that minority group students sense that, as individuals and as a group, they are being treated as well as others in the class. Teachers who are suspected of singling out students for negative treatment or comments that in any way seem tied to ethnicity or race may find it difficult to maintain the interest and cooperation of minority group students.

Students often measure a teacher's fairness by looking at how he handles episodes of misbehavior. The general rule is that the same category of misbehavior should be met by the same level of teacher response, regardless of who the offender is. That is, high-achieving students shouldn't get off more lightly than low-achieving students, white students shouldn't get off more lightly than minority group students, and so forth. When students feel the teacher dispenses justice equitably and holds all to the same standard, motivation levels increase, discipline problems diminish, and achievement levels improve.

Mixing Minority Group and Majority Group Students in Groups

When group work is planned, it is important that groups not serve as a vehicle for "resegregating" students on the basis of race or ethnicity. For one thing, individual groups sometimes are asked to do different things (e.g., some groups may be assigned more challenging academic tasks than others).

There is evidence that some groups are organized by teachers so that racial minorities are concentrated within a few groups (Rist, 1985). This is a mistake. Group instructional techniques must not be seen by learners as subtle covers for an instructional program designed to provide different (and perhaps lower quality) instruction to minority group students.

Additionally, a key purpose of secondary education is to help students adjust to living in a multicultural society. Given this priority, it makes sense to organize groups to encourage personal contacts among students from varying cultural and ethnic back-

Multicultural perspectives are encouraged when teachers assign students from different ethnic and cultural backgrounds within groups formed as part of small-group instruction.

grounds. Such practices break down group-to-group isolation and provide a way for students to become more familiar with perspectives different from their own.

Responding to Varying Learning Styles

Students vary in terms of their preferred learning styles. This means that some individuals learn better when they read about new information. Others learn better when they listen to someone explaining new content. Others are visual learners—people who master new content best when they are presented with examples they can see. Still others need opportunities to touch, handle, and otherwise manipulate physical objects.

Kinds of preferred learning settings also vary. For example, some individuals prefer to learn alone. Others do much better when they are organized into groups.

Researchers have found that students' cultural backgrounds affect their learning styles (Grant and Sleeter, 1989). This does not mean that individuals with similar cultural backgrounds do not vary. Rather, it suggests that more people from one cultural group may be characterized by a given learning style than people from another cultural group.

For example, researchers have found that students from African-American and Hispanic backgrounds do better when they are presented with a broad general overview of a situation first and then asked to think about how specific information relates to the general situation (Bowman, 1991; p. 22). (For example, it would be better to provide general information about the Civil War and then to ask about the relationship of the Battle of Gettysburg to the war in general.) Non-Hispanic white students, on the other hand, have been found to do well when complex situations are first broken down into small parts. These small parts are learned one at a time, and only in the end does a general picture emerge. (Given this orientation, a class might study individual battles of the Civil War one at a time and conclude with a description of their cumulative effective on the war in general.)

Establishing Relationships with Students' Families

To the extent possible, it is desirable for teachers to establish relationships with members of their minority group students' families. Although many relatives of minority students are very positively disposed toward the school and its programs, this attitude is not universal. Some of them did not have particularly good experiences in school themselves and may be inclined to lump teachers into a category that includes indifferent city hall bureaucrats, law enforcement officials, and other establishment figures that, in their view, have not always treated minorities fairly. People with these views may be reluctant to come to the school on open house nights or on other occasions, and teachers need to make special efforts to contact them.

Students' priorities and general attitudes are strongly influenced by those of their parents, grandparents, and other relatives, especially those living in the same household. If the teacher can establish a common ground with a student's family members that results in a consensus regarding what the student ought to be doing in school, the student may well benefit from a consistency of messages from the home and the teacher. It has been found that "school learning is most likely to occur when family values reinforce school expectations" (Ogbu, 1973; p. 27).

Multicultural Perspectives: Information Sources

Many sources of information are available to teachers who wish to increase their sensitivity to the perspectives of different ethnic and cultural groups. Current articles on this topic and on approaches for working successfully with minority group learners are listed in the *Education Index*, available in nearly all college and university libraries, as well as in many public libraries. A particularly good book that includes many useful instructional ideas is *Turning on Learning: Five Approaches for Multicultural Teaching—Plans for Race, Class, Gender, and Disability* by Carl A. Grant and Christine E. Sleeter.

Educational Extension Systems (P.O. Box 259, Clarks Summit, PA 18411) publishes an annual Ethnic Cultures of America Calendar. This calendar includes information about holidays and other celebrations that are meaningful to many different cultural and ethnic groups. Some additional places to write for information regarding perspectives of different cultural and ethnic groups are:

The Balch Institute for Ethnic Studies
18 South 7th Street
Philadelphia, PA 19106

Center for Migration Studies
209 Flagg Place
Staten Island, NY 10304

Center for the Study of Ethnic Publications
Kent State University
Kent, OH 44242

Institute of Texan Cultures
University of Texas
San Antonio, Texas 78294

Table 7.1   Summary Table

Main Points	Explanation
Changing Characteristics of Student Population	The student population is becoming more racially, ethnically, and culturally diverse. At the same time, non-Hispanic whites are increasing as a percentage of the total teaching population. This means that more and more teachers come from cultural and ethnic backgrounds different from those of their students.
School Learning of Minority Group Students	Minority group students have not had achievement scores in school as high as those of students from the non-Hispanic white majority. High school graduation rates of minorities are also lower. The gap between graduation rates of African-American and non-Hispanic students has narrowed. The rate for Hispanic students continues to lag far behind that for both African-American students and non-Hispanic white students.
Risk Factors for Students Who Do Not Do Well and Often Drop Out	Among the most important risk factors are (1) living with only one parent, (2) having parents who have not graduated from high school, (3) having limited proficiency in English, (4) coming from a household with an annual income below $15,000, (5) having a brother or sister who dropped out of school, and (6) spending more than three hours a day home alone. Minority group students, as a group, are characterized by more of these risk factors than are members of the non-Hispanic white majority.
Now-Discredited Explanations for Poor School Performance of Minority Group Students	
Genetic Deficit View	According to this view, minority students lack the basic intellectual potential to succeed at complex intellectual tasks. An implication of this position was that schools sensed little obligation to provide quality instruction to minority students. This was defended on the ground that such effort was fruitless given their "inability to learn."
Cultural Deficit View	The cultural deficit view, another outmoded blame-the-victim perspective, suggested that the intellectual environments in homes of minority students were so impoverished that these students came to school lacking attitudes and aptitudes needed for success on serious academic tasks.
Communication Process Difficulties	People who subscribed to this idea felt that language problems of minority students were so severe that it was fruitless to believe they were capable of understanding sophisticated instruction in the schools.

Table 7.1   Summary Table *(continued)*

Main Points	Explanation
The Importance of Cultural Context	The cultural context shared by individuals in a similar ethnic, racial, or language group helps to shape their view of reality and to establish for them what is important in life. For students to succeed in school, they need instruction that is consistent and responsive to their own cultural backgrounds. When this happens, they are likely to experience success. Success is a wonderful motivator that often breeds further success. Therefore teachers have a stake in learning nuances associated with the diverse cultural backgrounds of their students. Armed with this knowledge, they can plan learning experiences to which these young people are likely to commit and at which they are likely to succeed.
Comer-Model Schools	James Comer and his associates established a model for organizing, managing, and delivering instruction in schools that has proved very successful in high schools serving high percentages of inner-city African-American students. Comer-model schools operate on the assumption that "all students can learn." They feature shared decision making that involves parents, principals, teachers, and other key staff members.
Characteristics of High Schools That Graduate High Percentages of Hispanic Students	These schools have been found to share many of these features: (1) value is placed on the student's home language, (2) teachers' expectations are high, (3) school leaders have established education of Hispanics as a priority, (4) many courses and programs are available, (5) the counseling program pays attention to Hispanic students' needs, (6) active involvement by parents in their children's education is solicited, and (7) efforts are made to continue development of students' levels of proficiency in both English and Spanish.
What Educators Can Do to Help Minority Group Students Succeed	Among positive steps teachers can take are (1) assume all students can learn, (2) assign good teachers to classes enrolling large numbers of minorities, (3) encourage teachers to become aware of their own perspectives, (4) encourage teachers to avoid showing favoritism to certain groups of students in the classroom, (5) ask teachers to include a mixture of minority group and majority group students in each instructional group, (6) plan instruction to accommodate diverse learning styles, and (7) establish close relationships with families of minority group students.

Review of Key Ideas

- Ethnic and cultural diversity among the population of secondary students is becoming more pronounced at the same time ethnic and cultural diversity among teachers is decreasing. Non-Hispanic white teachers are accounting for an ever-larger proportion of the total population of teachers. This suggests that few teachers will have come from ethnic and cultural backgrounds similar to those of the students they will be teaching in their classrooms.

- School achievement levels of students from cultural and ethnic minorities have lagged behind those of non-Hispanic white students. High school graduation rates are poorer for both African-American and Hispanic students than for non-Hispanic white students. The gap has been narrowing between African-American and non-Hispanic white students. Graduation rates of Hispanic students are much worse that those of either African-American or non-Hispanic white students.

- Educators are greatly concerned about improving high school graduation rates of minority group students. Evidence abounds that future job opportunities will be much greater for college graduates than for high school graduates. Students lacking a high school education will be most disadvantaged of all in the job market.

- A number of risk factors have been identified that commonly characterize students who drop out of school. These include (1) living with only one parent, (2) having parents who are not high school graduates, (3) having limited proficiency in English, (4) coming from a household with less than $15,000 in annual income, (5) having a brother or sister who dropped out of school, and (6) spending more than three hours a day at home alone. Minority group students are much more likely to be characterized by two or more of these risk factors than are non-Hispanic white students.

- In times past, poor performance levels of minority students were attributed to such "causes" as genetic deficit. According to this now-discredited view, minority group children lacked the necessary intellectual resources to succeed academically; hence, it made little sense to worry too much about their failure to do well in school. Another outdated view suggested that minority students suffered from a cultural deficit (from intellectually sterile home environments) that failed to prepare them to do school work. Still another view was that minority students suffered a communication process problem. It was suggested that they had language characteristics that made it virtually impossible for them to grasp what teachers expected them to do. The genetic deficit, cultural deficit, and communication process views are now largely regarded as blame-the-victim excuses that allowed schools to avoid their responsibilities to provide quality educational services to minority group students.

- Students from different ethnic and cultural groups bring a variety of world views with them to school. Teachers need to understand these differences. Instructional programs need to be developed that take into account the many ways different groups perceive reality and establish personal priorities.

- James Comer and his associates have developed a program that has proved particularly successful in improving school achievement levels of African-American students in urban schools. These Comer-model schools feature shared decision making. Programs and policies are collectively and collaboratively planned by parents, principals, teachers, and selected school support people. A key premise is that all students can learn.

- Recently, efforts have been undertaken to identify characteristics of high schools that, contrary to prevailing national patterns, succeed in graduating high percentages of Hispanic students. These high schools have been found to share these characteristics: (1) value is placed on the home language and culture of the students, (2) teachers' expectations are high and are communicated to students in concrete ways, (3) school leaders have made education of Hispanic students a high priority, (4) staff-development activities help teachers and staff to effectively serve Hispanic students, (5) there are many courses and programs available to students, (6) a counseling program pays particular heed to Hispanic students' needs, (7) parents are encouraged to become actively involved in the education of their sons and daughters, and (8) efforts are made to continue the sophisticated development of students' language skills in both English and Spanish.

- A number of guidelines have been developed to help teachers promote better learning and better attitudes toward schooling among minority group students. These include: (1) providing minority students with good teachers, (2) insisting that teachers become aware of their own cultural perspectives, (3) encouraging teachers to avoid favoritism in the classroom, (4) including students from varied ethnic backgrounds in each group when students are divided into groups for instructional purposes, (5) varying teaching methods to accommodate different learning styles, and (6) developing close working relationships with students' families.

Follow-Up Questions and Activities

Questions

1. What general change patterns are occurring in the ethnic and cultural makeup of students and in the ethnic and cultural makeup of teachers?

2. How have performance levels of minority group students compared with those of non-Hispanic white students?

3. What are some risk factors associated with dropping out of school, and how are these distributed among minority group students?

4. What are some historic views of minority group students, and how might they have influenced school practices in the past?

5. Why is it important for teachers to appreciate the cultural context minority group students bring with them to school?

6. What evidence is there that minority group students have been treated differently in school than white, non-Hispanic students?

7. In what ways might the school curriculum influence attitudes of minority group students toward the school?

8. What are some characteristics of Comer-model schools and of high schools that have succeeded in graduating high percentages of Hispanic students?

9. Why is it desirable for teachers to approach their instructional task with the assumption that all students can learn?

10. Why are reactions of families of minority group students to the school and teacher important?

Activities

1. Interview a central office administrator from a school district that enrolls a culturally and ethnically diverse group of students. Ask this person to comment on high school graduation rate differences among the major cultural and ethnic groups enrolled. Also, solicit comments about any special programs the district has to encourage minority group students to stay in school. Share your findings in an oral report to your class.

2. Read some reports in professional journals (perhaps supplemented by other sources suggested by your instructor) that describe programs that have increased high school graduation rates of minority group students. From these articles, develop a list of features that seem associated with the success of these programs. Distribute these lists to others in your class, and use them as a basis for a discussion focusing on the topic: "Keeping Minority Students in Our Secondary Schools: What Works."

3. Many teachers who work successfully with students from diverse cultural and ethnic groups have taken time to familiarize themselves with how members of these groups "see the world." Compile a list of journal articles, books, and other sources of information that might be helpful to non-Hispanic white teachers interested in learning more about the cultural perspectives of members of selected minority groups. Share your list with others in the class.

4. Interview several members of minority groups about their own experiences in middle schools, junior high schools, and high schools. Ask them to comment on program features they liked and disliked. In particular, try to elicit any feelings they might have regarding whether members of their group were singled out for different treatment of any kind simply because they were not members of the non-Hispanic white majority.

5. Lay out a personal professional development plan for yourself that outlines what you might do over the next two years to better prepare yourself to plan instruction that truly is based on the assumption that all can learn. Specifically, describe what you will do to learn more about perspectives of cultural and ethnic minorities. What do you propose to read (name titles of specific articles, books, and other printed material) and do? Present your plan to your course instructor for review and comment.

References

ARMSTRONG, D. G.; HENSON, K. T.; AND SAVAGE, T. V. *Education: An Introduction.* 4th ed. New York: Macmillan Publishing Company, 1993.

BORICH, G. *Effective Teaching Methods.* 2nd ed. New York: Merrill/Macmillan Publishing Company, 1992.

BOWMAN, B. "Educating Language Minority Children: Challenges and Opportunities." In S. L. Kagan (ed.). *The Care and Education of America's Young Children: Obstacles and Opportunities.* Nineteenth Yearbook of the National Society for the Study of Education. Part I. Chicago: National Society for the Study of Education, 1991, pp. 17–29.

COMER, J. P. "Educating Poor Minority Children." *Scientific American* (November 1988), pp. 42–48.

ERICKSON, F. "Transformation and School Success: The Politics and Culture of Educational Achievement." *Anthropology and Education Quarterly* (December 1987), pp. 335–356.

GRANT, C. A. AND SECADA, W. G. "Preparing Teachers for Diversity." In R. Houston (ed.). *Handbook on Research in Teacher Education.* New York: Macmillan Publishing Company, 1989, pp. 403–422.

GRANT, C. A. AND SLEETER, C. E. *Turning on Learning: Five Approaches for Multicultural Teaching—Plans for Race, Class, Gender, and Disability.* New York: Merrill/Macmillan Publishing Company, 1989.

LUCAS, T.; HENZE, R.; AND DONATO, R. "Promoting the Success of Latino Language-Minority Students: An Exploratory Study of Six High Schools." *Harvard Educational Review* (August 1990), pp. 315–340.

MARSHALL, R. (CHAIR). *Education That Works: An Action Plan for the Education of Minorities.* Cambridge, MA: Quality Education for Minorities Project, The Massachusetts Institute of Technology, 1990.

OAKES, J. *Keeping Track: How Schools Structure Inequality.* New Haven, CT: Yale University Press, 1985.

OGLE, L. T.; ALSALAM, N.; AND ROGERS, G. T. (EDS.). *The Condition of Education, 1991: Volume 1—Elementary and Secondary Education.* Washington, DC: United States Government Printing Office, 1991.

OGBU, J. H. *Minority Education and Caste.* New York: Academic Press, 1973.

RIST, R. C. "On Understanding the Process of School: The Contributions of Labeling Theory." In J. A. Ballentine (ed.). *Schools and Society: A Reader in Education and Sociology.* Palo Alto, CA: Mayfield, 1985, pp. 88–106.

SAVAGE, T. V. AND ARMSTRONG, D. G. *Effective Teaching in Elementary Social Studies.* 2nd ed. New York: Macmillan Publishing Company, 1992.

SIMON-MCWILLIAMS, E. (ED.). *Resegregation of Public Schools: The Third Generation.* Portland, OR: Network of Regional Desegregation Assistance Centers and Northwest Regional Educational Laboratory, 1989.

TATUM, B. D. "Talking about Race, Learning about Racism: The Application of Racial Identity Development Theory in the Classroom." *Harvard Educational Review* (Spring 1992), 62, pp. 1–24.

8

Planning for
Exceptional Students

AIMS

This chapter provides information to help the reader to:

- List some events that have contributed to the increased diversity of learners found in secondary classrooms.
- Identify concrete actions that can be taken to respond to slow learners' needs.
- Explain key provisions of federal legislation dealing with the education of students with disabilities.
- Identify specific actions that can be taken to accommodate students with different disabling conditions.
- Describe some characteristics of students who are labeled "gifted and talented."
- Point out how teachers can facilitate the development of gifted and talented students.

FOCUS QUESTIONS

1. How have exceptional students been treated in the schools at various times in our nation's history?

2. How much diversity is there in the population of today's schools as compared to periods in our nation's past?

3. What are some things teachers can do to assist slow learners?

4. What are some key provisions of federal legislation having to do with providing educational services to students with disabilities?

5. What kinds of disabilities are teachers likely to find among the students enrolled in their secondary school classrooms?

6. What characteristics are associated with each type of student disability?

7. What are some specific things teachers can do to respond to needs of students with specific disabilities?

8. What problems have been encountered in selecting students for gifted and talented programs, and what are some selection criteria that experts recommend today?

9. What two major categories of programs have been devised to meet needs of gifted and talented students?

Introduction

The last students were filing out of the building at the end of the day. First-year teacher Jorge Maldonado slumped into the chair behind his desk. He fought exhaustion as he tried to prepare himself mentally to plan tomorrow's classes. He was finding it harder and harder to come up with ideas to motivate his students. No matter what he tried, some students simply didn't seem interested.

■ ■ ■

Many beginning teachers face problems similar to Jorge Maldonado's. A major contributor to this situation is the great diversity they find among students in their classrooms. Though many beginning teachers come from fine preparation programs that have provided excellent information about the range of students in today's schools, learning about this diversity in the congenial atmosphere of a college classroom is quite different from confronting it every day as a teacher.

Differences among students in secondary schools today are more profound than they have ever been. Middle schools, junior high schools, and senior high schools enroll students from many cultural and linguistic backgrounds. Intelligence levels vary enormously. Every socioeconomic stratum is represented.

In recent years, organized groups have recognized that some categories of students within this diverse mix have not been well served by the "traditional" secondary school program. Their efforts have supported the development of school programs for students with special needs. Among these needs are those of slow learners, students with various disabilities, and gifted and talented students.

A Brief History of Programs for Exceptional Students

For many years, the nation's secondary schools did not provide instructional experiences designed to meet the needs of special populations of students. Early secondary education in the United States was directed primarily at preparing sons of an aristocratic leadership to assume positions of responsibility in business and government.

With few exceptions, early secondary schools were unapologetically elitist. Talent was assumed to reside almost exclusively in the minds of the sons (but not the daughters) of the upper classes. A few people—Thomas Jefferson, for example—suggested that there might be such a thing as a "natural aristocracy" and that the sons of quite ordinary people might be a part of this group. Jefferson recommended the establishment of procedures to identify these students so that they could be provided with special training (Schnur, 1980). Jefferson seemed to build a case for a school system that would identify gifted and talented students and educate them to take maximum advantage of their talents. However, Jefferson's was an isolated voice. Further, he believed that the number of natural aristocrats to be found among the common people was very small.

The view that the major audience for secondary schools consisted of children of a narrow elite began to break down during the second and third decades of the nineteenth century. Horace Mann was especially influential in changing attitudes about the purposes of education. Mann was advocate of the "common school," an institution that would bring learners from all social classes together in the school. This kind of social mixing was, in Mann's view, an essential ingredient of a democracy that depended for its existence on mutual understanding among diverse groups. (Wilds and Lottich, 1964).

Although Mann's views, in time, greatly expanded the proportion of the population of young people who enrolled in both elementary and secondary schools, they tended to run counter to any effort to provide special programs for gifted and talented students. Such programs, when proposed, were often attacked on the grounds that they sought to impose an intellectual caste system on public schools—something that many viewed as incompatible with democratic values.

Reluctance of secondary schools to offer special programming for gifted and talented students was paralleled by a disinclination to provide special instruction for other groups as well. The idea that schools should be democratic suggested that no special programs should be implemented that might result in some students receiving more teacher attention than others.

For example, in 1919 the parents of a student with cerebral palsy attempted to enroll their child as a regular student in a Wisconsin school. The school denied the student admission, and the parents took their case to court. In its ruling, the Wisconsin Supreme Court upheld the decision of the school district, stating that the presence of a child with a disability in a regular classroom would have a "depressing and nauseating" effect on teachers and students and would require too much teacher time (Colachico, 1985).

The view that secondary schools should not provide special instruction for learners with unique needs began to be challenged during the first three decades of the twentieth century. One force influencing this change was the expansion in the numbers of young people who continued their education into the secondary school years. Throughout the nineteenth century, most students received only an elementary education. Most secondary students were academically talented young people who were preparing to go on to colleges and universities. Young people with disabilities and economic problems simply did not enroll in secondary schools. When a much broader range of students began to appear in the secondary schools, educators found themselves required to respond to students having special and unfamiliar needs.

The trend toward paying more attention to special student groups within the total secondary school population began to accelerate in the late 1950s. A key event during this period was the launch of the first Soviet earth satellite, Sputnik I, in 1957. This event prompted concerned citizens to look seriously at American educational practices. Some of them concluded that our schools were not preparing bright students well. Many new programs for gifted and talented students began appearing in the 1960s. Much less was heard about the old argument that special programs for bright students were "undemocratic."

The Vietnam War and its accompanying social upheavals had a great influence on school programs throughout the 1960s and into the 1970s. Violence in the nation's inner cities drew attention to the plight of economically deprived learners and learners from minority groups. Increasingly, schools attempted to mount programs designed to serve the special needs of these groups.

A very important result of the unrest of this period was a growing realization that organized pressure groups could achieve significant change. Increasingly, parents of students with special needs gathered together and lobbied politicians at the local, state, and federal levels to win support for programs designed to meet unique needs of various groups of learners. Many of these lobbying efforts were successful. Large numbers of new programs were established to the needs of slow learners, students with disabilities, economically deprived students, and gifted and talented students.

Slow Learners

Defining the term *slow learner* is difficult. Typically, this category has included those individuals who are not learning at a rate designated as average for a given grade level (Bloom, 1982). If the term *average* is used to indicate the mean of the population, by definition, one-half of the students in school will be below average and, therefore, "slow."

For many teachers, a slow learner is one who has difficulty keeping up with the pace of instruction provided to the class. An individual who might be labeled as slow in comparison to an exceptionally able group of learners might be perfectly normal if compared to a group of less-talented students. In addition, a learner who might be slow in grasping one concept or one subject might be very quick to grasp another content or body of knowledge.

Teachers can do several things to meet the needs of slow learners. An important first step is for them to realize that these students do not want to be slow learners. They want to do well in school and to be successful. However, many of these students have experienced so many failures that they have stopped trying. Some slow learners work hard to convince their teachers that they do not care and that school achievement is unimportant to them. Although this might be what these students say, it often is not an expression of their true feelings.

Box 8.1

Tracking is Essential

A critic of present secondary school practices recently made the following comments:

"The presence of less academically able students in secondary classrooms results in a waste of academic talent. Teachers have to gear instruction to the lowest common denominator, which slows down the progress of brighter students and leads to boredom. If we want significant reform in education we need to remove this handicap and encourage our more intelligent students. One way we can do this is to follow practices established in some other countries."

"Students could be tested as they enter high school and assigned either to an general track or a college track. Less able students would take general-track courses and not be asked to compete with brighter students in the college track. Students in the college track could be provided more challeng-

ing work. This system would simplify teachers' jobs. They would not have to plan for such a wide range of academic talent as they now must do in classrooms open to all."

What Do You Think?

1. Would everyone would benefit from this plan? Why or why not?

2. Describe possible negative effects of this idea.

3. What track would you have been in if you had been assigned to either a general track or a college track at the time you completed the sixth grade?

4. Point out any major flaws in this proposal.

Lack of success in the secondary classroom is often related to students' lack of prerequisite knowledge, experience, or skills. Since this is the case, teachers at this level need to work closely with slow learners to determine what they know before instruction begins on a new topic. When students are found to be weak in some areas, additional instruction on previously introduced material may be needed.

Another common problem of slow learners is an absence of good work habits and study skills. Many of these young people have not received help at home and may even have a home life that facilitates a careless and undisciplined approach to life. Some individuals simply do not know how to study or how to complete assignments. To remedy this situation, many teachers have found it useful to model appropriate learning and study techniques for these students. Showing these students concrete examples of properly completed assignments, giving them clear step-by-step instructions, and pairing them with successful students are among other approaches that can help improve inadequate work and study habits.

Many slow learners have not developed good thinking skills. They do not know how to approach a problem or to think about an issue. Thinking aloud is one way teachers provide help to students with this problem. To implement this procedure, the teacher identifies a problem similar to one that might be assigned to students. The teacher talks to students about the thinking processes he uses to identify key aspects of a problem and to work through to a reasonable conclusion.

Thinking aloud procedures are sometimes also used when teachers work with students to improve their abilities to take notes and to organize information. Some slow learners may appear "slow" because they seem unable to grasp the ideas and concepts presented to the class. One of the sources of difficulty may be that the material is not presented in a manner that is compatible with their personal learning styles. Some students can listen to verbal explanations and quickly grasp the material. Others need to see or visualize how it is organized. Still others require concrete illustrations and examples. To accommodate possible differences in student learning styles, teachers need to use a variety of presentation modes.

The pacing of the curriculum is another variable that may have to be considered in adapting instruction for the slow learner. The pace might be too fast for some individuals. As they become lost and frustrated, problems begin to mount. One way of altering the pacing is to emphasize key ideas to be learned fairly early in an instructional sequence. Once this has been done, questions can be asked of individual students to ascertain who has and who has not grasped the information. Students who have the new content in hand can be assigned enrichment activities calling on them to apply basic information that has been learned. Slower students can be grouped together and retaught the material. When this is done, ordinarily some attempts are made to vary teaching techniques somewhat from those used when the content was initially introduced to the whole class.

Slow learners often have negative self-concepts. To the extent possible, teachers of these students strive to provide opportunities for these individuals to succeed. Where possible, lessons are designed to take advantage of whatever academic strengths these students might have. Developing some instruction around areas of personal interest to these people often will increase their levels of motivation. As students experience more success, their levels of self-confidence go up. They feel better about themselves. This, in turn, makes them more likely to approach new learning tasks optimistically.

One way some teachers attempt to assure that slow learners experience some success is to reduce levels of competition among students in the classroom. Where competition is keen, slower learners often sense little possibility of achieving success. A few negative experiences may reinforce self-images that, even at the beginning of the school year, may not be positive. Cooperative learning activities often work well with these students. (For more information about cooperative learning, see Chapter 15, "Small Groups and Cooperative Learning.")

Students with Disabilities

Educators have a long history of concern for working with individuals with special needs. For years, students with disabilities received some training in public schools in so-called "special classrooms." Teachers interested in working with this population received special training and were assigned as special education teachers. In general, there was an assumption that these learners would not be present in regular classrooms or instructed by regular classroom teachers. This long-standing tradition began to be questioned seriously in the middle 1950s.

The beginnings of change trace to a famous court decision that had nothing to do with students with disabilities. This was the famous *Brown v. Board of Education* case that was decided in 1954. This decision involved the issue of racial segregation and declared that separate schools for white and black students were inherently unequal. The Supreme Court's decision included language that suggested the opportunity for an education was a right which was to be made available to all individuals on equal terms (Colachico, 1985).

Subsequent investigations revealed that many students with disabilities were not being served by the public schools. Many others were simply staying at home. There were concerns about the adequacy of the education being provided to those students with disabilities who were attending school. Critics pointed out that they were being unfairly isolated from contact with students having no disabilities and that this was discriminatory. Recommendations were made to include students with disabilities in regular classrooms to the extent possible. As a result, it was hoped that the self-esteem of students with disabilities would improve and that other students would come to accept them simply as "some of the people in my class."

Public Laws 94–142 and 101–476

As a result of a continuing interest in the needs of students with disabilities, the Senate in the early 1970s held a number of hearings on the status of education for these young people. Senators learned that more than one million students with disabilities were receiving no educational services whatever from the schools. These findings and continued pressure from constituencies representing the interests of students with disabilities led to the 1975 enactment of the Education for All Handicapped Children Act, Public Law 94–142. In 1990, P.L. 94–142 was reauthorized under the designation P.L. 101–476 and was retitled the Individuals with Disabilities Education Act (IDEA). This legislation has been called the "Bill of Rights for Students with Disabilities."

The original P.L. 94–142 was a new kind of federal legislation for educators. Before it was passed, most federal laws dealing with education went no farther than establishing certain goals or objectives. Means of achieving these goals or objectives were left largely to state and local school authorities. P.L. 94–142, on the other hand, not only specified goals and objectives but went on to speak in very specific terms about *how* schools should achieve them. Some of these required processes have resulted in dramatic changes in schools' responses to the needs of students with disabilities. To understand these changes and their implications for the regular classroom teacher, let us review some of the major provisions of P.L. 94–142 and its successor, P.L. 101–476.

1. *Each student with a disability will receive a free, appropriate education.* This means that the schools will assume the cost of educating the student. An "appropriate education" is one designed to meet the particular needs of individual students with disabilities.

2. *Students with disabilities will be educated in the least restrictive environment, alongside other students in regular classrooms when that placement is appropriate.* Responses to this provision of the law is often referred to as *mainstreaming*. This means that, whenever possible, these students are to be educated, or mainstreamed, in regular classrooms. The regular classroom teacher is expected to provide much of the instruction to students with disabilities.

3. *The instruction for students with disabilities is to be based on an Individualized Education Program (I.E.P.).*   The I.E.P. is a management tool. It requires school professionals and parents of students with disabilities to identify (a) short- and long-term goals for the students, (b) the resources to be committed to the program, (c) the dates when the services are to be rendered, (d) who is to deliver the instruction, (e) the extent to which the student is to be involved in regular education programs, and (f) how the student's progress is to be evaluated. The I.E.P. requirement imposes several responsibilities on classroom teachers. First of all, it requires participation in meetings to develop and monitor the I.E.P. In addition, teachers are expected to be capable of diagnosing entry-level achievement of the learners, identifying long- and short-term goals, delivering instruction to the students, and evaluating their progress. Some teachers have been frustrated by the time demands imposed by this portion of the law.

4. *Procedural safeguards were established to cover the identification, placement, evaluation, and due process rights of students with disabilities.*   Once a student with a disability is identified, both educators and parents must be involved in determining what constitutes an "appropriate" educational program. Often a committee known as an admissions, review, and dismissal (A.R.D.) committee is formed. This committee involves a representative of the district qualified to supervise or provide services to the student, the teachers of the student, the parents, and, sometimes, the student. Parents have a right to demand a hearing if they disagree with what is written in the I.E.P. Parents who are dissatisfied with diagnosis and prescription provided by the school district are usually allowed to demand an independent evaluation. This provision means that communication between the parents and the school must be kept open and that the school personnel must be very professional in their diagnosis and treatment of the student.

5. *Each school district must specify the procedures to be used to prepare personnel to work with students with disabilities.*   In addition, the law requires teacher education programs to better prepare future teachers to deal with the specific needs of students with disabilities.

Kinds of Disabilities

In general, the effort to include students with disabilities in regular classrooms has worked well. Research "findings indicate that mainstreamed students with mild disabilities may participate in academic lessons as well or nearly as well as their peers without disabilities" (Truesdell and Abramson, 1992; p. 392).

Teachers who work with mainstreamed students need some basic understanding of the kinds of disabilities they may encounter among students in their classrooms. Any attempt to categorize disabilities is risky. Broad categories often mask differences among individuals within each category. Also, students may have multiple disabilities. For example, someone who is visually impaired may also be emotionally disturbed.

In general, *students with disabilities* are defined as individuals who have a mental or physical condition that prevents them from succeeding in programs designed for people not having this condition (or these conditions). Various schemes have been developed for categorizing disabilities. We will discuss disabilities under these headings:

Box 8.2

SAMPLE INDIVIDUALIZED EDUCATION PROGRAM FORM

STUDENT: _____ SUBJECT AREA: _____

TEACHER: _____ ENTRY DATE: _____

SUMMARY OF ENTRY-LEVEL PERFORMANCE: _____

_____

_____

PRIORITIZED LONG-TERM GOALS: _____

_____

Behavioral Objectives	Materials or Resources Needed	Person Responsible to	Date Started	Date Ended	Date of Evaluation

Continuum of Services Hrs. Per Week Committee Members:

Regular Classroom _____   _____
Resource Teacher in
   Regular Class _____   _____
Resource Room _____   _____
Specialists (specify) _____   _____
Counselor _____   _____
Special Class _____   Date I.E.P. Approved _____
Others _____   Meeting Dates _____

- Mental retardation
- Hearing impairment
- Speech impairment
- Visual impairment
- Learning disability
- Attention Deficit Disorder
- Physical and health impairment
- Emotional disturbance

Mental Retardation

Mental retardation is a term that is difficult to define with any degree of precision. In general, people are described as mentally retarded with their intellectual development is (1) significantly below that of age-mates and when (2) their potential for academic achievement has been determined to be markedly less than that of so-called "normal" individuals.

In the past, IQ scores were often used to determine whether a person could be categorized as mentally retarded. A problem with using IQ for this purpose is that people who may appear to be mentally retarded on the basis of an IQ test may be perfectly capable of functioning in a normal fashion under other conditions. For example, people with low IQ scores may succeed in some job roles after leaving school. Because of this, the American Association of Mental Deficiency (AAMD) has long advocated that mental retardation be identified using broader and more diverse measures than a simple IQ test score. The AAMD suggests that people who are mentally retarded cannot function within the typical range of life situations. Individuals capable of functioning within this range should not be classified as mentally retarded, regardless their IQ test scores.

Several levels of mental retardation have been described. These include the categories of (1) educable, (2) trainable, and (3) severely or profoundly retarded. The type of student with mental retardation who is most likely to be assigned to spend part of the instructional day (or the entire instructional day) in a regular classroom is someone in the educable category. By far the largest percentage of individuals with mental retardation are educable.

It is difficult to speak authoritatively about what educable students can do. This is because there are tremendous differences among individuals in this category. In general, educable students can derive some benefits from the school program. Individual teachers must diagnose specific characteristics of educable students in their classes and, in cooperation with parents and other school officials, devise appropriate learning experiences for them.

Working with Educable Students.   Educable students often have short attention spans. They may become easily frustrated. By the time they reach their secondary school years, many have a history of failure in school. Often they lack confidence as they begin a new task. Frequently they experience difficulty grasping abstract ideas or complex sequences of ideas.

Some of the following principles make sense in planning instruction for educable students:

- Lessons should be short, direct, and to the point.
- Material should be introduced in short, sequential steps.
- Content introduced in prose form should be reinforced by additional visual and oral examples.
- It may be useful to assign a student who is not mentally retarded to work with the educable student as a peer tutor.
- Teacher directions should be delivered clearly, using vocabulary words educable students understand.
- Lessons should not place educable students in highly competitive situations, particularly those requiring them to compete against non-mentally-retarded students.

Box 8.3

Sensitive Treatment of Educable Students in the Regular Classroom

When you were in school, you probably had some educable students in your classes. To you and your fellow students, these people probably seemed simply to be young people who were much less bright than others in the room.

What Do You Think?

1. How did these students react to school? Were they active in extracurricular programs? Were they popular?

2. Have you kept track of what has happened to any of these people since you graduated from high school? What are they doing? Are some of them doing things you never would have predicted?

3. Based on what you know about educable students, how might you make assignments in your subject area that would give them a reasonable possibility of achieving success? Would everyone in the class be doing the same thing? If not, how might you manage different kinds of activities at the same time?

In addition, educable students often require more time to complete tasks than do their non-mentally-retarded fellow students. Teachers need to avoid imposing tight, restrictive deadlines when assigning tasks to educable students. It is better for these students to succeed at completing fewer tasks than for them constantly to be put in the position of failing to complete a larger number of them. Successful task completion is an important builder of self-esteem for these young people.

Hearing Impairment

Students who are hearing impaired fall into two key categories. One includes students whose hearing loss is so profound as to greatly inhibit their ability to acquire normal use of oral language. These individuals are classified as "deaf." In the second category are students whose hearing loss is serious, but not serious enough to prevent them from acquiring normal speech patterns. They are classified as "hard of hearing."

There are great differences among students who are hearing impaired. Some of them are unable to hear certain pitches. Others require different levels of amplified sound. Some have had a hearing loss since birth; others may have suffered a hearing loss after they were old enough to have acquired some oral-language proficiency. Despite individual differences, students who are hearing impaired generally experience difficulty developing great proficiency with the spoken language. School programs for these students place a heavy emphasis on helping them improve their oral-language proficiency.

About 5 percent of the school-aged population is estimated to suffer some degree of hearing loss. Of this 5 percent, only about $1\frac{1}{2}$ percent require special educational services. Even students who have quite severe hearing losses function well in regular classrooms.

Working with Hearing-Impaired Students.   Many students who have severe hearing losses have been taught to pay close attention to visual clues. Many know how to read lips. Because of their dependence on visual signals, students with hearing losses need to be provided with lessons that enable them to take advantage of their visual-learning skills. For example, teachers need to face these students directly when they give directions and present new information. It helps if teachers write information on an overhead transparency rather than on a chalkboard. (Teachers frequently talk about what they are writing when making notes for students. A teacher who uses an overhead continues to face students while writing; a teacher who uses a chalkboard faces away from the class while writing.) It is also a good idea for teachers with hearing-impaired students to remain relatively stationary while they are speaking. Trained lip readers find it difficult to understand a person who is in motion.

Assignments and other directions need to be provided in written form. (They can be oral as well, but the written information can help eliminate possible confusion among hearing-impaired students.) When a lecture is delivered, it helps to provide class members with a general printed outline that includes at least major topics and subtopics to be covered. Additionally, it is a good idea to provide students with lists of important (and potentially confusing) words before the lecture begins. This is particularly true when terms are to be introduced that have multiple meanings. (Consider the term *market* as it is understood in everyday conversation and how it is used by specialists in economics.) A discussion of special vocabulary before the lecture begins may help students who are hearing impaired (and other students as well) to better grasp the material.

All students do better when instruction is well organized and when point-to-point transitions are clear and smooth. Clarity in planning and delivering instruction is even more critical for hearing-impaired students than for the general population of secondary school learners. Students who are hearing impaired lack the multiple communication channels that other students sometimes use to "make sense" out of disorganized lessons.

Some hearing-impaired students wear hearing aids or other mechanical devices. Their teachers need to know how they work. For example, they should know how batteries are replaced in hearing aids. It may be a good idea to keep a supply of batteries on hand. Many school districts employ specialists in the education of students who are hearing impaired who can provide additional guidance regarding how these young people can best be served in the regular classroom.

Speech Impairment

Identifying students with clearly defined speech impairments is difficult. Even the most clear-cut definitions require a great deal of personal judgment. In general, individuals are thought to suffer from impaired speech when their speech differs significantly from that of others in the same age group. Speech problems encompass a range of difficulties. These relate to such things as voice quality, problems in articulating certain sounds, and stuttering.

Because speech impairments do not represent the obvious obstacles to learning as hearing impairment and visual impairment do, some teachers tend not take them as seriously as they should. An important side effect of speech impairment, and one that occurs in a distressingly high number of students suffering from this problem, is a low self-image. Because of the frustration they feel at not being able to speak normally, some of these students conclude that they are inferior or even incompetent. The dropout rate of students with speech impairments is high.

Working with Speech-Impaired Students.   Many students with speech impairments profit from work with a trained speech therapist. Many school districts have these specialists on staff. Classroom teachers also can help these students. In general, students with speech impairments need emotional support. Teachers need to avoid placing students with a speech impairment in situations that call unnecessary attention to this condition.

In classroom discussions, it makes sense to call on students with speech impairments only when they raise a hand and indicate a willingness to volunteer a response. When such students begin to speak, they should be allowed to finish what they have to say without interruption or correction. Praise and other kinds of reinforcement should be provided when these students volunteer a remark in class.

Teachers need to provide opportunities for speech-impaired students to speak with the teacher on a one-to-one basis. This provides an opportunity for the teacher to boost students' morale by making sensitive, supporting comments to them. Additionally, it affords students opportunities to talk to the teacher about course work (and other matters) without feeling that they will be embarrassed by a communication difficulty that might draw ridicule from others in the class.

Visual Impairment

The term *visual impairment* is used to describe a variety of conditions related to the sense of sight. Some visually impaired individuals have no sight whatever. However, most students in this category have some sight. Some see a world that is blurred, dim, or out of focus; others may see only parts of objects. About one percent of the school-aged population is visually impaired.

Working with Visually-Impaired Students.   Whenever assignments are written on the chalkboard or written information is distributed, teachers need to make special arrangements to assure clear communication with their students who are visually impaired. Sometimes oral explanations will suffice. At other times, teachers find it useful to provide these students with audio-recordings of information. Students can play back the tapes later to assure they have the needed information.

Personal mobility is a important problem for students who are visually impaired. Over time, many of these students develop good mental pictures of places they visit frequently. They require some experience in a new environment before a good mental picture develops. Teachers need to make time for visually impaired students to visit classrooms when classes are not being held. This will given them an opportunity to become familiar with placement of furniture and with other room features. If changes in room arrangements are made later, students who are visually impaired need time to become familiar with the new configuration.

Learning Disability

A student with a learning disability exhibits a disorder in one or more of the basic psychological processes involved in understanding or using spoken or written language.

The problem may be revealed in such areas as listening, writing, reading, spelling, or computing. Sometimes learning disabilities are referred to by such terms as *perceptual handicaps, minimal brain dysfunctions,* and *dyslexia.* Students who have learning disabilities have difficulty processing sensory stimuli.

People with learning disabilities often find it hard to follow directions. They may appear disorganized. Teachers often find these students unable to get started on assigned tasks. Often they have a low tolerance for frustration. They may become tense and appear incapable of doing anything when they feel the teacher is pressuring them. Handwriting of these students often appears disorganized. Letters within words may be inconsistent in size, and there may be letter reversals. Some students with learning disabilities have unusual speech patterns. For example, words may be spoken out of their proper sequence.

Working with Learning Disabled Students. Most students with learning disabilities need special help with organization. These students often find it difficult to distinguish between important and unimportant information. Teachers need to take time to highlight key ideas for them and to provide ways of organizing information into meaningful patterns.

Learning disabled students often have a hard time dealing with alternatives. Sometimes they become anxious when they are forced to make choices. Teachers need to limit options available for these students.

By the time they reach their secondary school years, many students with learning disabilities have experienced many years of frustration and failure in school. As a result, their self-esteem often is low. Anything teachers can do to help these young people develop more self-confidence should be encouraged. In a supportive classroom environment, these students *can* learn.

Attention Deficit Disorder

Attention Deficit Disorder (ADD) might be thought of as a specific type of learning disability. It bears special mention because students with ADD have been declared eligible for services under P.L. 101–476 (the successor to P.L. 94–142) "when ADD impairs educational performance or learning" (Lerner and Lerner, 1991; p. 1). Students with ADD have difficulty staying actively engaged on tasks assigned to them by their teachers and pursuing, paying attention to, and completing their school work. Sometimes they appear to be hyperactive, racing from one idea to another and producing extremely sloppy work as a result of a compulsion to finish quickly. At other times, these students give teachers the impression that they aren't listening to what is being said (Lerner and Lerner, 1991).

ADD is common. It accounts for fully half of all referrals of children to outpatient health clinics. More male students than female students suffer from ADD (Lerner and Lerner, 1991).

Working with Students with ADD. In working with these students, teachers need to modify the learning environment and the nature of assigned tasks. Students with ADD are easily distracted by noise. They have problems with tasks that are too difficult or when others in the class establish the learning pace. These students do better when tasks are self-paced.

In general, students with ADD require more structure in their lessons than other students. To help these students pay attention, their teachers often increase the potential for holding their interest by adding color, shape, and texture to learning materials. These students do better in small classes than in large ones, and they tend to profit more from direct instruction than indirect instruction (Lerner and Lerner, 1991).

Physical and Health Impairment

Physical and health impairment is a broad category. In general, it includes students who have limitations related to physical abilities or medical conditions that may interfere with their school performance. About half of the students in this group have suffered from a crippling disease.

Working with Students with Physical and Health Impairments.   The range of conditions in this category makes it impossible to provide recommendations appropriate for every student with a physical or health impairment. For teachers, the appropriate initial step is to gather complete information regarding the specific nature of the condition of each student in the class who falls into this general category. Counselors and parents often are able to provide specific descriptions of each student's special circumstances. Once this information is available to them, teachers can decide upon modifications of their programs that need to be made for each student with a physical or health impairment.

These modifications will vary greatly from case to case. For example, some conditions may make it impossible for affected students to complete tasks as quickly as others in the class. This may mean that time allowed for these students to complete work will have to be adjusted. For learners who have physical problems requiring the use of walkers or crutches, it may be necessary to rearrange classroom furniture to allow these students to move about the room.

In general, students with physical and health impairments are fully capable of meeting the intellectual challenges of regular classroom instruction. For the teacher, the major adjustment comes not in devising unique methods of instruction but in devising appropriate responses to accommodate special limitations imposed by particular physical and health conditions of these students. When the special needs of these students are met, many of them do extremely well in the regular classroom.

Emotional Disturbance

Emotionally disturbed students have "a marked deviation from age-appropriate behavior expectations which interferes with positive personal and interpersonal development" (Turnbull and Schulz, 1979; p. 41). Some emotionally disturbed students may be defiant, rude, destructive, and attention seeking. Others may be fearful and withdrawn.

Most emotionally disturbed students find it difficult to cope with their environments. As a result, they often experience difficulty making the kinds of adjustments needed to stay at school-related tasks. As a result, academic problems are common among these students. These frequently lead to low self-concepts. Many of these students become caught up in a negative cycle featuring poor academic performance, leading to diminished self-esteem, and resulting in poor attitudes that contribute to additional academic performance problems and a renewal of the same distressing sequence.

Working with Students Who Are Emotionally Disturbed.   Teachers need to attend to four key principles in working with emotionally disturbed students.

- Activities must be "success oriented." Students must sense that they have a reasonable chance of succeeding.
- Behavior expectations must be communicated with exceptional clarity, and they must be consistently enforced.
- Distractions must be minimized to reduce the probability of students' being distracted from their assigned work.
- Efforts need to be taken to assure that students understand that there is a clear and definite relationship between their behaviors and consequences flowing from these behaviors.

A concern that has some connection to each of these four major principles is motivation. By the time many emotionally disturbed students enter their secondary school years, they have experienced so much failure that they doubt they can master anything taught in school. Additionally, many of them suspect that school learning isn't particularly useful. As a result, many of these students go to great lengths to avoid serious engagement with academic tasks. All of this means that teachers must work hard to convince these students that mastery of school subjects will yield important personal benefits. These benefits need to be characterized by immediacy. It does little good to tell an emotionally disturbed student to "do this because it will help you get a better job in 10 years."

Instruction needs to be designed to maximize these students' potential for success. It helps to cut large complex tasks into smaller parts that appear less intimidating. As individual parts are mastered, the teacher needs to provide positive feedback to encourage students to stay on task. Additionally, teachers need to help develop these students' self-regulatory behaviors. There is some evidence that, with help, these students can be taught self-monitoring techniques that will help them behave in ways that will facilitate learning and assist them to develop more positive self-concepts (Graham, Harris, and Reid, 1992).

Teachers with students who are emotionally disturbed need to understand that such problems are not likely to disappear overnight. In many cases, emotional disturbance is a condition that has developed over many years. Even teachers who approach their emotionally disturbed students with sensitivity and compassion cannot expect quick results. Change may take months, or even years.

Gifted and Talented Students

In a status report prepared more than 20 years ago, the U.S. Commissioner of Education pointed out that only a few specific programs for the gifted and talented existed in the nation's schools. Stimulated by the considerable interest generated by this report,

Congress established the Office of Gifted and Talented within the U.S. Office of Education. Gifted and talented learners were defined by P.L. 91–230 as "children who have outstanding intellectual ability or creative talent, the development of which requires special activities or services not ordinarily provided by local education agencies" (United States Statutes at Large, 1971; p. 153). In 1974, Congress responded to additional public interest with P.L. 93–380, which provided federal funds to local and state agencies for the specific purpose of improving programs for the gifted and talented.

CASE STUDY

Dealing with Too Many Individual Student Needs

Rusty Llewellyn is in his first year of teaching sophomore English at Ponce de Leon Senior High School. The first semester went well. As Rusty told his parents during the holidays, "I still have some enthusiasm left even late on Friday afternoon, and every morning I can't wait to go to school to get started."

Since the beginning of the spring semester, Rusty's professional life has been more challenging. His biggest frustration has been dealing with some unhappy parents—not large numbers of them, but enough to raise some worries. To sort things out, he has decided to chat with Laura Suarez, the Vice Principal for Student Affairs. He and Laura have hit it off well, and he feels she is someone who'll really listen. After school last Tuesday, Rusty headed for Ms. Suarez's office, sat down, pulled the top off a soft drink from the machine, and began to talk.

"I need some help out of your trusted 'sage advice' file," Rusty began.

"Fine," said Ms. Suarez. "What's up?"

"Well, I'm taking a bit of flack from a few parents. Basically, I feel that some of them are pulling me one way, and others are tugging me off in a totally different direction."

"Can you be a bit more specific?" Ms. Suarez asked.

"Sure," Rusty replied. "I've got two or three students with disabilities working on special I.E.P.s we've developed for them, and their folks are after me to be sure that they learn what they're supposed to learn. Then, I have a few people from the gifted and talented group . . . you know, the ones we're supposed to provide enrichment lessons for. Some of their parents think I'm not giving these bright kids the kinds of challenging assignments they need. Then there are all of the kids in the middle . . . you know, the good, plodding B and C students. *I* don't think I'm paying nearly enough attention to them."

"If I'm reading you right, you're feeling stretched in so many directions that you don't feel you're doing anybody much good right now. Is that how it is?" asked Ms. Suarez.

"That's *exactly* the problem," said Rusty, nodding his agreement. "I feel I really need to be offering three, four, five, six, or even more separate instructional programs for these students. I just don't see how I can do this. But, if I don't try, then I feel I'm going to be in big trouble, first with these parents, and maybe later with you administrators. I'm really frustrated. Do you have any ideas?"

■ ■ ■

If you were Ms. Suarez, what are some suggestions that you might pass on to Rusty? How common do you think the situation he described is? Are there others in the school in addition to Ms. Suarez that Rusty might consult? What advice would you give him? What would you do yourself if you were faced with this situation?

Identifying Gifted and Talented Students

At one time, students were selected for gifted and talented programs almost exclusively on the basis of their scores on standardized intelligence tests. Critics charged that gifted and talented people had a wide range of abilities and that many of these were not revealed by intelligence test scores. Further, fears that standardized intelligence tests were culturally biased and, hence, tended to screen out minority group students drew additional negative attention to selection based only on test scores.

Through the years, there has been a broadening of the conception of characteristics of gifted and talented people. The work of Joseph Renzulli (1978), a leading expert in the education of these students, was especially important in gaining acceptance for the idea that selection should be based on multiple criteria. Renzulli argued that evidence should be gathered in three distinct categories of student characteristics when decisions were being made regarding who should be admitted to gifted and talented programs. These characteristics are:

- Intelligence
- Task commitment
- Creativity

Information related to intelligence should be gathered not just from standardized test performance. Other sources such as grades and comments from individuals who have had opportunities to observe academic work of students should be consulted.

The idea of task commitment refers to a person's ability to see through a project or activity to the end. People who are gifted and talented tend to finish things, even when there are frustrations along the way. They are not apt to bounce from one thing to another, leaving a lot of loose ends along the way.

Creativity refers to the ability to engage challenges and solve problems in unusual ways. Gifted and talented students tend to look at dilemmas in nontraditional ways and to use innovative (and sometimes surprising) techniques to respond to them.

How Gifted and Talented Students See Themselves

What are gifted and talented students really like? Certainly there are popular misconceptions. Consider, for example, the "Revenge of the Nerds" films and their images of bright students as eccentric misfits. Contrary to this view, most studies have found that gifted and talented students are well accepted by their peers. It is true that these students face some special kinds of pressure from other students. In particular, they may be pressured to do less and thereby keep the teacher from setting expectations too high for the class as a whole (Brown and Sternberg, 1990).

Some gifted and talented students have parents who expect too much of them. This leads some of these students to set unrealistic expectations for themselves and to feel bad when they fail to live up to them. Teachers can help these students by helping them focus on their accomplishments, not their shortcomings (Baum, 1990). These students need to be taught that everybody has strengths and weaknesses and that there is nothing to be ashamed of when they are less than outstanding in a given area.

Enrichment and Acceleration

Enrichment and *acceleration* are the two basic orientations of programs for gifted and talented students. Enrichment programs assume students will remain in the same classes and go through school at the same rate as other non-gifted and talented stu-

These students are perfecting a demonstration that will later be shared with science fair visitors.

"Your semester project proposals are always interesting, Schuyler. Last fall's light-hearted musical rendering of *The Scarlet Letter* certainly broke new ground. But, I ask you, is the world ready for *Silas Marner Meets Godzilla?*"

dents. However, there is an expectation that enriched programs will be provided for them that go well beyond the academic fare served up to the other students.

Acceleration programs increase the pace at which gifted learners complete their schooling. For example, in an accelerated program a gifted learner might complete the entire high school program in just two years. There is no attempt to keep gifted learners in classes with learners who are in the same age group. This often means that gifted learners are in classes where most of the others are older than they are.

Enrichment programs seek to provide learning experiences for gifted learners that are in addition to or that go beyond those provided to other learners. In enrichment programs, gifted learners remain as members in classes that include a mixture of gifted and non-gifted young people who are in the same general age group. They go through the school program at the same rate as all other learners.

Though there are loyal supporters of both enrichment and acceleration, today enrichment programs are much more common than acceleration programs. This is true because enrichment programs can be implemented with fewer administrative changes. Also, the possibility that some gifted and talented students in acclerated programs will be in classes with students who are much older than they are is a source of concern to some parents and educators and, hence, is a force working against the popularity of the acceleration approach.

Working with Gifted and Talented Students

Teachers who work with gifted and talented students must assure that what these students are asked to do is truly different from what is required of other students. It is particularly important that teachers do not simply ask them to do "more of the same." (For example, if all students are asked to do 10 homework problems, it is a mistake to ask gifted and talented students to do 15 problems from the same set.) If this is done, the teacher communicates to gifted and talented students that their condition is a "burden" for which they are "punished" by being required to do more school work than their classmates. Students are likely to see this as unfair. One result can be a diminished interest in school and a disinclination to "stretch" academically.

It is important to encourage development of gifted and talented students' creativity. To accomplish this, teachers can do the following:

- Encourage and support students' efforts to take risks.
- Make clear how students will be able to use new knowledge they have acquired (Sternberg and Lubart, 1991).

Risk Taking
Sometimes, school instructional practices discourage students from taking risks. For example, teachers often tell students exactly how to indicate that they have learned something. Or, they stipulate a specific kind of learning "product" that students are supposed to produce as a result of their involvement in a particular lesson. Through the years, many students have come to believe that a failure to prepare an essay when the teacher has asked for an essay or to turn in a set of note cards with summaries of outside reading when that is what the teacher has specified will result in nothing but trouble.

Teachers of gifted and talented students need to avoid "boxing students in" by laying out hard and fast rules regarding how learning will be assessed. Students need to understand that innovative, creative responses will be all right. They need to be challenged to develop unusual approaches that will stretch their imaginative and creative powers.

Establishing the Personal Importance of Learning
It is important that gifted and talented students are provided opportunities to pursue some issues they select themselves. These students need to be encouraged to redefine tasks provided by the teacher in ways that will make them more personally important.

Table 8.1   Summary Table

Main Points	Explanation
Historical Treatment of Exceptional Students	For many years, secondary schools were viewed as schools for an academic elite. Little effort was expended to provide special services for other students, including slow learners and students with disabilities. Only after the middle of the twentieth century were these attitudes seriously challenged. Today, schools enroll an extraordinarily diverse group of learners. Federal laws assure that students with disabilities receive as much instruction as possible in regular school classes.
Slow Learners	Slow learners include students who are not learning at a rate typical for their age or grade level. Many of these students have experienced many failures by the time they reach their secondary school years. Teachers need to exercise particular care to assure that students have the prerequisite knowledge needed to succeed on new tasks. Some of these students also need help in developing good study skills. Teachers also need to assist them in developing productive thinking skills. Instruction needs to be paced to allow slow learners to succeed. Perhaps the most important consideration in planning for slow learners is to build up their self-images by organizing instructional experiences that allow them to succeed.
Student Disabilities	These are conditions that have the potential to interfere with students' success at school.
Public Law 94–142	The Education for All Handicapped Children Act has been called the "Bill of Rights for Students with Disabilities." It requires schools to provide appropriate educational services for students with disabilities. One of its most important provisions calls for students to be educated in the least restrictive environment. This means that, to the extent possible, students with disabilities are intermingled with other students in regular classrooms.
Public Law 101–476	The Individuals with Disabilities Education Act essentially is a reauthorization of P. L. 94–142. It was passed in 1990.
Mental Retardation	This disability describes individuals (1) who have intellectual functioning that is significantly below that of age mates and (2) whose potential for academic achievement is considered markedly less than that of more typical students. Many of these students have short attention spans. Lessons need to be short, direct, and to the point. Information presented in written form needs to be reinforced orally and visually. Pacing needs to be adjusted so these students can follow point-by-point development of lessons. Vocabulary needs to be chosen carefully with a view to assuring these students understand what is expected of them.

Main Points	Explanation
Student Disabilities, *cont'd.*	
Hearing Impairment	Hearing impaired students often experience difficulty in developing proficiency with the spoken language. About 5 percent of the school population suffer from some degree of hearing loss. Many of these students have been taught to pay close attention to visual cues. It is important for teachers to face them directly when speaking. It also is helpful when spoken information is also introduced in written forms. Lip readers tend to find it easier to follow what is being said when the teacher stands relatively still when speaking.
Speech Impairment	Students who are speech impaired have patterns of speech that differ markedly from those of their age-mates. Many students with speech impairments need a lot of emotional support. They should not be interrupted when speaking. They need to be praised when volunteering to speak in class. It is important for the teacher to allow time for one-on-one conversations with these students.
Visual Impairment	About 1 percent of the total school population is visually impaired. Much information for these students needs to be provided orally. Some teachers provide students with audio recordings to play back at home to reinforce their understanding of what they are to do to complete assignments. Since many of these students develop a mental picture of the classroom, it is a good plan to invite them to visit the room when others are not there so they can learn locations of chairs, tables, and other room features.
Learning Disability	Individuals who are learning disabled exhibit a disorder in one or more of the psychological processes involved in understanding written or spoken language. They often find it difficult to follow directions and to get started on assigned tasks. Many of these students need help with organization. They need to be cued to distinguish between relevant and irrelevant information. Because sometimes they find it extremely difficult to make choices, numbers of choices should be reduced.
Attention Deficit Disorder	Students with this particular type of learning disability have difficulty staying actively engaged on school tasks. They may be hyperactive, racing from one activity to the next. Distractions for these students need to be minimized. These students do better in smaller classes, and they tend to profit more from direct than from indirect instruction.

Table 8.1   Summary Table *(continued)*

Main Points	Explanation
Student Disabilities, *cont'd.*	
Physical and Health Impairment	This broad category includes students who have physical or health limitations that may interfere with their school performance. Modifications teachers make are in response to the specific condition characterizing an individual student. In general, students in this category are fully capable of coping with the intellectual challenges of the regular classroom.
Emotional Disturbance	Emotionally disturbed students deviate noticeably from age-appropriate behaviors. Their behavioral patterns interfere with their personal and interpersonal development. They may be defiant, rude, destructive, and attention seeking. They also may be fearful and withdrawn. Activities for these students must be success oriented. Expectations regarding appropriate behavior must be communicated to them clearly. Distractions need to be minimized. These students must understand that there is a clear and predictable connection between their behavior and any resultant consequences.
Gifted and Talented Students	These students have outstanding intellectual or creative abilities. The development of these abilities is thought to require school services that go beyond those provided to other students. These students have a record of high academic achievement, creativity, and task commitment.
Enrichment Program	This category of programming for gifted and talented students keeps these students in classes with their age-mates. Their needs are met by teachers who provide them with special lessons and tasks that are designed to "stretch" their special intellectual and creative abilities.
Acceleration Program	This category of programming for gifted and talented students moves these students through school at a faster-than-typical pace. As a result, many gifted and talented students in accelerated programs find that they are much younger than some of the other students in their classes. Acceleration programs are less popular than enrichment programs.

Gifted and talented students are not motivated to stretch themselves in pursuit of arid academic goals that seem little connected to their own needs or interests. They may see such pursuits as "a stupid game" and simply refuse to play.

On the other hand, when these bright young people are encouraged to play an active part in identifying (or in at least redefining) the learning task, they often will commit their intellectual and emotional resources to it with great enthusiasm. This kind of commitment is essential. Without it, these special young people will fail to fully develop their outstanding creative, imaginative, and intellectual powers.

Review of Key Ideas

- Differences among students in secondary schools are more pronounced today than they have ever been before. Within this diverse group are students who are slow learners, students with various disabilities, and students who are classified as gifted and talented.

- Historically, secondary schools failed to serve many of the exceptional students who now enroll. Only in the latter part of the nineteenth century did large numbers of people begin to question the view that secondary schools could serve more than an elite few. Only after the middle of the twentieth century did schools begin to take seriously responsibilities for educating large numbers of students with disabilities. There were also few special programs for gifted and talented students prior to this time.

- The term *slow learner* is a slippery one. This is true because some students who may lag behind their age-mates in some subjects are able to do average (or even above average) work in other areas. To say that slow learners are "below average" is not helpful. By definition, half of the population is "below average"; however, few would argue that half of the people in the schools are "slow learners." In working with slow learners, teachers need to establish conditions that will allow them to succeed. Many slow learners in secondary schools lack confidence as a result of years of failure. Adjustments to assignments, mode of presentation, and pacing of instruction sometimes are helpful.

- For many years, many students with disabilities received no educational services from the schools. All this changed with the passage of Public Law 94–142, the Education for All Handicapped Children Act, in 1975. This act was renewed and retitled in 1990 with the passage of P. L. 101–476, the Individuals with Disabilities Education Act. These laws require that schools (1) provide each student with a disability a free, appropriate education, (2) educate these students in the least restrictive environment possible, (3) develop individual educational programs for each of these students, (4) establish safeguards covering identification, placement, evaluation, and due process rights of these students, and (5) specify procedures to be followed in preparing professional personnel to work with these students.

- Teachers today encounter many students with disabilities in their regular classrooms. These students may have disabilities including: (1) mental retardation, (2) hearing impairment, (3) speech impairment, (4) visual impairment, (5) learning disability, (6) Attention Deficit Disorder, (7) physical and health impairment, and (8) emotional disturbance. Today's secondary teachers are expected to be familiar with characteristics of students with these disabilities and to work with others in planning and delivering meaningful instruction to them.

- Federal laws support efforts of schools to provide special programs for gifted and talented students. Today, these students tend to be selected on multiple criteria. Often, these include measures of intellectual abilities, creativity, and task commitment (persistence). Despite some popular misconceptions, most gifted and talented students are well adjusted and get along well with other students. These students tend to be served either by enrichment programs or acceleration programs. In enrichment programs, gifted and talented students stay in regular classes and progress through school at the same rate as their age-mates. However, they are provided with instructional experiences appropriate to their superior abilities. In acceleration programs, these students go through the school program at a faster rate than other students. This means that gifted and talented students in these programs may be in many classes where they are much younger than the other students. Today, enrichment programs are more common than acceleration programs.

Follow-Up Questions and Activities

Questions

1. What kinds of students were served by early American secondary schools?
2. What are some characteristics of slow learners, and why is the very term *slow learner* difficult to define?
3. What are some approaches teachers can take to help students who are slow learners?
4. What are some key provisions of federal legislation relating to how schools must treat students with disabilities?
5. How has the mainstreaming requirement worked out in practice?
6. What kinds of mentally retarded students are secondary teachers likely to encounter in their classes, and what are some things they can do to help these young people learn?
7. What are some characteristics of students with hearing and speech impairments, and how can teachers help these students?
8. In what ways can teachers help students with learning disabilities, Attention Deficit Disorders, physical and health impairments, and emotional disturbance problems?
9. Why has selection of gifted and talented students sometimes posed problems, and what are some criteria commonly used today to identify these young people?
10. What are some differences between enrichment and acceleration approaches to providing for needs of gifted and talented students?

Activities

1. Invite a panel of five or six secondary school teachers to your class. Have them discuss experiences they have had in working with mainstreamed students in their regular classes. In particular, urge them to share ideas about how instruction has been modified to meet these students' special needs.
2. Interview an educational diagnostician or some other official from a school district with responsibility for working with teachers, parents, administrators, and others

to develop individualized education plans (I.E.P.s) for students with handicaps. Ask this person to explain how development of an I.E.P. proceeds. Summarize your interview in a short paper for your course instructor.

3. This chapter provides a few general suggestions for working with slow learners. Read some articles in professional education journals that contain additional ideas. Identify four or five specific ideas. Gather together all ideas found by members of your class. Produce a composite list titled "Working with Slow Learners: What Works," and give a copy to everyone in the course.

4. Organize a class debate on this topic: "Resolved that programs for the gifted and talented divert scarce educational resources away from other, more deserving students."

5. Use professional journal articles, interviews with specialists in the education of gifted and talented students, and other sources as a basis for a paper entitled: "Teaching the Gifted and Talented: Characteristics of Teachers Who Succeed with These Special Students."

References

BAUM, S. "The Gifted/Learning Disabled: A Paradox for Teachers." *Education Digest* (April 1990), pp. 54–56.

BLOOM, B. S. *Human Interaction and School Learning*. New York: McGraw-Hill, 1982.

BROWN, B. B. AND STERNBERG, L. "Academic Achievement and Social Acceptance." *Education Digest* (March 1990), pp. 57–60.

COLACHICO, D. *The Education for All Handicapped Children Act: Legislation for Academic Equality (A Historical Study of Public Law 94–142)*. Unpublished record of study, Texas A&M University, 1985.

GRAHAM, S.; HARRIS, K. R.; AND REID, R. "Developing Self-Regulated Learners." *Focus on Exceptional Children* (February 1992), pp. 1–16.

LERNER, J. W. AND LERNER, S. R. "Attention Deficit Disorder: Issues and Questions." *Focus on Exceptional Children* (November 1991), pp. 1–17.

RENZULLI, J. "What Makes Giftedness: Re-examining a Definition." *Phi Delta Kappan* (November 1978), pp. 180–184; 261.

SCHNUR, J. "Teachers for the Gifted—Past, Present, and Future." *Roeper Review* (May/June 1980), pp. 5–7.

STERNBERG, R. J. AND LUBART, T. I. "Creating Creative Minds." *Phi Delta Kappan* (April 1991), pp. 608–614.

TRUESDELL, L. A. AND ABRAMSON, T. "Academic Behavior and Grades of Mainstreamed Students with Mild Disabilities." *Exceptional Children* (March/April 1992), pp. 392–398.

TURNBULL, A. P. AND SCHULZ, J. B. *Mainstreaming Handicapped Students: A Guide for the Classroom Teacher*. Boston: Allyn & Bacon, 1979.

UNITED STATES STATUTES AT LARGE. 91st Congress, 1970–1971, Vol. 84, Part 1. Washington, DC: U.S. Government Printing Office, 1971.

WILDS, E. H. AND LOTTICH, K. V. *The Foundations of Modern Education*. 3rd ed. New York: Holt, Rinehart & Winston, 1964.

III

Organizing the Learning Environment

Teachers face two major organizational tasks in working with students in their class-rooms. They must develop plans and procedures related to instruction, and they must develop plans and procedures related to maintaining order (Doyle, 1986). Absent attention to either of these responsibilities, optimum student learning will not occur.

Planning for management requires teachers to consider students in a class in terms of how they interact as a group. Experienced teachers know that many individuals in their classes take on quite different patterns of behavior as members of groups than when they are involved in one-on-one relationships. To better understand how specific students will work within the many instructional situations they will encounter in the classroom, teachers work hard to know their students well. This is not always an easy task, and it is one reason that Theodore Sizer (1992) and others have recommended that ways be found to reduce numbers of individuals with whom secondary school teachers work each day.

The knowledge teachers gain about individuals in their classes helps them to plan learning experiences that will allow students to achieve success. Today's technologies have greatly expanded options available to teachers as they design instructional experiences for their students. Increasingly, secondary schools are incorporating new technologies to meet students' needs and to prepare them for the high-tech world they will encounter as graduates.

Part 3 answers questions people often have about secondary school teachers' responsibilities regarding organizing the learning environment. Among these questions are:

- What are some commonsense approaches to maintaining order in the classroom?
- What is meant by "individualizing" instruction?
- Is it really necessary for a teacher to prepare totally different individualized programs for each student in a class?
- In what ways are technologies helping today's secondary teachers do their jobs better?

Discussion related to these questions is introduced in three unit chapters:

Chapter 9: Management and Discipline

Chapter 10: Individualizing for Learning

Chapter 11: Enhancing Learning Through Technology

REFERENCES

DOYLE, W. "Classroom Organization and Management." In M. C. Wittrock (ed.). *Handbook of Research on Teaching*. 3rd ed. New York: Macmillan Publishing Company, 1986, pp. 392–431.

SIZER, T. R. *Horace's School: Redesigning the American High School*. Boston: Houghton Mifflin, 1992.

9

Management and Discipline

AIMS

This chapter provides information to help the reader to:

- Identify the relationship between instruction and classroom management.
- Point out some principles of management that can be applied to the classroom.
- Describe areas of management that need to be considered when organizing a classroom for instruction.
- State the basic goal of discipline.
- List some principles to be considered when disciplining students.
- Describe a range of responses that can be tried when responding to episodes of misbehavior in the classroom.

FOCUS QUESTIONS

1. How serious is the problem of discipline in the schools?

2. What do you believe needs to be done to overcome discipline problems?

3. What is the basic goal or purpose of discipline in the schools?

4. How does teacher leadership style influence student behavior?

5. Why is teacher consistency an important element in preventing discipline problems?

6. What elements in the physical environment need to be considered in efforts to establish conditions that will reduce the number of episodes of student misbehavior?

7. What should be considered by a teacher in choosing a particular method of responding to an episode of misbehavior?

Introduction

Teachers' success in the classroom depends on their competence in two key areas: instructing students and managing the classroom. Excellence in instructional planning, alone, will not suffice. Students in the classroom must be managed so that sound instructional ideas can be implemented.

Classroom management and discipline problems challenge teachers everywhere. Results of one study revealed that two-thirds of the teachers surveyed reported unmotivated and undisciplined students as causing problems in their classrooms. Fifty-eight percent of teachers in another study cited misbehavior of students as the primary cause of teachers' job stress (Baker, 1985; p. 485).

Classrooms that are not well managed can also intimidate students. In a study involving a survey of a huge number of secondary school students, 800,000 (or 8 percent of the total surveyed) reported that they failed to attend school at least one day a week because of fear of what they would encounter in the classroom (Baker, 1985; p. 483). Students who are fearful have difficulty learning even when they attend school. The failure of students to learn in poorly managed and controlled classrooms has an enormous cost in terms of lost student achievement.

Important economic costs are also associated with a lack of classroom discipline. For example, teachers who face extremely disruptive students and who fail to cope leave the profession after only a few years in the classroom. This represents a huge personal cost to them in terms of the time and money spent preparing to become teachers. Many of them will face additional costs when they return to higher education classrooms to prepare for other careers. Often vandalism is high in uncontrolled classrooms. These costs represent a drain on limited school resources that otherwise could be going to support quality instructional programs.

We do not wish to paint an excessively negative picture. However, we do believe it is important for prospective teachers to recognize that they have important responsibilities in the area of classroom management and discipline. There is a need to prepare for this dimension of the professional teacher's role as much as for instructional responsibilities.

Occasionally we find students in our teacher education programs who dismiss the need to take classroom management and discipline responsibilities seriously. Among myths we have often heard from undergraduate students of teaching are the following:

- "If your lessons are exciting, you won't have any problems."
- "I'm young, and I know how to relate to and understand high school students."
- "If you love the students and love teaching, everything will be fine."
- "Show the class who is the boss on the first day. Don't take anything from anybody. Come down hard on the first person who misbehaves, and make this person an example that tells the others you mean business."
- "The only way you can learn anything about managing a class is getting into the classroom as a teacher. There's nothing a book can teach you."

As with most myths, some of these statements do contain some elements of truth. But none of them reports the whole truth. Let's look at some of them to see what's missing.

Although everybody supports the view that good lessons may diminish the potential for discipline problems to occur, good lesson planning alone does not guarantee an absence of classroom control problems. Even the best organized lessons may be ruined by episodes of misbehavior.

Certainly it is desirable for the teacher to like the students and the profession of teaching. But personality variables among students are every bit as great as among the general population. No teacher enjoys a wonderful relationship everyday with every student. There will be times when some students will demonstrate behaviors that will be hard for the teacher to take.

Beginning teachers who are young soon become disabused of the idea that their youth confers any special advantages when it comes to managing students. In the minds of secondary students, the person on the other side of the desk is "the teacher." The teacher's age has little to with students' development of either positive or negative relationships with the teacher. The tone and pattern the teacher establishes is critical, not his age.

The idea of coming down hard on students in the beginning "to show them who the boss is" has some intuitive appeal. However, this kind of behavior can be taken as a challenge by students. Instead of being intimidated by the teacher, they may be challenged to become even more disruptive. This whole approach may prove to be counterproductive.

Certainly it *is* true that much learning related to classroom management and control occurs on the job. But the rate of initial learning can be speeded up tremendously when prospective teachers take time to master some fundamental principles before assuming the first teaching position. These principles provide beginners with a solid foundation upon which to base decisions which, in the context of day-to-day teaching, must be made quickly.

Box 9.1

Give Teachers More Authority?

Some people argue that the best way to improve discipline in the schools is to give teachers more authority. According to this view, present rules and regulations prevent teachers from doing what needs to be done to assure order in the classroom. The proposed remedy would give teachers power to establish rules, administer punishment, and permanently remove students from their classes without fear of recrimination from administrators or parents. Supporters allege that this would help students learn because disruptive individuals would not be present to interrupt the instructional process.

What Do You Think?

1. Do you agree with this idea? Why or why not?

2. What do you see as strengths and weaknesses of this argument?

3. What immediate consequences might result if a school board suddenly gave teachers this authority?

Some teachers experience few discipline problems. What is their secret? How do they prevent problems? How do they react to the few problems that do occur in ways that prevent them from getting out of hand? There are no easy answers. However, there are some principles that tend to guide responses of teachers who are particularly effective classroom managers. In this chapter, content relevant to these issues is introduced under these major headings:

- Classroom management
- Preventing problems
- Responding to problems: two key principles
- Responding to problems: a range of responses

Classroom Management

Classroom management refers to the way a teacher organizes and manages time, material, and space to promote smooth and efficient classroom operation. It also encompasses teacher actions designed to establish leadership and to motivate students.

Visitors to classrooms of teachers who are good managers often are unaware of specific management decisions the teacher has made. These classrooms sometimes seem "just to run themselves." In a systematic study, Emmer, Evertson, and Anderson (1980) found that smoothly functioning classrooms were not chance occurrences. They certainly also did not come about because of an individual teacher's "luck" in drawing a

"I think the disruptive behavior in our schools today is caused by the volume and intensity of rhetoric *about* discipline."

group of unusually well-behaved students. Rather, they resulted from careful teacher preparation and planning that began even before the start of the school year.

Teacher Leadership and Authority

Effective classroom management begins with the teacher. The teacher's philosophy, values, understanding of individual students, beliefs about learning, and leadership style all affect how she manages the social environment of the classroom.

Teachers who are effective classroom managers are willingly accepted as leaders by their students (Boles and Davenport, 1975). Teachers who are viewed as leaders are secure, confident, and optimistic people. They are not afraid of people who know things they don't know, and they are not easily discouraged when faced with students who initially reflect little enthusiasm for what they are teaching. Because of their confidence in their own authority, these personally secure educators avoid overreactions to minor episodes of student misbehavior.

Teachers' beliefs about students affect their development of a personal leadership style (Clark and Peterson, 1986). Individuals who believe that students are lazy and untrustworthy develop management and control patterns different from those who trust and respect students. Students are quick to recognize a teacher's negative attitude. When they sense that the teacher does not respect or trust them, they become very reluctant to accept the teacher as a leader. A negative classroom atmosphere often results.

In preparing to work with secondary students, it is important to remember that young people in this age group are striving to establish some sense of personal identity. As part of this effort, it is natural for them to engage in some testing of the limits of imposed authorities (parents, teachers, and others). Secondary students cannot be expected to defer quietly to every teacher demand, particularly if they sense an element of unfairness or something else that they feel is acting to diminish their self-concepts.

There are many sources that contribute to a person either being perceived as having or not having leadership authority. Some of these sources were identified by French and Raven (1959). They are:

- Expert power
- Referent or attractive power
- Legitimate power
- Reward power
- Coercive power

Expert Power

Individuals perceived by a group to have superior knowledge or skill are accorded some leadership authority. This is called *expert power*. It is effective because it is awarded out of respect, not because it is demanded. It helps teachers greatly to be accorded expert power by their students. Students consistently identify knowledge of content and ability to explain and clarify as attributes of teachers they like (Tanner, 1978).

To be accorded expert power by their students, teachers must be well prepared. They need a sound content background in their subjects. Further, they must come to class prepared. Careful planning and consistently good execution of lessons communicates a sense of expertise to students. This, in turn, often translates into expert power that can greatly assist the teacher in managing students.

Referent or Attractive Power

Individuals who are well liked often are accorded leadership status. Teachers who earn this *referent power* are seen as having the best interests of student at heart. This leadership power is based on the respect and trust of students. William Glasser (1990) considers this kind of leadership to be particularly important. He points out the need for teachers to create warm and personal classroom atmospheres where students believe they "belong" and where their needs are regularly met. Leadership stemming from referent power is not as widespread at the secondary level as it should be. A common reason secondary students cite for misbehaving is that they believe their teacher does not care for them.

Teachers can begin to build referent power by doing things such as learning students' names, encouraging them, and treating them respectfully. Fairness in testing and grading all play a role. Students are particularly troubled when they perceive the teacher as someone who designs irresponsible tests that seem more designed to trick them than to honestly measure what they have learned.

Legitimate Power

Some roles in our society carry with them a certain power and expectation of leadership, regardless of who fulfills those roles. The role of the teacher is an example. Although it is true that some leadership initially comes to a teacher simply because he is "the teacher," this kind of leadership power will be short lived if the individual does not quickly establish a pattern that students see as indicative of credibility, trust, and caring.

Legitimate power is helpful to teachers at the beginning of each new school term. Students tend to be on their best behavior during their first few days with a new teacher. During this time, teachers need to work hard to broaden their leadership authority by taking actions that will prompt students to accord them expert power and referent power.

Reward Power

People in positions of authority are able to provide certain benefits to members of groups they lead. This gives them *reward power*. Teachers dispense rewards that include grades, privileges, praise, and other kinds of attention.

There are important limitations to teachers' reward power. In some situations, the kinds of rewards teachers are in a position to give may not be valued by all students. For example, if a given individual attaches no importance to the grade she receives, she will not be motivated to work hard to get a high grade. In some cases, individual students tend to value the attention and praise they get from other students more than that they receive from their teacher.

Coercive Power

Individuals who hold positions of authority often are able to punish members of groups they lead. Teachers can exercise some *coercive power* over their students. However, there are some important limitations to coercive power as an effective remedy for classroom control problems.

Teacher-administered punishment may result in a temporary cessation of an objectionable student behavior. However, unless there is some support for an alternative, appropriate pattern of behavior, an even more unacceptable pattern may evolve. Also, teachers who rely too much on punishment to assert their authority sometimes encourage their students into a kind of combat. Students may feel challenged to outwit the teacher and "get away" with breaking rules. Vandalism, truancy, and student anger frequently characterize class members in classes taught by teachers who depend too much on punishment to maintain their authority.

In general, coercive power should be used as a last resort. Even then, its use is likely to be ineffective unless it is linked with referent power. Punishment has the best likelihood of working when it is administered by a teacher who is liked and who the recipient sees as basically fair and just.

Teacher Consistency

Teacher consistency is an important part of an effective management style. It involves consistent and fair application of rules and expectations (Savage, 1991). It is important for teachers to apply rules and expectations consistently. This means that behavior that is unacceptable on one day should be regarded as unacceptable on another.

In addition, rules and regulations need to be applied consistently to all students. A common complaint among problem students is that they are not treated fairly. Sometimes they have a valid point. Occasionally teachers will overlook and excuse behaviors of high-achieving or generally well-behaved students that would result in punishment for other students. This kind of selective enforcement undermines the teacher's credibility. This may result in student hostility and contribute to classroom control problems.

Managing the Physical Environment

The classroom's physical environment affects student behavior. In thinking about how to arrange furniture and other items in their classrooms, teachers often consider questions such as these: "Do I want to encourage interactions among students?" "Do I expect students to move from place to place during the class period?" "Do I want to focus students' attention on a specific part of the room?" In considering how to arrange the classroom, attention needs to be given to:

- Floor space
- traffic patterns
- location of the teacher's desk
- materials storage
- classroom ambiance

Floor Space

Arrangements of desks and other classroom furniture cue students to a teacher's expectations. Arrangements need to vary to accommodate different kinds of learning activities. For example, different patterns may be helpful when students are to listen to the teacher, work individually, work in small groups, or take part in a large-group discussion.

In determining a specific arrangement, the teacher begins by thinking about what students will be required to do. When the teacher plans to present new information, it is important that student desks be arranged in such a way that each student has an unobstructed view of the teacher. Further, it may be a good idea to separate individual desks as much as possible to discourage social interaction among students.

On the other hand, if the teacher plans to have students work individually on assignments, it makes sense to arrange classroom furniture so that the teacher can move quickly to help any student in the class. Ideally, the teacher should be able to move freely among all desks in the room. This kind of teacher mobility helps assure that the teacher can move quickly to help anyone experiencing a problem, and it also tends to promote on-task behavior. (Students know that the teacher will arrive quickly if a disturbance breaks out.)

When students are working in small groups, spaces between students in each group need to be decreased. This will allow papers and other materials to be seen by all group members, and it permits easy conversation among group members. It is helpful if all group members can easily see one another. (This is difficult if students are required to sit in rows.)

Traffic Patterns
Traffic patterns need to be considered when planning the arrangement of the classroom. High-traffic areas must be kept free of obstructions. These typically include areas around doorways, materials storage locations, and space close to the teacher's desk. Student desks should be placed so they do not interfere with high-traffic areas.

Teacher's Desk
In many classrooms, the teacher's desk occupies a position of importance in the front of the classroom. This may not represent the best locational choice. There are important advantages to placing the teacher's desk in the rear of the classroom.

Space between student desks allows for easy teacher movement to any part of the classroom.

Such a position makes it extremely difficult for the teacher to "teach from the desk." This is probably a good thing. Individuals who teach from their desks communicate a lack of enthusiasm to students. Additionally, it is difficult to monitor students properly when seated. As a result, students' attention may wander, and general behavior problems may increase.

There is also advantage for rear-of-the-room teacher desk placement when students are working individually on assignments. In this arrangement, the students are facing away from the teacher, who is seated at her desk. Under these conditions, students cannot be sure what the teacher is doing or, more importantly, who the teacher is watching. As a result, students tend to assume their behavior may be under scrutiny by the teacher. This assumed teacher monitoring encourages them to stay busy at the assigned task.

Regardless of where the teacher's desk is placed, the teacher should leave the desk area to go to where an individual student is seated rather than encouraging those seeking help to get out of their seats and walk to the teacher's desk. Students walking through the classroom may disrupt others. In addition, when students crowd around the teacher's desk, the teacher has a difficult time seeing and monitoring other students. Recently this problem was illustrated in a local news report aired by a station in Los Angeles. Some students in a class made a videotape of students rolling and smoking marijuana cigarettes in a class while the seated teacher's view was blocked by a crowd of students surrounding the teacher's desk.

Materials Storage

Secondary teachers use many kinds of materials to support their instruction. These need to be stored so they are easily accessible by the teacher but not by others. Because of scarce instructional time, these items should be placed in secure areas where the teacher can get to them in a hurry. If materials are stored in out-of-the-way locations, the momentum of a lesson may be lost when a teacher stops to get needed items. At such times, misbehavior problems may occur.

Classroom Ambiance

The ambiance of a place refers to its general atmosphere or "feel." The ambiance of an individual classroom helps shape students' attitudes. Some classroom environments are attractive and inviting; others are ugly and foreboding. A positive classroom ambiance results when the teacher pays attention to establishing an orderly overall classroom appearance and makes good decisions regarding nature of lighting, decoration of wall space, and control of temperature.

The ambiance of the classroom has been found to affect behavior patterns of both teachers and students (Weinstein, 1979). As the quality of the physical environment declines, teachers make more control statements and are less friendly. Students in such classrooms are less involved in lessons, and feelings of conflict among students increase.

Managing Time

Teachers who manage time effectively experience fewer classroom control problems than those who do not. Researchers have found there to be much unproductive time in many classrooms (Good and Brophy, 1991). Effective teachers are particularly skillful in maximizing the amount of time students spend on productive tasks. The operating principle here seems to be that "busy students don't have time to misbehave." These are some important considerations and decision points in managing time in the classroom:

- Establishing routines
- Beginning the class
- Managing transitions
- Providing assistance to students
- Lesson pacing

Establishing Routines

Procedures established to handle recurring events help keep lessons on track. They tend to increase the total time students spend on learning tasks. Routines need to be established for activities such as: (1) taking attendance, (2) making announcements, (3) using equipment, (4) distributing materials, (5) leaving the room, (6) asking questions, and (7) requesting assistance from the teacher. It is important to spend time with new groups of students, familiarizing them with classroom routines.

Beginning the Class

When the teacher starts class promptly, the number of discipline problems tends to decline. A prompt beginning gets students quickly on task and creates a businesslike atmosphere. Beginning-of-the-period management routines such as taking roll must be accomplished quickly. Actual instruction needs to start within a few minutes of the official start of the period.

Many teachers use a signal system that alerts students that a lesson is about to begin. This might be a visual system such as turning the lights quickly off and on. Or the teacher might identify a certain location at the front of the room which, when occupied by the teacher, means "pay attention, I'm going to start the lesson." When the agreed-upon signal is given, students are expected to pay attention to the teacher.

It is important that the lesson is not started until all students are paying attention. If the lesson starts while some students are talking or doing something other than focusing on the teacher, the teacher inadvertently is sending a message to the students that "this material is not really important; otherwise, I would insist you were paying attention before I start." In addition, information presented before all students are paying attention may result in wasted time when some students ask for material to be repeated. A refusal to teach until all are ready to listen encourages students to quiet down quickly. An insistence on this courtesy is a great aid to maintaining classroom control.

Managing Transitions

Transitions occur during gaps when students shift from one activity to another. For example, there is transition time involved when a science teacher concludes a lecture and directs students to move to lab tables to apply some of the ideas that have been introduced. There is the potential for much time to be lost during transitions, which is why it is important to plan for them so they can be accomplished quickly and efficiently.

Box 9.2

Preparing for Transitions

Discipline problems often occur during times of inactivity and confusion in the classroom. Ineffective teachers often create these conditions by failing to plan for smooth transitions. Transitions occur throughout the typical secondary school teacher's day. For example, there is a transition at the beginning separating roll taking and the actual start of instruction. There may be several transitions during a lesson, and there often is one toward the end of the period when instruction concludes and students begin putting away materials.

Look at the following questions and make decisions about how you would plan for the mentioned transitions.

What Do You Think?

1. How would you signal to the class that administrative duties at the beginning of the period have been completed and that you are ready to begin the lesson?

2. How would you manage a transition involving moving students from one part of the room to another?

3. How would you get students quickly and efficiently started on an application task after completing presentation of new information?

4. How would you handle end-of-the-period activities?

Teachers can do a number of things to shorten the length of transitions. For example, materials students will use during each phase can be carefully prepared and laid out in advance so students can begin work quickly. Procedures for gathering completed work can be designed to facilitate speedy completion of this process. When transitions require students to move from one area to another, precise directions can be prepared that tell students to move in a way that will minimize disruption and get them quickly located in the new location. As students proceed to a new phase of a lesson, the teacher can move quickly through the group to help any students who are confused about what they should be doing.

Providing Assistance

Assisting individual students can consume tremendous quantities of classroom time. One researcher who studied this matter concluded that many teachers spend more time than necessary working with each student in their classrooms (Jones, 1979). To remedy this situation, it was recommended that teachers begin by building an individual student's confidence by commenting positively about something he has done.

Next, the teacher should provide a brief and direct suggestion regarding what the student should do next. This should be a recommendation that leads the student to act; it is important that the teacher not do the work for the student. As the student begins working in response to this suggestion, the teacher should move quickly to assist another student (following the same process with this individual). If needed, the teacher can check back briefly with students who have been helped to see that work is being done correctly and to provide a few additional suggestions, if needed. This procedure has been found to allow teachers to spend no more than about 20 seconds working with each student (Jones, 1979).

The teacher does not always have to be the one providing the help. One junior high school teacher created "consultant" badges that were earned and worn proudly by a few students. These students were authorized to leave their seats to help students who requested assistance. The number of consultants was limited, and members of the class worked hard to win the honor for being among the "consultants for the week."

Lesson Pacing

Classroom control problems diminish when lessons are paced briskly and when a high percentage of students in the class are succeeding at the assigned tasks. Boredom has been found to contribute to classroom control problems. It often results when lessons "drag" and when teachers spend too much time going over and over minor points.

As they attempt to adopt an appropriate instructional pace, many effective teachers identify a reference group of students who they use to indicate general levels of class interest and understanding. Occasionally they direct questions to students in this group to check on levels of understanding. Sometimes, the teachers simply watch reactions of members of this group. Based on what they observe, the teachers will slow down, maintain, or accelerate the pace of their lessons.

Preventing Problems

Teaching is a decision-making activity. No canned set of prescriptions is equally applicable to all problem situations. Teachers need to think about the nature of the specific situation they are confronting and to generate responses consistent with a limited number of tested principles. Some of these are introduced in the subsections that follow.

The Purpose Is Self-Control

One of the most important purposes of schooling is helping young people learn how to exercise self-control (Savage, 1991). When teachers accept this premise, they tend to see episodes of misbehavior as learning opportunities that can help students develop more mature patterns of controlling their emotions. When responding to student misbehavior, effective teachers weigh alternative responses in terms of which will best promote development of self-control.

Respect the Student's Dignity

Secondary school students are working hard at establishing their own personal identities. They react negatively when they feel an adult is treating them disrespectfully or is not taking them seriously. Teacher efforts to deal with misbehavior that demean the dignity of the student will not succeed. It is important that teacher comments address the inappropriate-ness of the behavior, not any perceived deficiencies in the student as a human being.

Treat the Causes of the Misbehavior

A specific teacher response often will stop an immediate student misbehavior problem. However, unless some attention is given to dealing with the cause of the misbehavior, it may well occur again.

Unacceptable patterns of student behavior may result for many reasons. Sometimes poorly planned lessons or thoughtless teacher actions may be the source. Pressures from peers, family difficulties, high levels of stress, and drug or alcohol problems are among the common causes of student misbehavior. Efforts to identify reasons students are misbehaving can help the teacher to develop responses to prevent outbreaks of unacceptable behavior.

CASE STUDY

How Do You Establish Control?

Loretta Carter remembers dreaming about becoming a teacher. From her high school days, she recalls the thrill of encountering new literature and learning how to apply the insights of great writers to her own life. As an undergraduate student her enthusiasm for her subject increased, and she worked hard at perfecting the communications and planning skills she knew she would need to inspire high school students. She took her first job this past fall. All has not turned out as she had hoped.

For one thing, she has been assigned to work with students who are different from what she had expected. She had wanted to teach advanced secondary students who were capable of appreciating good literature. Instead, she finds herself teaching ninth-graders. These students seem to have little enthusiasm for academics. They are con-sumed by social and recreational interests. They view the classroom as a stage where they can show off and challenge her authority.

To remedy this situation, Loretta has tried several things, but nothing has worked. She started the year by trying to be friendly with all of the students. She took time to tell her students she trusted them and therefore didn't think a lot of rules were needed. Instead of being grateful and responsible, her students have taken this information as an invitation to do anything that pleases them.

In thinking about this situation, Loretta decided that motivation for learning was the culprit. She decided she needed to let her students know why it was important for them to know something about literature. She prepared a careful 10-minute talk on this subject, but her students rejected her logic. One student's statement summed up much of the reaction: "Look, you may like this stuff, but we think it is *really* boring. We'd much rather see a movie."

Her next approach was to build motivation around students' interests. But the more she thought about this approach, the less promising it seemed. "How," she wondered, "can I build a responsible literature program around student interests that seem limited to film stars, sports, and sex?"

Out of frustration, Loretta has moved on to try punishment as a means of getting students to do the work. When students fail to do their work or misbehave, she has started lowering grades. This has only seemed to make matters worse. Many of the students laugh when they get a poor grade. Some of them actually seem to be competing to see who can accumulate the most F's.

At this point, Loretta is about to give up. She has been telling her friends that "students have really changed since we were in school." She is thinking about looking for a job where she can just work with college-bound students. She said recently, "I would do *anything* to work with some students who cared."

■ ■ ■

What should Loretta do? Why do you think she is experiencing these problems? She has concluded that today's students are different from students in years *past*. Do you agree? Why or why not? Would a change of assignment really help Loretta? Are there others she should consult? If she has to stay in this school another year and work with a similar group of students, what changes should she make in the way she attempts to motivate and control students?

Responding to Problems: Two Key Principles

There are no sure-fire remedies or guaranteed fixes for behavior problems. What is effective in one setting and with one individual may not be effective in another. However, important principles have been developed to guide teachers as they decide what they should do when a student misbehaves. These two are among them:

- Private correction is better than public correction.
- Choosing misbehavior implies choosing its consequences.

The Benefits of Private Correction

Correcting misbehavior in private is an indicator of a teacher who respects students' dignity. Working with a misbehaving student in a setting where the teacher-student discussion cannot be observed by other students also removes the student from a situa-

Box 9.3

Reflecting on Personal Experience

Think about times when you or your friends were disciplined in school. Try to recall at least one time you thought the approach taken by the teacher was effective and one time when it was not. Consider these situations as you answer the following questions.

What Do You Think?

1. What did the teacher do when administering the effective discipline?

2. What made it effective?

3. Did this person apply any principles mentioned in this chapter? If so, which ones?

4. What made the actions of the other teacher ineffective in the other episode you remember?

5. What might this person have done differently to change the outcome?

tion where she may feel it necessary to take a firm stand in front of other class members. Private correction also affords opportunities for the individual student and the teacher to improve their personal relationship. This arrangement allows the teacher to communicate a general respect for the student while, at the same time, indicating disapproval of a particular unacceptable behavior.

Choosing Misbehavior Means Choosing the Consequences

To develop self-control, people must see the relationship between their actions and resultant consequences. Some secondary students have not made this connection. Sometimes they see negative consequences that result from their misbehavior as arbitrary actions of the teacher or even bad luck.

To help students grasp the connection between unacceptable behavior and consequences, teachers need to communicate clearly that unpleasant things that happen to a misbehaving student have come about directly as a result of his behavior. William Glasser (1965) has suggested that teachers ask students a series of questions to help them see the link between behavior and consequences. The first question is, "What are you doing?" The intent is to get the student to focus on and describe the inappropriate behavior. If a student is unable to do this, the teacher should explain carefully what the problem behavior is. The second question is, "What happens when people behave as you have done?" This begins to encourage students to think about the relationship between the behavior and its consequences. The final question is, "Is this what you want to happen to you?" This helps students reflect on what they have done and to begin thinking about whether they really want to face the consequences likely to befall them when they behave inappropriately.

Individual conferences with a student can also help her focus on the issue of consequences. During such a conference, the teacher may ask the students to identify some things that might happen as a result of misbehavior. If student ideas are unrealistic, the teacher can supply some acceptable alternatives.

Responding to Problems: A Range of Responses

Effective teachers anticipate typical problems that may occur and think through a range of responses. This section introduces things teachers do to maintain effective classroom control. Responses are ranked (1) from those that are less intrusive to those that are more intrusive and (2) from those that allow students to exercise self-control to those where the teacher takes a more direct role.

Choice of a particular response varies depending on the severity of the problem and the probability the student will be able to exercise self-control. In general, serious problems tend to demand more intrusive teacher responses than those that are less serious. In situations where an individual student persists in misbehaving over a period of time, the recommended pattern is for the teacher to begin with less intrusive responses and gradually escalate their severity until the problem is resolved.

Responses Supporting Self-Control

Responses in this category are designed to be nonintrusive. The hope is that actions taken by the teacher will not interfere with the flow of instruction and that students will self-correct their behavior when provided an opportunity to do so.

Reinforce Productive Behavior

A commitment to reinforce desirable behavior is essential to any discipline plan. Students need to know that there are rewards for productive, acceptable patterns of behavior. Positive reinforcement helps them to become more self-controlled. It is important, too, that students recognize they will receive some attention when they behave properly.

In some classrooms, students feel that the only way they will be recognized is to misbehave. A student in such a classroom once made this comment to one of the authors: "In this school everybody knows me because I'm not afraid of the teachers. What do you get for being good?" In the minds of some students, "being good" earns contempt from other students, an occasional nod from the teacher, and an expectation that they will be asked to do more work than others in the class.

Praise can take many forms. Some secondary students react negatively to excessive teacher praise in front of other class members. They do not want to be seen as "a teacher's pet." Individual comments, brief notes, and awards of special privileges are among the kinds of things teachers do. When the entire class has been working and behaving well, it also makes sense to provide the whole group with some positive reinforcement. Giving class members a few minutes to chat freely or inviting them to select a particular activity they enjoy are among alternatives that might be considered.

Nonverbal Signals

Minor misbehaviors are much more common than serious ones. Often a teacher can stop them through use of nonverbal signals. These include eye-contact (the famous "cold, hard stare"), nodding the head in the direction of the offending student, or using a hand gesture. All of these actions send a message to a student that a particular behavior has been noted and found to be unacceptable. This kind of nonverbal notification often is sufficient to cause the student to stop the unacceptable behavior.

Proximity Control

Proximity control is another technique teachers can use that sends a message to a misbehaving student without interfering with the flow of a lesson. It involves nothing more than a teacher's moving closer to the student while continuing the lesson. Many students find it difficult to continue misbehaving when the teacher is close at hand.

Using the Student's Name in the Context of the Lesson

When efforts to gain student attention through nonverbal techniques fail, sometimes a teacher can use a student's name in the context of a lesson to stop misbehavior and to refocus the student on what is being taught. The technique requires the teacher simply to insert the name of the student as part of the general flow of information that is being presented. ("If John were a member of a scientific team, he would need to know. . . .") Typically a student will perk up when the teacher says his name. He will recognize that the teacher has been watching, has found something unacceptable, and that the behavior should change.

Self-Monitoring

Students who have difficulty in the area of self-control often benefit from direct instruction on how to monitor their own behavior. One way of doing this involves the student making a list of her own desirable and undesirable behaviors. Together the student and the teacher can identify the kinds of reinforcers that might be employed to encourage the desirable patterns.

A teacher known to one of the authors had a student who regularly interrupted others. The teacher had this individual keep a tally of how many times this happened over a three-day period. Then, the student and teacher together established some goals and some accompanying "good things" that would result for the student when these goals were reached. This programs was successful, and the problem behavior was brought under control.

Some teachers also find it useful to teach students to ask themselves a series of questions when they sense they may be about to lose control. Questions might include:

"What will happen to me if I do this?" "Is it worth the risk?" "What should I be doing instead?"

Students who frequently experience self-control problems can be taught to take other kinds of actions when they find themselves becoming upset, anxious, or angry. For example, they might be encouraged to close their eyes, think of a favorite place or activity, and then refocus on their work.

Providing Situational Assistance

When responses designed to support student efforts at self-control are not effective, the teacher needs to become more involved. This means providing direct assistance to the student or restructuring the learning environment.

A Quiet Word

This response requires the teacher to move to the classroom area where the misbehaving student is located and to provide a quiet reminder of the expected behavior. This needs to be done quickly and quietly. The intent is to avoid distracting others in the class while drawing the attention of the offending student to exactly what is wrong and how it should be quickly corrected.

Rule Reminder

Sometimes the teacher finds it necessary to stop the lesson and remind the entire class or an individual about a classroom rule that is being violated. For example, a teacher might say something like this: "Angela, what are you supposed to do when you have a problem with an assignment and need help?" A rule reminder of this kind often stops inappropriate behavior. (When, in response to the question, a student professes ignorance of the rule, the teacher needs to quickly restate it.)

Implementing Logical or Natural Consequences

Sometimes nonverbal signals are not effective, a quiet word fails to get the job done, and a student contends that following rules is unimportant. When this happens, the student needs to experience negative consequences resulting from his failure to correct an inappropriate behavior. Consequences need to be clearly the result of the misbehavior. For example, if an entire class is failing to stay at task during a lesson, the teacher may insist that wasted time be made up later when, otherwise, the group would be engaging in an enjoyable activity. If a student destroys equipment, she should be required to make restitution. If a person cannot work productively in a group, he should be removed, required to work quietly at a desk, and carefully monitored by the teacher.

One teacher was having a problem with students getting to class late. When the bell rang at the beginning of the period, the teacher stacked all empty chairs in a corner. Late arriving students had to sit on the floor. Another teacher instituted a plan requiring students who failed to bring required materials to class to "rent" substitute materials from the teacher.

Responding with Clarity and Firmness

When other techniques fail or when a given behavior is seriously disrupting an entire class, the teacher needs to take quick action. Teacher responses need to be characterized by clarity and firmness. Clarity means that there should be a specific reference to who is misbehaving, what this person is doing that is unacceptable, and what an appropriate alternative behavior might be. The teacher might say something like this: "Susan and Jose, your whispering and note-passing is disrupting the class. Take out your lab manuals and begin the assigned work now."

Messages need to be firm. This means they should be sent in an "I mean business" manner. This can be accomplished through use of a steady, serious tone of voice, direct eye contact, an erect body posture, and by moving toward the offending student.

Removing the Student from the Situation

Students who continue to misbehave sometimes will develop more self-control when they are moved. Sometimes simply requiring a student to sit in a different seat will stop the undesirable behavior. This is particularly likely to be true if the problem is talking to another student while the teacher is introducing a lesson.

Often it is helpful to move the student closer to the teacher's desk. This permits the teacher to easily monitor the individual's behavior. Also, physical proximity to the teacher itself often prompts students to behave properly.

Student Conferences

A personal conference with a student who continues to misbehave often yields productive results. During such a conference, effective teachers manage to get students to do most of the talking and to make decisions regarding how their behavior might be changed for the better. Sometimes teachers use conferences as opportunities to develop informal "behavior contracts" with students. These specify what students are to do to improve their behavior, and they often reference some good things that will come to the students as a result of positive changes in their behaviors.

Conferences need to be conducted in a firm, businesslike manner. Often students will be upset when a conference begins. If the teacher fails to keep her own emotions under control, an unproductive exchange that might include angry accusations and unproductive debates can ensue. One of the teacher's responsibilities is to "cool" the situation, explain exactly what is amiss with the student's behavior, and work calmly to lay out some possible solutions.

Implementing Severe Consequences

When a student's misbehavior is especially persistent or serious, it may be necessary for relatively severe consequences to be imposed. These kinds of consequences ordinarily are imposed rarely. They should be implemented only after other less-intrusive measures have been tried and found to be ineffective.

Removing the Student from the Classroom

When misbehavior of a student has not responded to other actions, it may be necessary to remove the individual from the classroom. This can accomplish several things. First, it tells the student that the teacher is serious about maintaining order in the classroom. Second, since most students like to be with their friends and peers in the classroom, removal often takes them away from a social situation they find rewarding. Among other things, removal takes away the possibility that challenging the teacher will gain them status in the eyes of others in the class. Finally, removing a student from the class gives both the teacher and the student some "cooling-off" time. For the teacher, there is an advantage in gaining some time to think about productive next steps.

When students are removed from the classroom, they need to be sent to a supervised area. They should never simply be sent out into the hall. This puts students in an uncontrolled situation. If anything should go awry as a result, there may be serious legal complications for the teacher.

Students may be sent to a counselor's office, the principal's office, or to a special designated area set aside by the school (staffed by adult supervisors) for students who have been asked to leave class for disciplinary reasons. When a student has been sent out of the classroom, the teacher needs to notify personnel in the school's central administrative office. They will alert individuals in the appropriate office that the student is expected. If the student fails to arrive in a timely manner, many schools have guidelines calling for someone to look for the student and to accompany him to the designated area.

A few secondary schools have detention halls. When a student seriously misbehaves and is asked to leave class, she must report to the detention hall to make up a prescribed amount of time. This detention sometimes is served before school, after school, or, occasionally, even on Saturday mornings. Schools with detention halls often have specific guidelines about how to assign students to these facilities. Teachers need to become familiar with these important operational rules.

Conference with Parents or Guardians

When students seriously misbehave, their parents or guardians needed to be reached. Often a telephone call or a note will initiate actions at home that will encourage the student to change an unacceptable pattern. If serious misbehavior persists, a face-to-face conference needs to take place involving the teacher and the student's parent(s) or guardian. In preparing for such a meeting, the teacher needs to gather anecdotal records (brief summary accounts) of misbehavior. These should include dates and times of episodes of misbehavior and summaries of what has already been done to change this unacceptable pattern.

During the conference, the teacher should try to make the parents as comfortable as possible, conveying to them that the purpose of the meeting is to solve the problem so their son or daughter can change an unproductive behavior pattern and do better in school. It is important for the parent(s) or guardian(s) to share their perspectives on issues that are raised. If possible, the conference should conclude with a plan of action to which all agree. The teacher may wish to prepare a written summary of the meeting and mail a copy to the parent(s) or guardian(s).

After several days have passed, the teacher should initiate a follow-up communication with the parent(s) or guardian(s) to bring them up to date on how the student is doing and solicit any further comments or reactions. The idea is to build a common team approach to helping the student. Often, when the teacher and the parent(s) or guardian(s) are working in support of a common plan of action, a misbehaving student will channel behaviors into more productive channels. This will not happen overnight. Unacceptable patterns often have taken a long time to develop. Logically, it also takes time for more acceptable patterns to displace them.

Involving Other Professionals

In extremely serious cases, a group of other professionals may need to be brought in to develop a plan of action to help a student with a particularly difficult and persistent misbehavior problem. These professionals might include school administrators, counselors, psychologists, other teachers, and even representatives from youth and community services agencies outside the school. When this is done, the student's teacher needs to present a well-documented case to the group so members will have a clear picture of what has been going on. Recommendations of this group may result in a wide range of decisions depending on the specific circumstances of the case being considered.

Corporal Punishment

In looking over recommendations that have been introduced, you may have noticed that corporal punishment has not been mentioned. This is no accident. First of all, corporal punishment is illegal in some states. In others that permit it, its use often is banned by school district policy. Even where corporal punishment is permitted, stringent guidelines must be observed before it can be administered.

The case for not recommending corporal punishment, however, does not rest primarily on legal issues. It has not been recommended here for a much more basic reason: Corporal punishment is not effective. When it is used with secondary students, it tends to create anger and hostility. It makes adversaries of students and teachers, a relationship that is not at all conducive to learning. Corporal punishment provides no model that encourages students to develop patterns of self-control. In addition, it communicates to them that physical violence is an acceptable way of treating others. This is a miserable example to be giving to young people who, in a few years, will be having their own children. (Some have them already.) The dismal statistics on battered children suggest that all too many young people have "learned" that it is all right to beat others. The schools, we believe, should be no party to such a terrible social lesson.

Table 9.1   Summary Table

Main Points	Explanation
Teachers' Management Role Sources of Teachers' Authority	Effective teaching involves expertise both in instruction and in management. Unless students are controlled and the classroom is managed in a businesslike, professional manner, students cannot profit from instruction.
Expert Power	Expert power comes to individuals who are perceived to possess specialized knowledge or skill. It is a kind of authority that derives from respect. Expert power is highly desirable for teachers. To earn it, they must have solid grounding in subject matter and be capable of explaining material clearly to students.
Referent or Attractive Power	This comes to individuals who are well liked by their constituents. Teachers who have it enjoy students' trust and respect because they are viewed as having students' best interests at heart.
Legitimate Power	This kind of authority is conveyed to persons because of the particular position they occupy. Teachers' leadership power will be short lived if they do not work to establish their credibility as individuals who are believable, trustworthy, and caring.
Reward Power	Reward power comes to people who are in a position to dispense rewards to groups they lead. Teachers do enjoy some reward power. To be effective, they must understand precisely what individual students find rewarding.
Coercive Power	This power comes to people who are in a position to punish members of groups they lead. Teachers have some coercive power. It must be used appropriately and sparingly. If it is not, students probably will develop negative attitudes toward the teacher and, perhaps, the entire school program.
Teacher Consistency	Consistency is a hallmark of a teacher with an effective management style. It is particularly important that rules and guidelines be enforced in the same way for all students. Students who believe that some class members are not being treated fairly may develop negative attitudes toward the teacher.
Managing the Physical Environment	Good classroom control is facilitated when the physical environment of the classroom has been arranged to support instruction. Specific arrangements will vary depending on the subject being taught and the nature of individual lessons. In making decisions about the physical environment of the classroom, teachers consider (1) floor space, (2) traffic patterns, (3) the location of the teacher's desk, (4) materials storage areas, and (5) overall ambiance of the classroom.

Table 9.1   Summary Table *(continued)*

Main Points	Explanation
Managing Time	Time is a precious resource in the classroom. More time can be won for instruction when the teacher plans carefully for (1) procedures to be followed to accomplish routine tasks, (2) steps to be taken in starting instruction promptly, (3) ways to manage transitions between lesson parts efficiently, (4) pacing lessons appropriately to maximize learning, and (5) working quickly and effectively with individual students needing help.
Preventing Discipline Problems	Effective teachers work hard to prevent discipline problems before they occur. Part of their efforts are directed at helping students mature by becoming more self-controlled. They also recognize that responses to students need to respect their personal dignity. Students who feel personally diminished in the eyes of the teacher have the potential to become behavior problems. Finally, these teachers analyze potential causes for misbehavior and attempt to remedy them before the misbehavior occurs.
Two Principles for Responding to Misbehavior	Two principles are often followed by successful classroom managers as they decide how to respond to a particular episode of misbehavior. They are: (1) private correction is better than public correction, and (2) the student needs to recognize that when he or she chooses to misbehave, he or she simultaneously chooses the consequence of that misbehavior.
A Range of Responses to Misbehavior	The general idea here is that there should be a range of teacher responses that will vary depending on the nature of the misbehavior and its persistence. It makes sense to begin with less severe, less intrusive teacher actions and to employ more severe, more intrusive teacher actions only when the misbehavior persists.
Responses Supporting Self-Control	Responses designed to help students gain personal control over their behavior require fairly nonintrusive teacher actions. They include (1) reinforcing productive behavior patterns, (2) using nonverbal signals, (3) employing proximity control, (4) using the student's name in the context of a lesson, and (5) encouraging students' self-monitoring behaviors.
Providing Situational Assistance	Teacher responses in this category are recommended when efforts to help a student establish self-control do not work. Teacher actions in this category include (1) sharing a quiet word with a misbehaving student, (2) reminding a student about a rule, (3) implementing logical or natural consequences, (4) responding with clarity and firmness, (5) removing the student from the situation, and (6) taking time to have a personal conference with the student.

Main Points	Explanation
A Range of Responses to Misbehavior, *cont'd.*	
Implementing Severe Consequences	When a student's misbehavior is persistent or especially serious, it may be necessary for the teacher to initiate more drastic actions. These include (1) removing the student from the classroom, (2) scheduling a conference with the student's parent(s) or guardian(s), or (3) involving other professionals.
Corporal Punishment	Corporal punishment is *not* recommended as a teacher response to a student misbehavior. It is illegal in some states. Even where it is permissible, there are negative consequences associated with its use. It can poison teacher-student relationships. It also puts the teacher and the school in the unhappy position of modeling an undesirable behavior for future parents. Today's educators already deal with too many abused children; they do not want to be accused of communicating that it is all right to hit people.

Review of Key Ideas

- Challenges associated with maintaining decorum in the classroom confront teachers everywhere. Instructional effectiveness depends, in part, on teachers' classroom management skills. While there are no sure-fire recipes or tricks teachers can use that are universal remedies for discipline problems, there are some general principles teachers need to follow when making classroom management decisions.

- Teacher leadership and teacher authority contribute to preventing classroom management problems. Students are most willing to accept their teachers as leaders when they respect their expertise and perceive them as people sincerely concerned about learners' welfare.

- The physical environment of the classroom influences patterns of student behavior. Specific arrangements need to be varied by the teacher depending on the specific nature of a given lesson. Physical arrangement decisions require teacher attention to (1) floor space, (2) traffic patterns, (3) teacher's desk location, (4) materials storage, and (5) general ambiance of the classroom.

- Effective use of class time is a hallmark of teachers who are good managers. By attending to basic routines for recurring events, managing transitions, providing assistance to students, and maintaining a brisk pace in lessons, teachers help students to pay attention. As a result, the potential for unproductive and undesirable patterns of student behavior diminishes.

- An important objective of teacher actions to maintain discipline is developing students' self-control. Viewed in this way, episodes of student misbehavior can be seen as opportunities for the teacher to help students develop more mature patterns of controlling their emotions.

- Principles teachers need to observe in selecting a response to a behavior problem include (1) respecting the student's dignity, (2) identifying and treating the causes of the misbehavior, (3) using private correction when possible, and (4) helping the student understand the connection between the undesirable behavior and the resulting consequence. It is important that students come to appreciate that when they choose to misbehave, they also choose certain consequences.

- Many alternatives are open to teachers as they consider a response to a specific episode of student misbehavior. Their choices should be influenced by their perception of the individual student's ability to control his own behavior and the seriousness or persistence of the problem. In general, responses that are less intrusive should be used first; if they fail, then more direct, intrusive teacher responses may be initiated.

- Corporal punishment should not be used. In some places it is illegal. Even where corporal punishment is allowed, there is little to commend it as an approach to solving discipline problems. Its use often creates a negative relationship between the teacher and student. It fails to model an appropriate alternative behavior for the student. What it *does* model is the idea that it is all right in our society to hit other people. Given the high incidence of child abuse in this country, this is a terrible lesson to be transmitted to young people who, in just a few years, will be having children of their own. (Indeed, some secondary school students already are parents.)

Follow-Up Questions and Activities

Questions

1. How do the myths that are introduced at the beginning of the chapter interfere with efforts of beginning teachers to develop effective approaches to classroom management?

2. What are characteristics of the five types of leadership and power?

3. How might the classroom's physical environment affect students' behavior?

4. Why do some people argue that the teacher's desk should be put at the back of the room? What is your reaction to this view?

5. What might be done to create an attractive and businesslike classroom ambiance?

6. What are some recurring events in the classroom for which routines ought to be developed, and what are some examples of such routines?

7. How can a teacher demonstrate respect for students' dignity while, at the same time, communicating to them that certain behaviors are unacceptable?

8. How can teachers encourage students to grow in terms of self-control?

9. What are some characteristics of a teacher response to a misbehaving student that feature clarity and firmness?

10. Do you agree that corporal punishment has no place in secondary schools? Why do you take this position?

Activities

1. Take a few minutes to list some concerns you have regarding classroom management and discipline. What problems worry you the most? What beliefs do you have that might interfere with your ability to control students in your classes? Share your responses with others. Engage in a brainstorming activity with them to identify responses to your concerns. Share your concerns and the proposed responses with others in your class.

2. Make arrangements to observe a teacher working in a secondary school classroom. Note locations of student desks, materials storage areas, the teacher's desk, and other physical features of the room. Is this an optimal configuration? If not, what changes might you make? Make a sketch of what you observed and another sketch of your proposed changes. Share your ideas with your instructor.

3. Invite a panel of secondary teachers to visit your class. Ask them to comment on specific management and discipline problems they have confronted. What approaches have they found to be most productive? Are there specific things they tend to do when they get a new group of students? How serious do they feel classroom management and discipline problems are?

4. Think about your own experiences as a secondary school student. Then, review categories introduced in this chapter of teacher leadership and power. What patterns characterized teachers you had who experienced the fewest classroom management problems? Do they differ from those of your teachers who had trouble controlling their classes? Discuss your findings with others in your class.

5. Identify at least five rules you think you will need to manage your own classes successfully. Describe your reasons for wanting each rule. How will these rules be communicated to students? List possible consequences you might impose on students who violate these rules. (You might want to generate a list of initial, nonintrusive responses as well as a list of more intrusive responses to use if problem behaviors persist.) Distribute a copy of your rules to others in the class. As a group, discuss the appropriateness of rules class members have suggested.

References

BAKER, K. "Research Evidence of a School Discipline Problem." *Phi Delta Kappan* (March 1985), pp. 482–485.

BOLES, H. W. AND DAVENPORT, J. A. *Introduction to Educational Leadership*. New York: Harper & Row, 1975.

CLARK, C. M. AND PETERSON, P. L. "Teachers' Thought Processes." In M. C. Wittrock (ed.). *Handbook of Research on Teaching*. New York: Macmillan Publishing Company, 1986, pp. 256–296.

EMMER, E. T.; EVERTSON, C. M.; AND ANDERSON, L. "Effective Classroom Management at the Beginning of the School Year." *The Elementary School Journal* (May 1980), pp. 219–231.

FRENCH, J. R. R. AND RAVEN, B. H. "The Bases of Social Power." In D. Cartwright (ed.). *Studies in Social Power*. Ann Arbor, MI: University of Michigan Press, 1959, pp. 118–149.

GLASSER, W. *The Quality School: Managing Students Without Coercion*. New York: Harper & Row, 1990.

GLASSER, W. *Reality Therapy*. New York: Harper & Row, 1965.

GOOD, T. AND BROPHY, J. *Looking in Classrooms*. 5th ed. New York: HarperCollins, 1991.

JONES, F. H. "The Gentle Art of Classroom Discipline." *National Elementary Principal* (June 1979), pp. 26–32.

SAVAGE, T. V. *Classroom Discipline for Effective Teaching and Learning*. Englewood Cliffs, NJ: Prentice-Hall, 1991.

TANNER, L. N. *Classroom Teaching for Effective Teaching and Learning*. New York: Holt, Rinehart & Winston, 1978.

WEINSTEIN, C. "The Physical Environment of the School: A Review of the Research." *Review of Educational Research* (Fall 1979), pp. 577–610.

10

Individualizing for Learning

AIMS

This chapter provides information to help the reader to:

- Describe some reasons for using individualized approaches.
- Identify variables that can be altered to accommodate individual differences.
- Cite examples illustrating how the pace of instruction can be changed.
- Describe basic assumptions of the mastery learning approach.
- Point of characteristics of the content-of-learning variable.
- Suggest specific things a teacher can do to respond to students with differing learning styles.
- Explain how contracts can be used to modify goals of learning.
- List typical components of a learning activity package.
- Point out differences between learning centers and learning stations.
- Suggest how new technologies might affect approaches to individualizing instruction.

1. What is meant by the term *individualized instruction*?

2. How can learning centers and learning stations be compared?

3. What variables can be changed to accommodate individual student differences?

4. What do proponents of mastery learning view as the most important causes of differences in achievement levels of individual students?

5. Why do many teachers regard the learning activity package as a very flexible planning tool for designing instruction to fit students' individual needs?

6. What are some features of and relative strengths and weaknesses of learning centers and learning stations?

7. How can computers and other new technologies assist teachers to meet individual needs of students?

Introduction

Teachers have long puzzled over how to provide meaningful instruction for all of the students in their classes. Secondary students are a very diverse group. In fact, differences among secondary students are more profound than those among elementary students. As learners progress through school, bright and motivated students increase their distance from less able and less motivated students. Differences among twelfth graders are more pronounced than among students at any other grade level in the K-to-12 program.

Differences among secondary school students seem to make an iron-clad case in support of tailoring instructional practices to meet the needs of individual learners. Yet, surprisingly, much more individualized instruction goes on at the elementary school level than at the secondary level. Thomas Good and Jere Brophy (1991), two well-known compilers of educational research, note that investigators have found that about one-third of elementary school teachers make some attempts to individualize instruction, compared to only about one-fifth of secondary school teachers (p. 336).

Few question the theoretical merit of individualizing instruction. The reality, however, as Good and Brophy (1991) have pointed out, is a compromise between the desire to accommodate individual differences and pressures to deliver educational services inexpensively. Over time, this latter concern has resulted in the traditional practice of assigning teachers 20 to 40 students per class period. In groups this large, great differences in abilities and attitudes of individual students are inevitable.

Instruction geared to a class average may reach some of the students, perhaps even a majority, but it will not reach all of them. Exceptionally bright students have potential to become bored. Slower learners who are unable to maintain the pace established by the teacher may become frustrated and present teachers with discipline problems. Students from culturally different backgrounds may challenge the relevance of what the teacher is offering. All of these difficulties build a case supporting the idea that teachers should give some attention to individualizing their teaching.

This does not mean that all classroom instruction should be individualized. Some authorities argue that individualized instruction functions best as a component within a program featuring much cooperative and whole-group instruction (Johnson and Johnson, 1991). They argue that motivation for individualized instruction is enhanced when students know they will have opportunities to use what they have learned in large group settings (Johnson and Johnson, 1991). Individualized instruction represents just one of the tools at the disposal of professional educators.

Within the broad topic of individualized instruction, many specific approaches have been developed. Some of them are introduced in the sections that follow.

Altering Variables to Accommodate Individual Differences

The term *individualized instruction* is a slippery one. It has been used in so many ways that the term sometimes communicates very different things to various individuals. For example, for some people *individualization* suggests a program where all students are working independently on the same assignment. They are doing the same thing; only their rate of progress varies. This kind of individualization is sometimes called *continuous progress learning*. The phrase *continuous progress* implies that the rate of academic development of one learner will not be held up because others in the class may learn at a slower rate than he does.

Others see individualization focusing not on the rate of learning but on the content of instruction. These people see individualized programs as those where individual students study different topics, with the teacher acting as an overall learning manager. Individualized programs of this kind place a great deal of responsibility into the hands of individual students. The teacher functions as facilitator and a monitor.

Still other conceptions of individualization focus on issues such as the method of learning and the goals of learning. To appreciate the array of concerns that are implied by the general term *individualized instruction*, it is useful to consider each of the variables that can be changed to accommodate individual differences. These variables include:

- The rate of learning
- The content of learning
- The method of learning
- The goals of learning

"Our architect has come up with an interesting and novel building design concept that will allow us to reduce class size and really get serious about individualizing instruction."

Altering the Rate of Learning

The term *rate of learning* refers to the pace at which instruction occurs. In a class where all students are exposed to exactly the same instructional program, there is an assumption that all of them are capable of learning at the same rate. Proponents of individualized instruction point out that this assumption is false. Students vary tremendously in terms of the rate at which they can learn new material.

When the learning-rate or pacing variable is manipulated, the basic content remains the same, as do basic assignments for students. What is altered is the time teachers allow for the completion of the tasks. Arrangements are made that allow brighter students to move quickly through the material, while less able learners are allowed more time.

Altering the learning rate makes the most sense in situations where it is essential for all learners to master a given body of content. This form of individualization is reflected a number of instructional approaches. One of these is mastery learning. Mastery learning presumes that differences in students' levels of achievement are not the result of differences in their intelligence or aptitudes (Bloom, 1976, 1980). Rather, they result from variations in time required by individual students to learn. Provided the learning task is appropriate, Bloom (1976, 1980) suggests that nearly all students can achieve success on school tasks if they are provided with sufficient time.

The Personalized System of Instruction (PSI) represents an example of an application of mastery learning to individualized instruction (Guskey, 1985). Similar to other mastery learning programs, it features:

- Clearly specified learning objectives.
- Diagnoses of students' entry-level capabilities.
- Numerous and frequent assessment measures.
- Specification of mastery levels to be attained.
- A structured sequence of facts, principles, and skills to be learned.
- Frequent feedback to learners about their progress.
- Provision of additional time that allows students who fail to achieve mastery to study some more and master the content.

Mastery learning approaches such as PSI have drawn some criticism. For example, these programs do not always result in increased student motivation and achievement. In some applications in higher education settings, students have expressed a dislike of the format. Some have complained about the lack of opportunities to work with other students in the class. Sometimes monitoring has been lax, and progress has been slowed because students have procrastinated. Some teachers have resisted mastery learning approaches because preparation is very time consuming (Good and Brophy, 1991; p. 334).

Other criticisms have focused on procedural matters. Because mastery learning programs often divide large tasks into small pieces, sometimes a great deal of paperwork is involved. This feature, along with the frequent testing that goes on, often creates work for teachers that, in the view of some, goes beyond what they face in more traditional instructional programs (Good and Brophy, 1991).

Frequency of testing, a common characteristic of mastery learning programs, also has been attacked. Some critics charge that frequent testing results in assessments that focus on isolated pieces of content. Such tests may encourage students to lose sight of the larger dimensions of the subject. Some teachers have found that students may do well on mastery tests but experience difficulty in applying what they have learned to different settings (Good and Brophy, 1991).

In summary, mastery learning programs seem to work best when they focus on a relatively narrow band of content that is required of all students. They function better when the content lends itself easily to division into numerous smaller pieces that can be organized for purposes of teaching and testing. Under these circumstances, mastery learning programs can motivate some students who have developed chronic failure patterns in more traditional instructional programs. Success depends on careful teacher monitoring of students to assess levels of progress and to provide encouragement to stay on task. It is particularly important that students who have experienced few instances of success develop confidence in their own abilities to succeed. Teachers in mastery learning programs work hard to assure that this happens.

Altering the Content of Learning

Instead of focusing on the issue of pacing, some programs try to individualize instruction by altering the content studied by different students. Students who are pursuing common goals and objectives may work with very different learning materials. For example, a mathematics teacher may allow students interested in automobiles to study mathematics concepts in the context of car design. Students in the same class with interests in farming might study the same concepts in the context of agriculture.

A basic premise of programs that focus on changing the content of learning is that students will be more motivated when they study material that interests them. Supporters of this approach point out that many traditional programs fail to consider students' interests. For example, a textbook written by an author in New York City might contain examples and explanations that might not be of interest at all to students in Missoula, Montana, or Laredo, Texas. To accommodate this problem, supporters of altering the content urge teachers to provide learning options for students that do take into consideration individual interests.

When this approach to individualizing instruction is used, students often are given some flexibility in choosing the specific content they will study to meet the teacher's goals and objectives. The nature of student choice will vary from setting to setting. In some places, this basic concept has been extended so far as to create magnet high schools with unique emphases.

Each magnet high school has a special theme or special focus. For example, there may be a high school for mathematics and science, another one for music and the performing arts, and another one for classical studies. Students attend a given magnet high school by choice. Though each school teaches a number of required basic courses, instruction tends to be flavored in accordance with the theme of the school. Hence, students attending a high school for music and the performing arts might study mathematics in terms of its application to musical harmonies.

Magnet high schools are features of the nation's urban areas. These kinds of learning environments are not open to many of the nation's secondary students. However, this does not mean that many high schools deny students opportunities to learn in settings where the content is varied to meet individual interests. Many teachers make serious

Box 10.1

Altering What Students Study to Master Objectives

One variable that is manipulated in some individualized instructional programs is the content-studied variable. When this is done, all students seek to master a common set of objectives, but teachers provide them with alternative materials to study. The idea is to select materials that are well matched to individual student interests.

As an exercise, identify a specific learning objective for a subject you would like to teach. Identify three separate interests represented among students in your class. Suggest kinds of learning experiences that might help students with each of these interests to master the material.

OBJECTIVE: _____

INTEREST A _____

    Suggested Learning Experiences: _____

_____

_____

INTEREST B _____

    Suggested Learning Experiences: _____

_____

_____

INTEREST C _____

    Suggested Learning Experiences: _____

_____

_____

---

attempts to diagnose student interests and to make assignments consistent with them. The approach, however, is not without its difficulties.

One obvious problem has to do with the availability of learning materials and the diversity of student interests. Materials that would meet the interests of every student in a class would require an investment beyond what many school districts can afford.

Traditional teacher programs rarely spend a great deal of time preparing people to develop extensive sets of materials to accommodate individual student needs. Though prospective teachers are admonished to use instructional resources other than texts, there usually is an assumption that many students will be working with similar learning materials.

Another force militating against individualized programs that vary content is standardized testing. There is a trend for school quality to be assessed in terms of students' scores on standardized tests. When students study different kinds of learning material, some students may not come into contact with the kinds of content likely to be sampled on the test. Standardized tests act to encourage teachers to prepare instructional programs that expose all students to learning materials that closely parallel those that will be included in test items.

Though there are many problems in organizing and delivering individualized programs that are based on varying kinds of content studied by each student, there are teachers who use this approach successfully. When such programs are carefully planned, delivered, and monitored, they can greatly enhance students' levels of motivation.

Altering the Method of Learning

Individualized programs that focus on varying the method of learning attempt to respond to different learning styles or aptitudes of students. These programs presume that people vary in their aptitudes for specific tasks and in their preferred modes of learning. To maximize learning, teachers need to take these differences into account and to respond to them.

In programs of this kind, the objectives and content of learning remain the same for all students. The teacher directs students to learn the material in ways that are compatible with their aptitudes and learning styles. Sometimes teachers offer students several options and allow them to select the one they would prefer. For example, some students in a class might choose to read information from a textbook, while others might choose to view a filmstrip covering the same topic.

Adaptive instruction has been used as a general term to refer to approaches that attempt to alter the variable of instructional method to meet individual student needs (Glaser, 1980). Students are matched to instructional methods based on initial diagnoses of their needs and subsequent monitoring of their progress. Sometimes students who are initially matched to one instructional approach are switched to another based on teacher observation of their performance.

Altering the method of instruction poses several problems. For one thing, teachers must be familiar with a number of methods. For another, they need a variety of support materials and equipment to deliver the alternatives. Finally, they must be capable of diagnosing a wide variety of student needs. These constraints tend to put some limits on the number of instructional options that teachers can make available to students. Whatever options are selected must be delivered well. Abundant evidence supports the proposition that student learning correlates highly with well-designed and well-delivered instruction (Good and Brophy, 1991).

Research focusing on matching instructional methods to individual student characteristics is still in its infancy. The theoretical rationale for this practice is well grounded. However, there are practical issues to be addressed and resolved before altering the mode of instruction to fit individual student characteristics becomes a common feature of secondary school programs.

Altering the Goals of Learning

Instructional programs that alter learning goals to individualize are controversial. Perhaps for this reason, they also are rare. Much of the debate about the approach results from the great latitude given to students. In some programs of this type, students are permitted to make many decisions about what they want to learn. Teachers function as facilitators. They listen to students and help them clarify their personal goals. This approach presumes that each student is the best judge of her educational needs. There also is an assumption that, when given the freedom to do so, students will make intelligent choices.

A few examples of highly student-controlled programs of this type were implemented in a small number of schools during the late 1960s and 1970s in response to critics who charged that schools were imposing too many limitations on students. More recently, educational critics have been making quite a different argument. Many of them have suggested that schools have provided students with too many electives and that authorities should require a larger number of core courses for all students. These recommendations have acted to eliminate most of the highly student-controlled individualized learning programs of the type that appeared in some schools 20 or so years ago.

Some more common examples of altering-the-goals-of-learning approaches to individualized instruction are those where the goals are negotiated between teacher and students. One scheme of this type that has been used by many teachers is the *learning contract*. A learning contract is an agreement between the teacher and student. Its terms are negotiable. In most cases, the teacher has the final word as to what the contract will include. In general, a learning contract specifies what an individual student will do to satisfy a given learning requirement.

Among items often referenced in a learning contract are:

- A description of what steps the student will take to accomplish the learning objective.
- A list of learning resources that will be used.
- A description of any product(s) the student will be required to produce.
- An explanation of criteria that will be used in evaluating the student's work.
- A list of dates when different tasks are to be completed and submitted to the teacher for review.

Both the teacher and the student sign the contract. Its provisions become the curriculum for the student. When its terms are satisfied, a new contract is developed. Completed contracts document what the student has done and learned.

Though many teachers have had great success in using learning contracts, others are not so enthusiastic. Part of their resistance may stem from teacher preparation programs' failure to focus heavily on skills related to negotiating curriculum issues with students. Teachers who use contracts must be very good diagnosticians. They need to know what appropriate learning experiences for individual students are, and they need to be aware of the kinds of support materials that are available for them to use. Unquestionably, contract approaches require a great commitment of teacher time. In addition to preparing and monitoring a large number of individual instructional programs, teachers must manage a huge volume of paperwork. The daunting prospect of maintaining records on large numbers of students working on individual contracts has made some teachers shy away from the approach.

CASE STUDY

My Success Is Killing Me!

LaShandra Pettybird, following a long-standing routine, settled into a comfortable chair in the faculty lounge at William Henry Harrison Middle School and opened the small bag containing her lunch. She was joined by her good friend Leticia Bennett, chair of the school's English department.

"LaShandra, how are things in the wild and wonderful world of seventh-grade science?" Leticia asked as she made herself comfortable.

"Mostly good news to report. But I'm still keeping total perfection at bay, thank you. In fact, some of this 'wonderful stuff' we've been doing is about to do me in," replied LaShandra.

"How so?" asked Leticia.

"Well, you might remember that I was getting nothing from Robin Coleman. Finally, I sat him down and we hammered out the details of a learning contract. Then he got busy. To the amazement, I think, of both of us, he has done just outstanding work on the assignments specified in the contract. His test scores have been excellent. He's even telling other people that 'science is pretty neat.' "

After pouring herself another cup of coffee, Leticia commented, "It seems to me you hit the right button. Is there really a down side to this story?"

"Well, yes and no," LaShandra replied. "Robin's good work has turned his mother into one of my biggest fans. In fact, she has been telling all of her friends about my 'outstanding learning contract system.' Lots of these people are parents of some of my other students."

"It sounds as though you are getting some wonderful public relations out of all this," said Leticia.

"Well," continued LaShandra, "that's true. But the problem is that I now have 23 parents begging me to set up individualized contracts for their children. I just can't do it. The time involved to lay out individualized objectives, find special learning material, and prepare tailor-made tests that will be different for 23 people would require me to work 30 hours a day, seven days a week. Some of these people are coming to see me on Thursday afternoon. I know they expect me to be enthusiastic about setting up all these individualized contracts. I'm afraid I am going to disappoint them if I say no, and I'm afraid I'll never survive the year if I say yes."

■ ■ ■

What should LaShandra do when the parents come? Are there some others from whom she should seek advice before they arrive? Would it be possible to develop learning contracts for these students without placing an irresponsibly heavy burden of work on LaShandra? How might school administrators feel about all this?

Clearly, individualizing instruction poses problems for teachers. Issues such as availability of learning resources, teacher planning time, and record keeping are among some that have already been noted. Additionally, there may be difficulties for students of a psychological nature when they are asked to work independently for long periods of time. Secondary students are peer-oriented. They enjoy opportunities to work together on projects.

In our view, the term *individualized instruction* ought not to be considered synonymous with *independent learning*. We believe that individualized instruction represents an attempt by the teacher to respond to individual students in ways that recognize limitations of resources and planning time. Further, we suggest that careful analyses of students' individual needs often will result in a decision that these needs can best be met in a group setting of some kind, rather than by independent study. The key to successful individualized instruction is careful diagnosis of needs. Analyses of these needs may well lead to teacher development of programs for a given student that feature a good deal of large-group instruction, some small-group instruction, and perhaps a limited amount of independent study. Sections that follow introduce some approaches to individualized instruction that view the approach as broader than independent learning.

Learning Activity Packages

Learning Activity Packages (LAPs) are highly structured, self-contained guides to learning. Typically they are developed by teachers to meet the needs of specific groups of learners. LAPs break content into a series of small steps. Students accomplish each step and are tested on mastery of this material before they go on to the next step. Usually a summary test at the end covers all content that has been introduced.

Most often LAPs are used to supplement the regular instructional program. Ray Latta (1974), who has worked extensively with LAPs, has suggested three basic uses of this scheme for individualizing instruction. First, they may be appropriate for students who, for one reason or another, are not able to profit from instruction delivered in more conventional ways. Second, they may feature content that goes beyond what is introduced to every student in the class. LAPs of this kind are directed toward brighter learners. Finally, on some occasions, teachers may choose the LAP format as a vehicle for delivering instruction on a certain topic to all students in a class.

LAPs typically allow students to work at their own pace, although teachers do need to monitor students to assure that they are staying on task. Some LAPs provide alternatives from which students may choose in learning specific kinds of content. Others contain open-ended sections that encourage students to pursue issues of personal interest.

In short, the LAP format is extremely flexible. This feature makes them an attractive instructional option for many teachers.

LAPs vary somewhat in terms of their format. The following components are found in large numbers of them (Latta, 1974):

- Title
- Overview
- Rationale
- Objectives
- Pretest
- Instructional program
- Posttest

Title

A good title conveys the general theme of the LAP. For example, if the LAP is designed to teach the student content related to music theory, the title should make some reference to music theory. Developers of LAPs often try to create a title that stimulates student interest. For example, the music theory LAP might be called something like, "Beethoven to Heavy Metal: Explorations in Music Theory."

Overview

The overview provides a general description of what the student will be expected to do to complete the LAP. There often is an indication of the approximate time required to complete the work. The overview, further, identifies major concepts and principles to be introduced. The overview serves as an advance organizer—something that helps students develop a mental framework they can use as they begin completing their assigned tasks.

Rationale

The rationale briefly states why the LAP is important. Good rationales give students a "need to know" the information they will be studying. They help students see how new content fits in with what they have already learned. Additionally, the rationale points ahead to future learning.

Objectives

LAP objectives provide students with a sense of direction. They indicate specifically what they are expected to learn. Further, the objectives tell students what will be done to assure them that their learning has been successful. Good objectives eliminate ambiguity. They also function as motivators for students as they begin working through their LAPs.

Pretest

Students take the LAP pretest before they begin work on the material that introduces new content. The pretest has two functions. First, it is designed to determine whether students have the prerequisite knowledge needed to cope successfully with the new content to be introduced in the LAP. Second, results can be used to pinpoint information introduced in the "new" content LAP that the students might already know. When pretest scores reveal that students have already mastered some of the content that is to be introduced, the teacher usually will ask these individuals some questions to assure they really do have this content mastered. If they do, they will be encouraged to skip some of the instructional material in the LAP and begin where they encounter information that they do not know.

Instructional Program

The heart of the LAP is the instructional program. Often it is divided into a number of sections. Students are provided with instructions about what they must do to complete each section. There may be references to pages to be read, films to be viewed, audio tapes to be heard, and papers to be written. Any forms students are to complete are included.

Often the instructional program of a LAP will present students with several options from which they can choose to complete work in each section. This allows students to choose an alternative that interests them. Provision of choices often functions as an important motivator for students.

Often there are assessment activities at the conclusion of each section. Sometimes there are practice tests for students to take as part of their review for these section tests. When students do well on the practice test, they typically also do well on the section tests themselves. When they do poorly, they are encouraged to review the material that has been introduced and to retake the practice test until they achieve a higher score. This general procedure tends to result in fairly high levels of success on the section tests.

Posttest

The posttest is administered at the conclusion of the instructional program. It is given only after all sections have been completed. Scores provide an overall measure of student learning regarding the content introduced in the LAP. The best LAP posttests are constructed so that individual questions are tied to each of the content sections that have been introduced. This allows teachers and students to identify particular areas of weakness. For example, if a student's overall posttest score is relatively good but his score on items associated with the second section is low, the student might be asked to review information related to this section. This situation may also prompt the teacher to look at the way information was presented in this section. A low student score may indicate an inadequate instructional design in this section of the LAP.

■ ■ ■

LAPs provide a worthwhile alternative to group-paced instruction for some students. Students who use them may sense a gain in personal control over their own learning. They may feel less pressed for time. A LAP design featuring several options for accomplishing individual tasks may convince students of a teacher's sincere interest in their individual needs and interests.

Learning Centers

A learning center is a designated place within the classroom where a student goes to pursue either required or optional activities related to a single topic. A learning center provides a self-contained environment for learning all required information about a given subject. Centers typically will feature general information about the topic, a list of options students may pursue in mastering the material, needed materials, and information about tests or other assessment alternatives.

In response to the need to provide learning options for students, a center focusing on "Reasons for the Outbreak of World War I" might allow students to gain information by one of the following:

- Reading some material from one or two textbooks.
- Reading a transcript of a lecture on this topic.
- Viewing a filmstrip.
- Listening through headphones to a discussion of this issue on a cassette tape.

Sometimes classrooms feature several centers. However, each center is independent of all of the others. Completion of work at one center is not prerequisite for work at another.

General Guidelines for Using Learning Centers

Learning centers vary enormously in their complexity. Some may involve little more than a corner of a room featuring a bulletin board display, an instruction sheet, and descriptions of activities students will complete prior to taking a test on the content. More complex centers may require space for media equipment such as filmstrip projectors, video or audiotape players, overhead projectors, and computers. Shelving may be

Box 10.2

Layout of a Simple Learning Center with Directions for Users

This learning center has been designed to be set up on top of a table. Note that there are two alternatives for learning the material that students may select. One is in the box labeled *yellow*. The other is in the box labeled *blue*. In this learning center, the teacher assigns students either to work with the yellow materials or the blue materials. Assignments are based on diagnoses of individual student characteristics.

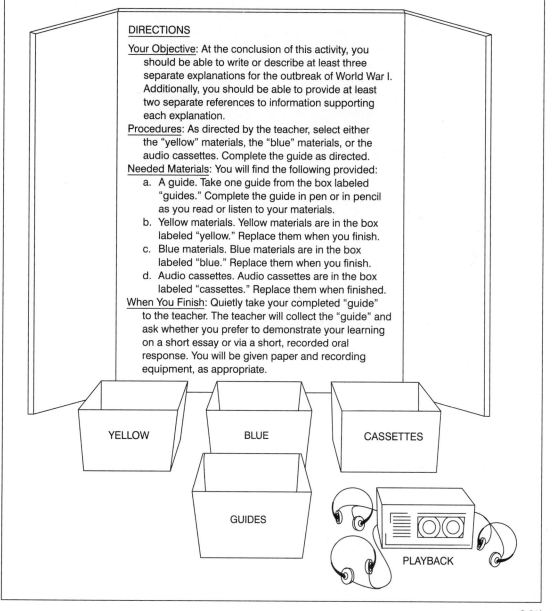

DIRECTIONS

<u>Your Objective</u>: At the conclusion of this activity, you should be able to write or describe at least three separate explanations for the outbreak of World War I. Additionally, you should be able to provide at least two separate references to information supporting each explanation.

<u>Procedures</u>: As directed by the teacher, select either the "yellow" materials, the "blue" materials, or the audio cassettes. Complete the guide as directed.

<u>Needed Materials</u>: You will find the following provided:

  a. A guide. Take one guide from the box labeled "guides." Complete the guide in pen or in pencil as you read or listen to your materials.

  b. Yellow materials. Yellow materials are in the box labeled "yellow." Replace them when you finish.

  c. Blue materials. Blue materials are in the box labeled "blue." Replace them when you finish.

  d. Audio cassettes. Audio cassettes are in the box labeled "cassettes." Replace them when finished.

<u>When You Finish</u>: Quietly take your completed "guide" to the teacher. The teacher will collect the "guide" and ask whether you prefer to demonstrate your learning on a short essay or via a short, recorded oral response. You will be given paper and recording equipment, as appropriate.

YELLOW

BLUE

CASSETTES

GUIDES

PLAYBACK

This teacher is providing assistance to a student who has gone to a learning center, received necessary information, and begun work on an individualized assignment.

needed to hold books, pamphlets, newspapers, filmstrips, audio and videotapes, compact disks, software, and even CD-ROM disks. These elaborate centers may take up quite a bit of classroom space.

Learning centers can be used for different purposes. Several learning center types are introduced in the subsections that follow.

The Alternate-Materials Center

The alternate-materials center focuses on content that is required of all students in the class. It responds to individual student needs by including a wide variety of learning materials related to the common topic. Students are allowed to select materials that are consistent with their own interests and abilities.

A problem faced by many secondary school teachers is that some students lack reading skills sufficient for them to profit from information in the course textbook. At an alternate-materials center, teachers respond to this dilemma by providing other learning options for students with reading problems. These might include less difficult reading materials, audio cassettes, filmstrips, computer-based programs, and other alternatives that treat information similar to that in the course text.

The Enrichment Center

The enrichment center is designed to challenge students who are capable of doing more sophisticated work than many of their classmates. Enrichment centers focus on a topic that is being studied by the entire class. However, only more able students are assigned to work at centers of this type, and assignments are designed to motivate them and to stretch their mental powers. Sometimes teachers use enrichment centers to maintain the interest of brighter students who finish regular assignments much more quickly than others in the classroom and who need to be assigned to an additional productive learning activity.

The Reinforcement Center

Reinforcement centers focus on a topic all students in a class have been studying. Their primary purpose is to provide students opportunities to review what they have learned. Hence, teachers typically set up reinforcement centers toward the end of a given instructional unit. Activities provide students opportunities to work again with difficult concepts that have been introduced and to practice new skills.

In preparing reinforcement centers, teachers often focus on aspects of content that have typically proved difficult for students. Sometimes, when a particularly large and difficult topic has been taught, several reinforcement centers will be developed. Each will focus on a particular area of the general topic.

Learning Stations

Learning stations, unlike learning centers, tend to divide a single topic into several parts. Each learning station provides experiences for students related to *one part* of a more general topic. Individual stations are interrelated.

In terms of their basic organizational features, individual learning stations are very much like learning centers. They typically will include general information, learning alternatives, needed materials, and details about what a student must do to demonstrate what she has learned. Depending on the nature of the focus content, it may be necessary for students to work through learning stations in a prescribed sequence. Where this is done, teachers often will assign numbers to each station and instruct students to work through them in numerical order. In other cases, where the material does not have to be presented in a sequential fashion, students can be assigned randomly to stations and told to work through them in any order.

Box 10.3

Example of General Student Instructions for Using Learning Stations

At the beginning of this unit, you will be assigned to work at one of the eight learning stations. Go directly to that station and begin. You will find instructions at that station telling you what to do. DO NOT GO TO ANY OTHER LEARNING STATION UNLESS SPECIFICALLY INSTRUCTED TO DO SO BY THE TEACHER.

When you complete each assignment at each station, secure it in this notebook. Place the notebook in the box for your period on the shelf along the west wall of the room.

When you have completed the work at the station to which you have been assigned, raise your hand. The teacher will come to you and check your work. If everything is in order you will be directed to go to another station. Please do *not* go to another station until you have been directed to do so by the teacher.

As you work through each of the stations, you may wish to keep track of your own progress. If that is the case, fill in information on the form below as you complete your work:

		Date Completed	Score (if appropriate)
Station 1:	Test on "Sinking of PT 109"	_____	_____
Station 2:	Vocabulary Test	_____	_____
Station 3:	Short paper on imagery	_____	_____
Station 4:	Short story I wrote	_____	_____
Station 5:	Six examples of personification I found	_____	_____
Station 6:	Completed crossword puzzles	_____	_____
Station 7:	Vocabulary Test	_____	_____
Station 8:	Six poems I wrote	_____	_____

General Guidelines for Using Learning Stations

Because a learning stations approach always requires development of several interrelated stations, preparation typically requires more teacher time than does development of a single learning center. In addition to deciding on which elements of a larger topic will be featured in each station, teachers also must think about how to manage student movement from station to station.

In planning a series of learning stations, the teacher's first task is to divide a proposed unit of work into a number of subtopics. Each of these becomes the focus for an individual station. Next, physical locations for the stations need to be identified. For each station, sets of student instructions must be developed, equipment and materials must be provided, and tests and other assessment procedures must be prepared. Additionally, guidelines must be developed regarding what students should do to indicate to the teacher they need help or to leave the station.

Planning for this last issue is important. Rules need to be established that prevent individual stations from becoming overloaded with students. Sometimes teachers establish a rule such as "no more than four students at a station at a given time." To make such a rule practical, students who have finished work at one station and who are waiting for someone to vacate a filled station must be given something productive to do. Some teachers handle this by developing guidelines at each station beginning with this phrase, "If you have finished all work at this station and there are too many people at the next station, do this until there is a vacancy at the next station: [specific instructions follow]."

Teachers who use learning stations tend to develop good record-keeping schemes. These allow them to keep track of the progress of individual students' progress through the various stations. This information helps them spot problems of individual students and identify general design deficiencies of a station that may be causing difficulties for a large number of learners.

Computers and New Technologies

One of the fast-growing approaches to individualizing instruction in secondary schools is computer-based instruction. Over the past decade, the number of computers in schools have increased at an explosive rate. Today, there are at least a few personal computers in virtually every middle school, junior high school, and high school in the nation. Many schools have large computer laboratories. Computers also are being placed in individual classrooms.

Increasing numbers of quality software packages are coming on the market. The better of these programs allow teachers to alter most of the important variables associated with individualized instruction to provide a learning experience that fits the needs of the individual student. For example, programs can be modified to allow students to work at their own pace. Some programs allow for variations in how new content is introduced. Many provide alternative ways for students to review content.

Hardware availability continues to plague many teachers who wish to make more extensive use of computers. Optimally, there should be a computer for every student. Many schools do not meet this standard. Consequently, availability of equipment continues to limit numbers of individualized instructional programs that depend on the use of personal computers.

Computers represent just one of the new technologies that have potential to help teachers individualize. Optical disk technologies are just beginning to enter the mainstream of public school use. Some of the more sophisticated optical disk applications allow for storage and retrieval of vast quantities of information and for highly flexible teacher control over the organization of learning experiences. A more comprehensive review of optical disk and other emerging technologies is provided in Chapter 11, "Enhancing Learning Through Technology."

Table 10.1   Summary Table

Main Points	Explanation
Individualizing Instruction	Individualized instruction is an effort to tailor instruction to meet the unique needs of each student. This does not mean that each student studies independently all of the time. Often, meeting individual needs involves group work. Today, more individualized instruction is provided in elementary than in secondary schools.
Altering Variables to Individualize	Among variables that can be altered to individualize instruction are (1) the rate of learning, (2) the content of learning, (3) the method of learning, and (4) the goals of learning.
Continuous Progress Learning	This approach to individualizing focuses on the rate-of-learning variable. Students pursue the same learning objectives, but each goes through required material at his or her own pace (or rate).
Mastery Learning	This approach to individualized instruction is founded on the belief that differences in student achievement do not result from differences in intelligence or aptitude but rather from variations in time required for them to learn the material. Mastery learning programs typically provide additional time for students who do not learn material the first time to restudy it and to have their learning reassessed. One approach to mastery learning is the Personalized System of Instruction (PSI).
Adaptive Instruction	This term describes approaches taken to alter instructional methods to meet the needs of individual students. Student needs are diagnosed, instruction is matched carefully to these needs, and teachers carefully manage their progress, making adjustments to the designed program as needed.
Learning Contract	Often used in altering-the-goals approaches to individualizing, the learning contract is an agreement between the teacher and a student. Typically it specifies (1) what a student must do to accomplish a specified learning objective, (2) learning resources to be used, (3) any student work that is to be produced, (4) criteria to be used in evaluating student work, and (5) key due dates.

Main Points	Explanation
Learning Activity Package	A Learning Activity Package, or LAP, is a highly structured, self-contained guide to learning. Typically, LAPS include (1) a title, (2) an overview, (3) a rationale statement, (4) a list of objectives, (5) a pretest, (6) an instructional program for the student to follow, and (7) a posttest.
Learning Center	A learning center is a designated place in the classroom that provides a self-contained environment for learning. Typically, a learning center will include (1) general information about the topic to be studied, (2) a list of learning options from which students may select, (3) needed learning materials, and (4) information about tests or other assessment alternatives.
Learning Stations	Learning stations consist of a series of self-contained learning environments. Each focuses on a specific aspect of a more general topic. To learn all aspects of this general topic, students move from station to station and follow the directions. Organizational features of individual learning stations parallel those found in learning centers.
Technology and Individualizing	New computer software and other emerging technological aids to instruction provide teachers with more options as they plan to meet the special instructional needs of individuals in their classes. Availability of equipment in many places poses some limits on what teachers can do to incorporate instruction based on these technologies into their planning. However, schools are working hard to deal with this problem, and in the future it is probable that many more individualized programs will draw upon computers, optical disks, and other technologies that have the potential to greatly extend teachers' options as they plan instruction for individual students.

Review of Key Ideas

- Differences among individual students increase with each year people are in school. Differences among twelfth-graders are most notable of all. The great diversity among secondary students suggests that secondary schools are ideal settings for individualized instructional programs. Interestingly, however, much more individualized instruction takes place in elementary than in secondary schools.

- Individualized instruction is not synonymous with independent learning. Rather, it implies attempts by teachers to fit instruction to the specific needs of individuals. This may well mean that a given student may spend a majority of her time in whole-group instructional settings.

- One approach to individualizing involves altering the rate of learning. When this is done, all students are exposed to the same basic instructional program, but the speed at which individual students progress through the program varies.

- Mastery learning is an example of altering the rate of learning to individualize instruction. Mastery learning presumes that observed differences in students' levels of achievement have little to do with differences in their levels of intelligence or in their aptitudes. Rather, differences occur because individuals vary in terms of how much time they need to do the required work. Proponents of mastery learning believe nearly all students can succeed on school tasks provided they are given enough time to complete them.

- Another approach to individualizing involves altering the content of learning. Goals pursued by all students may be the same, but specific content materials assigned to individuals vary in terms of their abilities and interests. This approach assumes that students' levels of motivation increase when learning materials are closely matched to their interests.

- Individualized programs that attend to learning style differences of learners often involve teachers in altering the method of learning. Objectives and content remain the same for all students, but individuals are allowed to pursue different paths as they seek to learn the material. For example, some students may read about it, others may listen to audio recordings, and still others may interview people and take notes.

- A fairly unusual approach to individualizing, at least in public school settings, involves altering the goals of learning. In this approach, great latitude is given to students to select the goals of instruction and to make other important decisions about what they wish to learn. There is an assumption that, given the freedom to do so, students will make intelligent choices.

- Some altering-the-goals-of-learning approaches feature more direction from teachers. The learning contract approach is an example. A learning contract is an agreement between the teacher and the student that describes specific objectives, what the student will do to reach them, and how learning will be assessed.

- Learning Activity Packages (LAPS) are highly structured, self-contained guides to learning. They break content into a series of small steps. LAPS often feature (1) a title, (2) an overview statement, (3) a rationale for the program, (4) a list of objectives, (5) a pretest, (6) an instructional program featuring complete directions for students, and (7) a posttest.

- A learning center is a designated place within a classroom where a student pursues learning activities related to a single topic. This self-contained environment for learning often provides general information about the topic, a selection of learning options for students, needed learning materials, and information about tests or other assessment alternatives.

- Learning station approaches subdivide large topics into important subtopics. Each station focuses on one part of the general topic. Organizationally, each learning station is set up much like a learning center. Learning stations require more teacher time to prepare than learning centers. This is true because several of them must be set up at once, and complete instructions and support materials must be provided for each.

- Emerging electronic technologies, particularly those based on computers, are providing more options for teachers who wish to individualize their instruction. In recent years, there have been great advances in software that can be used to generate instructional options suited to needs of individual students. In some places, hardware availability continues to be a problem for teachers wishing to incorporate more computer-based instruction into their plans to individualize instruction.

Follow-Up Questions and Activities

Questions

1. How do you define individualized instruction? Do you think your definition will satisfy everyone? Why or why not?

2. Under what conditions might you consider using a learning contract? What specific features would you include?

3. As you think about the issue of individualizing, do you think you would be more comfortable with an approach that (a) altered the rate of learning, (b) altered the content of learning, (c) altered the method of learning, or (d) altered the goals of learning? Why?

4. What is meant by mastery learning, and what do you see as some strengths and weaknesses of this approach?

5. What are some features of Learning Activities Packages, and how can they be used to individualize instruction?

6. What are some features of a typical learning center?

7. What are some features of a learning stations approach?

8. What are some differences in the planning and preparation of learning centers and learning stations?

9. What are some general problems teachers face when they try to individualize instruction?

10. How can the new electronic technologies help teachers to individualize their instruction?

Activities

1. Invite a teacher who has used learning stations with his or her students to visit your class. Ask for comments regarding preparation tasks, managing the flow of students from station to station, and maintaining control of students when learning stations are used.

2. Identify a specific topic you would cover in one of the courses you would like to teach. Develop a complete set of plans for a learning center devoted to this topic. Present your plans to your instructor for review.

3. Education's professional journals include many articles that report practical ideas for individualizing instruction. Begin an individualized instruction folder that includes reprints of at least 10 articles. You might begin by looking at entries in the *Education Index*. Your instructor may have other suggestions as you begin this project.

4. Proponents of mastery learning suggest that lack of sufficient time to complete an assigned task is a major barrier to student achievement. Do you agree? Prepare a position paper in which you either support or attack this assumption. Support your position with citations from the research literature. Consider looking at such sources as Good and Brophy's *Looking in Classrooms* and Wittrock's *Handbook of Research on Teaching*. Your instructor may wish to recommend other sources of information.

5. Select any chapter in this textbook. Then, prepare a complete Learning Activity Package (LAP) to teach the content. Alternatively, develop a LAP for a topic you would like to teach. Present your material to your instructor for review.

References

Bloom, B. S. *All Our Children Learning*. New York: McGraw-Hill, 1980.

Bloom, B. S. *Human Characteristics and School Learning*. New York: McGraw-Hill, 1976.

Glaser, R. "General Discussion: Relationships Between Aptitude, Learning, and Instruction." In R. Snow, T. Federico, and W. Montague (eds.). *Aptitude, Learning, and Instruction*. Volume 2. Hillsdale, NJ: Lawrence Erlbaum Associates, 1980, pp. 309–326.

GOOD, T. AND BROPHY, J. *Looking in Classrooms*. 5th ed. New York: HarperCollins, 1991.

GUSKEY, T. *Implementing Mastery Learning*. Belmont, CA: Wadsworth Publishing Company, 1985.

JOHNSON, D. W. AND JOHNSON, R. T. *Learning Together and Alone: Cooperative, Competitive, and Individualistic Learning*. 3rd ed. Boston: Allyn & Bacon, 1991.

LATTA, R. *A Practical Guide to Writing and Using Learning Activity Packages*. Bellingham, WA: Western Media Printing, 1974.

11

Enhancing Learning Through Technology

AIMS

This chapter provides information to help the reader to:

- Recognize the general impact technology is having on society and the schools.
- Explain some basic differences between modern electronics-based technologies and older mechanical-based technologies.
- Cite examples of earlier technological innovations and describe their impact on educational programs.
- Describe some general barriers to the adoption of technological innovations in the schools.
- Cite examples of emerging technological innovations that have already influenced or are beginning to influence secondary schools' instructional programs.

FOCUS QUESTIONS

1. Why are schools being pressured to place more emphasis on up-to-date technologies in their instructional programs?

2. In what ways can technology help teachers design programs to develop students' higher-level thinking powers?

3. What is the connection between technological competence and employment?

4. What characteristics of many of the newer technologies separate them from innovations of the past?

5. What barriers stand in the way of school and teacher adoption of new technologies?

6. How can use of data bases and electronic computer-to-computer linkages enrich instruction in secondary schools?

7. What are some possible instructional applications of CD-ROM technology?

8. What are some potential advantages of interactive distance learning technologies?

9. How is electronic satellite technology being used to enhance school instruction?

Introduction

The pace of technological change is accelerating. Increasingly, nations' standings in the world are being measured by the level of sophistication of their technology-based industries. Some critics of American schools charge that our secondary schools have taken too little action to assure that graduates have the technical skills needed in today's workplace (Barlow, 1992). Secondary schools today are under pressure to increase their use of technology to support instruction *and* to make students more personally familiar with emerging technologies.

The second part of this statement is important. It reflects a belief that graduates must have levels of expertise beyond a simple ability to use today's technology. What is needed is technological competence. This implies a sophisticated understanding of technologies that includes an ability to see novel applications and to extend the nature of the technologies themselves. Today's students are expected to leave schools (1) unafraid of new technologies, (2) with abilities to use some of the technologies, and (3) willing to confront a world in which they will be required to master new technologies as they become available.

Rationales for Use of Up-to-Date Technologies in School Programming

Computers and other electronic technologies extend the range of what teachers can do to develop students' higher-level thinking skills. Links to data bases of various kinds tremendously increase the raw material students have to work with. This allows teachers to develop wide-ranging assignments that are not limited by information contained in the textbook or in the school library. Further, these technologies allow students to test hypotheses, consider alternatives, and make decisions much more quickly than heretofore has been possible. Hence, possibilities for their active engagement on multiple sophisticated thinking tasks is extended.

Teachers at The School of the Future, a public secondary school in New York City that makes extensive use of technology, have noted that groups of students using computers to solve complex problems become much more sensitive to their own *metacognitive* processes. This means that they become much more aware of the thought processes they are using to approach a given problem and whether the selected processes are appropriate, given the nature of the problem (Soloman, 1992). Self-monitoring of mental processes is a hallmark of sophisticated thinkers.

Economic realities are also supporting expanded use of up-to-date technologies in school programs. New, electronics-based technologies have become pervasive in the work place. Education of employees in many industries increasingly depends on sophisticated technology. For example, as long ago as 1988, IBM estimated that about 60 percent of all of its internal employee education programs were delivered through communication satellites and educational television (Charp, 1988; p. 8).

Supporters of new technologies have pointed to successful educational applications in industry as evidence that these applications make sense for public schools as well. Computers and other technologies have become pervasive features of the world of work. Increasingly, employers expect new workers to be familiar with their use. The most rapid expansion of future jobs is predicted to occur in fields where technological know-how is a must.

National security fears are another important force behind the drive to expand the use of new technologies in the schools. One measure of a nation's political power is its economic strength. Economic strength depends, in part, on an educated citizenry that is highly familiar with the latest technologies. A nation with a weak economy may find it difficult to sustain a strong national defense system.

In addition to arguments related to national security, other proponents of technology in the schools recognize the personal benefits such programs bring to learners. As far back as the early 1980s the Education Commission of the States pointed out that in the future most American workers would not be engaged in the production of goods. Rather, the future will witness a time when "an increasing percentage of workers will be retrieving, processing, and transmitting information" (Education Commission of the States, 1983; p. 1). A concern that schools must more closely align programs with the technological demands of the workplace continued to be reflected at the 1992 National Forum and Annual Meeting of the Education Commission of the States (McKernan, Gifford, Nielson, and Tucker, 1992).

Some critics of school practices contend that schools have lagged far beyond other institutions in responding to technological change. James Mecklenburger (1990) argues that piecemeal adoption of technologies won't do. What is required is an enormous infusion of money to provide not just computers but well-stocked libraries of CD-ROM disks, electronic ties to national data bases, and interactive video links. Only when all the pieces are in place will the advantages of the new technologies really begin to be felt.

This will be enormously expensive. However, supporters of this approach argue that long-term costs will be high if we continue to turn out high school graduates who have not personally benefited from instruction supported by the best-available technologies and who are generally not familiar with them.

Box 11.1

Are Employers Ducking Their Financial Responsibilities?

These comments appeared recently in the letters-to-the-editor section of a local newspaper.

I see our school board has approved another enormous contract for the purchase of personal computers. A couple of technicians have been hired to service this equipment. A total of $50,000 has been spent over the past several years to train teachers to use computer and other electronic technology. This is a mistake.

The school board has caved in to demands of employers. *Of course* employers want new employees who will be as highly trained as possible. This has always been true. But, in the past, employers expected that training new employees to use special equipment was part of their cost of doing business. Not today. Employers have discovered that taxpayers will foot this bill. All they have to do is hint that "our schools are technologically not up to

par" and our free-spending board will rush in to buy expensive new equipment and to pay for high-cost staff training.

What this all boils down to is a rip-off of the taxpayers. We're tired of this expensive practice, and we want it stopped *now*!

What Do You Think?

1. Should private employers assume more responsibility for training new employees in expensive technologies?

2. What do you see as the strongest points in this letter to the editor? Its weakest points?

3. If you were a member of the school board in this community, how would you respond to these comments?

The Nature of the New Technologies

Computers represent only one of the many new technologies that are increasingly being used in secondary schools. Others include CD-ROM, interactive video, videocassettes, optical disks, on-line data systems, and electronic bulletin boards. Each of these innovations has its unique characteristics. However, they all share a common characteristic that suggests they are quite different from earlier technological innovations. Specifically, each of them depends on electronic as opposed to mechanical technologies. This has important implications for costs and maintenance.

By way of contrast, many older technologies made very heavy use of mechanical technologies. Consider, for example, the motion picture projector and the typewriter. Each has dozens of moving parts. These moving parts produce vibration. Mechanical wearing of part on part results in relatively frequent breakdowns. Maintenance costs have been high where this equipment has been heavily used.

Innovations depending on electronic innovations have many fewer moving parts (Hawkridge, 1983). One result is that there are fewer limits on their speed of operation. Electronic technology depends on an ability to control the flow of electrons through elaborate circuits. This circuitry has been made possible through application of discoveries in microelectronics. These discoveries have led to the production of extremely small electronic devices, especially switches and circuits. Today, thousands of circuits and switches can be embedded on extremely small chips. Sophisticated production lines allow the manufacture of these microchips by the millions. Once a production line is in operation, it is relatively inexpensive to produce countless duplications of the same circuit. This production system and the high degree of competition in the business have acted to produce electronic devices that are small and relatively cheap.

Since much of this equipment has few moving parts, maintenance costs often are low. For example, the keyboard on a microcomputer is one of its few moving parts. Maintenance on moving parts of microcomputers often is a fraction of that required for a busy office typewriter.

Forces Opposing the Spread of New Technologies in the Schools

Barriers facing introduction of new electronic technologies are generally similar to those that have often confronted new innovations through the years. Larry Cuban (1986) has made an extensive study of innovations in the schools. He found that innovations proposed for use in the schools often go through four distinct phases. First is the exhilaration phase. This phase features announcements by school authorities of marvelous positive changes that will accompany or result from the innovation's introduction. Cuban (1986) found that these announcements often have been made been individuals who, themselves, would not be required to work with the innovation on a day-to-day basis in the classroom.

The next phase is the scientific-credibility phase. At this point in the process, school officials work hard to discover a research base that supports the innovation's effectiveness. Often there are reports that installation of the change resulted in improvement of student scores as compared to outdated "traditional" methods. If no score improvement can be documented, sometimes there is a reported finding that equivalent scores resulted from use of the innovation at less cost than those achieved when traditional approaches were used.

The studies surveyed during the scientific-credibility phase frequently are used to convince authorities to adopt an innovation. Once this decision has been made and the innovation has been introduced, often the innovation is used less extensively than had been hoped. Often, too, its overall effectiveness falls short of initial hopes. This leads to what Cuban (1986) has aptly described as the disappointment phase.

Disappointment frequently is felt most acutely by people who were the strongest supporters of the change. This is particularly likely to be true of administrators who have taken a public stand to back the innovation. This disappointment often leads to a search for explanations about why the innovation failed to live up to expectations. Sometimes teachers are blamed. When this happens, Cuban (1986) suggests that the innovation-introduction cycle has entered the teacher-bashing phase. When this happens, teachers are sometimes depicted as unbending conservatives who have deliberately stood in the way of an innovation that is "basically sound." Had teachers embraced the innovation enthusiastically, so the argument goes, wonderful results would have been achieved.

Cuban (1986) argues that it is unfair for teachers to be blamed for the failure of many technological innovations to take root. Failure more logically can be attributed to (1) methods used to introduce the change, (2) the nature of the individual innovation, and (3) the character of teachers' working conditions.

Historically, introduction of innovations has often been a top-down process. This means that supporters of innovations such as instructional films, educational television, and programmed instruction did not initially consult with teachers. Rather, they attempted to influence school boards to adopt these technologies. Once convinced, school boards ordered administrators to implement the change, and administrators passed along these instructions to teachers. This pattern left teachers out of the picture until policy decisions mandating innovation adoption were made.

As a result of this process, most teachers had little background knowledge about the innovations. Further, they had little emotional commitment to them. Frequently, with very little (if any) training, teachers were expected to include these new technologies in their day-to-day instructional planning. There was an assumption that teachers would be able to adapt easily to these changes. But, "little in the formal training and early years of a teacher's career . . . nurtures the use of the newer forms of technology" (Cuban, 1986; p. 60).

Many environmental variables have interfered with secondary teachers' successful use of innovations. For example, instructional programs requiring the use of educational films and educational television depend on the availability of special equipment. Further, this equipment must be in good working order. Teachers who have planned lessons only to find needed equipment is missing or out of order often have become frustrated with technological innovations. Such stand-bys as chalkboards and textbooks may not be flashy, but they are highly dependable instructional resources. The perceived reliability of traditional instructional technologies as compared to their suggested replacements has contributed to some teachers' reluctance to commit strongly to some of the newer technologies.

Some of the early attempts to introduce computers into school programs featured large computers that forced teachers to take students to special classrooms for instruction. Today, personal computers are available in individual classrooms. Although this represents an improvement, teachers often are still concerned about the inability to involve larger numbers of students on this equipment at the same time. Experts in classroom applications of computers have recognized this problem, and they have developed some instructional approaches that are specifically designed for groups of students working with a single computer.

The issue of flexibility of use is very important to teachers. Some recommended innovations have placed great constraints on teachers. This has been particularly true in terms of their flexibility to vary scheduling of different learning experiences. Educational television, especially when first introduced on a large scale in the 1950s and 1960s, was an example of a particularly restrictive technology. Broadcast schedules generally required all interested teachers to have their classes prepared to view programs

Box 11.2

Teacher Survey on Low-Tech and High-Tech Innovations

Larry Cuban (1986) argues that many high-tech innovations are not well matched to conditions teachers face in their classrooms. To test this view, interview several teachers about four instructional technologies: textbooks, overhead projectors, videocassette players, and personal computers. Take notes about their responses to each question. Share information with your instructor.

1. As a teacher, how easy do you and your students find each of the following to use?

   • Textbooks

   • Overhead projectors

   • Videocassette players

   • Personal computers

2. As a teacher, how would you rate the flexibility of each of the following? That is, how free are you to schedule the occasions and times of use?

   • Textbooks

   • Overhead projectors

   • Videocassette players

   • Personal computers

3. How dependable do you find each of the following to be?

   • Textbooks

   • Overhead projectors

   • Videocassette players

   • Personal computers

at prearranged times. This took away planning flexibility. Consequently, many teachers found it difficult to integrate educational television into their instructional programs.

More recent innovations have not been so constraining. For example, videotapes of television programs can be used by individual teachers whenever they deem them appropriate (provided, of course, the needed playback equipment and television receivers are available and in working order). In general, it is fair to say that the newer technologies seem to be responding to teachers' desires to exercise more personal discretion over times and occasions of their use.

For example, educational television has evolved into a highly flexible instructional technology. This has been especially true since the invention of affordable videotaping equipment. This equipment has placed programming control directly into the hands of individual teachers. Teachers can record and replay programs as they see fit.

Additionally, video cameras have allowed teachers to prepare videotapes of programs of their own making. Many physical education teachers use this equipment. The technology has been enormously beneficial to them in teaching and critiquing complicated skills—for example, in tumbling classes. This technology provides teachers with a means of providing students with immediate visual feedback about their performances.

The newer electronic technologies lend themselves well to decentralized use. More than ever before, teachers are able to use them for purposes they identify and at times of their own choosing. This flexibility allows wider use of some of the newer technologies than of the less flexible innovations introduced before the age of the microchip.

CASE STUDY

Implementation of Technological Innovations and One Teacher's Integrity

Joan Pescoli teaches in a well-to-do suburb of one of the nation's largest cities. Parents take pride in their schools and like to think that theirs are among the finest in the state. At the same time, they are well aware of what these schools cost them, and they keep a close eye on budgets. There are many people who feel their school taxes are already too high.

Administrators in the district have felt themselves pressured to have school programs featuring up-to-date technology. At the same time they have had to contend with taxpayers who again and again have expressed a reluctance to pay higher school taxes. One response of school leaders in this district has been to concentrate high technology resources in just a few schools. Joan Pescoli teaches eighth-grade United States history in one of these schools, Washington Irving Middle School. Recently, Joan wrote this letter to her old college roommate, Rene LaPointe.

> Rene, I feel I'm in an emotional bind. The district has just been great to me. They paid for me to go to the advanced computer-networking workshop last summer, and they've gone along with this on-line set up where my kids exchange information once a week with classes in England and in British Columbia. They also let me buy 20 new computers, and they've said I can subscribe to any data bases I want. The program has been going great with my students, and I'm getting some of them turned on to school who never really seemed to care much about it before.
>
> The problem is that my class has become a kind of permanent showcase for the district. Hardly a day goes by without a central office administrator trooping in with two or three taxpayers in tow. What gets me down is that these people are getting the impression that this school is "typical" of what is going on in this district. It's not. We've got resources other schools in the district hardly know exist. Some of my friends in the other buildings are less than thrilled when they see media reports about technology and learning here at Irving.
>
> I *know* the district can't afford to buy this kind of equipment for all the schools. I just wish the district leadership had the courage to play it straight with the public on this issue. I feel I'm nothing but a star player in public relations effort designed to obscure a much less wonderful reality. I don't think the district is being professional; I don't feel like *I* am being professional when I leave visitors with the impression (hinted at, but not directly stated) that our program typifies education throughout the district.
>
> I'm giving serious thought to resigning at the end of the year. The wonderful equipment I have here just doesn't compensate for the strain of being part of a dubious public relations effort.

■ ■ ■

What do you think Joan should do? What arguments can you make in favor of her staying at this school? What arguments can you make in favor of her leaving to take a job elsewhere? Who should Joan talk to before making a final decision? Have you ever been in a situation where you felt you were being asked to gloss over the truth? How did you feel? What did you do?

Examples of Technologies and Their Uses in Secondary Schools

The categories of technological applications introduced in this section are not meant to be all-inclusive. They are provided as examples of those being used in today's secondary schools. The following are some applications of technology now being used in many secondary schools:

- Personal computers
- CD-ROM
- Interactive videodisks
- Interactive distance learning
- Videocassettes
- Optical disks
- Electronic satellite links

Personal Computers

The decade of the 1980s witnessed a tremendous growth in the number of personal computers in the schools. From a modest number at the beginning of the decade, numbers of schools with microcomputers soared to over 90 percent by the middle 1980s (Cuban, 1986). By the early 1990s, virtually all of the nation's secondary schools had at least a few personal computers available for student use.

The great growth in the total number of personal computers in the nation's schools has by no means meant they have "taken over" secondary school courses. In many places, there are not sufficient numbers of machines. To deal with this situation, a number of firms have begun marketing devices that project images from microcomputer screens onto large wall screens. This equipment has made it possible for teachers to use some programs with the entire class.

In recent years, group learning techniques have been growing in popularity. Research by such scholars as David and Roger Johnson of the University of Minnesota and Robert Slavin of Johns Hopkins University has supported the idea that students often learn better in groups than they do when they do work individually (Johnson,

Johnson, Holubec, and Roy, 1984; Slavin, 1990). (For additional information about the benefits of group learning, see Chapter 15, "Small Groups and Cooperative Learning.")

When group learning techniques are used, several students often can be assigned to work with a single personal computer. This allows computer technology to be used when there are fewer personal computers than students. Results of group-oriented work with personal computers have been encouraging. In commenting on group work with computers at The School of the Future in New York City, Gwen Soloman declares, "when [students] work collaboratively, the result is greater than what each individual could learn alone. If they are not pleased with the work, the group must evaluate the task, the process, and its ability to function" (1992; p. 11).

Early instructional software in many curricular areas was poor. Today, this situation has greatly improved. Excellent software is now available to support instruction across all areas of the secondary school curriculum. The availability of good instructional software and the ability to electronically link individual schools to data bases and electronic linking systems have greatly changed the ways computers are used in the schools.

Data Bases

Today, phone lines allow personal computers in schools to be connected to data bases of all kinds. The PRODIGY Service, jointly sponsored by IBM and Sears, is a subscription system that allows users to gain access to a wide array of data in exchange for a monthly fee. Hundreds of categories of information are available, including an electronic encyclopedia, extensive geographic information, and science content derived from the NOVA public television series.

Quantum Computer Services is another provider of data to electronically linked personal computers. Quantum Computer Services has available data bases designed both for owners of IBM (and compatible) computers and Apple computers. Services include America OnLine (for owners of Apple computers) and PC-Link (for owners of IBM compatible computers) (Grunwald, 1990). Users can look up information in an electronic encyclopedia and access other information-retrieval sources as well.

Electronic Computer-to-Computer Linking Systems

An electronic bulletin board allows for exchanges of information among personal computer users at widely scattered locations. Individual computers are equipped with modems that permit links to the bulletin boards using telephone lines. Bulletin boards afford opportunities for information exchanges of many kinds.

Electronic ties are also opening up other possibilities for linking widely separated personal computers. These electronic ties allow instructional possibilities that were undreamed of a few years ago. For example, a group of students in Massachusetts regularly communicate with students in the Canadian province of Saskatchewan. Among other things, students exchange information about local geographic features and climate (Watson, 1990). Some students in West Virginia have become pen pals with students in Russia.

An especially ambitious use of electronic computer linkages has been promoted by the American Association of Teachers of French. This scheme uses a service called EDU-TEL-Classe that is made available by Minitel, a French telecommunications system. The program matches schools in the United States with those in France. Using the French

"What do you mean your students *accidentally* tapped into the main computer at the Pentagon?"

language as the medium of exchange, students in both countries undertake joint research projects in civics, science, and mathematics ("American Students Learn French," 1991).

The possibilities offered by these linkages have prompted an interest in creating "global classrooms." These are classrooms that are electronically linked to classrooms in other countries. Such organizations as GTE, AT&T, the National Geographic Society, and the FrEdMail Foundation are among those facilitating linkages of classrooms in different countries. GTE's World Classroom project links students and teachers and facilitates communication in these five areas: welcome, science, social studies, language arts, and special projects. One participating school in Virginia recently linked with other classrooms in California, Texas, Mexico, and Argentina (Kurshan and Dawson, 1992). Information about global classroom projects is available from the following groups:

AT&T Learning Network
P.O. Box 6391
Parsippany, NJ 07054

Computer Pals Across the World, Inc.
P.O. Box 1206
Lake Oswego, OR 97035

FrEdMail Foundation
Box 243
Bonita, CA 91908-0243

Global Common Classroom
c/o John Whiteley
Program in Social Ecology
University of California
Irvine, CA 92717

Global Laboratory
TERC Communications
2067 Massachusetts Avenue
Cambridge, MA 02140

Teleclass International
c/o Dr. John Wollstein
1103 9th Avenue
Honolulu, HI 96816

World Classroom
GTE Directories Corporation
1411 Greenway Drive
P.O. Box 165008
Irving, TX 75016-5008

CD-ROM

CD-ROM stands for "compact disk, read-only memory." This powerful technology allows integration and management of tremendous quantities of digital, audio, and visual information. A single CD-ROM disk can store as much information as 250 large reference books (Phillipo, 1989). Information is recorded on a CD-ROM disk by a light beam that burns small pits on its surface. Information is retrieved by a system that uses a computer to interpret and store reflections produced by a laser beam bouncing off the surface of the disk.

Students can use CD-ROM disks in different ways. For example, they can flip through an electronic encyclopedia much as they would turn pages in a printed version in the school library. They can find specific information by cueing the system to look for key words or phrases. They can transfer information, both words and graphics, from the CD-ROM disk to a regular computer floppy disk or hard disk. Information of different types can be easily edited and customized. For teachers, CD-ROM technology offers the possibility of producing learning materials for students that are designed to respond to the unique needs of individuals in a given class.

The following firms market CD-ROMs specifically designed for use by teachers and schools:

Broderbund Software, Inc.
17 Paul Drive
San Rafael, CA 94903

Encyclopedia Britannica Educational Corp.
Britannica Centre
310 S. Michigan Avenue
Chicago, IL 60604

Grolier Electronic Encyclopedia
Sherman Turnpike
Danbury, CT 06816

Microsoft Corp.
Box 97017
Redmond, WA 98073

PC SIG Inc.
1030 Duane Avenue, Suite D
Sunnyvale, CA 94086

Tri-Star Publishing Company
475 Virginia Drive
Ft. Washington, PA 19034

Interactive Videodisks

This technology allows visual and audio information to be stored on plastic disks. Most videodisk systems use laser beams to convert stored information to visible images or sound. Interactive videodisks allow users to determine exactly which bits of stored information they wish to play back. They can edit material to serve their own needs. All of this is accomplished by linking basic videodisk technology and computer technology.

Interactive videodisks have great potential as instructional tools. They allow teachers to prepare customized lessons that organize certain parts of stored information to respond to interests and needs of individual students. This technology also can be used to help students develop their own creative thinking powers as they prepare learning "products" of their own design.

One particularly notable application of this technology is GTV. GTV is an interactive program focusing on United States history. It is designed for use by students and teachers in grades 5 through 12. The program features two total hours of video. This material has been divided into a total of 40 segments. Each lasts between three and five minutes. Teachers or students who use GTV can sequence these segments in any way they wish. For example, they might decide to pursue a common theme across a number of sequences. The system includes a word processing feature that allows users to prepare written materials to accompany selected content. Information regarding GTV is available from:

National Geographic Society
Department GTV
Washington, DC 20077-9966

Interactive Distance Learning

Distance learning refers to a system of instruction designed to serve students who are located at a considerable distance from the place the instruction is delivered. Distance learning can be delivered in many ways. Some of these use technologies that certainly are not new. For example, correspondence courses depend on the mails to provide a communication link between teacher and students. Radio has been used for many years, particularly in Australia where many students in remote interior sections of the country live far from their teachers. Some distance learning programs utilize television signals of various kinds.

Traditionally, much distance learning has been one way. That is, students have been able to receive information *from* the teacher, but have had no way to immediately communicate questions and concerns *to* the teacher. New technologies are making this kind of two-way communication possible.

Compressed video signals are being used in many places to enable instructors and students to see one another and communicate with one another. This technology makes it possible for a teacher to have a group of students in a classroom where the instruction is physically delivered and other students in remote sites who can see and hear the instructor and who, themselves, can be seen and heard by the instructor. Often fax

Interactive video technology allows a teacher in one location to teach students in his or her own classroom as well as students at remote sites. This teacher can both see and talk to students at the remote sites. They also can both see and talk to the teacher.

machines provide a supplementary link from the teacher to students in the remote locations. This allows hand-outs to be sent. Further, tests and other examples of student work can be faxed to the teacher. There is evidence that students in remote sites perform as well on examinations as students present in the classroom where the instruction originates (Washor and Couture, 1990).

Technologies that make interactive distance learning possible have the potential to remove many educational disadvantages faced by students in remote areas. New technologies make it feasible for students everywhere to profit from instruction from superior teachers and to interact with them much as if they were together in the same room.

Videocassettes

Videocassette technology is now almost as widespread as television itself. Large numbers of playback units are available in secondary schools. The number of educational programs available on videocassettes has increased tremendously over the past decade.

Videocassettes are well adapted to school settings. They can provide instruction that formerly required use of educational films. Further, they can do so at a much reduced cost. A typical half-hour color instructional film may cost as much as $500. Often a videocassette of the same film can be purchased for less than one-tenth of this figure. With reasonable care, a videocassette will last for many years. Videocassettes are not nearly so vulnerable to the kinds of breaks and tears that often afflict 16mm films.

Many teachers have found videocassettes to be easy to use and easy to integrate into their instructional programs. A single playback unit in a classroom can serve the needs of an entire class of students, provided that television monitor screens are reasonably large and that student chairs are properly arranged. The videocassettes themselves are not bulky, and they lend themselves easily to storage in classroom cabinets.

In addition to playing back prerecorded videocassettes, many teachers are now using combination video-camera/video-recorder equipment to make video recordings of their own. Increasingly this equipment is becoming light, portable, and affordable. Teachers use it to make video recordings of such things as student activities on field trips, art students' first attempts to raise a pot using a potter's wheel, high school wrestlers' performances during matches, and so forth. They are particularly useful when instruction focuses on a specific skill. Video recordings can be replayed immediately after they are made and can provide very useful feedback to students.

Optical Disks

Optical disks are of two basic types: audio disks (often simply called *compact disks*) and videodisks. There are several ways information is stored and retrieved. Increasingly, laser beams are used. As the disks rotate, laser beams "read" information that has been stored. This information is converted to audio signals, in the case of audio disks, and to both audio and visual signals in the case of videodisks. Since only the laser beam strikes the disk, there is no physical abrasion. Optical disks will not wear

Box 11.3

Planning for Use of Videotaping Technology

Today many schools have videotaping equipment. Teachers use it to make video recordings of students. It is particularly useful when students are demonstrating a skill. Students can be videotaped and the tape played back so they can view their performances while the teacher critiques them.

Think about two or three lessons in your own teaching area in which you might use videotaping. Identify the topic and the specific skills you would be looking for.

Topic 1. _____

   Relevant Skill(s) _____

   _____

   _____

Topic 2. _____

   Relevant Skill(s) _____

   _____

   _____

Topic 3. _____

   Relevant Skill(s) _____

   _____

   _____

out as a conventional record will after repeated playing because of friction from the tone-arm needle.

Quality of audio-disk sound reproduction is superb when they are played through a sophisticated system. In some schools, they are used in the music department by instructors who wish to expose students to the best possible reproduction of the sounds of professional musicians. Generally speaking, however, audio disks have not been widely used in other secondary school subject areas.

Videodisks store both sight and sound signals. They are an attractive medium because tremendous quantities of information can be recorded on a single disk. Disks are easily stored.

Though still not widespread, videodisks may have potential to support instruction in many secondary school subjects. This is especially true of interactive videodisk systems. These are distinguished from other, non-interactive systems, which operate much like traditional record players. A videodisk is inserted, and it is simply played back in a predetermined sequence from beginning to end. Interactive units, on the other hand, allow users to vary the other, the speed, and the composition of the information that is played back.

Interactive videodisks involve a combination of videodisk technology and computer technology. They provide users with a great deal of flexibility. For example, specific portions of recorded programs can be identified quickly. Action can be slowed down so students can see how specific parts of complex processes are accomplished. Action can be stopped to permit time for student questions. Sequencing of information that is presented can be varied to meet the needs of specific lessons.

The flexibility of interactive videodisk technology suggests that it may play a larger role in secondary school programs in the years ahead. Present costs for the equipment are quite high, which is slowing the adoption processes. However, as the size of the market and the volume of production increase, prices may well go down. This is likely to be accompanied by increased purchases by middle schools, junior high schools, and senior high schools.

Electronic Satellite Links

Satellite technology is beginning to serve a number of technologies relevant to supporting instruction in the schools. For example, some interactive television signals are now transmitted from up links at sending stations, to communication satellites, and then down again to down links at receiving sites. A particularly interesting initiative using satellite technology is an effort begun with Project VSAT.

Project VSAT, which ended in June 1992, established the foundations for a nationwide interactive telecommunications network devoted to education ("Project VSAT," 1992). *VSAT* stands for "very small aperture terminal." VSAT technology makes possible the free exchange of data, voice, and video information. Since 1993, all PBS stations in the United States have been equipped with VSAT technology. Possible classroom applications of VSAT include:

- Classroom projects related to PBS broadcast programs.
- Use of educational data bases, including reference materials of interest to both students and teachers.
- Exchange of electronic mail among students and teachers throughout the nation.
- Downloading curriculum guides that have been prepared to help teachers make better classroom use of PBS programming.
- Providing a mechanism to facilitate interactive voice and data exchange among teachers and students in distance learning courses.

Table 11.1   Summary Table

Main Points	Explanation
Technological Competence	*Technological competence* implies a sophisticated understanding of new technologies. Students who are technologically competent when they leave school are (1) unafraid of new technology, (2) able to use technology, and (3) willing to master new technology as it becomes available. Increasingly our society requires employees to be technologically competent.
Rationales for Using Up-to-Date Technologies in Schools	These technologies greatly broaden teachers' instructional options as they seek to develop students' sophisticated thinking skills. These technologies also help students to become more aware of and more selective in their use of particular thinking strategies as they attempt to solve individual problems. Economic realities of today's workplace are placing increasing demands on workers to understand new technologies. Critics of the schools argue that schools have lagged far behind businesses and governmental offices in utilizing modern technologies.
The Nature of Newer Electronic Technologies	Many newer innovations have fewer moving parts than earlier innovations. This is because they depend on movement of electrons, not movement of mechanical parts. As a result, maintenance costs for some electronic innovations are less than for those developed in earlier years that featured large numbers of moving, mechanical parts.
Forces Opposing the Spread of New Technologies in Schools	Failures of teachers and schools to adopt some new technologies result from several reasons. Sometimes, people who introduce and recommend the innovations do not have to work with them on a daily basis. Some innovations, by their very nature, have tended to reduce teachers' instructional flexibility (e.g., some have required teachers to use the technology at preset times or to follow a prescribed sequence). Insufficient and undependable equipment has occasionally also caused teachers to lose faith in new technologies.
Examples of New Technologies	
Personal Computers	Personal computers have become available in nearly all secondary schools. Educational software has improved in quality tremendously in recent years. Computer-based learning techniques, particularly recent ones involving small-group instruction, are being used in growing numbers of secondary schools. Special computer data bases and electronic bulletin boards have allowed teachers and students to access quantities of information that were undreamed of a few years ago.

Main Points	Explanation
Examples of New Technologies, *cont'd.*	
CD-ROM	CD-ROM technology allows for the integration and management of tremendous volumes of information. A single CD-ROM disk can store as much information as a 250-volume set of reference books. Information from CD-ROM disks can be selectively retrieved and specifically tailored to meet the needs of individual students.
Interactive Videodisks	This technology allows visual and audio information to be stored on plastic disks. Specific bits of stored information can be retrieved and organized according to the needs of the teacher or learner. This allows lessons to be designed specifically for an individual student or a small number of individuals in a given class.
Interactive Distance Learning	Distance learning involves instruction that is delivered to students in a location other than where the instructor is teaching. Today, compressed video and other electronic means allow the teacher and the students to see and talk to one another. This technology makes it possible for students even in remote locations to be taught by outstanding instructors.
Videocassettes	Videocassette technology is now extremely widespread. Nearly all secondary schools have some videocassette playback units. The technology is very user friendly. Videocassettes are largely displacing 16mm instructional films. The cassette versions are much less expensive. Educational supply catalogs now contain tremendous numbers of videocassettes that have been specifically prepared for the secondary education market.
Optical Disks	Both audio and video versions of optical disks are available. The audio versions are generally referred to simply as *compact disks.* Laser beams "read" information on the disks as they rotate. Quality of sound reproduction is superb when signals are played back through sophisticated systems.
Electronic Satellite Links	Satellite technology is being used to connect many different kinds of instructional technologies. It allows a free exchange of information among teachers and students at a variety of geographic locations. VSAT technology is now in place at all PBS stations. It provides the foundation for a nationwide telecommunications network devoted to education.

Review of Key Ideas

- Because of international competition and changes in the workplace that are resulting in demands for employees with sophisticated technical skills, secondary schools are under increasing pressure to produce graduates who are technologically competent. This means that they should (1) be unafraid of new technologies, (2) be able to use new technologies, and (3) be prepared to master new technologies as they become available.

- Computers and other technologies increase the options available to teachers as they seek to develop students' sophisticated thinking abilities. There is some evidence that technology-based programs make students more aware of their own metacognitive processes. This means that students become more sensitized to their own thinking processes and more attuned to selecting processes appropriate to the assigned thinking task.

- Some critics allege that secondary schools have lagged behind private business and governmental agencies in adopting new technologies. There is some feeling that up-to-date technologies cannot be implemented one small step at a time. To maximize the potential of new technologies, heavy investment enabling electronic links among many related technologies and technological devices is needed.

- Many of the newer innovations depend on electronic rather than mechanical technologies. This feature allows for great speed of operation. Because electronic innovations lack the physically moving parts of innovations dependent on mechanical technologies, maintenance costs for these innovations are often lower.

- Historically, many innovations have failed to take root in the schools, despite glowing initial reports regarding their potential. Problems often have been associated with (1) methods used to introduce the change, (2) the peculiar nature of the individual innovation, and (3) the nature of teachers' working conditions. In particular, innovations have run into trouble when they have not been dependable and when they have tended to reduce teachers' flexibility regarding when and how the innovation should be used.

- Personal computers are among the most important and most widely used technological innovations in the schools today. Early concerns that too many machines would have to be purchased and that software was not particularly good have largely been overcome. Today, there are many group learning activities (allowing a number of students to use just one personal computer) available for teachers to use, and the quality of educational software has improved tremendously. Electronic data bases and systems to link computers at different sites through the use of electronic bulletin boards have greatly extended the instructional options of teachers who incorporate the use of computers into their lessons.

- CD-ROM is a powerful technology that allows integration and management of vast quantities of audio and visual information. Entire libraries of books can be stored on a single CD-ROM disk. Many private sector vendors now market CD-ROM disks that are specifically designed for use by teachers and students.

- Interactive videodisks allow audio and video material to be stored on disks. Linking videodisks to computers allows users to select particular parts of the stored information for playback. Teachers and students can develop learning materials that are designed to serve their own instructional and learning purposes.

- Advanced interactive distance learning systems allow teachers and students to see and talk to one another even though they may be separated by many miles. Hence, it is now feasible for students even in very remote locations to receive instruction from superior teachers and to interact with them much as if they were together in the same room.

- Other electronic technologies are also widely used in secondary schools. Videocassettes, optical disks (including both audio disks—usually called *compact disks*—and videodisks), and electronic satellite links are examples.

Follow-Up Questions and Activities

Questions

1. What is meant by the term *technological competence?*
2. What are some rationales for supporting an expanded emphasis on technology in secondary school programs?
3. How are many newer technological innovations different from those that appeared 10 or more years ago?
4. What are some phases or cycles that educational innovations often go through?
5. Why do some innovations that initially appear to have great promise fail to take root in the schools?
6. How can electronic data bases and electronic bulletin boards enrich secondary school instruction?
7. How is information recorded on CD-ROM disks?
8. What are some advantages of interactive distance learning systems for students in remote areas?
9. What are some instructional applications of videodisk technology?
10. In what ways may teachers and students benefit from VSAT technology?

Activities

1. Interview a principal (or a central office administrator who is familiar with school budgets). Ask this person to comment on the costs associated with purchasing personal computers and other electronic hardware and software to support instruction. How have these items been paid for? Have additional costs, if any, been worth it? Ask the person you interview to explain his or her answer to this last question.

2. Invite a panel of teachers to visit your class. Ask them to discuss ways they are now using personal computers in their work. Be sure to inquire about any problems they may be confronting now (and have confronted in the past). How have they responded to these problems?

3. New technologies to support instruction are becoming available with increasing frequency. Do some reading in the professional literature, then write a paper for your instructor on this topic: "The Technologically Up-to-Date Classroom in the Year 2010: What It May Look Like."

4. Some people argue that schools have been too slow to adopt new electronic technologies. Others take the contrary position, suggesting that schools often have rushed to buy technologically advanced equipment before it has demonstrated its merits. Organize a debate on this issue: "Resolved that schools' efforts to purchase technologically advanced equipment is driven more by a political fear that they will appear backward than by a real need for this equipment."

5. Make arrangements for four or five people in your class to contact several school district directors of personnel. (Exact titles may vary. You are looking for the person in charge of hiring new teachers.) Have these people inquire about personnel directors' expectations of new teachers in the area of technology. For example, try to find out which specific technologies new teachers are expected to be able to use beginning with their first day on the job. Present your findings to your class in a group report.

References

"American Students Learn French Using Telecommunications Link to France." *Tech Trends* (Number 5, 1991), p. 10.

BARLOW, J. "High Schools Aren't Working." *Houston Chronicle.* August 2, 1992, p. E1.

CHARP, S. "Editorial." *Technological Horizons in Education Journal* (August 1988), p. 8.

CUBAN, L. *Teachers and Machines: The Classroom Use of Technology Since 1920.* New York: Teachers College Press, 1986.

EDUCATION COMMISSION OF THE STATES. *Issuegram* No. 17. Denver: Education Commission of the States, 1983.

GRUNWALD, P. "The New Generation of Information Systems." *Phi Delta Kappan* (October 1990), pp. 113–114.

HAWKRIDGE, D. *New Information Technology in Education.* Baltimore, MD: The Johns Hopkins University Press, 1983.

JOHNSON, D. W.; JOHNSON, R. T.; HOLUBEC, E.; AND ROY, P. *Circles of Learning: Cooperation in the Classroom.* Alexandria, VA: Association for Supervision and Curriculum Development, 1984.

KURSHAN, B. AND DAWSON, T. "The Global Classroom: Reaching Beyond the Walls of the School Building." *Technology and Learning* (January 1992), pp. 48–51.

MCKERNAN, J. R., JR.; GIFFORD, B.; NIELSEN, B. S.; AND TUCKER, M. S. "Educating a World-Class Work Force." Program session presented at the National Forum and Annual Meeting of the Education Commission of the States, Cincinnati, OH. August 7, 1992.

MECKLENBURGER, J. A. "Educational Technology Is Not Enough." *Phi Delta Kappan* (October 1990), pp. 105–108.

PHILLIPO, J. "CD-ROM: A New Research and Study Skills Tool for the Classroom." *Electronic Learning* (June 1989), pp. 40–41.

"Project VSAT Linking America's Classroom by Satellite." *Tech Trends* (No. 1, 1992), p. 37.

SLAVIN, R. E. *Cooperative Learning: Theory, Research, and Practice*. Englewood Cliffs, NJ: Prentice Hall, 1990.

SOLOMAN, G. "Technology and the Balance of Power." *The Computing Teacher* (May 1992). *19*, pp. 10–11.

WASHOR, E. AND COUTURE, D. "A Distance Learning System that Pays All Its Own Costs." *T.H.E. Journal* (December 1990), pp. 62–64.

WATSON, B. "The Wired Classroom: American Education Goes On-Line." *Phi Delta Kappan* (October 1990), pp. 109–112.

Promoting Learning and Thinking

Demands being placed on graduates of the nation's high schools are higher than they have ever been before. In the future, they are likely to be higher still. Recently, a state task force on high school education made these comments.

> The traditional goals of a high school education—basic knowledge of academic subjects coupled with good citizenship and marketable skills—are not sufficient for the coming century. During the next century graduates will have to handle diverse information, perform effectively in cooperative work groups, solve complex problems, and continue to learn in a rapidly changing world and workplace. High quality, meaningful performance in these real world activities will be required of all graduates in the coming century. (*One Student at a Time*, 1992; p. 5)

Secondary school teachers increasingly are being asked to produce students who can think in sophisticated ways and participate with others to solve complex problems. Part 4 introduces a variety of approaches teachers can use to develop students' learning and thinking skills. Material in this part provides answers to questions such as these:

- What basic considerations go into all effective instructional planning?
- Under what conditions should direct instruction and indirect instruction approaches be used?
- What purposes can be served by cooperative learning and other small-group approaches, and what are the mechanics of implementing these approaches?
- What are teachers' responsibilities regarding students' attitudes and values?

Discussion related to these questions is introduced in five unit chapters:

Chapter 12: The Elements of Instruction

Chapter 13: Direct Instruction

Chapter 14: Indirect Instruction

Chapter 15: Small Groups and Cooperative Learning

Chapter 16: Affective Learning

REFERENCE

One Student at a Time (Executive Summary). Report of the State Board of Education Task Force on High School Education. Austin, TX: Texas Education Agency, October 1992.

The Elements of Effective Instruction

AIMS

This chapter provides information to help the reader to:

- Identify several of the key elements of effective teaching.
- State how key elements of instruction can be applied in the classroom.
- Point out implications the elements of good instruction have for lesson planning.
- Suggest ways in which basic principles of motivation can be applied to teaching.
- Explain the relationship between verbal and nonverbal communication.
- Point out the importance for teachers of self-evaluation.

FOCUS QUESTIONS

1. Do you believe teaching is basically an art or a science?
2. What are special characteristics of a proactive teacher?
3. How does teaching for multiple outcomes affect what teachers do?

4. How does prior knowledge affect what a student learns from an instructional sequence?

5. What is meant by "balancing depth and breadth" in the curriculum?

6. Why are some students motivated to learn in school while others are not?

7. What are some characteristics of verbal and nonverbal communication that can either make a message more clear or less clear?

8. What are some things teachers must do to use classroom questions to stimulate student thinking?

9. Why is the conclusion a particularly important part of a lesson?

10. What methods of self-evaluation can teachers use?

Introduction

How should people be prepared to teach in secondary schools? This question has been much debated. Some people argue that sound preparation in subjects to be taught is all that is needed. Supporters of this view sometimes question the value of professional education courses.

Another point of view holds that teaching is essentially an art. One is either born a "good" teacher or he is not. People who subscribe to this position also often question the value of courses in professional education. Their view is that good teaching abilities cannot be taught. If good teaching is not part of a person's basic personality structure, the individual will never become a good teacher by taking professional education courses.

Others reject both the idea that good teaching is a matter of mastering academic subjects and the idea that teaching is an art that cannot be taught to someone who is not born with the ability. They do acknowledge the importance of good subject matter knowledge, and they appreciate that personality variables may make it easier for some people to master effective teaching practices than others. Their most fundamental commitment, however, is to the idea that effective teaching skills can be taught and mastered; these skills, by and large, are not competencies people are born with.

A growing body of research literature is identifying teacher behaviors that are associated with good student learning. Research on teaching effectiveness has some limitations. Because educators work in many different settings, teach different subjects, work with diverse groups of students, and pursue a wide range of goals, principles associated with good teaching probably will never been as precisely defined and universally applicable as those in the physical sciences. However, research in this area has pinpointed some promising general patterns of teacher behavior. Evidence, too, mounts that these patterns can be transmitted to people interested in entering the teaching profession.

Box 12.1

Can a Person Be Taught to Become a Teacher?

These comments were made by a critic of teacher education programs:

Teacher education is frivolous. It takes students away from valuable courses in the academic subjects they will be expected to teach in the schools. Teaching is something that is intuitive. Individuals either have the ability or they don't. People who are 'born teachers' don't need the courses. People who lack this native ability won't benefit from them. Today's teachers should receive more training in their subject areas. They should take few, if any, education courses.

What Do You Think?

1. Is there a body of knowledge regarding teaching that is taught only in education courses?

2. Is lack of background in the subjects they teach a problem for many beginning secondary teachers? Why or why not?

3. What is your general reaction to the proposition that teaching competence is an innate ability that can be little influenced by courses in education?

This chapter identifies some general categories of effective teaching. This information is not a list of steps or recipes that will guarantee success. As noted in Chapter 3, teaching is a decision-making enterprise. Whether procedures outlined in the following sections are effective depends in the quality of the teacher's decisions. These are the sections:

- Proactive Teaching
- Goal-Directed Teaching
- Taking Prior Knowledge into Account
- Using the Social and Cultural Dimensions of the Class
- Scaffolding
- Balancing Depth and Breadth
- Motivating
- Clear Communication
- Teacher Questioning
- Reinforcement and Praise
- Practice
- Monitoring and Adjusting
- Lesson Conclusion
- Self-Evaluation

Proactive Teaching

Many teachers who experience success in the classroom are proactive. The proactive teacher is an active processor of information and a decision maker. This person accepts responsibility for content selection, planning, lesson presentation, and students' learning. For example, proactive teachers make many of their own decisions about content selection and sequencing. They monitor their students carefully and take care to design evaluation activities of their own to assess students' progress.

Proactive teachers enjoy their work and are confident both in their own ability to teach and their students' ability to learn (Rohrkemper and Good, 1987). They are committed to the idea that delivery of academic content is one of their primary responsibilities. Proactive teachers are task-oriented people who approach their work in a businesslike manner.

Goal-Directed Teaching

That teaching should be goal directed may seem obvious. However, there is evidence that some teachers present content without giving much thought to the overall purposes of their instruction (Good and Brophy, 1991). For example, a chemistry teacher might assign students to learn certain aspects of the periodic table with very little reflection as to why students need this information and what important longer-term goal might be served by lessons with this focus.

Instructional methods tend to be more effective when they are part of a comprehensive plan that features clear goals. Learning is particularly facilitated when goals are explained to students and when aspects of individual lessons are introduced in terms of their relationship to these goals.

Goal-directed instruction features lessons that incorporate teaching approaches and evaluation procedures that are appropriate to the goal. It provides a rationale for rejecting instructional approaches that are not suitable, given the nature of the goal that has been identified. For example, if a goal is selected requiring students to apply a skill, an evaluation procedure that required no application of the skill but simply some responses on a true-false test would not be appropriate.

Goal-directed teaching by no means implies that teachers are free to select one or two narrow goals and to focus all instructional planning on helping students achieve them. The kinds of skills, knowledge, and attitudes students need are complex. Hence, teachers must be prepared to direct their instruction toward large numbers of goals and toward many different kinds of goals.

The kinds of teaching practices useful for helping students reach some goals are quite different from teaching practices that help them achieve other goals. For example, lessons designed to teach students how to compare and contrast positions on a controversial issue are very different from those needed to teach them how to perform a psychomotor task such as throwing a pot on a potter's wheel.

Taking Prior Knowledge into Account

The prior knowledge students bring to the classroom clearly influences subsequent learning. The kinds of knowledge people have about subjects and the individual schemas or mental maps they have constructed to organize information influence what they learn from their lessons in school. Experts in learning psychology have found that students' failure to learn often is not a matter of their lacking essential information. Rather, they have failed to make new information fit into their preconceptions of how the world is. That is, the new knowledge may not make sense in light of what they already believe to be true; hence, they fail to master it (Leinhardt, 1992). This implies a clear need for teachers to present information in contexts that have meaning for their students.

Teachers, then, need to know not just how much prior knowledge about a topic students have, but how students have organized what they already know. This means that teachers must take the initiative to learn what their students believe reality to be. As a beginning point, instruction needs to tie to what students believe to be true. This kind of a link is a key to helping students master new information and, in time and as appropriate, to modify their conceptions of reality.

Using the Social and Cultural
Dimensions of the Class

Each class is a social system that has its own culture of ideas, meanings, norms, and accepted procedures. Teaching is not a matter of the teacher interacting with a single learner. Rather, the teacher's communication occurs within the social system context of her classroom. Peers can greatly influence students' reactions to instruction. It is clear that teaching approaches that take into account the social structure and the collective perspectives of students have more potential for success than techniques that fail to consider these variables.

For example, many students are more comfortable in learning situations that allow them to talk with and actively interact with other students. This social reality may account for the success many teachers have experienced when using cooperative learning and other small-group techniques, such as those introduced in Chapter 15.

Though there are important differences in the social characteristics of individual classes, many secondary school classes feature a culture that is more negatively disposed toward independent seat work and teacher lecture than toward activities demanding more active participation by all students. In general, students perceive interactive teaching to have more value than teaching that involves mostly a one-way channel of communication from teacher to students. This suggests a need for secondary school teachers to develop sound discussion leadership and group management skills as well as a solid grounding in the academic content of their subjects.

Scaffolding

In the context of teaching, a *scaffold* refers to a technique teachers use to help students bridge the gap between previous knowledge and new content. Scaffolds can take many forms. They may include such things as outlines of content to be covered, lists of questions in the form of think sheets (questions designed to help students tie new content to previous learning), and lists of questions organized on cue cards.

The specific scaffold used varies depending on lesson content and purpose. For example, a scaffold for a lesson in a high school literature class might include questions or prompts related to:

- Theme
- Main character
- Obstacles to be overcome
- How obstacles were mastered
- Implications

Students writing an essay might be provided with a think sheet prompting them to respond to a series of questions, including:

- What personal information do I already have about this topic?
- Why am I writing this?
- Whom am I writing this for?
- What am I supposed to explain?
- What is may main point?

A secondary science teacher might provide students with a set of cue cards as a prompt to help them write up experimental observations. Questions might include some of the following:

- What was the procedure?
- What was observed?
- What happened when I (we) did . . . ?
- How does this relate to what we have already learned?
- What probably caused this?
- What would happen if . . . ?
- What do I still not understand?

Scaffolds are best used when students have the needed prerequisite ability and skills for the new content but need some teacher guidance to master the material (Rosenshine and Meister, 1992). It is useful for the teacher to model the use of scaffolds before asking students to use them for the first time. An example should be provided, and the teacher should think aloud his probable responses to the prompt questions provided.

Some teachers find it useful to have students work in groups as they respond to scaffolding questions. This format allows students to talk to one another and for all to benefit from insights of others. Insecure students often benefit greatly from this approach. With some practice, students often are able to develop excellent prompt questions of their own. When this is done, they develop an important sense of ownership in the resultant learning activity.

Balancing Depth and Breadth

Depth of understanding is an important goal of effective teaching. This implies that it is better to treat fewer topics in some depth than to treat a larger number of topics superficially. The intent is to develop sophisticated thinking skills and to move learners beyond simple recall of large numbers of isolated facts.

Teaching that emphasizes depth of understanding requires teachers to focus on the most important ideas and to skim over or omit the rest (Brophy, 1992). This means that teachers must play an active role in selecting the content they include in their lessons. Textbooks and other learning resources often introduce enormous volumes of information. It is the teacher's task to pinpoint content that is really critical, to develop lessons that will enable students to grasp key principles and explanatory generalizations, and to decide exactly what information will be omitted entirely from lessons.

Development of sophisticated understanding takes time. Students cannot be expected to develop a sophisticated understanding of every item of content introduced in texts (and in other learning resources); there simply is not enough time. Teachers must make choices and establish priorities. These decisions are not easy.

For example, in many places students are required to take standardized tests. Newspapers often report scores, and often these scores are taken by the public as indicators of school quality. Standardized tests usually cover many topics. Teachers who restrict their content coverage to a small number of topics about which they expect students to develop sophisticated levels of understanding may well be concerned that their students will not score well on standardized tests that feature questions on topics their students have not been taught. Teachers in this kind of a situation need to be prepared to take a public position in support of the idea that teaching for sophisticated understanding and teaching for high standardized test scores are incompatible.

There is increasing evidence that students benefit more from instructional programs that develop sophisticated thinking skills and understandings than from those focusing on more superficial knowledge of a broader array of topics. Today's educators are encouraging development of assessment procedures that will provide better measures of the depth of students' understanding and the maturity of their thinking skills (Wiggins, 1989). In time, these more authentic assessment procedures may well displace some of the standardized tests that are still used in many school districts. For a more detailed explanation of authentic assessment, see Chapter 17, "Measuring Student Progress."

Motivating

Motivation is a key component of effective teaching. It is related to the kinds of academic tasks a student initiates, the direction he takes in pursuing it to completion, the intensity of work on the task, and the persistence to stay at the task until it is completed (Good and Brophy, 1991).

Many teachers today often say their students do not seem to be as highly motivated as those they had in the past. What these teachers are really saying is that these students do not seem as interested in the *things required of them in school*. There is no such thing as an unmotivated person. Everyone is motivated to do something. The problem teachers face is finding what motivates individual students and determining how these motivations can be used to interest students in school-related activities.

Despite the importance of motivation to learning, researchers have found that relatively few teachers take specific actions to motivate their students. Researcher Jere Brophy (1987) reported results of several key studies in this area. In one study, investigators found fewer than 5 percent of teachers took time to explain the purposes of their

This teacher is using an interesting artifact to interest students. Novel or unusual items often work well as motivators.

presentations to students. Another study found that none of the teachers who were observed took time to explain purposes of their presentations to students. In another investigation, researchers found that teachers failed to suggest to students that they might derive some personal satisfaction from learning the material. Researchers reported that in one long study involving observations in classrooms totaling more than 100 hours, there were only nine observed instances of teachers specifically trying to motivate students when new learning tasks were introduced.

The motivational problem is complex. What appears to be motivating to one group of students may be met with indifference by another group. However, there *do* appear to be some general concerns teachers can consider as they attempt to identify what motivates individual students and groups of students. These are:

- The unique interests and needs of the individual student.
- The perceived difficulty of the task.
- The degree to which the student perceives herself capable of succeeding at the assigned task (Klinger, 1977).

Needs and Interests

Students' personal needs and interests attract their attention and encourage them to focus their energies. Students are attracted to school lessons that they view as being responsive to their needs and interests. Teachers who develop such lessons often find that their classroom control problems diminish. Students who believe their teachers are trying to meet their needs rarely cause discipline problems. In his discussion of characteristics of quality schools, William Glasser (1986) emphasizes the importance of meeting students' needs in this way:

> A good school could be defined as a place where almost all students believe that if they do some work, they will be able to satisfy their needs enough so that it makes sense to keep working. (p. 15)

Students have been found to place three types of values on educational tasks that are assigned to them. These value categories include attainment value, interest or intrinsic value, and utility value (Eccles and Wigfield, 1985).

Attainment value refers to the importance of being successful for the purpose of meeting needs of power, attention, achievement, and enhancement of a person's self-concept. The general feeling of satisfaction a student gets from successfully completing an assignment also relates to attainment value. For example, some students spend time trying to succeed in such areas as drama or athletics. When they do, they accrue attainment value that is reflected in increased attention from others and in boosted levels of self-confidence. Because attainment value is important, teachers need to help students understand how successful completion of school learning tasks can improve their sense of personal power.

Interest or intrinsic value refers to the satisfaction a person gets from the process of engaging in a task. People do many things simply because the act of doing them is pleasant. For example, people play golf and other games even when they have no real expectation that their scores are going to improve as a result. (They're often happy when scores rise, but their willingness to continue playing is not contingent on this happening. They play because they enjoy the activity.) In the classroom, learning activi-

"I'll say one thing for that new economics teacher. He sure lowered *my* interest rate!"

Box 12.2

Responding to Students' Interests

A common complaint of secondary teachers is that their students are hard to motivate. Researchers have found that students' motivation increases when they see lessons at school tied to their interests and values. Consider this point as you respond to the following questions.

What Do You Think?

1. In general, what categories of things do you feel would appeal to middle school, junior high school, and senior high school students?

2. How might you use this information to generate interest in content of your subject area?

3. Can you cite some specific examples of how you might use the principles of attainment value, intrinsic value, and utility value to motivate your students?

---

ties that call upon students to talk to one another often have intrinsic value. The success of cooperative learning techniques (see Chapter 15 for details) may be largely attributed to its requirement that students talk to one another.

Utility value concerns students' perception of the importance of a given activity as an aid to achieving a larger purpose or goal. Schools sometimes have done a much better job of focusing on utility values in areas not directly tied to academic learning. For example, sometimes high schools prominently display pictures of graduates who went on to become athletic stars at major universities. This practice establishes an important attainment value link between hard work on school athletic teams and potential future success in college and university athletics. Perhaps schools should also consider displaying photographs of former graduates who are scientists, engineers, attorneys, physicians, and engaged in other roles requiring a strong academic background. Such photographs may help students see the utility of doing good academic work in their secondary school years.

The utility value is often reflected in questions students ask teachers such as: "Why do we have to do this?" "What good is this to me?" "Is this really relevant anymore?" Teachers need to be prepared for questions such as these. They need to have thought through how their subjects connect to their students' futures. A teacher response that tells a student nothing more than "you need to know this for the test" has little utility value for students. Few students will find this kind of a response a compelling reason to work hard to master the assigned content. Teachers who can provide students with more concrete examples of how mastery of content will be of some genuine personal value to students will have much better luck in getting students to take their learning tasks seriously.

Perceived Effort Required for Success

Even when students perceive a task as having value for them in terms of their own unmet needs, they may not engage the task seriously if they perceive the required effort to be too great. People have limited quantities of time and energy. Hence, they must make choices. In general, they choose activities that appear to provide the greatest benefits with the least effort. If a proposed task seems to require a too much effort, they often seek alternative ways to satisfy their needs.

Teachers need to pay close attention to students' perceptions of task difficulty. If large numbers of students are viewing a task as "too hard," it may make sense to reduce its complexity and length. Often this can be done by breaking a large task into smaller parts. This response often convinces students that the effort required to complete the task is more reasonable. Teachers who outline a task and carefully talk the class through some general approaches to the assignment tend to reduce anxieties students may have regarding task complexity and difficulty.

Once work on the task has begun, frequent teacher encouragement and feedback helps to assure students that they are capable of doing the assigned work. This kind of communication tends to maintain their momentum and helps them to complete what they have been asked to do.

Probability of Success

Few factors motivate people more than success. Everybody has a need to feel competent. It is important that each student feels "yes, I can do that" when the teacher assigns new work. Students who lack this kind of confidence may have come to this conclusion in several ways. Some students may simply feel that they lack sufficient intelligence to do the work. Others may be unsure of their abilities to compete successfully with others in the class. Still others may feel that they lack the necessary resources to do the work. This latter condition is particularly prevalent among students from low-income homes where money may not be available to purchase desirable supplementary materials (books, magazines, computer software, and so forth). These students may not do some assignments simply because they know they lack the resources and refuse to be publicly embarrassed by turning in work that will compare unfavorably with that of other students.

Students are particularly likely to develop concerns about their personal probability of success when grading procedures and learning activities are highly competitive. Some students conclude that such arrangements establish ground rules that will allow for only a few students to emerge as "winners." If a given student does not see himself as being among this elite group, he may lose interest in the learning task and even refuse to participate at all. More cooperative learning arrangements that are designed to make all group members responsible for transmitting key elements of content to every student sometimes help students to gain confidence in their abilities to succeed.

It makes sense, too, for teachers to be explicit about the criteria that will be used in evaluating success. When these criteria are explained clearly and when they are accompanied by supportive teacher comments regarding students' abilities to do the work, students tend to lose some of their fear of failure. Sometimes, too, it makes sense for the teacher to engage in interim assessments of students' progress. These allow students to receive feedback that assures them they are on the right track and making appropriate progress.

In establishing learning tasks, teachers work to develop assignments that are neither too easy nor too hard. Tasks that are too easy quickly lead to boredom, and boredom is a sure precursor of classroom control problems. Tasks that are too difficult lead to task avoidance, and they can poison student attitudes in ways that also can lead to management difficulties. Establishing appropriate levels of difficulty requires teachers to know their individual students well and to plan learning approaches that will maximize the learning effort of the largest number of students and genuinely extend students' levels of understanding.

Causal Attributions

Motivation is also influenced by students' feelings about what contributes to their successes and failures. Sometimes students attribute levels of performance to internal factors such as intelligence or unique physical characteristics. Sometimes they feel external factors such as "bad luck" or even "fate" play an important role.

Researchers have found that effort and persistence, two factors closely associated with motivation, are greater among students who attribute their levels of performance to internal rather than to external factors (Weiner, 1984). Students who believe that their successes and failures are due to bad luck, the whims of the teacher, or bad karma often will be reluctant to put forth much effort when new work is assigned. In their view, there is little relationship between how hard they work and what they learn; achievement is a matter largely out of their control.

Teachers need to help students develop clearer understandings of the relationship between their own levels of effort and learning. These are some of the things that teachers can do:

• Emphasize the relationship between effort and outcome. Make sure that effort has a payoff by establishing a clear connection in the grading system to make-up work, homework assignments, extra credit work, and other assigned tasks.

• Build students' self-confidence by emphasizing that they have the ability to succeed. Provide positive feedback when students successfully accomplish small steps en route to completing a larger goal.

• Allow students to set realistic goals for themselves.

• Help students take responsibility for learning through learning contracts or through other devices that establish time lines that encourage completion of assigned tasks.

• Allow opportunities for self-evaluation that help students to develop clear criteria for judging the adequacy of their progress.

- Provide instruction on learning how to learn.
- Help students to appreciate that ability is not a fixed trait and that it can be improved with learning and practice.
- Provide remedial instruction and plenty of support for discouraged students.

Clear Communication

Communication is the basis of all teaching. In the communication process, a sender has a message that needs to be sent. It is encoded in some way, and a channel for sending it is selected. It might be sent verbally, through the written or spoken word, or nonverbally through gestures, facial expressions, or touch. A sent message needs to be concise and logically organized. A spoken or written message must be free from ambiguous or vague terms, and it should be delivered with some intensity.

The receiver has to recognize that a message is being sent, and then he must decode or interpret it. Some students have difficulty in recognizing the teacher is sending an important message. This is true because the typical classroom is filled with large numbers of verbal messages that include a confusing mixture of important and unimportant information. For this reason, effective teachers often use marker expressions to alert students that something they are saying is especially important. ("The key idea here is. . . ." "You'll want to remember that. . . ." "It is important that we remember that. . . ." "Before we can go on to the new procedure tomorrow, everybody needs to be thoroughly familiar with this idea. Now listen carefully and ask questions if you don't understand.")

Students may have trouble interpreting some messages because the words and symbols may be unfamiliar or outside their range of experience. This is particularly troublesome when terms are used in highly specialized ways in certain subject areas but are used somewhat differently in ordinary conversation. For examples, the term *market* has a much more restricted meaning for economists that it does for most of us in our everyday speech. It is important for key terms to be defined and explained clearly to students.

Sometimes noise hinders the ability of listeners. Noise is defined as anything that interferes with the message. Sometimes spoken words are misunderstood. At other times, the sender's mannerisms confuse the listener and distort the message. Sometimes the person speaking is not well organized, goes off on tangents, and fails to move smoothly from point to point. When this happens, listeners may be very confused as to what the intended message was. Sometimes, too, noise from external sources makes it difficult for listeners to hear (a jet aircraft passing over a classroom, for example).

Effective teachers are well aware of problems associated with noise. To deal with this difficulty, they often include a feedback loop in their communication process. This is a fancy term for something that really is quite simple. After communicating with students, they tend to pause and ask someone in the class to summarize what has been said. This provides an opportunity for the teacher to check on student understanding and to correct any mistaken impressions resulting from noise interference of various kinds.

Box 12.3

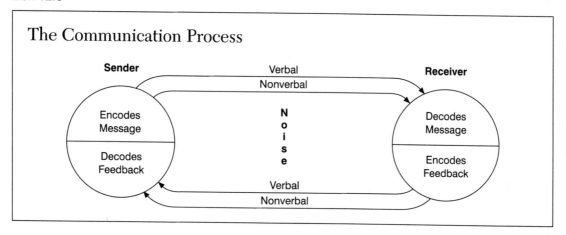

The Communication Process

Sender   Verbal   **Receiver**
Nonverbal

Encodes Message   **N o i s e**   Decodes Message

Decodes Feedback   Encodes Feedback

Verbal
Nonverbal

Nonverbal communication is very important in the classroom. Nonverbal communication often works in tandem with verbal communication to make up a complete message. Speakers' facial expressions, eye contact, gestures, body posture, rate of speech, and voice tone all affect the meaning obtained from verbal communication. It is particularly important that contents of the verbal message be consistently supported by accompanying nonverbal behaviors. When this does not happen, students tend to be confused and even to feel uneasy. For example a student might well be unsettled after a scowling teacher said, "I'm just delighted with the work you did on this project."

Nonverbal aspects of our behavior send important messages to students. For example, teachers' expectations of individual students often are revealed through nonverbal behavior. Teachers tend to stand further away from students for whom they hold low expectations and to display fewer positive nonverbal behaviors toward them than toward students for whom they hold high expectations (Smith, 1987).

Listening is another key communication skill for teachers. Good listening skills imply an ability to attend to both nonverbal and verbal messages. Teachers who are good listeners maintain good eye contact with students who are speaking, use facial expressions and gestures that imply an interest and understanding, use a relaxed body posture, and either lean toward or move toward the person who is speaking (Moore, 1992).

Active listening or paraphrasing is an important part of the listening process. This means that the listener sends back to the sender her interpretation of what has been said. Examples include phrases such as "Are you saying . . . ?" "I hear you saying . . ." and "The message I get is. . . ." Teachers who are good active listeners have trained themselves to pay close attention to what students have said. They must do this to summarize what has been said in a paraphrase that is repeated so the student can tell the teacher that he has understood the student's message correctly. Teachers who are good active listeners signal to students that they are taking their learners' comments seriously and that they sincerely want to base their reactions on an accurate understanding of what students have said.

Teacher Questioning

Good questioning behaviors have long been associated with effective teaching. As long ago as 1903, it was suggested that to question well was to teach well (DeGarmo, 1903). Years later, Mary Jane Aschner (1961) described teachers as "professional question askers."

Researchers, however, have found that the simple act of asking questions does not facilitate learning. Other associated variables play an important role. For example, the number of questions teachers ask during a class period has been found to influence learning. In one study, investigators found that more effective junior high school mathematics teachers asked an average of 24 questions during a 50-minute class period; less effective teachers asked an average of only 8.6 questions (Rosenshine and Stevens, 1986). It may be that frequent questions keep students alert. This is particularly likely to be true when, during a single class period, the teacher asks a high percentage of students in the class questions.

Through the years there have been many attempts to identify the characteristics of "good" questions. One approach has sought to classify questions in terms of their difficulty as measured by the sophistication of the student thinking they are designed to elicit. Questions that require only recall of previously learned information have been described as low-level questions (e.g., "What is the capital of Utah?" "Who wrote the story?"). More intellectually demanding questions have been referred to as higher-level questions ("How would you compare and contrast the advantages and disadvantages of the North and South at the beginning of the Civil War?" "What implications does this story have for our lives today?" "Which of these two policy alternatives is better, and what evidence supports your view?"). Although sometimes it is useful to make distinctions between lower-level and higher-level questions, it does not follow that higher-level questions are always "better" than lower-level questions. In some situations, lower-level questions are better instructional choices. In general, the excellence of a questioning strategy relates to each of the following:

- The purpose of the question
- The clarity of the question
- The nature of the student response
- The length of the wait time

Question Purpose

A question that is appropriate under one set of conditions may be inappropriate under another. Researchers have found that if the teacher's purpose is to check students' understanding of basic information, then most questions should be lower level. There should be a simple pattern involving (1) a lower-level teacher question, (2) a student answer, and (3) immediate feedback from the teacher in response to the student.

The cycle reflected in this pattern should be repeated at a brisk pace. This is true for several reasons. Lower-level questions tend to be short. Students require little thinking time before responding. Typically answers are short and to the point. This allows the teacher to ask many questions. When the teacher maintains a brisk pace students stay alert, and the teacher can direct questions to a high percentage of class members. This allows the teacher to gain important insights into levels of understanding of large numbers of students.

When the purpose is to stimulate critical or creative thought, a different pattern of questioning that includes use of higher-level questions is appropriate (Redfield and Rousseau, 1981). This kind of questioning requires teachers to pay close attention to students' prior knowledge. It may be necessary to ask some lower-level questions to establish an adequate information base before asking higher-level questions. Once a necessary information base has been established, higher-level questions should clearly signal to students what is expected of them. Because higher-level questions require complex thought, students need time to think about them before responding. Hence, the pace of questioning is slower than when lower-level questions are used as a quick check on students' recall.

Several authorities have described ways of categorizing higher-level questions. One framework involves eight different types of higher-level questions. They are (Marzano, 1992):

- Comparison questions
- Classification questions
- Induction questions
- Deduction questions
- Error-analysis questions
- Constructing-support questions
- Abstracting questions
- Analyzing-perspectives questions

Comparison questions focus students' attention on similarities and differences. It includes questions such as: "How would you compare these two things? How are they the same? How are they different?"

Classification questions require students to group items according to characteristics they share. Questions in this category include examples such as: "Which items could be grouped together and why?" "What are common characteristics of items in this group?" "What rules could you state that would tell what qualities something must have to be included in this group?"

Induction questions ask students to draw conclusions or make inferences based on their study of specific information. Students are required to seek relationships among specific items and to develop explanatory principles or generalizations. These are some questions of this type: "How can you explain the similarities and differences you have observed?" "What general rule would explain what you have discovered?"

Deduction questions might be thought of as requiring a pattern of thinking that reverses that required to answer induction questions. In an induction question, students begin by examining isolated pieces of information and then go on to develop a general explanation. In an deduction question, students begin with a general explanatory principle and then determine whether specific pieces of information are consistent with it. Here are some examples of questions of this type: "Based on the principle that each action has an equal and opposite reaction, what would you expect if we . . . ?" "What examples of adaptation did you observe in the film?"

Error-analysis questions require students to look for possible errors of logic or procedure. Questions in this category can help students identify propaganda and other examples of data distortion. Here are some examples: "In what ways is the conclusion in error?" "What would be a more defensible procedure for finding an answer?" "What critical information has been ignored by the person who arrived at this conclusion?" "What evidence would contradict this conclusion?"

Constructing-support questions ask students to look for information to support a position that has been taken. Examples include: "What other evidence would support this claim?" "Under what conditions might the argument be valid?" "What logical arguments could support this conclusion?"

Abstracting questions ask students to identify patterns and to relate them to new or different content. Often these questions include analogies and metaphors. Here are some examples: "What patterns did you notice in the development of the plot of the short story we finished yesterday, and how are these patterns similar to those we've encountered so far in the one we've read today?" "How is identifying a good idea in a paragraph like panning for gold?" "How might the old saying 'Love is blind' apply to this situation?"

Analyzing-perspectives questions ask students to identify their personal positions and to consider the merit of other views. Questions in this category help students to focus on the particular values different individuals prize. Some examples include: "What are the assumptions you make when you take that position?" "How would your conclusion differ if you held another set of assumptions?" "If you were a Native American living in the nineteenth century, how might you have viewed Manifest Destiny, and why?"

Question Clarity

"Good" questions must be stated clearly. Unclear questions confuse students because many plausible answers are possible. Consider this question: "Who was the first President of the United States?" Because of the imprecision of the question, students logically might answer "a man," "a Virginian," "a general," "a farmer," or "George Washington."

Students would have been much better served had this question been phrased in a way that better cued them to the teacher's real intention. For example, the teacher might have asked: "What was the name of the first President of the United States?" This version is likely to elicit the kind of answer the teacher is looking for.

Box 12.4

Developing Clear Questions

Vague and ambiguous questions confuse students. Such questions can be a real hindrance to learning.

Observe a class and write down several questions that are asked. From your list of questions, choose five examples of poorly phrased questions. Identify the problem with each, and rewrite it to enhance its clarity.

1. Original question: _____

    _____

    Problem: _____

    Revision: _____

    _____

2. Original question: _____

    _____

    Problem: _____

    Revision: _____

    _____

3. Original question: _____

    _____

    Problem: _____

    Revision: _____

    _____

4. Original question: _____

    _____

    Problem: _____

    Revision: _____

    _____

Clarity is enhanced when the teacher sets the stage and establishes a context for a question (Cazden, 1986). For example, the teacher might begin with a low-level question to help students develop a general focus on a broad topic ("Where is Chicago located on the map?"). This could be followed by a higher-level question related to this general topic ("How do you account for Chicago's development at that particular geographic spot?").

Asking multiple questions before giving students opportunities to answer poses problems. When teachers do this, students often become confused because they don't know which question the teacher really wants them to answer. Discussions are much more productive when teachers ask a single question and listen to and comment on student answers before asking new questions.

Nature of Student Responses

A successful questioning strategy features participation by a high percentage of students in the class, and most student responses are correct or appropriate. When the teacher's purpose is to review material with students, at least 80 percent of students' responses should be correct. If the success rate is lower, the teacher may have assumed students know more than they do and may need to spend more time preparing them for the review. A low success rate sometimes also is an indication that the teacher's questions are not clearly stated.

Wait Time

What a teacher does after asking a question has an important influence on how much students profit from a lesson featuring teacher questions. *Wait time* refers to the time after the teacher asks a question and (1) a student is recognized and answers, (2) the teacher goes to another student who answers, or (3) the teacher rephrases the question or gives up and asks another question. Mary Budd Rowe, who has conducted extensive research on wait time, has found that teachers' wait time, on average, is less than one second. There is evidence that increasing wait time tends to do the following (Rowe, 1986):

- Increase the probability a student will answer the question.
- Increase the length of student responses.
- Increase the likelihood that student responses will involve speculative thinking.
- Improve students' self-confidence.
- Increase the number of student-initiated questions.
- Increase the total number of students participating in a discussion.

Increasing wait time also seems to affect teachers' behavior as well. Teachers who increase their wait times tend to ask more higher-level questions and to develop more positive attitudes toward students.

Reinforcement and Praise

Proper use of reinforcement and praise can contribute to the development of a positive learning environment. Individuals who feel they receive some personal benefit from what they have done tend to persist in the behavior pattern that yielded this result. In schools, reinforcers can help build more positive attitudes toward learning. Praise is a particular type of reinforcement that works well with many learners.

Reinforcement

An important learning principle associated with reinforcement is that a behavior that is followed by a desirable consequence will be strengthened and is likely to occur again. Successful reinforcers in the classroom help students develop more positive attitudes toward their teachers, learning, and themselves. There are important characteristics of reinforcers that teachers need to know in preparation for using them with their own students.

First, what is reinforcing to one person may not be reinforcing to another. What the teacher views as a "desirable consequence" may not be seen in that light at all by some students. Efforts to encourage certain student behaviors by using reinforcers that are not prized by students will not be successful. Indeed, they can lead students to behave in undesirable ways (Good and Brophy, 1991). An implication of this finding is that teachers need to know their students well. They must understand individual student likes and dislikes. Armed with this information, they can select reinforcers students will prize.

In general, reinforcers that involve natural social behavior reactions tend to be more effective than tangible rewards. For example, it is more appropriate for a teacher to make natural, positive comments to students who do well than to toss bits of candy to them as a reward for good work. Secondary students often will reject such obvious efforts at manipulation. They are much more likely to respond well to encouraging words from a sincere teacher whose opinions they have come to value.

The peer group is a particularly important source of reinforcers for adolescents. Many students react much more enthusiastically to reinforcers they receive from their friends than those received from adults, including teachers. This by no means implies teachers cannot use reinforcement effectively. It does suggest, however, that there are competing sources of reinforcers that many students, initially at least, may value more than those provided by teachers.

Praise

Praise is a commonly used form of reinforcement. Used properly, praise can exert a positive influence on students' behaviors. To be effective, however, certain guidelines must be followed. For example, too much gushy teacher praise to a student in front of his peer group may result in taunts from fellow students that completely undo the teacher's intent. Also, praise that is highly generalized and not tied to a specific student action may have little impact at all.

Researchers have found that some teachers give praise when it is not deserved. This is particularly likely to happen when the teacher is working with low-achieving students or with individuals identified as "problem students" (Good and Brophy, 1991). When this is done, these teachers may be operating under the assumption that these students need some positive rewards and that they are unlikely to earn them by engaging in behaviors characterizing better students. There are important problems with this approach.

If a student is praised occasionally for a behavior that is not meritorious, she receives little guidance regarding what good or appropriate behavior is. The reinforcement is not directed at promoting a consistently productive way of behaving. Second, undeserved praise often is recognized as such by the receiving student and by his friends. This can lower the student's self-esteem. The real message the teacher appears to be sending is that this individual is incapable of doing really good work.

Good and Brophy (1991; p. 213) suggest some guidelines for using praise effectively in the classroom. They include these ideas:

- Deliver praise naturally without gushing or over-dramatization.
- Be "genuine" when praising students.
- Identify the specific student behavior that is being praised. (Avoid general praise statements such as, "You did a good job.")
- When possible, praise students in private to avoid embarrassment.
- Praise students for behaviors over which they can exercise personal control. (This builds a sense of self-control in support of appropriate behaviors.)
- Use a variety of praise statements to avoid dulling the impact of what is said through overuse of the same words and phrases.
- Combine verbal praise with consistent nonverbal behaviors that signal approval.

Practice

Some practice is required for students to master new knowledge. Important principles that can make practice more effective include:

- Practice should include some novelty or variety. Otherwise, students are likely to become bored.
- Spaced practice is superior to massed practice. Breaking practice tasks into smaller parts and distributing time of practice greatly enhances motivation.
- Practice with supervised reactions from the teacher should precede independent practice. This allows the teacher to correct mistakes.

WHAT SCHOLARS SAY

The Effectiveness of Homework

Some critics of education contend that American teachers require too little homework. They point out that much more is required in other nations, where students often have done better on tests of learning than have American students. This concern has led some people to use amount of homework required as one measure of a school's overall quality.

What is the role of homework in learning? How much homework is best? These questions were addressed in a review of research completed by Herman Cooper (1989). Cooper found evidence that homework generally has a positive influence on student achievement, but that this effect varies depending on students' ages. Homework seems to have the most impact on the achievement of senior high school students. It has somewhat less of an effect on middle school and junior high school students. For pupils in elementary schools, the amount of homework assigned has only a marginal relationship to what these young children learn.

Length of homework assignments also makes a difference on what students learn. For junior high school students, academic achievement generally increases when length of homework increases to somewhere between one and two hours a night. Longer homework assignments for these students do not continue to be associated with improved learning. Senior high school students' improvement continues to be evident even when homework assignments require more time than those that seem to be at the outer limit of benefits for junior high school students.

Monitoring and Adjusting

As they teach lessons, effective teachers carefully monitor students and make necessary adjustments to assure students are understanding the new content. Monitoring for understanding can be accomplished in several ways. For example, the teacher may ask questions of individual students or ask them to paraphrase what they have learned. Students of differing ability levels need to be involved so the teacher gains a sound appreciation of general levels of understanding of all class members. When these actions reveal misunderstandings, the teacher needs to take time to clarify information.

Adjusting or reteaching is necessary when the teacher determines that students are failing to grasp the new information. Adjustments may take several forms. For example, it may be sufficient for basic information simply to be repeated. Sometimes, an entirely new approach to presenting information may be required. (For example, if students were asked to read new material the first time, the teacher may find a short lecture, supported by a few visual aids, more appropriate during an adjusted version of the lesson.)

Lesson Conclusion

Prospective teachers sometimes fail to appreciate the importance of the conclusion of their lessons. Students often remember best information that is presented at the very end of an instructional sequence. Hence, it is important that the lesson conclusion (sometimes called the lesson *closure*) be well planned. Key points students will be expected to remember should be highlighted at this time. Often teachers call upon individual students to recall and share their recollections of important information. The teacher corrects and supplements details provided by the students.

The lesson conclusion also helps build a bridge to content to be introduced in the next lesson. This helps to establish continuity across the instructional program and assists students to recognize relationships among the various content components of a complete instructional unit.

Good lesson conclusions require time. This time needs to be anticipated in teacher planning. It is a mistake for an entire instructional period to pass without setting aside time at the end for a conclusion that will help students draw new information into a coherent whole and to anticipate the relevance of what has been studied now for what is to follow.

Self-Evaluation

Effective teachers are reflective teachers. Reflective teachers engage in a continuous process of self-evaluation. The process of self-evaluation is a simple one. Often, it involves little more than systematic attention to several questions, such as:

- Did the students learn what I expected them to learn?
- How do I *know* what they learned?
- What went well today? What did the students find confusing? How might I eliminate this confusion in a future lesson?

Some teachers find it convenient to write answers to these questions (and others they might devise) on the lesson plan form that guided their instruction. These forms can be reviewed later and any needed changes can be built into future planning.

Sometimes teachers find it useful to engage in more formal efforts to gather information about their teaching. This might be done by making audiotapes or videotapes of lessons. These can be reviewed later and critiqued. Sometimes other teachers are invited to observe and take notes. Their reactions can also be an important data source in the self-evaluation process.

Table 12.1   Summary Table

Main Points	Explanation
Proactive Teaching	Proactive teaching features a teacher who is an active decision maker who willingly accepts responsibility for content selection, planning, lesson presentation, and student learning.
Goal-Directed Teaching	Goal-directed teaching is planned, delivered, and evaluated in terms of its relevance for important goals that are part of a comprehensive plan guiding the instructional program.
Taking Prior Knowledge into Account	Students have certain preconceptions they bring with them to any lesson. These preconceptions act as filters that tend to shape their understanding. Teachers need to understand these preconceptions, correct them when they are causing mistaken understandings, and take advantage of any features of these unique student characteristics that may facilitate learning.
Using the Social and Cultural Dimensions of the Class	To some extent, students' reactions to instruction are influenced by the general attitudes of other students in the class. Effective planning takes into consideration these important peer pressures. In many classrooms, there is a peer consensus around the idea that highly interactive group learning is preferable to whole-class instruction that is dominated by the teacher. For this reason, cooperative learning techniques often work well.
Scaffolding	Scaffolding techniques are used by teachers to build bridges between students' previous knowledge and new content. Scaffolds include lists of questions, cue cards, and content outlines.
Balancing Depth and Breadth	Encouraging students to acquire in-depth understanding of topics they have been taught is an important teaching aim. Learning for depth of understanding takes time, and time is a limited commodity in the schools. This means that teachers must establish priorities and assign more time to those topics that are considered particularly worthy and which students should learn especially well. To achieve depth, there must be some sacrifice of breadth of coverage. In general, it is preferable to reduce the number of total topics taught to allow students to develop sophisticated levels of understanding than to introduce a tremendous number of topics that can be mastered only superficially.
Motivating	Motivation is a component of teaching that influences how students apply themselves to their tasks and what they learn. It is greatly influenced by students' needs and interests, the perceived difficulty of the assigned tasks, and whether students really believe themselves capable of completing the work.
Clear Communication	Clear communication is an essential ingredient of effective instruction. Verbal and written messages to students need to be clear, concise, and free from ambiguous or vague terms. It is important that "noise," anything that interferes with the message, is minimized and that verbal and nonverbal communication are consistent.

Table 12.1   Summary Table *(continued)*

Main Points	Explanation
Teacher Questioning	Good questioning behaviors have long been associated with effective teaching. Among variables related to questioning that influence student learning are: (1) the number of questions teachers ask, (2) the consistency of the question with the teacher's purpose, (3) the length of teacher wait time (time after a question has been asked before (a) a student answers, (b) the teacher calls on someone else, or (c) the teacher rephrases the question, asks another question, or answers his or her own question), and (4) the clarity of the question. Among kinds of questions teachers ask are the following: (1) comparison questions, (2) classification questions, (3) induction questions, (4) deduction questions, (5) error-analysis questions, (6) constructing-support questions, (7) abstracting questions, and (8) analyzing-perspectives questions.
Reinforcement and Praise	Reinforcement is a learning principle that states that a behavior followed by a desirable consequence will be strengthened and will be likely to occur again. Praise is a type of reinforcer widely used in the classroom. To be effective, reinforcement of all kinds, including praise, needs to be provided in support of clearly desirable patterns of behavior. What reinforces one student may not reinforce another. This suggests that teachers need to diagnose characteristics of individuals in their classes to learn what kinds of responses will be considered reinforcing by each student.
Practice	Students must practice what they have learned to make new content truly their own. Researchers have discovered these principles: (1) practice should include some novelty or variety, (2) spaced practice of relatively short duration is preferable to longer periods of massed practice, and (3) practice should begin with teacher supervision before students are asked to practice independently.
Monitoring and Adjusting	Effective teachers carefully monitor students while they teach. By calling on and observing individuals, they learn how well they are getting through to students. As needed, they adjust their instruction when they determine students are not understanding.
Self-Evaluation	Effective teachers engage in a good deal of self-evaluation. This involves reflection on what they have done in the classroom with a view to self-improvement. Some questions that typically guide self-evaluation include: (1) "Did the students learn what I expected them to learn?" (2) "How do I know what they learned?" and (3) "What went well today? What did the students find confusing? How might I eliminate this confusion in a future lesson?"

Review of Key Ideas

- Effective teaching requires a good grounding in what is to be taught. In addition, there is some artistry involved in the process. Researchers have identified elements of good teaching that can be learned by individuals planning to enter the profession. Even people with high levels of natural ability as teachers can be taught to perform at higher levels.

- Proactive teachers are active information processors and decision makers. They take personal responsibility for selecting what is taught, organizing presentations, and student learning. They do not rely on others (e.g., textbook authors and so forth) to make these decisions for them. They are confident in their own abilities to make decisions that are "right" for students.

- Instructional methods are more effective when they are part of a comprehensive plan featuring clear goals. Students do better when teachers explain goals to them and when their planning clearly reflects attention to these goals. Goal-directed teaching helps teachers to select instructional approaches that are well-matched to the goals that are pursued.

- The prior knowledge students bring with them to any learning situation affects what they will learn when new content is introduced. Effective teachers work to understand the schemas or mental maps their students have constructed to explain reality. They try to link instruction to students' understanding and to help students modify patterns of understanding that interfere with accurate interpretations of new information.

- Classroom instruction takes place within the cultural context of the classroom. The influence of a student's peers greatly affects the student's attitudes and what she learns. In many classrooms, the prevailing culture strongly supports instructional approaches that are highly interactive and that involve opportunities for students to talk as members of work groups. When appropriate, it makes sense for teachers to design lessons to take advantage of the cultural characteristics of their classrooms.

- The term *scaffolding* is used to describe specific steps teachers take to build bridges between students' previous knowledge and new content. These may include outlines of content to be covered and lists of questions that help students see relationships between new material and what they have learned previously.

- One purpose of effective teaching is to promote depth of understanding. Researchers have found that this is most likely to occur when a small number of topics are studied intensively than when a large number of topics are studied more hastily. Sophisticated levels of understanding take time to develop.

- Motivation is a key characteristic of effective instruction. Despite its importance, researchers have found that few teachers take actions that are specifically designed to motivate students. In thinking about what to do to motivate members of a class, teachers need to consider (1) the unique interests and needs of individuals, (2) how difficult individual students are likely to perceive a given assigned task to be, and (3) the degree to which individual students perceive themselves as capable of succeeding at the assigned task.

- Clarity of oral and written communication is a hallmark of effective teachers. They select words carefully to avoid ambiguity, check with students to make sure they have grasped the essentials of the message, and take action to eliminate noise (environmental factors of various kinds that interfere with clear reception of a message).

- Questioning is an important component of many teaching strategies. Teachers who are good questioners are careful to assure that their questions tie closely to their instructional purposes, are stated clearly, are appropriate given the level of thinking sought, and take into account student responses. These teachers also provide sufficient wait time, silent time that allows the student to think about what has been asked before responding aloud to the teacher.

- Teachers who use appropriate reinforcement and praise in the classroom create positive environments for learning. In planning to use reinforcers, teachers should recognize that something that will be seen as reinforcing by one student may not be reinforcing to another. This means that teachers must take time to learn about likes and dislikes of individual members of their class. Praise is a form of reinforcement that is effective with many students. To be effective, praise must be tied to a specific behavior. ("You got all the math problems right. Congratulations!" *not* "Good work.") To be effective, praise must be genuine. Often it is best to deliver it privately. Some students may experience negative reactions from fellow students if the teacher lavishes praise on them in front of the whole class.

- Providing opportunities for students to practice what they have learned enhances their levels of competence. Effective practice requires students to do something new or novel with the information, not to simply parrot what they have been taught. Practice that is dosed out in small quantities over a longer period of time is more effective than long periods of concentrated practice in a shorter period of time. It is best for initial practice to take place under conditions where the teacher can monitor students and provide corrective feedback when mistakes are made.

- Effective teachers carefully monitor students at the same time they introduce new material. They may ask questions or take other actions to assure that the class is grasping the information. When problems are observed, the teacher makes adjustments in the lesson to reintroduce material that students have failed to understand.

- The conclusion of a lesson is a critical component of the instructional sequence. Students often remember best what they experience at the end of a lesson. At this time, it makes sense for the teacher to reemphasize key points and to check with individual students to assure they have understood. In planning lessons, teachers should allocate time for the conclusion and avoid the temptation to use this time for another purpose. When teachers overlook the need to summarize important information for students in a systematic way at the end of a lesson, students' levels of learning are not likely to be as high as they otherwise might be.

- Effective teachers are reflective teachers. They engage in a continuous process of self-evaluation, asking questions such as: "Did the students learn what I expected them to learn?" "How do I know?" "What might I do better next time?" Sometimes teachers record their classes or have another teacher sit in and take notes. Information from these sources is considered as the teacher thinks carefully about the effectiveness of his performance.

Follow-Up Questions and Activities

Questions

1. What is meant by *proactive teaching*?
2. Why is it important for teachers to take into account students' prior knowledge?
3. What are some influences on student learning of the social and cultural dimensions of the classroom?
4. Why is scaffolding important?
5. Why is motivating students difficult, and what do teachers need to consider as they try to motivate their students?
6. What are some things that interfere with clarity of communication, and what can teachers do to overcome them?
7. This chapter introduces types of questions teachers ask. Which of these types do you think are asked most often, and why?
8. Why do you think it is so hard for teachers to wait for a student answer after they have asked a question?
9. Why is it important for teachers to know characteristics of individual students when deciding on which reinforcers to use?
10. What do you think could be done to help teachers become more reflective?

Activities

1. Interview a teacher who teaches in your area of interest. Ask the teacher to comment on specific kinds of misconceptions and misunderstandings students have often had. How has the teacher responded to these understandings? Share your information in your class as part of a general discussion on approaches to dealing with students' prior knowledge.

2. As an observer in a secondary school classroom, look for examples of teacher attempts to motivate students. How many such instances did you observe? At what points of the lesson did they occur? How did students respond? Specifically, what did the teacher do in each case? Prepare a short written report for your instructor.

3. Interview several secondary students. Ask them this question: "What does it take to get good grades in your school?" Share responses with members of your class. If large numbers of students you interview have attributed good grades to luck or to

something other than hard personal effort, what might a teacher do to encourage students to seriously commit to assigned learning tasks? Share your views with others in the class.

4. Look at each of the eight question categories introduced in this chapter. Using a subject you wish to teach as a source of content, develop one question of each type. Share them with others in the class, and ask them to critique them for clarity.

5. Design a procedure you might use to evaluate your own teaching. Be sure your design will provide information related to topics that are of real concern to you. Make arrangements to have someone videotape you while you teach a lesson. Have someone use your procedure to provide information to you regarding your performance. Critique your lesson in terms of the design you developed.

References

ASCHNER, M. J.; GALLAGHER, J.; PERRY J.; AND ASFAR, S. *A System for Classifying Thought Processes in the Conduct of Classroom Verbal Interaction.* Urbana, IL: The University of Illinois, 1961.

BROPHY, J. "On Motivating Students." In D. C. Berliner and B. V. Rosenshine (eds.). *Talks to Teachers.* New York: Random House, 1987.

BROPHY, J. "Probing the Subtleties of Subject-Matter Teaching." *Educational Leadership* (April 1992), pp. 4–8.

CAZDEN, C. "Classroom Discourse." In M. Wittrock (ed.). *Handbook of Research on Teaching.* 3rd ed. New York: Macmillan Publishing Company, 1986, pp. 432–463.

COOPER, H. "Synthesis of Research on Homework." *Educational Leadership* (November 1989), pp. 85–91.

DeGARMO, C. *Interest in Education: The Doctrine of Interest and Its Concrete Application.* New York: Macmillan, 1903.

ECCLES, J. AND WIGFIELD, A. "Teacher Expectations and Student Motivation." In J. Dusek (ed.). *Teacher Expectancies.* Hillsdale, NJ: Erlbaum, 1985.

GLASSER, W. *Control Theory in the Classroom.* New York: Harper & Row, 1986.

GOOD, T. AND BROPHY, J. *Looking in Classrooms.* 5th ed. New York: HarperCollins, 1991.

KLINGER, E. *Meaning and Void: Inner Experiences and the Incentives in People's Lives.* Minneapolis, MN: University of Minnesota Press, 1977.

LEINHARDT, G. "What Research on Learning Tells Us About Learning." *Educational Leadership* (April 1992), pp. 20–25.

MARZANO, R. *A Different Kind of Classroom: Teaching with Dimensions of Learning.* Alexandria, VA: Association for Supervision and Curriculum Development, 1992.

MOORE, K. *Classroom Teaching Skills.* 2nd ed. New York: McGraw-Hill, 1992.

REDFIELD, D. AND ROUSSEAU, E. "A Meta-Analysis of Experimental Research on Teacher Questioning Behavior." *Review of Edcational Research* (Summer 1981), pp. 237–245.

ROHRKEMPER, M. AND GOOD, T. L. "Proactive Teaching." In M. Dunkin (ed.). *The International Encyclopedia of Teaching and Teacher Education.* New York: Pergamon Press, 1987, pp. 457–460.

ROSENSHINE, B. AND MEISTER, C. "The Use of Scaffolds for Teaching Higher-Level Cognitive Strategies." *Educational Leadership* (April 1992), pp. 26–33.

ROSENSHINE, B. AND STEVENS, R. "Teaching Functions." In M. Wittrock (ed.). *Handbook of Research on Teaching*. 3rd ed. New York: Macmillan Publishing Company, 1986, pp. 376–391.

ROWE, M. B. "Wait Time: Slowing Down May Be a Way of Speeding Up." *Journal of Teacher Education* (January-February 1986), pp. 43–50.

SMITH, H. "Nonverbal Communication." In M. Dunkin (ed.). *The Encyclopedia of Teaching and Teacher Education*. New York: Pergamon Press, 1987, pp. 466–475.

WEINER, B. "Principles for a Theory of Motivation and Their Application within an Attributional Framework." In R. Ames and C. Ames (eds.). *Research on Motivation in Education. Volume 1: Student Motivation*. Orlando, FL: Academic Press, 1984.

WIGGINS, G. "Teaching to the (Authentic) Test." *Educational Leadership* (April 1989), pp. 41–47.

13

Direct Instruction

This chapter provides information to help the reader to:

- Define *direct instruction*.
- Cite some claimed advantages and disadvantages of direct instruction.
- Identify kinds of objectives for which direct instruction is appropriate as well as those for which it is not appropriate.
- Explain each component of the direct instruction model.
- Apply the direct instruction model to specific instructional situations.

FOCUS QUESTIONS

1. Are there some teaching approaches that are better than others in all situations? Why or why not?
2. What distinguishes a direct instruction lesson from other kinds of lessons?

3. What types of objectives are best served by direct instruction?

4. What kinds of students have been found to profit most from direct instruction?

5. What is the purpose of a daily review?

6. What does a teacher need to consider when planning ways to introduce content to a specific group of students?

7. How should a teacher respond to different types of student responses to questions?

8. What are some alternative ways a teacher can check for student understanding?

9. Why should guided practice precede independent practice?

Introduction

Direct instruction is probably the most widely used instructional approach. A large body of research supports its effectiveness in certain situations (Good and Brophy, 1991). In part, the popularity of direct instruction stems from its effectiveness in teaching students the basic information often evaluated on standardized tests. Direct instruction features a teacher-centered mode of presentation that closely parallels what many teachers experienced as college and university students. Parents remember this kind of teaching from their own school days, and many of them presume that tradition has imbued this approach with a certain legitimacy.

In preparing for the content in this and the chapters that follow, you might wish to review concepts in previous chapters. In Chapter 3, "Teaching and Decision Making," you can review decisions about classroom presentations. Chapter 4, "Content Selection and Organization," discusses types of content that need to be included in the instructional program. In Chapter 5, "Writing Objectives," information about different categories of objectives teachers develop to guide their instruction can be reviewed.

We by no means wish to suggest that direct instruction is the best approach to classroom instruction. *No* single approach is most appropriate for all situations. Properly, the instructional approach should vary depending on the content to be taught, the nature of students to be served, the kinds of objectives selected, the expertise of the teacher, and the availability of particular kinds of instructional support materials.

This chapter will define *direct instruction*, suggest where its use is appropriate and inappropriate, and introduce the basic components of a direct instruction model. We have followed some elements in the direct instruction model in writing this chapter. After you have finished the chapter, you may wish to revisit the chapter to see how parts of the model have been incorporated.

What is Direct Instruction?

What we have chosen to identify here as *direct instruction* sometimes has been referred to by other names. *Systematic teaching, explicit teaching,* and *active teaching* are among other labels that have been used (Rosenshine, 1987). Regardless of the label used, this approach to teaching is highly teacher centered. The teacher clearly controls identification of content, delivery of content, pacing of lessons, and patterns of classroom interaction. Information is delivered in a systematic, step-by-step fashion. The teacher works with students until they master one idea before introducing another. The approach features whole-class or large-group instruction rather than individualized or small-group learning.

Direct instruction has several advantages. Because lessons are presented to the class as a whole, teacher planning is simplified. One lesson plan suffices for the entire group; hence, planning time is less than when alternative plans must be developed for individuals or small groups. Direct instruction puts the teacher in a controlling position. Some teachers feel a greater sense of security under these conditions than when they are able to exercise less sure control over actions of individuals.

Direct instruction's focus on transmitting important elements of teacher-selected content allows teachers to prepare students well for tests. This is viewed as a particular advantage in schools and districts where there are pressures for students to achieve high scores on standardized achievement tests. (For more information about standardized tests in the schools, see Chapter 17, "Measuring Student Progress.")

Researchers have found that students score well on achievement tests when they have been exposed to direct instruction in their classrooms. Direct instruction seems to increase the amount of student engagement with the kind of content that is featured on tests (Good and Brophy, 1991; Rosenshine and Stevens, 1986).

There are also some potential negatives associated with direct instruction. For example, it tends to work best when the intent is to transmit specific content items to students. Direct instruction may be less effective when the intent is to develop students' abilities to reflect on complex problems and develop solutions of their own. Successful direct instruction also requires the teacher to have excellent presentation skills. Teachers must be well organized, able to identify an appropriate pace, and quick to gauge levels of student interest and adapt instruction, as needed, to keep students engaged.

Because such a heavy volume of information can be disseminated in a relatively short period of time during a direct instruction lesson, a teacher who is insensitive to students' reactions may overwhelm them. This can lead to high levels of student frustration and undermine students' confidence. When this happens, both motivation and achievement levels may decline.

■ ■ ■

At this point, stop and take a minute to write your own brief definition of direct instruction. Compare your version with that of another person in your class who is also reading this chapter.

"History repeats itself. History repeats itself. History repeats itself. History . . ."

Basic Characteristics: An Elaboration

Some of the basic characteristics of direct instruction deserve some elaboration. Direct instruction is *not* just another name for lecturing. Indeed, the teacher may not present a formal lecture at all in some direct instruction lessons. (There may be teacher demonstrations, teacher comments and questions as slides are projected, and so forth; the key is not the presence of a lecture but, rather, direct teacher control over the flow of new information.) To be designated as a direct instruction lesson, these characteristics must be present:

- Academic focus.
- Formal delivery to the whole class.
- Constant monitoring to check for understanding.
- Controlled classroom practice.

Academic Focus

Direct instruction lessons have an academic focus that is maintained throughout the lesson. The teacher usually has developed explicit instructional objectives, and the lesson centers on providing students with the content needed to master these objectives. Digressions from the content focus are discouraged. When these occur, the teacher acts quickly to get students to deal with content associated with the lesson objectives. Independent seat work activities follow teacher presentation of information related clearly to content that has been introduced. These activities tie directly to behaviors stated in the instructional objectives.

Formal Delivery to the Whole Class

Direct instruction features systematic and formal presentation of information by the teacher to the whole class. Material is presented in a logical, step-by-step fashion. Typically, students are asked to demonstrate their understanding of each step before the teacher goes on to the next. The teacher controls classroom interactions and the rate at which content is introduced. Under optimal conditions, the teacher maintains as brisk a pace as possible consistent with students' ability to grasp what is presented. It is important to note that clear teacher control of the classroom does not mean an absence of active student participation. On the contrary, when direct instruction is effectively implemented, there is a high degree of student involvement associated with actions the teacher takes to assure they are understanding the new material.

Direct instruction lessons feature many teacher-to-student questions. A large number of these tend to be recall questions, and when the instruction is effective, students are able to respond to a high percentage of them (Rosenshine and Stevens, 1986). Questions often focus either on a request for specific answers or a request for an explanation of how a student arrived at an answer (Rosenshine, 1987). The general pattern that is followed has been described as "factual question-student response-teacher feedback" (Stallings and Kaskowitz, 1974).

The large number of questions asked during a direct instruction lesson affords opportunities for the teacher to interact with large numbers of students. This tends to keep all students in the class alert and actively involved. Questions from the teacher

Box 13.1

Whole-Group Versus Individualized Instruction

An educator recently made this statement:

I do not like direct instruction and teaching that is planned for the whole group of students in a class. Students each have their own interests and learning styles. They vary tremendously in their aptitudes. The only way these differences can truly be accommodated is through individualized instruction. I think direct instruction of the whole group is not educationally sound.

What Do You Think?

1. What are the strengths of this person's argument?

2. What do you see as weaknesses in the position this person takes?

3. What kind of a personal response would you make to this individual?

give students opportunities to repeat and practice what they have learned. This condition facilitates student learning of the new content.

Constant Monitoring to Check for Understanding

During a direct instruction lesson, the teacher regularly asks questions and takes other actions to assure that students are understanding. Students' responses cue the teacher to adjust the pace of the lesson and to spend more time dealing with content aspects that students find difficult. Sometimes teachers find it necessary to reteach some material. This is likely to occur when the teacher discovers that large numbers of students have missed some key points.

Controlled Classroom Practice

Effective direct instruction lessons feature substantial opportunities for students to engage in controlled practice. The key word here is *controlled*. Before students are allowed to engage in application activities requiring the use of information the teacher has presented, the teacher checks to assure that students have the necessary understanding to successfully complete the application exercises.

■ ■ ■

Stop reading at this point. Summarize the main ideas that have been introduced so far in the chapter. How is a complete direct instruction lesson different from a lesson in which the teacher just lectures? What would a teacher who does nothing but lecture need to do to change her practices to make them consistent with characteristics of effective direct instruction?

Appropriateness of Direct Instruction

Direct instruction is more appropriate for meeting some kinds of instructional objectives than others. It also seems to be more effective with some kinds of students than with others. Researchers have extensively studied both the issue of kinds of contents and kinds of students that are well served by direct instruction (Savage, 1989).

Let's look first at the issue of subject matter content. Direct instruction seems to be most effective when students are asked to master a well-defined body of content or a skill that can be broken down into parts and taught one step at a time (Rosenshine and Stevens, 1986). Several studies have found the approach to be particularly beneficial in helping students to learn basic skills (Savage, 1989). These studies suggest that direct instruction makes sense as an approach to provide students with the basic information they will need as a prerequisite to engaging in complex higher-level thinking and problem-solving activities.

Conversely, direct instruction appears not to be well suited to teaching content for which constituent parts and learning steps cannot be clearly identified. Instructional objectives calling on students to engage in higher-level cognitive thinking at levels such as application, analysis, synthesis, and evaluation are not well served by direct instruction. The same is true of affective objectives. Instruction that seeks to engage students' higher cognitive processes and that is aimed at affective outcomes needs to include approaches that go beyond direct instruction.

Let's consider now the issue of student characteristics and direct instruction. Researchers have found the approach to be particularly effective with younger students, students who are having academic difficulty, and students who are in the introductory phases of learning a specific body of content (Rosenshine and Stevens, 1986). Direct instruction has been found to work well with students from lower socioeconomic backgrounds and for those who have an external locus of control (Savage, 1989). (Students with an external locus of control tend to attribute their successes and failures in school to chance factors or to factors they perceive as being beyond their personal ability to control.)

Approaches other than direct instruction seem to be more effective with high-achieving, task-oriented students who have an internal locus of control. (Students with an internal locus of control perceive school failures and successes to be directly connected to their own, controllable behaviors.) These students seem to benefit from instructional approaches that give them more choices in the classroom and that feature an instructional pace that is less subject to direct teacher control.

■ ■ ■

Box 13.2

Appropriate Uses of Direct Instruction

More Appropriate for . . .

Content that can readily be divided into parts

Teaching basic skills

Low-achieving students

Students with an external locus of control

Introductory material

A prescribed body of content

Less Appropriate for . . .

Content for which constituent parts are difficult to define

Teaching higher-level thinking

High-achieving students

Students with an internal locus of control

Affective outcomes

Learning demanding creative thinking

In summary, what questions do you have about general characteristics of direct instruction? Write down your questions and share them with several others. Present a master list of questions from your group to your instructor, and ask your instructor to react to them.

A Model for a Complete Direct Instruction Lesson

The term *direct instruction model* refers to a list of characteristics researchers have found to be included in complete direct instruction lessons. A number of common elements in lessons of these kinds have been identified (Good and Brophy, 1991; Rosenshine, 1987). Although these elements need to be present in a lesson, they do not have to appear in the same sequence (Hunter, 1986). Deciding how and when each component should be implemented depends on the circumstances of the particular learning situation. These components have been widely identified as necessary features of a sound direct instruction lesson:

- Daily review
- Presentation of new material
- Guided practice
- Provision of feedback and correctives
- Independent practice
- Periodic reviews

Daily Review

The daily review usually occurs at the beginning of a lesson. During this time, the teacher goes over material students have learned previously. The idea is to provide opportunities for additional practice on this information and to make sure the students have mastered the prerequisite information needed for them to accomplish the lesson objective.

Correction of homework often is part of the daily review process. This enables the teacher to identify errors and to spend a little time reteaching content that has not been well understood.

Rosenshine and Stevens (1986) recommend some of the following ideas for making the daily review component of a lesson effective:

- Administer a short quiz over previously introduced material.
- Have students correct one another's homework.
- Ask students to summarize the main points of content introduced during the previous lesson.
- Assign students to prepare questions for each other based on previously introduced content.
- Require students to review content of the previous lesson in small groups.

Student interest is enhanced when teachers use a variety of procedures to review previous work. It is also important that the daily review be accomplished quickly. Specialists Thomas Good and Jere Brophy (1991) recommend that review take up no more than eight minutes of total lesson time.

■ ■ ■

Take a minute to write down some key ideas that need to be considered by teachers when they implement the daily review component of a lesson.

Presentation of New Material

Presentation of new information is central to direct instruction. In deciding how to introduce material clearly and logically, teachers need to ask themselves questions such as these:

- How should the material be sequenced?
- How rapidly should information be presented?
- What examples will work well with this group?

Answers to these questions will vary somewhat with the nature of students in the class, the kind of content to be introduced, and the nature of the lesson's instructional objectives. Good presentations feature many of the characteristics introduced in the following subsections.

Provide Students with a Statement of Objectives

It is important that students understand what will be expected of them as a result of their exposure to lesson content. This can be easily accomplished by providing them with a list of lesson objectives. These objectives cue students as to what content the teacher sees as important and what they will be expected to do to demonstrate mastery once the lesson has been taught.

Provide an Overview or Structure

A lesson structure or overview helps students see relationships between various parts of a lesson. This kind of information can be presented to students in several ways. For example, the teacher might project an outline from an overhead transparency, list main topic headings of the lesson on the chalkboard, or provide students with an incomplete lesson outline to fill out as new information is provided to them.

This teacher has provided a basic outline of information to be covered in the lesson on the chalkboard. This outline will help students follow the lesson's point-by-point development.

Step-by-Step Progression

Good direct instruction lessons proceed one step at a time. These steps are presented at a pace sufficiently rapid to maintain student interest but not so rapid that they fail to keep up. Effective teachers learn to "read" their students and alter their pace as needed to maintain levels of motivation and maximize learning.

Individual lesson steps are identified before instruction begins. This requires the teacher to identify all the things the students must be able to do to master the lesson objectives. Once all these things are identified, the teacher arranges them in a sequence that is logically consistent and compatible with students' characteristics.

Frequent Checking for Understanding

In a well-taught direct instruction lesson, the teacher takes time to check for student understanding after each part of the total presentation has been introduced. This is done to assure that students understand before the teacher moves on to introduce additional material.

Checking for understanding is accomplished in several ways. A common approach is for the teacher to ask students questions about what has been covered. When this is done, it is important to involve a broad range of students so the teacher can get an accurate idea of how the class, as a whole, has grasped the material. Sometimes teachers check for understanding by asking students to work out a problem requiring use of the new information. On other occasions, students may be asked to work in pairs and take turns summarizing what has been learned.

Include Demonstrations and Models

During teacher presentations, student learning is enhanced when teachers use concrete examples, illustrations, or demonstrations. Providing new information in a variety of ways helps students with different learning styles master the material. Some students learn best through observation, others through manipulation of objects, others through listening, others through reading, and still others through a combination of these and additional approaches.

Highlight Main Points

Students retain critical information better when it is highlighted for them during teacher presentations. Students' attention can be drawn to key points in a variety of ways, including writing main points on the chalkboard, repeating important information several times, and using marker phrases such as "now pay attention to this . . . this is especially important."

■   ■   ■

Summarize what you understand to be important considerations for teachers as they present new material to their students during a direct instruction lesson. Share your observations with others in your class and ask them to help you check the accuracy of your understanding.

Guided Practice

During the guided practice phase of a direct instruction lesson, students engage in an activity, under the supervision of their teacher, that requires them to use information they have learned. The purpose of guided practice is to provide students with an opportunity to receive corrective feedback from the teacher that will help clear up any misunderstandings. Important aspects of guided practice are:

- Frequent practice and checking for understanding.
- Assuring high levels of success.
- Reteaching.

Frequent Practice and Checking for Understanding

During guided practice, students benefit from working with parts of the material that is being presented at frequent intervals during the lesson. These practice intervals need to be kept brief enough to allow time for remaining content to be taught and for a practice period at the end of the lesson.

Short questions sometimes function well. On other occasions, it is appropriate for a few students to perform brief activities at the chalkboard or on an overhead projector transparency. Short problems for students to work on while the teacher circulates also often are used as brief practice activities. These quick practice sessions allow teachers to check on students' levels of understandings and correct mistaken impressions.

High Level of Success

During the guided-practice phase of a direct instruction lesson, it is important that students experience a high degree of success. To optimize their learning, researchers have found that students should respond to questions and perform other guided practice activities with about 80 percent accuracy before the teacher goes on to introduce additional new information (Rosenshine and Stevens, 1986).

Reteaching

In reteaching, the teacher goes over material that has already been introduced because students have failed to understand. It may occur at any point during the guided practice phase of the lesson when the teacher discovers that students are making a lot of mistakes.

■ ■ ■

How would you describe the purpose of guided practice? Why is it an important part of a directed instruction lesson?

Provision of Feedback and Correctives

During a direct instruction lesson, teachers regularly provide feedback and correctives to students. These signals either tell students they have correctly understood the material, or they point out errors and help students correct them. The specific kind of feedback or corrective provided depends on the nature of a student's response. The following four categories of student responses have been identified (Rosenshine and Stevens, 1986):

- A correct and quick student response.
- A correct but hesitant student response.
- An incorrect student response due to carelessness.
- An incorrect student response due to lack of knowledge or skill.

A Correct and Quick Student Response

This kind of student response signals to the teacher that students have properly understood the material. The teacher's reaction should be aimed at keeping the lesson moving along at a brisk pace. Ordinarily, a brief comment to students affirming the appropriateness of their answer will suffice. It is important that teacher reactions not be so long that they interfere with the momentum of the lesson.

A Correct but Hesitant Student Response

This student response is correct, but it is given so slowly and hesitantly that the teacher suspects the student has some doubts about the accuracy of what he has said. The teacher response should be directed at removing the student's uncertainty. For example, the teacher might affirm the accuracy of the student answer while briefly reviewing reasons the response is correct. All of this must be accomplished relatively quickly so that the basic flow and pace of the lesson is maintained.

An Incorrect Student Response Due to Carelessness

Experienced teachers develop a feel for when a student's mistake is simply a careless slip and not evidence of misunderstanding. Asking a student to explain her answer often will reveal whether the mistake resulted from a lack of understanding or from carelessness. The ability to distinguish between a careless response and a true lack of understanding is an important teaching skill. It allows the teacher to quickly correct the careless mistake without interrupting the flow of the lesson to reteach something the student really knows. A quick comment or two from the teacher before formal instruction resumes ordinarily is enough to help the student who has made a careless mistake.

An Incorrect Student Response Due to Lack of Knowledge or Skill

When a student mistake clearly reflects a lack of understanding, some reteaching is required. If only a few students are having difficulty, the teacher sometimes continues on with the rest of the lesson content, makes assignments to the entire group, and calls together students having difficulty and reteaches them the aspects of content they are finding difficult to understand. Sometimes students who have mastered these content elements are put to work as peer tutors to work with these students. Peer tutoring works well so long as the teacher has confidence in the abilities of the tutors. It allows the teacher to monitor the work of others in the class while the tutors provide assistance to students who need some additional help mastering basic information that has been introduced.

■ ■ ■

What do you see as the major purposes of feedback and correctives? How could they be applied in a lesson you might teach in your own subject area?

Independent Practice

Practice promotes permanence of learning. The idea of independent practice is to give students sufficient experience in working with new information and skills so that their responses become quick and automatic. Independent practice often occurs during the latter part of a lesson. Often it takes the form of seat work or homework.

To assure that students stay continuously engaged with the lesson content, the teacher needs to actively monitor students during independent practice. This requires movement through the room to respond to student questions and provide other kinds of assistance. Independent practice facilitates learning only when students have a good grasp of the information they will be asked to use. If they don't, the practice activity can reinforce mistaken impressions and can stand as a barrier to appropriate learning. Ideally, independent practice requires students to apply newly learned content in novel and interesting ways.

■ ■ ■

What are some ways independent practice might be implemented in your subject area? What major concerns does a teacher need to consider in developing an independent-practice activity?

WHAT SCHOLARS SAY

New Directions in Research on Instruction

Much of the research supporting the use of direct instruction was conducted during the 1970s and 1980s. Many studies used scores on standardized tests as the relevant measure of student behavior. As is noted in this chapter, large numbers of studies confirmed that direct instruction prepares students quite well for standardized tests.

In recent years, critics have suggested that the kinds of student behaviors measured by standardized tests are excessively narrow. They are calling for more authentic assessment tools, particularly those that will require more sophisticated student thinking and task performance (Leinhardt, 1992).

Other critics suggest that it may no longer be appropriate to search for approaches that claim to work well in all subject areas. Indeed, today there is much less research directed toward trying to determine the general appropriateness of broad approaches such as direct instruction (Brandt, 1992). Instead, researchers are turning their attention to the task of identifying approaches that may be particularly good for teaching some specific subjects, but not others (Brophy, 1992). There are suspicions, for example, that what constitutes effective teaching in science may not be effective at all in English or in other subject areas.

In addition to looking for teaching procedures that are particularly well suited to teaching specific subjects, researchers also are interested in what students *do* with information they have learned. Efforts are underway to discover how students relate separate elements of content they are taught, how they use information in the classroom, and, most importantly, what they do with school learning in their daily lives.

Results of these exciting new lines of inquiry are just starting to be reported in education's professional journals. Findings may well challenge some present practices. They are certain to stimulate broad discussion among teachers and the entire national community of educators.

Sources: Brandt, R. "On Research on Teaching: A Conversation with Lee Shulman." *Educational Leadership* (April 1992) pp. 14–19; Brophy, J. "Probing the Subtleties of Subject-Matter Teaching." *Educational Leadership* (April 1992), pp. 4–8; Leinhardt, G. "What Research on Learning Tells Us About Teaching." *Educational Leadership* (April 1992), pp. 20–25.

Periodic Reviews

Periodic reviews occur when a series of direct instruction lessons are being taught. These allow the teacher to help students recall critical aspects of content topics that have been introduced. Teachers often schedule regular times for periodic-review activities. For example, some of them set aside the first few minutes of their class periods on Mondays to review what was learned the previous week. Once a month they may review main points covered during an entire month of instruction (Good and Brophy, 1991).

Periodic reviews reinforce learning and help students maintain levels of expertise. They also help students see that they are making progress. This kind of evidence helps enhance their self-images by allowing them time to reflect upon their academic accomplishments.

Box 13.3

Instructional Implications of Dimensions of Direct Instruction

DAILY REVIEW
- Provide students with additional practice and review of needed prerequisite information.
- Communicate information to students about the correctness/appropriateness of their responses.
- Note patterns of errors made by individual students; assess general levels of student understanding.
- Reteach specific items of information, as necessary.
- Use a variety of methods during the review process to maintain student interest.

PRESENTATION OF NEW MATERIAL
- Provide students with a statement of objectives.
- Provide students with an overview or summary of material to be learned.
- Present material in a logical step-by-step or point-by-point sequence.
- Check for understanding by asking questions about basic facts and processes and provide opportunities for controlled practice.
- Use a variety of presentation modes and ways to check for understanding to maintain student interest.
- Employ models and demonstrations as content is introduced.
- Highlight main points.
- Reteach specific areas of content, as needed.

GUIDED PRACTICE
- Allow frequent opportunities for students to practice new learning while observing their work.
- Make frequent checks for understanding.
- Assure students are experiencing high levels of success.
- Reteach specific areas of content, as needed.

FEEDBACK AND CORRECTIVES
- Provide abundant and specific feedback.
- Gear responses to individual students so they are consistent with the nature of responses other students have provided.
- Correct mistaken responses in a positive way.

INDEPENDENT PRACTICE
- Allow independent practice only when students have achieved high levels of success during guided practice.
- Avoid practice that students find boring or that seems to create negative attitudes.
- Use practice activities featuring novelty or other high-interest activities.
- Stay active during practice to encourage students to stay alert and keep on task.

PERIODIC REVIEWS
- Review key points periodically, perhaps weekly and monthly.
- Use variety during review sessions.

To review some of your own learning, return now to the focus questions at the beginning of the chapter. How many of them can you answer? What other questions might you include in a quiz over contents of this chapter? You might also want to review focus questions from other chapters you have read. Can you still remember key ideas from those chapters?

This Chapter as an Example of Direct Instruction

We attempted to use some elements of direct instruction in organizing content in this chapter. You may recall that an important element in a direct instruction lesson is a review of previously introduced material to assure that prerequisite information has been learned. The chapter introduction referred you to parts of other chapters containing content helpful in understanding the place of direct instruction in secondary school classrooms.

The direct instruction approach calls on instructors to provide students with information about objectives as well as with an overview and structure for the new learning. We began this chapter with a statement of aims, a series of focus questions, and a formal introduction. (This same approach is followed throughout the text.)

Direct instruction lessons break content into small pieces or steps. Content in this chapter is broken into major sections as well as subordinate subsections. At the end of many of these chapter divisions, we checked for understanding by asking you to reflect on what you had read by responding to questions, summarizing the content, checking your reactions with someone else, or generating questions of your own.

Direct instruction lessons often feature examples, illustrations, or models. Illustrations are provided at various points throughout this chapter, and the general layout of the chapter generally is consistent with a direct instruction format.

Authors of a text are not really in a position to see that guided practice takes place. (Since they are not with you in the classroom, they cannot listen to you, watch what you do, and react to your comments in person.) However, it is hoped that some of the practice activities scattered throughout the chapter as well as those at the end will allow your instructor to monitor your progress as you engage in various guided practice activities.

Some of the end-of-the chapter activities are designed to provide you opportunities for independent practice. They call on you to apply what you have learned and to extend your understandings of the material. Ideally, an independent practice experience related to direct instruction would be for you to prepare and deliver a direct instruction lesson to a group of students.

In summary, we hope the way we have introduced direct instruction in this chapter has helped you to grow in your understanding of this approach. Its success is something you will have to evaluate for yourself. If you now feel fairly comfortable about your knowledge of the essentials of a direct instruction lesson and reasonably confident in your ability to design and deliver this kind of instruction, we will have met our own aims. We hope you think we have succeeded.

Table 13.1   Summary Table

Main Points	Explanation
Direct Instruction	This instructional approach is highly teacher centered and focuses on whole-group instruction. The teacher controls patterns of interactions, is the primary dispenser of information, and manages the pace of the lesson. The focus is on transmission of academic content. This content is broken into relatively small parts that are taught one step at a time. The teacher takes specific action to assure students understand each step before going to the next. Indeed, continuous monitoring is an important general characteristic of this approach.
Claimed Advantages of Direct Instruction	Direct instruction is thought by some teachers to facilitate classroom management. In part, this is true because the approach requires the teacher to act in a highly controlling manner. Also, the whole-group instruction focus somewhat simplifies planning. The focus on key points embedded within academic content helps students prepare to do well on standardized tests.
Claimed Disadvantages of Direct Instruction	Direct instruction is limited in terms of the kinds of content and objectives for which it is appropriate. Direct instruction does not work well to develop students' higher-level thinking powers. Additionally, it is not a good approach when instruction is directed toward affective outcomes. Direct instruction requires particularly good teacher knowledge of students who receive the instruction. The approach has potential to overwhelm students with more information than they can handle. Teachers who are not sensitive to students' backgrounds and abilities may not adjust the instructional pace appropriately and, hence, make students feel they are set up for failure. This can greatly undermine students' confidence, and it can also lead to classroom management problems.
Components of a Model for Direct Instruction Lessons	Components of direct instruction lessons include the following: (1) daily review, (2) presentation of new material, (3) guided practice, (4) provision of feedback and correctives, (5) independent practice, and (6) periodic reviews.

Review of Key Ideas

- There is no one best method for teaching. Various approaches are appropriate for helping students master different kinds of objectives. For some purposes, direct instruction has proved to be a desirable way to organize and deliver instruction.

- Direct instruction is a teacher-centered approach in which the teacher controls selection and delivery of content, mode of presentation of content, pace of lesson development, and patterns of classroom interaction. Continuous monitoring throughout the lesson assures students are understanding. The focus is on transmission of academic content. Instruction is provided to the class as a whole, not to individual groups of students. Complex content is broken into parts, and each part is introduced sequentially, one step at a time. The teacher takes pains to assure students grasp information associated with one step before going on to the next.

- There are some claimed advantages for direct-instruction. Because the teacher works with the whole class, planning is somewhat simplified. Planning assumes all students will be exposed to basically the same instruction. The teacher is very much in a central, controlling position during direct instruction lessons. Some teachers feel this enables them to maintain classroom control more effectively than in lessons where, by design, there is less direct teacher control of interactions. Direct instruction allows for a clear focus on specific academic content. Some people feel the approach functions well as a means of preparing students for standardized tests.

- Some criticisms of direct instruction have been made. Although the approach has merit as a way to help students recall specific information, it is less effective in helping students develop higher-level thinking skills that require them to reflect on complex issues and generate solutions of their own. Some teachers, too, lack the ability to diagnose needs of their students and student reactions as instruction is being delivered. This is a particular problem when direct instruction is being used. Because it is so teacher centered, an unaware teacher can overwhelm students with content and completely undermine their interest in what is being taught.

- Direct instruction is more appropriate for meeting some kinds of instructional objectives than others. It works best when the content to be covered lends itself to be broken down into small parts that can be presented in sequential steps. Researchers have found that direct instruction works particularly well when the intent has been to teach skills. On the other hand, it has been found less appropriate when lesson objectives call on students to engage in higher-level thinking and problem-solving activities. It also is not a favored approach when instructional plans are guided by affective objectives.

- Some kinds of students seem to profit more from direct instruction than others. It has been found especially effective with younger students, students who are having academic difficulty, and students who are just beginning to work with a new content area. Studies have found that direct instruction lessons often are effective with students from lower socioeconomic backgrounds and with students with an external locus of control.

- Several models that list elements of a complete direct instruction lesson have been developed. A typical model includes these components: (1) daily review, (2) presentation of new material, (3) guided practice, (4) provision of feedback and correctives, (5) independent practice, and (6) periodic reviews.

Follow-Up Questions and Activities

Questions

1. What are some reasons for the popularity of direct instruction?
2. What are some basic characteristics of direct instruction?
3. What advantages and disadvantages have been claimed for direct instruction?
4. What is meant by the statement that "direct instruction lessons feature a strong academic focus"?
5. How would you explain the phrase *controlled classroom practice*?
6. For what kinds of learning outcomes does direct instruction seem most appropriate?
7. What elements would you expect to see in a complete direct instruction lesson?
8. Some people argue that direct instruction is rigid, cold, and likely to create negative student attitudes. How do you react to this contention?
9. How would you feel if an administrator told you that he expected you to be using a direct instruction approach every day?
10. What problems, if any, do you envision as you think about implementing direct instruction in your own teaching?

Activities

1. Review your content field. Identify three or four topics that might be appropriately delivered using a direct instruction approach. For each topic, identify a series of parts or steps you would use in presenting information to students. Share your ideas with your instructor, and ask for a critique of your work.
2. Take time to look over parts of the model of direct instruction introduced in this chapter. Observe a teacher in a secondary school who is using a direct instruction approach to introduce information. To what extent did you find each of the elements of the model used? Write up your findings in the form of a brief report, and submit it to your instructor.
3. Organize a debate on this topic: "Resolved that too much direct instruction occurs in today's secondary schools." Hold the debate during a regular class session. When it is over, engage the entire class in a discussion of this issue.

4. With assistance from your instructor, identify some summaries of what researchers have found about the effectiveness of direct instruction. (For example, you might wish to look at Thomas Good and Jere Brophy's book, *Looking in Classrooms*.) Prepare a short oral report for class members in which you summarize what researchers have found.

5. For a topic in your own subject area, prepare a complete lesson plan based on direct instruction. Share it with others in your class, and ask them to suggest places your plan might be improved. You might also solicit reactions from your instructor.

References

BRANDT, R. "On Research on Teaching: A Conversation with Lee Shulman." *Educational Leadership* (April 1992), pp. 14–19.

BROPHY, J. "Probing the Subtleties of Subject-Matter Teaching." *Educational Leadership* (April 1992), pp. 4–8.

GOOD, T. AND BROPHY, J. *Looking in Classrooms*. 5th ed. New York: HarperCollins, 1991.

HUNTER, M. "Madeline Hunter Replies: Develop Collaboration; Build Trust." *Educational Leadership* (March 1986), p. 68.

LEINHARDT, G. "What Research on Learning Tells Us About Teaching." *Educational Leadership* (April 1992), pp. 20–25.

ROSENSHINE, B. "Direct Instruction." In M. Dunkin (ed.). *The International Encyclopedia of Teaching and Teacher Education*. New York: Pergamon Press, 1987, pp. 257–262.

ROSENSHINE, B. AND STEVENS, R. "Teaching Functions." In M. Wittrock (ed.). *Handbook of Research on Teaching*. 3rd ed. New York: Macmillan Publishing Company, 1986, pp. 376–391.

SAVAGE, M. K. *The Impact of Different Instructional Models on Teacher Performance Scores as Measured by the Texas Teacher Appraisal System*. College Station, TX: Unpublished doctoral dissertation, 1989.

STALLINGS, J. AND KASKOWITZ, D. *Follow-Through Classroom Observation Evaluation, 1972–1973*. Menlo Park, CA: Stanford Research Institute, 1974.

14

Indirect Instruction

AIMS

This chapter provides information to help the reader to:

- Implement several metacognitive techniques that can help students derive more benefits from indirect instruction.
- Describe characteristics of inquiry teaching.
- Suggest how comparing, contrasting, and generalizing might be used in the classroom.
- Use the Suchman inquiry strategy.
- Describe implementation procedures for and differentiate among purposes of creative thinking, critical thinking, problem solving, and decision making.

FOCUS QUESTIONS

1. How is indirect instruction distinguished from direct instruction?
2. Why is it desirable for students to learn how to monitor their own thinking processes, and how can metacognitive techniques help them learn how to do this?

3. How can the Suchman inquiry technique help students learn to focus on the important dimensions of a problem situation?

4. What are some conditions necessary for creative thinking to take place?

5. How do the rules of brainstorming help participants to consider as much information as possible?

6. Compare and contrast characteristics of creative thinking and critical thinking.

7. For what kinds of situations is the problem solving technique an appropriate instructional choice?

8. In what ways does decision making differ from problem solving?

Introduction

Direct instruction describes a broad category of instructional approaches that promote on-task behavior by students through centralized teacher control (Corno and Snow, 1986). For example, the teacher carefully oversees patterns of communication as well as the substance and rate of presentation of new information. Researchers have found direct instruction techniques to be particularly useful for helping students master basic information and skills (Good and Brophy, 1991).

Indirect instruction places more responsibility on students to control their own behavior. Learning experiences for which indirect instruction has proved especially well suited often require students to engage in sophisticated thinking (Borich, 1992). Lessons featuring indirect instruction may call on students to "go beyond the givens" and develop conclusions that require careful analysis of quite challenging content. In indirect instruction, the teacher acts as a manager who presents the task to be accomplished, provides the basic information students will need to use as they work toward a conclusion, and helps nurture students' thinking processes when they engage the assigned problem.

Because of the emphasis on promoting more sophisticated levels of student thinking, many indirect instructional approaches focus heavily on teaching certain thinking skills to students. Instruction that emphasizes how to think is just as worthy of school time as instruction that focuses on the traditional academic subjects (Beyer, 1987, 1988). Not only are sound thinking skills needed for students to benefit fully from school subjects, these thinking skills are also needed as they cope with challenges they will face throughout their adult lives (Ruggiero, 1988). This chapter introduces several of them under these headings:

- Metacognition
- Inquiry Teaching
- Creative Thinking

- Critical Thinking
- Problem Solving
- Decision Making

Metacognition

Metacognition refers to thought about the process of thinking. It involves bringing to a conscious level the kinds of procedures we follow as we think. Metacognitive processes serve an important monitoring function. When people are aware of the steps they are taking as they think, they can make more conscious choices about whether approaches they have selected for a given task are appropriate.

Instructional experiences can be provided that help students monitor and that modify their own patterns of thinking. Several approaches have been designed to achieve these purposes. Two that have been used by a number of teachers are teacher modeling and visualizing thinking strategies.

Teacher Modeling

Modeling has long been known to be a powerful instructional tool. As applied to metacognition, teacher modeling seeks to help students recognize that people who successfully think about challenging issues carefully monitor their own thinking processes. They engage in a type of silent personal dialogue as they confront relevant issues. They may speculate about alternatives, consider numerous responses, evaluate available evidence, weigh the relevance of competing views, and get deeply involved in other considerations pertinent to the issue at hand. To help students understand how such thinking processes operate, it sometimes is helpful for teachers to model these processes by thinking aloud as they attack a given issue.

The idea is to cue students to thinking patterns that might be useful when they are called on to perform a similar task. By observing the teacher, they will note general approaches to the issue that have proved to be productive. They will see the importance of thinking carefully about their own approaches to the task. After a teacher has thought aloud, students often will perform better on an assigned task than when the teacher has assumed students already know how the task should be approached.

Suppose a teacher in an English class were teaching a unit on descriptive writing. Each student might have been asked to write a two- to three-page paper on tourist attractions of a selected world place. After an initial draft, the teacher might expect students to think about what they had written and to rewrite the material. A simple teacher directive to "rewrite what you have written" would not cue students to the kinds of thought processes that should be used as they approach the task of revision. A more productive way to get students successfully started on the revision task would be for the teacher to model what students should do.

For example, the teacher might have prepared an overhead transparency from a first-draft of the same assignment prepared by a student from a previous semester. The teacher could think aloud with students in this way:

> All right, now look at this draft of a paper on Easter Island. Now, if this were my paper and I were about to revise it, these are some of the things I would want to do.
>
> First of all, readers are going to be reading lots of literature about lots of different places. They will be turned off by anything that has been written hastily without careful attention to spelling and grammar. The first thing I'll want to look for is spelling errors. Then, I'll want to be sure that verb tenses are correct and consistent throughout.
>
> I will want to hold the attention of my reader. I don't want to lose anyone with long, complicated sentences. As a quick check on this, I'll read the paper aloud. Anytime I run out of breath before I finish a sentence, I am going to mark that sentence. Later, I will go back and cut these long sentences into shorter ones. Also, as I read I will try to spot any places where I am using the same word too frequently. If I find any excessive repetition, I will make a note to correct this situation in a revision.
>
> As I read through the material, I will mark every sentence that has as its main verb some part of the verb "to be." This tends to be a very weak, dull verb for the reader. As I rewrite the material, I will try to replace these verbs with more action-oriented words.
>
> Look at this sentence: "The giant statues are visited by many tourists." There are two serious problems here. First of all, the verb is in passive voice, a weak, uninteresting construction. Second, the reference to the statues simply being "visited" is not particularly exciting. I would rewrite the sentence to eliminate the passive voice and to add some color. One possibility might be a sentence something like this: "The giant statues of Easter Island challenge tourists' views of so-called 'primitive' peoples."

Students who listened to this teacher think aloud about the thought processes to be followed in revising the sample paper have a model to follow as they begin to work on their own revisions. Modeling can also plant the idea that thinking about what the task requires is an essential prerequisite to beginning to address the task. This perspective is one that teachers hope will take root in students as a result of thinking aloud demonstrations.

Visualizing Thinking

Another technique to encourage students to monitor their own thinking processes is visualizing thinking. This approach is designed to help students think about the nature of an assigned task, consider the kinds of thinking they will be required to engage in, and identify the nature of the information they will need to gather. Once they have decided on their responses to these issues, students are encouraged to develop diagrams. The diagrams will help them to take and organize notes consistent with the requirements of the assigned task.

Suppose a teacher decided to have class members read the following material from their text:

Box 14.1

Designing a Thinking-Aloud Approach

In a thinking-aloud approach, the teacher models a thinking sequence appropriate for a given task. Think about a topic you would like to teach and a particular learning assignment you might develop for students. Briefly outline a thinking-aloud strategy you might use. Begin by identifying the focus for your assignment ("identifying unknown compounds," "writing a position paper," "looking for bias in a political speech," and so forth). Then, briefly describe steps you would follow in your thinking-aloud approach.

Focus:

Step 1:

Step 2:

Step 3:

Step 4:

Step 5:

Step 6:

(The number of steps needed may be more or less than the six indicated here. Develop as many steps as you will need given your focus.)

Early Spanish Explorers of the Caribbean

In the year 1492, the Spanish explorer Christopher Columbus landed on San Salvador Island, a rather small island in the West Indies. San Salvador is in the group of islands that we know today as the Bahamas. Columbus later explored many other Caribbean islands. He set up a fort on one of the largest islands in the region, Hispaniola. Today, Hispaniola is occupied by the countries of Haiti and the Dominican Republic.

Another well-known early Spanish explorer was Nicolas de Ovando. In the year 1502, he was sent out from Spain to become Governor of Hispaniola. He brought a large number of colonists with him. These colonists sought to make their fortunes in two ways. Some of them attempted to strike it rich in gold mining. Others started large plantations. A common problem all of these early Spanish colonists faced was a lack of a large supply of local workers.

In response to this situation, the colonists initially tried to make slaves of the local Indians. This was not successful. The Indians did not take to slavery, and many of them died. Once the local supply of Indians on Hispaniola had been exhausted, the Spanish for a time tried bringing in Indians from other Caribbean islands. They, too, died. Later, slaves from Africa were brought to the island. Though many of these slaves survived, Hispaniola continued to have a need for more workers than could be supplied.

As a result of this labor shortage, many Spanish colonists began moving from Hispaniola to other islands in the region. One of the other large islands that attracted a number of Spanish settlers was Puerto Rico. The first settlers arrived there in 1508 under the leadership of Ponce de Leon. The Spanish moved into Jamaica in 1509 when Juan de Esquivel led a group of settlers there. Cuba, the largest island in the region, was reached by Spanish settlers in 1514. In time, it became the most prosperous of Spain's Caribbean territories.

Because of differences in ability levels of students, the teacher might wish some students to focus on different aspects of this material than others. For example, the teacher might have decided that some students should read for the purpose of accomplishing this learning task:

Task: Who were four famous Spanish explorers who made discoveries in the Caribbean between 1492 and 1514, and what large islands were occupied by Spain during this period?

To help these students focus on this task as they read the material and took notes, a visual-thinking diagram something like this might be developed:

Leaders and Islands

Leaders	*Islands*
_____	_____
_____	_____
_____	_____
_____	_____

Others in the class might be asked to read the material to accomplish this task:

Task: What actions were taken by the early Spanish settlers of Hispaniola to solve the labor shortage, and what happened as a result?

To help students focus on this task as they read the material and took notes, a visual-thinking diagram something like this might be developed:

Why Laborers Were Needed

_____

_____

_____

_____

What Was Tried First?	*What Was Tried Second?*
_____	_____
_____	_____

What Were the Results?   *What Were the Results?*

_____   _____

_____   _____

_____   _____

Final Outcome

_____

_____

_____

_____

Note that, although all students were asked to read the same material, the thinking task assigned to some students was different from the thinking task assigned to other students. These differences are reflected in the visual-thinking diagrams. Use of such diagrams can help students focus on information that is relevant to a specific assigned task.

When this approach is used for the first time, teachers usually provide students with these diagrams. Once they get used to working with them, students can develop visual-thinking diagrams of their own. The process of constructing the diagrams forces them to think about the nature of the task and about the nature of thinking that will be required in responding to it.

Use of the diagrams helps students to monitor and adjust their own thinking processes as they work with assigned materials. As a result, their work is likely to be more productive and their levels of achievement and self-satisfaction higher.

Inquiry Teaching

Inquiry approaches have been used by teachers for many years. Many models of inquiry teaching have been developed. Nearly all of them introduce content to students inductively. Inductive learning proceeds from the specific to the general. A simple example will illustrate the general procedure. Suppose a teacher wanted to teach a group of learners the concept *fish*. She might provide them with photographs of different fish. Through a series of questions, students would be led to identify common features of the things in the individual photographs. To conclude the exercise, the teacher would urge students to develop their own description of the concept *fish* and would ask them to name its necessary defining characteristics.

Inductive or inquiry thinking involves students in the creation of new knowledge. This is true because students develop their own conclusions after considering independent pieces of evidence. The process of knowledge production is thought to be motivating for many students. Additionally, the basic processes of considering evidence and arriving at reasoned conclusions represent the kind of rational thinking ability students will be called upon to exercise throughout their adult lives. In short, supporters of inquiry thinking are as much interested in students' mastering the *processes* of thinking as in students' mastering the academic content that provides the focus for a given inquiry lesson.

Basic Steps in Inquiry Teaching

Inquiry teaching in American schools traces back to a famous book published by the eminent American educational philosopher, John Dewey. In *How We Think*, originally published in 1910, Dewey suggested basic steps for sequencing inquiry instruction. With some variation, the following steps, derived from Dewey's work, are featured in many inquiry lessons:

- Identify and describe the essential dimensions of a problem or situation.
- Suggest possible solutions to the problem or explanations of the problem or situation.
- Gather evidence related to these solutions or explanations.
- Evaluate possible solutions or explanations of the problem in light of evidence.
- Develop a conclusion that is best supported by the evidence.

The basic steps of inquiry involve nothing more than the application of the scientific method to a wide variety of problems. Inquiry lessons can be developed in many subject areas.

Suppose a high school humanities teacher were interested in probing the relationship between urbanization and life expectancies of American women. An inquiry lesson with this focus might develop along these lines:

STEP ONE

FOCUS: The teacher might begin by writing the following statistics* on the board.

Percentages of Females in Three Age Groups			
Year	Under 30	30 to 50	51 or Older
1850	71%	20%	9%
1910	61%	25%	14%
1970	50%	23%	27%

*Data adapted from U.S. Bureau of the Census. *Historical Statistics of the United States, Colonial Times to 1970*, Bicentennial Edition, Part I, Washington, DC: 1975, pp. 16, 19, and 11–12.

Median Age of U.S. Females in Three Years

Year	Median Age
1850	18.8 years
1910	23.9 years
1970	27.6 years

Percentages of U.S. Urban and Rural Population in Three Years

Year	Rural	Urban
1850	84.7%	15.3%
1910	54.3%	45.7%
1970	26.5%	73.5%

TEACHER: Look at this information. What trends do you see? Notice that women seem to be living longer in each of the three years. Notice, too, that more people seem to be living in cities. Now, I want you to think about two questions. First, what might be the connection between longer lives for women and the trend toward living in cities? Second, are there other possible explanations for women living longer in the later years?

STEP TWO

Students provide answers to each question.

QUESTION 1:   What might be the connection between longer lives for women and the trend toward living in cities?

A Sample of Possible Student Responses

- People in cities might have earned more. Women may eaten better and stayed healthier in the cities.
- Women in cities may have had better access to newspapers. They may have read more about good health standards.
- There may have been better access to doctors in the cities. Thus, women may have begun to live longer because they were more likely to get treated when they were sick in cities than when they were sick in rural areas.

- Cities tended to bring more medical scholars and researchers together. This resulted in an explosion of new information about health and medicine. This new information increased the life spans of all people in the later years.

QUESTION 2:   Other than the move from rural areas to the cities, what other things might have led to higher percentages of women in older age groups in the later years?

A Sample of Possible Student Responses

- Women could have started having fewer children. If this happened, fewer would have died in childbirth, and more would have lived to an older age.
- In the earlier years, a high percentage of women could have been immigrants. Immigrants tend to be younger. This would account for higher percentages of younger women in the earlier years.
- There could have been some fatal diseases that killed women in their twenties and thirties for which cures became available in later years.
- In earlier years, society may not have cared as much for older women as it did in later years. There could have been a deliberate failure to care for older women in the earlier years.

STEP THREE

During this phase of the lesson, the teacher would direct students to gather evidence supporting or refuting each of the possible explanations they had generated in response to the two questions. They would be directed to additional resource materials containing information. Students would be told to gather as much relevant information as possible.

It is important to have specific sources of information readily available for student use. Directions to students to "go to the library and find it" are a sure prescription for failure. Many will give up. Even those who do not will be frustrated. These kind of negative attitudes can undermine the motivational potential of a good inquiry lesson.

STEP FOUR

During this phase, the responses to the focus questions are reexamined in light of the additional information that has been gathered. The nature and reliability of the evidence is discussed. Once all information related to a given explanation has been considered, the class decides whether to accept, reject, or revise the explanation.

The teacher concludes this phase of the activity by writing on the board those explanations for which the most evidential support has been found.

STEP FIVE

Students are asked to look at the explanations for which they have found good support. The teacher may ask questions such as these:

Given all of the evidence you have seen supporting these explanations, what do you think is the single best explanation for more women living longer in 1910 than in 1850 and in

1970 than in 1910? Why do you make this choice? How confident are you that it is correct?

When the students make a final choice, the teacher reviews the supporting evidence. Students are reminded that this conclusion should not be regarded as final. It may be revised should additional information become available.

■ ■ ■

This description has been compressed for purposes of illustration. Good inquiry lessons require time, and issues addressed are often complex. It takes time for students to master skills associated with logical thinking. If time is at a premium and the primary objective is content coverage rather than teaching the inquiry process, an inquiry approach may not be the best choice.

Comparing, Contrasting, and Generalizing

Many inquiry lessons seek to improve students' abilities to compare, contrast, and generalize. Organization of the data into a format that students can easily understand can help students accomplish tasks requiring these complex thinking processes.

One approach to organizing data for learning activities requiring students to compare, contrast, and generalize is the retrieval chart. A retrieval chart is basically a matrix that includes basic concept categories under which relevant information can be listed.

A lesson using a retrieval chart might develop along these lines. Suppose an English teacher had assigned students to read a novel called *Mines and Dreamers* that featured many interactions among the five major characters: Joe Carmody, Luella McPhee, Tony Marino, Gordon Duffy, and Selma Steele. In planning a lesson designed to promote students' abilities to compare, contrast, and generalize, the teacher might develop a chart that students could use to organize basic information from the novel. The chart could require them to organize information about each character under these major headings:

• Family background

• Education

• Occupation

• Basic motives

Students might be asked to gather information individually. Or members of the class might develop the information as part of a group discussion focusing on the novel. In either case, the result would be a completed data chart. This might take the form of a large chart in the front of the room, a chart prepared on an overhead transparency and projected on a screen, or individual charts that would be printed and distributed to each student. An example of such a chart with data filled in might look something like this:

	Family Background	Education	Occupation	Basic Motives
Joe Carmody	divorced parents; reared by mother	Grade 8	union organizer; former coal miner	improving of lives of the working poor
Luella McPhee	divorced parents; reared by mother	Grade 10	owner of successful real estate firm	personal social advancement; wants to hide nature of her family background
Tony Marino	upper middle class; reared by both parents	college graduate	attorney	betterment of conditions of the working poor
Gordon Duffy	upper middle class; divorced parents; reared by father	college graduate	attorney	promotion of his own economic self-interest; insensitive to needs of others
Selma Steele	upper class; reared by both parents	college graduate	business manager	believes that what is good for her business is, in the long run, good for everyone else too

The completed chart can be used as a basis for a discussion designed to prompt students to compare, contrast, and generalize. The teacher would begin such an exercise by asking students to look carefully at the information on the chart and to respond to this sequence of questions:

1. What are some similarities you see among these characters?

Possible responses:

- Joe Carmody, Luella McPhee, and Gordon Duffy were reared in one-parent homes.
- Joe Carmody and Luella McPhee have less than a high school education.
- Tony Marino and Gordon Duffy are attorneys.
- Joe Carmody and Tony Marino are both interested in improving the lot of the working poor.

(These are simply examples. Students may identify additional and different responses.)

2.   What are some differences you see among these characters?

Possible responses:

- Their educational levels are different.
- They come from a variety of home backgrounds.
- Some of them are basically out for their own interests.
- Some of them are interested in improving the lot of others.

(These are simply examples. Students may identify additional and different responses.)

3.   From looking at this information, what general statements can you make about what this author may believe to be true?

Possible responses:

- There is not necessarily a connection between a person's occupation and his or her sensitivity to the needs of others.
- The kind of home a person grows up in as a child does not necessarily predict the kinds of attitudes toward others he or she will have as an adult.

(These are simply examples. Students may develop different and additional generalizations from the information in the chart.)

The generalizations developed in this exercises are developed from consideration of a very limited amount of information. The teacher should remind students that they should be regarded as only tentatively true. As students study other material, they can be urged to test the accuracy of these generalizations in the light of new information.

Building a Basis for Sophisticated Thinking Through Delimiting and Focusing

Students sometimes find themselves overwhelmed with the volume of available information when they confront a task demanding higher-level thinking. They need a way of sorting through all of the available data to get to the relevant information. Part of an inquiry strategy developed by J. Richard Suchman can be used to help students develop their abilities to delimit the amount of information they need as they think about a given issue.

Suchman had several major concerns as he developed his approach. First of all, he wanted a system that would prevent students from arriving at premature conclusions. Indeed, he wished to promote the view that knowledge is tentative and that even the best grounded generalizations can be revised in the light of new and better information (Suchman, 1962).

Suchman's approach builds on students' natural curiosity about puzzling situations. He called these puzzling situations *discrepant events*. These can be prepared in many secondary school subject areas. One that has been employed in many science class-

Box 14.2

Identifying Discrepant Events

Discrepant events are puzzling situations that are used as focal points for an inquiry procedure developed by J. Richard Suchman. Think about a subject you are preparing to teach. Then, identify six different discrepant events that you could use in lessons based on Suchman's approach.

Discrepant Event 1: _____

Discrepant Event 2: _____

Discrepant Event 3: _____

Discrepant Event 4: _____

Discrepant Event 5: _____

Discrepant Event 6: _____

rooms uses a short film to introduce the discrepant event. The film features a man who is looking inside a bell jar. In the middle of the bell jar, there is a beaker of water that is boiling furiously. The man makes a show of putting on elbow-length asbestos gloves. He removes the bell jar, gingerly lifts the beaker with the boiling liquid, and slowly drinks it, showing no evidence of any discomfort. The film stops at this point. Students are asked how the man was able to do this. (Good luck. You figure it out.)

The following steps are modified from those developed by Suchman:

- Students are presented with a puzzling or perplexing situation. (Suchman called this a *discrepant event*.)
- They are encouraged to try to explain it by asking the teacher questions about it.
- They are told the questions they ask must be framed in such a way that they can be answered by a "yes" or a "no."
- The exercise ends with a general discussion of explanations that have been suggested and of the processes students followed in arriving at them.

With practice, students come to understand that by asking large and broad questions they can eliminate enormous categories of information. (For example, a question such as "Is this a chemical substance?" regardless of whether the teacher answers "yes" or "no" provides students with much more information than a narrow questions such as "Is this fluorine?") Classes that have had a little experience with the Suchman approach tend to develop a strategy of beginning with broad questions that delimit the range of content they must consider. This provides a focus for their thinking that allows them to disregard information that, early on, is identified as irrelevant.

Creative Thinking

The world confronts people with a never-ending supply of serious problems. Throughout history, solutions often have come from people who have responded to them in unusual, creative ways. Problems would not be "problems" if conventional solutions could be easily applied. It takes a person who has the curiosity, insight, and emotional security to try a novel approach. Often, creative solutions have resulted when people have made unusual associations between very different kinds of things.

This student is writing information that will be used as part of an inquiry lesson.

For example, Ruggiero (1988) points out that the inventor of the fork-lift truck got the idea from watching mechanical fingers lift donuts out of an oven. He goes on to note that Gutenberg's invention of the printing press resulted, in part, from his observation of a wine press.

Creative thinking is stimulated when people are able to defer final judgment and when they do not have fear of failure (Ruggiero, 1988). The ability to generate creative new information is not widespread among students (Perkins, 1981). Part of the problem may well be that students experience little systematic instruction designed to develop their creative thinking skills.

A number of instructional techniques have been developed to enhance students' creative thinking powers. One that is widely used is *brainstorming*.

Brainstorming is designed to stimulate original solutions to problems. It seeks to unleash mental power in ways that discourage students from relying on ordinary and conventional responses. It places a premium on the ability to generate large numbers of creative responses.

Brainstorming developed in the world of business. Concerned leaders noticed that junior-level managers tended to shy away from proposing novel solutions to problems. Often, they simply parroted positions of senior executives. As a result, insights of these younger executives rarely got a hearing. The brainstorming technique was developed to encourage a broad sharing of innovative ideas. The technique ensures that all ideas will be heard and considered.

Rules for conducting a brainstorming exercise are simple:

- Students are provided with a problem to consider. ("Suppose all books were printed with an ink that would disappear after six months. What would happen if that were true?")
- Students are invited to call out their ideas as rapidly as possible. A student is free to speak whenever an opening of silence occurs. The idea is to generate a rapid outpouring of ideas. Students are told to say whatever comes to their minds so long as it is relevant to the problem.
- Students are cautioned not to comment positively or negatively on any ideas suggested by others. All ideas are accepted. This rule helps break down students' fear of "saying something stupid."
- The teacher or a designated record keeper writes down every idea. This person should not be concerned about neatness. He needs to be someone who can write fast. Student ideas come at a very rapid rate.
- The exercise should be stopped when there is a noticeable decline in the rate of presentation of new ideas.
- A general discussion of the ideas concludes the exercise.

Brainstorming can be applied in a number of secondary curriculum areas. It is an effective technique for stimulating students to produce new ideas rather than rehash old ones or react to views of others.

"I've been looking over a 'product' of one of your creative thinking lessons, Ms. Devon, and frankly I have some concerns."

Critical Thinking

Whereas the primary function of creative thinking is to generate ideas, the primary function of critical thinking is to *evaluate* ideas. Critical thinking always involves judgment. Critical thinking judgments are more than simple exchanges of uninformed opinion. Properly, judgments are made in terms of defensible criteria (Lipman, 1988).

Sometimes teachers link activities calling for creative thinking and critical thinking. When this is done, the creative thinking activity takes place first. During this phase of the lesson, students produce ideas. During the second phase, they use critical thinking approaches to evaluate these ideas.

A basic procedure for brainstorming was introduced in the section introducing creative thinking. An analytic brainstorming approach has been developed by Dunn and

Dunn (1972). This procedure applies critical thinking to the initial creative results of the first part of a brainstorming activity. An analytic brainstorming lesson might develop along these lines:

- The teacher poses a problem in the form of a statement about what an "ideal" solution to a problem might be: "The best thing we could do to prevent pollution of Gulf Coast beaches would be to. . . ." (Students brainstorm appropriate responses. Their answers are written so they can be easily seen by all students.)

- With responses developed during the preceding step in full view, the teacher asks students why the "best things" mentioned have not already taken place: "What things are getting in the way of those 'best things' we could do to prevent pollution of Gulf Coast beaches?" (Students brainstorm responses.)

- The next phase features a question about what might be done to overcome obstacles noted in responses to the question posed in the previous step: "How could we overcome difficulties that keep us from doing what we have to do to prevent pollution of Gulf Coast beaches?" (Students brainstorm appropriate responses.)

- Next, the teacher asks students to point out difficulties of implementing ideas noted in the previous step: "What might stand in the way of our efforts to overcome difficulties that keep us from taking necessary action to prevent pollution of Gulf Coast beaches?" (Students brainstorm appropriate responses.)

- Now, the teacher asks students to decide what should be done first to begin a realistic solution to the problem: "Considering all of our thinking, what steps should we take first? Be prepared to explain your choices." (Students respond and defend their choices by reference to appropriate criteria.)

In general, critical thinking involves approaches to making evaluative judgments that are based on logical consideration of evidence and application of appropriate criteria. Barry Beyer, a leading proponent of teaching thinking skills to students in the schools, points out that critical thinking does not result from following a specific sequence of steps. Rather, critical thinking involves the use of a number of mental operations including the following (Beyer, 1988):

- Distinguishing between statements of verifiable facts and value claims.
- Distinguishing relevant from irrelevant information, claims, or reasons.
- Determining the factual accuracy of a statement.
- Determining the credibility of a written source.
- Identifying ambiguous claims or arguments.
- Identifying unstated assumptions.
- Detecting bias.
- Identifying logical fallacies.
- Recognizing logical inconsistencies in a line of reasoning.
- Determining the strength of an argument or claim.

Box 14.3

Using Diagrams to Help Students Visualize Their Reasoning

One task of critical thinking is to help students recognize logical fallacies. Sometimes students are taught to use *syllogisms* as they analyze phenomena of various kinds. A syllogism is a formal argument that consists of a major premise, a minor premise, and a conclusion.

Sometimes students master the forms but make errors because their premises are faulty. This can lead to inaccurate conclusions. Natalie Yeager (1987) suggests using diagrams to help students visualize their logic.

The media has made much of Japan's technological excellence and the proficiency of Japanese students in mathematics. An unsophisticated student who meets an exchange student from Japan named Toshi Nakimura might use the following syllogism to conclude that Toshi is a strong mathematics student.

Major premise: All Japanese students are good at mathematics.

Minor premise: Toshi is a Japanese student.

Conclusion: Toshi is good at mathematics.

This relationship can be diagrammed as follows. In the diagram, the largest circle, "a," includes all people who are good at mathematics. The second circle, "b," includes all Japanese. It is totally within the "a" circle because the assumption is that all Japanese are good at mathematics. The third circle, "c," indicates Toshi. It suggests that Toshi is Japanese and, hence, good at mathematics.

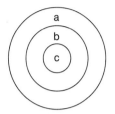

In time, it may become evident that Toshi finds mathematics difficult. This information would suggest a flaw in the original argument. A new argument that takes into account the new information about Toshi might be diagrammed in this way:

Circle "a" still denotes all people who are good at mathematics. Circle "b" continues to identify all Japanese students. Note, though, that now some Japanese students are among those who are good at mathematics and some are among those who are not. The circle "c" continues to identify Toshi. He is represented now as one of those Japanese students who are not good at mathematics.

Encouraging students to diagram their arguments helps them to understand the flow of their logic. The exercise is particularly useful when new information challenges an erroneous assumption. A comparison of diagrams helps to clarify differences separating the initial line of logic from the line of logic developed once initial errors have been corrected.

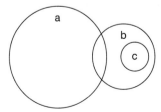

Problem Solving

Problem-solving approaches are used when students are asked to think about problems for which there is likely to be a "best" or "correct" solution. This does not necessarily mean that, in every case, these solutions may not at some future time be held up to question. However, they are considered "best," "correct," "right," or "appropriate," given the evidence that is available at the time the problem is considered. These are examples of issues that might be addressed using a problem-solving approach:

- What is causing the leaves on my house plants to turn yellow and fall off?
- Why is it colder in the winter months in Minneapolis than in Juneau, even though Juneau is much farther north?
- Why do people in Maine and Alabama speak with different accents?
- Why don't armadillos live in California?
- What has caused twentieth century English to differ more from seventeenth century English than twentieth century French differs from seventeenth century French?

When students are introduced to problem solving, often they are taught to follow certain steps. The following four-part sequence includes steps similar to those found in many problem-solving models.

Step 1: Identify the problem

Step 2: Consider possible approaches to its solution

Step 3: Select and apply approaches

Step 4: Evaluate the adequacy of the conclusion

Suppose a high school algebra teacher wished to apply this model. This is how a lesson following these steps might unfold.

Step 1

TEACHER: All right, class, I want each of you to solve this equation. [On the board, the teacher writes this equation: $2X^2 - 46 = 116$.] Now, does everybody understand what I want you to do? [Student raises a hand.] Ruby?

RUBY: You want us to solve for X, right?

TEACHER: Right.

Step 2

TEACHER: Now, before you start, I want someone to tell me how you're going to go about it. John, how about you?

JOHN: Well, we're going to have to get this thing down to a simpler form. The first thing I would do is get rid of the $2X^2$ by dividing both sides by 2.

TEACHER: O.K. That makes sense. What would need to be done next? Gabriella?

GABRIELLA: I think we'll need to arrange it so we'll have the X^2 on one side and all of the numbers on the other.

TEACHER: Fine. Now what do we need to remember about the sign of a number when we move it from one side of an equation to the other? I mean, if I had the equation X - 3 = 4, what would happen if I moved the minus three to the other side? Kim?

KIM: The minus three would become a plus three. So you would end up with X = 4 + 3, or 7.

TEACHER: Excellent. Remember the sign changes when we move from one side to the other. Now, once you had moved all the numbers to one side, what would you have to do to solve for X? Jean?

JEAN: You would need to add all of the numbers together and then take the square root of the total.

STEP 3

TEACHER: We seem to have the basic procedures well in mind. Now I want each of you to solve the problem. If you get stuck, raise your hand, and I will try to help you. [Students individually begin working on the problem.]

STEP 4

TEACHER: I see that everybody has come up with an answer. Now let's check our work to see whether the answers are correct. Jennifer, tell me how we might do that.

JENNIFER: I'm not sure.

TEACHER: Anyone have an idea? Raoul?

RAOUL: We could substitute our answer for X in the original equation to see if it works.

TEACHER: Good idea. Let's try that. Raoul, what did you get as your answer?

RAOUL: 9.

TEACHER: Fine, now let's substitute 9 for X in our original equation. [Teacher writes following sequence of substitutions on the board:]

$$2X^2 - 46 = 116$$
$$2 (9 \times 9) - 46 = 116$$
$$2 (81) - 46 = 116$$
$$162 - 46 = 116$$
$$116 = 116$$

Your answer seems to be correct. Does everybody see what I have done here? [Teacher goes on to answer questions and to emphasize the importance of checking the accuracy of answers to problems.]

Box 14.4

Sometimes Solutions to Problems Are Short Lived

Solutions to problems based on excellent evidence may not always be "permanently correct." New information may become available. There may also be unforeseen consequences of a solution that made perfectly good sense when it was initially developed.

For example, in the 1870s, planters in Jamaica were searching desperately for a way to control hordes of rats in their sugar cane fields. They tried many approaches without success. Then, in 1872, nine mongooses from India were set loose in the sugar cane fields. The mongooses prospered. In a few years, rats

ceased to be a problem. But, there was an unintended consequence.

The mongooses continued to multiply. They began attacking chickens. In time they became a threat to the agricultural economy of Jamaica. Today, the decision to bring the mongoose to the West Indies as a "solution" to the rat problem is recognized as a terrible blunder.

Think about other solutions to problems that, in the short run, seemed to make good sense but, in the long run, proved not to be desirable. Prepare to share two or three examples with the class.

Example 1:

Example 2:

Example 3:

Decision Making

Not all problems have answers that are clearly right, correct, or appropriate. They are questions for which there are no necessarily "best" alternatives. In this situation, people often must make choices from among a variety of acceptable alternatives. This process involves a thinking skill known as *decision making* (Beyer, 1988). Because it involves choices from among a number of competing appropriate responses, decision making involves consideration of personal values and relevant evidence.

The thinking model for decision making varies from that used in problem solving. The major reason for this difference is that value judgments play a much more important role in decision making than in problem solving. The following seven-step model is an example of an approach used in decision-making lessons:

1.   Describe the basic issue or problem.
2.   Point out alternative responses.

3. Identify evidence supporting each alternative.

4. Identify values reflected in each alternative.

5. Point out possible consequences of each alternative.

6. Make a choice from among available alternatives.

7. Identify evidence and values considered in making this choice.

CASE STUDY

Why Don't Ms. Levin's "Good" Students Like Decision Making?

Naomi Levin is midway through her fourth year of teaching. Her subject is American history, and she teaches 11th-graders in a high school in a medium-sized city in the Rocky Mountains. Last summer, she attended a special institute on higher-level thinking skills, and she came back determined to use some of these techniques in her own classes.

She decided to emphasize decision-making skills in a unit on the Great Depression. She selected these focus questions:

• What should the government have done (that it didn't do) to prevent the Depression?

• What should the government have done to end the Depression sooner?

To help students gather information about these questions and likely alternative responses, Naomi worked closely with the school librarian. A special shelf of resource materials was organized for members of Naomi's class to use. After she gave students a general orientation to the decision-making approach, students dug into the materials.

After students had had a chance to think about the questions, some possible responses, and some more-or-less final conclusions that made sense to them, Naomi led the class in a general discussion centered on the focus questions. She said that the intensity of student interest and the level of involvement was outstanding. She thought everything had gone very well. This view changed when some of her "A" students dropped by to talk after school.

These students reported that they had really enjoyed what was going on in class, but that they had some concerns. Most of them indicated that they were going on to college and that the class had spent a lot of time just on one topic. They indicated that they were worried about not covering other topics that they might need to know about to do well in college.

Also, they felt very uneasy about what kind of test they would be facing when "all this discussing and speculating ends." Though they didn't say so in so many words, they seemed to be indicating that they knew how to get A's when content was taught in a more traditional way, but that they weren't sure about how their performances would stack up when they were evaluated on "this decision-making stuff." Several students strongly hinted that they would prefer to go back to a more familiar way of dealing with course content.

Naomi has always counted on her good students for support. She has been disappointed that these class leaders have expressed concerned about an approach that, in her mind, works well. She is in doubt as to what she should do.

■   ■   ■

How concerned should Naomi be about this situation? Do you think it possible that any change from a familiar pattern will result in student concerns of this kind, or is there something attached specifically to the decision-making technique that brought it about in this situation? One of the concerns seems to relate to content coverage. Is it acceptable to cover less content at more depth, or does such a decision irresponsibly deny students access to important information they should have? What kinds of assessment might be appropriate when the emphasis has been on developing students' decision-making proficiency? How might they vary from tests given at the conclusion of approaches featuring more direct instruction (lecture, assigned readings with questions to answer, and so forth)? Who could Naomi ask for advice?

The following example illustrates an application of this seven-step model.

STEP 1

A local school board has taken under consideration a proposal to require every student to take four years of mathematics. The issue or problem might be framed like this: "Should students be required to take four years of mathematics in high school?"

STEP 2

In this case, there are just two basic alternatives. Alternative one is to support a requirement for all students to take four years of mathematics in high school. Alternative two is to oppose such a requirement.

STEP 3

Some of the following evidence might be gathered to *support* a four-year mathematics requirement:

- SAT scores in mathematics have failed to reach levels achieved by students in the 1960s.

- The nation is facing an impending shortage of engineers and other technical people who must have sound backgrounds in mathematics.
- Students will begin college-level mathematics instruction at higher levels because of better high school backgrounds.
- The requirement will improve the general quality of the high school curriculum by making the whole program more rigorous.

Some of the following evidence might be gathered to *oppose* a four-year mathematics requirement:

- The requirement will weaken existing math courses. This is true because all high school students do not have the talent for the math courses that, given the new requirements, they will be required to take.
- The requirement will result in an unfortunate reduction in the number of available electives.
- Not all high school graduates go to college.
- Not all occupational fields, even for college graduates, demand an extensive background in mathematics.

STEP 4

The following values might be among those cited by individuals who *support* a four-year mathematics requirement:

- Mathematics courses are difficult, and they provide a needed element of rigor to the high school program.
- Too much electivity in high school is not good.
- Society needs more technically trained people, and it is the school's job to provide them.

The following values might be among those cited by individuals who *oppose* a four-year mathematics requirement:

- Individual choice is an important part of the high school experience.
- Mathematics is not necessarily more rigorous than other subjects it might displace.
- The society should not go overboard in imposing its priorities on individuals.

STEP 5

The following consequences might be cited by a *supporter* of a four-year mathematics requirement as logically resulting from implementation of such a policy:

- Quantitative SAT scores may be expected to rise.
- High school graduates will be better prepared for college.
- The nation will be better able to compete with such technologically oriented nations as Japan.

The following consequences might be cited by an *opponent* of a four-year mathematics requirement as logically resulting from implementation of such a policy:

- The drop-out rate among high school students will increase as academic frustrations become too much for some students.
- Discipline problems will increase among students who remain because many who are not talented in mathematics will sense that they have been put in a no-win situation.
- Because vocationally oriented electives will decrease in number, some employers will begin to attack the schools for failing to provide relevant instruction.

Step 6

At this point, a decision is made. In this case, since there are only two alternatives, a choice would be made either to (1) support the decision to require four years of mathematics, or (2) to oppose this decision.

Step 7

A person *supporting* the decision might identify the pieces of information and values relevant to his conclusion in this way:

> I was impressed by the data showing the decline in quantitative SAT scores since the early 1960s. The growing shortage of engineers and technicians also impressed me. Thinking back on my own high school experience, I concluded that high school students lack the maturity to choose electives wisely. In the long run, they would be better served by a more prescriptive curriculum. Finally, I think the schools *do* have a responsibility to require students to take courses in areas where we have a critical national shortage.

A person *opposing* the decision might identify the pieces of information and values relevant to her conclusion in this way:

> It is clear to me that requiring four years of mathematics will reduce the number of electives available to students. Many vocational electives in the high school program do a fine job of responding to needs of students who will go to work once they graduate. We need to preserve these programs. Finally, I don't think we should allow needs articulated by bureaucratic federal agencies to force content on students in the schools. Local control and freedom of choice are a cherished part of our educational heritage.

Table 14.1   Summary Table

Main Points	Explanation
Indirect Instruction	In indirect instruction, the teacher acts as a learning manager and encourages students to accept a great deal of responsibility for their own behavior. Many indirect instruction lessons call on students to deal with challenging content and go beyond the givens.
Metacognition	*Metacognition* refers to thought about the processes persons use as they think. Metacognitive techniques are designed to help people to become more aware of their own thought processes. In particular, they seek to assist them in determining whether their approaches are appropriate for a particular thinking task.
Teacher Modeling	Teacher modeling is a metacognitive approach that asks students to observe, listen, and otherwise become aware of thought processes used by teachers in solving problems of a type they will be asked to solve themselves. The idea is to inform students about patterns of thinking that are appropriate for a given learning task.
Visualizing Thinking	Visualizing thinking encourages students to monitor their thinking processes by generating visual models they can use to organize responses to an assigned task.
Inquiry Teaching	Inquiry teaching embraces instructional techniques based on inductive learning principles. Students are exposed to specific examples. They are encouraged to develop general explanatory principles based on their analyses of the features of these examples. Basic steps include (1) identifying essential features of a problem, (2) developing proposed solutions, (3) gathering evidence related to these proposed solutions, (4) evaluating proposed solutions in light of this evidence, and (5) developing a conclusion that is supported by evidence.
Data Retrieval Chart	The data retrieval chart is often used to organize data used in inquiry lessons. It consists of a matrix featuring basic headings at the top and specific items of information under each. A completed data retrieval chart allows for visual inspection of a large quantity of information at one time. The data can be used by students as they attempt to formulate conclusions about a problem being used as a focus for an inquiry lesson.

Table 14.1   Summary Table *(continued)*

Main Points	Explanation
Inquiry Teaching, *cont'd.*	
Suchman Strategy	Developed by J. Richard Suchman, this strategy is designed to help students quickly focus on essential features of a puzzling situation — something Suchman labeled a *discrepant event.* Students play an active role. They ask the teacher questions about the discrepant event that must be capable of being answered by "yes" or "no." This technique helps students quickly eliminate huge categories of nonrelevant explanations and to narrow their focus on issues clearly connected to a possible explanation for the discrepant event.
Creative Thinking	*Creative thinking* refers to thought processes directed at solving problems in unusual, innovative ways. It has been found to be stimulated when people are able to avoid the temptation to reach quick conclusions and do not have a strong fear of failure. Brainstorming is a classroom technique directed at promoting creative thinking in students.
Critical Thinking	The primary function of critical thinking is the evaluation of ideas. It always involves judgments. It *should* involve judgments made in light of defensible criteria.
Problem Solving	This kind of thinking is directed at the solution of problems for which there exists a "best" or "correct" solution. These solutions need not be best or correct in an absolute sense, but rather they are "best" or "correct" in terms of the available evidence. Steps in problem-solving lessons often include (1) identifying the problem, (2) considering possible approaches to solving it, (3) selecting and applying these approaches, and (4) evaluating the adequacy of the solution.
Decision Making	This kind of thinking is appropriate when there tends not to be a clearly evident "best" or "correct" solution. It requires people to make choices from among several competing (and attractive) alternatives. Steps include (1) describing the issue or problem, (2) pointing out alternative solutions, (3) identifying evidence supporting each alternative, (4) identifying values reflected in each alternative, (5) pointing out possible consequences of each alternative, (6) making a choice from among possible alternatives, and (7) identifying the evidence and values considered in making this choice.

Review of Key Ideas

- There is much less centralized teacher control in indirect instruction than in direct instruction. Indirect instruction places more responsibility on students to control their own behavior. Indirect instruction often is directed at developing students' higher-level thinking skills. The teacher functions as a manager who presents them with a problem and assists them, as needed, as they work toward a conclusion.

- *Metacognition* refers to thought about the process of thinking. Metacognitive instructional approaches seek to help students become conscious of their own thought processes and to select those that are relevant for solving particular problems and tasks with which they are confronted. Examples of these metacognitive approaches include teacher modeling and visualizing thinking.

- *Inquiry teaching* is based on inductive learning. Inductive learning proceeds from the specific to the general. This means that students first are presented with specific examples that they are asked to study; from this study, they derive general explanatory conclusions or principles. Inquiry teaching involves students in the creation of new knowledge. Approaches typically follow a logical, step-by-step sequence that is thought to develop students' rational thinking powers. Creative thinking frees people to develop unusual or novel solutions. It involves unique insight. Creative thinking is thought to be stimulated when people are able to defer final judgment until many alternatives have been considered and when they do not fear failure. Brainstorming is an example of a classroom technique that is designed to elicit creative thinking.

- *Critical thinking* focuses on the evaluation of ideas. It aids students in making judgments. Further, these judgments are based on the consideration of evidence. The analytic brainstorming approach developed by Dunn and Dunn (1972) is an example of a classroom technique designed to encourage the development of critical thinking abilities.

- *Problem-solving approaches* are designed to help students consider problems for which a single "best" answer is thought to exist. This does not mean that this best answer will be right for all time. It simply implies that it is best, given presently available evidence. These steps are included in many problem-solving approaches: (1) identifying the problem, (2) considering alternative approaches to solving it, (3) selecting and applying one or more approaches, and (4) making a final judgment regarding the best approach (or solution).

- *Decision making* refers to thinking sequences that are relevant when problems with which students are confronted have no generally agreed-upon correct or right answers. A number of appropriate answers may be identified. The alternative selected reflects both a consideration of evidence and of values. Value judgments play an important role in lessons requiring students to engage in decision making.

Follow-Up Questions and Activities

Questions

1. How might you explain the general differences between direct instruction and indirect instruction?

2. Teachers today feel obligated to cover a great deal of academic content in the courses they teach. Given this reality, should they devote class time to instruction designed to help students develop appropriate metacognitive processes? Why or why not?

3. Both the Suchman inquiry approach and visualizing thinking presume that students have trouble making sense out of the enormous volume of information that confronts them. Is this true? If so, are the Suchman technique and visualizing thinking sound approaches to helping them deal with it?

4. Why are relatively few people creative thinkers, and what might you do in the classroom to prompt more creative thinking from students?

5. What are some key features of approaches designed to elicit critical thinking?

6. How would you describe differences in the purpose of a traditional brainstorming approach and the variant called *analytical brainstorming*, developed by Dunn and Dunn (1972)?

7. Under what conditions would a problem solving approach be an appropriate instructional choice?

8. Why do different people arrive at quite different conclusions when a decision making approach is used to consider an issue?

Activities

1. Secondary teachers are always pressed for time. As a result, the issue of how scarce class time should be used is an important concern. Some people argue that time devoted to teaching students learning processes and thinking skills (e.g., metacognitive approaches, creative thinking skills, problem-solving skills, critical thinking skills, decision-making skills, and so forth) take valuable time away from content instruction. Find another student in your class to work with you on a project to prepare arguments related to this question: "Is taking class time to teach thinking skills to students responsible?" Make an oral presentation to your class in which one of you presents evidence supporting a "yes" answer and one of you presents evidence supporting a "no" answer.

2. Select a topic from a subject you are preparing to teach. Describe how you might incorporate one of the following into a lesson related to this topic:

   • Inquiry teaching

   • Problem solving

   • Creative thinking

- Decision making
- Critical thinking

Present this information to your instructor in a short paper.

3. Interview teachers who have incorporated inquiry teaching into their instructional programs. Ask them to describe pluses and minuses of this approach. Share your findings with others in the class as part of a general discussion of inquiry in the secondary school classroom.

4. Prepare a portfolio of articles from professional journals in education that describe practical classroom applications of inquiry and creative thinking approaches. You may wish to use the *Education Index* to locate article titles and journals. Your course instructor may also provide you with some ideas. Try to include at least 10 articles. Present them to your instructor for review. Keep these materials as a resource to use when you begin teaching.

5. Invite several department heads from a local secondary school to visit your class. If this is not possible, try to get a director of secondary education, a director of secondary curriculum, or another central school-district office administrator to come. Ask about the relative emphasis on inquiry instruction and on teaching thinking skills to students. Specifically, ask whether teachers are encouraged to use these approaches and whether any effort is made to provide inservice training to help teachers become more proficient in implementing them.

References

BEYER, B. K. *Developing a Thinking Skills Program*. Boston: Allyn & Bacon, 1988.

BEYER, B. K. "Practice is Not Enough." In M. Heiman and J. Slomianko (eds.). *Thinking Skills: Concepts and Techniques*. Washington, DC: National Education Association, 1987, pp. 77–86.

BORICH, G. D. *Effective Teaching Methods*. 2nd ed. New York: Merrill/Macmillan Publishing Company, 1992.

CORNO, L. AND SNOW, R. E. "Adapting Teaching to Individual Differences Among Learners." In M. C. Wittrock (ed.). *Handbook of Research on Teaching*. 3rd ed. New York: Macmillan Publishing Company, 1986, pp. 605–629.

DEWEY, J. *How We Think*. Boston: D. C. Heath, 1910.

DUNN, R. AND DUNN, K. *Practical Approaches to Individualizing Instruction: Contracts and Other Effective Teaching Strategies*. New York: Parker Publishing Company, 1972.

GOOD, T. AND BROPHY, J. *Looking in Classrooms*. 5th ed. New York: HarperCollins, 1991.

LIPMAN, M. "Critical Thinking—What Can It Be?" *Educational Leadership* (September 1988), pp. 38–39.

PERKINS, D. *The Mind's Best Work*. Cambridge, MA: Harvard University Press, 1981.

RUGGIERO, V. R. *Teaching Thinking Across the Curriculum*. New York: Harper & Row, 1988.

SUCHMAN, J. R. *The Elementary School Training Program in Scientific Inquiry*. Report to the U.S. Office of Education, Project Title VII, Project 216. Urbana, IL: University of Illinois, 1962.

YEAGER, N. C. "Teaching Thinking to Teach Literature While Teaching Literature to Teach Thinking." In M. Heiman and J. Slomianko (eds.). *Thinking Skills: Concepts and Techniques*. Washington, DC: National Education Association, 1987, pp. 134–144.

15

Small Groups and
Cooperative Learning

AIMS

This chapter provides information to help the reader to:

- Identify some functions of small-group learning.
- Point out claimed advantages of cooperative learning.
- Implement activities designed to make students more effective small-group participants.
- Explain procedures to be followed in implementing selected small-group learning approaches.
- Describe several instructional approaches that fall under the general heading of "cooperative learning."

FOCUS QUESTIONS

1. What arguments are there in support of small-group learning?
2. How can students be prepared for small-group learning?

3. How might a teacher organize a class so that students could efficiently be organized into groups of varying sizes on different days of the week?

4. How might you compare and contrast investigative groups, tutorial groups, and team learning groups?

5. Why might a teacher who has studied the relevant research be inclined to support the use of cooperative learning activities in his classroom?

6. Why is Jigsaw appropriate for fewer instructional situations than Learning Together?

7. What incentives are built into such cooperative learning approaches as Student Teams-Achievement Divisions, Teams-Games-Tournaments, Jigsaw, and Learning Together to encourage each student to develop an interest in the learning of each group member?

Introduction

Secondary school teachers often organize class members into small groups. The term *small group* has been defined in different ways. For our purposes, we'll regard a small group as

> a group of from 3 to 15 students who have been organized to pursue a specific task in a way that requires participation of all group members and that encourages high levels of interaction among group members.

Depending on the specifics of the individual situation, instruction provided to these small groups may be direct or indirect. Though researchers have studied whole-class versus small-group instruction, findings have not consistently favored one organizational pattern over the other (Brophy and Good, 1986). However, there do appear to be certain situations where small-group instruction has certain advantages. Brophy and Good (1986) have suggested that small-group instruction makes sense when critical basic skills are being taught and when there are tremendous differences in abilities, interests, and backgrounds of learners in a given class. When students are organized in small groups, teachers are better able to provide learning experiences tailored to individual needs and to monitor the progress of each student.

Small-group instruction places more demands on the teacher than whole-group instruction. Because students in different groups often are not doing exactly the same thing, the teacher must plan for several concurrent activities rather than for just one (as would be the case in a lesson featuring whole-class instruction). Further, monitoring can be a problem. The teacher has to develop ways of helping individuals in one group while maintaining some contact with students in other groups. Simply getting around to all groups can pose a challenge. As Brophy and Good (1986) have pointed out, small-

Box 15.1

Is Small-Group Learning a Time-Waster?

A first-year teacher recently overheard these comments being made by a veteran teacher.

I've been to some of these small-group workshops. In fact, I've tried some of the ideas in my own classes. The students really liked the activities. But, then, why shouldn't they? I mean, this kind of an arrangement just invites lots of talk. I think all small-group instruction does is give students the idea that the teacher has awarded a 'free talking' period. They know I can't keep tight reins on what they're doing. I just don't think it is responsible for me to organize students in this way, and I won't do it again.

What Do You Think?

1. Suppose some of this teacher's comments are true. What might you do when organizing your own students for small-group work to eliminate some of the problems this person mentions?

2. Is careful monitoring of students possible when they are doing small-group work?

3. In general, how do you react to this teacher's views?

group instruction often is more successful in situations where teachers have an instructional aide available to share monitoring tasks.

Elizabeth G. Cohen (1986), a well-known sociologist who has conducted extensive research on group learning in schools, has identified two key characteristics of successful groups. The first involves delegation of authority by the teacher to the group. This means that students are given a general task to accomplish, but are allowed to make decisions on their own regarding exactly how they should proceed and what each group member should do.

Second, the group project is designed so that each group member must participate if the task is to be satisfactorily accomplished. This feature assures that all members will contribute to the successful completion of the assigned task. The potential for intense personal involvement of all students in small-group instruction is greater than that in whole-group instruction.

Learning in groups has also been promoted on the grounds that it allows students to talk to one another. As Cohen (1986; p. 3) has noted, "the process of group interaction is enormously interesting to students. Students who usually do anything but what they are asked to do become actively involved with their work."

A special category of instructional approaches that often involves group work is cooperative learning. Cooperative learning techniques have become very popular in recent years. Cooperative learning approaches often feature schemes that reward students for cooperative or collaborative work, rather than for individual effort (Brophy and Good, 1986). They have been found to increase students' levels of motivation and their commitment to such prosocial behaviors as helping others and sharing expertise (Brophy and Good, 1986; Slavin, 1990). This chapter introduces some examples of small-group approaches and some illustrations of techniques associated with cooperative learning.

Preparing for Small-Group Learning

Students do not just take to small-group learning automatically. There are special kinds of behaviors that are required of students who function well in small groups, and these sometimes vary considerably from what learners have become used to in whole-group instruction. In particular, there is a need for students to understand that *each* group member has a responsibility to participate and that sharing of information is important. When students have been conditioned over many years to think of themselves as individuals who have a personal and highly competitive relationship with others in their classes, this perspective represents an important shift away from familiar patterns.

Often students who have experienced success in classes where whole-group instruction has been the norm are initially reluctant to get actively involved in small-group work. They sometimes see small-group settings as a potential threat to their academic status. To win students' support for small-group work, teachers often put members of their classes through exercises designed to teach functional group-work behaviors, particularly those associated with sharing and collaborating. Two such techniques are:

- Two-by-Twos
- Inside and Outside

Two by Twos

Many secondary students have not done much group work since they were in the earlier elementary school grades. Often, their classes have featured primarily whole-group instruction; in the typical class, the teacher has worked with all class members at the same time. Two-by-Twos is an exercise that some teachers have found useful in preparing students for small-group instruction.

General Background

Small-group instruction works best when students know and feel comfortable with one another. Particularly at the beginning of a new semester or school year, many students in a class of 25 to 30 will not be well acquainted. Two-by-Twos functions as an icebreaker. The technique helps students to learn something about each student in the class. Because it involves intense verbal interaction, it conditions the students to speak up and work productively together.

Implementing

The technique involves a series of steps that starts with small groups of two people and continues in a sequence that ultimately involves the whole group working together. If a teacher had a group of 32 students, the exercise might proceed along these lines:

STEP 1:   [The teacher gives these directions.] "I want each of you to stand up and walk over to someone you don't know well. Try to find a perfect stranger. You'll have 30 seconds to find someone." [Students quickly find a partner.]

STEP 2:   [The teacher gives these directions.] "I want each of you to find out three things about your partner. One—what is your partner's name? Two—when is your partner's birthday? Three—what would your partner do today if he or she received an unexpected gift of $1,000?" [Students follow these directions.]

STEP 3:   [Teacher gives these directions.] "Now, I want each pair of you to meet with another pair to form a group of four. Do the same thing in the group of four that you did with your partner. Take turns until all four of you know the answers to the three questions for each member of your new group." [Students follow these directions.]

STEP 4:   [Teacher gives these directions.] "Now life begins to get interesting. I want each group of four to get together with another group of four. Do the same thing in your new group of eight that you did before." [Students follow these directions.]

STEP 5:   [Teacher gives these directions.] "We are about to find out who the real memory champs are. I want each group of eight to join with another group of eight to form a new group of 16. Follow the same process as before. I'll give you enough time so everybody can share the necessary information." [Students follow these directions.]

STEP 6:   [Teacher gives these directions.] "This is the hard part. Let's get everybody together in one group of 32. Let's get in a big circle to do this. Try and learn everyone's answers to the three questions." [Students follow these directions.]

STEP 7:   [The teacher gives these directions.] "Is anybody ready to chance it? Will any of you try to give answers to the three questions for *everybody* in the group?" [Usually, several students will try, and several will be successful.]

Debriefing

This exercise is designed to make students comfortable with one another by getting to know more about each member in the class. After the exercise is over, the teacher may wish to ask some follow-up questions such as these:

- Were answers to any one of the three questions more difficult to remember than others? If so, which one, and why?
- Did you feel you had enough time during each part of the exercise?
- Do you feel you know people in the class better now than you did at the beginning?

Inside and Outside

Most group work requires verbal interaction with others. Some verbal behaviors contribute more to overall group performance than others. Inside and Outside is a technique that can make students aware of effective individual behaviors in small groups.

General Background

This technique calls students' attention to behaviors of group members that provide psychological support to others and that help the group complete an assigned task. Students have opportunities to observe actions of others who have been organized into groups and to participate in groups themselves. A follow-up discussion centers on kinds of individual behaviors that facilitate overall group functioning.

Implementing

Suppose a teacher has 32 students in a class. To start the Inside and Outside activity, 16 chairs are organized in a circular fashion. Half of the students are assigned to sit in them. This is the "inside" group. Members of the "outside" group arrange themselves around this circle of chairs. Each member of the outside group is assigned to observe and take notes on behaviors of a single member of the inside group. They are asked to note information related to what their assigned person did in terms of the following:

- Taking an active part in the discussion.
- Making comments that built logically on those of the previous speaker.

"Learning in groups is a sound approach in general. As for this particular lesson, well . . . ?"

- Summarizing something said by a previous speaker.
- Saying something to prevent the group from arriving at a premature conclusion.
- Supporting a comment made by someone else.
- Providing evidence to back up what he or she said.

The teacher provides the inside group with a controversial issue to discuss. For example, the insiders might be told to discuss the following idea:

> Since most teenage crime occurs between midnight and 6:00 A.M., there should be a law that makes it illegal for anyone under age 18 to be on the street between those hours, unless he or she is accompanied by someone who is 18 or older.

Once the topic is given, the insides discuss it for about 10 minutes. Then the groups switch, and the old insides become outsides, and the old outsides become insides. The discussion picks up again and continues for another 10 minutes.

Debriefing

Debriefing focuses on notes students took when they were in the outside role. It focuses on such issues as these:

- What kinds of verbal behaviors were most supportive of others?
- What kinds of statements tended to inhibit others from speaking up?
- What did some people do that helped the group to move toward a conclusion?
- What did some people say that interfered with the group's ability to resolve the issue?
- What general kinds of verbal behaviors do you think are most appropriate for someone who is involved in a group activity?

■ ■ ■

Two-by-Twos and Inside and Outside are examples of activities that have been designed to help students develop behaviors that will help them to perform well in groups. Elizabeth Cohen's book, *Designing Groupwork*, includes an appendix that describes many other useful approaches for training students to work in groups.

Scheduling Small-Group Learning

Few teachers organize students in their classes into small groups every day. Suppose a teacher has about 30 students in a class. On some days, she might want the group organized into six 5-student groups. On other days, the teacher probably will want to provide learning experiences to all 30 students organized as a single large group. On still other occasions, the teacher might wish to have 15 or 20 students engaged in activity A and 15 or 10 others engaged in activity B.

Box 15.2

An Example of a Weekly Schedule Illustrating Different Grouping Arrangements on Each Day

Monday	Groups A, B, C, D, E, and F meet together as one large group	(Total of 30 students meeting together for whole-group instruction).
Tuesday	Group A — small-group activity Group B — small-group activity Group C — small-group activity Group D — small-group activity Group E — small-group activity Group F — small-group activity	(Six small groups of 5 students each work as assigned by the teacher.)
Wednesday	Groups A, B, and C work with teacher on unit review.	(Total of 15 students work with the teacher.)
	Groups D, E, and F work on assigned task in the school library.	(Total of 15 students work in the library.)
Thursday	Groups A, B, and C work on assigned task in the school library.	(Total of 15 students work in the library.)
	Groups D, E, and F work with teacher on unit review.	(Total of 15 students work with the teacher.)
Friday	Groups A, B, C, D, E, and F meet together as one large group.	(Total of 30 students meeting together for whole-group instruction.)

Note: These are just examples of possible arrangements. Using this basic scheme, a teacher could put together many different arrangements by clustering two or more of the five-student groups.

To conveniently schedule a variety of group sizes within a single classroom, the teacher might begin by thinking about the class not as a single group of 30 students but rather as six groups with five students apiece. As an aid to planning, the teacher might designate these groups with letters of the alphabet, as follows:

Group A: 5 students

Group B: 5 students

Group C: 5 students

Group D: 5 students

Group E: 5 students

Group F: 5 students

This arrangement makes it relatively easy to plan an instructional week featuring somewhat different grouping arrangements on each day.

This approach to small-group and whole-class planning merely identifies names of groups (A, B, C, D, E, F); it does not indicate the names of students who are assigned as members of each group. The teacher is free to assign students to groups, as required. Depending on what is being taught, the ability levels of the students, and the desires of both students and teacher, students might be assigned to the same group for a considerable period of time. Under other conditions, the teacher may wish to make fairly frequent changes in the student makeup of individual groups.

Examples of Small-Group Learning Experiences

Though activities such as Two-by-Twos and Inside and Outside are designed to prepare students to work well in group settings, they by no means guarantee that students will work productively in just any small group. Researchers have found that small-group activities themselves must be well organized and that students must be also be taught desirable group work behaviors in the context of a "real" small-group learning experience.

Many instructional formats for small-group instruction have been developed. Three examples are introduced here. They are:

- The investigative role group
- The tutorial group
- The team learning group

The Investigative Role Group

Many school assignments require students to solve problems of various kinds. The investigative role group organizes students so that each group member has a specific assigned responsibility.

General Background

Because assignments requiring students to solve problems are featured in many different kinds of classes, the investigative role group can be used in many subject areas. It can be used by teachers in English, social studies, and science classes, among others.

Specialization is a common feature of modern life. Complex problems rarely are addressed by individuals working alone. For example, an issue such as water pollution may require the expertise of individuals with backgrounds in biology, hydraulic engineering, physics, law, medicine, and other areas as well. The investigative role group seeks to help students learn the wisdom of breaking complex problems into smaller parts and assigning individuals to work on only a few aspects of a problem that, in its totality, may be too difficult or intimidating for one individual to handle.

Implementing

To facilitate the development of reasonable solutions to problems or vexing situations that are posed as a focus for investigative group work, teachers' directions often feature a systematic decision-making scheme. Such a plan might proceed according to these steps:

STEP 1:   Identifying the focus issue.

STEP 2:   Breaking the issue into parts and assigning specific students to each one.

STEP 3:   Students gather information about specific parts of the problem to which they have been assigned.

STEP 4:   Students share information with one another; basic points are recorded by the group chair.

STEP 5:   Discussion with the teacher, emphasizing strength of evidence that has been gathered and culminating with a tentative conclusion.

Suppose a teacher had decided on this statement as a focus for an investigative group activity:

What might happen if the United States banned the import of all cars from Japan?

If the teacher envisioned an investigative group of four members, this issue might be broken down into these four parts:

• What would be the impact on Japan's ability to pay for merchandise manufactured in the United States, and what might happen to U.S. workers producing these goods?
• What might happen to the U.S. trucking firms and railroads that presently ship Japanese autos from U.S. ports to the nation's interior?
• What might happen to U.S. autoworkers?
• What might happen to the quality of automobiles produced in the United States?

In a four-student group, each student would be assigned to become the "expert" on a specific issue. One of these students also might be designated as the group chair, the person responsible for seeking help from teacher (as needed), assisting group members to find appropriate information, and taking notes on what group members found.

Successful implementation of this method requires identifying a problem that is of interest to students, assigning individuals to parts of the problem based on their particular interests and motivations, and the availability of learning resources that will provide the information individual students will need to accomplish their specific tasks. If learning materials are not readily available, students will become frustrated, and the group exercise will not succeed.

As students do their work, the teacher circulates among them to provide general assistance and guidance. An encouraging word or two from the teacher can be an important confidence-builder for students.

This teacher is helping students gather information needed as part of their work as members of an investigative role group.

Debriefing

When groups have finished, the teacher engages each in a debriefing discussion. Sometimes the entire class, perhaps consisting of six or more groups, listens and participates. Sometimes the teacher works with groups one at a time during this phase of the lesson.

During debriefing, the teacher does the following:

- Elicits from each student his or her findings regarding the part of the larger problem he or she was assigned to investigate.
- Sensitively asks students to consider the quality of their conclusions. (This must be done carefully. Some secondary students have had little experience generating interpretations of their own, and teachers' comments must not be so negative as to inhibit students' willingness to think about possible solutions to complex problems.)
- Asks the group as a whole to come up with a tentative conclusion about the major focus problem.
- Challenges group members to think about how the adequacy of this conclusion might be tested in the future.

Throughout the debriefing phase, the teacher underscores the point that complex issues do not have simple solutions. It is particularly important for students to understand that there may well be potential solutions to the problem other than those that came out during the discussion.

The Tutorial Group

Sometimes teachers want to present information and interact with students in a way that is quite similar to patterns used in whole-group instruction but that assures more intense student involvement. Tutorial groups serve this purpose well. Basically, a tutorial group instruction is whole-group instruction scaled down to fit the special needs of a small group of learners. Numbers of students involved range from about four to about six.

General Background

Tutorial groups are particularly useful in helping (1) students who may find it difficult to pay attention and learn from whole-group instruction, and (2) students who can profit from exposure to content that supplements or in other ways goes beyond information introduced to the entire class during whole-group instruction. Said in another way, tutorial groups can serve either remediation or enrichment needs.

During tutorial group instruction, students are encouraged to ask questions and make comments. Because of the relatively small numbers of students involved, there is more teacher-student interaction than in whole-group instruction. This allows for better teacher monitoring of individual students' levels of understanding, something researchers have found to be closely associated with how much students learn (Good and Brophy, 1991). Students often feel more comfortable in speaking up and becoming active participants in small tutorial groups than in large groups of 25 or 30 students. Often, too, this instructional format sparks more student interest than the more impersonal whole-group instruction setting.

Implementing

Students have few adjustments to make when a teacher decides to organize them into a tutorial group. In many respects, what they do will be quite similar to the familiar behavior patterns to which they have long been accustomed in whole-group instructional situations. Initially, some students may feel a bit exposed because there is not much room to hide in a small tutorial group. Typically, supportive comments from the teacher relieve any anxieties, and students soon become quite comfortable with this format.

For the teacher, planning for a tutorial group is not too different from getting ready for whole-group instruction. However, there is one key difference. Once work with a given tutorial group has begun, students in this group will demand the undivided attention of the teacher. This means that careful plans must be prepared for students who are not members of the tutorial group with which the teacher is working. These students must be provided with clear directions regarding what they are to do. If this is not done, there will be frequent interruptions from students not in the tutorial group, and the quality of the lesson being introduced to tutorial-group students will suffer.

Debriefing

Debriefing a tutorial-group lesson parallels what teachers do when they conclude a lesson and review key points during whole-class instruction. The key difference is that a much higher percentage of tutorial-group students can be called on during lesson debriefing than is possible during whole-group instruction. In many cases, it will be possible for the teacher to call on each student (perhaps several times). This feature of tutorial-group instruction enables the teacher to have a clear understanding of what each student has learned and to clear up misconceptions and review difficult points.

The Team Learning Group

The kinds of content to which students are exposed within a given course vary enormously. Some content features basic, highly structured information that may be laid out in considerable detail in the course text. In reviewing this kind of content and elaborating on it, a whole-group instructional technique (for example, a lecture) might be a reasonable choice. On the other hand, as a means of helping students master content that requires them to "go beyond the givens" and use thinking skills requiring them to apply, synthesize, interpret, and judge, small-group techniques make sense (Borich, 1992). Team learning groups are particularly well adapted for instructional programs that smoothly integrate whole-group and small-group instruction.

General Background

The team learning approach was initially described more than 20 years ago (Dunn and Dunn, 1972). It blends together whole-group and small-group instructional approaches by dividing lessons into two principle phases. Individual students work in groups to develop answers to key questions. This phase is followed by a general discussion that is led by the teacher and includes the whole class.

Students generally react positively to work in team learning groups. In part, their satisfaction results from the opportunity this format gives them to talk to one another—something they cannot ordinarily do during whole-group instruction. Additionally, team learning requires the teacher to incorporate student responses generated during the small-group phase in the second, whole-group part of the lesson. There is evidence that using student ideas promotes higher levels of student engagement in the learning process (Evertson, Emmer, Sanford, Clements, and Worsham, 1989).

Implementing

Students are divided into a manageable number of groups. Each group should have between four and six members. The teacher provides each group with the same set of focus questions. These questions should require students to make interpretations and inferences about basic information to which they have already been exposed. Group members are allowed to look at texts and any other available resource materials that might help them as they try to answer the questions. (If a great deal of specialized material has been introduced that individual students do not have, a supply of this information should be conveniently available for the use of each group.)

Suppose a high school English class had just finished reading *The Merchant of Venice*. Members of team learning groups might be provided with questions such as these:

- Is it possible to make a case for Shylock as a hero? If so, what arguments might be made?
- Is it really true that the quality of mercy is not strained?
- Are there some lessons or morals in this play that are still relevant for us today? Can you identify at least two possibilities? What are they?

The general sequence of events in a team-learning activity follows this basic pattern:

PHASE ONE: Small-Group Teamwork

- Teacher organizes students into small groups, and each group is provided with the set of focus questions.
- One student in each group is assigned to be the recorder. This person will take notes on responses to the focus questions.
- Students are told they may talk to anyone in their own group, but they are not to talk to people in other groups.

PHASE TWO: Whole-Group Discussion

- The teacher calls the whole class to attention. (It may not be necessary for students to move. In many cases, they will be able to participate comfortably in a whole-group discussion from where they have been working as members of individual small groups.)
- The teacher starts with the first question on the list of focus questions. The teacher calls on each group for a response. The response is provided by the recorder. (Other members of individual groups are encouraged to speak up if they disagree with what the recorder has said or wish to add some additional comments.)
- Brief summaries of responses are written by the teacher (or by a student assigned to do this) on the board or on an overhead projector transparency.
- This same procedure is followed until responses have been gathered from all groups and written down where all can see them.
- The activity concludes with a discussion of the relative merits of the individual responses that have been made to each focus question.

Debriefing

The debriefing activity is really an extension of the final part of the whole-group discussion. It might feature such questions as these:

- Do you think that people could ever agree on right or correct answers to questions such as these?
- If there are no answers that are necessarily right or correct, does this mean that any answer is as good as any other?
- What other questions could we have looked at as we thought about what the *Merchant of Venice* really has to say to us today?

Cooperative Learning

Cooperative learning is defined as "students working together in groups (often following a teacher-prepared lesson), with group goals but individual accountability" (Willis, 1992; p. 1). Each student's evaluation depends, in part, on the success of the entire group in completing an assigned task. This feature helps students develop a prosocial commitment to helping others (Slavin, 1990), and it replicates the kind of productive group work featured in the adult workplace (Willis, 1992).

Cooperative learning has been gaining rapidly in popularity over the past 10 to 15 years. Among leading proponents of cooperative learning are Robert Slavin of Johns Hopkins University and David Johnson and Roger Johnson, who are co-directors of the Cooperative Learning Center at the University of Minnesota. Slavin recently estimated that about 10 percent of the nation's teachers now use cooperative learning approaches (Willis, 1992).

Researchers have found that cooperative learning methods that incorporate group goals and individual accountability result in improved levels of academic achievement. These approaches also have been found to have positive effects on:

- Students' self-esteem.
- Generating peer support for academic achievement.
- Increasing the amount of time students spend on academic tasks.
- Students' attitudes toward the class.
- Students' feelings toward other class members. (Slavin, 1990)

There are several approaches to organizing students for cooperative learning activities. Many of them share some characteristics. Typically, students are organized into groups or teams. Members of each team work together to accomplish a set of tasks. Rewards to individuals often are based largely on the accomplishment of the team. This builds an incentive for students to work productively together.

One important consideration for the teacher in planning a cooperative learning lesson is the issue of reward for performance. The selected reward system must encourage cooperation. At the same time, it needs to provide for individual accountability so that the contributions of each group member can be properly appreciated.

Most cooperative learning schemes provide students with considerable autonomy. Team members exercise a great deal of freedom as they decide how to deal with the assigned task or problem. Sometimes teams even have the right to determine when members are ready to take a test or present their final product to the teacher.

Many cooperative learning approaches have been developed. We will discuss four that are widely used. These are:

- Student Teams-Achievement Divisions
- Teams-Games-Tournaments
- Jigsaw
- Learning Together

Student Teams-Achievement Divisions (STAD)

Student Teams-Achievement Divisions was developed by the Johns Hopkins Team Learning Project (Slavin, 1980). It is one of the easiest cooperative learning models to implement. It can be used in many different kinds of secondary school classrooms.

General Background

This approach involves students in a learning format designed to promote cooperation and active participation by all students. The scoring system used gives each student a vested personal interest not only in his own learning, but in the learning of every other group member as well.

Implementing

Students are assigned to learning teams consisting of four or five members. Each team has a mix of high, average, and low achievers. If the class has a diverse ethnic make-up, the teacher makes an effort to achieve a reasonable ethnic balance among members of each team. There is also an attempt to have a gender mix on each team that closely approximates the percentages of males and females in the whole class.

Ordinarily, the teacher introduces new content using traditional whole-group instruction. Then, individual teams go to work on task sheets provided by the teacher. These provide students with directions for what is to be done. Tasks relate to the content introduced during the whole-group-instruction phase of the lesson.

Next, team members work on assignments explained on the task sheets. They do all work as a team. Individual team members take responsibility for assuring that each student understands the content. When they believe every member has as good grasp of the material, they take a test. During testing, team members may not help one another.

A special system of scoring is used to promote cooperation and active participation of all group members. Test scores are provided for each student, but each student's score also plays a role in deriving a total score for the entire team.

Box 15.3

Example of One Group's Score in Student Teams-Achievement Divisions

Student	Base Score	Quiz Score	Team Points
Raoul A.	57	64	7
LaShandra C.	63	60	0
Joyce R.	40	55	10
LaRue T.	83	88	5
Samuel W.	75	95	10

An individual team member, depending on how well she did on the test, may add from 0 to 10 points to the total team score. The teacher looks at how well each member of a team did on the previous test. For example, suppose one student scored 15 points (out of 30 possible) on the previous test and 20 points (out of 30 possible) on this test. The difference between 20 and 15 (new test score minus old test score, or base score) is 5. Five points would be added to the team score as a result of this student's performance.

Each student may provide a maximum of 10 points to the overall team score. There are two ways this 10-point maximum can be earned. Ten points is awarded if the student scores 10 or more points on the present test as compared to the last test. Ten points are awarded for any perfect paper regardless of what the student received on the last test. This is an incentive to maintain the active participation of brighter students.

Box 15.3 illustrates an array of scores for one group of students in a biology class where Student Teams-Achievement Divisions were used. Notice that Joyce R., who received the lowest grade on the quiz, still contributed the maximum of 10 points to the total group score. This occurred because her quiz score of 55 was significantly higher than her base score of 40.

Student Teams-Achievement Divisions encourages less-able students. These students have an incentive to do as well as they can. Even though their individual scores may not be high, they can make important contributions to the total score of their team. Brighter students are encouraged to help less-able members of their group because all group members benefit when these less-able students exceed the expectations reflected in their base scores. Each member of a group has a stake in the learning of every other member. Thus, every student has a reason to want to help all group members to learn, and improvement of all team members becomes the goal as team members strive to increase their overall team scores. Teachers usually arrange for some special recognition to be provided to high-scoring teams at the end of grading periods, perhaps once every six or eight weeks.

Debriefing

Debriefing in Student Teams-Achievement Divisions tends to focus heavily on the quality of interactions the teacher has observed among individual team members. Team scores are shared, and the teacher reemphasizes the importance of every group member helping every other group member. The debriefing phase of the lesson provides an opportunity for the teacher to single out for special recognition students who have done well themselves and who also have been observed working well to help others to learn.

Teams-Games-Tournaments

Teams-Games-Tournaments is another approach developed by the Johns Hopkins Group (Slavin, 1980). It requires somewhat more time to plan and implement than Student Teams-Achievement Divisions. Teams-Games-Tournaments can be used in a wide variety of secondary school classes.

General Background

Teams-Games-Tournaments is basically an extension of Student Academic-Teams Divisions. In this approach, the teacher periodically creates new groups of students who participate in academic tournaments.

Implementing

As a first step, the teacher organizes students into teams. Each team has from four to six students. As is the case when Student Teams-Achievement Division groups are organized, each team represents a cross section of ability levels, ethnic groups, and gender. Members of each group study assigned material together. Team members are encouraged to help each other master the content. Instead of receiving team points based on test performance, members of each team participate in weekly academic tournaments.

The format for the tournaments requires the teacher to organize students into tournament groups. Three students, each from a different team, constitute a group. Each group sits around a table. If there are 24 students in a class, there will be eight tables of tournament-group students. Questions are drawn, and students attempt to respond to them. Points for correct answers are awarded to the team to which each tournament group member belongs. At the end, scores for each student are examined.

When the first tournament is held, the teacher simply assigns students to sit at particular tables based on their past performances. For example, in a class of 24 students, the top three individuals will be assigned to table 1, the next three to table 2, and the next three to table 3. The process continues until the bottom three students are assigned to table 8.

Following the initial week, students are assigned to tables based on their performance at the previous week's tournament. The high scorer at each table moves up to the next table (e.g., the high scorer at table 3 would move to table 2). The low-scorer moves down one table (e.g., the low scorer at table 3 would move to table 4). The person who came in second at each table retains his or her place at the same table for the next tournament. Over time, this system tends to equalize competition.

The Teams-Games-Tournaments approach combines cooperative and competitive activities. The format tends to keep competition among students at approximately the same level. Students find this system to be fair. Teachers have reported that even quite reluctant learners have become interested in school when the approach has been used (Slavin, 1980).

Debriefing

Debriefing focuses on the processes students have followed in their groups to learn content. The teacher makes comments to encourage collaborative behavior of students. Any issues relating to the fairness of the teachers' assignment to individual groups are also addressed at this time. It is important that the students understand that the teacher is attempting to create groups in such a way that the average ability (as reflected by past performance) in each group will be about the same.

Jigsaw

Jigsaw is a cooperative learning method that can be used in many different kinds of secondary school subjects. It requires a topic that can be conveniently divided into several major components. It is also helpful if information related to each component can be organized under a common set of headings. For example, if a sixth grade class is studying South America, the components might be the individual countries. Information about each might be organized under the common headings of (1) physical features, (2) population size and ethnic makeup of the population, (3) major languages, (4) major economic activities, and (5) education and literacy.

General Background

Before deciding to use the Jigsaw technique, it is important for the teacher to assure that the topic lends itself to being divided into major subtopics. If possible, the teacher goes on to develop a common set of headings under which students can organize information gathered about each subtopic. A well-constructed Jigsaw lesson helps students to focus on relevant information, to master it, and to share it with others in their team.

Implementing

A Jigsaw lesson begins by the teacher assigning students to teams of approximately six persons each. Academic material to be studied is broken into a number of parts. For example, suppose a teacher wanted to focus on "A Comparison of the Literary Work of Selected Twentieth-Century American Writers." This large topic could be divided into a number of subordinate topics such as: (1) Theodore Dreiser, (2) Eudora Welty, (3) F. Scott Fitzgerald, (4) Ernest Hemingway, (5) Willa Cather, and (6) Joyce Carol Oates. If the teacher had organized students into five 6-person teams, then one student from each team would be assigned to become an "expert" on one of these individuals. In this situation, each six-person team would include one Theodore Dreiser expert, one Eudora Welty expert, one F. Scott Fitzgerald expert, one Ernest Hemingway expert, one Willa Cather expert, and one Joyce Carol Oates expert.

Once individual experts are identified for each of these original or home teams, these teams break up. Members from each team who have been assigned to become experts on a given subordinate topic meet together. For example, all Theodore Dreiser experts meet together. (There will be five of these people, one from each home team of six.) Members of the five-person expert teams meet together. They are given directions about learning resources to be used. (These often will include their own notes and rec-ollections from previous class sessions as well as books and other materials furnished by the teacher.) If the teacher chooses to provide them, members of each group might organize information under certain common headings. For example, students might be asked to generate ideas under these categories: (1) novels written and major themes treated, (2) short stories written and major themes treated, (3) poetry and other writings and major themes treated, and (4) general reactions of critics to this person's work.

When the expert teams have finished their cooperative study, the original home teams are reconstituted. The experts on each subordinate topic teach what they have learned to other members of the home group. In this way, members of each home group receive information related to all subordinate topics. Since the criterion test at the end of the lesson will cover the entire topic, there is an incentive for home group members to listen carefully to presentations by experts on each topic and for them to insist that experts share all of their information.

Jigsaw requires careful teacher monitoring of the work of the expert teams. Mem-bers of each expert group must understand all of the necessary information, and each student must learn it well enough to pass it on to members of his home group.

Jigsaw lessons designed to last several days pose problems. If a student from one home team is absent during part of the time she is supposed to be attending an assigned expert group, then this person's home group may lack important information. The teacher, in such a case, must step in and provide the missing information to the home group. There are particular difficulties when several students are absent. Gener-ally, there are fewer problems when a topic that can be concluded in a single class ses-sion is used as a focus for a Jigsaw exercise.

Debriefing

Debriefing in a Jigsaw lesson often takes the form of a general discussion involving class members working as a single large group. Information teams have gathered is reviewed. Students are asked to take notes on ideas introduced by members of other groups that were not brought up in their own group meetings. Debriefing affords an opportunity to fill in information gaps and to encourage higher-level thinking. For example, in the lesson focusing on the American authors, the teacher might ask ques-tions such as these:

• In what ways is the literary work of some of these people similar?

Box 15.4

Organization of Home Groups and Expert Groups for a Jigsaw Lesson Focusing on a Comparison of the Literary Work of Selected Twentieth-Century American Writers

Focus: A Comparison of the Literary Work of Selected American Writers

Home Groups

GROUP 1	GROUP 2	GROUP 3
Anna (Dreiser)	Paul (Dreiser)	Yu (Dreiser)
Rodney (Welty)	Sondra (Welty)	Monica (Welty)
Juan (Fitzgerald)	Norman (Fitzgerald)	Lee (Fitzgerald)
LaRue (Hemingway)	Sally (Hemingway)	Helmut (Hemingway)
Spencer (Cather)	Nora (Cather)	Rene (Cather)
Agnes (Oates)	Raoul (Oates)	Roy (Oates)

GROUP 4

Sarana (Dreiser)
Ming (Welty)
Kara (Fitzgerald)
Renaldo (Hemingway)
Price (Cather)
Travis (Oates)

GROUP 5

Tasha (Dreiser)
Karl (Welty)
Courtney (Fitzgerald)
Toshi (Hemingway)
Rocky (Cather)
Cole (Oates)

Expert Groups

Dreiser Group	Welty Group	Fitzgerald Group
Anna	Rodney	Juan
Paul	Sondra	Norman
Yu	Monica	Lee
Sarana	Ming	Kara
Tasha	Karl	Courtney

Hemingway Group	Cather Group	Oates Group
LaRue	Spencer	Agnes
Sally	Nora	Raoul
Helmut	Rene	Roy
Renaldo	Price	Travis
Toshi	Rocky	Cole

- In what ways is it different?
- How might you explain these differences?
- How might we account for differences in how critics have viewed each of these people?
- What does each of these authors have to say to us today?
- Do you think some of these authors will be better regarded 50 years from now than the others? If so, which ones and why?

Learning Together

Some cooperative learning approaches include more incentives than others for students to support the work of all group members. Learning Together places an especially high premium on students helping students (Johnson, Johnson, Holubec, and Roy, 1984).

General Background

Learning Together can be used in many secondary school subject areas. It does not require, as does Jigsaw, content that can be easily broken down into a set of clearly identifiable parts or subtopics.

Implementing

To implement Learning Together, the teacher organizes students into teams that include a cross section of ability levels. Each team is given a task or project to complete. The approach works best when the assignment requires a wide variety of talents. Individuals on each team work on a part of the overall project that is compatible with their own interests and abilities. The idea is to maximize strengths of individual students to get a better overall group effort.

Roles of individuals in Learning Together teams can be quite varied. For example, if the final product is to be a short play, one or more students might assume roles such as (1) head writer, (2) manuscript editor, (3) manuscript production chief, (4) set designer, and (5) and sound and light planner.

Each team is responsible for gathering the information and materials needed to complete its assigned task or project. Final assessment is based on the quality of the team's performance. Each student on a team receives the same grade. This is encourages individuals to pool their talents in such a way that work of each student adds the greatest possible contribution to the effort.

Some teachers have expressed concern about the fairness of giving each team member the same grade. This issue has been researched. Johnson and Johnson (1985) reported that, though students tend to favor competitive grading before they engage in cooperative tasks, after they have completed a cooperative learning project they commit to the idea that awarding every group member the same grade is a fair approach.

CASE STUDY

Cooperative Learning Blues

"I went to this cooperative learning workshop last summer. It was great. There were teachers there who were using cooperative learning in their own classrooms, and they talked us through some of the pitfalls. I left really pumped up and ready to try some of the ideas myself." The speaker was Nora Bennington, a second-year English teacher at J.V. Ortonsen High School. Rene Wu, Nora's former college roommate and herself now also a high school teacher, listened attentively.

"So how has it gone?" Rene asked.

"Well, I got off to a smoother start than I really had expected," Nora responded. "Having those teachers work with us helped a lot. I picked up some good tips, and I managed to avoid some stupid mistakes I probably would have made otherwise. Also, I decided to start with Learning Together, one of the techniques that isn't just a killer when it comes to planning."

Nora continued, "The students were a bit reluctant at first, but now they're really into it. I tend to mix it up a bit. We do Learning Together a while, and then we do a day or two of large-group work. By and large, I think I'd have a revolution on my hands if I went back to using large-group work all the time."

"No real problems, then?" Rene asked.

"Well," replied Nora, "there *has* been a glitch. I have had one parent on my back constantly since I started using Learning Together. She's come to see me, and she's complained to the principal."

"What's her complaint—an unhappy son or daughter, or what?" Rene inquired.

"No, that's not it at all. Her son, Eric, is really bright. He has gotten into the swing of things, and he tells me he likes the small-group work. His mother has a real problem with the grading thing. You know, each student in the group gets the same grade."

"And, I suppose," put in Rene, "that she's convinced that her Eric is doing everybody else's work."

"Yes, that's part of it. But there's a bit more. Everytime she calls me I get this big lecture about how competitive the world is and that this kind of learning just isn't preparing students for the real world. She also makes pointed remarks about how each student has to take the Scholastic Aptitude Test *alone* and that his or her personal score is what will be evaluated. She says this small-group stuff will make our students too dependent on others. She thinks the lazier ones will find somebody bright to carry the load and never really develop their own talents."

"Did they give you any information from the research this summer that you might use as ammunition?" asked Rene.

"As a matter of fact, they did," Nora replied. "And I've shared some of this information with her, but she's not impressed. I think she feels the researchers were people with a vested interested in cooperative learning. Since the results don't square with her biases, she questions the researchers' real motives.

"Rene, I didn't mean to ramble on so long about this, but I'm in a bit of a quandary. I just don't know how to respond to this person. I hate to give up a program I believe in and the kids like. But, I am afraid Eric's mother is going to make my professional life very uncomfortable unless I give up on Learning Together."

■ ■ ■

What should Nora Bennington do? Can you think of some other arguments that might make sense to this parent? To what extent should other professionals be brought into the picture? What might these people do? Is it fair that one parent's concern might lead Nora to change her instructional program? Or, should she change only if a number of parents complain? Do you think the complaints of all parents would be equally weighed by school administrators? If not, which parents would be listened to most? What would *you* do if you were faced with this situation?"

Debriefing

Debriefing involves the teacher in helping students to focus on the process they used in their groups to produce their product. The teacher often asks questions such as these:

- What are some things you did in your groups that helped you to accomplish your task?
- Without naming names, what are some things that went on that were not helpful? How did you handle this situation?
- How do you feel about the quality of what you produced?
- If we were to do this again, what might we do differently?

Small-group and cooperative learning techniques, in addition to their academic benefits, help prepare students for today's workplace. Increasingly employers seek people who know how to work together for a common purpose. This is precisely the kind of experience students get in small-group and cooperative learning activities.

Table 15.1   Summary Table

Main Points	Explanation
Small Group	A small group is made up of from 3 to 15 students who have been organized to pursue a specific task in a way that requires participation of all group members and that encourages high levels of interaction among group members.
Major Characteristics of Small-Group Instruction	This instructional arrangement features (1) some delegation of authority to the group by the teacher, and (2) rules that require each group member to participate.
Techniques for Preparing Students for Small-Group Instruction	
Two-by-Twos	The Two-by-Twos technique works as an icebreaker. Students go through a series of exercises that help them to become well acquainted with class members.
Inside and Outside	Inside and Outside helps students focus on how they can become more effective members of a small group. Students alternatively watch behaviors of others who participate in small groups and participate, themselves, as small-group members.
Scheduling Small-Group Learning	One useful administrative procedure requires the teacher to think of the whole class as a number of 5-student groups. For example, a class of 30 might be viewed as being composed of six 5-student groups. These might be labeled A, B, C, D, E, and F. On days when the whole class is to meet as one group, the teacher's planning simply shows groups A–F meeting together. On days when the teacher wants half of the class to work on one thing and half on something else, planning will reflect groups A–C doing activity one and groups D–F doing activity two. On days when all students will be working in small groups, students will be organized in six separate groups, as assigned. This general approach makes it easy for a teacher to plan a week's activity with different grouping configurations on each day.
Selected Examples of Small-Group Techniques	
Investigative Role Group	This small-group technique organizes students to solve an assigned focus problem. The problem is broken into parts, and each individual is responsible for gathering information about one part and sharing it with the group. Participants learn that issues that may be too complex for one individual to handle often yield to the collective wisdom and effort of a group of people who each take responsibility for working on a particular aspect of the problem.

Table 15.1   Summary Table *(continued)*

Main Points	Explanation
Selected Examples of Small-Group Techniques, *cont'd*.	
Tutorial Group	In the tutorial group arrangement, teachers present information and interact with students much as they do when delivering large-group instruction. The advantage is that numbers of learners are small, and teachers can be more sensitive to the concerns and learning difficulties of individuals. Also, because numbers are small, students are likely to be more intensely involved in the learning experience than during whole-group instruction.
Team Learning Group	Team learning allows for a smooth blending of whole-group and small-group instruction. During the small-group phase, students are organized into groups and given focus questions to answer. Students in each group are allowed to talk and work together to develop a common set of answers. During the follow-up, whole-group phase, questions are reviewed, and students take notes to fill in any information gaps.
Cooperative Learning	*Cooperative learning* refers to a number of small-group techniques that are organized in such a way that each student's evaluation depends, in part, on the success of the group to which the student is assigned.
Student Teams – Achievement Divisions	In Student Teams–Achievement Divisions, students are organized into groups to study assigned material. A scoring system, based on students' test performances, is used to give each student a vested interest not only in his or her personal learning, but in the learning of every other group member as well.
Teams-Games-Tournaments	This extension of Student Teams–Achievement Divisions begins with groups organized for group study. This phase is followed by an arrangement of new teams, which include representatives from the original teams. These new teams participate in academic tournaments in which students are required to answer content-related questions. Successes of individuals during these tournaments are credited to the participants' original teams.

Main Points	Explanation
Cooperative Learning, *cont'd.*	
Jigsaw	The Jigsaw cooperative learning technique requires as a focus a topic that can be conveniently divided into subtopics. One student in each of these home groups is assigned to become an expert on one subtopic. Next, new groups are formed consisting of students from the home groups assigned to the same subtopic. Members of these expert groups work together to learn as much as possible about their assigned subtopic. Then, home groups are reconstituted. Each expert shares information about his or her subtopic with other members of the home group.
Learning Together	This cooperative learning technique places a particularly heavy emphasis on each student supporting and encouraging learning of all group members. To encourage this kind of behavior, each Learning Together group member receives the same grade. This gives each student a vested interest in the quality of learning of everyone and in the quality of the final learning product produced by the group as a whole.

Review of Key Ideas

- A small group is a group of from 3 to 15 students who have been organized to pursue a specific task in a way that requires participation of all group members and that encourages high levels of interaction among members. Small-group instruction is especially useful when critical basic skills are being taught and when there are important differences in abilities, interests, and backgrounds of students.

- Successful small groups frequently have been organized so that (1) some authority has been clearly delegated to the group by the teacher, and (2) rules require all members to actively participate.

- Many secondary students have not worked extensively in small groups since they were in the early elementary grades. Consequently, teachers often use some preliminary activities to help them better understand how to work more effectively in groups. Two examples of these preliminary activities are (1) Two-by-Twos and (2) and Inside and Outside.

- Many teachers find it useful to develop an administrative plan that allows them to vary ways in which students are grouped on different days of the week. One way this can be done is to think of the class as composed of clusters of five students. For example, in a 30-student class, there might be six such clusters, labeled A, B, C, D, E, and F. Depending on how the teacher wishes to organize the class, each day's schedule can indicate whether individual groups are to meet together or separately. This scheme makes it easy for the teacher to organize anything from a class featuring six clusters of five meeting together as a whole group of 30 to six independent groups of five students each meeting separately.

- Many formats for small-group work have been developed. To function well, activities must be well organized, students must understand how they should behave in groups, and group work should be carefully monitored by the teacher. Three examples of small-group techniques are (1) the investigative role group, (2) the tutorial group, and (3) the team learning group.

- *Cooperative learning* is a general term used to describe small-group learning techniques that bases each student's evaluation, in part, on the overall level of performance of her group. Researchers have found cooperative learning approaches to have positive effects on (1) students' self-esteem, (2) generating peer support for academic achievement, (3) increasing the amount of time students spend on academic tasks, (4) students' attitudes toward the class where cooperative learning has been used, and (5) students' attitudes toward other students.

- There are many different cooperative learning techniques. Among those that are widely used are (1) Student Teams-Achievement Divisions, (2) Teams-Games-Tournaments, (3) Jigsaw, and (4) Learning Together.

Follow-Up Questions and Activities

Questions

1. If both small-group and whole-group instruction can be used to transmit information to students, why do some people make a case for including at least a minimal amount of small-group work in the instructional program?

2. Why do some secondary students need instructional experiences specifically designed to help them understand how to behave in small groups?

3. What planning and management challenges do teachers face when working with small groups?

4. How can a teacher plan for work with student groups of different sizes on different days of the week?

5. What kinds of learning outcomes do you think might be well served by (a) investigative groups, (b) tutorial groups, and (c) team learning groups?

6. How is *cooperative learning* defined?

7. What effects on learners have researchers found associated with students' involvement in cooperative learning?

8. Why has the grading procedure associated with Learning Together sometimes spawned controversy?

9. What kinds of special preparation might be required of a teacher who decided to use Teams-Games-Tournaments?

10. How does the design of techniques associated with cooperative learning encourage students to be concerned about the learning of each group member?

Activities

1. Many small-group techniques have been developed. Whole books have been written about the subject. Go to the library and locate information about four small-group techniques not mentioned in this chapter. (You might wish to look in the *Education Index* for periodical articles on this topic.) For each small-group technique, prepare a short summary sheet in which you organize information under these headings:

   • General description of the technique

   • How to implement it in the classroom

   Make copies of your information for all members of your class.

2. Interview one or more secondary teachers regarding how they use small groups in their classes. In particular, ask them to describe how they integrate whole-group instruction with small-group instruction. Request information about such practical matters as moving students into small groups quickly and efficiently, selecting students to go in specific groups, and monitoring small-group learning activities. Present your findings in a brief oral report.

3. Invite a panel of three secondary teachers who have used small-group methods to your class. Ask them to discuss candidly what they like and dislike about the techniques and advice they might offer teachers who were thinking about using small-group methods for the first time. Allow time for class members to ask questions.

4. Robert Slavin and the two Johnson brothers, Roger and David, have written extensively about cooperative learning. With a group of three or four other students, read some of the articles they have written about cooperative learning. Share information with others in your class regarding the kinds of research they have done on cooperative learning, suggestions they provide regarding implementation, and any other information that would contribute to a better understanding of cooperative learning.

5. Using content in this chapter as a focus, organize a Jigsaw scheme that members of your class could use to review chapter content. Share your design with your course instructor and, if he or she is agreeable, implement the technique during one of your class sessions.

References

BORICH, G. *Effective Teaching Methods*. 2nd ed. New York: Merrill/Macmillan Publishing Company, 1992.

BROPHY, J. AND GOOD, T. "Teacher Behavior and Student Achievement." In M. C. Wittrock (ed.). *Handbook of Research on Teaching*. 3rd ed. New York: Macmillan Publishing Company, 1986, pp. 328–375.

COHEN, E. G. *Designing Groupwork*. New York: Teachers College Press, 1986.

DUNN, R. AND DUNN, K. *Practical Approaches to Individualizing Instruction: Contracts and Other Effective Teaching Strategies*. New York: Parker Publishing Company, 1972.

EVERTSON, C.; EMMER, E.; SANFORD, J.; CLEMENTS, B.; AND WORSHAM, M. *Classroom Management for Elementary Teachers*. Englewood Cliffs, NJ: Prentice Hall, 1989.

GOOD, T. AND BROPHY, J. *Looking in Classrooms*. 5th ed. New York: HarperCollins, 1991.

JOHNSON, R. T. AND JOHNSON, D. W. "Structuring Conflict in Science Classrooms." Paper presented at the annual meeting of the National Association of Research in Science Teaching. French Lick, IN: April 1985.

JOHNSON, D. W.; JOHNSON, R. T.; HOLUBEC, E.; AND ROY, P. *Circles of Learning: Cooperation in the Classroom*. Alexandria, VA: Association for Supervision and Curriculum Development, 1984.

SLAVIN, R. E. *Cooperative Learning: Theory, Research, and Practice*. Englewood Cliffs, NJ: Prentice Hall, 1990.

SLAVIN, R. E. *Using Student Team Learning*. Baltimore: Johns Hopkins Team Learning Project, Center for Social Organization of the Schools, Johns Hopkins University, 1980.

WILLIS, S. "Coop. Learning Shows Staying Power." *Association for Supervision and Curriculum Development Update* (March 1992). 34, pp. 1–2.

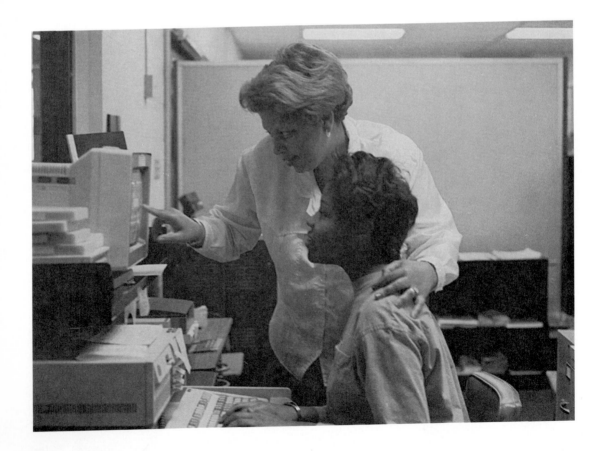

16

Affective Learning

AIMS

This chapter provides information to help the reader to:

- Point out the importance of including the affective dimension in instructional programming.
- State several reasons that lead some teachers to avoid dealing with affective issues.
- Identify several techniques for helping students to develop more positive attitudes toward school.
- Cite some basic issues associated with dealing with values in the classroom.
- Describe some methods that can be used to deal with value issues in secondary school classes.
- Point out differences involved in dealing with values and moral issues.
- Describe a framework that can be used to deal with issues of morality in the classroom.
- Define and describe several types of moral discourse.
- Describe each of Kohlberg's stages of moral development.

- Point out how moral-dilemma discussions can lead students to higher levels of moral reasoning.

FOCUS QUESTIONS

1. In what ways does education involve more than transmission of information?

2. What are some things teachers can do to improve students' attitudes toward school?

3. If teaching values is controversial, why should teachers be concerned about it?

4. What is the purpose of values clarification, and what processes are associated with valuing as defined by this approach?

5. What are the four components of James Rest's framework for analyzing morality, and how may they be incorporated into secondary school lessons?

6. What are some features of a moral-discourse lesson?

7. How might some of Lawrence Kohlberg' ideas be incorporated into the secondary school classroom?

Introduction

Transmission of information is only one of education's purposes. Emotional or affective components are important too. John I. Goodlad, Roger Soder, and Kenneth A. Sirotnik (1990; p. xii) explain that "teaching the young has moral dimensions . . . simply because education—a deliberate effort to develop values and sensibilities as well as skills—is a moral endeavor. The teacher's first responsibilities are to those being taught."

Kenneth Strike (1991), who has studied the moral role of schooling, points out that schools have an important role as an agency charged with helping the young develop a commitment to the democratic political aspirations of our country. He points out there is a view that "sees the task of creating free people as a matter of creating a harmony between individual aspirations and social institutions" (Strike, 1991; p. 425). This means that teachers must strike a delicate balance between their desires to help students develop as individuals and their interests in having them commit to core social values.

Helping students develop as individuals and helping them to understand the importance of shared social values is promoted when teachers themselves manifest an attitude of caring. This caring is not soft-minded. It reflects a deep and abiding teacher concern for students as individual human beings. The "ethnic of caring does not preclude or exclude competence or motivation; in fact, it implies a concern for both." (Rogers and Webb, 1991; p. 180). The quality of the relationship between students and teachers can importantly influence what students learn and how they feel about school.

Teachers' concerns about education's affective aspects center on several key areas. Among them are:

- Students' attitudes toward their subjects and toward school in general.
- The personal values students develop as they progress through the school program.
- The nature of the sense of morality students develop as they mature.

"Mr. Dingle, your willingness to take personal action to relate to the feelings, attitudes, and perspectives of *all* of our students is appreciated; however . . ."

Attitudes Toward Subject and School

Development of positive attitudes toward learning is critical. New knowledge evolves at a truly incredible rate. To keep abreast of new developments, people must commit to becoming lifelong learners. Educators have an obligation to help students grasp the idea that they need to continue study and learning throughout their lives.

Many teachers are sincerely interested in what they teach. They appreciate the power that mastery of their subjects has given them to grapple successfully with many of life's complexities. Many teachers would be unhappy if students left their classrooms intensely disliking what they had been taught.

Personal Values

Personal values and attitudes are important to everyone. Values are bedrock beliefs that give direction to a person's life. Individuals prize, cherish, and act in ways that are consistent with these convictions. Values help people make decisions about how to choose among competing demands for their time, talent, and money.

There are two major categories of values. The first concerns values related to standards of behavior expected by society in general. The second focuses on personal values that guide individuals' actions (Scriven, 1966). Educators face the difficult task of helping students appreciate widely held community values that enable us to live together while, at the same time, helping students recognize personal values they will use as a basis for decision making. In our pluralistic society, educators recognize that "while uniqueness must be respected, certain commonalities must also be taught" (Friesen and Boberg, 1990; p. 172).

Values help people find meaning in their lives. A person who is confused about personal values may be confused and inclined to act in inconsistent or self-destructive ways. An awareness of our personal values helps us to recognize who we are and what is important in our lives. Secondary schools have an obligation to deal with personal values. Students must be confronted with value decisions and value choices. They need to be helped to reflect on their values and to understand how these values affect their decisions.

Morality

Although the values a person holds are related to morality, moral behavior involves more than just value considerations. Morality concerns issues of right and wrong. Moral questions often focus on themes such as justice, equality, fairness, compassion, responsibility, and truth. James Rest (1983) suggested that morality includes those behaviors that help others, conform with social norms, arouse empathy and guilt, stimulate thought about social justice, and lead people to put the interests of others ahead of their own. Preparing individuals for life in their society is an important mission of the schools. Hence, issues relating to morality, which influence patterns of social behavior, deserve attention in secondary school classrooms.

Developing Positive Attitudes Toward Subjects and the School

Successful schools engender positive student attitudes toward school subjects and toward the general school experience. These attitudes tend to develop when schools feature an accepting, supportive environment, encourage students to accept responsibility for school affairs, and direct personal attention toward students (Stedman, 1987). Two approaches that show promise as ways to create the kinds of environments that will lead to positive student reactions to the school and learning are:

- Nondirective teaching
- Classroom meetings

Nondirective Teaching

Carl Rogers' Nondirective Teaching Model is an extension of this famous educator's perspectives on counseling (Rogers, 1983). Nondirective teaching requires teachers to accept the proposition that students are capable of understanding and of coping with their own problems. It requires teachers to yield some power to students and to respect their feelings and attitudes. In nondirective teaching, teachers try to view the world through the perspective of the student. Learning is viewed as an activity involving teacher-student partnerships.

These general steps are followed in nondirective teaching:

- Defining the situation
- Exploring the problem
- Developing insight
- Planning and decision making
- Integration

Defining the Situation
The first step in nondirective teaching is defining the situation. This step is designed to focus the discussion on pressing issues or concerns. The teacher plays an important role during this step. He must work with students to help them clearly understand critical issues, key terms, and ground rules for participating in the discussion. During this phase, teachers typically make a special effort to assure students that they will be free to express their genuine feelings throughout the discussion.

Exploring the Problem
During the second step, students are encouraged to share their own ideas about the issues under discussion. The teacher encourages all students to participate. The intent is to bring out into the open all perspectives and feelings held by students in the group.

Developing Insight

During this third phase, teachers seek to help students develop new insights about the issue under discussion and about their own feelings regarding the issue. The teacher attempts to do this by using nondirective, nonthreatening questions. ("What do you think about that reaction?" "How do you feel when that happens?" "Why do you think you feel that way?") The teacher is careful not to make judgments about students' answers. The idea is to get students to clarify and reflect on their own feelings.

Sometimes teachers may need to provide some guidance and to render interpretations to keep the discussion moving. In taking these actions, the teacher works to avoid suggesting that a given student answer is right, wrong, good, or bad. Interpretations often are provided to students in the form of tentative hypotheses. ("Are you saying that the reason you feel this way is . . . ?" "Do I understand you to be saying . . . ?" "Is it fair to say that you are doing this because you don't believe anyone listens to you?")

The purpose of these interpretive statements is to elicit additional responses from students. Students are the ones who must develop insights into their own feelings and behaviors. Thus, the teacher works hard to avoid making judgments. She must have confidence in students' abilities to work out their own views on issues and problems.

Planning and Decision Making

In the fourth step, the teacher tries to move students toward developing a plan of action or toward making decisions. The students should do the actual planning, not the teacher. The teacher prompts students by asking them what actions they might take. As students make tentative decisions, the teacher asks probing questions to assure that they adequately understand the issues to which they are responding. Further, the teacher tries to keep them from arriving at decisions prematurely. He works to get students to consider alternative courses of action before they commit to a final plan.

Integration

The fifth phase, integration, occurs when the students implement their decisions and reflect on their feelings and on the consequences of their decisions. They report on actions taken and try to develop additional insights as they analyze what has occurred. In light of these analyses, they plan additional actions.

The integration phase of nondirective teaching is a particularly delicate one. If it is to succeed, the teacher must be sure that students sense the emotional climate to be safe. They must feel free to report mistakes in judgments as well as decisions that worked out well. Students need to understand and accept that a certain amount of failure is a part of life. It is not the failure that is critical but rather what one does in response to it that is the key issue. A successful integration phase can help students grow emotionally. They can develop more confidence in their abilities to develop long-term solutions to difficulties that, in the short run, appear to be particularly intractable.

Box 16.1

Is There Time to Build Students' Self-Images?

Recently, a teacher was overheard making these comments:

I feel that I am absolutely pushed to the wall to cover the academic content. And I *do* have to cover it. Our district has become very concerned about standardized test scores. These scores reflect on me and my teaching. The tests don't care a whit about how students feel about themselves. Special lessons designed to help students develop more positive images are great in theory. But the realities I face in the classroom just don't allow time for this kind of thing.

What Do You Think?

1. Is this teacher philosophically opposed to lessons that are designed to improve students' sense of competence and self-worth?

2. How real are the constraints this teacher mentions?

3. Why have test scores become so important?

4. What are your own feelings about the issues raised by this teacher?

In summary, the nondirective teaching model suggests a pattern teachers can follow in dealing with issues involving students' emotions and feelings. The procedure can help students cope with their feelings and to grow in self-confidence. It builds their ability to express their feelings and to develop their own solutions to problems of all kinds. This kind of personal empowerment is associated with the development more positive student attitudes toward teachers and schools.

Classroom Meetings

Classroom meetings have great potential for improving students' attitudes toward school, themselves, and others (Glasser, 1969). William Glasser believes that regular use of classroom meetings can help students learn how to accept social responsibility. Glasser says students have a need to develop a "success identity," a perception of themselves as competent individuals. He points out that the home and the school are the only places students can acquire this perspective. He suggests that education for social responsibility should be part of every school program (Glasser, 1969, 1990.)

The classroom meeting features a discussion of something important and takes place with the teacher and students grouped in a circle. Glasser (1969) identifies three basic types of classroom meetings. The social-problem-solving meeting focuses on behavioral or social issues that are facing class members. The educational-diagnostic meeting centers on curriculum content and its meaning for students. The open-ended meeting encourages students to bring up and discuss any issues that are bothering them.

This teacher has organized these middle school students in a way that allows for free, easy, and comfortable communication.

Successful classroom meetings require a warm and trusting classroom climate. Students must sense that the teacher accepts and is genuinely concerned about them. They must feel completely free to express their own views without fear of eliciting negative teacher judgments.

In making the physical arrangement for a classroom meeting, chairs should be placed in a tight circle. The idea is to make face-to-face discussion possible and to decrease space separating individual students. The teacher occupies one of the seats in the circle. Her role is to act as a facilitator of the discussion, but a facilitator who is also an active group member and participant. Meetings should not go on too long. Thirty minutes should be viewed as an outside limit.

The following basic steps are some used by many teachers as they conduct classroom meetings:

- Establishing the focus for the discussion
- Making a personal choice or value decision
- Identifying alternative courses of action

- Making a public commitment
- Following up

Establishing the Focus for the Discussion

This step is designed to direct the group's attention on the issue or issues to be discussed. Depending on the type of classroom meeting, this step may be initiated either by the teacher or by the students. For example, if an educational-diagnostic meeting is planned, the teacher may seek to establish the focus by using questions, introduction of an example, description of a problem, or explanation of an event. Students may well initiate the focus in open-ended meetings.

During this phase of the meeting, one task of the teacher, who acts as a facilitator, is to make certain that the basic issue or problem is described completely. All students need to understand what is to be discussed. This might necessitate explanation of specific information—for example, meanings of certain terms. Once students understand the issue, the teacher encourages group members to state their individual reactions and views. All reactions are welcome. The teacher should intervene if some students begin to criticize opinions of others. These students need to be reminded that all views are welcome.

Another task of the teacher is to help students recognize their own relationship to a situation or problem. Students need to learn to identify ways in which their personal behaviors may have contributed to the development of a problem. The idea is to promote the idea that socially responsible people recognize the consequences of their behavior and are willing to be accountable for it.

Making a Personal Choice or Value Decision

Specific teacher actions during this phase of a classroom meeting will vary, depending on the type of meeting that is taking place. For example, during social-problem-solving meetings focusing on problem behaviors, the teacher may solicit information from students about the personal values that led them to act as they did. The group may discuss social norms governing this kind of behavior and may consider the degree to which individual group members accept these norms.

In educational-diagnostic meetings, the teacher may have students identify value issues related to academic content that has been discussed. The discussion may move on to consider the general value or worth of the content that is being taught. The idea is to engage students in an active consideration of the value choices that have given shape to individual lessons and to the general school program.

Identifying Alternative Courses of Action

During this phase, the teacher encourages students to explore alternative courses of action. One responsibility of the teacher is to prevent students from making judgments too quickly. They should be encouraged to give sincere consideration to a number of alternatives.

Suppose a group of students had been involved in a social-problem-solving meeting. The teacher might ask questions designed to help them identify alternative behaviors that might avoid similar problems in the future. As a result of an educational-diagnostic meeting, members of the group may come to the conclusion that parts of the school curriculum are "irrelevant." The teacher might ask probing questions designed to elicit from students ideas about what might be done to make the program relevant. If in an open-ended meeting students expressed concern about a political issue, the teacher might work to get students to identify specific actions they might take as citizens to influence this issue in a desired direction.

Making a Public Commitment

During this step, the teacher seeks to move the discussion to the level of a personal commitment to act from participants. The attempt is to bridge the gap between talk and performance. The purpose of this step is to keep the responsibility on the students. It seeks to prevent students from giving facile, insincere answers that simply "sound good." During this phase, teachers might ask questions such as "What are you going to do about it?" and "What are you willing to commit to personally?"

Following Up

This step does not occur immediately following the preceding four. It takes place several days, or even longer after the conclusion of the classroom meeting. At this time, the teacher asks individual students if they have taken the actions they had stated they were prepared to take. They are asked to reflect on the consequences of these actions. Sometimes, a discussion of these consequences provides the basis for another classroom meeting.

■ ■ ■

Glasser (1969) sees a number of advantages of regular classroom meetings. They help students feel important. They provide them with a sense that they exercise some power over what goes on in the classroom and over their personal lives. They provide opportunities for teachers to bridge the gap between life at school and life in the "real world." They develop students' abilities to express themselves and encourage the development of higher-level thinking skills. They have the potential for building positive attitudes toward schools and teachers.

WHAT SCHOLARS SAY

Teaching Attitudes Through Example

Students' attitudes are not shaped only by teachers' planned instructional experiences. Students also learn by observing what their teachers do. Gary D. Fenstermacher, Dean of the College of Education at the University of Arizona, has noted the importance of the teacher's manner on influencing what students prize and value. He writes:

Nearly everything that a teacher does while in contact with students carries with it the moral character of the teacher. The moral character can be thought of as the *manner* of the teacher.

Manner is an accompaniment to everything teachers do in their classrooms. Chemistry can be taught in myriad ways, but however it is taught, the teacher will always be giving directions, explaining, demonstrating, checking, adjudicating, motivating, reprimanding, and in all these activities displaying the manner that marks him or her as morally well developed or not. Teachers who understand their impact as moral educators take their manners quite seriously. They understand that they cannot expect honesty without being honest or generosity without being generous or diligence without themselves being diligent. Just as we understand that teachers must engage in critical thinking if they expect students to think critically in their presence, they must exemplify moral principles and virtues in order to elicit them from students. (Fenstermacher, 1990; pp. 134–135)

Source: Fenstermacher, G. D. "Some Moral Considerations on Teaching as a Profession." In J. I. Goodlad, R. Soder, and K. A. Sirotnik (eds.). *The Moral Dimensions of Teaching.*" San Francisco: Jossey-Bass Publishers, 1990, pp. 130–151.

Values and Value Analysis

The teaching of personal values in schools is controversial. Some critics argue that, since values are deeply held personal beliefs, schools should not intrude in this area. Others have argued that some personal beliefs are socially destructive. Hence, the schools have an important role to play in assuring that certain basic acceptable social values become part of the values repertoire of each student.

Few argue that a individual might hold personal values that are socially destructive and should be countered by instruction in the school. For example, no influential group in our society supports the freedom of one citizen to murder another citizen simply because he has committed to a personal value that sanctions killing. The real problem for the secondary teacher is identifying those common values that should be taught. Although a majority of people in this country generally support the idea that some values should be promoted by the school, there are violent disagreements about the list of values that should be taught.

In addition to debates about which values should be taught, controversy also rages about *how* they should be taught. Should teachers provide experiences that are specifically designed to teach values directly? Or, should lessons focus on letting students acquire them indirectly by helping them clarify the values they do hold and providing them with opportunities to freely reject or accept specific values?

We believe that the most responsible approach for a teacher in a democratic society is the second approach. Any effort to impose a rigid set of values smacks of indoctrination. This is inconsistent with core American commitments and with the need for students to recognize that they have broad personal responsibility for the values to which they have committed.

Issues, Values, and Consequences Analysis

The technique of issues, values, and consequences analysis is designed to help students appreciate that the decisions individuals make reflect their values. These are the general steps typically followed in an issues, values, and consequences analysis lesson:

- Identifying the general issue.
- Describing faction A.
- Identifying relevant alternatives open to faction A.
- Identifying possible consequences for each alternative.
- Repeating steps 2, 3, and 4 for faction B (and any other remaining factions).
- Comparing the values, alternatives, and probable consequences of all factions.
- Making a choice.

Step One: Identifying the General Issue

During this step, the teacher works with the entire class to assure that all students understand the issue. The teacher may do this by introducing students to a problem. ("During the 1950s China was not a member of the United Nations. Some people thought it was strange that the world's most populous nation was not a member. Others feared that admitting China would give additional voting power to nations with Communist governments. There was much debate over whether China should be admitted to the U.N. We are going to be working with this issue today.")

Step Two: Describing Faction A

Controversial issues used as a focus for lessons of this kind are controversial because different individuals or groups have different opinions about what should be done. Every controversial issue has at least two contending factions associated with it. Some have more.

During this phase, students are assigned to work in groups. They are asked to gain as much information as possible about the people supporting one of the factions. ("All right, I want John's group to think about the motives of people who wanted to admit China to the U.N. What did they see as potential benefits to China? To the United States? To the world? What kinds of things seemed to have been very important to these people? What values did they esteem?" And so forth.)

Step Three: Identifying Relevant Alternatives Open to Faction A

During this phase of the lesson, students are asked to think about alternative courses of action open to members of the faction they are considering. Sometimes teachers have students brainstorm their ideas. This tends to open up a number of possibilities, and it tends to prevent students from restricting their thinking to an extremely limited number of alternatives. ("What are some kinds of things that supporters of China's admission to the U.N. might have done? Let's develop a long list of plausible possibilities.")

Box 16.2

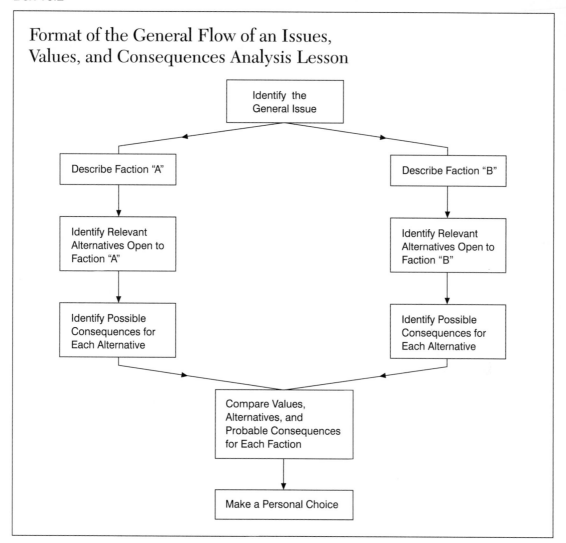

Format of the General Flow of an Issues, Values, and Consequences Analysis Lesson

Step Four: Identifying Possible Consequences for Each Alternative
Alternative courses of action may produce different results or consequences. During this step, the teacher encourages students to look at each alternative course of action with a view to identifying consequences that might have followed a commitment to this option. ("We have identified seven distinct possible courses of action for people who supported China's admission to the U.N. Let's look at these one at a time. What might have happened if these people had decided to follow this first alternative?" [Same pattern continues for each of the remaining listed options.])

Step Five: Repeating Steps 2, 3, and 4 for Faction B
(and Any Other Remaining Factions)

The teacher takes students through the same sequence of activities for each of the remaining factions. For example, students might be instructed to consider the motives of people opposed to admitting China to the U.N., the action alternatives open to these individuals, and the probable consequences of each option.

Step Six: Comparing the Values, Alternatives,
and Probable Consequences of All Factions

This step helps students grasp the point that many policy arguments involve value conflicts. To help students see differences in value priorities, the teacher helps students review differences that have come to light during previous phases of the lessons. ("What are similarities and differences in action alternatives that were open to people favoring and opposing China's admission to the U.N.? What things were considered to be especially important to those favoring China's admission? To those people opposing China's admission? How would you summarize the values that were most important to people in each faction?")

Step Seven: Making a Choice

At this point in the exercise, the teacher challenges students to make a personal decision about the issue that has been considered. Students are encouraged to consider the values of individuals associated with each faction as well as their own values. ("What should have been done in the 1950s about admitting to China to the U.N.? I want you to let me know your decisions. Then, I am going to ask you what your decisions tell us about the values you consider to be especially important. We will want to compare your values to those of people associated with each of the factions we have studied.")

■ ■ ■

In summary, issues, values, and consequences analysis is designed to help students appreciate that decisions are not made just by dispassionate consideration of evidence. Students are taught that individual values also play an important role. The technique helps students to examine carefully the values that are reflected in decisions of others. Additionally, students come to appreciate relationships between their own values' priorities and those of others.

Values Clarification

Values clarification is an approach developed during the 1960s by Louis Raths, Merrill Harmin, and Sidney Simon (1966). A basic premise of this approach is that teachers have no right to impose values on students. Rather, teachers are urged to use an approach that helps students to clarify or recognize their own values, think about alternative value positions, and act on those values that are highly prized.

Raths et al. (1966) suggest that the valuing process has three major components: (1) choosing a value, (2) affirming or prizing a value, and (3) acting on a value. There are criteria associated with each of these major components. Choosing a value requires that the person (1) choose the value freely, (2) choose the value with full knowledge of the alternatives, and (3) choose the value with knowledge of the consequences.

Affirming or prizing a value requires that the individual be (1) glad about the choice, and (2) willing to affirm the choice publicly. Acting on a value requires that the individual (1) do something with the chosen value, and (2) act repeatedly in a manner consistent with the value so it becomes a permanent part of her behavior.

Proponents of values clarification have developed large numbers of teaching activities. One of them is values ranking. This simple procedure is designed to help students recognize their own values priorities. It requires the teacher to provide members of the class with a situation with a number of alternative responses. Each response tends to reflect a different value. Students are asked to rank the listed responses in terms of their personal preference. Note this example:

Teacher: "Read over the explanation of the general situation. Then, rank each option in terms of your own preference. Place a 1 in the blank before your favorite choice, a 2 in the blank before your next favorite choice, and so forth. Conclude with a 9 in the blank before your least favorite choice."

The Situation: You have just discovered that you have inherited $1 million (tax free). The same day, you learn that you have an incurable disease. You will die within the next six months. How will you spend your time?

_____ Going to church or synagogue.

_____ Identifying and giving money to worthy charities.

_____ Traveling to places I always wanted to visit.

_____ Establishing scholarships for the urban poor.

_____ Giving lavish parties.

_____ Building new homes for my relatives.

_____ Buying an expensive wardrobe of designer clothes.

_____ Having a car custom built just for me.

_____ Reading all the books I always wanted to read.

Students rank these items independently. In the follow-up discussion, the teacher and students work identify values associated with the various options on the list. The teacher takes care to assure students that there is no right or wrong way to prioritize items on the list. The purpose is to get students to think about what they personally value. As part of the exercise, the teacher may wish to invite students to share and talk about their personal rankings, but this must be a completely optional decision. Students' rights to privacy must be respected. Those students who are willing to talk about their own values and choices provide additional information that can help sensitize students to value commitments different from their own.

Many examples of lessons associated with values clarification are available in education's professional literature. Two books that are widely held in college and university libraries that discuss a number of techniques are *Values and Teaching* by Louis E. Raths, Merrill Harmin, and Sidney B. Simon and *Values Clarification* by Sidney B. Simon, Leland W. Howe, and Howard Kirschenbaum.

Morality

Morality focuses on right and wrong. It concerns such ideas as justice, equality, fairness, compassion, and responsibility. Individuals' values play a role in their understandings of what constitutes moral behavior.

Some of these values are very widely shared. For example, all world cultures hold human life to be sacred. Murder is considered an immoral act everywhere. Many widely held values tend to be of a type that are called *prosocial values*. These values relate to patterns of behavior that members of a culture must endorse if their society is to survive.

James Rest's Framework

James Rest (1983) has developed a four-level framework that can be used in preparing lessons that focus on morality. The four levels of Rest's approach are:

- Moral sensitivity
- Moral judgment
- Moral decision making
- Moral action

Moral Sensitivity

At this level of moral awareness, individuals begin to appreciate that issues under discussion have a moral dimension. Teachers attempt to help students understand that moral considerations may lead to decisions different from what they might be if people considered only "the facts." For example, some evidence may suggest that wiretaps can assist law enforcement officials in their efforts to apprehend criminals. But, the moral issue involving invasion of privacy also must be considered.

At this level, teachers' actions generally involve asking students questions that are designed to help them focus on moral dimensions of issues. ("Jose correctly points out that tripling fees on the turnpike will reduce the volume of traffic. This, as he mentions, will reduce wear and tear on the roadway, will reduce the number of accidents, and will save lives. Before we commit to Jose's solution to the problem of the deteriorating turnpike roadbed and the high accident rate, are there some moral issues we need to look at?")

Moral Judgment

The second level in Rest's model flows logically from the first. Moral sensitivity seeks to plant the idea that issues have a moral dimension that must be considered. Moral judgment requires individuals to think of the moral consequences that might flow once a decision about a given issue has been made.

During this phase of a lesson, teachers take care to help students understand that people may have different value priorities and, hence, different conceptions of morality. ("Let's suppose that the state adopted Jose's solution to triple users' fees on the turnpike. What sorts of things might be most important to people supporting this decision? How might they defend the action on moral grounds? What sorts of things might be most important to people opposing this decision? How might they support their opposition to the decision on moral grounds?")

Moral Decision Making

At this level, students are asked to make decisions of their own. Facts relevant to a given issue are reviewed. Value positions of a number of factions posing alternative solutions are reviewed. Then, students are asked to make their own decisions and to comment on the possible consequences of the choices they make.

("We have talked about several solutions to the problem of turnpike wear and the high accident rate. We have also thought about the values reflected in the positions of a number of alternative solutions. Among these solutions were (1) tripling user's fees, (2) rationing turnpike use by allowing cars with even-numbered license plates to use it on even-numbered days and cars with odd-numbered license plates to use it on odd-numbered days, (3) committing funds to add additional turnpike lanes and to resurface the entire highway, and (4) requiring all cars to carry a minimum of four passengers. Now, I want each of you to think about these ideas and about any other solutions that occur to you. I want you to be able to make a decision, point out some possible consequences of the decision, and explain the personal values you hold that led to the decision you chose.")

Moral Action

During this phase, students are asked to go beyond verbalization of their decision to act. The moral action level calls for a considerable depth of commitment. The purpose of lesson components directed at moral action is to help students recognize that it is easier for people to talk about their conceptions of morality than to act upon them. During this phase, teachers take care not to coerce students to act. The purpose is not the action itself but rather the recognition that different people have different levels of commitment to moral issues they support.

("Let's think about the decisions you have made about this issue. I don't want you to feel a need to answer 'yes' to these questions unless you really want to. Now, how many of you would be willing to write a letter to the editor supporting your decision? How many of you would write a letter to the Director of the Turnpike Authority? How many of you would come to a meeting after school to start a pressure group? Now why do you think some of you were willing to do these things and others weren't? Can you think of examples where people sometimes talk about their support for something but aren't too interested in acting on their convictions? Why is it that we humans are like this?")

Moral Discourse

The term *moral discourse* refers to a discussion focusing on issues having a moral dimension (Oser, 1986). A wide variety of topical areas can be used as subjects of moral-discourse lessons. Fritz Oser (1986) suggests that such discussions might focus on such issues as (1) moral role taking and moral empathy, (2) taking "right" moral action, (3) norms of the group, (4) moral values in relationship to school programs, (5) changing personal values, (6) theoretical moral knowledge, and (7) moral conflict and moral judgment.

Lessons directed at moral role taking and moral empathy encourage students to see issues from the perspectives of others. They are encouraged to analyze both issues and values commitments of individuals whose perspectives they attempt to reflect. Often lessons take the form of role-playing activities.

Taking right moral action lessons focus on the gap that sometimes exists between what people say and what they do. The focus is very much on the word *action*. Lessons help students to identify what people say is good and moral and compare their actions to these statements. Students consider causes of inconsistencies between verbalized commitments and actual behaviors.

Lessons focusing on norms-of-the-group issues consider the broadly accepted moral principles that guide individuals' behavior in their society. Society-wide principles as well as those of local communities and peer groups may be investigated. Sometimes moral discourse of this type focuses on changing community standards over time.

Moral values in relation to school programs discussions help students to focus on moral dilemmas raised in such areas as literature, government, and history. Sometimes a study of these moral conflicts can help students to clarify their own values. Sometimes moral discourse lessons of this type also focus on the content of the school program. Students and teachers may wish to consider the implicit moral messages embedded in what authorities have decided students should study in school.

Moral discussions focusing on changing personal values help students to reflect on their own values and views of morality, particularly as they may change over time. Students need to understand that all individual values are not rigidly fixed. Changing conditions may modify personal perspectives and alter conceptions of what constitutes a "moral" act or decision.

Occasionally, moral-discussion lessons focus on theoretical moral knowledge. These lessons are designed to help students identify and apply varying theories of moral philosophy. The intent of such lessons is to help students discover relationships between differing value systems. For example, they might be taught to recognize conflicts between ethical relativism and universal principles of morality. The goal is to help them understand the premises of people making moral arguments on one side or the other of an issue.

Lessons focusing on moral conflict and moral judgment direct students' attention to issues where two or more value and moral positions might be taken. The idea is to familiarize them with alternative moral orientations and to help them articulate the values and moral principles that undergird their own judgment. Lawrence Kohlberg (1980) has developed a scheme for engaging students in this kind of learning.

Kohlberg's Moral Reasoning

Lawrence Kohlberg (1980) argues that individuals' responses to issues vary in terms of their stages of moral development. He has developed a theory that includes six stages of moral development. According to the theory, individuals progress sequentially through these stages. This means, for example, that a person cannot be at stage three without at some earlier time having been at stage one and stage two. Further, people vary in terms of where their moral development stops. Some stop at lower stages; only a few progress to the highest stage. These are the six stages Kohlberg's (1980) scheme:

- Stage one: Punishment and obedience orientation
- Stage two: Instrumental relativism
- Stage three: Interpersonal concordance
- Stage four: Law and order orientation
- Stage five: Social-contract, legalistic orientation
- Stage six: Universal ethical principle orientation

Stage One: Punishment and Obedience Orientation

A person at the punishment and obedience orientation stage makes decisions about what is right and wrong based on respect for power. The individual chooses out of a fear that an inappropriate decision will result in punishment for this action. Logic used by people at this stage is very egocentric. They do not take into account consequences of their actions for others. They worry only about whether punishment will be directed at them personally.

Stage Two: Instrumental Relativism

Reasoning of people at the instrumental relativism stage is also very egocentric. The basis for decisions, though, is different from that of people at the punishment and obedience orientation stage. Instead of fear of punishment, people at the instrumental relativism stage make decisions after they have calculated the likely personal benefits of the alternatives. The rightness or wrongness of a decision depends on whether it will bring personal benefits to the decision maker.

Logic at this level often reflects a you-scratch-my-back-and-I'll-scratch-yours mentality. Sometimes people at this level do things that may *appear* to be very altruistic in nature. On closer examination, their decisions always are calculated to provide a personal benefit. For example, a wealthy business owner might give money to a worthy cause. The action may not be taken out of a commitment to the cause but rather out of a conviction that the resultant publicity will increase his personal profits.

Stage Three: Interpersonal Concordance

Individuals at this stage make decisions based on their assumptions about what others in their group believe to be right and wrong. Many parents of secondary school-aged children have encountered this kind of logic from their children. ("Mom, *nobody* else has to

Box 16.3

Recognizing Differences in Logic Used by People at Different Stages of Moral Development

Students often present their teachers with a variety of excuses when they are caught cheating. Look at these examples. Then, decide what levels of moral reasoning the students are using to defend their actions to a school counselor.

1. "I really shouldn't have done it, but my dad said he would whip me if I flunked another test."

2. "I'm trying to get into this special club. To get in, I have to have cheated on a test."

3. "I just knew the test was not going to be fair. I mean, I don't mind studying for a fair test, but not for one where the cards are stacked against me at the beginning. I've been a pretty good student. I thought if word got around that I was so frustrated that I had to resort to cheating somebody might take action. The teacher really needs to be told to prepare tests that have something to do with the content we've studied."

be in at 11:00. The other parents think 1:30 A.M. is just fine.") Standards of the peer group strongly influence patterns of behavior of people at this stage of moral development.

Stage Four: Law and Order Orientation

People at this stage base their decisions on respect for established rules and regulations and long-standing traditional social practices. They are strongly influenced by formal authority. What the law says tends to dictate their behavior, even though they may not always agree the law is correct. In a conflict between legal authority and other considerations, they will reject the other considerations. This kind of thinking was reflected in the trials at Nuremberg following World War II. When asked about atrocities against the Jews, many former Nazis simply stated that they were just obeying orders.

Stage Five: Social-Contract, Legalistic Orientation

At this stage, reasoning about moral issues moves beyond a simple consideration of the dictates of established authority. Legal authority is considered, but so are some general, less formal guidelines and some personal values. Authority is not always perceived as right. A kind of social contract between those in power and the individuals in the society is presumed. There are times when those in power may exercise control in ways that violate the social contract. In such cases, people may determine that a decision of constituted authority is wrong.

At this stage, people take action to change laws, regulations, and other practices of constituted authorities that they believe may violate the social contract that should govern relations between leaders and citizens. Conceptions of right and wrong are often based on what individuals see as good for the society, as opposed to what is consistent with the views of those in power.

Stage Six: Universal Ethical Principle Orientation

At this stage of moral development, individuals base decisions on certain universal principles to which they have decided to commit. Among these are respect for justice, freedom, personal dignity, and the sanctity of human life. Decisions about right and wrong are based on the dictates of individual conscience. Decisions of conscience take precedence over formal rules, wishes of the peer group, and legal frameworks for altering rules. An example of someone at this stage of moral development would be a conscientious objector who chooses not to serve in the military in time of war out of a personal conviction that taking human life is wrong under all circumstances.

■ ■ ■

The movement of individuals from a lower stage of moral development to a higher stage is thought to be influenced by the nature of their experiences. When a person comes into contact with others who make decisions based on a conception of morality consistent with a moral stage one stage higher than her own, then this individual may begin to move toward this next higher stage. If, however, this same person is exposed to people whose reasoning is based on logic consistent with moral stages two or more stages higher than hers, she may have great difficulty understanding the logic of these people. To create an environment that will systematically expose individuals to logic at levels one step higher than their own, Kohlberg (1980) has developed a "moral dilemma discussion" approach.

Moral Dilemma Discussion

There are four basic steps to the approach, as follows (Kohlberg, 1975):

- Introducing the moral dilemma.
- Asking students to suggest tentative responses.
- Dividing students into groups to discuss reasoning.
- Discussing reasoning and formulating a conclusion.

Step One: Introducing the Moral Dilemma

This first step requires the teacher to identify an issue that poses a clear moral dilemma. The best issues are those that are of high concern to students. (Should students inform their parents about another student's attempt to provide them with illegal substances at a party? Should a student skip school to help a worried friend talk through a serious personal problem? Should a student who finds a wad of one-hundred dollar bills report this find to the police? And so forth.)

Dilemmas can be introduced in a variety of ways. The teacher might provide students with a written scenario that highlights key aspects of the situation. Films or cassette tapes might be used. Role-playing a situation represents another useful approach. Once the dilemma is introduced, the teacher takes time to conduct a short discussion for the purpose of highlighting key issues.

Step Two: Asking Students to Suggest Tentative Responses

This step begins with a teacher request to the students to write short summaries of what they would do if faced with a similar situation. They are asked to specify reasons that would lead them to respond in this way. The reasons provide cues to students' individual stages of moral development. The specific decisions are not nearly so important as the kinds of logic individual students use to defend them.

Step Three: Dividing Students into Groups to Discuss Reasoning

At this time, students are divided into a number of small groups. Members of each group are asked to share the course of action they would take and the reasons for their choices. Chances are that reasons will reflect several levels of moral reasoning. Possibilities are excellent that many students will hear arguments based on moral reasoning that is just one stage higher than their own. This exposure, according to Kohlberg (1975), can facilitate their growth toward this higher stage.

These discussions should be kept fairly brief. The teacher should take action to assure that students engage in open exchanges of ideas, not confrontational debates about the merits of the various positions that are taken. As a concluding part of this step, members of each group should try to come to a collective decision about what action should be taken. Next, group members should identify two or three of the best reasons that were brought up in support of this action.

Step Four: Discussing Reasoning and Formulating a Conclusion

During this step, the teacher asks a spokesperson from each group to share its decision and supporting logic. The decisions and the supporting logic should be written on the chalkboard, on a large chart, or on an overhead projector transparency. After all information has been recorded, the teacher leads a discussion focusing on reasons and actions chosen by the different groups.

After students have shared ideas during this discussion, the teacher asks each person to write down the best reasons supporting a decision he does *not* personally endorse. Then, students are asked to write down the strongest reasons supporting a decision they do support. These activities require students to carefully consider the logic of others.

■ ■ ■

In summary, moral reasoning discussions help students consider the logic and moral reasoning of others. By exposing them to the logic of people operating one moral stage higher than their own, there is a good possibility that their move to the next higher moral-reasoning stage will be facilitated. Such movement is unlikely to occur after participation in only a single moral reasoning discussion. Growth in moral reasoning may require many other experiences and a good deal of personal introspection.

Kohlberg (1980) himself is cautious on the issue of how much moral development can be expected of students in schools. He suggests that, as a realistic goal, schools might strive to develop students to the law and order stage of moral development (Kohlberg, 1980; p. 463). Others may move higher. Certainly, it is hoped that as they grow to adulthood and have broad-ranging experiences, many will become higher-stage moral reasoners.

Table 16.1   Summary Table

Main Points	Explanation
Importance of Affective Components of Education	Transmission of information is only one of the purposes of education. Schools also have an obligation to help students commit to the basic values of our society and to develop their own capacities to think independently within a democratic context. Much of affective education is concerned with caring about students as individual human beings.
Developing Positive Attitudes Toward School and Learning	One important purpose of affective instruction is to help students develop positive attitudes toward the school and toward the idea that learning is a lifelong process.
Developing Personal Values	Another purpose of affective instruction focuses on helping students recognize both personal and society-wide values. These values influence the kinds of decisions they make.
Morality	Instruction focusing on morality seeks to help students work with issues associated with justice, equality, fairness, compassion, responsibility, and truth.
Nondirective Teaching	This approach, developed by Carl Rogers, assumes students are capable of solving their own problems. It requires teachers to yield some power to their students and to respect students' feelings and attitudes.
Classroom Meetings	Developed by William Glasser, the classroom meeting approach is designed to help students learn how to accept social responsibility. Teachers and students organize themselves in a circle and focus on an important issue.
Issues, Values, and Consequences Analysis	This technique is designed to help students understand that the decisions individuals make reflect their values. It requires them to consider a controversial issue from several perspectives and to identify values positions associated with each.

Table 16.1 Summary Table *(continued)*

Main Points	Explanation
Values Clarification	This approach, developed by Louis Raths, Merrill Harmin, and Sidney Simon, is designed to help students identify, clarify, and recognize their own values. They are encouraged to think about alternative value positions and to act on values that they prize highly. A premise of this approach is that teachers have no right to impose values on students.
James Rest's Moral Education Framework	James Rest has developed a four-level framework that can be used in planning lessons focusing on morality. The framework includes the categories of (1) moral sensitivity, (2) moral judgment, (3) moral decision making, and (4) moral action.
Moral Discourse	Fritz Oser developed this scheme for dealing with issues having a moral dimension. Moral discourse discussions seek to help students see issues from perspectives of others.
Kohlberg's Moral Reasoning	Lawrence Kohlberg argues that people respond to issues in terms of their respective stages of moral development. These are the stages in Kohlberg's scheme: (1) punishment and obedience orientation, (2) instrumental relativism, (3) interpersonal concordance (4) law and order orientation (5) social-contract, legalistic orientation, and (6) universal ethical principle orientation. The movement of people from one stage to another is facilitated by their interacting with people operating at higher stages.
Moral Dilemma Discussion	Based on Lawrence Kohlberg's stage theory, moral dilemma discussions organize students into small discussion groups. The process is designed to expose group members to various levels of moral reasoning, with a view to promoting the development of individuals at lower levels to higher moral reasoning stages.

Review of Key Ideas

- Teachers' responsibilities are not only associated with the transmission of content knowledge. They have obligations in the attitudinal or moral realm as well. They need to strike a reasonable balance between an obligation to help students develop as individuals and to promote their acceptance of core social values (tolerance, respect for the dignity of others, and so forth) that provide a context for individual behavior in our society.

- Teachers' concerns in affective areas often focus on (1) students' attitudes toward their subjects and school in general, (2) personal values students develop as they go through the school program, and (3) the view of morality students develop as they mature.

- Nondirective teaching, a model developed by Carl Rogers, views learning as a teacher-student partnership. It requires teachers to yield some power to students and to attempt to see the world through the perspectives of their students.

- Classroom meetings, a technique pioneered by William Glasser, seek to help students learn how to accept social responsibility. Meetings focus on discussions of important issues. The technique assumes that education for social responsibility should be a part of every school program.

- The issues, values, and consequences analysis technique is designed to help students understand that the decisions people make are not made only on the strength of the available evidence. Value considerations also come into play. This technique encourages students to identify alternative solutions to problems and to recognize value priorities associated with each view.

- The values clarification approach was developed by Louis Raths, Merrill Harmin, and Sidney Simon. It is designed to help students recognize their own values, consider alternative values, and commit to actions consistent with their own value priorities. A basic premise is that teachers should refrain from imposing their own values on students.

- James Rest has developed a framework that can be used in preparing lessons focusing on morality. Categories of the framework include (1) moral sensitivity, (2) moral judgment, (3) moral decision making, and (4) moral action. Another scheme for dealing with issues having a moral dimension is Fritz Oser's moral discourse approach.

- Lawrence Kohlberg argues that there are stages of moral development people pass through. From lowest to highest these are (1) the punishment and obedience orientation stage, (2) the instrumental relativism stage, (3) the interpersonal concordance stage, (4) the law and order orientation stage, (5) the social-contract, legalistic orientation stage, and (6) the universal ethical principle orientation stage. Individuals' movement from lower to higher stages is thought to be facilitated by their exposure to reasoning of people at stages one or two stages higher than their own. The moral dilemma discussion technique has been developed as a means of promoting higher-level moral development by exposing individual students to arguments reflecting patterns of thought consistent with moral development stages higher than their own.

Follow-Up Questions and Activities

Questions

1. Why are the affective dimensions of education important?

2. In what ways are personal values important to people?

3. Are teachers in a position to do something about students' attitudes toward the school and toward learning in general? If they are not, why is this so? If they are, what are some things they can do?

4. Is it true that schools have a responsibility to teach every student social responsibility? Explain your answer.

5. Teaching values in school is controversial. Indeed, some people suggest it should be avoided altogether. How do you feel about this issue, and why?

6. This chapter introduced the issues, values, and consequences analysis technique? Would this procedure be something you could use in a subject you would like to teach? Why or why not?

7. To what degree should values clarification be emphasized in secondary school programs? Why do you think so?

8. What are the components of James Rest's framework for teaching lessons focusing on morality? Would his scheme be adaptable to your own subject area? Why or why not?

9. What are the stages in Kohlberg's moral development scheme?

10. How can moral dilemma discussions be used to help students move to higher moral development stages?

Activities

1. Some proponents of affective education assert that our society's survival depends on its citizens' commitment to certain basic values or principles. They suggest that these values or principles function as a "social glue" that holds us together. Prepare a short paper in which you identify 10 key values or principles that all people, including students, should support. Include a justification for the inclusion of each key value or principle you identify.

2. One of the assumptions of the values clarification technique is that teachers should never impose their personal values on students. Is this true, or are there some values teachers should strive to engender in those they teach? Organize a debate on this topic: "Resolved that a teacher should never attempt to impose any values on students."

3. Invite a panel of teachers and administrators to visit your class. Ask them to discuss such questions as these:

- Have you ever experienced a problem when values or attitudes reflected in school lessons have conflicted with those of community members?
- Should teachers be held responsible for passing on values associated with good citizenship?
- To what extent is affective instruction emphasized in the classroom?

4. Value issues often come up when school boards make decisions about how to spend educational-programming resources. Interview several school board members. Ask them to cite examples when organized groups, with different values priorities, have taken contending positions on proposed new programs.

5. Organize about five members of your class into a group. At a regular class meeting, seat this group at the front of the room and present them with a problem that a secondary school teacher might face in dealing with a student (such as student chronically late to class, student fails to do assigned work, or student lies). Give members of the group about five minutes to suggest responses. Then, as a class, review statements that have been made in terms of their "fit" with Kohlberg's individual moral development stages. Be sure to point out that the appropriateness of suggested responses will depend, in part, on the level of moral development of the student with whom the teacher is working.

References

FENSTERMACHER, G. D. "Some Moral Considerations on Teaching as a Profession." In J. I. Goodlad, R. Soder, and K. A. Sirotnik (eds.). *The Moral Dimensions of Teaching*. San Francisco: Jossey-Bass Publishers, 1990. pp. 130–151.

FRIESEN, J. W. AND BOBERG, A. L. *Introduction to Teaching: A Socio-Cultural Approach*. Dubuque, IA: Kendall/Hunt, 1990.

GLASSER, W. *The Quality School: Managing Students Without Coercion*. New York: Harper & Row, 1990.

GLASSER, W. *Schools Without Failure*. New York: Harper & Row, 1969.

GOODLAD, J. I.; SODER, R.; AND SIROTNIK, K. A. "Preface." In J. I. Goodlad, R. Soder, and K. A. Sirotnik (eds.). *The Moral Dimensions of Teaching*. San Francisco: Jossey-Bass Publishers, 1990. pp. xi–xvii.

KOHLBERG, L. "The Cognitive-Developmental Approach to Moral Education." *Phi Delta Kappan* (June 1975), pp. 670–675.

KOHLBERG, L. "Education for a Just Society: An Updated and Revised Statement." In B. Munsey (ed.). *Moral Development, Moral Education, and Kohlberg*. Birmingham, AL: Religious Education Press, 1980, pp. 455–470.

OSER, F. "Moral Education and Values Education: The Discourse Perspective." In M. Wittrock (ed.). *Handbook of Research on Teaching*. 3rd ed. New York: Macmillan Publishing Company, Inc., 1986, pp. 914–917.

RATHS, L; HARMIN, M.; AND SIMON, S. B. *Values and Teaching*. Columbus, OH: Charles E. Merrill Publishing Company, 1966.

REST, J. "Morality." In P. Hussen (ed.). *Handbook of Child Psychology*. Volume 4. New York: John Wiley, 1983, pp. 556–629.

ROGERS, C. *Freedom to Learn for the '80s*. New York: Merrill/Macmillan Publishing Company, 1983.

ROGERS, W. AND WEBB, J. "The Ethnic of Caring in Teacher Education." *Journal of Teacher Education* (May–June 1991). *42*, pp. 173–181.

SCRIVEN, M. "Student Values as Educational Objectives." *The Alberta Journal of Educational Research* (June 1966). *12*, pp. 89–103.

SIMON, S. B.; HOWE, L. W.; AND KIRSCHENBAUM, H. *Values Clarification*. New York: Hart Publishing Company, 1972.

STEDMAN, L. "It's Time We Changed the Effective Schools Formula." *Phi Delta Kappan* (November 1987), pp. 215–224.

STRIKE, K. A. "The Moral Role of Schooling in a Liberal Democratic Society." In G. Grant (ed.). *Review of Research in Education*. Vol. 17. Washington, DC: American Educational Research Association, 1991, pp. 413–483.

V

Measuring and Evaluating

"Was the test fair?" If you ask this question to an average group of secondary students who have just received their grades, answers will vary. Those who received A's may answer with an enthusiastic "Yes!" Students getting D's or F's may express grave doubts about the fairness of the test and, by extension, of the teacher who prepared it.

Assessment of all kinds generates controversy. Sometimes views are highly personal. They are shaped by whether people see themselves as being fairly treated. Other people, who take a more general view, may wonder whether evaluations really measure important behaviors. They may ask, "Are items on tests there because they are the best ones that can be devised, or are they there because they are easy to write and correct?"

Discussions about evaluation often lead different people to different conclusions. Consider these statements:

- Objective tests featuring multiple-choice, true-false, and matching items are good because large numbers of questions can be asked in a short period of time. This allows a broad sample of the content that has been introduced to be tested.

- Objective tests are bad because they focus on superficial understandings and do not require sophisticated student thinking. Essay examinations are much better because they allow students to express what they really know and enable them to engage in higher-level thinking.

- Teachers should be evaluated based on what their students learn. The most important obligation of teachers is to transmit content to students. Students who perform well on tests have been well taught. As a result, their teachers should receive outstanding evaluation reports.

- What students learn depends on many things other than the actions of their teachers. A teacher may be doing an outstanding job but lack the kinds of learning materials and the kind of classroom environment needed to help students learn well. Also, students may learn content that allows them to make high test scores from sources other than their teacher. For a variety of reasons, teachers' evaluations should not be based on how well their students do on tests.

Content in Part 5 focuses on the multiple purposes of and multiple approaches to evaluation both of students and teachers. Material in this section provides answers to questions such as these:

- What is *authentic assessment*?
- What are some formats that can be used for formal and informal assessment techniques?
- What approaches can be used to gather information about teachers' classroom performance?
- What might be included in a teaching portfolio?

Discussion related to these questions is introduced in two unit chapters:

Chapter 17: Measuring Student Progress
Chapter 18: Evaluating Teachers' Performance

Measuring Student Progress

AIMS

This chapter provides information to help the reader to:

- Distinguish between measurement and evaluation.
- Describe what is meant by authentic assessment, and cite some advantages of this approach.
- Point out some uses of informal approaches to assessment, and describe examples of these informal techniques.
- Point out strengths and weaknesses of selected formal evaluation techniques.
- Explain formatting techniques for constructing matching, essay, multiple-choice, completion, and true-false tests.

FOCUS QUESTIONS

1. How might you explain differences between the terms *measurement* and *evaluation*?

2. What purposes are served, respectively, by formative evaluation and summative evaluation?

3. How might a proponent of authentic assessment dispute the accuracy of this statement: "The teacher should not teach to the test"?

4. How does what students are asked to do on an authentic test vary from what they are often asked to do on more traditional classroom tests?

5. What are some informal approaches to gathering assessment information about students?

6. What are some formal approaches to gathering assessment information about students?

7. What kinds of circumstances help teachers to decide whether to select an informal approach or a formal approach?

8. What are some formatting guidelines for rating scales, essay items, completion items, matching items, multiple-choice items, and true-false items?

Introduction

"Is my program working well?" "Are my students learning anything?" These questions are of great interest to teachers. As professionals, they want to know about the impact of their teaching. Students often have a related set of questions. "How am I doing in this course?" "What are my areas of strength and weakness?" "Am I doing as well as others?" Students' parents often share many of these same concerns.

To get information about the general impact of their programs and to provide information to students and parents, teachers use measurement and evaluation techniques. Though the terms *measurement* and *evaluation* are closely related, they are not synonyms. *Measurement* refers to the process of gathering information. Measurement is nonjudgmental. When the term is applied to instruction, information that is collected generally relates to student performance.

Evaluation refers to the process of drawing conclusions from a study of data gathered as a result of measurement. Evaluation, unlike measurement, is judgmental (Scriven, 1967). Evaluation requires interpretation. The measurements almost never "speak for themselves."

How individuals interpret measurements is closely related to their views about standards of student performance. For example, teachers favoring norm-referenced evaluation prefer to evaluate students in terms of how their work compares to that of others in the class. Teachers favoring criterion-referenced evaluation believe students' work should be evaluated in terms of a preestablished standard of performance.

Today, evaluation activities occur more frequently in schools than they did 40 and more years ago. Early measurement specialists placed a heavy emphasis on assessing

"It's an interesting theory, Fred, but the power to give grades is *not* terrorism."

students only at the end of an extended unit of instruction (Tyler, 1949). The idea was simply to determine whether or not the students had mastered the content.

More recent thought on evaluation has modified this approach. Michael Scriven (1967), a leading thinker on issues related to measurement and evaluation, pointed out that summary evaluation at the end of a block of instruction provided little information that could help students learn the content. The content had already been taught. By the time the test was given, the teacher was preparing to introduce new material.

Scriven (1967) proposed that teachers should assess students not only at the conclusion of a unit of instruction but at various times while the unit is being taught as well. He used the term *formative evaluation* to describe the periodic evaluation that takes place while new material is being taught. This evaluation is designed to provide ongoing feedback to students. It seeks to identify and remediate learning problems as the instructional sequence is being taught. Scriven (1967) used the term *summative evaluation* to refer to the traditional testing at the conclusion of an instructional sequence. Today, evaluation experts support instructional programs that include both formative evaluation and summative evaluation.

A critical issue associated with the whole area of assessment concerns whether the behavior evaluated truly relates to what teachers want students to learn. Critics of commonly used school testing practices charge that too often the behaviors that are evaluated are selected because they are easy to assess on tests that can be quickly scored, not because they are what the teacher truly considers to be important (Wiggins, 1989a). As an alternative to these practices, a growing number of critics are urging that teachers commit to practices associated with authentic evaluation (Kulm, 1990; Shepard, 1991; Wiggins, 1989a; Wiggins, 1989b).

Authentic Evaluation

"Teachers should not teach to the test" is a time-honored bit of folk wisdom in education that rarely has been challenged. Proponents of authentic evaluation say the time has come to reconsider this issue. The phrase seems to make sense because most tests clearly fail to measure what teachers really consider to be important. Supporters of authentic evaluation argue that the problem here is not teaching to the test but, rather, it is teaching to an *inappropriate* test. If tests could be designed that really required students to demonstrate the kinds of learning teachers consider to be important, it would make good sense to teach to the test.

Authentic tests are designed in such a way that students must demonstrate the kinds of learning that have been emphasized in class. Many school tests do not do this. Rather, they select samples of content to which students have been exposed and give them opportunities to demonstrate their recall abilities. Only infrequently do they call upon students to engage in complex performances that reflect sophisticated levels of understanding and competence.

An authentic test requires students to perform in ways consistent with how experts in the subject area perform as they go about their work. An expert in this area, Grant Wiggins (1989b), argues that

> authentic assessments replicate the challenges and standards of performance that typically face writers, businesspeople, scientists, community leaders, designers, or historians. These include writing essays and reports, conducting individual and group research, designing proposals and mock-ups, and so on. (p. 704)

This view of testing sees the test as the standard setter for the school. If tests are sophisticated and require students to engage in complex performances, then there will be incentives for students to work hard so they will be able to do well on these tests. On the other hand, if tests require students to engage in performances that require little academic effort and that fail to replicate the real demands faced by experts in the subjects they are studying, then students' development in school will fall short of what it might be.

CASE STUDY

Do Parents and Administrators Really Want Authentic Evaluation?

Joe Plinney, who is in his second year of teaching journalism at Parson Weems Senior High School, is talking about his work with Roy Lee, a long-time friend.

"When my students leave my class, I want them to be able to get the job done. After all, they're all juniors and seniors. I screened them before they came into this advanced journalism section. They're bright people. As far as I'm concerned, they should be able to go to work for a paper and even begin doing some real investigative reporting, right from the start."

Roy Lee nodded and said, "Sounds great to me. So what's your problem?"

"Well," Joe responded, "I've done a pretty fair job of analyzing what an investigative reporter has to do. And I've checked my ideas out with an editor or two. There's more to it than you might think. These people have to know what kinds of questions to ask. They have to figure out who to talk to and how to get them to open up. When something controversial comes up, they have to find someone reliable to corroborate what they have learned. And, of course, they've got to be able to stitch the story together so it not only is logical but also interests the general reader."

"That makes sense," Roy said. "How do you get the students to get a handle on all that?"

"It's both simple and difficult," Joe replied. "I've figured out that the way to get these students to really take seriously what I tell them investigative reporters do is to evaluate them on their ability to do all of these things. For all that we like to talk about 'learning for learning sake,' most of these kids don't pay much attention to anything that's not connected to a grade. So, basically all I have to do is give them an investigative reporting assignment and check carefully on how well they execute it. That sounds easy, but it really takes a lot of time.

"Especially," continued Joe, "since to make the thing work I have to base students' whole grade on how well their behavior compares to what real investigative reporters do. If I deviate from this and throw in some Mickey Mouse tests over basic terms, for example, students think the real purpose of the class is passing the test rather than learning how to operate as a reporter. Unfortunately, some of my parents and a couple of my building administrators don't agree with me."

"What's their concern?" asked Roy.

"A couple of things," answered Joe. "For one thing, basing a grade only on how a student can perform a complex activity such as investigative reporting is foreign to their experience. They remember pop quizzes, midterm examinations, questions from the text, and that sort of thing. What I want to do is quite different.

"And the administrators, though they won't come right out and say so, think my students won't score well on the standardized tests we give at the end of the year. They're afraid that, because these students won't have had exposure to traditional tests in my class, they'll freeze up when they have to take these exams. If our scores go down, I'll be in trouble. It will be especially bad if we don't stack up well against scores of other schools in the area. I'm sensing a lot of pressure to back off from what I want to do and to go back to more traditional tests."

"What do you think you'll do?" Roy asked.

Joe answered, "Right now, I'm on the fence. On the one hand, I think my priority should be to teach these young people how reporters function in the real world. On the other hand, I can understand that it will be bad for everybody if my approach angers parents and that the school may suffer a real public relations disaster if my students' standardized test scores take a dive."

■ ■ ■

What should Joe do? What positives and negatives do you see if he decides to base all of his evaluation on students' abilities to discharge the role of an investigative reporter? What positives and negatives might result from a decision to go back to a more traditional testing and grading procedure? From whom should Joe seek additional advice? Might anything be done to convince parents and others that traditional ways of evaluating and grading students may not have served students' long-term interests well?

Authentic assessment procedures require teachers to devote considerable time to test preparation. This time can be defended by thinking of authentic assessments as a legitimate component of instruction. These assessments are designed to teach as well as to reveal what students know.

Traditional Data-Gathering Techniques

Though support is growing for more authentic testing in schools, many traditional techniques for gathering assessment data and judging students are still in use. These divide into two broad categories: informal approaches and formal approaches.

Informal Approaches

When they hear references to "measurement and evaluation," many people immediately think of multiple-choice tests, true-false tests, or other formal testing approaches. Certainly pencil-and-paper tests are important. But by no means are they the only available alternatives. For example, depending on what they are teaching, some teachers might wish their students to demonstrate their proficiencies by doing things as

Box 17.1

Sample Authentic Assignment

The assignment that follows is an example of authentic assessment for a grade 7 social studies class. As you look over this material, consider how this kind of evaluation differs from what you experienced as a seventh-grader.

A STORY BASED ON LOCAL HISTORY: ASSESSING A LESSON IN A GRADE 7 STATE HISTORY COURSE

Write a true story describing how some aspect of our community has changed from 1950 to today. Focus on any aspect you like. Some possibilities might include: changes in the schools, changes in how people make a living, changes in where people do most of their shopping, changes in how the downtown area looks, changes in the places people live, and changes in what people do when they're not working. Interview long-time residents. Use microfilm copies of the local newspaper available in the school library. Write a two- to three-page paper describing your findings. You must also be prepared to tell others in the class what you found.

After you begin work, identify two major ideas about why changes have occurred. Then, develop three questions for each idea; try to answer the questions to test the accuracy of your ideas. Include your ideas, the questions you asked about them, and your findings in your paper.

EVALUATION GUIDELINES FOR THE TEACHER
In assessing work of individual students, consider:

- Whether the student identified two tentative ideas to explain the reported change.
- Whether three questions were generated for each idea.
- Whether the student drew on interviews and newspaper accounts to respond to these questions.
- Whether the people selected to be interviewed had the necessary background to provide information related to the change the student was investigating.
- Whether the student, in reflecting upon what was said in interviews or what was read in newspaper accounts, was able to distinguish between fact and opinion.
- Whether the student based conclusions on evidence that was clearly relevant to the position being taken.
- Whether there was a logical, point-by-point development in both the student's written work and in her oral presentation to the class.

---

diverse as baking a cake, playing a difficult selection on a French horn, or rebuilding a carburetor and installing it in an automobile.

The choice of the assessment procedure depends largely on what kind of information about the student the teacher is seeking. Often, informal procedures provide valuable insights regarding students' attitudes and levels of proficiency. Informal techniques tend to be used more for the purpose of formative evaluation than summative evaluation. They yield information teachers can use to identify and respond to problems learners may be experiencing as they attempt to master new content.

There are many kinds of informal evaluations. Those included here represent just a small sample of the many kinds of things that teachers do to keep track of students' progress.

Teacher Observation

Teacher observation refers to a number of things teachers do to assure students are performing assigned tasks properly. For example, a geometry teacher may walk systematically through the classroom once assignments have been made to identify students having problems and to clarify misunderstandings. An art teacher may observe students who are learning to use the potter's wheel and make helpful comments as they try to center the clay properly. An English teacher may listen to the words used by a student during an oral presentation to determine the extent of his vocabulary. A physical education teacher may watch students carefully to assure that required exercises are being done correctly.

Often informal observation results in a teacher giving specific directions to a student about what needs to be done to complete a task successfully. Sometimes, teachers make notes about specific difficulties individual students have been experiencing. These observation notes serve several purposes. For example, they can provide a continuing record to which the teacher can refer to see whether a given student is improving over time. A review of observation notes can also help a teacher identify problems being experienced by a number of students. When several students have failed to understand, the teacher may decide that instructions were not well understood and that some additional effort to clarify expectations with the entire class is in order.

Headlines and Articles

This informal technique is an appropriate procedure for assessing students' abilities to describe essential features of a large body of information. A good newspaper headline provides a concise summary of the article that follows. A writer of effective headlines must be thoroughly familiar with the article's content.

In the secondary school classroom, some teachers assign students to write headlines for a hypothetical article focusing on content they have studied. The headlines provide an informal assessment of students' understanding of general points raised in materials that have been studied. For example, a member of a social studies class that had been studying the coming end of Britain's Hong Kong lease might write a headline such as: "Brits Out—Chinese In: Hong Kong's Uncertain Future." Or, a student in a biology class might write: "Keeping Fit: Darwin's Theory a Survivor in Scientific World."

Student-produced headlines provide only general indications that basic information has been understood. They are not intended to provide teachers with insights about students' grasp of content specifics. However a headline-writing activity can be a good choice for the limited purpose of informally assessing students' abilities to summarize information accurately.

Some teachers find it useful to have students prepare short articles to accompany their headlines. These articles provide additional opportunities for them to summarize what they have learned.

Teacher-Student Discussion

Teachers often make informal judgments based on information gleaned from personal discussions with students. These conversations sometimes reveal a great deal about students' understandings, interests, and feelings. Such information can provide teachers with valuable insights. These discussions give teachers opportunities to check the accu-

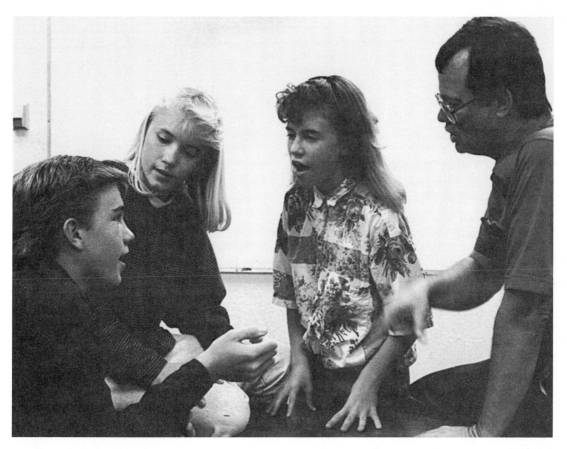

This teacher is using a classroom discussion to determine what individual students have learned and what misconceptions will need to be addressed.

racy of their assumptions about how individual learners are understanding content that is being introduced.

There are some important limitations to the teacher-student discussion approach. As a practical matter, it is difficult for teachers to engage in frequent one-on-one conversations with each student regarding all issues that are raised in class. There simply is not enough time. Hence, the levels of understanding of individual students cannot be sampled frequently. Informal evaluations resulting from teacher-student discussions need to be augmented by evaluations based on information gathered in other ways.

Student-Produced Tests

By the time students begin their secondary school years, they will have taken hundreds of teacher-prepared tests. Few of them will ever have had the opportunity to prepare a test of their own. Some teachers find that students enjoy assuming the role of the teacher and preparing test items over what they have been studying. Often teachers who ask their students to prepare tests agree to use a selection of these student produced items on a real test over the material. These teachers usually retain the right to add and modify items to assure the test adequately samples the content.

Student-produced tests provide a good indirect measure of what students have learned. Such tests also reveal which elements of content different members of a class have deemed important. This information can help the teacher to pinpoint students who need additional help with some content areas and others who may have faulty understandings of material that has been introduced.

Other Techniques

The informal procedures introduced here represent only a few that teachers use. Among others that are widely used are sorting activities of all kinds. Frequently, these activities provide opportunities for students to identify major content categories and to point out elements of content properly associated with each category.

Observation of students during a classroom debate can be used as an informal evaluation technique. Positions taken by individual students and their skill in using evidence to support points can reveal much about what they have learned. Crossword puzzles and other simple vocabulary exercises sometimes are used to provide general information about students' grasp of key concepts.

The great majority of teachers make some use of informal evaluation techniques. The specific procedures they use vary. Selection depends on the kinds of information about a student's progress that the teacher wants and on the capacity of a given informal technique to provide it.

Formal Approaches

Formal approaches seek to make judgments about students' progress based on evidence gathered through the use of carefully planned measurement devices. Formal evaluation techniques take many forms. Multiple-choice tests, true-false tests, matching tests, completion tests, essay tests, rating scales, and checklists are among the types commonly used in secondary schools.

Formal evaluation tests fall into two broad categories. These are (1) standardized tests and (2) teacher-made tests. Standardized tests are prepared by professional evaluation specialists for use with large numbers of students. Some of them are designed to assess general aptitudes of students. Others test student understanding of content related to subjects—for example, United States history.

The Scholastic Aptitude Test (S.A.T.), taken by many high school seniors and used by colleges and universities in their admissions screening process, is a well-known example of a standardized test. The National Assessment of Educational Progress administers standardized tests throughout the country to determine average levels of subject matter of students at different grade levels. Some states require teachers to administer standardized tests that focus on basic skills and, in some cases, on individual academic skills. The results provide general indications of the effectiveness of school programs and sometimes point to curricular areas that need special attention.

Box 17.2

Debating the Value of Standardized Tests

Standardized tests have engendered a great deal of public debate. Supporters claim that these tests provide a means of gathering important baseline data about performances of large numbers of students. Scores, they suggest, can be used to pinpoint and remediate general weaknesses in the curriculum. They also foster accountability by providing the public with a means of identifying particular schools where performance levels are dramatically above or below national averages.

Some critics suggest that standardized tests often examine students over content they have not studied. Further, it is alleged that standardized test scores fail to differentiate among the capabilities of individual schools to provide instruction. For example, wealthy schools may have sophisticated science laboratories.

Poorer schools may have woefully inadequate facilities.

Finally, some opponents of standardized tests say they encourage teachers to teach to the test. This may result in emphasis on memorization of content likely to be sampled on the test rather than on more complex thinking skills.

What Do You Think?

1. What are the greatest strengths of arguments of individuals who support standardized testing?

2. What are the greatest strengths of arguments of individuals who oppose standardized testing?

3. What are your own feelings about standardized testing?

Standardized tests are designed to measure the performance of a single student as it compares to the performances of all other students in similar circumstances. For example, a standardized reading test given at the seventh-grade level provides a score for each student that indicates how the student's performance compared with reading achievement of all seventh-graders.

Students' scores on standardized tests are rarely used for grading purposes by teachers. This is true because items on these tests often do not accurately sample the content that individual teachers have introduced in their own classrooms. Teacher-prepared tests are much more likely to have test items that tie closely to the content to which students have been introduced.

Because most teacher evaluation uses teacher-prepared rather than standardized tests as data sources, prospective teachers need to understand techniques for creating these materials. Guidelines for using a number of teacher-prepared assessment techniques are introduced in the following subsections.

Rating Scales

Some instructional objectives require students to engage in tasks that cannot be easily assessed with paper-and-pencil tests: using laboratory equipment, delivering speeches, completing art projects, and turning finials on a lathe are examples. A rating scale is a measurement tool that can be used to record information about student proficiency on tasks of this type.

Typically, a rating scale identifies a specific set of characteristics or qualities. Indications made along the scale make it possible for the teacher to note the degree to which the indicated qualities are present. The developer of a rating scale must take care to ensure that the qualities identified on the rating scale are consistent with those referenced in the instructional objectives. In addition, clear descriptions of the kind of performance implied by each point on the rating scale are essential. Otherwise, the rater will have difficulty deciding exactly where along the scale a mark should be made to note the quality of an individual student's performance.

Suppose a music teacher wanted to know how well a student could sight-read a given piece of music. She might develop a rating scale inducing the following directions and sample item:

Directions: Circle the appropriate number for each item. The numbers represent the following values.

> 5 = outstanding
> 4 = above average
> 3 = average
> 2 = below average
> 1 = unsatisfactory

1.   To what extent does the person play the appropriate notes?

> 5   4   3   2   1

This rating scale does not give the rater much specific information about what is implied by each rating. For example, what specifically, separates "outstanding" from "above average," "above average" from "average," and so forth? The item might be improved somewhat by changing the descriptors for each rating point as follows:

> 5 = always
> 4 = frequently
> 3 = occasionally
> 2 = seldom
> 1 = never

Some confusion may remain about which rating a given performance ought to be given, but these descriptors are more informative than the original set. (For example, few would have difficulty distinguishing between "always" or "never." There may be problems with making clear separations among "frequently," "occasionally," and "seldom," but these problems probably pose fewer difficulties than distinguishing among "above average," "average," and "below average.")

Sometimes it is helpful to add descriptive phrases at various points along the scale to indicate behaviors that students should demonstrate to earn a given rating. Suppose that a teacher was evaluating performances of students who were giving speeches. He might use a rating scale something like this:

5	4	3	2	1
Demonstrates a continuous unity of thought. Points are clear and related to the topic.		Demonstrates a generally logical flow. There are occasional drifts from the main topic.		Rambles consistently. Presentation lacks coherence. Topic never comes into focus.

Inclusion of these descriptors contributes to the accuracy of the rating process. Also, if this scale is shared with students before they give their speeches, it provides them with useful cues as they prepare for their presentations.

In summary, rating scales are useful for making judgments about the kinds of student performance that cannot be assessed by pencil-and-paper tests. A particular challenge for teachers in developing rating scales is providing clear descriptions of the performance that will merit a rating at each point on the scale.

Evaluative Checklists

Checklists share some characteristics with rating scales. Both are used to evaluate students on behaviors that do not lend themselves readily to traditional pencil-and-paper testing. Both require the focus behaviors to be clearly observable. (The teacher must be able to see or hear what the student is doing to make a judgment and note information on the rating scale or checklist.)

A major difference between rating scales and checklists is that rating scales generally provide teachers with more flexibility in determining the degree of adequacy of a given student's performance. Although nearly all rating scales allow teachers to make judgments at any one of a number of points along a scale (for example, on a five-point scale, a teacher might choose to mark any one of the following: 5, always; 4, frequently; 3, occasionally; 2, seldom; 1, never), most checklists allow only for a yes/no decision. Thus, checklists typically are used when there is an interest only in the presence or absence of a given behavior. When the behavior is present, the checklist format does not allow for judgments to be made regarding the relative quality of the behavior.

Suppose a teacher wanted to monitor the progress of individual students on a term-paper project. A checklist such as the following might be developed:

STUDENT'S NAME_____

	yes	*no*
Topic has been selected and approved	_____	_____
Rough outline turned in	_____	_____
Final outline turned in	_____	_____
Note cards turned in	_____	_____
First draft turned in	_____	_____

Essay Items

Essays are powerful because they can be used to assess students' thinking at virtually any level of the cognitive taxonomy (knowledge, comprehension, application, analysis, synthesis, and evaluation). Though essays are capable of testing students' thinking skills at many levels of sophistication, as a practical matter they are best suited to assessing thinking at the higher levels (application, analysis, synthesis, and evaluation) than at the lower levels (knowledge and comprehension). Alternative testing approaches—for example, multiple-choice, matching, and true-false tests—are available to assess lower-level thinking. These require much less correction time than essays.

A problem teachers face in preparing essays has to do with content coverage. Because of the time required for students to respond to essay questions, typically only a few essay items are included on a single examination. This can result in a very limited sampling of content unless great care is taken in selecting the essay questions to which students are asked to respond.

Maintaining a consistent pattern of scoring when correcting essays is difficult. Correction takes a long time, particularly when large numbers of students are involved. Fatigue often interferes with grading consistency even when the teacher intends to apply the same standards to the last paper as to the first.

Though problems of content selection and correction consistency are difficult, they can be overcome. First of all, care must be taken in structuring the essay task for the student. This means that teacher directions regarding what must be included in the essay should be as precise as possible. Notice the differences in the two following sets of instructions:

Write an essay in which you discuss the chromosome hypothesis and the gene theory.

Write an essay, about five pages in length, in which you compare and contrast the chromosome hypothesis and the gene theory. In your answer, provide specific references to (1) essentials of each position, (2) modifications that have been made to each position since it was initially adopted, and (3) strengths and weaknesses that have been attributed to each view by leading experts.

A student receiving instructions similar to those in "A" may be inclined to ramble. The language used to describe the task is imprecise. (The word *discuss*, for example, is a vague guide to the student regarding what she should be writing about.) Further, there are no references to how long the response should be. A student might write a paragraph or eight or nine pages. In light of these imprecise instructions, the teacher may receive papers that are difficult to evaluate because individual students have interpreted the assignment in different ways.

The set of instructions in "B" is better. Students get a clear idea of what subjects should be covered in their response. In addition, a length condition is imposed ("about five pages"). Because of the specificity of these guidelines, students receiving the "B" instructions are not forced to do nearly as much guessing about what the teacher wants as students receiving the "A" instructions.

Box 17.3

Improving the Quality of Essay Test Questions

Below are a number of poorly written essay questions. Try your hand at rewriting each question to turn it into a better item. Be prepared to tell the instructor why your rewritten version is superior to the original.

1. Compare and contrast the underhanded versus the overhanded method of shooting a free throw.

2. Analyze the president's policy on Iran.

3. Suggest possible changes in the nature of plane geometry theorems that might result in a new geometry based on the assumption that parallel lines meet at some point this side of infinity.

4. Contrast alternative explanations for the growth of suburbs.

5. Contrast the two poets' use of alliteration.

6. Analyze critically the theory of plate tectonics.

What Do You Think?

Write an essay question that you might give to students focusing on a subject you might be teaching. Be sure that your essay requires thinking beyond the levels of knowledge or comprehension. Ask your instructor to comment on the adequacy of your item.

In addition, correcting the set of papers received from students receiving the "B" directions should be easier. At a minimum, the teacher can look to see whether each essay (1) compares and contrasts the chromosome hypothesis and the gene theory, (2) outlines essentials of each, (3) notes changes in each position since it was first postulated, and (4) describes strengths and weaknesses of each position as viewed by leading experts. These common "must-be-included" features help the teacher to look at each essay in the same way. They help the teacher to maintain a consistent correction pattern from paper to paper.

Completion Items

Like essays, completion items requires students to write responses in their own handwriting. (Sometimes students are allowed to use personal computers or typewriters.) However, completion items are much less powerful in terms of the kinds of thinking they can assess. Generally they are most useful for assessing student thinking at the lower cognitive levels of knowledge and comprehension. It is difficult to prepare completion items capable of testing students' higher-level thinking abilities.

Completion items are easy to construct. They can be used to sample a broad range of content. Individual items do not require much time to correct. Hence, many completion items can be included on a given test or examination.

There is a problem in scoring completion items. It is difficult to construct items for which a single answer is the only one that is logically correct. It is particularly difficult to decide what to do about student answers than are partially correct. To get some perspective on this issue, look at the following completion-type item:

> The person who succeeded Margaret Thatcher as Prime Minister of the United Kingdom was _____.

Probably, the answer the teacher had in mind was "John Major." Other plausible alternatives exist, however. For example, students might have included answers such as "a conservative," "a Tory," or even "a man."

To avoid correction problems, a completion item should be written so that the type of response desired is clear. For example, the item above could easily be rewritten to narrow the range of plausible answers. A revised version might look like this:

> The name of the individual who succeeded Margaret Thatcher as Prime Minister of the United Kingdom was _____.

It is important that an individual completion item have only one blank. This blank ought to come toward the end of the item. This arrangement gives the student time to pick up relevant cues regarding the nature of the expected response. An item with many blanks that are placed at random is almost certain to result in confusion. Consider this horrible example:

> _____ affects _____ independently of _____ except on those occasions when _____ and _____ are inversely related.

To eliminate scoring problems, teachers often provide students with a selection of answers, some correct and some incorrect, from which they are to draw their responses. Students must use only answers provided on the list. Thus, they can be held accountable both for correct word choice and for spelling (the word is there; the student has only to copy the word correctly to spell it right).

But this kind of revision alters the format of the completion item into a modified matching item. Further, it introduces the possibility of being able to guess at the right item. However, some teachers are willing to accept this exchange to simplify their correction chores. An example of this kind of modification is provided here:

> Student's Name _____

> Completion Item

Directions: A number of blanks appear in the following short paragraph. Below the paragraph you will find a list of terms. Select appropriate terms from this list and print them carefully in the proper blanks. Include only terms included in the list at the bottom of the page. You will be expected to spell these terms correctly.

> In recent years, there has been a trend for people to move away from the core of a city toward the surrounding suburbs. Sociologists call this movement _____. Another

urban phenomenon involves movement of people from one social class to a part of the city occupied by people in another social class. This is termed _____. When a new group in a society succeeds in taking over a neighborhood, a situation termed _____ results. When minority members of a community are removed by majority members, we have a situation called _____. When this causes married couples to move to a locale where neither set of parents is resident, their new family residence is said to be _____. The group an individual interacts with over time on a more or less continuous basis is called a (an) _____.

List of Terms

recurrent	suburbanization	succession
allotropic	invasion	concession
neolocal	separation	expulsion
patrilocal	segregation	deviance

In general, completion items do not represent a particularly good technique for assessing students' proficiencies. In most cases, multiple-choice, true-false, and matching items are better. These items have the capacity to assess knowledge- and comprehension-level thinking, as do completion items; however, they are much easier to correct than completion items.

Matching Items

Matching items are typically used to measure students' thinking at the levels of knowledge and comprehension. They are easy to construct, they can be corrected quickly, and there is little danger that one student's test will be graded according to a standard different from that used for another student's test.

Difficulties associated with the use of matching items usually have to do with item construction. These problems can be overcome by designing these tests according to a few basic principles.

First, all terms in a giving matching item should focus on a single topic or theme. Students become confused when they are confronted with a matching item containing a mixture of unrelated terms and definitions. Focusing on a single topic or theme remedies this problem. The focus of the item should be listed at the beginning of the matching item. For example, a test including names of Confederate generals on one side and a number of exploits associated with them listed on the other might be labeled "Matching Quiz: Confederate Generals."

As a rule of thumb, the list on the right-hand side (the one providing alternative descriptions or definitions from which students are to select answers) should contain approximately 25 percent more items than the list on the left-hand side. For example, if there were 10 items on the left side, there might be 12 or 13 alternative choices on the right side.

The practice of placing more options on the right makes it possible for a student to miss one question without being forced, as a result, to miss another. When there is an identical number of items in both left- and right-hand lists, the double penalty for a missed question comes into play. (For example, a student who incorrectly identifies term *e* as the response to item 1 instead of the response to item 3, which is correct, will end up having wrong responses both to item 1 and item 3.)

The entire matching item should be printed on one page. It is unacceptable for any portion of either the left-hand list or the right-hand list to be carried over to a second page. When this formatting error occurs, many students fail to realize that part of the test is on another page, and they make mistakes as a result.

Directions on matching tests must be clear. Students must be provided with directions that direct them specifically to place the letter identifying a particular alternative in the right-hand column in the blank before the appropriate item in the left-hand column. When explicit directions are not given, students often draw lines connecting items in the two columns. This results in a confusing spider web of lines that makes correction difficult. In addition, directions should make clear to students that only one correct response is provided in the right-hand column for each item in the left-hand column.

Multiple-Choice Items

Multiple-choice items can be adapted to a variety of subject matter content. They can be scored easily. They have the capacity to test not only for knowledge and comprehension but for some higher-level thinking abilities as well.

In terms of basic format, a multiple-choice item consists of two basic parts: (1) a stem and (2) some alternative choices, only a few of which (usually only one) are logically related to the stem. Among the alternative choices there are some correct answers and others that are called distractors. The difficulty of the item depends in large measure on the level of sophisticated thinking required to distinguish correct answers from the distractors.

It is not easy to prepare multiple-choice items featuring distractors that appear to be plausible answers. Carelessly written distractors tend to give away the correct answer, even to students who do not really know the content. Good distractors take time to develop; hence, high-quality multiple-choice tests cannot be prepared hastily.

A number of principles guide development of sound multiple-choice items. First, it is important that the stem be clear and that all distractors be written in a way that assures grammatical consistency with the stem. Consider this example:

Nils Johannsen, in his novel of the Canadian Prairies, *West from Winnipeg*, called trapping an

   a.   science.

   b.   art.

   c.   duty.

   d.   nuisance.

A student totally unfamiliar with this novel who read the question carefully would identify *b* as the correct answer simply because it is the only choice grammatically consistent with the article *an* at the end of the stem. To correct this problem, the writer of the item might have concluded the stem in this way: ". . . called trapping a (an)." This revision makes any of the four alternative answers grammatically plausible.

Box 17.4

Sample Matching Test

MATCHING TEST: YOUR NAME: _____
TENNIS TERMINOLOGY

Directions: Find the term in the right-hand column that is defined by the definition in the left-hand column. Place the letter identifying this term in the blank space provided before its definition. Only one term is correct for each definition. Please do *not* draw lines connecting definitions to terms.

_____ 1. The point that, if won, wins the match for a player.

_____ 2. The area between the net and the service line.

_____ 3. Hitting the ball before it bounces.

_____ 4. Stroke made after the ball has bounced, either forehand or backhand.

_____ 5. The line that is perpendicular to the net and divides the two service courts.

_____ 6. The initial part of any swing. The act of bringing the racket back to prepare for the forward swing.

_____ 7. A ball hit high enough in the air to pass over the head of the net player.

_____ 8. A ball that is served so well that the opponent fails to touch it with his or her racket.

_____ 9. A shot that bounces near the baseline.

_____ 10. Start of play for a given point.

a. ace

b. backswing

c. center service line

d. deep shot

e. forecourt

f. set point

g. lob

h. match point

i. serve

j. volley

k. dink

l. ground stroke

A stem that is too brief fails to cue students regarding what kind of information they should be looking for in the list of alternatives. Consider this example:

Roger Williams

   a.   sailed on the Mayflower.

   b.   established the Thanksgiving tradition.

   c.   founded the Rhode Island colony.

   d.   developed the New World's first distillery.

Because the stem is so incomplete, students are really faced with four true-false items to ponder rather than with one good multiple-choice item. A far better way of formatting this question would be as follows:

The founder of the Rhode Island colony was

a. Sir Walter Raleigh.

b. John Winthrop.

c. Roger Williams.

d. William Bradford.

As noted earlier, multiple-choice items can be designed to test students' abilities to think at a number of cognitive levels. Let's look at some examples of multiple-choice questions designed to assess thinking at different levels of sophistication.

Knowledge Level.   Recall that knowledge-level thinking requires students to recall specific information. The following is an example of a knowledge-level multiple-choice item:

A belief that an individual has the right not only to succeed but also has the duty or obligation to succeed is referred to by sociologists as the

a. multiplier theory.

b. mobility ethic.

c. transference syndrome.

d. neolocal tendency.

Comprehension Level.   Multiple-choice tests designed to assess comprehension-level thinking require an understanding of several pieces of information that are related to one another in a systematic way. Comprehension requires students to demonstrate their ability to perceive interrelationship. The following is an example of a comprehension-level multiple-choice item:

Directions: Look at the following table. It provides information about the percentage of males in three different groups who were employed in four different years. The groups include (1) men who left high school after completing grades 9, 10, or 11, (2) men who graduated from high school, and (3) men who graduated from college. Study the table, then respond to the question that follows it.

Percentage of Men Employed by Education Level

Year	Left high school* after finishing grades 9, 10, or 11	Graduated from high school	Graduated from college
1971	87.9%	93.6%	92.5%
1980	77.7%	87.0%	93.4%
1985	76.0%	86.1%	92.2%
1990	75.9%	88.6%	93.1%

*Data are from Laurence T. Ogle, Nabeel Alsalam, and Gayle Thompson Rogers (eds). *The Condition of Education, 1991*. Volume 1—Elementary and Secondary Education. Washington, DC: U.S. Government Printing Office, 1991, p. 306.

Question: From 1971 to 1990, there was a tendency for the percentage of employed men who left high school after completing grades 9, 10, or 11 to do what as compared to the percentage of employed men who had completed college?

a. The percentage of employed men who left high school after completing grades 9, 10, or 11 rose, whereas the percentage of employed men who were college graduates went down.

b. The percentage of employed men who left high school after completing grades 9, 10, or 11 rose, as the percentage of employed men who were college graduates went down.

c. There was no change in the percentage of employed men who left high school after completing grades 9, 10, or 11 and the percentage of employed men who were college graduates.

d. The percentage of employed men who left high school after completing grades 9, 10, or 11 went down, while the percentage of employed men who were college graduates stayed about the same or rose slightly.

Application Level.   Application-level multiple-choice items require students to take information learned in one setting and use it correctly in another. Suppose that students had been exposed to the concept of "horizon of worker expectation." An application-level test item related to this concept might look like this:

In a social system where workers are allowed to vote on how profits of their employing firms are to be spent, we logically would expect a worker near retirement to:

a. Support expenditures for plant improvement projects rather than expenditures for workers' benefits.

b. Support expenditures for workers' benefits rather than for plant improvement projects.

c. Support nearly all efforts of younger workers to improve efficiency.

d. Support nearly all efforts of younger workers to gain agreements to improve working conditions, beginning 10 years after a contract settlement had been reached.

Analysis Level.   Analysis requires students to make inferences. That is, they are asked to go beyond what is given. To accomplish this, they examine information that may provide relevant clues and that will serve as a data base for their analytical thinking activities. Analysis-level multiple-choice questions are difficult to construct. They require considerable time to prepare. For this reason, some teachers prefer to use essay examinations when testing for analysis-level thinking. An example of an analysis-level multiple-choice item is provided here:

Ellison had the flair of genius, but he was not a genius. Though pedestrian in his approaches, he was yet a phenomenon. His was a talent of concentration, not of innovation. No other man of his time rivaled his ability to shunt aside irrelevancies to focus on a problem's essentials. For him, non-critical considerations were a trifling bit of detritus to be swept away in a moment. His resolute attack on the nuggety essence of an unresolved issue obviated even the serious probability of egregious error. Contemporaries described his reasoning as "glistening." Only an audacious few ventured public challenges to his positions. It is not too much to say that he lived out his days surrounded by a nervously approving silence. Later generations have seen his conclusions as less than revolutionary. But, in his own time, Ellison's ability to "will" an impeccable solution to a complex issue made others seem small figures who were destined ever to walk lightly in the dark shadows of a giant.

One assumption revealed in the preceding paragraph is:

a. Ellison was truly competent, but he had a flair for impressing people with the logical structure he built to support his solutions.

b. Ellison really was a genius whose "glistening" logic resulted in novel solutions to problems.

c. Today, people tend to be more impressed with Ellison than they were in his own day.

d. Ellison's form probably was a more significant contributor to his reputation than was the substance of his thought.

Synthesis Level and Evaluation Level.   It is possible to prepare multiple-choice questions at levels higher than analysis. However, they are very difficult to write. Many teachers prefer essay items for assessing synthesis-level and evaluation-level thinking.

True-False Items

True-false items, though most frequently used to assess knowledge-level thinking, do have some limited applications at a few higher cognitive levels. True-false items can be prepared relatively quickly. They provide a format that ensures consistency of grading from student to student. True-false items do not require much time to correct.

There are also some disadvantages of true-false items. For one thing, they encourage guessing. Since there are only two choices, students have a 50:50 chance of getting an item correct even when they have no grasp of the content being tested. True-false items require teachers to prepare statements that are absolutely true or absolutely false. Much course content tends more toward gray than black or white. For this reason, some teachers feel constrained by the true-false format, which, they feel, forces them to steer away from the main focus of their instruction to find the odd example that indeed is absolutely true or absolutely false.

When a teacher decides to develop a true-false test, several basic principles need to be followed. Items selected must be clearly true or false. Further, specific instructions must be provided for students regarding how they should record answers.

Often, true-false tests are prepared with blank spaces in front of each item. Students are asked to write answers in the blanks. When this approach is used, students should be directed to write the entire word *true* or *false* or the use symbols such as "+" for true items and "-" for false items. It is *not* a good idea to instruct students to write the letter *t* in the blank before true items and the letter *f* in the blank before false items. Some students may produce hybrid letters that, when looked at in one way, appear to be a *t* and, when looked at in another way, appear to be an *f*.

Box 17.5

Sample Comprehension-Level True-False Test

Data to Be Used in True-False Test

Projected Demand for New Elementary and New Secondary Teachers*

	Number of New Teachers Needed (in thousands)	
Year	Elementary	Secondary
1990	165	75
1991	163	92
1992	163	103
1993	161	112
1994	157	123
1995	157	120

Directions: Use the data above as you respond to the following true-false items. If the statement is true, circle the word *true*. If the statement is false, circle the word *false*.

true   false   1. In none of the years listed is there expected to be a demand for more secondary teachers than for elementary teachers.

true   false   2. The decline in demand for new elementary teachers is predicted to begin before the decline in the demand for new secondary teachers.

true   false   3. There will be a greater growth in demand for elementary teachers than secondary teachers in the years between 1990 and 1994.

true   false   4. The greatest year-to-year growth in demand for new secondary school teachers will occur between 1993 and 1994.

true   false   5. There will be a demand for more new elementary teachers in 1995 than in 1990.

---

*Data are from Joyce D. Stern (ed.) and Marjorie O. Chandler (assoc. ed.), *The Condition of Education*, 1987 edition. Washington, DC: U.S. Department of Education. Center for Education Statistics, 1987, p. 46.

Correction problems associated with how students fill in blanks can be eliminated by doing away with the blanks. In their place, the words *true* and *false* can be printed to the left of each item. When this is done, students are asked to circle the correct word.

As noted at the beginning of this discussion, most true-false tests seek to test students' knowledge-level thinking. With some work, true-false tests can be developed to test other levels of thinking.

Table 17.1   Summary Table

Main Points	Explanation
Measurement	Measurement refers to the process of gathering information. In and of itself, measurement is nonjudgmental.
Evaluation	Evaluation is the process of drawing conclusions and making judgments based on data gathered through measurement activities.
Formative Evaluation	Formative evaluation occurs as an integral part of instruction. It is designed to provide continuous feedback to the teacher and to students. Results help teachers modify instructional practices to help students master the content.
Summative Evaluation	Summative evaluation occurs at the conclusion of an instructional sequence. It is designed to provide a more or less final measure of what students have learned from a completed block of instruction.
Authentic Evaluation	Authentic evaluation requires students to perform in ways that are consistent with how experts in subjects they have studied perform. The idea is to test students in terms of what the real demands of the subject are, not in terms of those aspects that can be conveniently measured. Proponents of authentic evaluation believe that testing of this sort will result in students who are able to engage in more complex and sophisticated thinking than students exposed to more traditional classroom tests.
Informal Data-Gathering Approaches	Informal data-gathering approaches allow students to demonstrate what they have learned by engaging in activities that do not involve traditional pencil-and-paper testing.
Teacher Observation	In this informal approach, teachers base their judgments about what students can do on what they observe the students doing in the classroom.
Headlines and Articles	This approach, often used to assess students' abilities to identify essential features of a large body of information, requires students to develop mock newspaper headlines that highlight main points and to prepare articles relating to these headlines. The articles elaborate on key information.
Teacher-Student Discussion	In this approach, the teacher makes inferences about what the student knows from listening carefully to what he or she says in a personal conversation with the teacher.

Main Points	Explanation
Informal Data-Gathering Approaches, *cont'd.*	
Student-Produced Tests	Teachers gain insights into what students have learned by having the students develop test items related to what they have studied.
Formal Data-Gathering Approaches	These approaches include a wide variety of pencil-and-paper assessment techniques.
Rating Scales	A rating scale allows a teacher to make a qualitative judgment about a given student's performance. Each rating point is defined by a particular quality or standard. The teacher determines the degree of this quality or standard through observation and assigns an appropriate rating to each student.
Checklist	A checklist is a modified version of a rating scale used when the teacher has an interest only in noting the presence or absence of a given behavior or quality.
Essays	The essay is a powerful assessment tool that can be used to assess many different kinds of student thinking. Because correcting essays takes time, many teachers reserve essay questions for occasions when they are assessing students' higher-level thinking abilities (i.e., their ability to think at the levels of application, analysis, synthesis, or evaluation). Students prepare better essays when directions are very clear regarding the kinds of information the teacher is looking for.
Completion Items	Completion tests gather information about students' abilities to think at the levels of knowledge and comprehension. Scoring can be a problem because there are no clear rules for handling synonyms and misspellings. A variant of the basic completion test format features a list of terms that includes a mixture of both correct and incorrect responses to individual questions. Students are expected to use terms in the list in their answers.

Table 17.1   Summary Table *(continued)*

Main Points	Explanation
Formal Data-Gathering Approaches, *cont'd.*	
Matching Items	Matching tests usually are used to assess thinking at the levels of knowledge and comprehension. Grading is relatively simple, and such issues as synonyms and misspellings are not a problem when this approach is used. Good matching tests focus on a single topic or theme. Clear directions regarding how answers are to be recorded are essential.
Multiple-Choice Items	Multiple-choice items can be prepared to assess knowledge, comprehension, and some higher levels of thinking as well. Care must be taken to provide sufficient information in the stem of a multiple-choice item to cue students to the basic context of what is being asked. Care, too, must be exercised in developing plausible distractors (incorrect answer choices).
True-False Items	True-false items most frequently are used to assess knowledge-level thinking. They have limited applications at a few higher cognitive levels. Their construction challenges teachers to prepare statements that are either absolutely true or absolutely false. This somewhat limits the range of content that can be sampled because much of what teachers deal with tends to be in shades of gray rather than in black or white. Explicit directions for recording answers are important. It is recommended that the words *true* and *false* be written to the left of each question or that students be asked to circle the printed word of their choice.

Review of Key Ideas

- Measurement refers to the process of gathering information; *evaluation* refers to the process of drawing conclusions based on data gathered through measurement activities.

- Formative evaluation consists of the periodic assessment activities that occur as part of the instructional process. Formative evaluation occurs while new material is being introduced. Summative evaluation involves testing and other assessment activities that take place at the conclusion of an instructional sequence.

- Authentic evaluation refers to the idea that assessment should require students to demonstrate the important kinds of learning that have been emphasized in an instructional sequence, not just samples of content selected for ease of measurement. Ideally, authentic assessment calls on students to demonstrate their abilities to perform in ways that are consistent with patterns used by experts in subjects the students have studied.

- Informal assessment techniques embrace non-paper-and-pencil approaches teachers use to gather information about what students have learned. Many informal procedures provide insights into student attitudes as well as about their abilities to perform certain tasks.

- Many alternatives are available to teachers who wish to gather information using informal approaches. Among them are (1) teacher observation, (2) headlines and articles, (3) teacher-student discussions, and (4) student-produced tests.

- Formal approaches to gathering assessment information seek to gather evidence through the use of carefully designed measurement devices. These tend to sort into two major categories: standardized tests and teacher-made tests. Standardized tests are prepared by professional measurement specialists, and they are often used to provide general information comparing students in one place to those in other places. Teacher-made tests are prepared by teachers to assess how well students have mastered specific content they have taught in their own classrooms.

- Formal approaches to evaluation include (1) rating scales, (2) evaluative checklists, (3) essays, (4) completion items, (5) matching items, (6) multiple-choice items, and (7) true-false items.

Follow-Up Questions and Activities

Questions

1. What are the relationships between the terms *measurement* and *evaluation*?
2. What are the advantages for students of an instructional program that features carefully planned formative evaluation?
3. How might authentic evaluation result in student learning that is more complex and sophisticated than student learning occurring in classrooms where authentic evaluation is not used?
4. What are some barriers to wider use of authentic evaluation?
5. How should a teacher select a given assessment procedure?
6. What options are available to teachers who are interested in using an informal approach to gathering assessment information?
7. What is a basic characteristic of data-gathering procedures associated with formal approaches to gathering assessment information?
8. How are standardized tests and teacher-made tests distinguished?
9. How can a teacher assure consistency of grading from student to student when an essay has been used to gather information about what students have learned?
10. Compare strengths and weaknesses of completion tests, matching tests, and multiple-choice tests.

Activities

1. Do some additional reading on authentic evaluation. For periodical articles, consult the *Education Index*. Your instructor may also be able to direct you to some specific information sources. Design a complete authentic evaluation procedure for a lesson you would like to teach. Present it to your instructor for review.

2. Think about a topic you would like to teach. Then, develop a portfolio of ideas that describes specific informal assessment procedures you might follow to gain insights into students' understandings and attitudes.

3. Prepare a position paper in which you take a stand in favor of or in opposition to this statement:

   School tests irresponsibly direct students' attention to content that is easy to test but essentially trivial.

4. Invite one or more teachers to visit your class. Ask them to describe the kinds of tests they use, problems they have experienced in assessing students, and their ideas for improving the ways students are tested.

5. For a subject you would like to teach, prepare examples of properly formatted (1) completion tests, (2) multiple-choice tests, (3) true-false tests, (4) matching tests, and (5) essay tests. Ask your instructor to critique your formatting of these materials.

References

KULM, G. "New Directions for Mathematics Assessment." In G. Kulm (ed.). *Assessing Higher Order Thinking in Mathematics*. Washington, DC: American Association for the Advancement of Science, 1990, pp. 71–78.

OGLE, L. T.; ALSALAM, N; AND ROGERS, G. T. (EDS.). *The Condition of Education, 1991. Volume 1—Elementary and Secondary Education*. Washington, DC: United States Government Printing Office, 1991.

SCRIVEN, M. "The Methodology of Evaluation." In R. W. Stake and others. *Perspectives on Curriculum Evaluation*. AERA Monograph Series on Curriculum Evaluation, No. 1. Chicago: Rand McNally, 1967, pp. 39–83.

SHEPARD, L. A. "Psychometricians' Beliefs About Learning." *Educational Researcher* (October 1991), pp. 2–16.

TYLER, R. W. *Basic Principles of Curriculum and Instruction*. Chicago: The University of Chicago Press, 1949.

WIGGINS, G. "Teaching to the (Authentic) Test." *Educational Leadership* (April 1989a), pp. 41–47.

WIGGINS, G. "A True Test: Toward More Authentic and Equitable Measurement." *Phi Delta Kappan* (May 1989b), pp. 703–713.

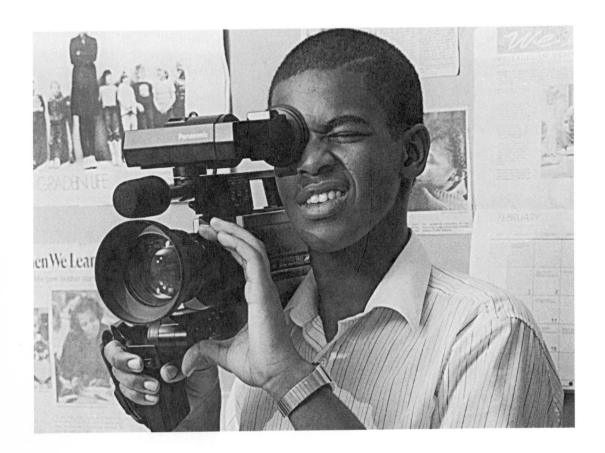

18

Evaluating Teachers' Performance

AIMS

This chapter provides information to help the reader to:

- State the purposes of teacher evaluation.
- Identify the strengths and weaknesses of different types of teacher evaluation.
- Overcome some anxieties traditionally associated with evaluation of teaching performance.
- Identify multiple data sources that can be used for evaluating teaching.
- Explain several observational approaches that can be used to gather information about teachers' classroom performance.
- Describe the elements of a teaching portfolio.

FOCUS QUESTIONS

1. What are some benefits of teacher evaluation?

2. What role do you think student-achievement information should play in evaluating a teacher?

3. Are ratings students make of their teachers valid indications of the quality of the teaching of these individuals?

4. What needs to be done to make self-evaluation worthwhile?

5. Why should supervisors evaluate teachers over whom they have authority?

6. What can be done to reduce teachers' anxieties when they are facing an evaluation by a supervisor?

7. How is peer coaching different from mentoring?

8. What are some important ingredients of successful peer coaching?

9. What is a teaching portfolio?

10. Should more reliance be placed on teacher-prepared portfolios during the evaluation process? Why or why not?

Introduction

Throughout this book, there has been an emphasis on teaching as a process demanding reflection and decision making. This implies a need for teachers to have access to data regarding what they have done in the classroom. Absent such data, reflection is impossible. Under these conditions, judgments teachers make about what they have done may be seriously flawed.

Teacher effectiveness researchers Thomas Good and Jere Brophy (1991) point out that teachers' personal recollections of what happened during lessons they have taught are not reliable. This is true because things happen quickly in the complex milieu of the typical classroom. Unless some systematic attempt to gather reliable information has been established, teachers' recollections are likely to reflect personal biases, past experiences, and other filters that often result in erroneous recollections regarding what *really* happened.

To eliminate this difficulty, sound data are required. Some data can be generated by teachers who take pains to gather information themselves. Others can be provided to them by other professionals who observe them in the classroom. Many school districts require principals and other supervisors of teachers to periodically evaluate teachers' classroom performances and to provide feedback to teachers regarding what they have done. This information often provides teachers with useful "snapshot" views of their behaviors during the act of teaching. Self-gathered data and data from supervisors collectively have the potential to provide teachers with great quantities of useful information that can be used as the basis for sound reflection on the quality of their instruction.

Box 18.1

Should Pay Be Based on Performance?

In response to pressure from teachers for improvements in salaries, some state legislators have demanded evidence that teachers are doing good work in the classroom. In some places, state legislatures have chosen not to increase salary levels of all teachers, only salaries paid to those who "deserve more money." Various kinds of merit-pay or career-ladder schemes have been devised to pay some teachers more than others.

Supporters of these plans contend that introducing competition into teaching increases teachers' incentives to do well. These plans, among other things, have greatly increased the amount of supervised evaluation of teachers in schools with merit-pay or career-ladder plans. This is true because laws usually require that

decisions resulting in higher pay levels for some teachers must be based on objective measures of their classroom performance. In some places, annual expenditures for gathering evaluation information about teachers are high.

What Do You Think?

1. Do you agree that schemes that foster competition among teachers lead to improved teacher performance?

2. What do you see as the positive and negative aspects of merit-pay and career-ladder proposals?

3. Is it possible to identify expected standards of performance against which individual teachers should be judged?

Purposes for Evaluating Classroom Performance

There are two basic purposes for evaluating teachers' classroom performance. One purpose is developmental. This kind of information is designed to help teachers analyze what they are doing and modify and improve any patterns that are not as good as they might be. Developmental evaluation data encourage teachers to think about what they have done and to consider ways to improve. This kind of evaluation falls under the general formative evaluation category that was introduced in Chapter 17, "Measuring Student Progress." Formative evaluation may be based on data gathered through teachers' own self-evaluation procedures, or it may involve feedback provided to the teacher by someone else—for example by another teacher, an administrator, or a supervisor.

The second purpose for gathering data about teachers' performance is to make a summary judgment regarding the general quality of a teacher's performance. This is what was described as summative evaluation in Chapter 17. Often, this kind of evaluation is gathered by administrators and teachers' supervisors. These individuals have professional and ethical obligations to assure that teachers for whom they are responsible are performing at an acceptable level.

This kind of evaluation stirs great debate among educators. Much of this controversy results from difficulties professionals have had in agreeing on what constitutes "satis-

"Does this mean my evaluation was good or bad?"

factory" performance. There have been instances where judgments about teachers have been made on the bases of flawed data or biased judgments. Much work has been done to improve these kinds of evaluations, and school districts are working hard to assure that principals and supervisors are using well-defined standards and are applying them uniformly to the teachers they observe.

Data used for either formative evaluation or summative evaluation purposes can be provided from several sources. Teachers can establish procedures of their own to generate this kind of information. Other teachers, acting as peer coaches or mentors, can provide useful information. Additionally, data often are provided by principals and others who hold supervisory positions in the schools.

Categories of People Providing Evaluation Data

Before we look at three categories of individuals who are in a position to provide useful data to teachers, let's pause to define evaluation. *Evaluation* is judging something on the basis of criteria. The judgment based on *criteria* is what separates evaluation from mere opinion.

The appropriateness of the criteria is an important consideration. To be defensible, these criteria must relate clearly to the purpose of the evaluation. When teachers are being evaluated, it is important to keep in mind that a key purpose of the exercise is to determine the extent to which the teacher's performance facilitates students' learning.

If criteria do not tie clearly to this issue, they may be inappropriate, and the results of the evaluation may be spurious.

Consider this example. Suppose an evaluator decided to focus attention on such issues as the attractiveness of the room, the quality of bulletin boards, and the orderly arrangement of desks. Unless this person has hard evidence that there is a clear connection between these criteria and student learning, the criteria make no sense as standards against which to judge the quality of the teacher's performance.

Complaints teachers make about evaluations often result when inappropriate criteria have been selected. One teacher the authors know once received a negative evaluation because the observer felt the grouping of student seats into small circles in various parts of the room made the custodian's job difficult. With utter disregard for the highly effective small-group instruction this person was using, the evaluator sent a signal to this teacher that "good" teaching, by definition, featured whole-group instruction with all students seated in chairs arranged in neat rows.

Comments in this section need to be understood in light of the need for appropriate criteria. This is an imperative regardless of whether the evaluation is (1) self-evaluation, (2) peer evaluation, or (3) supervisor evaluation.

Self-Evaluation

During self-evaluation, the individual teacher gathers data, identifies criteria to be used in making a judgment, and arrives at a conclusion about the quality of her teaching performance. Self-evaluation data can come from several sources. Often teachers consider information related to student achievement. Student attitudes and opinions often are included as well. Some teachers make audio recordings as they teach and use them to review what they did during a lesson. Video recordings may also be used (although the paraphernalia to obtain them may introduce an unfamiliar element into the classroom and, hence, change the more typical classroom environment).

Several reasons support the importance of this kind of evaluation. First of all, self-evaluation may occur much more frequently than either peer evaluation or supervisor evaluation. In one recent survey, only 34 percent of secondary teachers reported being observed even once during the their first year of teaching for more than five minutes (Good and Brophy, 1991). A lack of evaluation information has been reported as a source of dissatisfaction among teachers (Wise, Darling-Hammond, McLaughlin, and Bernstein, 1985). Since the individual teacher controls the frequency of self-evaluation, this approach can fill the information gap resulting from infrequent peer or supervisor evaluation.

A second rationale for using self-evaluation is that people are more inclined to change their behavior pattern when they personally identify something they do not like and resolve to change. Responding to self-evaluation gives teachers a sense of personal control over their own needs and how these needs should best be accommodated (Rodriguez and Johnstone, 1986).

Third, self-evaluation is a nonintrusive way of gathering information and making judgments about teacher behavior. It requires no disruption of regular classroom procedures. This distinguishes the approach from peer evaluation and supervisor evaluation, both of which introduce outside observers into the classroom. As a result, information gathered during self-evaluation may be a more accurate reflection of how the teacher behaves under typical classroom conditions than information gathered by either peer observers or supervisors.

Finally, regular self-evaluation builds confidence. Over time, teaching behavior that has been modified as a result of regular consideration of self-evaluation information reflects a pattern of careful introspection. This helps teachers to articulate a rationale for what they typically do in the classroom.

There are also some negatives associated with self-evaluation. It can be haphazard and unsystematic. Unless care is taken to gather information that clearly represents what the teacher did, judgments about teaching performance may be faulty. When teachers are unable to describe and defend procedures they have followed in gathering information about their teaching performances, their conclusions have been found to correlate poorly with the findings of outside observers (Brown, 1983).

Teachers may find it difficult to make accurate records of what goes on during a lesson. Classrooms are fast-paced environments. So much happens within a class period that the teacher cannot possibly reconstruct from memory everything that happened. Using audiotapes or videotapes to record lessons can help overcome this difficulty. Teacher-effectiveness specialists Thomas Good and Jere Brophy (1991) report that researchers have found teachers' instruction to improve more from recording and evaluating their own lessons once every two weeks than from receiving feedback from an outside observer who watched them teach.

Audio and video recordings do not provide an absolutely complete record of what went on during a lesson. Audio recordings provide no information about non-audio aspects of teacher and learner behavior. Also, often individual students' comments are difficult to pick up. This is a particular problem if several students have been speaking at the same time.

Video recordings often do not focus on the entire room. Behaviors out of range will not be picked up. Also, often all students will not be clearly in focus. Sometimes expressions of certain students will be missed as they react to different aspects of the lesson. Even with all of their limitations, however, audio recordings and video recordings can provide useful information for teachers interested in self-evaluation.

Once a decision has been made about how information is to be gathered, the teacher must decide on exactly what kind of information is needed. Focus questions, generated by the teacher, help to pinpoint kinds of needed information. Focus questions such as these might be developed:

- How many different students did I involve in the discussion?
- Did my lesson follow a logical sequence?
- How often did I praise students, and whom did I praise?
- How long did I wait for students to respond after I asked a question?
- What did I do when I asked a question and nobody responded quickly?
- What did I do to highlight key points of the lesson?
- How often did I make control statements?

Box 18.2

Is Self-Evaluation Possible?

One school administrator made this response to a question about self-evaluation:

I don't believe self-evaluation has value. Studies show little correlation between self-evaluations and evaluations conducted by students or colleagues of a teacher. This is only logical. People don't see themselves as others see them. When we think about ourselves, we see what we want to see and ignore what we don't like. In addition, teachers simply will not conduct worthwhile self-evaluation on a regular basis. It tends to be haphazard and threatening. It is easier to avoid the task and, at the same time, escape the need to confront evidence that improvement may be needed.

What Do You Think?

1. What are the strongest points made in this statement?

2. On what points do you disagree?

3. What could be done to make sure that self-evaluation is worthwhile?

- How did I deal with misbehavior?
- What did I say to make a smooth transition from one part of the lesson to another?
- What did I do to accept students' ideas and feelings?
- What did I do to make sure students understood tomorrow's assignment?

Responses to the focus questions serve as the data pool the teacher considers in determining whether anything he did during the lesson fell short of his expectations. If so, the teacher can develop a personal action plan. For example, if one of the teacher's interests was to maximize the number of students participating in a discussion, and a review of what actually happened revealed that only a few took part, then the teacher could take action during future discussions to assure involvement of more students. Recordings or other means of gathering data can be used during subsequent lessons to verify that intended behaviors are being implemented.

Peer Evaluation

Collaboration with a respected peer sometimes provides teachers with valuable insights into their behaviors and with ideas about how their instruction might be improved. Collaborative work with other teachers often has an important psychological benefit. It breaks down the sense of isolation teachers sometimes feel when they work alone in their classroom with no adult company. When a teacher's work is observed by a colleague, there is an opportunity for a rich debriefing discussion that brings to bear the collective insights of two trained professionals.

Several approaches to peer collaboration have evolved. Two that are commonly used are peer coaching and mentoring.

This teacher is listening as a colleague provides feedback following an observation session. Both of these teachers are members of a peer coaching group.

Peer Coaching

Peer coaching is defined as a situation in which two or more individuals voluntarily work together to help each other to solve problems and grow professionally. In a peer coaching situation, no individual is regarded as superior to another. All members of a peer coaching team are viewed as having abilities and skills that may be valuable to others.

Successful peer coaching groups require members to know one another well and to have a relationship based on mutual trust and respect. When such groups first form, members often spend considerable time sharing ideas about teaching and exchanging perspectives that help each member of the team to better understand others. In time, members begin sharing and critiquing lesson ideas and instructional materials they are considering. Every effort is made to assure that comments are made in as positive and supportive a manner as possible. This continues to build members' confidence in perspectives of others and to enhance their sense of professional self-worth.

When members arrive at a point where they feel quite comfortable with one another, they start observing each other's teaching performance in the classroom. Research has established that the anxieties of teachers who are observed diminish considerably when observations are conducted by people they view as credible and trustworthy (Bang-Jensen, 1986).

When members of a peer coaching group start observing members' classroom teaching, a formal supervision cycle often is followed. This involves these elements:

- Preconference
- Observation
- Postconference

During the preconference, the teacher and the individual (or individuals) who will be observing plan the observation experience together. The teacher informs the observer(s) about the lesson objectives and other features of the lesson plan. The group discusses kinds of information that the observers should gather as the lesson is taught and procedures to be followed in obtaining this information.

During the observation itself, information is gathered using procedures agreed to during the preconference meeting. Observers may also take notes on other matters that they feel ought to be shared with the teacher. Comments are written in positive terms with a view to supporting the efforts of the teacher.

Information is shared with the teacher during the postconference. Observations are presented in a nonjudgmental fashion, and the teacher is invited to look for patterns and draw her own conclusions. Every effort is extended to urge the teacher to reflect on what was done and to spend a good deal of the postconference sharing her own perceptions. Those involved in gathering observation information can affirm what was done well and suggest a few ideas the teacher might like to try in the future. Ideally, the postconference involves a sharing of information among equals.

There are some constraints on the use of peer coaching. The approach takes time. Schedules sometimes do not permit teachers to observe others, much less engage in needed preconferences and postconferences. Also, peer coaching depends on mutual trust. If school administrators force teachers to organize into peer coaching teams or build teams of people who do not like or respect one another, nothing good will result. Little change and improvement results unless everybody on a peer coaching team trusts and respects each member (Bang-Jensen, 1986).

Mentoring

Mentoring involves the tutoring of a less skilled person by a more skilled person. The mentor serves as guide, adviser, role model, or consultant (Odell, 1990). There is a clear hierarchical relationship assumed in mentoring. One person is viewed as having more advanced knowledge than the other. This person uses this knowledge to assist the less skilled person with whom he works. In teacher education programs, there is often a mentoring relationship between the supervising teacher and the student teacher.

For mentoring programs to succeed, there must be mutual trust and respect between the mentor and the mentee (the person being helped). Ideally, mentoring relationships, like peer coaching relationships, are given adequate time to develop. This is particularly true when administrators assign one person to be the mentor of another. It is important that there be adequate time for the mentor and mentee to get to know one another well. When this is the case, the mentee is much less likely to feel threatened and is more open to the mentor's suggestions.

WHAT SCHOLARS SAY

Is Peer Collaboration Worthwhile?

Interest in peer collaboration is increasing. This kind of cooperative involvement of teachers breaks a more typical pattern in which teachers operate in isolation from one another (Feiman-Nemser and Floden, 1986). This traditional arrangement has tended to isolate teachers from their peers and has made it difficult for them to assist one another to grow professionally.

Not all teachers are enthusiastic about peer collaboration. Some teachers enjoy working alone in their classrooms and view too much direct involvement by others as interference. Some see collaboration as a potential threat to their professional autonomy.

Good and Brophy (1991) have summarized findings of many researchers who have studied the impact of peer collaboration. They report that this approach generally has been found to help teachers to improve their instructional practices. In one study involving 19 secondary teachers who taught low achievers, some individuals worked collaboratively in an effort to increase the amount of time their students spent on assigned instructional tasks. Others worked alone to achieve a similar objective. Students of those who worked collaboratively increased their time on task the most.

In another study, teachers who worked collaboratively were found to benefit in ways they had not anticipated. A number of them reported that they acquired many useful ideas as a result of opportunities to observe other teachers in the classroom. Also, the observations of other teachers prompted them to think more seriously about how they were organizing and presenting their own lessons.

In general, research has confirmed that large numbers of teachers welcome opportunities to collaborate with their peers. Further, this kind of collaboration often has been associated with improved teaching. In summary, for many teachers, collaborative work has been shown to have positive benefits on both teacher attitudes and performance.

Sources: Feiman-Nemser, S. and Floden, R. "The Cultures of Teaching." In M. Wittrock (ed.). *Handbook of Research on Teaching*. 3rd ed. New York: Macmillan Publishing Company, 1986, pp. 505–526; Good, T. and J. Brophy. *Looking in Classrooms*. 5th ed. New York: HarperCollins, 1991, p. 535.

Supervisor Evaluation

Supervisor evaluation occurs when someone in a position of authority is given the responsibility for evaluating a subordinate. In school settings, when teachers are evaluated by their superiors (often by school administrators) results of evaluations may have

purposes going beyond those usually associated with self-evaluation or peer cooperation. Both self-evaluation and peer-cooperation efforts are almost uniformly focused on
helping the teacher to become a more proficient instructor. This is also a key purpose of
supervisor evaluation. However, supervisor evaluation also sometimes is used to provide a rationale for firing or retaining a teacher, awarding a teacher tenure, or assigning
a teacher to a higher salary category.

The varied purposes of supervisor evaluation sometimes make teachers more nervous about this kind of evaluation than about self-evaluation or peer evaluation.
Despite these concerns, researchers have found that teachers want and value evaluation by their supervisors (McLaughlin and Pfeifer, 1988). One teacher who reflected on
this finding indicated general agreement, but also noted an important condition: "We
need people to come in and check on us just like anybody else. As long as it is done in a
positive and constructive manner, all it can do is benefit education" (McLaughlin and
Pfeifer, 1988; p. 63). When supervisors provide positive and constructive feedback,
they often succeed in helping teachers overcome some of their fears and defensiveness
about the evaluation process.

Supervisor evaluation tends to be done in more formal and systematic ways than self-
evaluation or peer collaboration. Supervisors often use formal evaluation instruments that
have been developed by trained specialists. Some evaluations are scheduled in advance.
Sometimes this scheduling is done to allow the supervisor an opportunity to view instruction related to particular lesson. At other times, supervisors may drop in unannounced.
Observations often are followed by a formal conference between the supervisor and the
teacher. This allows opportunities for the supervisor to share comments with the teacher
and to engage the teacher in a general discussion about the lesson.

In preparing for supervisor evaluations, many teachers find it useful to review the
data-collection instruments supervisors will use. This allows them to better understand
the categories of behavior that will be assessed. If the teacher disagrees with the categories reflected on the instrument, it may be possible to discuss this situation in
advance with the supervisor. As a result, some compromise might be reached.

Whether supervisors ever see a truly representative sample is a matter of some
debate. The presence of a supervisor alters the classroom environment. Changes can be
both positive and negative. On the plus side, many teachers feel their students behave
better when a supervisor is present and that they are more responsive to the lesson
than usual. On the other hand, the supervisor's presence often makes teachers a bit
nervous, and this may affect their typical patterns of behavior.

The degree of nervousness a teacher feels is closely related to how she regards the
purpose of the evaluation process and the motives of the supervisor. If the teacher feels
evaluation is being used as a means of finding data that will support a dismissal decision, obviously this person's attitude is going to be more negative than if she feels the
only agenda is to provide information that can be used to improve instruction.

Responsible supervisors recognize this problem, and they take pains to assure teachers that their agenda is positive staff development. Teachers are not always receptive to
this message. Some researchers have found that the most difficult problem associated
with supervisor evaluation is overcoming teachers' negative feelings about the integrity
and purposes of the process (McLaughlin and Pfeifer, 1988).

Data Sources for Teacher Evaluation

Responsible teacher evaluation incorporates data from multiple sources. Each data source offers information that differs in some way from information provided by others. The chances that judgments will accurately reflect what a teacher does in the classroom are greatly enhanced when data from multiple sources are considered. Regrettably, some appraisals of teacher performance are made on the basis of data from an extremely small number of sources. When this is the case, teachers have reason to be concerned about the validity of observers' conclusions.

Data sources that are potentially useful for teacher evaluation sort into three categories. These are:

- Data about student learning
- Data from student opinions
- Data from classroom observations

Data About Student Learning

Since promotion of learning is a fundamental obligation of teachers, it is not surprising that student achievement information is often used in evaluating teachers. Although student-learning data are important, there are reasons this kind of information is not the only thing considered in judging teachers' effectiveness. For one thing, an exclusive emphasis on achievement might encourage teachers to use unethical means to produce increases in student scores on such things as basic achievement tests. For example, students might be threatened with harsh punishments if they failed to perform well.

It is also true that some important objectives of education do not lend themselves conveniently to being measured on traditional kinds of tests. This tends particularly to be true for affective outcomes that focus on changes in students' attitudes and values. For example, encouraging students to use rational thinking processes might be an extremely important learning outcome. It is difficult to measure this kind of a commitment directly. If a teacher evaluation procedure depends only on student achievement data from tests, the good work of a teacher who is exceptionally good in helping students develop strong commitments to rational thinking processes would not be recognized.

Using student achievement data to evaluate teachers assumes that students have learned subject matter content from their teacher. This is not always the case. For example, some bright students may well get high scores on tests even when the instruction they have received from their teacher is terrible. They may have learned tested information on their own.

Despite these limitations, there is a place for student achievement data in teacher evaluation. However, achievement information must come from well-designed procedures. It is also important that tests or other data sources adequately sample information that students have been taught. Specific information about procedures for preparing good tests is provided in Chapter 17, "Measuring Student Progress."

Teacher evaluations based on achievement data, ideally, involve more than a review of students' test scores. Samples of student's daily work and other products of student learning often are used for this purpose.

A recognition that their evaluations will depend, in part at least, on student achievement information encourages teachers to assume professional responsibility for students' learning. This practice fosters a commitment to the idea that all students can learn. It encourages a positive cycle in which the realization that student achievement data plays a role in evaluation stimulates a sincere interest in meeting the special needs of all students. This, in turn, often results in enhanced student performance levels, which help teachers to earn high marks when they are evaluated.

A focus on student learning helps teachers to reflect on their practices. Questions such as these sometimes are used by teachers interested in what students have learned from specific lessons:

- What did students learn, and what did they fail to learn?
- What specific things did I do to promote learning in those parts of lessons most students learned well?
- What specific things did I not do to promote learning in those parts of the lesson students failed to learn well?

Answers to questions such as these provide the teacher with ideas for modifying instructional procedures in subsequent lessons.

Data from Student Opinions

Students are the teacher's clients or customers. They come into contact with the teacher every day they are in class, and they have a perspective on his teaching that cannot be duplicated by anyone else. For this reason, opinions of students sometimes are included when teachers are evaluated.

Some cautions must be observed in designing student rating scales for evaluating teachers. It is important that students be asked to rate only behaviors they are qualified to comment on. For example, items related to the teacher's apparent organization, ability to highlight key points during lecture, and skill in involving large numbers of individuals in a discussion are behaviors students are likely to have seen and about which they may logically be expected to share a knowledgeable opinion. On the other hand, few students have sufficient background to make meaningful judgments about such things as the depth of the teacher's subject-matter knowledge or the quality of the teacher preparation program in which he at one time was enrolled.

Second, rating scales should feature items over which the teacher can exercise some personal control. Items related to acoustic quality of the classroom or the nature of overhead lighting are not appropriate. Though these environmental variables may influence student learning, they often cannot be altered by personal intervention of the teacher. Teachers should not be held accountable for things they can do nothing about.

Box 18.3

Are Student Ratings Worthwhile?

A teacher recently commented in this way about using student ratings as a source of information about teaching performance:

A system that weighs student ratings in considering the relative excellence of as teacher's performance makes little sense. Such ratings can actually undermine really 'good' teaching. Because ratings pit teachers against one another in a popularity contest, there is an incentive for teachers to give easy assignments and lots of high grades. Though immature students may reward these practices with high teacher ratings, in the long run students lose when teachers do these things. The bottom line is that students simply lack the qualifications needed to judge whether a teacher's performance is good or bad.

What Do You Think?

1. What are the strong and weak points of this teacher's position?

2. Are students unable to make any reliable judgments about the quality of their teachers' instruction, or are there some areas in which they have the expertise needed to make sound judgments?

3. How do you feel personally about the use of student ratings to evaluate teachers? On what do you base your position?

Finally, interpretation of students' reactions sometimes is a problem. It is important that conclusions drawn from a review of rating scale responses focus on what the majority of respondents have indicated. In any class, there are likely to be a few individuals with opinions that are at odds with the preponderance of opinion. Individuals who pay too much attention to these out-of-the-mainstream views may draw some false conclusions about the adequacy of their teaching.

Data from Classroom Observations

Formal classroom observations often provide information useful in evaluating the quality of instruction. Various techniques that provide data can be used to shed light on such issues as students' attitudes, student performance on assigned tasks, and levels of student involvement.

Good classroom observation procedures provide for systematic data gathering. Typically, there is an emphasis on a specific set of focus behaviors. Data are gathered as they relate to these behaviors. This allows the observer to focus on a relatively small sample of what a teacher does. Under these circumstances, it is possible for the observer to keep up with the rapid interchanges that frequently characterize classroom instruction. Without this kind of a focus, it is easy for observers to fall behind and "get lost" in their futile attempt to keep track of everything that happens.

The accuracy of information obtained from classroom observations can also be influenced by the personal background of the observers. Observers with little formal training in proper observation procedures may bring perspectives to their work that they may not even recognize. For example, they may have formulated impressions about what constitutes "good teaching" based solely on their recollections of their experiences as students. What appealed to them may not appeal to other learners; hence, these personal definitions of good teaching may be at odds with what careful researchers have identified as characteristics of sound instructional practice. Clearly, observers who are familiar with findings of teacher-effectiveness research and who clearly understand procedures to be followed in gathering information are likely to provide more valid and reliable information about what a teacher does than observers who do not have this kind of background.

A number of approaches are taken by trained observers as they collect data about a given teacher's performance. Many formal observation instruments have been developed. Space limitations prohibit an extensive discussion of these approaches, but, to illustrate kinds of procedures used by trained observers, we will introduce a few that they often employ.

List of Focus Questions

Observers often develop a list of focus questions to guide their observations. Sometimes these are worked out cooperatively with the teacher to be observed. The observer uses these questions to guide his data-gathering as the lesson is taught by the teacher. Figure 18.1 shows an example of a list of focus questions.

Clearly these questions are just examples of those that might be used. Some teachers and observers, for example, might be interested in issues such as lesson pacing, the efficiency of transitions from one part of the lesson to another, the relative degree of participation by male and female students, and the amount of on-task behavior demonstrated by individual students during independent study. A general guideline in preparing questions is the list should not be too long. More useful information ordinarily results when observers gather extensive information about a fairly small number of focus questions.

Verbatim Record

Another approach observers sometimes use in gathering information is the verbatim record. In this procedure, a small number of teacher behavior categories are identified. Usually no more than three are selected for a given lesson. As the lesson is taught, the observer writes down everything the teacher says that relates to each selected category. Sometimes the observer identifies the focus categories. Sometimes the observer and the teacher jointly agree on them before the lesson begins.

This approach also lends itself to self-evaluation. To use it in this way, the teacher arranges to record the lesson. Then, she plays back the recording and notes everything she said in each focus category.

A verbatim record form is shown in Figure 18.2.

Sometimes additional categories are added by the observer as the lesson is being taught. For example, the observer might note that the teacher is overusing the word *good* when students respond correctly to a question. To point out this pattern to the teacher, the observer might add a new category, "Specific Statements Made to Students

LESSON OBSERVATION

Teacher: _____ Date: _____

Lesson Topic: _____

Course: _____ Period: _____

Number of Males _____ Number of Females _____

1. What routines were used to get the instructional phase of the class period started?

2. What did the teacher do to draw students' attention to the content of the lesson?

3. What was the sequence of activities?

4. How did the teacher check for student understanding?

5. How were students actively engaged in the lesson?

6. Was there evidence of reteaching to help students having trouble with some of the lesson content?

7. Were key points highlighted? If so, how was this done?

8. How were student questions answered?

9. If there was discussion, how many students participated? Were their answers responsive to the questions?

10. What appeared to be the objective of the lesson? What evidence was there that it was achieved?

11. Were students given opportunities to engage in independent study activities related to the lesson objective?

12. What were some examples of general student reactions or attitudes toward the lesson?

13. How did the teacher handle episodes of misbehavior?

Figure 18.1
Sample focus questions

Answering Correctly," and write the word *good* under this heading every time the teacher uses the word for this purpose. The long string of *goods* that result can be shared with the teacher in debriefing the lesson.

In debriefing lessons for which a verbatim record has been made, well-trained observers try not to be judgmental. Ideally, information is shared with the teacher, and the teacher decides whether the pattern revealed is consistent with his intentions. If it is not, then the teacher may resolve to change certain things he did when teaching future lessons.

VERBATIM RECORD

Teacher: _____ Date: _____

Lesson Topic: _____

Course: _____ Period: _____

Number of Males _____ Number of Females _____

All comments of the teacher will be written down exactly as they are said so long as statements are related to one of these focus categories:

1. MOTIVATING STUDENTS

    Time   *Statement*

2. PRAISING STUDENTS

    Time   *Statement*

3. CONTROLLING STUDENTS

    Time   *Statement*

Figure 18.2
A sample verbatim record form

Frequency Count

Another easy-to-use procedure for gathering useful information during a classroom observation is the frequency count. It is basically a checklist that is used to note the number of times something occurs. Its usefulness is restricted to kinds of behaviors that may recur several times during a lesson.

One limitation is that the issue of duration is ignored when the focus is on tallying the number of times an individual behavior occurred. For example, in one class, a teacher might have criticized students on 10 separate occasions. In another, a teacher might have criticized them only three times. This does not necessarily mean more *total* criticism was going on in the first teacher's class. For example, in the first class, criticism statements might have been very short, and the total time taken up by criticism might be less than five minutes. In the second class, each episode of criticism might have taken an average of six minutes. This would mean 18 minutes of class time was taken up in this way, more than three times the amount of criticism time in the first class.

A frequency count scheme might look something like the example in Figure 18.3.

FREQUENCY OF SELECTED TEACHER BEHAVIORS

Teacher: _____ Date: _____

Lesson Topic: _____

Course: _____ Period: _____

Number of Males _____ _____ Number of Females _____

Directions: Tally the frequency of the following kinds of teacher behaviors:

1. Statements designed to motivate students in the topic of the lesson.

2. Questions requiring factual recall.

3. Questions requiring higher-level thinking (questions above cognitive levels of knowledge and comprehension).

4. Females called on by the teacher.

5. Males called on by the teacher.

6. Positive teacher comments directed toward females.

7. Positive teacher comments directed toward males.

8. Negative/critical comments directed toward females.

9. Negative/critical comments directed toward males.

Figure 18.3
A sample frequency count scheme

Many other kinds of items can be included on checklists. New ones may be added if the observer notes a category of behavior the teacher should know about. For example, if the observer notes that a teacher has a pattern of calling only on students in the front of the room, focus categories labeled "students seated in front half of the room called on" and "students seated in the back half of the room called on" can be added.

Portfolios

Interest is increasing in gathering and packaging more complete information about teachers' instructional performances than can be generated by traditional observation procedures. The idea is for the teacher to organize information of many kinds to provide a fairly comprehensive picture of her teaching behavior.

Information might include evidence attesting to the teacher's professional work such as instructional units she has designed, tests prepared for students, other teacher-developed materials, examples of assignments, samples of papers and other instructional products prepared by students, data gathered by observers using formal evaluation, and video or audiotapes of lessons. Collectively, all of these things comprise the teacher's portfolio. A teacher's portfolio is prepared to demonstrate her work much in the same way that artists prepare portfolios to show others what they have been capable of accomplishing.

Portfolios often include several basic categories of information. Many of them feature separate sections for each of the following:

- Material prepared by the teacher
- Material gathered from others
- Examples of student work

Material Prepared by the Teacher

This section often features a statement by the teacher describing his views regarding elements of "good" teaching. Specific information about courses that are taught and relevant state or local requirements is typically included here. Often there are references to course objectives or at least to what the teacher hopes to accomplish with students in each course.

Preferred instructional methodologies also may be referenced in this section, along with preferred evaluation procedures. Often, there are examples of instructional units, teacher-prepared tests, and lesson plans. Sometimes teachers include examples of below-average, average, and above-average work that they have graded. This is done to showcase the teacher's abilities to differentiate among learners whose performances reflect varying achievement levels. There may be an explanation of specific actions the teacher has taken to deal with exceptional students and with others with special learning characteristics and needs. Some teachers include self-evaluation data in this part of the portfolio.

Material Gathered from Others

This section of the portfolio may include data gathered through peer evaluation and supervisor evaluation. The peer evaluation materials may include comments from colleagues who are willing to provide written comments about the teacher's work. It is particularly common for other members of the teacher's department to provide information for the portfolio. Student opinionaires and other reactions from students may be featured in this section. Comments from parents sometimes also are included in this section. In some cases, information is included that has been gathered from college and university people who have worked with the teacher's students.

Examples of Student Work

Student test scores on quizzes and examinations often are featured in this section. Essays students have written, models they have built, projects they have completed, term papers they have written, and other examples of student products reflecting learning are included. Testimonials from students' employers that attest to the impact the teacher has had on their lives might be included here. There may be letters from students who have gone on to do advanced work in a subject the teacher has taught and who have written to express appreciation for the fine background in the subject they received from the teacher.

Assessing Portfolios

Similar kinds of information do not appear in every portfolio. Hence, assessment procedures, to some degree, need to be tailored to the specific portfolio that is being evaluated. Despite differences from portfolio to portfolio, each tends to have an identifiable organizational scheme. This can be used by individuals charged with evaluating the portfolio to develop assessment guidelines. Portfolio assessment is basically a matter of consistency analysis. The evaluator looks for clues regarding the teacher's hopes and priorities. Then, she looks through the portfolio for examples that confirm behaviors are consistent with these hopes and priorities or that suggest behaviors are at odds with them.

For example, the teacher's description of what constitutes "good teaching" can be used as a backdrop for considering evidence considered throughout the portfolio. What evidence is there that the data presented are consistent with this person's vision of good teaching? Does the provided information support the view that the teacher's practices have been consistent with her stated priorities?

This kind of evaluation has important advantages over more traditional schemes that depended on data gathered from one or two classroom observations. Information is gathered over a considerable period of time. It includes information from many sources. There is an attempt to provide a comprehensive view of the teacher's behavior.

Potentially, at least, portfolio evaluation can provide a much more complete picture of what the teacher does than procedures that encourage observers to make inferences based on more limited data. Portfolio assessment is an idea gathering increasing support in the profession. It is likely to be used by larger numbers of schools in the years ahead.

Table 18.1 Summary Table

Main Points	Explanation
Evaluation	Evaluation is defined as "making a judgment about something in the light of criteria." The element of criteria is particularly important. Without it, judgments may be made on the basis of unsupported opinion and, therefore, may lack a solid evidentiary base.
Reasons for Evaluating Teachers' Instructional Effectiveness	There are two basic purposes of teacher evaluation. First of all, evaluation provides information to teachers that they can use to improve their behavior. Second, evaluation data can be used to make summary judgments regarding the overall quality of teachers' performances.
Self-Evaluation	Self-evaluation involves the individual teacher in gathering data, identifying appropriate criteria, and arriving at a conclusion about his or her performance. Since no others are involved, it is a very nonintrusive kind of procedure. Often teachers use video or audio recordings of what they have done when teaching lessons. Self-evaluation can occur as frequently as a teacher wishes to use it. Good self-evaluation focuses on specific questions a teacher wishes to have answered about his or her behavior.
Peer Evaluation	Peer evaluation involves collaborative work with others, typically teachers, who offer to provide feedback regarding a teacher's lesson(s). It involves nonjudgmental feedback that is designed to bring the collective insight of two or more professionals to bear on an individual teacher's classroom performance.
Peer Coaching	In this kind of peer evaluation, two or more individuals voluntarily work together to help each other solve problems and grow professionally. To be effective, members of a peer coaching group must know one another well and trust one another. Comments that are shared are designed to be as positive and supportive as possible. There is a concerted effort to increase each member's sense of professional self-worth. When formal observations occur, they typically follow a three-part cycle including (1) a preconference, (2) an observation, and (3) a postconference.
Mentoring	Mentoring is defined as "the tutoring of a less skilled person by a more skilled person." In this kind of peer evaluation, the mentor serves as a guide, advisor, role model, or consultant. It features a hierarchical relationship in which the mentor is perceived to possess more advanced knowledge than the person being helped. This knowledge is used to help the less skilled person to become more proficient. Successful mentoring requires mutual respect between the mentor and the person being helped.

Table 18.1   Summary Table *(continued)*

Main Points	Explanation
Supervisor Evaluation	Supervisor evaluation occurs when someone in authority evaluates a sub-ordinate. In schools, this often occurs when an administrator evaluates a teacher. Results of evaluation may have consequences other than provid-ing suggestions for improvement. For example, they sometimes are used as a basis for termination or salary decisions. Teachers tend to be more nervous about this kind of evaluation than about peer evaluation. Despite this concern, researchers have found that many teachers want to be evalu-ated by their supervisors.
Data Sources Used in Teacher Evaluation	Data from different sources often are incorporated in teacher evaluation. Often information gathered includes (1) data regarding student learning, (2) data from student opinions, and (3) data from classroom observations.
Student Learning Data	Information about what students have learned is important because teach-ers have a primary mission to transmit information to members of their classes. This kind of information must be interpreted cautiously. For exam-ple, some tests may not adequately sample what students have learned. In addition, students' scores may reflect what students have learned from sources other than school lessons. Ideally, student learning data takes into account products of learning that go beyond scores on tests.
Student Opinion Data	Opinions of students regarding how well their teachers have performed sometimes form part of teachers' evaluations. Though not everyone agrees this should be done, some research evidence indicates students' opinions of a teacher go up as their amount of learning from a teacher's instruction goes up. It is important that students be asked to comment only on issues on which they can be expected to have some real expertise.
Classroom Observation Data	Classroom observation information is gathered by observers during their observations of teachers in their classrooms. Various techniques are used to accomplish this purpose. Among them are (1) lists of focus questions, (2) verbatim records, and (3) frequency counts.
Portfolios	Portfolios are a means of compiling quite comprehensive evidence regard-ing a teacher's capabilities. A portfolio includes various materials that, taken together, provide a general picture of his or her level of expertise. A teacher's portfolio is designed to present his or her work to the world much in the way an artist's portfolio evidences his or her expertise to a wider audience. Teacher portfolios often include (1) material prepared by the teacher, (2) material gathered from others, and (3) examples of student work.

Review of Key Ideas

- One reason teachers need feedback about their classroom performance is that the rapid pace and complex milieu of the classroom make it extremely difficult for teachers themselves to recall accurately what went on during a given lesson.

- There are two basic purposes for evaluating teachers' classroom performances. First of all, evaluation data help to identify specific actions teachers may wish to modify in subsequent lessons. Second, evaluation attempts to provide a summary judgment of teachers' general levels of excellence at a particular time.

- In self-evaluation efforts, teachers gather data, identify criteria to be used in making judgments, and draw conclusions about their own teaching. Self-evaluation can be initiated as often as a teacher wishes. There is some evidence that teachers who engage in self-evaluation grow in their sense of personal control over their own professional growth and development. Finally, self-evaluation is nonintrusive. It does not introduce an outsider into the classroom as an observer. On the negative side, unless teachers take care, self-evaluation can be haphazard. It is sometimes difficult for teachers to gather data about what they are doing while they are teaching their lessons.

- Peer evaluation involves teachers working collaboratively with fellow teachers to gather insights about their behaviors. It tends to break down the isolation many teachers feel as they work alone in their own classrooms. In peer coaching, a popular form of peer evaluation, a group of individuals voluntarily agree to work together to solve problems and help one another grow professionally. Each member of the peer coaching team is viewed as having abilities and expertise of value to the whole group. In mentoring, another form of peer evaluation, one person—the mentor—is perceived as having more knowledge than the other member of the group. The mentor has an obligation to assist the other person to grow professionally.

- Supervisor evaluation occurs when someone in a position of authority over a teacher conducts his evaluation. Results of supervisor evaluation sometimes go beyond providing data the teacher will use for self-improvement. Results in some instances are used to support dismissal decisions or to support salary and promotion actions. In general, teachers tend to be more nervous about supervisor evaluation than about either self-evaluation or peer evaluation.

- Student achievement information is often used in making judgments about teachers' instructional effectiveness. There are some limitations to relying too much on test scores. For example, some tests may not adequately sample content that has been taught. Further, some students may have learned information that is tested from sources other than their teacher. Student achievement information ought to include information from a variety of sources, including student essays, projects, and other products reflecting what they have learned.

- Data from student opinionnaires sometimes are used in evaluating teachers. Not everyone agrees this practice is sound, but some research has supported a correlation between high student ratings of a teacher and high student academic achievement scores on tests over content taught by the teacher. It is not sound practice to ask for student opinions about subjects for which they lack expertise or an adequate experiential base.

- Classroom observational data of many kinds often are included as part of teacher-evaluation schemes. Techniques have been developed that are capable of providing information about many dimensions of teachers' classroom performance. Examples of these procedures include (1) lists of focus questions, (2) verbatim records, and (3) frequency counts.

- Teaching portfolios are increasingly being used in teacher evaluation. A teaching portfolio includes a variety of information about a teacher's performance. Evidence in a portfolio typically provides a quite comprehensive picture of a given person's patterns of behavior as a teacher. It is designed to demonstrate a teacher's work much as artists' portfolios show others what they have been able to do. Teaching portfolios often include (1) material prepared by the teacher, (2) material gathered from others, and (3) examples of student work.

Follow-Up Questions and Activities

Questions

1. Why is it desirable to collect information about what teachers do in a systematic way rather than simply relying on their recollections?

2. What are two key purposes of teacher evaluation?

3. What are some advantages and disadvantages of self-evaluation?

4. What are some similarities and differences between peer coaching and mentoring?

5. What purposes of supervisor evaluation tend to make it different from either self-evaluation or peer evaluation?

6. What are some limitations of relying exclusively on students' test scores to evaluate teachers?

7. On opinionnaires, should students be asked to provide information about any topic whatever? Why or why not?

8. How are focus questions prepared, and what are some advantages of using them to gather information about what a teacher does in the classroom?

9. What procedures are followed by an observer who wishes to prepare a verbatim record?

10. Why do some people think that portfolios represent a particularly useful way of presenting a comprehensive picture of a teacher's classroom performance?

Activities

1. Ask some administrators in several schools to share with you instruments used to gather information about teachers' classroom performance. Based on your analysis of these instruments, what kinds of teacher behaviors seem to be of interest to users of these instruments? How important do you feel these behaviors to be? Prepare a short paper for your instructor in which you comment on these questions.

2. Use one of the observation instruments introduced in this chapter (or another provided by your instructor) to observe a class. Consider the information you gather. How useful is it for providing information to the teacher that might lead to improved teaching practices? Share your reactions in an oral report to the class.

3. Develop a rating scale that you think might be useful for your students to use to give you information about the quality of your teaching. Be prepared to defend the importance of items you include on your instrument. Share this material with others in your class, and request their reactions.

4. Interview a local administrator about the schedule of teacher evaluation that is followed. How often is information collected? Are new teachers evaluated more often than teachers who have been employed for some time? What do observations emphasize? How is information shared with teachers? What kinds of problems have new teachers most frequently been found to have? Share this information with others in your class.

5. Develop a peer coaching plan with one or two others in your class. Each person in the group should teach a lesson. Others should hold a pre-conference with the "teacher" before the lesson is taught and provide feedback after the lesson has been taught. How did you feel about this process? Share your reactions with others in the class.

References

BANG-JENSEN, V. "The View from Next Door: A Look at Peer Supervision." In K. K. Zumwalt (ed.). *Improving Teaching*. 1986 ASCD Yearbook. Washington, DC: Association for Curriculum Supervision and Curriculum Development, 1986, pp. 51–62.

BROWN, R. "Helpful and Humane Teacher Evaluations." In W. Duckett (ed.). *Teacher Evaluation: Gathering and Using Data*. Bloomington, IN: Phi Delta Kappa, 1983, pp. 9–26.

FEIMAN-NEMSER, S. AND FLODEN, R. "The Cultures of Teaching." In M. Wittrock (ed.). *Handbook of Research on Teaching*. 3rd ed. New York: Macmillan Publishing Company, 1986, pp. 505–526.

GOOD, T. AND J. BROPHY. *Looking in Classrooms*. 5th ed. New York: HarperCollins, 1991.

MCLAUGHLIN, M. AND PFEIFER, R. *Teacher Evaluation: Improvement, Accountability, and Effective Learning*. New York: Teachers College Press, 1988.

ODELL, S. "Support for New Teachers." In T. Bey and C. Holmes (eds.). *Mentoring: Developing Successful New Teachers*. Reston, VA: Association of Teacher Educators, 1990, pp. 3–23.

RODRIGUEZ, S. AND JOHNSTONE, K. "Staff Development Through a Collegial Support Group." In K. Zumwalt (ed.). *Improving Teaching: 1986 ASCD Yearbook*. Alexandria, VA: Association for Supervision and Curriculum Development, 1986, pp. 87–99.

WISE, A.; DARLING-HAMMOND, L.; McLAUGHLIN, M.; AND BERNSTEIN, H. "Teacher Evaluation: A Study of Effective Practices." *Elementary School Journal* (September 1985), pp. 61–121.

VI

Professional Concerns

People entering teaching today will experience enormous changes during the 30 or 40 years many of them will spend in professional education. Some changes will confound the best efforts of today's professional forecasters. Others can be predicted with relative confidence. For example, we know that, absent totally unforeseen circumstances, white Americans will become a minority of the total U.S. population sometime close to the year 2050.

Our system of laws and common law precedents helps us respond to change. Teachers today work within legal constraints that have evolved in response to social conditions that are different from those of 20 and 30 years ago. It is imperative that teachers be prepared for future changes that will result as our legal system helps us adapt to new conditions in ways that accommodate individual rights and preserve social order.

The preparation phase of a teacher's development represents a beginning point of a career-long obligation to keep current. Teaching is no career for people seeking a calm retreat from the world. It requires engaged professionals who are keenly committed to life-long learning.

Content in Part 6 focuses on the legal milieu within which secondary school teachers and students operate and on teachers' need for career-long development. Material provides answers to questions such as these:

- To what extent can school authorities place limits on teachers' out-of-school behavior?
- What is the *in loco parentis* doctrine, and what has happened to it in recent years?
- What are some ways teachers can pursue professional development?
- As teachers' needs and interests change, what are some other roles they might play within professional education?

Discussion related to these questions is introduced in two unit chapters:

Chapter 19: Legal Issues Affecting Students and Teachers
Chapter 20: Professional Development

Legal Issues Affecting Students and Teachers

AIMS

This chapter provides information to help the reader to:

- Define and explain the *in loco parentis* doctrine.
- State some conditions under which officials may place controls over the contents of student publications.
- Explain basic principles that have tended to guide courts in cases involving freedom of conscience.
- Differentiate among different types of teaching contracts.
- Point out teachers' responsibilities in reporting suspected cases of child abuse.
- Define different types of teacher negligence.
- Explain some limitations that legally can be placed on teachers' out-of-school behavior.
- Describe some implications of copyright law for teachers.

1. What has happened to the doctrine of *in loco parentis*, as applied to public school settings, over the past several decades?
2. How much power do school officials have to regulate student publications?
3. If, as a result of a decision in a Supreme Court case, a given school practice is declared to be unconstitutional, does this practice automatically cease to exist in all schools? Why or why not?
4. What are some implications of due process as they relate to disciplining students?
5. What tests ordinarily have courts applied in determining whether a personal search of a student is justified?
6. Under what conditions can a teaching certificate be revoked?
7. What are some types of teaching contracts?
8. What kinds of limits can be legally placed on teachers' academic freedom?
9. What provisions of the copyright law influence teachers' selection and use of material in their classrooms?
10. To what extent can school districts place limitations on the personal, as opposed to the professional, behaviors of teachers?

Introduction

In times past, legal issues related to schools and schooling were rarely matters of concern to secondary school teachers and principals. They exercised an authority over students that was infrequently challenged. Professional employees were viewed as authorities who were expected to make and enforce rules, and students were expected to follow them. Individuals who failed to conform to school rules could be summarily dismissed. Expelled students had no standing in courts to challenge school authorities' decisions.

Times have changed. Over the past 20 years, court decisions have defined students as citizens enjoying constitutional rights. Further, it has been determined that schooling is an arena in which those rights merit full legal protection. Cases such as the *Tinker v. Des Moines Independent School District* case in 1969 and *Goss v. Lopez* in 1975, among many others, extended constitutional guarantees contained in the Bill of Rights and in other constitutional amendments to public school students.

There have also been changes in recent years in teachers' legal standing. In times past, school districts were able to put many restrictions on teachers' personal behavior. Their deportment in all areas of life was expected to be impeccable, and it was possible for teachers to be publicly criticized, even lose their jobs, because of complaints related to such issues as irregular church attendance, alcohol and tobacco use, and changes in marital status. Today, legal protections afforded to citizens in general, for the most part, also apply to teachers.

Many teachers, regrettably, are not as knowledgeable as they should be about legal issues relevant to their profession. Lack of understanding of some legal principles is dangerous. In a 1975 case, the United States Supreme Court ruled that teachers and administrators could be held personally liable and required to pay monetary damages for violating students' constitutional rights (Fischer, Schimmel, and Kelly, 1991). It is in teachers' self-interest to have an understanding of some legal guidelines that today govern relationships among school leaders, teachers, and students.

Legal Issues Affecting Students

Few issues in secondary education have generated as much controversy as has the issue of student rights. In recent years, the legal relationship between students and school authorities has been greatly altered. Changes began during the 1960s and continued through much of the 1970s. By the 1980s, students had come to enjoy legal rights generally comparable to those extended to all adult citizens.

In Loco Parentis

The traditional legal doctrine governing the relationship between school and students was *in loco parentis*. This is a Latin phrase meaning "in place of the parent." According to this doctrine, school authorities were expected to treat students as wise parents would, and the protections extended to parents also were extended to school authorities. Common law precedents related to the parent-child relationship generally meant that courts would not hear a case brought by a young person complaining about an "unjust" parental directive. As extended to school authorities, the doctrine of *in loco parentis* protected school authorities from having to justify actions taken against students who had broken rules. Legally, actions taken against a student were regarded by courts as part of the school's role as a surrogate parent acting in the long-term best interest of the student.

The assumptions undergirding the *in loco parentis* doctrine began to break down in the 1960s. It was first challenged at the university level. Later court cases challenged it successfully at the secondary and elementary levels. Attacks on the doctrine came at a time when many traditional assumptions were coming under attack. There were particular concerns about the long-term personal and social consequences of expelling students and, thereby, denying them permanent access to educational services. A key case in the effort to extend full constitutional protections to school students was the landmark case of *Tinker v. Des Moines Independent Community School District* in 1969.

The *Tinker* case evolved out of a situation that developed in Des Moines, Iowa. Children from several families who opposed the Vietnam War decided to express their protest to the war by wearing black arm bands to school. When school officials discovered this was going to happen, they quickly adopted a policy forbidding the wearing of these arm bands in school. According to this policy, a student who came to school wearing an arm band would be asked to remove it. Failure to comply would result in suspension.

Three students defied this regulation, arrived at school wearing arm bands, refused to remove them, and were suspended. Suit was brought on behalf of the students, and the case ultimately worked its way to the United States Supreme Court. In its decision in the *Tinker* case, the high court ruled that wearing arm bands to school as a protest constituted symbolic speech. Since free speech and expression is protected by the First Amendment of the United States Constitution, the Court ruled the wearing of arm bands was protected and that the school authorities had erred in passing and enforcing the anti-arm band regulation.

The many post-*Tinker* case decisions that, collectively, have acted to extend the constitutional rights of citizens to school students have focused on two key areas. First, there have been many cases focusing on the limits of school authorities' power to interfere with students' actions. Second, many cases have centered on the appropriateness or fairness of procedures school authorities have used in making decisions affecting students.

In reviewing information related to students' rights cases, it is important to keep in mind that each case is considered by the courts on its own merits, as well as in light of laws and decisions in previous, related cases. Laws and precedents change over time. Hence, the general direction the courts have taken must not be regarded as applying to every new case. Indeed, it is possible that, for reasons that cannot be discerned at present, future courts may take quite different views of some of these matters.

Freedom of Speech and Expression

The *Tinker* case dealt with the important area of freedom of speech and expression. It was one of many cases that have helped to define the limits of school authorities' power over students' freedom of expression rights. An area that has prompted much concern and litigation is the authority of school officials to limit what is printed in official student publications as well as "underground" or unauthorized student newspapers.

In general, the nature of school administrators' power to regulate publication has been found to depend on whether the publication in question is sponsored by the school in some official way. In general, courts have supported more administrative control over student newspapers that are written by students as part of a regular journalism course than publications that are not officially connected with the school. An important precedent in this area was established in 1988 in the case of *Hazelwood School District v. Kuhlmeier*.

This case involved a situation in which a school principal had deleted two articles from the school newspaper. One article referred to teen-age pregnancy. Though names in the article had been changed to mask the true identities of pregnant students, the principal felt that many readers might be able to identify them. In the second article, a

Box 19.1

Freedom of Expression in Student Publications

Suppose a group of high school students decided to print their own unofficial newspaper to "expose" what is "really going on" in their school. Their first issue features an article in which the principal is described as "dead from the neck up." The principal sees a copy of the paper and takes immediate action to ban its distribution on two grounds.

First, she contends, the articles are unsigned and it is unclear that writers have any connection with the school. Second, she believes that the school administration has the right to control distribution of anything passed out at school and that no one granted approval authorizing distribution of this publication.

What Do You Think?

1. How do you react to the argument that publications that may have been written by individuals who are not students in the school can be banned?

2. How would the courts be likely to react to this principal's position?

3. In your opinion, should there be any limits regarding what students publish and distribute at school?

student had written a complaint about her father, but the father had not been given an option to respond. The principal felt the treatment was unbalanced and, hence, unfair. In its decision, the court upheld the right of the principal, noting that educators have the authority to exercise considerable control over school-sponsored publications.

In the case of school-sponsored publications, educators generally have the right to reject articles that are poorly written, insufficiently researched, clearly biased, vulgar, or otherwise unsuitable for immature audiences. They may prohibit articles that advocate unacceptable (and often illegal) social practices such as alcohol or drug abuse and irresponsible sexual activities. Control can be exercised when actions taken by school leaders are undertaken to assure some consistency with the ongoing instructional responsibilities of the school.

Authority to limit the content of school publications does not extend to censorship of controversial issues or of views that may be unpopular with administrators, teachers, or parents. Officials must be prepared to demonstrate that actions taken to censor content are taken for valid educational reasons, not for capricious, convenient, or punitive reasons.

Underground and other publications that are produced without formal school recognition and support generally lie outside the control of school officials. These publications ordinarily cannot be regulated unless their contents can be challenged on grounds that would invite legal actions against publications of any kind. Though articles criticizing school administrators and teachers may be highly irritating, they do not constitute legal grounds for barring publications containing them from the school campus nor for punishing the writers.

It is possible for school officials to exercise some limited control over the distribution of underground publications. They can define how and where they can be distributed, but they cannot lay down guidelines so restrictive that they actually bar distribution.

The issue of vulgar oral speech has also led to court cases. In one situation, administrators removed a student from the school's graduation ceremony after he had used language filled with sexual innuendo during a campaign for a school office. Attorneys sued on behalf of the student. At the District Court level and on appeal at the Ninth Circuit Court, decisions came down supporting the student's contention that his freedom of speech rights had been violated. However, on further appeal to the United States Supreme Court, this decision was overturned. The high court supported the actions of the school administrators, noting in the decision that students may be subject to punishment when language they use in school and in school-related activities goes "beyond the boundaries of socially appropriate behavior" ("Chalk Talk," 1987; p. 124).

Cases in the area of freedom of expression and speech tend to consider the special circumstances of the situation being litigated. Generally, however, a pattern has been established of courts supporting the idea that students enjoy constitutional free-speech and free-expression rights. Though administrators can exercise some control over these rights, their attempts to do so must made with reference to a legitimate educational concern and not simply to limit student criticism of school officials or discussion of controversial issues.

Students' Freedom of Conscience

Legal questions focusing on the issues of separation of church and state and the place of religious expression in schools have generated much controversy. Two basic First Amendment principles often have been involved in these disputes. One principle guarantees the right to free exercise of religion; the other bars the government from establishing any religion.

Courts have consistently affirmed the idea that freedom of religion cannot be abridged unless the state and its officials demonstrate an overwhelmingly compelling need to do so. This means that school officials cannot arbitrarily require all young people in the school to do something that may interfere with the fundamental religious principles of some students. For example, court cases have upheld the right of individual students to refrain from participating in daily pledge of allegiance exercises on the ground that their participation conflicts with their religious beliefs. In pledge of allegiance cases, the courts have taken the position that a refusal to recite the pledge does not threaten any major public interest; hence, the state has no compelling interest in compelling *all* students to participate in this activity.

On the other hand, a religious group might claim teaching students to read was contrary to the group's fundamental religious convictions. It is doubtful courts would excuse students who belonged to this group from reading instruction. The state probably would be able to demonstrate that there is a compelling public interest in teaching future citizens to read.

Courts often have ruled that students' religious views may excuse them from certain parts of the school program. For example, courts sometimes have upheld students' rights to refrain from dancing and viewing films, based on the students' religious convictions. In recent years, there have been challenges by parents to literary works such as *The Wizard of Oz* and *Macbeth* on the grounds that they promote witchcraft. For the most part, courts have supported school officials' contentions that familiarity with these works is essential to the complete educational development of students, something in which the state has a compelling interest. Litigation in this area is continuing.

Student Dress and Appearance

Regulations governing student dress and appearance have often led to confrontations between students and school officials. Though many court cases have dealt with this issue, few consistent patterns are revealed in the decisions. Basically, courts have recognized that schools do enjoy some rights to govern what students wear to school (Fischer et al., 1991). However, school officials do not enjoy unrestricted power in this area. In the case of *Bannister v. Paradis* in 1970, the court ruled that a school can exclude students whose clothing is unsanitary or whose clothing violates obscenity standards. However, this logic by no means suggests that school leaders have blanket authority to ban wearing of blue jeans or other clothing on the grounds that it is too informal for school wear.

What the courts seem to be saying is that dress standards established by a school district cannot be capricious or arbitrary. Standards must bear some reasonable relationship to the educational process or to health or safety of students. For example, requirements barring students from wearing floppy clothing in a machine shop may well be defended on safety grounds. Courts probably too would be inclined to uphold regulations forbidding students to wear shirts with slogans that might lead to a disruption of the instructional process by prompting fights or other unrest. In recent years, courts have tended to uphold school regulations banning the wearing of clothing associated with gang membership such as certain kinds of caps, earrings, jewelry, and other emblems.

Hairstyle and grooming standard regulations have been the subject of numerous court cases. Some courts have held that hairstyle is a more fundamental right than clothing style because regulations to control it are more invasive of personal freedom. Where regulations have been upheld, they typically have been designed with a clear focus on students' health and safety and on the issue of potential interference with the educational process. In general, schools today give students much broader latitude in the area of personal grooming and dress than was the case a quarter of a century ago.

Due Process

Due process is a principle requiring certain procedures and safeguards to be followed when individuals are charged with breaking rules, regulations, or laws. Until the late 1960s, school attendance was widely regarded as a privilege rather than as a right meriting due process protection. A legal precedent extending due process safeguards to public schools was established in the *Goss v. Lopez* case in 1975. In its decision in this case, the court noted that while the United States Constitution does not require states to establish public schools, once they are established, students' rights to attend them is a constitutionally protected property right. Therefore, efforts to deny students access to schooling through such measures as expulsion and suspension must be accompanied by due process procedures in conformity with the Fourteenth Amendment to the Constitution.

There are two basic components of due process. The first, or *substantive component*, consists of the basic set of principles upon which due process is based. The second, or *procedural component*, delineates procedures that must be followed to assure that due process rights have not been violated.

The following are included in the substantive component of due process:

- Individuals are not to be disciplined on the basis of unwritten rules.
- Rules must not be unduly vague.
- Individuals charged with rules violations are entitled to a hearing before an impartial body.
- Identities of witnesses are to be revealed.
- Decisions must be supported by substantial evidence.
- A public or private hearing can be requested by the individual accused of a rule violation.

The following steps are consistent with guidelines to be followed by schools to assure compliance with the procedural component of due process:

- Rules governing students' behavior are to be distributed in writing to students and their parents/guardians at the beginning of the school year.
- Whenever a student is accused of a serious violation of rules that can lead to the loss of a right, charges must be provided in writing to the student and to his/her parent/guardian.
- Written notice of the hearing to consider the alleged violation must be given, with sufficient time for the student and his or her representatives to prepare a defense. However, the hearing must be scheduled in a timely manner (usually within two weeks).
- A fair hearing must include the following:
  Right of the accused to be represented by legal counsel.
  Right of the accused to present a defense and to introduce evidence.
  Right of the accused to face his or her accusers.
  Right of the accused to cross-examine witnesses.
- The decision of the hearing board must be based on evidence presented and must be rendered within a reasonable time.
- The accused must be informed of his or her right to appeal the decision.

Box 19.2

Does Due Process Keep "Bad" Students in School?

A parent recently commented as follows at a school board meeting:

My son is in an algebra class with a student who disrupts the class constantly. He interrupts the teacher, asks irrelevant questions, makes stupid remarks, and seems to work hard at keeping the teacher from doing any real teaching. As a result, my son is not learning anything.

I've complained to the principal who told me legally it is very difficult to remove a misbehaving student. I want you to know that I am extremely unhappy about this situation. I think you and your attorneys should get busy and draft a policy to get these troublemakers out of school so others can learn. This is the kind of thing that drives us to put our kids in private schools.

What Do You Think?

1. Does due process place such severe restrictions on school administrators that situations such as this are just a fact of life today?

2. What sort of action do you think could be taken in this case that would resolve the situation and still be consistent with due process considerations?

The need to comply with due process requirements requires school officials to exercise great care in initiating actions against a student who is suspected of having violated an important rule or regulation. Due process requirements, for example, must be carefully followed when school administrators take actions to suspend or expel students.

Suspension is defined as a temporary separation from school. A suspension of less than 10 days duration is considered to be a short-term suspension. When a student is faced with a potential short-term suspension, only minimal due process guidelines must be observed. In such cases, the student to be suspended must receive (1) at least an oral (preferably a written) notice of the specific charges that led to the suspension decision, (2) an explanation of the evidence supporting these charges, and (3) an opportunity to provide her version of facts relevant to the situation. When the result of action of school officials is to be short-term suspension, it is not required that legal counsel be present to represent the student's interest when he is apprised of the relevant charges and provided with an opportunity to challenge their accuracy.

A suspension exceeding 10 days in length is considered to be a long-term suspension. Long-term suspension has the potential to seriously interfere with a student's ability to profit from school instruction. Hence, school officials are obliged to follow all of the guidelines noted under the procedural component of due process.

Expulsion is very serious. It permanently separates a student from the school. In situations where expulsion is likely to be the end result of actions initiated against a student by school authorities, strict due process procedures must be followed. Usually, teachers and administrators at an individual school do not, by themselves, have the authority to make an expulsion decision. This tends to be a prerogative of the highest governing officials of the school district. This tends to be true because unless very careful procedures are followed to assure that a student's interests have been adequately protected and represented, potentially expensive legal action could be initiated against the school district and the school board by the student or her representatives.

There are important implications of due process for teachers. First, they need to recognize that their students have been legally defined as citizens whose rights are protected by the U.S. Constitution. This means teachers and other educators must proceed in a fair and appropriate manner in making and enforcing school rules. The need to observe due process guidelines by no means diminishes teachers' abilities to control students in their classrooms. The courts have affirmed teachers' rights to establish and maintain a safe and orderly educational environment for their students.

The following are some guidelines many teachers have found useful in considering whether rules they have developed are fair and appropriate:

- Is the purpose behind the rule clear?
- Is the rule consistent with local, state, and federal laws?
- Is the rule stated in clear and precise language?
- Does the rule bear a clear relationship to the need to maintain an orderly educational process and to prevent disruptions?
- Do all students know that the rule has been established?

Gender Issues

Gender discrimination has been a topic of great interest in recent years. Landmark legislation in this area was Title IX of the Education Amendments of 1972. This legislation provided that any educational program or activity that received federal financial assistance could not exclude individuals from activities on the basis of gender. Many state legislatures subsequently enacted equal rights acts of their own to cover general gender discrimination issues in their respective states.

As a result of Title IX, related legislation, and court decisions, it is no longer permissible to exclude individuals from any part of the school curriculum on the basis of their gender. However, this does not mean that students may not be separated for instruction in some particularly sensitive topic. When this is done, however, school officials must be prepared to respond to potential court challenges that would require them to provide strong reasons in support of decisions to separate students by gender.

In recent years, the issue of separate schools for students of different genders has occasionally come up. In general, schools for single sexes have been found to violate gender discrimination laws. There are exceptions, however. In one case, a school system maintained one high school for academically talented boys and another one for academically talented girls. Since attendance at either school was voluntary and the two schools were genuinely equal in terms of their size, prestige, and quality of academic programs, the courts allowed the arrangement to continue (*Vorcheimer v. School District*, 1977).

The biggest impact of Title IX has been in the area of athletics. Both genders must have equal access to noncontact sports. There may be separate teams for each gender if a school can fund two teams. If only one team is funded, students from both genders must be eligible to participate. Although funding for teams of different genders does not need to be equal in terms of dollar amounts allocated, team schedules, equipment, and support must be roughly "comparable."

Another gender issue that, at one time, was the source of considerable controversy concerned school policies that barred married or pregnant students from attending the same schools as other students (or even from attending school at all). In times past, many schools required these students to attend alternative schools or to stay home and continue their studies by taking correspondence courses. Over the years, these regulations have been struck down by court decisions that, in general, have argued that the presence of married or pregnant students has not been demonstrated to have an adverse impact on the overall educational environment of the school.

Rights of married students to participate in extracurricular activities have generally been supported by the courts. In an Ohio case, a local school district adopted a policy barring married students from participating in school-sponsored athletic events. This policy was challenged. In its decision, the court affirmed that participation in these activities was an important part of students' overall educational opportunities and that a policy excluding married students represented an illegal deprivation of their rights (*Davis v. Meek*, 1972).

In summary, court decisions, by and large, have greatly reduced the number of school policies and practices that have discriminated against students on the basis of gender. This by no means suggests that no such policies or practices remain. In our legal system, there are no "educational police" going about the country checking to see that procedures everywhere are consistent with what courts have decided. A practice or policy in a given location may continue until it is challenged in a court of law. Only then may local officials be obliged to bring their policies into conformity with what courts, generally, have found to be legally defensible practice. Policies that discriminate against students on the basis of gender are likely to remain in place for a long time in places where school leaders believe there is little likelihood that such policies will be challenged in court.

Search and Seizure

Concerns about drugs and weapons on school campuses have prompted much interest in the issue of search and seizure. For example, school authorities often have wished to conduct searches of school lockers, automobiles parked in student lots, possessions of students, and sometimes students themselves. The need to conduct searches to find drugs, weapons, and other illegal items that potentially can threaten the general student population has had to be weighed against the Constitutional guarantees against unreasonable search and seizure as outlined in the Fourth Amendment.

In general, court decisions in this area suggest that school officials must apply four basic tests as they attempt to decide whether a proposed search is appropriate. The first test relates to the nature of the material or object they will be looking for. The greater its potential danger to the health and safety of students, the stronger the justification for the search. For example, a gun or bomb poses a tremendous danger to all students in a school, and a search certainly could be justified in response to this potential threat to safety. On the other hand, a stolen book generates no immediate threat. As a result, a highly intrusive search probably could not be justified.

The second test used in determining the potential legality of a proposed search has to do with the quality of the information that has led to the search decision. In deciding the issue of information quality, the reliability of individuals providing supporting evidence must be weighed. If several reliable people provide similar information, a stronger case for a search can be made than if information comes from a tip from an anonymous caller. If a search is to be particularly "invasive" (that is, if it involves a search of a person, his clothing, or possessions such as purses and wallets that are generally viewed as "private"), then school officials must demonstrate probable cause. This calls for a very high standard of evidence as a justification for the search and is equivalent to what courts require before issuing a search warrant.

The third test concerns the nature of the place to be searched. If this is an area where there is a high expectation of privacy, school officials need extremely reliable information to justify the search. This would be the case if there were an intent to search a student's person, a student's clothing, or a private possession such as a purse or wallet. On the other hand, there is much less of an expectation of privacy for an area such as a school locker. A search of a locker can be justified on slimmer evidence than a search of a student's person.

The fourth test concerns the nature of the proposed search. Highly intrusive searches require considerable evidence before a search can be justified. Additionally, the age and sex of the individual being searched needs to be considered. Some interesting cases will illustrate the importance of this and the other three tests.

In one case, a fifth-grade student reported that three dollars was missing from his coat pocket. The principal tried to get someone to confess. When this effort failed, boys and girls were separated and strip searched. Angry parents took legal action against the school. The court ruled that the strip search was unreasonable (*Bellnier v. Lund*, 1977). The object of the search (the money) posed no immediate threat to students. The search was extremely intrusive and invaded areas where people have a high expectation of privacy. Information leading to the search came from one well-meaning youngster, but it was not of sufficient quality to provide solid evidence that any members of the class had taken the money. (In fact, it was later discovered that the student had misplaced the money.)

In another case, *Doe v. Renfroe* (1980), search dogs used in the school to sniff out drugs alerted to "Diane Doe." This action suggested to school officials that she possessed narcotics. She was required to empty her pockets and purse. When no illegal substances were found, "Diane Doe" was strip searched. Again, nothing was found. "Diane Doe," infuriated at her treatment, filed suit against the school district.

In its decision, the court held that the use of sniffing dogs did not, in and of itself, constitute search; hence, it was permissible. The court also ruled that, when the sniffing dogs alerted to "Diane," there was reasonable suspicion that an illegal substance was present. Hence, actions school authorities took to require her to empty her purse and pockets were justified. However, the court held that the strip search was an extreme invasion of privacy that could not be justified given the evidence the school authorities had available.

Accidents in science classes
may lead to legal action
being taken against the
teacher and the school.

The case of *New Jersey v. T.L.O.* set some important search and seizure precedents. In this case, a vice principal questioned a girl suspected of smoking, a behavior not permitted by school rules. At the principal's request, the girl opened her purse. It contained not only cigarettes but also drug paraphernalia. This led the principal to do a thorough search of her purse. The girl took legal action. The case ultimately ended up in the Supreme Court. In its decision, the court stated that the initial suspicion that the girl had been smoking and might have cigarettes in her possession was sufficient reason to ask her to open her purse. Once this was done, the physical evidence of drug paraphernalia provided sufficient justification for the extensive search of her purse that followed.

The ruling in *New Jersey v. T.L.O.* seemed to give school authorities considerable latitude in search and seizure situations. However, there are important limits to what they can do. For authorities to act, they must have reasonable suspicion that a student has violated a specific rule. General "fishing expeditions" are not permitted, and, when undertaken, are likely to be viewed by courts as illegal invasions of students' privacy rights.

Family Rights and Privacy

Over the past 30 years, there has been a great increase in concern about potential misuses of school records. Much of the discussion of this issue has focused on long-term damage to students that might occur as a result of their being stigmatized by comments made about them in school records.

In 1975, the federal Family Educational Rights and Privacy Act was passed in response to this concern. This legislation requires schools to protect students' privacy rights by denying access to their files to anyone except individuals immediately concerned with these students' education. Files can be opened to others only with the consent of students' parents or, in the case of students who are 18 years old or older, of the students themselves. The law also gives parents free access to school files and records pertaining to their children. Students who are 18 years of age and older have similar rights to see this information. After parents have viewed files and records of their children (or after students who are 18 years of age and older have viewed their records), they may request to amend any record they believe to be (1) inaccurate, (2) misleading, or (3) in violation of privacy rights.

The access to student records by parents and by students 18 and older authorized by the Family Educational Rights and Privacy Act means that teachers need to exercise care when placing information in these files. Comments should be descriptive rather than judgmental. It is particularly important to avoid malicious or other kinds of general comments that might be construed as a negative summary judgment about a student. Such comments may be grounds for a legal action against the teacher (Connors, 1991).

Teachers also need to be careful about the kinds of comments they make to others about individual students. A person who knowingly spreads false information that hurts another's reputation (for example, that of a student) has committed slander, a punishable offense.

Legal Issues Affecting Teachers

Legal issues concerned with schools and schooling include more than students' rights issues. There also are important legal dimensions related to the rights and obligations of teachers. These include issues related to such areas as conditions of employment, contracts, freedom of expression, academic freedom, drug and alcohol abuse, copyrights, and professional performance of duties.

Conditions of Employment

Generally, teachers must possess a valid teaching certificate as a condition of employment.* Some states prohibit school districts from paying salaries of teachers who do not hold a valid certificate. Several court cases have declared that people who sign contracts and perform teaching duties without possessing valid certificates are "volunteers" who

---

* The term *certificate* is one term used for the official authorization a state provides to individuals who are legally qualified to teach. Other terms—for example, *credential* and *license*—are used in some areas.

"Another of his colleagues just got slapped with a teacher-liability suit."

have donated their services to the district. It is important for beginning teachers to assure their certificates are in order prior to beginning their work in the classroom.

Certification is a state responsibility. Each state has its own requirements for people who wish to teach in its schools. Because of differences in requirements from state to state, a person who graduates from a teacher-preparation program and is certified in one state may not necessarily meet certification requirements in other states. Individuals who are interested in teaching in other states should contact the Teacher Certification Office in the State Department of Education in the state where they wish to seek employment. This office will be able to provide information about procedures to be followed to qualify for a certificate.

Teaching certificates are not guaranteed for the life of the holder. They may be terminated for a variety of reasons, and states can establish conditions that must be met to renew them or keep them in force. In many states, certificates have fixed expiration dates. Renewal often requires teachers to enroll in college or university courses or to participate in other professional development opportunities. Certificates may be revoked for conviction of a felony, public displays of immorality, incompetence, or extreme examples of socially unacceptable behavior. The courts have held that teachers, because of their daily contact with impressionable young people, can be held to higher standards of personal conduct than the population as a whole.

Teachers' Contracts

Teachers' contracts are important documents. They contain information related to such issues as conditions of employment, salary levels, sick leave policies, insurance provisions, and grievance procedures. For a contract to be valid, it must include these four basic features (Fischer et al., 1991):

- Language that reflects a meeting of the minds of the signatories.
- Signatories who are competent parties.
- Obligations from each of the signatories to the other(s).
- Definite and clear terms delineating what is to be done and by whom.

The phrase *meeting of the minds* means that all parties must agree on the contents of the contract. One party must offer the contract, and the other must accept it. (There may be some negotiation of provisions before acceptance occurs.) In the case of teaching contracts, the formal process of offer and acceptance is not officially over until the contract is approved by action of the school board.

For a contract to be between "competent parties," the individual signatories must be of legal age and be legally and intellectually able to engage in and conclude needed negotiations. A prospective teacher must have a teaching certificate to be competent to enter into a contract.

CASE STUDY

Completing the Employment Application

Rodney Harte started a business after he graduated from college. The business prospered, but the work didn't satisfy his need to be involved in more service-oriented work. Rodney always had enjoyed working with young people and, after talking to several of his friends who were high school teachers, he started taking courses at a local university to qualify for a teaching certificate.

Rodney proved to be an excellent student. He completed the required course work, and he did his student teaching. As a result of his outstanding performance, he received excellent recommendations from his supervising teacher and from the university professor who worked with him during the student teaching semester. At this point, he made an official application for a teaching certificate.

When he was completing the application form, he noted a question asking for information about any prior legal problems. Many years earlier, Rodney had been convicted of shoplifting. He noted this information on his application, being careful to explain the circumstances and that many years had passed since this unhappy episode. After some follow-up correspondence regarding this matter, the state department of education granted Rodney a teaching certificate. He began looking for a teaching position.

During his job search, he was interviewed for a position that he felt was ideal. It was in a good school district, not too far from his home, and offered opportunities to teach and assist coaches in the school's athletic program. During the interview, he was asked whether he had ever been convicted of a felony. He reflected on this matter before answering. He considered the state department of education's review of his situation and its decision to award him a teaching certificate. As a result of these deliberations, he concluded that there was no need for the school district to know about his prior conviction, and he told the interviewing official that his record was clear.

He was hired for the position and began teaching at the beginning of the fall term. At the end of September, he received a note from the school district's central office requesting him to report immediately to the Director of Personnel. When he arrived, he was told that his employment was being terminated immediately. The school district had learned of his felony conviction, and he was being dismissed for failing to report this information.

■ ■ ■

What should Rodney Harte do? Did the district have a right to ask him questions about a possible felony conviction? Did he have an obligation to provide this information given that the matter had not result in a denial of teaching certificate by the state? Was it fair for him to be held accountable for something that had occurred many years ago? What do you think a court of law might decide were Rodney Harte to hire an attorney and contest the dismissal action?

Teaching contracts are legal documents that, if broken, can result in legal action against the party breaking the agreement. A school district may sue to collect monetary damages from a teacher who breaks a signed and approved contract. Similarly, a teacher can sue a school district for salary lost because of action taken by the district to break a signed and approved contract.

There are circumstances that make it possible for contracting parties to agree to dissolve their signed and approved agreement in an amicable fashion. When a teacher has a compelling reason to be released from a signed and approved contract, the appropriate procedure is to make a formal request to the school district to be released from the contract. There is no legal obligation on the part of the school district to agree to this request, but often it will be honored. As a practical matter, school districts do not want people working for them who would really prefer to be doing something else. Sometimes school districts require some compensation from teachers who are released from contracts. This is particularly likely to be the case when teachers are scarce and the district will find it difficult to hire a replacement.

There are several types of teachers' contracts. Typically, new teachers are offered a term contract. A term contract offers employment for a specified term, usually for one school year. At the conclusion of the term, a decision is made about renewing the contract. The term contract allows either party (the school district or the teacher) to negotiate new terms of employment when, and if, the contract is renewed. In some places, term contracts are issued to all teachers. In others, regulations require that term contracts be issued only to new teachers. Usually, after they have taught for a given number of years, teachers must be offered a different type of contract.

A second type of contract is the continuing contract. Unlike term contracts, basic employment provisions of continuing contracts do not have to be renewed after a specified term. (Ordinarily there are allowances for adjustments of salaries.) This kind of a contract is automatically renewed at the end of each year. This means that teachers holding continuing contracts enjoy more security of employment than do teachers holding term contracts. Continuing contracts ordinarily require the school district to adhere to strict procedural guidelines before the services of a teacher can be terminated.

A third type of contract is the tenure contract. Like a continuing contract, a tenure contract stays in force from year to year. Usually teachers holding tenure contracts can be dismissed only when they have been found guilty of violating state statutes governing behavior of teachers. The school board has the burden of proving that there is legal cause for dismissing a teacher.

Tenure contracts tend not to be awarded to teachers until they have worked successfully in a given district for several years, often for three. During their initial years of service, teachers are issued term contracts. Laws that established tenure contracts were passed, in part, to protect teachers from political interference on the part of parents or others who might take issue with what they were teaching in their classrooms and try to get them dismissed. Tenure laws also represented attempts to provide more stability to the group of teachers working a particular school by offering teachers considerable employment security.

Some critics have attacked tenure contracts on the grounds they guarantee lifetime employment for teachers. This is a misconception. Tenure does not guarantee permanent employment. What it does guarantee is that due process procedures will be followed in any proceedings that might lead to a dismissal and that dismissal will occur only when certain conditions have been met. Among reasons tenured teachers can be fired are (1) evidence of gross incompetence, (2) physical or mental incapacity, (3) neglect of duty, (4) immorality, (5) unprofessional conduct, and (6) conviction of a crime.

Teacher Dismissal and Due Process

There is no general answer to the question of whether teachers always have the right to challenge nonrenewal of their contracts or dismissals from their positions. Legal discussions of this matter have focused on two basic rights, liberty rights and property rights.

Liberty rights free individuals from having personal restraints imposed on them. These rights give them, among other things, opportunities to engage in the common occupations of life (*Meyer v. Nebraska*, 1923). Court decisions in this area have established that school districts cannot use unconstitutional reasons to deny teachers employment. As a result, teachers cannot be dismissed for such things as their religious beliefs.

Property rights, among other things, give individuals rights to enjoy benefits associated with their employment. Courts have wrestled with the question of whether teaching, as defined in a teacher's contractual agreement with a school district, is a property right. In general, the answer depends on the kind of contract a teacher holds and the specific language it contains. Sometimes this issue becomes quite murky. For example,

Box 19.3

Should Tenure Contracts Be Banned?

A member of a state legislature made these remarks during a hearing of a committee considering education legislation.

We should repeal present teacher-tenure legislation. All tenure does is keep marginal teachers on the job. People in other lines of work don't have this protection. Good teachers will never lose their jobs. They don't need this kind of protection.

What Do You Think?

1. Do tenure laws make it difficult to hold teachers accountable for their actions?

2. Would the quality of teaching improve if tenure laws were removed?

3. How would you respond to the position reflected in this legislator's remarks?

---

term contracts ordinarily terminate a teacher's employment on a given date. On the face of it, it would appear that the teacher would have no property right to employment by the district after the termination date of the contract. However, in places where it has become customary for districts to almost automatically reissue new term contracts to teachers, teachers may enjoy some property rights to employment going even beyond the strict terminology in their contracts. The courts tend to weigh questions about such matters in terms of the specifics of the particular cases they consider.

In situations where there is agreement that teachers have either liberty rights or property rights meriting legal protection, actions undertaken by school districts to interfere with these rights (typically actions taken to dismiss teachers) must follow strict due process guidelines. Teachers must be given notice of charges against them, have an opportunity to state their position in a hearing, be provided with a chance to respond to charges made against them, and be allowed to be represented by legal counsel. Some states require even stricter procedures, including opportunities for teachers to remediate any deficient behaviors before the formal dismissal proceeding can go forward.

AIDS and Drug-Abuse Testing

In recent years, there have been proposals in some areas that all teachers be tested for AIDS and for use of illegal drugs. These proposals raise serious legal issues. Some people believe that this kind of universal testing of teachers may violate their constitutional rights. In general, courts have insisted that procedures follow strict constitutional guidelines and that they be implemented only when schools demonstrate a "compelling interest" in results of the tests.

To demonstrate a compelling interest, schools have to be able to show that teachers with AIDS or teachers who use illegal drugs pose a clear threat to the health and safety of students. Because most evidence suggests that AIDS cannot be transmitted through the types of teacher-student interactions characterizing school classrooms, it has been extremely difficult for districts to demonstrate a their compelling interest in having all teachers tested for AIDS. Often, districts have also had difficulty defending universal testing of teachers to identify likely users of illegal drugs.

One school district decided to require urine analyses for teachers being considered for tenure. The idea was to use test results to identify illegal drug users. Teachers in this district challenged the policy in court. The court ruled that it constituted an unconstitutional invasion of teachers' privacy rights (*Patachogue-Medford Congress of Teachers v. Board of Education*, 1986).

Reporting Suspected Child Abuse

Public concern about child abuse continues to grow. As a result, all 50 states now have legislation requiring people in certain positions to report suspected cases of child abuse. Educators are included among the group of people with special legal obligations to report cases of suspected child abuse and neglect.

No state requires that a teacher be absolutely certain a child is being abused before reporting suspicions to the appropriate authorities. A teacher does not need to know "beyond a reasonable doubt" that a student is being abused before filing a report. All that is needed is a "reasonable suspicion" of abuse (Monks and Proulx, 1986).

Each state has a set of specific procedures that are to be followed when reporting cases of suspected abuse. It is important for teachers to become familiar with these guidelines. Some states have established a 24-hour telephone "hot line" to make it easier for suspected cases to be reported. In most cases, there is a requirement that an oral report be followed by a written report within a few days (often from about one to three days). Many school districts provide teachers with forms they can use in preparing reports of suspected cases of abuse.

All states provide teachers with some immunity from lawsuits for reporting suspected child abuse. This offers protection to individuals who may, otherwise, hesitate to file a report out of fear of reprisals. Immunity from lawsuits is not unlimited. Immunity is guaranteed only when reports are filed in good faith. If there is evidence that the teacher has filed a report for the purpose of maliciously harming the child's parents, the teacher may be sued by the parents.

Many states have established penalties for individuals who suspect a child is being abused but fail to report it. Penalties range from fines up to about $1,000 to jail terms of up to one year. These penalties and the long-term negative consequences of abuse on a child's development make it imperative for teachers to recognize signs of potential abuse and to become familiar with proper reporting procedures.

Legal Liability

The volume of litigation involving teachers has increased in recent years. One major category of liability faced by teachers is tort liability. A *tort* is a civil wrong against another that results in either personal injury or property damage. There are many categories of torts, including negligence, invasion of privacy, assault, and defamation of character. The areas that result in the largest number of lawsuits against teachers are (1) excessive use of force in disciplining students and (2) negligence.

Excessive Use of Force

Many court cases have centered on the issue of using physical punishment as a means of disciplining students. In the case of *Ingraham v. Wright* (1977), the United States Supreme Court ruled that teachers could use reasonable but not excessive force in disciplining a student. The justices further noted that corporal punishment did not constitute "cruel and unusual punishment," and, therefore, did not violate students' constitutionally protected rights.

The decision in the *Ingraham v. Wright* case hinted at the need to define the phrase *reasonable force*. No single subsequent case has done this. However, collectively, court decisions seem to suggest that the following factors should be considered in determining the reasonableness of force used in a specific situation:

- The gravity of the offense.
- The age of the student who is punished.
- The gender and size of the student who is punished.
- The size of the person administering the punishment.
- The implement used to administer the punishment.
- The attitude of the person administering the punishment while it is being administered.

With regard to this final factor, courts have looked more favorably on disciplinarians who were not angry or seeking revenge at the time they punished a student.

It is worth noting that cases such as *Ingraham v. Wright* have not made corporal punishment legal in all instances. Several states have passed laws forbidding the use of corporal punishment in public schools. Some school districts have similar policies applying to local schools.

Even where corporal punishment is technically allowed, often teachers must follow strict guidelines before administering corporal punishment. For example, they may be required to ask an administrator or some other designated person to act as a witness.

It is always possible for legal action to be taken against teachers who use corporal punishment, even where it is allowed. Allegations of excessive force by students or their legal representatives may result in criminal assault and battery charges being filed against the teacher. In such situations, juries often decide cases on whether or not, in their view, the teacher acted as a prudent parent would have acted.

Corporal punishment in discipline is an extremely controversial topic. In light of recent concerns about child abuse and the possibility of legal action against teachers who are deemed to have gone too far in administering corporal punishments, many educators today have concluded that the risks associated with corporal punishment outweigh any potential benefits.

Negligence

Negligence is a failure to use reasonable care and/or to take prudent actions to prevent harm from coming to someone. These are the three basic types of negligence:

- Nonfeasance

- Misfeasance

- Malfeasance

Nonfeasance occurs when an individual fails to act when she has a clear responsibility to act. Many lawsuits filed against teachers fall into this category. Ordinarily they stem from a situation where something bad has happened to a student when the teacher has been absent from his assigned place of responsibility. For example, if a student is injured in the classroom of a teacher while the teacher has slipped out to have a quick cup of coffee across the hall, the teacher might be found guilty of nonfeasance. Another nonfeasance suit might result if a teacher had information that a fight was about to occur between two students, failed to act to stop it, allowed the fight to go on, and one student was hurt.

This by no means suggests that there are no circumstances under which a teacher can legally be away from her designated area of responsibility. If there are compelling reasons for this to happen, the teacher is not guilty of nonfeasance. For example, if someone in the hall lit papers in a wastebasket, the teacher left the room to put out the fire, and a student was injured in the room while the teacher was away, it would be highly unlikely the teacher would face a nonfeasance suit. Even if one were filed, there would be little likelihood the teacher would be found guilty.

Misfeasance occurs when an individual fails to act in a proper manner to prevent harm from coming to someone. In the case of misfeasance, the person acts, but the action taken is not proper or correct. Misfeasance suits against teachers often result from their failure to take appropriate precautions when having students work with potentially dangerous equipment or materials. To avoid misfeasance suits, teachers must provide clear and specific instruction to students regarding such issues as equipment safety and proper uses of chemicals and equipment. Students must also be properly supervised when working with potentially dangerous equipment and materials.

Malfeasance occurs when a person deliberately acts in an improper manner and, thereby, cases harm to another. In school situations, a teacher might be charged with malfeasance who, in an effort to stop a fight, used too much physical force and injured a student as a result.

Academic Freedom and Freedom of Expression

Academic freedom issues often involve conflicts between (1) teachers' rights to conduct their classes according to their best professional judgment, and (2) school authorities' responsibilities to see that the authorized curriculum is taught. Court decisions in this area do not always reveal a consistent pattern.

However, one principle that has generally been supported by the courts is that school officials do have the right to impose some limitations on teachers' academic freedom. For example, school districts can require teaches to teach the subject-matter content of courses to which they have been assigned. A mathematics teacher cannot avoid mathematics content and promote his political views on the grounds that such instruction is an expression of his academic freedom.

On the other hand, the courts usually have decided that school districts cannot require teachers to avoid dealing with controversial issues in their classes. In one case, the right of an American history teacher to use a simulation exercise that evoked strong racial feelings was upheld (*Kingsville Independent School District v. Cooper*, 1980). In another case, the court supported a teacher who challenged an administrative ruling that forbade her from using a particular book. In this decision, the court ruled that the book was appropriate for high school students, contained nothing obscene, and that the decision to ban its use had violated the teacher's academic freedom rights (*Parducci v. Rutland*, 1979).

In the *Parducci* case, the court noted that the right to teach, evaluate, and experiment with new ideas was fundamental to a democratic society. In other cases, however, courts have upheld the rights of school boards to prohibit use of certain books, even literary classics. Decisions in this area have tended to be very responsive to specific characteristics of the work in question, the age and sophistication of the students, and the nature of the local community.

Freedom of expression refers to the rights of individuals to state their views on a subject without fear of reprisal. Court cases in this area that have involved teachers often have resulted from situations in which school authorities have attempted to punish teachers for out-of-classroom speech.

A landmark freedom expression case is *Pickering v. Board of Education of Township School District 205, Will County* (1968). Pickering, a teacher, wrote a letter to the editor of the local newspaper criticizing the way school funds were being allocated. Members of the school board were outraged. They claimed Pickering had made untrue statements in the letter and, thereby, had damaged the reputations of school board members and leading school administrators. The board took action to dismiss Pickering. Pickering took exception to this decision and challenged it in court. The case ultimately made its way all the way to the United States Supreme Court.

In arriving at its decision in the Pickering case, the high court considered two key issues. The first centered on whether a teacher could be dismissed for making critical comments about the school district and its policies in public. On this issue, the Court ruled that teachers have a right to speak out on school issues as part of a general effort to provide for a more informed public. The second issue the Court considered had do with whether a teacher could be dismissed for making false statements. In this particular case, the Court found that Pickering had made only one false statement in his letter. In the absence of any information that Pickering had knowingly or deliberately made the false statement, the Court decided in favor of Pickering. In other cases, dismissal actions taken against teachers have been upheld when evidence has been presented that they knowingly made false statements with a clear understanding they were recklessly disregarding the truth.

Freedom of expression rights of teachers generally extend to their criticism of their immediate superiors provided it is focused on significant issues related to the operation of the school or to matters of clear public concern. For example, in one recent case, several teachers challenged the actions taken by their employing school district to dismiss them after they wrote a letter to the state department of education complaining about the failure of another teacher in the building to implement provisions of legislation regarded to educating students with disabling conditions. The school officials who initiated the dismissal action contended that the matter referred to in the letter was an internal matter that should have been referred to district leaders and that the letter to the state board of education made the school district "look bad." The court rendered a judgment supporting the teachers, arguing that, by writing the letter, they were simply act-

Box 19.4

Academic Freedom in the Classroom

Issues related to academic freedom prompt great interest and, sometimes, heated exchanges. Some parents contend that, although they want the school to provide a quality education for their children, they, as parents, want to be sure that students are not taught values and ideas conflicting with those taught at home. To assure this does not happen, some parents want to exercise considerable control over books and other materials used in school classrooms.

On the other hand, many teachers contend that students should be confronted with diverse values and ideas, including some that may be quite different from those held by their parents. These teachers argue that giving parents veto power over books and materials would result in the elimination of virtually all educational materials. One or two parents may well find something objectionable in virtually every available text. Allowing parents this kind of control would paralyze the operation of the schools and greatly diminish the quality of school programs.

What Do You Think?

1. Have schools been too insensitive to parents' values?

2. What should teachers and school officials do to respond to some parental concerns while at the same time maintaining the academic integrity of school programs?

3. What topics might be controversial in your own subject area? How would you respond to parents concerned about exposing their children to this kind of content?

---

ing as responsible citizens in reacting to a matter of public concern (*Southside Public Schools v. Hill*, 1987).

This case by no means extends teachers' rights to complain publicly about everything. There are some activities of schools and school districts that may not be seen as matters of public concern by the courts.

Copyright Law

Copyright law seeks to protect the works of authors and artists. Federal copyright law covers use of materials copied from books, journals, computer programs, and videotapes.

The doctrine of fair use is an exception to copyright law that has implications for teachers. Fair use seeks to balance the rights of a copyright owner with the public's interest in having easy access to new ideas and information. The fair use doctrine makes it permissible for teachers to make single copies of book chapters, articles from journals, short stories or poems, or charts and graphs for their own scholarly research or as part of their preparation for teaching lessons. Multiple copies (not to exceed one for each student in a class) may be made if guidelines related to (1) brevity, (2) spontaneity, and (3) cumulative effect are met (Committee on the Judiciary, 1976).

Brevity (as the term applies to fair use) for different kinds of materials is defined as follows:

- A complete poem may be used if it is not more than 250 words and not more than two pages in length.

- An excerpt from a longer poem may be used consisting of no more than 250 words.

- A complete article or story may be used that is less that 2,500 words long.

- From a longer work, an excerpt may be used that is less than 1,000 words in length or that consists of no more than 10 percent of the length of the total work, whichever is less.

- One chart, diagram, picture, or cartoon per book or periodical may be used. (Committee on Judiciary, 1976)

The issue of spontaneity refers to situations where the teacher's inspiration and need to use the work is so close to the time when it must be provided to students in her class that it would be unreasonable or impossible to request and receive permission to use it before this time.

Criteria applied to meet the cumulative effect standard include the following:

- The material is used for only one course.

- Not more than one short poem, article, short story, or essay or two excerpts from works by the same author and not more than three excerpts from the same collective work or periodical volume may be used without permission.

- There are not more than nine instances of such multiple copying for one course during one term.

Unless these fair use guidelines can be met, teachers are obligated to secure permission from authors, artists, or other copyright holders before making and distributing copies. Teachers who fail to do so may face legal action brought by the copyright holders or their representatives.

It is also important to note that computer software programs are not covered by the fair use doctrine. It is illegal to make copies of commercially produced programs and to use them on different computers in the classroom unless specific permission has been granted. Many software vendors will sell a site license to a school or business authorizing the purchaser to make and distribute a given number of copies of a given program.

There are special copyright provisions that apply to videotaping for educational purposes. A copyrighted program may be videotaped, provided that the teacher uses it for instructional purposes within 10 days and keeps the videotape for no more than 45 days. The only legal use that can be made of the videotape between the tenth and the forty-fifth day is evaluation of its contents. Teachers who wish to keep a given program for some time and to use it repeatedly in their classes need to secure written permission from the copyright holder.

Failure to abide by provisions of copyright regulations can result in significant penalties. There may be an award to the copyright holder equivalent to a loss of profits resulting from the infringement or an amount of money determined by the court ranging between $500 and $20,000. If the court determines that the violator acted willfully, it can increase monetary damage to an amount as high as $100,000. On the other hand, if the violator can prove the infraction was unintentional, the court can scale back damages to a figure as low as $200.

Teachers' Private Lives

The case of *Board of Trustees v. Stubblefield* (1971) helped to establish the point that limitations can be placed on the behavior of people in certain professions, such as teaching, that are higher than those placed on other citizens. With regard to teachers, the argument is made that, because they work with impressionable young people, teachers should be held to high personal standards.

Courts have heard many cases in which there have been allegations of immoral behavior by teachers. Typically, courts have dealt quite harshly with teachers who have been found to be "immoral." The difficulty in deriving general principles from a review of these cases is that the terms *moral* and *immoral* tend to take on different meanings from place to place.

A thread that runs through many of these cases has to do with the perceived impact of a given teacher's behavior on his classroom performance and standing in the local community. When a teacher has been dismissed for an alleged immoral behavior and there has been evidence the behavior clearly has violated prevailing community standards, courts have tended to support the dismissal action. On the other hand, when the alleged immoral behavior has been shown to have little if any impact on the teacher's ability to teach effectively and has elicited little negative reaction in the community, courts have often held for the teacher and against the school officials who initiated the dismissal action.

Courts have dealt severely with teachers whose immoral behaviors have involved students. Courts have upheld dismissals of a male teacher who was found playing strip poker with a student in a car, of another teacher whose offer to "spank" two female students was interpreted as a sexual advance, and of a teacher who tickled and used suggestive language to female students on a class field trip.

In still another case, a teacher was dismissed when a high school girl he had been dating became pregnant. He admitted to having an affair with the student, but contended that since the girl was not a student at the school where he taught there was no adverse impact on his teaching. The teacher felt he should be reinstated. The court that heard his case disagreed (*Denton v. South Kitsap School District No. 402*, 1973). The court argued that no evidence of interference with the classroom performance of this individual was needed. The relationship between a teacher and any student constituted sexual misconduct that was inherently harmful to the school district.

Other cases in which teacher dismissal actions have been upheld have involved situations in which teachers have been arrested for public intoxication, being convicted of drunk driving, being found guilty of shoplifting, lying about being sick to collect sick leave pay, allowing students to drink in the teachers' homes, taking school property, and engaging in welfare fraud. Conviction for any serious crime, such as a felony, ordinarily is grounds for dismissal.

In summary, because of the sensitive roles they play as nurturers of young people, teachers are expected to reflect standards of personal behavior that are higher than those expected of average citizens. Hence, teachers are expected to be careful monitors of their own behavior. Particularly, they must avoid personal behaviors that can be demonstrated to interfere with their abilities to function as effective leaders or that clearly conflict with standards of morality prevalent in the communities where they teach.

Table 19.1   Summary Table

Main Points	Explanation
Student Issues	
In loco parentis	*In loco parentis* is a legal doctrine stemming from English common law that means "in place of the parent." As applied to education, this traditional doctrine suggested that teachers had the obligations and rights of a wise parent. The assumption was that teachers would always act in the best interest of the student. In recent years, court cases have basically overturned this doctrine, and today students generally enjoy constitutional protection as citizens. Unlike the "right to custody" students had when *in loco parentis* applied, today they have the rights of citizenship.
Freedom of Speech and Expression	In general, students enjoy the same constitutional rights to free speech and expression as all citizens. School authorities can place some limitations on the contents of school-sponsored publications, but constitutional rights associated with free expression cannot be abridged. School officials have much less authority to place restrictions on student publications that are not officially sponsored by the school or are not associated with school courses.
Freedom of Conscience	Issues in the area of freedom of conscience frequently concern separation of church and state. Freedom of religion is a constitutionally protected right that must be respected unless the state is able to demonstrate a compelling need to do otherwise. This means school officials cannot require students to do something that interferes with their basic religious principles unless there are convincing reasons to do so (e.g., a reason associated with preserving students' health, safety, or some other widely accepted public interest).
Dress and Appearance	Schools are limited in terms of the dress and appearance standards they can enforce. They can bar unsanitary clothing or clothing with obscene graphics or messages. Items of clothing (caps, earrings, specific kinds of jewelry) associated with gangs can also be banned. In general, courts have ruled that restrictions on dress and appearance must bear a demonstrable relationship to the educational process or to students' health or safety.
Due Process	Due process rights stem from the Fourteenth Amendment to the U.S. Constitution. They require that fair and just procedures be followed in any circumstance that has the potential to result in a negative judgment against someone accused of a violation of a rule, regulation, or law. These rights have been extended to students in schools.

Table 19.1   Summary Table *(continued)*

Main Points	Explanation
Student Issues, *cont'd.*	
Gender Discrimination	Title IX of the Education Amendments of 1972 provided that any educational activities receiving money from federal sources could not exclude individuals from participating on the basis of gender. This landmark federal legislation was followed by laws in many states extending similar protections to students in programs receiving support from state and local funding sources. This issue continues to generate controversy, particularly with regard to participation by students of both sexes in common athletic programs.
Search and Seizure	Court cases, by and large, have consistently found that school authorities have the right to search lockers, students, or students' possessions if they have evidence that items posing a threat to students or to the school may be found. The legality of their search depends on factors such as the nature of the potential threat, the place to be searched, the quality of evidence available to the authorities, and the intrusiveness of the search.
Family Rights and Privacy	Students who are 18 years old or older and students' parents have a right to see students' school records. After parents of a student (or a student who is 18 years old or older) have viewed his or her record, they may request to amend any record that is (1) inaccurate, (2) misleading, or (3) in violation of privacy rights. This legal access to records means teachers must exercise care when they write in student records. Comments should be descriptive rather than judgmental. Teachers can be sued for defamatory statements they make in student records.
Teacher Issues	
Conditions of Employment	Generally, teachers must possess a valid teaching certificate to legally accept a teaching position. A person who is found to have signed a teaching contract and who begins teaching without a certificate may be legally declared a nonpaid volunteer. Teaching certificates are issued by state authorities. Individual states establish specific conditions related to such issues as duration of an individual certificate and conditions that must be met to keep it in force.
Teachers' Contracts	A teaching contract is a binding legal agreement negotiated between a teacher and the employing district. It includes obligations that must be met both by the teacher and by the school district. To become valid, the contract has to be approved by official action of the school board of the employing district. There are several kinds of teachers' contracts. These include term contracts, continuing contracts, and tenure contracts.

Main Points	Explanation
Teacher Issues, *cont'd.*	
Teacher Dismissal and Due Process	Courts have generally established the principle that teachers cannot be dismissed on grounds that represent a violation of their basic constitutional rights. For example, teachers cannot be fired solely on the grounds of their religious convictions. Whether all teachers enjoy general due process protections in situations where they may be facing dismissal cannot be answered in a general sense. The answer tends to vary depending on the specific kind of teaching contract the teacher has and on the specific language contained in the contract.
AIDS and Drug-Abuse Testing	AIDS and drug tests have been viewed as a form of search. School districts cannot require them unless they can provide evidence of a compelling interest for doing so. In general, this requires evidence of clear potential danger to students' health or safety or to clear threats to the integrity of the instructional process.
Reporting Suspected Child Abuse	All states require teachers to report cases of suspected child abuse. Teachers who take such action in good faith are granted immunity from prosecution by potentially angry parents. Many states have established penalties for individuals who suspect child abuse and fail to report it.
Tort Liability	Teachers face tort liability (liability for a wrong resulting in personal injury to another or damages to another's property) for a number of possible circumstances, including negligence and excessive use of force. In the area of negligence, teachers may be sued for nonfeasance (failure to act when there was a clear responsibility to act), misfeasance (failure to act in a *proper* manner to prevent harm from coming to someone), or malfeasance (deliberately acting in an improper manner and, thereby, bringing harm to someone). Excessive-use-of-force cases often involve corporal punishment. Whether teachers used excessive force tends to be determined by reference to such things as (1) the gravity of the offense, (2) the age of the student punished, (3) the gender and size of the student punished, (4) the size of the person doing the punishing, (5) the implement used, and (6) the attitude of the punisher. Some states bar corporal punishment; others establish strict guidelines. Many educators believe that the negatives associated with corporal punishment outweigh any benefits.

Table 19.1   Summary Table *(continued)*

Main Points	Explanation
Teacher Issues, *cont'd.*	
Academic Freedom and Freedom of Expression	In academic freedom cases, courts have balanced (1) teachers' rights to teach classes according to their own best professional judgments, and (2) the need for teachers to teach the authorized curriculum. Court cases generally have supported the rights of school officials to insist that the prescribed curriculum be taught. On the other hand, courts have supported teachers when administrations have attempted to prevent them from dealing with controversial issues in their classes. Though court findings have reflected patterns varying somewhat depending on particulars of individual cases, in general teachers have been found to have the right to speak publicly on issues related to the operation of the schools or on other matters of clear public concern.
Copyright Law	Copyright law seeks to protect the rights of creators of intellectual properties including books, journal articles, computer programs, works of art, and radio and television programs. In general, teachers must obtain written permission to make copies of these materials. The fair use doctrine allows them to make some use of copyrighted material provided that certain strict guidelines are adhered to.
Teachers' Private Lives	Because teachers work with young people, courts generally have agreed that they should be held to higher standards of morality and personal conduct than other citizens. Dismissals for immoral behavior have been upheld most frequently when it has been established their behavior undermined their credibility in the local community and interfered with their abilities to function effectively in the classroom. Courts have been particularly prone to support school districts that have initiated dismissal actions against teachers who have behaved in immoral ways with students.

Review of Key Ideas

- Today teachers need to have an understanding of important legal issues that may affect them personally or professionally. The changing legal environment within which they work requires knowledge of students' rights as well as the rights and responsibilities of teachers.

- At one time the doctrine of *in loco parentis* (in place of the parent) governed the relationship between school authorities and students. According to this view, the student had a right to custody that was exercised by the teacher and school officials who acted as surrogate parents who were charged with looking after the student's interests. Under this doctrine, students had no legal standing in court to contest actions taken against them by school authorities. Over time, this legal doctrine has been overturned. Today, students in schools generally enjoy rights of citizenship and, hence, have extended to them the constitutional protections enjoyed by all citizens.

- Students enjoy considerable freedom-of-expression rights. Administrators have limited rights to oversee contents of student publications that are produced as part of the regular school program, but they may not censor materials simply on the grounds they are controversial or on other grounds that clearly violate students' constitutional rights. Administrators have even less authority over student publications not produced under the auspices of the school. They may indicate when and where such publications may be distributed, but these guidelines may not be so restrictive that they bar dissemination of the materials. Students' oral speech behaviors are also constitutionally protected.

- Many freedom-of-conscience cases have involved conflicts between students' religious beliefs and required school activities or course assignments. In general, the courts have allowed students' religious beliefs as grounds for excusing them from school activities that cannot be shown to be essential to students' health or welfare or essential to the general society. In practice, this has meant that religious beliefs have been viewed as grounds for excusing students from pledge of allegiance ceremonies, but not as grounds from excusing them from instruction in a basic school subject as reading (viewed as an essential survival skill in our society).

- Regulations regarding dress and appearance have been supported most frequently when courts have found a demonstrable connection between a student's dress or appearance and (1) safety or health of the student body or (2) disruption of the instructional process. Recent cases have also supported decisions to ban items of dress associated with gang membership.

- The Fourteenth Amendment of the United States Constitution guarantees due process rights to citizens. These have now been extended to schools. These provide that certain procedures and safeguards be in place whenever decisions are considered that might result in negative consequences for students. There are two key components of due process, the substantive component and the procedural component. The substantive component identifies basic principles upon which due process is based. The procedural component delineates procedures to be followed to assure due process rights have not been violated.

- Gender discrimination was banned from school programs receiving federal support by Title IX of the Education Amendments of 1972. In general, state legislation and other actions have now extended this protection to all school programs. Today, schools usually cannot ban students from school programs based on gender. Litigation in this area is continuing. There is considerable interest in cases involving the question of whether all athletic teams need to be open to both males and females.

- Search and seizure cases have considered the authority school officials have to search students, students' property, and such areas as school lockers. In determining whether a given search has been warranted, courts generally have considered (1) the nature of what is being looked for, (2) the quality of evidence leading to the decision to conduct a search, (3) the degree of expectation of privacy associated with the place to be searched, and (4) the nature or intrusiveness of the search.

- The federal Family Educational Rights and Privacy Act gives parents and students who are 18 years of age or older rights to look at school records. Further, the law prohibits records from being shown to anyone not immediately concerned with students' education. Parents (or students who are 18 or over and who ask to see their files) can request that records be amended to change information that they believe is (1) inaccurate, (2) misleading, or (3) in violation of privacy rights. Teachers can be sued if parents (or students 18 or over) believe they have written defamatory information in a record. This means teachers need to be careful about their entries. In general, information should be descriptive rather than judgmental.

- As a condition of employment, teachers must have a teaching certificate. This is a document issued by the state that attests that a teacher has met basic qualifications for teaching. A teacher who signs a contract without a certificate and who is later found out may find herself declared an unpaid volunteer who has agreed to provide free instructional services.

- Teachers' contracts are documents that establish a legal working relationship between teachers and the districts that employ them. Typically, contracts include the obligations of both teachers and their employing districts. To become valid, a contract must be approved by the school board of the employing district. There are several kinds of teaching contracts. Among them are term contracts, continuing contracts, and tenure contracts.

- Dismissal procedures that must be followed when a school district decides to release a teacher vary depending on several factors. Generally, dismissal actions cannot be initiated for reasons that are inconsistent with constitutional guarantees of citizenship. For example, a school district cannot dismiss a teacher solely on the grounds of his personal religious beliefs. Processes to be followed when there are concerns about teachers' academic performance or other issues thought to impair their effectiveness vary somewhat depending upon the types of contracts the individuals have and the specific language these contracts contain.

- General "fishing expeditions" involving required school district testing of all teachers for AIDS or for drug abuse generally have not been allowed. To be legal, districts must be able to show that the district has a clear and compelling interest in the results of such tests.

- All states have laws requiring teachers to report suspected child abuse. These laws provide some legal protection against reprisal for teachers who make such reports in good faith. There are penalties in many states for teachers who recognize a potential child-abuse situation and fail to report it. Hence, it is important for teachers to recognize signs of child abuse and to know procedures to follow in reporting it.

- Teachers may be held liable for certain types of actions. Many teacher liability suits have resulted from charges of (1) excessive use of force when disciplining students or (2) negligence. In considering whether excessive use of force was involved, courts have considered such variables as the gravity of the student behavior, the age of the student, the gender and size of the student, the size of the person administering the punishment, the implement used in punishment, and the attitude of the punisher. Negligence cases often have focused on issues related to nonfeasance (a failure of the teacher to act when she had a responsibility to act), misfeasance (a failure of the teacher to act in a proper manner to prevent harm from coming to a student), and malfeasance (a deliberately improper action of the teacher that causes harm to a student).

- In considering academic freedom issues courts have weighted both teachers' rights to conduct their classrooms according to their own best professional judgment and needs of school district administrators to see that the prescribed curriculum is taught. In general, courts have supported actions of administrators to assure mandated content is taught. On the other hand, courts have supported teachers when cases have involved administrative attempts to stifle consideration of embarrassing or controversial issues in the classroom. In general, teachers have been found to have the right to speak out publicly on issues associated with schools and schooling as well as on other topics of broad public concern.

- Copyright regulations are designed to protect the interests of the developers of intellectual property such as books, journal articles, works of art, computer programs, and radio and television programs. In general, teachers need to request and receive written permission for making and distributing multiple copies of these materials. Fair use guidelines allow some limited classroom use of copyrighted material without securing permission; these guidelines must be adhered to strictly. Teachers have been successfully sued for copyright law violations.

- Actions teachers take in their private lives sometimes come to the attention of the courts. The courts have declared that, because of their potential influence on young people, teachers can be held to higher moral and behavioral standards than citizens in general. Dismissal actions against teachers have frequently been upheld when courts have found their actions to undermine their credibility in the community and to make them ineffective as instructional leaders. Courts have been particularly likely to support dismissal actions when teachers have engaged in immoral behavior with students.

Follow-Up Questions and Activities

Questions

1. What was the relationship between teachers and students when the prevailing legal doctrine was *in loco parentis*, and how has this doctrine changed?

2. What basic principles of due process must be followed before a student can be suspended or expelled?

3. What implications did the decision in the famous *Tinker* case have for school authorities' rights to control the content of student publications?

4. What are some examples of school activities from which you think a student might logically be excused on freedom-of-conscience grounds?

5. What issues have courts tended to consider in deciding whether a given search by school authorities was justified?

6. What has been the general pattern of legislation and court decisions related to gender discrimination, and what issues in this general area are still be actively disputed?

7. Why do you think the Family Education Rights and Privacy legislation was passed, and do you think this legislation was needed?

8. Why is it difficult to generalize about the kinds of due process procedures that are to be followed when school districts wish to dismiss a teacher?

9. Why are laws related to teacher tenure controversial?

10. Why are teachers expected to conform to higher standards of behavior than other citizens? Is this fair?

Activities

1. Review newspaper articles that have appeared over the past several months dealing with legal issues related to education. Organize articles into groups according to the issue addressed. Write a short summary of issues being litigated. Present your information to the class in a brief oral report.

2. Interview a high school principal about procedures followed in his or her school when it becomes necessary to expel a student. In particular, ask the principal to share information regarding due process guidelines that are followed. Prepare a short summary of your interview for your course instructor.

3. Invite a personnel officer from a local school district to visit your class. Ask this person to bring an example of a teaching contract and to discuss its provisions with the class.

4. Obtain information regarding laws in your state pertaining to reporting child abuse. Your instructor may be able to suggest where this information is available. Share your findings with others in the class.

5. Organize a class debate on this question: "Resolved that teacher tenure laws undermine educational quality by making it too difficult to remove ineffective teachers."

References

Bannister v. Paradis, 316 F. Supp. 185 (d. N.H. 1970).

Bellnier v. Lund, 438 F. Supp. 47 (n.d. N.Y. 1977).

Board of Trustees v. Stubblefield, 94 Cal. Rptr, 318, 321 (1971).

"Chalk Talk: The Right of Free Speech in Public Schools: Bethel v. Fraser." *Journal of Law and Education* (Winter, 1987), pp. 119–124.

COMMITTEE ON THE JUDICIARY. H.R. No. 94–1476, 94th Congress, 201 Sess. 68–70 (1976).

CONNORS, E. *Educational Tort Liability and Malpractice*. Bloomington, IN: Phi Delta Kappa, 1991.

Davis v. Meek, 344 F. Supp. 398 (n.d. Ohio 1972).

Denton v. South Kitsap School District No. 402, 516 P.2d 1080 (Wash 1973).

Doe v. Renfrow, 631 F.2d 91 (7th Cir. 1980), cert. denied, 451 U.S. 1022 at 1025 (1981).

FISCHER, L.; SCHIMMEL, D.; AND KELLY, C. *Teachers and the Law*. 3rd ed. New York: Longman, 1991.

Goss v. Lopez, 419 U.S. 565 (1975).

Hazelwood School District v. Kuhlmeier, 484 U.S. 260 (1988).

Ingraham v. Wright, 430 UY.S. 651 (1977).

Kingsville Independent School District v. Cooper, 611 F.2d 1109 (5th Cir. 1980).

Meyer v. Nebraska, 262 U.S. 390, 399 (1923).

MONKS, R. AND PROULX, E. *Legal Basics for Teachers*. Fastback No. 235. Bloomington, IN: Phi Delta Kappa, 1986.

New Jersey v. T.L.O., 105 5. CT. 733 (1984).

Parducci v. Rutland, 316 F. Supp. 352 (m.d. AL 1979).

Patchogue-Medford Congress of Teachers v. Board of Education, 505 N.Y.S. 2d 888 (NY App. Div., 1986).

Pickering v. Board of Education of Township School District 205, Will County, 225 N.E. 2d 1 (1967); 391 U.S. 563 (1968).

Southside Public Schools v. Hill, 827 F.2d 270 (8th Cir. 1987)

Tinker v. Des Moines Independent Community School District, 343 U.S. 503 (1969).

Vorcheimer v. School District, 531 F.2d 880 (3rd Circ. 1976), aff'd, 430 U.S. 703 (1977).

20

Professional Development

AIMS

This chapter provides information to help the reader to:

- Explain the need that teachers have for career-long preparation.
- Point out how experiences prospective teachers have had can influence their reactions to teacher-preparation programs.
- Describe characteristics of individuals at the fantasy stage.
- Explain components of a typical preservice program for teachers.
- Suggest some approaches teachers can use to deal with induction-year problems.
- Cite examples of career-growth opportunities for teachers.
- Point out employment opportunities other than classroom teaching for individuals who have completed teacher certification programs.

FOCUS QUESTIONS

1. How does student teaching prepare a person for teaching?

2. How do different components of the total teacher-preparation program contribute to a teacher's education?

3. Why do teacher-preparation programs fall short of providing a total preparation for newcomers to the profession?

4. What are some problems that teachers often experience during the induction year?

5. How do staff-development programs contribute to teachers' growth?

6. Why do teachers often find it desirable to take additional college courses to grow professionally after they begin teaching?

7. What is meant by the term *merit pay*?

8. How does a career ladder work?

9. What are some opportunities within education other than classroom teaching?

10. Why is preparation for teaching also a good preparation for positions outside of education?

Introduction

At the end of their teacher-preparation programs, different people often have different attitudes about their preparation for teaching. Some of them are convinced that they have been well prepared. Large numbers of others often feel that, somehow, they were short-changed. When they confront difficulties in the classroom, they may feel that important content was left out of their preparation program. These feelings are particularly likely to result when the students they face during their first year of teaching are different from those they encountered as student teachers.

The first year or two of teaching are difficult. Commonly, teachers find at least some things for which they feel they were not well prepared. Many people simply decide teaching is not for them during their initial years in the profession, and they turn to other occupations. The failure of large numbers of people who have prepared to teach to stay in the classroom has been a major concern of educational leaders.

Explanations for this problem vary. What does seem clear is that teachers who develop a long-term commitment to the profession recognize early that their preparation does not end with the kind of training they received in their initial certification program. They understand that success in the classroom requires preparation that is career long.

Preparation for Entry into Teaching

There are two phases in the preparation of individuals seeking to become teachers. They are:

- The pretraining phase
- The preservice phase

The Pretraining Phase

Teachers' initial attitudes toward teaching and what constitutes "good" or "appropriate" teaching behavior are strongly influenced by experiences they have had prior to beginning formal preparation programs. For example, they often are affected by the experiences they have had as students and by the personalities and teaching styles of teachers who taught them. One researcher discovered that the typical person entering a teacher preparation program has spent more than 10,000 hours in classrooms with teachers (Nemser, 1983). They have probably taken classes from more than 50 different teachers (Ryan, 1986).

Recollections prospective teachers have of classes they took as students and teachers they worked with can have both positive and negative effects. These prior experiences often suggest that certain kinds of teacher behaviors are "good" or "bad." It is dangerous to make these kinds of generalizations. Behaviors that may be either good or bad in certain circumstances may have quite the opposite effect in others.

In addition to the possibility of making mistaken judgments about what constitutes effective teaching, too much reliance on personal memory sometimes convinces beginning teachers that they do not need much formal training. Individuals who subscribe to this view often think that they can use their memories as guides and simply do in their own classrooms what they remember their own teachers as having done. People with this kind of orientation often are a bit too ready to make quick analyses and recommend ill-conceived, sure-fire solutions to difficult problems.

Too much reliance on their own personal experiences in secondary schools can leave prospective teachers with a set of inflexible attitudes as they begin their preparation programs. They may feel they already know what good teaching is and approach their classes not as opportunities to learn but as obstacles to be overcome. This kind of attitude often leads them to an insufficient commitment of intellectual resources to important education classes. When this happens, the formal teacher-preparation program may have little influence on how they behave in the classroom once they begin teaching.

Many individuals who fail to appreciate the intellectual demands associated with a serious commitment to their teacher-preparation courses are at what sometimes has been labeled the *fantasy stage* of professional development (Ryan, 1986). People at this stage develop mental pictures of themselves functioning in idealized ways in the classroom. They often have visions of themselves teaching as their own favorite teachers did. They imagine themselves succeeding with every student. Even when these future teachers briefly picture reluctant learners, they tend to develop mind pictures in which young people fall quickly under the pedagogical spells woven by caring young teachers who "really understand students." Often these individuals assume that discipline problems are challenges faced by bad teachers and that there will be no such difficulties in their own classrooms.

Because of their failure to take courses in their preservice program seriously, the failure rate of individuals at the fantasy stage is high. This is particularly true during

Box 20.1

Individual Students and "Effective" Teachers

A businessperson described "good" teachers in this way:

"Good" teachers work hard to prepare students for college. They are subject-matter experts who give students demanding assignments. They favor essay tests and are known as hard graders. These teachers don't hesitate to fail students who do not perform up to minimum expectations. They refuse to tolerate misbehavior. They are people who are clearly in charge, and they don't waste time dealing with nonessential content.

What Do You Think?

1. In general, do you agree or disagree with this view?

2. What kinds of students would be most likely to profit from instruction delivered by the kind of teacher this person describes?

3. What biases or values does this person reveal?

4. How would you define a "good" teacher?

5. What does your definition tell us about your biases and values?

---

student teaching when they are confronted with teaching realities that are far different from the happy visions they have created.

Fortunately, relatively few people who are preparing to teach have a dysfunctional commitment to the roseate view of educators' work associated with the fantasy stage. However, it is common for prospective educators to begin their work with some preconceptions about the world of teaching. This is only natural. The important point for future teachers is to test these preconceptions against evidence. Information presented in preservice courses and, later, from student teaching can help shape perspectives and promote patterns of behavior that are well matched to the real demands of teaching today.

The Preservice Phase

The preservice phase of professional development occurs prior to certification and entry into the "service" of teaching. During this phase, prospective teachers follow a course of study (usually at a college or university) that leads to initial teacher certification.

Members of the general public who are not familiar with how teachers are prepared sometimes assume that people preparing to teach spend the majority of their college or university time taking education courses. This is not true. In most secondary teacher-preparation programs, the professional education component—including student teaching—comprises only about one-fifth of a student's total preparation program (Kluender, 1984). By far the largest portion of students' preparation programs is devoted to general studies courses and to courses in subjects they are preparing to teach.

Though there are differences in how programs are organized at individual institutions, many of them share common features. In part, this similarity results from guidelines and standards imposed by state and national accrediting bodies such as the National Council for Accreditation of Teacher Education (NCATE). A typical preservice program consists of three parts: (1) a general studies component, (2) an academic major or teaching specialization, and (3) a professional education component (Kluender, 1984).

The General Studies Component

In addition to having depth in the subjects they teach, teachers are also expected to be familiar with general information associated with the expected store of knowledge of educated people. The general studies component of the preparation program is designed to accommodate this need.

General studies knowledge often exposes students to a cross section of information from the liberal arts, the social sciences, mathematics, and the sciences. This information helps future teachers to deal with students from a variety of backgrounds and with many kinds of personal interests. These courses, too, point out that many important problems require people to draw information from a variety of academic disciplines. They help future teachers to see important relationships across subject lines and to develop sensitivity to historical, scientific, cultural, and technological issues (DeLandsheere, 1987). This kind of content helps future teachers appreciate that schools do not exist in isolation from the larger culture of which they are a part.

The general studies component often comprises about 40 percent of the total preparation curriculum of prospective secondary teachers. Important social changes often increase pressures to emphasize particular kinds of content. For example, the changing racial and ethnic makeup of the public schools has resulted in the infusion of more courses with a multicultural emphasis within the general studies component. In many places, additional courses are being added to help students deal with young people who have backgrounds in a language other than English.

A problem in some places is that instruction in general studies courses is not consistently good. At some institutions, general studies courses have not been staffed by the best instructors. The Holmes Group, an organization of major research universities that are trying to improve the quality of teacher-preparation programs, made these comments about this problem: "Few of those teaching university courses know how to teach well, and many do not seem to care. The undergraduate education that an intending teacher—and everyone else—receives is full of the same bad teaching that litters American high schools" (Holmes Group, 1986; p. 16).

The Academic Major or Teaching Specialization

Academic majors or areas of teaching specialization are included in all secondary teacher preparation programs. Nearly 40 percent of programs are devoted to this kind of content. This is appropriate, given that secondary teachers are expected to have depth in areas they are to teach. These courses are designed to provide teachers with a sophisticated grasp of content they will teach.

An abiding concern of education specialists is that many university courses in subjects future teachers will teach do not treat content that matches up well with secondary school curricula. For example, some people who major in English spend most of their time at the university studying literature. In some programs, no formal instruction in composition is provided after the freshman year. Yet, English teachers in middle schools, junior high schools, and senior high schools are expected to spend a considerable amount of time teaching students how to write.

Not everyone supports the idea that university courses should be closely related to the kinds of content teachers must teach to secondary students. They argue that the university courses have a broader mission to provide future teachers with exposure to patterns of serious scholarship in the discipline. University courses, they allege, should be as much directed toward developing future teachers' abilities to analyze, synthesize, evaluate, and otherwise engage in serious thinking as to providing them with "practical" information they need in working with secondary students.

The debate between individuals favoring and opposing university courses that are closely matched to secondary school curricula has raged for years. It seems destined to continue. Prospects are that some university courses will bear quite close relationships to what teachers must do when instructing secondary school students; others will have a tenuous connection, at best. Given the tradition of academic freedom in the nation's colleges and universities, it is unlikely that a common set of practices will evolve that will be endorsed by all departments and instructors.

The Professional Education Component

The professional education component includes courses specifically designed to provide teachers with the instructional and management skills they will need as they assume their roles in the schools. Most, sometimes all, of these courses usually are offered by professors in schools, colleges, or departments of education.

As noted previously, professional education courses typically account for only about one-fifth of the total course work a person takes as part of a secondary-level teacher preparation program. It has been increasingly difficult for teacher educators to disseminate the growing volume of knowledge about teaching in just a few professional educational courses (DeLandsheere, 1987). In some places, there have been efforts to extend the length of teacher-preparation programs to allow more time for professional education content to be taught.

The volume of knowledge presently available about effective teaching practices and the high rate at which new knowledge is being produced underscore a key point. No teacher, regardless of the excellence of her preparation program, is going to know everything worth knowing about teaching at the end of the preservice program. Professional development today has no neat and precise end point. It is an ongoing process that professionals accept as a career-long obligation. At best, student teaching, certification, and the first job offer are the end of the beginning.

Though it certainly should not be regarded as a culminating professional-development experience, student teaching continues to play an important role in preservice teachers' professional development. It provides an opportunity for beginners to apply what they have learned in classrooms filled with real secondary school students. It also allows supervisors to assess student teachers' classroom performance and make final recommendations regarding whether they have demonstrated enough expertise for them to be safely placed with students.

Box 20.2

What You Need to Know About What You Teach

Specific courses people must take to qualify to teach individual subjects vary somewhat from state to state and from university to university. These requirements are shaped by a number of influences. National specialty organizations serving teachers of English, social studies, mathematics, science, music, physical education, foreign languages, and other subjects issue guidelines that state authorities consider. Traditional practices also influence those who make decisions about what should be required. Graduation requirements of individual colleges and universities also sometimes are a factor.

Ask your course instructor to help you locate some guidelines from a national professional organization that describe kinds of courses that, in the organization's view, teachers in its subject area should take before being certified to teach. Alternatively, identify minimum requirements in your state for someone preparing to teach a subject area that interests you.

What Do You Think?

1. How do requirements established by your own college and university for people wishing to teach your subject compare either with those of the relevant national professional organization or with minimums prescribed by your state?

2. If there are differences, how do you account for them?

3. Compare the content of courses you are required to take to qualify for teacher certification in your subject area with the content secondary school teachers in your subject area actually teach. What are similarities and differences? If you find differences, what accounts for them?

4. If you find that courses you are required to take fail to provide you with all the subject matter background you will need, what might you do to fill in your knowledge gaps?

As important as student teaching is, it still tends to be "sheltered reality" (Ryan, 1986). It is an experience shaped to a large extent by the practices and expectations of the supervising teacher. Usually, the student teacher comes into a classroom that features an established classroom climate and culture. Students and school administrators know that the supervising teacher retains ultimate responsibility for what goes on. As a result of this set of conditions, even the best student teaching experiences fall short of mirroring everything new teachers face when they assume their first teaching positions.

Growing as a Teacher

Successful teachers are flexible. They recognize changing conditions in their classrooms and adapt to them, as appropriate. They recognize that effective teaching requires a commitment to an ongoing process of self-improvement, not to mastery of a fixed set of ideas.

The Induction Year

The first year of teaching is sometimes called the *induction year*. It is a critical period in a teacher's professional development. During this period, for the first time the teacher accepts a full range of professional responsibilities.

It is common for students who have completed student teaching, qualified for certification, and accepted an initial teaching position to assume that the first year of teaching will place fewer demands on them than student teaching. The pressures of the first year often come as an unpleasant surprise. For example, many new teachers find themselves stressed because of the hard work associated with maintaining classroom control. Others find it difficult to motivate students. Still others are surprised at the amount of time that must be spent at home preparing lessons and correcting students' work. Problems teachers face during the first few years of teaching lead some of them to conclude that teaching is not for them, and they leave the profession.

Potential problems teachers face during the induction year are better recognized today than they used to be. Interest in keeping teachers in the classroom once they are trained and certified has led many school districts to develop programs to assist new teachers. For example, in some places each new teacher is assigned a mentor who is charged with helping the newcomer. In other places, careful attention is given to providing new teachers with needed support materials. Reduction of class loads and assignments of new teachers to classes where their potentials for success are high represent other approaches that have been taken to help beginners have a successful induction year.

Many things contribute to challenges teachers face during the first year. For one thing, the support from supervising teachers and university supervisors that was available during student teaching is no longer available. Difficult decisions cannot be passed on to someone else. Often, too, record keeping and other paperwork requirements demand much more attention than beginning teachers expect. These obligations plus those associated with mandatory meetings, monitoring of student activities, and other responsibilities often leave beginners with the feeling that they simply cannot do everything that is expected of them. Stress, feelings of fatigue, and even loneliness often result.

There are several things beginning teachers can do to make these challenges more manageable. First of all, they can develop realistic expectations. In particular, they need to recognize that development of excellence in teaching takes time. They need not feel bad if every lesson does not work out well. Negative self-judgments should be avoided. Even highly experienced teachers have bad days.

Second, if the school district or school administration does not have a formal procedure for assigning new teachers a mentor, it makes sense for beginners themselves to seek out experienced people on the faculty. Every teacher in the building was once a beginning teacher, and many of them well remember adjustments they had to make as newcomers to the profession. Many of them will willingly reach out to befriend and help beginners. This kind of support can be invaluable to first-year teachers as they struggle to gain confidence.

It is also important for first-year teachers to recognize that the first year of teaching is a unique time in their professional lives (Ryan, 1986). Even when preservice preparation has been excellent, much remains to be learned. An extraordinary volume of professional learning occurs during the induction year. This new knowledge, taken together with what beginners already know, often allows them to approach subsequent years of teaching more competently and confidently.

The professional growth that takes place during the first year is so great that we strongly counsel frustrated beginners to teach at least two years before making a final decision to leave the profession. Individuals who depart after only one year really have not given their developing expertise a chance to blossom and be tested in the classroom.

Teaching is a people-intense activity. Day-long interactions with others can produce stress. It makes sense for teachers to develop outside activities that serve as a counterbalance to the challenges associated with classroom instruction. Exercise programs and other activities that free the mind from job-related concerns often add a much-needed dose of psychological serenity.

WHAT SCHOLARS SAY

What Types of Support Do New Teachers Need?

Successful induction programs respond effectively to the needs of first-year teachers. One study attempted to identify these needs by soliciting responses from 86 first-year teachers. Analyses of responses from these teachers identified a number of distinct kinds of needed support. The top four needs will be briefly introduced here.

One kind of needed support has to do with collecting and locating materials necessary to support instruction. New teachers often are not familiar with all materials available in the school or district. As a result, many of them spend great quantities of time just trying to locate needed items.

A second category of need concerns help with instruction. New teachers want help with their teaching strategies. This is a need that seems to persist throughout the entire induction year. In fact, it seems to increase during the second semester. Perhaps this is true because, by this time, new teachers have become relatively comfortable with basic management tasks and are more interested in focusing on issues related to instruction.

A third category of need involves emotional support. New teachers need to have someone available who can listen to their problems and who will share ideas with them. In particular, they need someone who will be sympathetic and supportive.

A fourth category of need concerns classroom management and discipline. Many newcomers continue to feel somewhat inadequate in this area. Interestingly, however, this need does not rank as high as the previously mentioned needs for locating materials, dealing with instructional issues, and identifying someone with whom to share frustrations and exchange ideas.

Source: Odell, S. "Induction Support of New Teachers: A Functional Approach." *Journal of Teacher Education* (January–February 1986), pp. 26–29.

Professional-growth opportunities that become available during the induction year often suggest productive new ways of approaching content and interacting with students. These experiences broaden the range of options available to newcomers and enhance their confidence. Among them are:

- Staff-development activities
- College and university course work
- Professional organization work

Staff-Development Activities

Staff-development activities typically are opportunities provided by local school districts that are designed to improve the quality of educational programming in the schools. Most are directed at teachers. Sometimes staff-development activities are referred to as *inservice education*. In many districts, the school calendar is developed in such a way that students are dismissed from school on several days throughout the school year so teachers can participate in staff-development opportunities.

Sometimes teachers are required to attend specific staff-development sessions; in other circumstances attendance may be optional. In some places, teachers receive staff-development credits for their participation. When teachers accumulate enough of these, they qualify for salary increases.

"And now to the most important point of all about teaching . . . relevance!"

Staff-development activities take a variety of forms. Frequently sessions include speakers, workshops put on by teachers with special expertise, and opportunities for teachers in given content areas to share ideas. Though not all staff-development activities provide useful information for every teacher, for newcomers to the profession they often provide opportunities to learn new instructional and management techniques. This kind of knowledge can be a valuable addition to expertise beginners have when they assume their initial teaching positions.

College and University Course Work

Many teachers continue to take college and university courses while they are teaching. To serve this market, many institutions of higher learning offer courses at night so local teachers can attend. In some places, Saturday classes are available. Some school districts place limits on the number of classes teachers can take during the academic year. They do this out of a concern that teachers who carry too heavy a load of college and university courses will be unable to devote an adequate amount of time to their own teaching.

In addition to the knowledge that can be gained from college and university courses, credits earned often help a teacher move to a higher level on the salary schedule. In many parts of the country, teachers' salaries go up as (1) number of years they have taught increase and (2) number of academic credits earned increase. A key assumption of salary schedules that are constructed this way is that academic credits are a measure of teachers' knowledge. As this knowledge increases, their expertise as teachers should improve. Because of this view, school districts may have restrictions on the kinds of courses they will count for credit for salary purposes. For example, a high school mathematics teacher who takes a college course in ceramics might find his district unwilling to accept these credits (for salary purposes).

In some parts of the country, teachers' needs for college courses, particularly for courses offered at night, have spawned some dubious practices. Fly-by-night campuses, extension courses staffed by people not on regular faculties, and other schemes have been hatched. The quality of instruction delivered by some of these irresponsible operations is low. Indeed, a few of them are not even accredited. Some teachers who have taken their "courses" find school administrators unwilling to accept their credits. It makes sense for teachers to check with school administrators before committing their time and money to college and university courses.

In addition to helping teachers develop more competence in areas related to what they are teaching, many college and university courses can be applied toward advanced degree programs. Teachers often can qualify for master's degrees after taking courses for several years in the evening and attending several summer sessions. Because advanced degree programs include specific course requirements, it is important that interested teachers seek advice from a university advisor before enrolling in courses.

We do not recommend that teachers begin work on an advanced degree during their first year of teaching. As noted, there are very specific course requirements associated with many advanced degrees. If a college or university course is to be taken, it is better to select it on the grounds of its potential to meet a specific instructional need of the teacher rather than on its applicability to a degree. Further, courses in an advanced degree program are more meaningful when individuals bring a background of several years' classroom experience to their classes.

Box 20.3

Professional Growth

This chapter stresses the importance of career-long professional development. Think about your own present strengths and weaknesses as well as your personal goals as you respond to the following questions.

What Do You Think?
1. How do you feel about your need to participate in professional-development activities throughout your teaching career? Some teachers are not enthusiastic about professional-development opportunities. Why do you think they feel this way?

2. If you were to take additional college or university courses after you begin teaching, what kinds of courses do you think would best serve your professional-development needs?

3. What kinds of help do you think would be most useful during your first year? What actions might you be able to initiate to assure such help is available?

4. What long-term career goals do you have? What are some things you must do to attain them?

Professional Organization Work
Professional organizations regularly sponsor events that include sessions designed to improve teachers' levels of expertise. They provide opportunities for teachers to interact with others sharing similar interests. Beginning teachers often find an association with a professional organization to be very beneficial. More specific information about teachers' professional groups is introduced in the next section.

General and Specialty Organizations

There are two broad types of teachers' professional organizations. They are (1) general organizations and (2) specialty organizations. The two largest general organizations, the National Education Association (NEA) and the American Federation of Teachers (AFT), seek their members from the total national pool of teachers. Members include teachers working at all grade levels and in all subject areas. Specialty organizations focus their attention on teachers interested in certain subject areas or categories of learners. Both general organizations and specialty organizations have publications of interest to teachers.

General Organizations

The NEA and AFT are particularly interested in issues associated with teachers' working conditions. In many parts of the country, local affiliates of the NEA and AFT represent teachers in efforts to negotiate salary and working conditions with representatives of the school board and administration. At the state and national level, representatives of these organizations lobby for passage of legislation of interest to teachers.

Representatives often also serve as members of accrediting agencies charged with examining and certifying the adequacy of practices within given school districts. They sometimes also serve as members of bodies considering curriculum changes. In general, representatives of the major general professional organizations may be found in any venue where issues related to major concerns of teachers are being considered.

Teachers who belong to these organizations are in a position to learn more about issues affecting the profession in general. For information about these organizations and their programs, write to:

National Education Association
1201 16th Street, N.W.
Washington, D.C. 20036

American Federation of Teachers
555 New Jersey Avenue, NW
Washington, D.C. 20001

Specialty Organizations

There are dozens of specialty organizations in education. They provide opportunities for professional educators to exchange ideas and share perspectives with others with interests in similar subjects or in similar kinds of students. Thousands of the nation's teachers belong to these groups.

Specialty organizations facilitate professional growth in several ways. Most of the large organizations have annual meetings that bring together educators from throughout the country to share ideas and discuss issues. Many of these national groups also have state and local affiliates. Many of these state- and local-level groups also sponsor meetings. Typically, these meetings include presentations designed to inform other teachers about promising approaches to instructing and managing students.

Most of the nation's large specialty groups publish one or more professional journals for their members. These journals provide teachers with up-to-date research findings, descriptions of innovative teaching practices, and discussions of other relevant issues. New teachers often find these journals an important source of new teaching ideas.

Many specialty groups allow people who are preparing to become teachers to join at reduced rates. Membership in these groups allows preservice teachers to meet teachers and encounter ideas that may not be treated in depth in their courses. Active participation can provide them with experiences that will serve them well during student teaching and beyond.

The subsections that follow introduce a number of specialty groups. This listing is by no means comprehensive. These groups have been selected to point out the broad range of concerns of specialty groups in education.

American Alliance for Health, Physical Education, Recreation, and Dance (AAHPERD)

This large national specialty group addresses the interests of educators specializing in health, physical education, recreation, and dance. Membership is drawn from elementary and secondary teachers, elementary and secondary school administrators, college and university professors, and others with an interest in the subject areas that provide a focus for this group.

AAHPERD publishes several professional journals. The *Journal of Physical Education, Recreation, and Dance* is published nine times a year. *Health Education* appears six times each year. The group's monthly publication, *Update*, keeps members up-to-date on ongoing activities. Research results appear in *Research Quarterly for Exercise and Sport*. For more information, write to:

American Alliance for Health, Physical Education, Recreation, and Dance
1900 Association Drive
Reston, VA 22091

Council on Exceptional Children (CEC)

This group is dedicated to promoting better education for students with disabilities and for students who are gifted. Membership includes teachers, administrators, college and university professionals, and others sharing an interest in the group's focus.

CEC publishes two major journals. *Exceptional Children* comes out six times a year, and *Teaching Exceptional Children* is published quarterly. For more information, write to:

Council for Exceptional Children
1920 Association Drive
Reston, VA 22091

International Council for Computers in Education (ICCE)

As its name suggests, this organization is dedicated to assuring computers are used effectively in schools. The organization promotes cooperation among various groups and individuals interested in improving instruction through application of computer technology.

ICCE produces two regular publications. *The Computing Teacher* is issued nine times a year. *The SIG Bulletin* comes out quarterly. For more information, write to:

International Council for Computers in Education
University of Oregon
1787 Agate Street
Eugene, Oregon 97403

International Reading Association (IRA)

The International Reading Association is one of the nation's largest specialty groups in education. It has about 90,000 members and has approximately 1,200 local chapters scattered throughout the country. Its membership includes teachers, reading specialists, administrators, consultants, educational researchers, college and university professors, and others interested in reading.

IRA publishes several journals. *The Reading Teacher*, published nine times a year, features articles of primary interest to elementary teachers. *The Journal of Reading*, also published nine times a year, focuses on the theory and practice of reading as applied to middle school, junior high school, senior high school, and adult learning situations. *Reading Research Quarterly*, published four times a year, disseminates the findings of researchers in reading. IRA also publishes a quarterly journal in Spanish, *Lectura y Vida*. For more information write to:

International Reading Association
800 Barksdale Road
P.O. Box 8139
Newark, DE 19714

Music Teachers National Association (MTNA)

This group seeks to improve music instruction, performance, and understanding. Members include teachers in the schools as well as music teachers with private tutoring practices.

Several publications are sponsored by MTNA. *The American Music Teacher* appears bimonthly. *The Directory of Nationally Certified Teachers* comes out once each year. For more information write to:

Music Teachers National Association
2113 Carew Tower
Cincinnati, OH 45202

National Art Education Association (NAEA)

The National Art Education Association promotes better instruction in the visual arts in schools. It is the leading national organization for art teachers. Membership includes anyone with a direct connection to or an interest in art education in the schools.

NAEA publishes several journals. The first of these, *Art Education*, appears bimonthly. The group also publishes *Studies in Art Education*, a quarterly that reports findings of researchers with interests in art education. For more information write to:

National Art Education Association
1916 Association Drive
Reston, VA 22091

National Association for Gifted Children (NAGC)

As its name implies, this group serves individuals who are interested in improving the education of gifted students. Membership includes educators and parents. It conducts training sessions for members and engages in lobbying activities in support of federal and state legislation that will provide better programs for gifted students.

The National Association for Gifted Children publishes *Gifted Child Quarterly*. For more information write to:

National Association for Gifted Children
4175 Lovell Road, Suite 140
Circle Pines, MN 55014

National Council for the Social Studies (NCSS)

The National Council for the Social Studies is the largest specialty group serving the needs of social studies teachers. Members include classroom teachers, curriculum directors, state-level social studies specialists, college and university professors, and others with interests in social studies instruction in the schools.

Several journals are published by NCSS. The most widely circulated of these is *Social Education*. It appears seven times a year and contains articles focusing on all aspects of teaching and learning social studies content in grades K through 12. *Theory and Research in Social Education* is a quarterly publication that reports the findings of social studies researchers and theoreticians. For more information write to:

> The National Council for the Social Studies
> 3501 Newark Street, NW
> Washington, DC 20016

National Council of Teachers of English (NCTE)

The National Council of Teachers of English is dedicated to improving instruction in English in the nation's schools. This large group has many state and local affiliates. Membership is open to individuals who teach English or language arts at any level or who have an interest in this part of the curriculum.

NCTE sponsors the publication of several journals. The *English Journal* appears eight times a year. Its primary audience includes middle school, junior high school, and senior high school teachers of literature, language, and composition. *Research in the Teaching of English* is a quarterly journal that reports research into the teaching and learning of English. NCTE also publishes several other specialty journals. For more information write to:

> National Council of Teachers of English
> 1111 Kenyon Road
> Urbana, IL 61801

National Council of Teachers of Mathematics (NCTM)

The National Council of Teachers of Mathematics is a large group that includes more than 200 state and local chapters. It is dedicated to the improvement of mathematics teaching in the schools. Membership is open to anyone committed to the group's objectives.

Several journals are sponsored by NCTM. *The Mathematics Teacher* appears five times a year and serves mathematics teachers at the secondary school and two-year college levels. The *Journal for Research in Mathematics Education* reports findings of researchers with interests in improving mathematics instruction. For more information write to:

> National Council of Teachers of Mathematics
> 1906 Association Drive
> Reston, VA 22091

National Science Teachers Association (NSTA)

The National Science Teachers Association is the largest national group serving the interests of science teachers. It draws its membership from teachers, administrators, curriculum specialists, state-level program supervisors, college and university professors, and others with interests in improving science teaching in the schools. It has numerous state-level and local-level affiliates.

The National Science Teachers Association publishes several journals. *Science Scope*, published five times a year, focuses on issues of primary concern to middle school and junior high school science teachers. The *Science Teacher*, issued nine times a year, serves the needs of junior and senior high school science teachers. The *Journal of College Science Teaching* focuses on issues of concern to people teaching science courses in higher education settings. For more information write to:

National Science Teachers Association
1742 Connecticut Avenue, NW
Washington, DC 20009

Summary Comments About Specialty Groups

Organizations that have been profiled here are typical of those that draw much of their membership from among the nation's teachers. These groups help members build a common community of concern. They function as catalysts for political action. Many federal and state laws that influence school programming had their impetus from lobbying and other actions of these groups. For example, present laws relating to working with students with disabilities can clearly be traced to pressures initially brought to bear on legislatures by organizations committed to better serving the needs of this special student population.

Career Options

People who are pursuing college and university programs leading to teacher certification often fail to recognize that there are many career options within education. Many of these are open only to individuals who have, first, trained as teachers and spent some time actually working as classroom teachers. Some of these positions require individuals to leave classroom teaching entirely.

Merit Pay and Career Ladders

Merit pay and career ladders really are not career options. Rather, they are responses to a concern that the lure of higher salaries will lead good people to accept positions that will take them away from the classroom.

Merit pay refers to a practice of paying some teachers more than others because of the high quality of their teaching performance. This approach has great appeal for many people outside of education. Merit-pay proposals, on the other hand, have been generally opposed by most large organizations representing teachers' interests. The objection of many teachers to merit pay has to do with the difficulty of defining and measuring "high-quality teaching." Teachers fear that, absent agreement on what high-quality teaching is and how it should be measured, merit-pay proposals invite abuse. There are concerns that teachers who are judged to be "meritorious" will be identified on such extraneous variables as their personalities or on the nature of their relationships with administrators.

Opponents of merit pay argue that since decisions regarding who gets merit pay may be awarded for reasons other than high-quality teaching, there are no incentives in merit-pay schemes for teachers to become more effective teachers. Rather than acting to improve instruction, there are fears that merit-pay schemes will promote dissension, jealousy, and distrust among teachers. This may well result in a negative intrapersonal atmosphere and lead to poorer overall teaching in a given school. In summary, merit plans continue to be controversial. Debates about the worth of this approach continue.

Career-ladder approaches are somewhat less controversial than merit pay. Unlike merit-pay schemes where increased salaries are supposed to be allocated to individuals who have been identified as high-quality teachers, career-ladder schemes are designed to increase salaries of teachers who take on increased special responsibilities. This approach is based on the idea of *differentiated staffing*. This means that not all teachers do the same kinds of things. In addition to teaching classes, some teachers, depending on their experience and expertise, are assigned special roles including curriculum development, staff supervision and leadership, working with student teachers, mentoring beginners, and so forth.

Career ladders typically have several rungs or steps. Many of them have about three of these. Individuals on career-ladder step one ordinarily are beginning teachers. As these individuals grow and develop increased competence, their performances are reviewed. Some of them are advanced to step two and given opportunities to work with student teachers, participate in curriculum development work, and take on other responsibilities not assigned to step-one teachers. Step-three teachers are selected from experienced step-two professionals. Those chosen are given still additional duties related to such things as helping other teachers develop professional growth plans and participating in making general policy decisions within the school. In some places, teachers at step three may be assigned a reduced teaching load to allow time for them to perform other assigned duties.

The credibility of career-ladder systems is closely tied to the criteria used to evaluate individuals who are promoted to higher steps. Because duties associated with each step tend to be more clearly defined than the somewhat vague reference to "high-quality teaching" used in many merit-pay plans, career-ladder schemes have not drawn as much active opposition from teacher groups as merit-pay plans. More career-ladder programs than merit programs have been adopted. Teachers, however, continue to monitor such schemes carefully to assure that promotion decisions are made on relevant criteria.

Department Chair

The department chair in a secondary school is the person designated to exercise leadership in a specific subject area (English, social studies, mathematics, science, and so forth). Duties vary, but often they include responsibilities in areas such as ordering supplies for department members, evaluating new faculty, coordinating staff development opportunities, and disseminating information about school policies. In general, the department chair functions as a liaison between school administrators and faculty members in her department.

Typically, department chairs are selected from among the most experienced teachers in their respective departments. They tend to be individuals who have credibility both with their teaching colleagues and with school administrators. Often, department chairs teach a reduced load to allow them time to perform other assigned duties. They sometimes receive extra salary, and often they must work more days each year than regular classroom teachers.

Opportunities for people to become department chairs are limited. Only one chair is appointed for each department. In some schools many years go by before a new chair needs to be appointed. One potential advantage of the department chair's role is that it allows an individual to assume some administrative and supervisory responsibilities while he continues to teach. Elevation to the position of department chair is one of the few promotions in education that does not remove a teacher completely from the classroom.

Curriculum Coordinator

This position often goes by one of a number of titles other than *curriculum coordinator*. Among them are *curriculum director, curriculum supervisor*, and *curriculum leader*. By whatever title it is known, this position requires the designated individual to assume leadership in such areas curriculum planning, inservice planning, and instructional-support planning. In small school districts, the curriculum coordinator may have responsibilities for several subject areas and may even continue to teach part-time. In larger districts, curriculum coordinators do not teach. Typically, curriculum coordinators have their offices in the district's central administrative headquarters.

Curriculum coordinators are individuals with a great deal of knowledge about up-to-date trends in the subject area (or areas) for which they are responsible. They are in a position to influence the nature of the instructional program throughout the district in their areas of responsibility. Many curriculum coordinators hold advanced degrees. Often curriculum coordinators work a longer school year than teachers, and they are paid more. Their primary audience is teachers in the district. Especially in medium- and large-sized districts, curriculum coordinators only infrequently work with students in the classroom.

School Administrator

Nearly all school administrators begin their work in education as classroom teachers. By taking advanced courses, often including completion of at least a master's degree and relevant administrative certification requirements, they qualify for administrative positions. These positions exist both at the school level and at the central district administrative level. Some typical administrative positions at the school level are assistant principal and principal. Positions often found in central school administrative headquarters are director of personnel, assistant superintendent, and superintendent.

Administrators have responsibilities requiring some skills that are different from those required of classroom teachers. Much of their work involves preparing budgets, scheduling plans, paperwork related to state and federal guidelines, and evaluation reports on teachers.

Administrators function as official representatives of the schools to the community; hence, administrators must have good public relations skills. School administrators almost always work a longer school year than classroom teachers. They are paid higher salaries than teachers. Because demands of administration are quite different from those of teaching, some individuals who are outstanding teachers may not much care for administration.

School Counselor

Another possible career option for people who begin as classroom teachers is school counseling. In most parts of the country, school counselors must take additional graduate training to qualify for a counseling certificate. Many counselors obtain master's degrees with a school-counseling emphasis. Counselors usually work a longer school year than teachers, and they are paid more. Some teachers who go into counseling choose this option because this role allows them to continue to work directly with students.

In addition to personal and academic counseling, many school counselors also are expected to perform a number of administrative tasks. Sometimes counselors are responsible for establishing the master teaching schedule for a school. Often they are in charge of all standardized testing. They must spend a great deal of time attending special meetings. Time available for working with individual students often is surprisingly limited.

State Education Agency Employee

All states have education departments or agencies that are largely staffed by professionals with backgrounds in education. State education agencies hire people with a variety of backgrounds and for diverse purposes. There often are subject area specialists who are charged with coordinating curriculum guidelines and inservice training throughout the state for teachers in specific subjects (English, social studies, music, science, mathematics, vocational education, physical education, and so forth). There often also are assessment specialists who coordinate statewide testing programs. Teacher education specialists work with colleges and universities to assure that teacher-preparation programs are providing new teachers with appropriate backgrounds.

School counselors are good communicators.

Employees of state education agencies often have had considerable prior experience working in the schools. Most of these positions require people to have at least a master's degree, and some of them require a doctoral degree. Often considerable travel is required. Employees of state education agencies work all year long. Levels of remuneration typically are considerably higher than those of classroom teachers.

Teacher Educator

Individuals who have taught successfully sometimes seek opportunities to share their expertise with future teachers. One way for them to do this is to become a teacher educator. Most teacher educators are faculty members of colleges and universities. A few are employed by large school districts.

Almost always, a teacher educator must hold a doctoral degree. Since most teacher educators are members of college and university faculties, this degree is essential for the teacher educator to meet employment and tenure standards at most institutions of higher learning.

The role of the teacher educator is more varied and complex than is sometimes imagined by those viewing it from the outside. Although exemplary teaching certainly contributes to success as a faculty member in teacher education, still more is necessary. Faculty members must also demonstrate initiative in improving preparation programs, keep up-to-date on findings of researchers, conduct research, write for publication, seek opportunities to make presentations at regional and national meetings, maintain good working relations with other departments and with the schools, serve on large numbers of committees, maintain good links with state education agencies, and counsel students. All of these obligations require processing of massive quantities of paperwork.

A person who enters a doctoral program must devote considerable time to intensive study. About three years of full-time study after the award of the master's degree is typical. Many institutions require that prospective doctoral students spend at least one full year as resident, full-time students on the campus. This means that a teacher interested in doing this must leave her teaching position for at least one year. Many who do decide to pursue a doctorate resign their positions to devote their full attention to their studies. Most universities have graduate assistantships and fellowships that provide modest financial support to individuals doing advanced doctoral work.

Teacher educators typically are employed for nine months a year. Many of them also have opportunities to work during the summer months as well. Salaries are not particularly high. In fact, some beginning teacher educators are paid less than some experienced public school classroom teachers. However, although beginning salaries of teacher educators tend to be modest, top salaries for experienced teacher educators tend to be higher than those paid to classroom teachers.

Individuals considering pursuing a doctoral program and becoming a teacher educator should seek information from reputable and accredited universities that offer doctorates. Some universities that offer doctorates are not widely respected, and an individual holding such a degree is going to have difficulty finding employment as a teacher educator. Discussions with practicing teacher educators can provide useful information. Once several possible universities have been identified, it makes sense to write to them for information about the specific features of their doctoral programs in education. There are important institution-to-institution differences, and someone considering advanced study should look for one that is compatible with his own objectives. For example, one university may have an outstanding program in mathematics education, and another would have special strengths in social studies education.

Opportunities Outside Education

For a variety of reasons, some teachers decide to leave the classroom after just a few years. Does this mean their preparation was wasted? Not at all. There are employment options outside of the public schools for individuals with backgrounds in teaching.

Many large private firms employ people with good teaching and curriculum-development skills to work in their employee training programs. Education in industry is becoming big business. Many large corporations have special training divisions. The term *human resource development*, often abbreviated "HRD," is often used to describe the corporate training function. There is a large national professional organization, the American Society for Training and Development (ASTD), that is devoted exclusively to promoting the interests of its members who are educators in industry. The group produces a fine journal titled *Training and Development*. People interested in the possibility of working as an educator in industry should look through several issues to get a feel for the kinds of things corporate trainers do.

In addition to working as educators in the private sector, teacher preparation provides individuals with the kinds of communications and interpersonal relations skills needed in many other fields. Educational materials sales people, for example, often are individuals who once were classroom teachers. Many occupations that demand face-to-face contact with the general public have proved attractive to former teachers.

Final Comments

Teaching is complex. Changing student populations, federal and state education regulations, public expectations, and knowledge about what works in the classroom require teachers to commit to career-long professional development. Preparation for teaching is not something that is begun and ended. It is a process that may take unexpected twists and turns but that, regardless of unanticipated conditions, goes resolutely onward. Teachers who enter the profession embracing the idea that change will be their constant companion will find they have made a highly satisfying career choice; those who anticipate an ordered and predictable world will be disappointed.

Teachers must make dozens of decisions each day. Our intent in this book has been to provide some principles that have been followed by teachers known to make good decisions. We hope some of these ideas will help you. We also recognize that not everyone should be a teacher. If it turns out you are one of these people, that is certainly all right. We wish you well in whatever career path proves satisfying for you.

For those of you who do decide to teach, we hope you will enjoy some of the same exciting moments and rewards we have experienced as teachers. We are proud of our profession. We look forward to welcoming you to one of civilization's proudest roles—that of the teacher.

Table 20.1   Summary Table

Main Points	Explanation
Career-Long Preparation	Preparation for teaching does not end with completion of the preservice program and the award of the teaching certificate. It is a process that goes on as long as an individual remains working as a classroom teacher.
Pretraining Phase	Prospective teachers pick up many attitudes about teachers and teaching even before beginning their formal preparation programs. Often they wish to model themselves on teachers they particularly liked when they were in school. These influences are to be expected. However, in a few instances, preservice teachers assume that all they need to do to succeed in the classroom is repeat behaviors of their own favorite teachers. When this position is taken, preservice teachers sometimes start their programs falsely assuming they already know everything they need for success in the classroom. Individuals who enter programs with this assumption and who fail to commit their best effort to their preservice course work often do not do well during student teaching.
Preservice Phase	The preservice phase is the formal preparation program a prospective teacher goes through. Most preservice programs are offered through colleges and universities.
General Studies Component	Comprising about 40 percent of the typical preservice program, the general studies component exposes preservice teachers to a broad array of content drawn from mathematics, the humanities and social sciences, science, and English. The purpose is to develop their sensitivity to historical, scientific, cultural, and technological issues.
Academic Major or Teaching Specialization	Courses in this area provide preservice teachers with depth of knowledge in the subject or subjects they are preparing to teach. These courses account for about 40 percent of the teacher preparation program for future secondary school teachers.
Professional Education Component	The professional education component includes courses designed to provide future teachers with the instructional and management skills they will need in the classroom. The courses comprise about 20 percent of the teacher-preparation program for future secondary school teachers.
Induction Year	The term *induction year* is applied to the first year of full-time teaching. During this time, the teacher is formally "inducted" into the profession. For many teachers, the first year is difficult. They must assume all responsibilities of the teacher. Unlike student teaching, regular help is no longer available from a supervising teacher or a university supervisor. Some school districts recognize the stresses associated with induction-year teaching and assign mentor teachers (teachers with several years experience) to work closely with newcomers. In some districts, first-year teachers are assigned somewhat lighter teaching loads than other staff teachers.
Staff-Development Activities	Many staff-development options are available to teachers. Inservice education programs sponsored by the school districts or other education agencies are one option. College and university courses are another. Many professional associations also provide staff-development opportunities either through their meetings or their professional journals.

Main Points	Explanation
General Teachers' Organizations	General teachers' organizations attempt to serve the interests of teachers in all subject areas and grade levels. They do so in various ways, including lobbying federal and state lawmakers to support legislation favorable to teachers' interests. The two largest general teachers' organizations are the National Education Association (NEA) and the American Federation of Teachers (AFT).
Specialty Teachers' Organizations	Specialty teachers' organizations serve the interests of teachers working in a single subject area or teachers interested in working with special kinds of students. These organizations serve their members in various ways. They sometimes engage in lobbying activities. They sponsor national, regional, state, and local meetings that provide opportunities for teachers to learn about new techniques and to hear reports of recent research. They publish journals that disseminate information of interest to members or subscribers throughout the country.
Merit Pay	The merit-pay approach to improving education seeks to identify high-quality teachers and pay them more. Many teachers' groups oppose this approach. Their contention is that high-quality teaching is hard to define and measure. Hence, people identified as "meritorious" may be selected for such reasons as their pleasant personalities or their close friendship with administrators.
Career Ladders	The career-ladder approach to paying some teachers more than others assumes that some teachers logically may be assigned to do things that are different from other teachers. As teachers are assigned new and more taxing responsibilities (for example, special curriculum-development assignments), they may be elevated to a higher step on the "ladder." This means that they will be paid more out of a recognition of their increased span of responsibility. Though schemes vary, many career ladders have about three steps. Step-two teachers are selected from the best step-one teachers. Step-three teachers are selected from the best step-two teachers.
Department Chair	The department chair heads an academic department. He or she may be relieved of some instructional responsibilities to allow time for other duties to be discharged. The department chair often works a longer school year than other teachers. Responsibilities frequently include such things as ordering materials for the department, evaluating new faculty members, and serving as a general liaison between department members and school administrators.
Curriculum Coordinator	A curriculum coordinator (sometimes known by other titles including *director of curriculum* and *curriculum specialist*) often works out of a school district's central administrative offices. He or she is responsible for leadership of all kinds in areas related to the subject or subjects for which he or she is responsible. Curriculum coordinators typically have advanced degrees and come from a background of successful classroom teaching.

Table 20.1   Summary Table *(continued)*

Main Points	Explanation
School Administrators	There are administrators in school districts both in individual buildings and in the central administrative offices. Administrators are individuals who have pursued advanced academic training to qualify for administrative certificates. Usually they also have advanced degrees. Most administrators begin their careers in education as classroom teachers. They work longer school years than the typical teacher.
School Counselor	A school counselor has responsibility for personal and academic advising of students. In addition, counselors also perform some administrative tasks. For example, they often have extensive responsibilities for administering the standardized testing program. Typically counselors have pursued an advanced program of academic study leading to certification as a school counselor. Often they hold advanced degrees. Many, though not all, school counselors have worked as classroom teachers.
State Education Agency Employee	Each state has its own education department or agency. These organizations employ large numbers of education professionals. Often these are individuals from public school backgrounds who have taken advanced course work. Many have master's degrees and doctoral degrees. They have statewide leadership responsibility for areas under their supervision. Often much travel is required of people holding these positions.
Teacher Educator	Most teacher educators are members of college or university faculties. Generally they are expected to hold doctoral degrees. Typically, they hold nine-month contracts, though many of them have opportunities to work during the summer months as well. Today, most teacher educators have spent some time as classroom teachers before going on to do their doctoral work.
Employment Outside Education	Some people who have been trained as teachers are not employed by school districts. Large numbers of them work in training divisions of businesses. Their public relations and communications skills make them attractive to employers in businesses of all kinds where meeting the public is an expectation.

Review of Key Ideas

- Professional development of a teacher is a career-long obligation. The teacher-preparation program is only a beginning. Successful teachers tend to be people who are comfortable with their need to be life-long learners.

- Teachers' attitudes toward the profession frequently are strongly influenced by what they have experienced even before beginning a teacher-preparation program. Often, for example, behaviors of teachers they particularly liked strongly affect their attitudes. These experiences sometimes lead prospective teachers to assume they already know all they need to become effective classroom practitioners. When this happens they may fail to fully commit their intellectual resources to their preparation program. Individuals who do this often experience difficulty during student teaching.

- Preservice preparation programs for prospective teachers typically include three basic components. The general studies component exposes them to information from liberal arts, the social sciences, mathematics, and the sciences. The academic major or teaching specialization includes courses in the subject or subjects the prospective teacher is preparing to teach. The professional education component, comprising only about one-fifth of the program total, includes courses focusing on the instruction and management skills a teacher needs to work with students in secondary school classrooms.

- The first year of teaching is sometimes called the induction year. Many beginners find this to be a particularly difficult year. For the first time, they have all the responsibilities of the classroom teacher with no built-in support system (e.g., services of student-teacher supervisors and university supervisors are no longer available). Time management often is a particularly vexing problem. Today, many school districts recognize the challenges facing first-year teachers. Often they provide mentor teachers to work with beginners. Sometimes first-year teachers are assigned somewhat lighter teaching loads than more experienced teachers.

- Many kinds of staff-development activities are available for teachers. Medium- and large-sized districts often offer their own inservice education programs. These may include opportunities for teachers to hear speakers, participate in workshops, and share ideas with others. Sometimes teachers are required to participate in staff-development activities; sometimes they are optional.

- Many teachers continue to take college and university courses while they teach. In many school districts, higher salaries are paid to teachers who have completed prescribed amounts of academic work. Many courses are offered in the evening so teachers can take them during the school year. Even more courses for teachers ordinarily are available during the summer months. Some districts place restrictions on the number of courses that first-year teachers can take during the school year.

- Professional organizations regularly offer opportunities for teachers to improve their skills. Annual meetings regularly feature sessions where experts demonstrate techniques and share research findings. Many of these organizations publish journals that also are an important source of professional-development information.

- There are two basic types of professional organizations. General organizations such as the National Education Association and the American Federation of Teachers represent interests of the entire teaching profession. Members are drawn from all grade levels and subject areas. Specialty organizations such as the National Council for the Social Studies, the Council for Exceptional Children, and the Music Teachers National Association serve interests of teachers working within a given subject area. Affiliation with these groups helps teachers develop a common community of interest. Newcomers to the profession find membership provides them with numerous opportunities to learn more about their chosen field.

- Merit pay is a controversial approach that seeks to improve education by paying high-quality teachers more than others. A difficulty with this effort concerns defining precisely what is meant by *high quality*. Absent agreement on the meaning of this phrase, there are concerns that teachers may be identified as meritorious based on their personalities or on their relationships with administrators.

- Career ladders are schemes that allocate higher salaries for teachers who have been assigned specialized duties that go beyond those expected of all teachers. They are based on the idea that all teachers need not do exactly the same things. For example, some teachers may have special curriculum development responsibilities not expected of others. Teachers selected for higher steps on the career ladder have more responsibilities than teachers at lower steps.

- In many secondary schools, each department has a department chair. This person acts as the head of the unit. She may have responsibilities including ordering materials, evaluating new faculty members, coordinating staff development opportunities, and disseminating policy information. The department chair acts as a liaison between department faculty members and school administrators. Often department chairs have a reduced teaching load. Frequently they work a longer school year than classroom teachers.

- Curriculum coordinators ordinarily work out of central administrative offices. These specialists have responsibility for academic programming either for one or more subjects or for students in specific grades. Ordinarily, curriculum coordinators are individuals who have been teachers and who have taken advanced academic training. In many places, curriculum coordinators must hold at least a master's degree.

- Nearly all school administrators begin their work in education as classroom teachers. They go on to take additional course work leading to administrative certification and, usually, to an advanced degree. They typically work a longer school year than classroom teachers.

- School counselors are individuals who have taken special graduate-level training in counseling. Most of them are former classroom teachers. They typically work a longer school year than classroom teachers. In addition to personal and academic counseling, school counselors often perform some administrative duties related to such things as academic scheduling, standardized test scheduling, and administration.

- State education departments and agencies employ large numbers of individuals with backgrounds in professional education. Many of these individuals have been classroom teachers, and they tend to hold advanced degrees. Many are subject-area specialists who are responsible for coordinating curriculum guidelines and inservice training throughout the state for teachers in their specialty areas. Many positions with state education departments and agencies require considerable travel.

- Teacher educators most frequently are members of college and university faculties. Ordinarily, to qualify for a full-time faculty position in education at a college or university a person needs a doctoral degree. Many institutions will not hire people who have not had a certain minimum number of years working as a classroom teacher. Entry-level salaries of teacher educators are often lower than those paid experienced classroom teachers. However, experienced teacher educators tend to be paid more than experienced classroom teachers. Salaries vary considerably from place to place.

- Today, many people with backgrounds in teacher education do not work in the schools. Many work in training and development departments in industry. The kinds of public relations and communications skills people exiting teacher education programs have often make them attractive to employers in all kinds of businesses where contact with the public is frequent.

Follow-Up Questions and Activities

Questions

1. Why is it important for teachers to regard professional development as a career-long obligation?

2. How might beliefs prospective teachers have acquired before beginning their teacher-preparation programs interfere with their professional development?

3. Of what value is the general education component of a teacher preparation program?

4. Do courses a prospective teacher takes as part of the academic major component of his professional preparation program always closely match what he will be expected to teach?

5. What kinds of things are emphasized during the professional education component of a teacher-preparation program for future secondary teachers?

6. Some critics have alleged that far too large a portion of future teachers' time is spent taking professional education courses. Is this a valid criticism?

7. Why do many beginners experience problems during their induction year?

8. Some school districts restrict the number of college and university courses that may be taken at night during the school year by first-year teachers. Are such policies wise?

9. How would you respond to this statement: "The best thing we could do improve our schools would be to institute a rigorous merit pay system"?

10. What are some career options both within and without education for individuals who have followed a teacher-preparation program?

Activities

1. Take a few minutes to write down some ideas you have about characteristics of "good" teaching. Where did your ideas come from? How might you check to see

whether others would support your ideas? Are your ideas based only on personal opinion, or do you have some other kinds of evidence to back them up? Share your views with your instructor.

2. Visit some administrators in a local school district. Ask if the district does anything special to help first-year teachers. Share your findings with others in your class.

3. Interview some students who are doing their student teaching. What kinds of responsibilities have they been given? To what extent do they find help is available from their supervising teachers? From college and university supervisors? How adequate do they think their student teaching experience is as a preparation for the first year of teaching? How closely are they supervised? Report your findings to others in your class.

4. Interview several teachers about their first year of teaching. What surprised them? What things might have been done to make their first year easier? Team up with several others who have conducted similar interviews. Reporting as a panel, share your findings with others in your class.

5. Do some research on career-ladder and merit-pay schemes that have been adopted in various places. Report on specific provisions of two or three examples of each. Prepare a written report in which you comment on the strengths and weaknesses of each of your examples.

References

DeLandsheere, G. "Concepts in Teacher Education." In M. Dunkin (ed.). *The International Encyclopedia of Teaching and Teacher Education*. New York: Pergamon Press, 1987, pp. 77–83.

Holmes Group. *Tomorrow's Teachers*. East Lansing, MI: Holmes Group, 1986.

Kluender, M. "Teacher Education Programs in the 1980's: Some Selected Characteristics." *Journal of Teacher Education* (July–August 1984), pp. 33–35.

Nemser, S. "Learning to Teach." In L. Shulman and G. Sykes (eds.). *Handbook of Teaching and Policy*. New York: Longman, 1983.

Odell, S. "Induction Support of New Teachers: A Functional Approach." *Journal of Teacher Education* (January–February, 1986), pp. 26–29.

Ryan, K. *The Induction of New Teachers*. Fastback #237. Bloomington, IN: Phi Delta Kappa, 1986.

Name Index

Abramson, T., 196, 215
Alsalam, N., 7, 11, 13–14, 25, 167–168, 186, 474, 482
Anderson, L., 224, 248
Armstrong, D. G., 34, 49, 89, 97, 169, 171, 175, 186
Aschner, M. J., 320, 334
Asfar, S., 334
Ayers, W. C., 54, 71

Baker, K., 222, 247
Bang-Jensen, V., 493
Barlow, J., 278, 298
Barr, R., 79, 83, 97
Barry, T. N., 6, 25
Baum, S., 207, 215
Berliner, D. C., 63, 71
Bernstein, H., 489
Beyer, B. K., 360, 376, 380, 389
Bloom, B., 112, 125–126, 192, 215, 255, 274
Boberg, A. L., 426, 449
Boles, H. W., 225, 247
Borich, G., 173, 186, 360, 389, 403, 419
Bowman, B., 166, 171, 186
Brandt, R., 351, 357
Braun, C., 58, 71
Briggs, L. J., 34, 49, 155, 162
Brophy, J., 32, 34, 38, 49, 55, 58, 62–63, 65, 68, 71,
    74–75, 79, 89, 97, 231, 248, 252, 255, 258, 275,
    308, 311–312, 325–326, 334, 338–339, 344–345,
    351, 357, 360, 389, 392–393, 402, 419, 486,
    489–490, 494
Brown, B. B., 207, 215
Brown, R., 490
Bruner, J., 84, 97

Cazden, C., 324, 334
Chandler, M. O., 12–13, 26, 477, 482

Charp, S., 279, 298
Clark, C., 130, 142–143, 162, 226, 248
Clements, B., 61, 71, 403, 420
Cohen, E. G., 393, 397, 419
Colachico, D., 191, 215
Comer, J. P., 172–173, 186
Connors, E., 528, 549
Cooper, H., 327, 334
Corno, L., 360, 389
Couture, D., 291, 299
Cuban, L., 281–282, 285, 298

Darling-Hammond, L., 489
Davenport, J. A., 225, 248
Dawson, T., 287, 298
DeGarmo, C., 320, 334
DeLandsheere, G., 555–556, 580
Denton, J. J., 34, 49
Dewey, J., 366, 389
Donato, R., 173, 186
Doyle, W., 218–219, 248
Dunn, K., 375–376, 389, 403, 419
Dunn, R., 375–376, 389, 403, 419

Eccles, J., 313, 334
Eggen, P., 133, 162
Egnatuck, T., 10, 25
Emmer, E., 61, 71, 224, 248, 403, 420
Erickson, R., 169, 186
Evertson, C., 61, 71, 224, 248, 403, 420

Feiman-Nemser, S., 494
Fenstermacher, G. D., 432–433, 449
Ferre, A., 104, 126
Fischer, L., 517, 521, 530, 549
Floden, R., 494

French, J. R. R., 226, 248
Friesen, J.W., 426, 449

Gagné, R. M., 34, 49, 155, 162
Gallagher, J., 334
Georgiady, N. P., 10, 25
Gifford, B., 279, 298
Glaser, R., 258, 274
Glasser, W., 226, 236, 248, 313, 334, 429, 432, 449
Good, T., 32, 34, 38, 49, 55, 58, 62, 65, 68, 71, 74–75,
    79, 89, 97, 231, 248, 252, 255, 258, 275, 308, 312,
    325–326, 334, 338–339, 344–345, 351, 357, 360,
    389, 392–393, 402, 420, 486, 489–490, 494
Goodlad, J. I., 424, 449
Graham, S., 204, 215
Grant, C. A., 166, 179–180, 186
Gronlund, N., 105, 126
Grunwald, P., 286, 298
Guskey, T., 255, 275

Harmin, M., 436–438, 449
Harris, K. R., 204, 215
Hawkridge, D., 280, 298
Henderson, J. G., 57, 59, 71
Henson, K. T., 171, 186
Henze, R., 173, 186
Hidi, S., 64, 71
Hoffman, M. S., 25
Holubec, E., 286, 298, 412, 420
Howe, L. W., 438, 450
Hunter, M., 33–34, 49, 155, 162, 344, 357

Jarolimek, J., 84, 97
Johnson, D. W., 253, 275, 285–286, 298, 405, 412,
    420
Johnson, R. T., 253, 275, 285–286, 298, 405, 412, 420
Johnstone, K., 489
Jones, R. H., 232, 248

Kaskowitz, D., 341, 357
Kauchak, D., 133, 162
Kelly, C., 517, 521, 530, 549
Kirschenbaum, H., 438, 450
Klinger, E., 313, 334
Kluender, M., 554–555, 580
Kohlberg, L., 440–441, 443–444, 449
Krathwohl, D., 116, 126
Kulm, G., 458, 482

Kurshan, B., 287, 298

Latta, R., 261, 275
Leinhardt, G., 309, 334, 351, 357
Lerner, J. W., 202–203, 215
Lerner, S. R., 202–203, 215
Levin, T., 55, 71
Lipman, M., 375, 389
Long, R., 55, 71
Lottich, K. V., 191, 215
Lounsbury, J. H., 9, 25
Lubart, T. I., 209, 215
Lucas, T., 173, 186

McKernan, J. R., 279, 298
McLaughlin, M., 489, 495
Marshall, R., 12–13, 25, 167, 176, 186
Marzano, B., 321, 334
Masia, B., 126
Mecklenburger, J. A., 279, 298
Meister, C., 310
Meyer, A. E., 154, 162
Millies, P., 53, 71
Monks, R., 534, 549
Moore, K., 107, 126, 319, 324
Morse, J. A., 104, 126
Muth, C. R., 10, 25

Nemser, S., 553, 580
Nielsen, B. S., 279, 298

Oakes, J., 171, 186
Odell, S., 493, 559, 580
Ogbu, J. H., 171, 180, 186
Ogle, L. T., 7, 11–14, 25, 167–168, 186, 474, 482
Olsen, R., 104, 126
Oser, F., 440, 449

Perkins, D., 374, 389
Perry, J., 334
Peterson, P., 142–143, 162, 226, 248
Pfeifer, R., 495
Phillipo, J., 288, 299
Piaget, J., 17–19
Popham, W. J., 111, 126
Popper, S. H., 9, 26
Posner, G., 34, 49, 89, 97, 153–154, 162
Proulx, E., 534, 549

Raths, L., 436–438, 449
Raven, B. H., 226, 248
Redfield, D., 321, 334
Reid, R., 204, 215
Renzulli, J., 206, 215
Rest, J., 426, 438, 450
Reynolds, A., 57, 59–60, 63, 71
Rist, R. C., 178, 186
Rodriguez, S., 489
Rogers, C., 427, 450
Rogers, G. T., 167–168, 186, 474, 482
Rogers, W., 424, 450
Rohrkemper, M., 308, 334
Romano, L. G., 10, 25
Rosenshine, B., 310, 320, 334, 339, 341, 343, 344–345, 348–349, 357
Rousseau, E., 321, 334
Rowe, M. B., 324, 335
Roy, P., 412, 420
Ruggiero, V. R., 360, 374, 389
Russell, D., 33–34, 49, 155, 162
Ryan, K., 553, 557–558, 580

Sanford, J., 61, 71, 403, 420
Savage, M. K., 343, 357
Savage, T. V., 34, 49, 169, 171, 186, 228, 233, 248
Schimmel, D., 517, 521, 530, 549
Schnur, J. U., 191, 215
Schubert, W. H., 54, 71
Schulz, J. B., 203, 215
Scriven, M., 426, 450, 456–457, 482
Secada, W. G., 166, 186
Shavelson, R., 52, 71
Shepard, L. A., 458, 482
Simon, S. B., 436–438, 450
Simon-McWilliams, E., 171, 186
Sirotnik, K. A., 424, 449
Sizer, T. R., 8, 26, 218–219, 248
Slavin, R. E., 286, 299, 393, 405–406, 409, 420
Sleeter, C. E., 179–180, 186
Smith, H., 319, 335

Snow, R. E., 360, 389
Soder, R., 424, 449
Soloman, G., 279, 286, 299
Stallings, J. A., 341, 357
Stedman, L., 427, 450
Stern, J. D., 12–13, 26, 477, 482
Sternberg, L., 207, 215
Sternberg, R. J., 209, 215
Stevens, R., 321, 335, 339, 341, 343, 345, 348–349, 357
Strike, K. A., 424, 450
Suchman, J. R., 371, 389

Taba, H., 84, 97
Tanner, D., 7, 26
Tanner, L. N., 7, 26, 226, 248
Tatum, B. D., 168–169, 186
Tillman, M. H., 109, 126
Tisher, R. P., 126
Truesdell, L. A., 196, 215
Tucker, M. S., 279, 298
Turnbull, A. P., 203, 215
Tyler, R. W., 457, 482

Vars, G. E., 9, 25

Washor, E., 291, 299
Watson, B., 286, 299
Webb, J., 424, 450
Weiner, B., 317, 335
Weinstein, C., 230, 248
White, R. T., 126
Wigfield, A., 313, 334
Wiggins, G., 311, 335, 458, 482
Wilds, E. H., 191, 215
Willis, S., 405, 420
Wise, A., 489
Worsham, M., 61, 71, 403, 420

Yeager, N. C., 377, 389
Yinger, R. A., 130, 142, 162

Subject Index

ABCD format for preparing objectives, 107–110
Academic learning time, 63
Acceleration programs, 207–209
Active teaching. *See* Direct instruction
ADD. *See* Attention deficit disorder
Affective domain, 114–119. *See also* Affective
    learning
Affective learning, 423–444
    classroom meetings, 429–432
    issues, values, and consequences analysis, 434–436
    Kohlberg's moral reasoning, 441–443
    moral dilemma discussion, 443–444
    moral discourse, 440
    nondirective teaching, 427–429
    Rest's model for teaching morality, 438–439
    values clarification, 436–438
African-American students. *See* Minority students
AFT. *See* American Federation of Teachers
AIDS testing, 533–534
Aims, 101–102
Allocated time, 62
American Alliance for Health, Physical Education,
    Recreation, and Dance, 41, 564
American Association of Mental Deficiency, 198
American Federation of Teachers, 562–563
American Music Teacher, 565
American Society for Training and Development, 573
American Vocational Association, 41
Art Education, 565
Association for Childhood Education International, 41
Attainment value, 313
Attention deficit disorder, 202–203
Authentic evaluation, 458–460

Bannister v. Paradis, 521, 549
Behavioral objectives. *See* Preparing objectives

Bellnier v. Lund, 526, 549
Bilingual programs, 14, 173–174
Black students. *See* Minority students
Board of Trustees v. Stubblefield, 540, 549
Brainstorming, 374–375
Breadth and depth of content, 82–84
Brown v. Board of Education, 194–195

Cardinal principles of secondary education, 8
Career ladders, 567–568
CD-ROM, 288–289
Certificates. *See* Teaching certificates
Child-abuse reporting, 534
Chronological sequencing, 91
Classroom management, 221–242, 327–328
    corporal punishment, 242
    monitoring, 327–328
    physical environment, 228–230
    preventing problems, 233–235
    principles to guide responses, 235–237
    sequential escalation of responses, 237–242
    teacher consistency, 228
    teacher leadership and authority, 225–227
    time, 230–233
Classroom meetings, 429–432
Clear communication, 318–319, 322–324
Coercive power, 227
Cognitive domain, 112–114, 474–476
Comer, James P., 172–173
Comer-model schools, 172–173
Commission on Reorganization of Secondary
    Education, 1918, 8
Committee of Nine. *See* National Education
    Association Committee of Nine
Committee of Ten. *See* National Education
    Association Committee of Ten

Common school, 191
Completion items, 469–471
Comprehensive high school, 8
Computers, 269, 285–286
Computing Teacher, 564
Concepts, 84–85, 137–139
Conditions of employment, 528–529
Content breakdown, 84–88
    concepts, 84–85
    facts, 84
    generalizations and principles, 86–87
    structure of knowledge, 84–87
Content selection, 77–89
    breadth and depth decisions, 82–84
    content breakdown, 84–88
    influences on decisions, 80–82
    opportunity to learn, 79
Continuing contract, 532
Contracts. *See* Teaching contracts
Cooperative learning, 405–414
    jigsaw, 409–412
    learning together, 412–414
    student-teams-achievement, 406–408
    teams-games-tournaments, 408–409
Copyright law, 538–539
Corporal punishment, 242
Council on Exceptional Children, 41, 564
Counseling, 35–36
Creative thinking, 373–375
Credentials. *See* Teaching certificates
Critical thinking, 375–376
Cultural minorities. *See* Minority students
Curriculum coordinators, 569
Curriculum development role of teachers, 38–40

Data bases, 286–288
Data retrieval charts, 369–371
Davis v. Meek, 525, 549
Decision making, 51–71, 132–135, 380–384
    factors influencing instructional decisions, 53–57
    using research findings, 57–65, 68
    variables influencing planning, 132–135
Denton v. South Kitsap School District No. 402, 540, 549
Department chairs, 568–569
Developing objectives. *See* Preparing objectives
Dewey, John, 366
Diagnosing students, 31–32
Differential staffing, 568

Direct instruction, 338–353
    appropriate use, 343–344
    basic characteristics, 340–343
    model for a lesson, 344–353
    positives and negatives, 339
Directory of Nationally Certified Teachers, 565
Disabilities of students, 194–204
    attention deficit disorder (ADD), 202–203
    Education for All Handicapped Children Act, 195
    emotional disturbance, 203–204
    hearing impairment, 199–200
    Individuals with Disabilities Education Act, 195
    learning disability, 201–202
    mainstreaming, 195
    mental retardation, 198–199
    physical and health impairment, 203
    Public Law 94–142, 195
    Public Law 101–476, 195
    speech impairment, 200–201
    visual impairment, 201
Disciplining students. *See* Classroom management
Dismissal of teachers, 532–533
Distance learning, 290–291
Doe v. Renfrow, 526, 549
Drug-abuse testing, 533–534
Due process, 521–524, 532–533
    applied to teacher dismissal, 532–533
    expulsion, 523–524
    procedural component, 522
    substantive component, 522
    suspension, 523

Educable students, 198–199
Education for All Handicapped Children Act, 195–196
Education Index, 42, 180
Electronic satellite links, 293
Emotional disturbance, 203–204
Engaged time, 62–63
English Journal, 566
Enrichment programs, 207–209
Essay items, 468–469
Ethnic groups. *See* Minority students
Ethnic minorities. *See* Minority students
Evaluating students, 35, 111, 141, 195–197, 209, 263–269, 452–477
    authentic evaluation, 458–460
    completion items, 469–471

essay items, 468–469
evaluation checklists, 467
formal approaches, 464–477
headlines and articles, 462
informal approaches, 460–464
matching items, 471–472
multiple-choice items, 472–476
rating scales, 465–467
standardized tests, 464–465
student-produced tests, 463–464
teacher observation, 462
teacher-student discussion, 462–463
true-false items, 476–477
Evaluating teachers, 486–504
data from classroom observation, 498–503
data about student learning, 496–497
data from student opinions, 497–498
mentoring, 493–494
peer coaching, 492–493
peer evaluation, 491
portfolios, 503–504
providers of data, 488–495
purposes, 487–488
self-evaluation, 489–491
superior evaluation, 494–495
Evaluative checklists, 467
Exceptional Children, 564
Exceptional students, 189–219
attention deficit disorder (ADD), 202–203
Education for All Handicapped Children Act, 195–196
emotional disturbance, 203–204
gifted and talented students, 204–212
hearing impairment, 199–200
history of programs, 191–192
Individuals with Disabilities Education Act, 195–196
learning disability, 201–202
mental retardation, 198–199
physical and health impairment, 203
slow learners, 192–194
speech impairment, 200–201
students with disabilities, 194–204
visual impairment, 201
Excessive use of force, 535
Expert power, 226
Explicit teaching. *See* Direct instruction
Expulsion, 523–524
External constraint sequencing, 91

Facts, 84
Family Educational Rights and Privacy Act, 528
Fantasy stage of professional development, 553–554
Financing secondary education, 6–7
First year of teaching, 558–559
Formal approaches to evaluating students, 464–477
completion items, 469–471
essay items, 468–469
evaluative checklists, 467
matching items, 471–472
multiple-choice items, 472–476
rating scales, 465–467
true-false items, 476–477
Formative evaluation, 457
Fourteenth Amendment to the U.S. Constitution, 522
Fourth Amendment to the U.S. Constitution, 525
Freedom of speech and expression, 518–520

Gagné and Briggs lesson model, 155–156
Gender issues, 524–525
Generalizations, 86–87, 137–139
Gifted Child Quarterly, 565
Gifted and talented students, 204–212
acceleration programs, 207–209
enrichment programs, 207–209
evaluating, 209
identification, 206
Office of Gifted and Talented, 205
Public Law 91–230, 205
Public Law 93–380, 205
Glasser, William, 226, 236, 313, 429, 432
Goal-directed teaching, 308–309
Goals, 101
Goss v. Lopez, 516, 521, 549

Hazelwood School District v. Kuhlmeier, 518, 549
Health Education, 564
Hearing impairment, 199–200
Hispanic students. *See* Minority students
History of secondary schools, 6–11, 191–192
cardinal principles, 8
comprehensive high school, 8
junior high school, 8–9
middle school, 9–11
programs for exceptional students, 191–192
senior high school, 6–8
HRD. *See* Human resource development
Human resource development, 573

Hunter, Madeline, 33–34, 155
Hunter and Russell lesson model, 155

IDEA. *See* Individuals with Disabilities Education
       Act
IEP. *See* Individualized education program
Independent learning, 261
Indirect instruction, 359–383
   brainstorming, 374–375
   creative thinking, 373–375
   critical thinking, 375–376
   decision making, 380–384
   inquiry teaching, 365–373
   metacognition, 361–363
   problem solving, 378–380
Individualized education program, 195, 197
Individualized instruction, 251–269
   altering content, 256–258
   altering goals, 257–260
   altering method of learning, 258
   altering rate, 254–256
   independent learning, 261
   learning activity packages (LAPs), 261–264
   learning centers, 264–267
   learning contracts, 259–260
   learning stations, 267–269
Individuals with Disabilities Education Act, 195–196
Induction year, 558–559
Informal approaches to evaluating students, 460–464
   headlines and articles, 462
   student-produced tests, 463–464
   teacher observation, 462
   teacher-student discussion, 462–463
Ingraham v. Wright, 535, 549
In loco parentis, 512, 517–518
Inner city programs, 172–173
Inquiry teaching, 365–373
   basic steps, 366–369
   comparing, contrasting, generalizing, 369–371
   decision making, 380–384
   delimiting and focusing, 371–373
   visualizing thinking, 377
Inservice education, 560–561
Inside and outside, 395–397
Instructional approach selection, 33–34. *See also*
       Teaching techniques
Instructional decision making. *See* Decision making
Instructional objectives. *See* Preparing objectives

Instructional tasks, 30–35, 51–71, 77–91, 100–121,
      130–157, 189–212, 221–242, 251–269,
      277–293, 302–328, 338–353, 423–444,
      452–477
   affective learning, 423–444
   balancing breadth and depth, 311
   choosing and implementing instructional
      approaches, 33–34
   classroom management, 221–242, 327–328
   clear communication, 318–319
   concluding lessons, 328
   content selection, 77–91
   cooperative learning, 405–414
   decision making, 51–71
   developing objectives, 32–33, 100–121
   diagnosing students, 31–32
   direct instruction, 338–353
   effective instruction elements, 302–328
   electronic technologies, 277–293
   evaluating students, 35, 111, 141, 195–197, 209,
      263–269, 452–477
   exceptional students, 189–212
   goal-directed teaching, 308–309
   indirect instruction, 359–383
   individualized education program, 195, 197
   individualizing instruction, 251–269
   information sources, 54–57
   learning students' characteristics, 309
   lesson planning, 63–68, 132, 150–157
   matching students to the program, 88–89
   modeling, 193
   monitoring, 327–328, 342
   motivating students, 59–61, 312–318
   organizing content, 77–91
   praise, 325–326
   providing for practice, 326
   reinforcement, 325
   scaffolding, 310–311
   sequencing content, 89–91
   small group learning, 394–405
   teacher questioning, 320–324
   unit planning, 131–132, 135–150
   using research findings, 57–65
Instructional technology, 269, 277–293
   CD-ROM, 288–289
   characteristics of electronic technologies,
      280–281
   computers, 285–286

data bases, 286–288
electronic satellite links, 293
forces opposing new technologies, 281–283
interactive distance learning, 290–291
interactive videodisks, 289–290
optical disks, 291–293
rationale, 278–279
videocassettes, 291
Instructional units, 135–150
elements of a unit, 136–142
formatting, 143–150
planning process, 142–143
sample unit, 144–150
Intellectual development patterns, 17–19, 22
Interactive distance learning, 290–291
Interactive videodisks, 289–290
Interest value, 313–314
International Council for Computers in Education, 42, 564
International Reading Association, 42, 564–565
Intrinsic value, 313–314
Investigative role group, 399–402
Issues, values, and consequences analysis, 434–436

Jefferson, Thomas, 191
Jigsaw, 409–412
Journal of College Science Teaching, 567
Journal of Physical Education, Recreation, and Dance, 564
Journal of Reading, 565
Journal for Research in Mathematics Education, 566
Junior high school, 8–9

Kalamazoo case, 6
Kingsville Independent School District v. Cooper, 537, 549
Kohlberg, Lawrence, 440–441, 443–444
Kohlberg's moral reasoning, 441–443

LAPs. *See* Learning activity packages
Latino students. *See* Minority students
Learning activity packages, 261–264
Learning centers, 264–267
Learning contracts, 259–260
Learning disability, 201–202. *See also* Disabilities of students
Learning objectives. *See* Preparing objectives
Learning stations, 267–269

Learning theory, 55
Learning together, 412–414
Lectura y Vida, 565
Legal issues affecting students, 517–528
dress and appearance, 521
due process, 521–524
family rights and privacy, 527–528
freedom of conscience, 520–521
freedom of speech and expression, 518–520
gender issues, 524–525
in loco parentis, 512, 517–518
search and seizure, 525–527
Legal issues affecting teachers, 528–540
academic freedom, 536–538
AIDS testing, 533–534
conditions of employment, 528–529
copyright law, 538–539
dismissal and due process, 532–533
drug-abuse testing, 533–534
excessive use of force, 535
freedom of expression, 536–538
liability issues, 534–536
negligence, 535–536
reporting child abuse, 534
teachers' private lives, 540
teaching certificates, 528–529
teaching contracts, 530–532
tort liability, 534–536
Legitimate power, 227
Lesson planning, 63–68, 132, 150–157, 194–204
clarity, 64
enhancing achievement, 65
formats, 156–157
Gagné and Briggs model, 155–156
gifted and talented students, 209–212
historical models, 153–154
Hunter and Russell model, 155
modern-day formats, 154–155
pacing, 68
process, 152–153
students with disabilities, 194–204
Licenses. *See* Teaching certificates

Magnet high school, 256
Mainstreaming, 195
Management role of teachers, 37–38
Mann, Horace, 191
Matching items, 471–472

Matching students and instruction, 88–89, 130–132, 134
Mathematics Teacher, 566
Measuring and evaluating. *See* Evaluating students
Mental retardation, 198–199
Mentoring, 493–494
Merit pay, 567–568
Metacognition, 361–365
    teacher modeling, 361–362
    visualizing thinking, 362–365
Meyer v. Nebraska, 532, 549
Middle school, 9–11
Minority students, 12–14, 166–180, 194–195
    Comer-model schools, 172–173
    enrollment changes, 12–13
    exemplary school programs, 172–174
    helping students succeed, 174–180
    historic views, 169–172
    language issue, 14, 173–174
    patterns of school learning, 167–169
    school achievement issue, 13, 167–169
    sources of materials, 180
    successful programs for Hispanics, 173–174
    suggestions for helping minority students learn, 174–180
Modeling, 193, 361–362
Monitoring, 327–328, 342
Moral dilemma discussion, 443–444
Moral discourse, 440
Moral reasoning, 440
Morality, 438–444
Motivating students, 59–61, 312–318
Multiple-choice items, 472–476
Music Teachers National Association, 42, 565

National Art Education Association, 42, 565
National Association for Gifted Children, 42, 565
National Council for the Social Studies, 42, 566
National Council of Teachers of English, 42, 566
National Council of Teachers of Mathematics, 42, 566
National Education Association, 7–8, 562–563
National Education Association Commission on Reorganization of Secondary Education Report of 1918, 8
National Education Association Committee of Nine, 7–8
National Education Association Committee of Ten, 7
National Science Teachers Association, 42, 566–567
Negligence, 535–536

malfeasance, 536
misfeasance, 536
nonfeasance, 535–536
New Jersey v. T. L. O., 527, 549
Nondirective teaching, 427–429
Non-school roles of teachers, 43–44
Non-sequential topic sequencing, 91

Objectives. *See* Preparing objectives
Office of Gifted and Talented, 205
Opportunity to Learn, 79
Optical disks, 291–293

Parducci v. Rutland, 537, 549
Part-to-whole sequencing, 89–90
Patachogue-Medford Congress of Teachers v. Board of Education, 534, 549
Pedagogical assumptions, 53–54
Pedagogical personality, 53
Pedagogical repertoire, 54
Peer coaching, 492–493
Peer evaluation, 491
Personal experiences of teachers, 54–55
Physical development patterns, 14–16
Physical and health impairment, 203
Piaget's developmental stages, 17–19, 22
Pickering v. Board of Education of Township School District 205, Will County, 537, 549
Portfolios, 503–504
Practice, 326
Praise, 325–326
Preparing objectives, 32–33, 100–121, 139
    ABCD format, 107–110
    affective domain, 114–119
    cognitive domain, 112–114
    description of objectives, 103–104
    evaluation and objectives, 111
    goals, 101
    necessary steps, 105–107
    psychomotor domain, 119–121
    relationships among goals, aims, objectives, 100–105
    types of objectives, 111–121
Principals, 86–87
Proactive teaching, 308
Problem solving, 378–380
Professional-development role of teachers, 41–43
Professional organizations in education, 41–42, 562–567

American Alliance for Health, Physical
  Education, Recreation, and Dance, 41, 564
American Vocational Association, 41
Association for Childhood Education
  International, 41
Council for Exceptional Children, 41, 564
International Council for Computers in
  Education, 42, 564
International Reading Association, 42, 564–565
Music Teachers National Association, 42, 565
National Art Education Association, 42, 565
National Association for Gifted Children, 42, 565
National Council for the Social Studies, 42, 565
National Council of Teachers of English, 42, 566
National Council of Teachers of Mathematics, 42,
  566
National Science Teachers Association, 42,
  566–567
Psychomotor domain, 119–121
Public Law 91–230, 205
Public Law 93–380, 205
Public Law 94–142, 195–196
Public Law 101–476, 195–196
Public relations role of teachers, 40–41
Purposes of secondary education, 7–8, 11, 101–102
  aims, 101–102
  cardinal principles, 8
  comprehensive high school, 8
  goals, 101
  National Education Association Commission on
    Reorganization of Secondary Education
    Report of 1918, 8
  National Education Association Committee of
    Nine, 7–8
  National Education Association Committee of
    Ten, 7

Questioning. *See* Teacher questioning

Rating scales, 465–467
Reading Teacher, 565
Referent power, 226
Reflective teaching, 57, 328
Reinforcement, 325
Research Quarterly for Exercise and Sport, 564
Research on teaching, 56–65, 230–233, 251–269,
  302–328, 338–353, 359–389, 423–444
  affective learning, 423–444
  beliefs about students, 57–59

clear communication, 318–319
  direct instruction, 338–353
  indirect instruction, 359–389
  individualized instruction, 251–269
  motivating students, 312–318
  practice, 326
  praise, 325–326
  presenting good lessons, 63–65, 68
  proactive teaching, 308
  reinforcement, 325
  scaffolding, 310–311
  stimulating student interest, 59–61
  teacher questioning, 318–319
  time management, 230–233
  using student contributions, 61–62
  using time effectively, 62–63
Research on the Teaching of English, 566
Rest's model for teaching morality, 438–439
Retarded students, 198
Retrieval charts, 369–371
Review of Educational Research, 56
Reward power, 227
Risk factors for students, 167–168
Rogers, Carl, 427
Roles of teachers. *See* Teachers' roles

Scaffolding, 310–311
School administrators, 86–87, 569–570
School counselors, 570
Science Teacher, 567
Search and seizure, 525–527
Sequencing content, 89–91
  chronological sequencing, 91
  external constraint sequencing, 91
  non-sequential topic sequencing, 91
  part-to-whole sequencing, 89–90
  whole-to-part sequencing, 90
SIG Bulletin, 564
Slow learners, 192–194
Small group learning, 394–405
  inside and outside, 395–397
  investigative role group, 399–402
  scheduling, 397–398
  team learning group, 403–405
  tutorial group, 402–403
  two by twos, 394–395
Social Education, 566
Southside Public Schools v. Hill, 538, 549
Speech impairment, 200–201

State education agency employees, 570–571
Structure of knowledge, 84–87, 137–139
    concepts, 84–85, 137–139
    facts, 84
    generalizations, principles, and laws, 86–87,
        137–139
    role in content-selection decisions, 87
*Stuart v. School District No. 1 of the Village of
    Kalamazoo*, 6, 26
Student characteristics, 6, 11–19, 22, 166–180,
        194–212
    enrollment patterns, 11–13
    gifted and talented students, 204–212
    intellectual development patterns, 17–19, 22
    minority students, 166–180
    physical development patterns, 14–16
    Piaget's developmental stages, 17–19, 22
    risk factors, 167–168
    students with disabilities, 194–204
Student dress and appearance, 521
Student freedom of conscience, 520–521
Student-teams-achievement divisions, 406–408
Studies in Art Education, 565
Suchman inquiry technique, 371–373
Summative evaluation, 457
Supervisor evaluation, 494–495
Suspension, 523
Systematic teaching. *See* Direct instruction

Talented students. *See* Gifted and talented students
Teacher educators, 571–572
Teacher questioning, 320–324
    nature of student responses, 324
    question clarity, 322–324
    question purpose, 320–321
    wait time, 324
Teachers' academic freedom, 536–538
Teachers' career options, 568–573
    curriculum coordinator, 569
    department chair, 568–569
    human resource developer, 573
    school administrator, 569–570
    school counselor, 570
    state education agency employee, 570–571
    teacher educator, 571–572
Teachers' freedom of expression, 536–538
Teachers' private lives, 540
Teachers' professional development, 552–563
    induction year, 558–559

graduate courses, 561–562
    preservice phase, 554–557
    pretraining phase, 553
    professional organization work, 562
    staff development activities, 560–561
Teachers' roles, 30–48, 51–71, 77–91, 100–121,
        130–157, 189–212, 221–242, 251–269,
        277–293, 302–328, 338–353, 359–383,
        423–444, 452–477
    classroom management, 221–242
    cooperative learning, 405–414
    counseling, 35–36
    curriculum development, 38–40
    decision making, 51–71
    direct instruction, 338–353
    discipline, 221–242
    evaluating students, 452–477
    indirect instruction, 359–383
    individualizing instruction, 251–269
    instructional tasks, 30–35, 51–71, 77–91, 100–121,
        130–157, 189–212, 221–242, 251–269,
        277–293, 302–328, 338–353, 394–414
    management function, 37–38
    modeling, 361–362
    non-school roles, 43–44
    professional development, 41–43
    promoting affective learning, 423–444
    public relations, 40–41
    small group learning, 394–405
Teaching certificates, 528–529
Teaching contracts, 531–532
    continuing contracts, 532
    tenure contracts, 532
    term contracts, 531–532
Teaching Exceptional Children, 564
Teaching techniques, 251–269, 277–293, 306–328,
        338–353, 359–384, 394–414, 423–444
    affective learning, 423–444
    brainstorming, 374–375
    classroom meetings, 429–433
    cooperative learning, 405–414
    creative thinking, 373–375
    critical thinking, 375–376
    data retrieval charts, 369–371
    direct instruction, 338–353
    goal-directed teaching, 308–309
    indirect instruction, 359–383
    individualizing instruction, 251–269
    inquiry teaching, 365–373

inside and outside, 395–397
investigative role group, 399–402
issues, values, and consequences analysis, 434–436
jigsaw, 409–412
Kohlberg's moral reasoning, 440
learning activity packages, 261–264
learning centers, 264–267
learning contracts, 259–260
learning stations, 267–269
learning together, 412–414
modeling, 361–362
monitoring, 327–328
moral dilemma discussion, 443–444
moral discourse, 440
motivating students, 312–318
nondirective teaching, 427–429
proactive teaching, 308
problem solving, 378–380
reinforcement and praise, 325–326
Rest's model for teaching morality, 438–439
scaffolding, 310–311
small groups, 394–405
student-teams-achievement divisions, 406–408
Suchman inquiry, 371–373
teacher questioning, 320–324
team learning, 403–405
teams-games-tournaments, 408–409
tutorial group, 402–403
two by twos, 394–395
values clarification, 436–438
visualizing thinking, 362–365, 377

Team learning, 403–405
Teams-games-tournaments, 408–409
Technology. *See* Instructional technology
Tenure contract, 532
Tenure laws, 532
Term contract, 531–532
Theory and Research in Social Education, 566
Tinker v. Des Moines Independent School District, 516–518, 549
Title IX of the Education Amendments of 1972, 524–525
Tort liability, 534–536
Trainable students, 198
Training and Development, 573
True-false items, 476–477
Tutorial group, 402–403
Two by twos, 394–395

Unit planning. *See* Instructional units
Update, 564
Utility value, 313, 315

Values. *See* Affective learning
Values clarification, 436–438
Videocassettes, 291
Visual impairment, 201
Visualizing reasoning, 362–365, 377
Vorcheimer v. School District, 524, 549

Wait time, 324
Whole-to-part sequencing, 90